PRAISE FOR *LAWYERS' EMPIRE*

Never one to equivocate, Wes Pue opens this book with a flourish. The past, he insists, is a "foreign place that can never be known." Unmasking lawyers as "energetic purveyors of historical myth," Pue then turns his considerable talents toward the "pursuit of better myth." Read this and marvel at his insight, his painstaking research, and his incomparable wit. These essays, boldly ranging across Britain and its Empire, brilliantly substantiate Wes Pue's "larger than life" reputation as one of Canada's most fascinating legal historians.

– CONSTANCE BACKHOUSE, Professor of Law at the University of Ottawa

A superb collection of essays from a scholar who eschews the obvious, yet attacks the crux of the issue without rubbing your nose in it. No one lays out for the reader such clarity of proffered understandings with such fascinating histories. There is a cinematic sense about Professor Pue's approach. He begins with a close-up on the individual specific, then withdraws to global view, with a short flashback, before setting the story in full play. This releases us from "given" theory such as the "sterile" view of the history of legal education as a battle between the profession and the academy and enables a deeper, more nuanced understanding that also enlightens the problems of today.

– AVROM SHERR, Woolf Professor of Legal Education Emeritus, Institute of Advanced Legal Studies, University of London

For decades Wesley Pue has stood at the forefront of the world's leading scholars on the politics of legal professions. This outstanding blending of his writings into a unified whole reveals at once the scope and imagination of his always fertile search for new and enlightening corners of lawyers' activities at work and collectively. He moves seamlessly and with great intellectual dexterity across the centuries from the heart of the British Empire to its edges, from one colony or post-colony to another. He unearths long-forgotten archives and melds disparate materials into rich theoretical motifs. *Lawyers' Empire* recasts our thinking about empire and the cultural politics of lawyers.

– TERENCE HALLIDAY, Research Professor and Co-Director, Center on Law and Globalization, at the American Bar Foundation

LAW AND SOCIETY

Law and Society Series
W. Wesley Pue, General Editor

The Law and Society Series explores law as a socially embedded phenomenon. It is premised on the understanding that the conventional division of law from society creates false dichotomies in thinking, scholarship, educational practice, and social life. Books in the series treat law and society as mutually constitutive and seek to bridge scholarship emerging from interdisciplinary engagement of law with disciplines such as politics, social theory, history, political economy, and gender studies. For a complete list of titles in the series go to www.ubcpress.ca. Recent titles include:

Sarah Turnbull, *Parole in Canada: Gender and Diversity in the Federal System* (2016)
Amanda Nettelbeck, Russell Smandych, Louis A. Knafla, and Robert Foster, *Fragile Settlements: Aboriginal Peoples, Law, and Resistance in South-West Australia and Prairie Canada* (2016)
Adam Dodek and Alice Woolley, eds., *In Search of the Ethical Lawyer: Stories from the Canadian Legal Profession* (2016)
David R. Boyd, *Cleaner, Greener, Healthier: A Prescription for Stronger Canadian Environmental Laws and Policies* (2015)
Margaret E. Beare, Nathalie Des Rosiers, and Abby Deshman, eds., *Putting the State on Trial: The Policing of Protest during the G20 Summit* (2015)
Dale Brawn, *Paths to the Bench: The Judicial Appointment Process in Manitoba, 1870-1950* (2014)
Dominique Clément, *Equality Deferred: Sex Discrimination and British Columbia's Human Rights State, 1953-84* (2014)
Irvin Studin, *The Strategic Constitution: Understanding Canadian Power in the World* (2014)
Elizabeth A. Sheehy, *Defending Battered Women on Trial: Lessons from the Transcripts* (2014)

Lawyers' Empire

Legal Professions and Cultural Authority, 1780-1950

W. WESLEY PUE

UBCPress · Vancouver · Toronto

25 24 23 22 21 20 19 18 17 16   5 4 3 2 1

Printed in Canada on FSC-certified ancient-forest-free paper (100% post-consumer recycled) that is processed chlorine- and acid-free.

Library and Archives Canada Cataloguing in Publication

Pue, W. Wesley, author
Lawyers' empire: legal professions and cultural authority, 1780-1950 /
W. Wesley Pue.

(Law and society series)
Includes bibliographical references and index.
Issued in print and electronic formats.
ISBN 978-0-7748-3309-7 (hardback). – ISBN 978-0-7748-3311-0 (pdf)

1. Lawyers – England – History. 2. Law – Study and teaching – England – History. 3. Practice of law – Social aspects – England – History. 4. Lawyers – Canada – History. I. Title. II. Series: Law and society series (Vancouver, B.C.)

H-KD460 P83 2016   340.023'42   C2016-903105-5
C2016-903106-3

Canada

UBC Press gratefully acknowledges the financial support for our publishing program of the Government of Canada (through the Canada Book Fund), the Canada Council for the Arts, and the British Columbia Arts Council.

UBC Press
The University of British Columbia
2029 West Mall
Vancouver, BC V6T 1Z2
www.ubcpress.ca

FOR JOANNE

Contents

PART 3
ETHICS, REGULATION, AND THE BUSINESS OF LAW

PART 4
CHALLENGING THE STATUS QUO: COMMUNISTS AND LIBERALS

PART 5
DOMINION AND COLONIAL LAWYERING

Foreword

It is an honour and pleasure to be invited to contribute a foreword to this notable collection of essays. That Wes Pue deserves recognition for his outstanding scholarship is without question. This book amply manifests Wes's considerable stature as an academic lawyer and his substantial and enduring contributions to the study and development of law-and-society style legal history. It also affords us an opportunity to reflect on what he has achieved.

In his work, Wes has developed a distinctive, wide-ranging, and subtle cultural approach that places centre stage the role and significance of law, the legal profession, and law schools in shaping, transmitting, and normalizing our assumptions regarding ethnicity, masculinity, class, progress, and colonization. He makes a strong case for seeing law and legal professionalism and education as a means of representing and thus helping to create professional, national, religious, ethnic, and cultural identities. Following those commentators who accord a central place to law in the colonizing process, Wes argues that law, legal education, and the socialization of lawyers seek nothing less than the transformation of souls. For him, legal institutions, practices, and thought are often best understood not simply as instrumental to some set of guild interests, economic self-interest, or even societal change but also as factors that promote and protect images of identity. By examining the legal profession and legal education in their political and, especially, cultural contexts, Wes identifies important questions concerning societal governance.

Wes depicts Canadian lawyers as energetic purveyors of historical myth, building worlds out of words. He identifies key historical errors in a professional apologetics founded on history. Acknowledging the mythic dimensions inherent in the use of history, he seeks to lay the foundations for what he terms "better myth." In these and other ways, he enhances our understanding of the use of history by the legal community.

That his essays are consistently insightful and adroit is also evidenced in the detailed attention he lavishes on the margins of, and the marginalized in, society. As perhaps befits one who spent his formative career living and teaching in the periphery of the United States and Canada, Wes is passionate about the significance of this periphery – from Canada as a mere dominion within the British Empire and the prairie west of Canada, to Queen's College (Birmingham, UK) and Nigeria – and the ways by which they might illuminate the centre. He has sought to show, for example, that lawyers west of Ontario, notably in Manitoba, spearheaded the movement that created modern legal professionalism and education in Canada. It seems likely that this has been much overlooked because it took place in Winnipeg, not Toronto, and during a period (the early decades of the twentieth century) before there was much focus on these matters in Canada. Wes charts Manitoba's effort to adopt the Socratic method and the casebook, sustained by British and American influences but underpinned by the particularities of Canada. More generally, he challenges assumptions by uncovering a neglected or suppressed voice.

His admirable penchant for de-centring extends to those within the legal professional firmament treated as "outsiders" and "folk devils." His series of essays investigating English barristers who sought to reform English legal education and legal institutions, and who were demonized for doing so, was a first in the modern literature. This work proved revelatory: it has become an important benchmark and role model for other scholars, and remains the most extensive and important set of case studies of its kind. Similarly, his discussion of lawyers and political liberalism in eighteenth- and nineteenth-century England problematizes the conventional dualisms that have traditionally separated the English Bar from its Parisian cousin. Wes argues that English barristers, like their counterparts in other countries, were frequently drawn to political action. Although English barristers were less activist than the Parisian bar, neither the political quiescence of barristers nor their supposed conservatism should be overstated. Others topics rescued from the condescension of "winner's history" include attempts at legal, professional, and educational reform that failed and paths that were not taken. Wes analyzes the earliest attempts to implement the recommendations of the 1846 Select Committee on Legal Education, and the difficulties encountered by Queen's College and Manitoba in seeking to provide a legal education that transcended mere vocationalism. And in a telling essay, the exclusion of an individual from the legal profession in British Columbia solely because he was a communist provides a striking case study that advances our understanding of professional autonomy and its sensitivity to locale and period.

As will be evident from my wave-of-the wand treatment of this book, Wes took care to frame his research in a way that was sensitive to the local and the international before this perspective became more widely adopted. The material that he has brought together on legal education and the legal profession in Canada and Britain is unique. It sheds new light on the commonalities, similarities, and the differences that characterized both sides of the Atlantic, while registering their entangled histories. The same is true of his scholarship on Canadian lawyers in the context of the history of the imperial profession – and of Canada as a British dominion – and its impact on the history of the Canadian legal profession. Although too few people outside Canada pay attention to Canada, Wes demonstrates why they should.

Originally appearing in assorted and sometimes obscure publications, these essays have been revised to produce what I believe is a revelatory work that will become a milestone in the study of legal history and the interplay between law and society. Like most cutting-edge scholarship, it raises as many questions as it answers, but in so doing it successfully highlights important themes and issues for future scholarship to consider and assess.

It is remarkable to realize that the essays in this book are but a relatively small proportion of Wes's published output, and that he has devoted much of his professional life to building institutions and creating the conditions in which scholarship can flourish. Besides being an exceptional scholar, Wes is also an outstanding academic leader, institution builder, and initiator of national and transnational scholarly associations and networks. He founded and is the general editor of the UBC Press Law and Society series (with more than ninety books published since 2001). He has served on national and international bodies, including the American Society for Legal History, the North American Association for Australia and New Zealand Studies, and, as president for two terms, the Canadian Law and Society Association. He has been a leading light in the International Working Group on Comparative Legal Professions – the principal international body in the field – including establishing and co-chairing subgroups on the "Cultural History of the Legal Professions" and "Lawyers and Imperialism." He has played a prominent role in creating an international network of scholars on the rule of law and lawyers in British colonial and postcolonial nations, and in organizing conferences and publications that have brought together scholars from Africa, Asia, Australia, Canada, Europe, New Zealand, and the United States. He has been a leader in mentorship and program innovation (including initiating new courses and degree programs, such as the first internationally developed and taught World Wide Web–based law course, "Legal History: Law, State and

Society in Canada and Australia," with colleagues in Canada and Australia) and an indefatigable university administrator (most recently Provost and Vice Principal, University of British Columbia, Okanagan Campus; Vice-Provost and Associate Vice President, Academic, University of British Columbia; and Associate Dean for Graduate Studies and Research, Faculty of Law, University of British Columbia). Above all, perhaps, he has touched an astonishing number of lives as a teacher, colleague, mentor, and friend.

This makes the quality and breadth of Wes's scholarship all the more remarkable. It testifies to his selfless public-spiritedness and his strong commitment to public education, to broadening and deepening legal scholarship and education, and to bringing people together across national and allied boundaries. Hence, the publication of this book is an occasion to mark Wes's outstanding contributions across a wide range of roles, and to acknowledge his commitment to the values of collegiality, constructive critique, interdisciplinarity, openmindedness, international dialogue, and transnational perspectives. I am truly privileged to have known Wes as a colleague and friend for over thirty years.

DAVID SUGARMAN, F.R.Hist.S.
Professor Emeritus of Law, Lancaster University Law School, UK;
Senior Associate Research Fellow, Institute of Advanced Legal Studies,
School of Advanced Studies, University of London

Acknowledgments

In the making of this book, the contributions of three individuals were indispensable. First, Peter Milroy, Director Emeritus of UBC Press, discussed the idea with me at length and helped me to formulate the approach and structure of the book. His input, advice, and assistance have been pivotal. His publishing expertise, encouragement, and practical assistance have also made the project possible. Second, Heather Pue served as a research assistant. Her background in the humanities and in book publishing was very helpful at every turn. This book would not have been possible without her many and varied contributions. She also took the photograph that appears on the cover of the book. Third, David Sugarman provided a gracious foreword, but went well beyond that, reading every chapter and making helpful suggestions at many points.

I am of course grateful for the intellectual stimulation, scholarship, or advice of many others. The notion that academic work is produced by scholars working in splendid isolation or on projects conceived entirely in their own minds is a myth. Most scholarship emerges from active engagement with the ideas of others and I wish to pay tribute to all of those who have influenced my work. This includes the many participants in law and society or legal history conferences in North America, the Antipodes, Britain, Europe, and Asia, who have profoundly influenced the questions I have sought to address and how I have chosen to do so.

A complete list is impossible, but notable mentors, colleagues, and sources of inspiration and encouragement include Alison Diduck, Alvin Esau, Anne McGillivray, Annie Rochette, Barry Wright, Bernard Hibbitts, Blaine Baker, Cameron Harvey, Carolyn Strange, Chidi Oguamanam, Constance Backhouse, Dale Brawn, Dale Gibson, David Bell, Dawna Tong, Doug Harris, Doug Hay, Elizabeth Comack, Emma Cunliffe, Eve Darian-Smith, Fred Zemans, Gerald Friesen, Graham Price, Hamar Foster, Harold Dick, Harry Arthurs, Harry

Glasbeek, Jim Phillips, Joan Brockman, John McLaren, Jon Swainger, Judith Grbich, Karen Busby, Karen Pearlston, Kim Economides, Lee Gibson, Lou Knafla, Lucien Karpik, Lyndsay Campbell, Margaret Thornton, Mary Jane Mossman, Nick Blomley, Philip Girard, Pooja Parmar, P.S.C. Lewis, Raymond Cocks, Renisa Mawani, Rick Abel, Robert Diab, Robert Gordon, Roderick Macdonald, Roland Penner, Russell Smandych, Sarah Ramshaw, Steve Brickey, Susan Binnie, Susan Boyd, Tony Lemon, and William H. Hurlburt. Special thanks are due to Avrom Sherr, David Sugarman, Ian Duncanson, Rob McQueen, Stuart Scheingold, Terri Halliday, and Wilfrid R. Prest.

Books do not produce themselves, of course. UBC Press has a top-notch team working on everything from book acquisitions to turning a manuscript into a book. Especial thanks go to the following for their exceptional efforts on this one: Alexa Love (cover design), Frank Chow (copy editor), Holly Keller (Assistant Director, Production and Editorial), Irma Rodriguez (design and typesetting), Nadine Pedersen (permissions), and Randy Schmidt (Acquisitions Editor, Law and Society Series).

To all of the above, I am extremely grateful.

Finally, and most importantly, thanks to my family. Each has put up with schedules and absences that were inconvenient on many, many occasions – their understanding and toleration of this has been enormous.

PART 1

History in Professional Apologetics

1

The Use of History in the Development of Lawyers' Mythologies

> What distinguishes the barrister from the insurance adjuster? The real estate conveyancer from the real estate agent? Tradition!
>
> – J. de P. Wright, "The Value of Tradition"[1]

> [A]ll invented traditions, so far as possible, use history as a legitimator of action and cement of group cohesion ... All historians, whatever else the objectives, are engaged in this process inasmuch as they contribute, consciously or not, to the creation, dismantling and restructuring of images of the past which belong not only to the world of specialist investigation but to the public sphere of man as a political being.
>
> – E. Hobsbawm, "Inventing Traditions"[2]

Lawyers are history buffs, much enamoured with the traditions of their profession. Some may look to history for solace or for inspiration: the retreat to an objective and knowable past that speaks to the uncertainties of the present by providing incontrovertible proof that the entire cultural logic of our civilization mandates a particular form of professional organization, training, or conduct. Others may look to history for critique, perhaps recalling the adage that those who forget history, who fail to heed its "lessons," are condemned to repeat it.[3] There are also, no doubt, skeptics who wonder what possible contemporary relevance there can be in the actions or thoughts of long-dead lawyers.

This last position, I have to admit, is one to which I am drawn. Though I hope there is good reason to study history, and the histories of legal professions in particular, it seems to me to be both naïve and wildly optimistic to seek a singular moral "truth" in history. It is absurd to think that history repeats itself, if only because, as every litigator and every expositor of legal doctrine knows all too well, no fact situation or problem ever repeats itself in exactly the same way as it appeared before. Even were this plausible, events can never recur because historical context itself changes. Nineteenth-century London or New York is not the same place as late-twentieth-century Calgary or St. John's. Winnipeg in 1919 is not the same place as Edmonton in 1989. Edmonton in June 2016 is not the same as Edmonton in June 2015. The past – even the recent past – is always a foreign place. We can read travelogues but can never go there. We may remember but can never investigate first-hand. It is a foreign place that can never be known. Anyone who has booked a package holiday or returned to an old haunt knows this to be true. If you can never "go home," you most assuredly cannot fully know the past.

The Importance of Professional Myth

History is not irrelevant, however. The stories told about the past speak powerfully to the self-image of the storyteller. Collective stories define collective identities. Speaking about the past, we make ourselves for the present and project a future. Canadian cultural commentator Northrop Frye explained:

> We move in time with our backs to what's ahead and our faces to the past, and all we know is in a rear-view mirror ...
>
> The question "Where are we going?" assumes that we already know the answer to the question "Where are we now, and how did we get here?" We certainly don't know the answer to that one, and in fact all our really urgent, mysterious and frightening questions have to do with the burden of the past and the meaning of tradition.[4]

All of this would remain rather abstract and esoteric were it not the case that Canada's lawyers are, in fact, energetic purveyors of historical myth. The principal oracles of mythic knowledge are professional associations and mysterious communications from lawyers who have attained the glory of the judicial bench.

It will, I hope, be understood that in speaking of professional "myths" I am using that term in a quite precise way. I do not in the least intend to offend. The term carries no pejorative connotation, and I certainly do not wish to be taken as implying anything at all resembling bad faith or a dissembling attitude on the part of professional apologists. Rather, I am content in understanding "mythology" as the active and communal process of "building worlds out of words."[5] Lawyers, like novelists, journalists, poets, comedians, or scholars, are word spinners. As such, we are simultaneously liegeman to and empress of the cultural uses and social functions of language. "Nobody," according to Frye, "can create, think or even act outside the mythology of his time, but a mythology is not some kind of prison; it is simply the whole body of material we work with. Like science, it is being recreated all the time, partly by critics and scholars and partly by literature itself, because every new writer recreates something already in literature."[6]

The task for lawyers, then, cannot be to transcend myth. It is futile to seek some objective "truth" beyond the bounds of place, time, and culture – myth. We should, however, expect more rather than less thoughtful professional myth making. Our most immediate goal should be to resist sanctifying our own unexamined assumptions, lest we risk the wilful suppression of knowledge and a descent into an abyss walled by "a complete and mostly phony mythology, made up of cliché and prejudice and stock response."[7]

In pursuit of better myth, this chapter seeks to explore, to tease out, the mythic narratives that underlie some important professional writings in Canada. By and large, I have confined myself to the publications of professional organizations, and limited my review to common law jurisdictions out of respect for the variations in forms of professional organization and mythic foundations of professional culture that distinguish common law from civil law traditions in Canada. Even with these limitations, there is certainly room for a more comprehensive exploration of myth in Canadian lawyers' professional rhetoric. This project could – probably should – have been expanded to encompass sources such as judicial pronouncements, academic writings, the *Street Legal* television show, jury addresses, newspaper articles, "talking head" television interviews, and so on. These, however, are much beyond the ambit of this chapter. Much less do I hope to explore the deeper "mythologies of modern law" that may at a much more profound level ground European-derived legal systems in their entirety.[8]

After identifying the major outlines of contemporary professional myth in Canada, I will critique the composite I have sketched. My purpose is not to present "objective" historical fact against professional myth but only to illustrate the ways in which commonplace narratives are cluttered with unfounded prejudices, assumed histories, clichés, and stock responses. To appropriate Peter Fitzpatrick's language for my own purposes, I seek here to subvert portions of received narratives "by heightening the contradictions and suppressions involved in their construction."[9]

Contemporary Lawyers' Mythologies

Although anthropology and other human sciences offer competing definitions of "myth," a number of components recur with some frequency:

1 Myths are often stories dealing with "origins and identity, and in particular here with the origins and identity of a group or a people."
2 Myth often provides "the basis for claiming ... a superiority for the group."
3 "The point of origin is sacred – set apart, made transcendent and beyond encompassing in profane experience."
4 "Such a self-generating, sacred force imposes and sustains an order from above. The ability to do this is often transferred in part to agents such as the first man made in the image of God."
5 Agents and forces mediate between the sacred and the profane. "Such mediations locate the profane, mortal world within the sacred, providing members of the group with guidance and orientation to a reality which is perceived and lived through myth."
6 "Myth both sets the limits of the world, of what can be meant and done, and transcends these limits in its relation to the sacred."
7 Contradictions and incoherencies might be obfuscated by "placing contradictory elements in distinct but related myths ... This is a relation of dependence of a myth on other myths for the revelation of its 'full' meaning."[10]

Most of these elements of "myth" recur with some frequency in Canadian professional apologetics.[11] Professional apologetics is constructed within a web of interconnecting myths relating to self-regulation, independence of the profession, adversarial justice, and public service.

A Note on Sources of Professional Mythology

In seeking out contemporary accounts of professionalism, I conducted a mail survey of lawyers' professional organizations across Canada in 1994.[12] Each was approached with a request for information covering just about any sort of considered statement relating to the role of the legal profession in Canadian society. Specifically, I asked these organizations to provide me with copies of any documents such as "position papers, submissions to government commissions, public education pamphlets or such-like" speaking to any of the following sorts of matters:

- the social role of the legal profession,
- professional ethics,

> - principles of self-regulation and/or the independence of the legal profession,
> - the adversarial process,
> - the public service orientation of a profession or the meaning of "professionalism"
>
> ...
>
> The sort of material that would be helpful to me relates to policy assessments, public statements or philosophical positions rather than the "hands-on" work that all professional organizations in Canada engage in with respect to the development of ethical codes or the application of rules in particular cases.

The responses were varied. Four professional organizations responded with brief letters indicating that they had not prepared any such documents.[13] The Nova Scotia Barristers' Society explained that, as "a small society, we tend to rely on the work of the larger jurisdictions to assist us in this area,"[14] but kindly provided me with a draft "objects clause" then under active consideration, and with a copy of their new *Legal Ethics Handbook*. The Law Society of Saskatchewan sent me four publicity pamphlets,[15] and I received an extremely interesting, very helpful thirty-five-page document prepared by the Law Society of Newfoundland.[16] The Law Society of British Columbia provided me with a copy of a paper prepared by its chief executive officer in 1993, and with a more recent "public briefing paper."[17] I found it very helpful to be able to review the *Submission of the Law Society of Manitoba in Response to the Law Reform Commission of Manitoba Discussion Paper on the Future of Occupational Regulation in Manitoba.*[18]

I received an interesting package from the Law Society of Alberta – including the final report of its "Futures Committee,"[19] an article by one of its former presidents,[20] and other material. I also received copies of both an important government report and the law society's rather poorly constructed response – a document that spoke powerfully to the role of professional rhetoric in the world of myth.[21]

In addition, the Barreau du Québec, the Chambre des notaires du Québec, the Law Society of Ontario ("Upper Canada"), and the Federation of Law Societies inundated me with voluminous and very interesting documentation.

The results of my survey provided me with nearly comprehensive professional documentation for a critical period of time in the evolution of thinking about the roles, functions, and organization of the legal professions in Canada. Although discussions have moved on somewhat, the core emphasis on legal professionalism as both historically embedded and bearing peculiar relationship with the conditions of freedom in modern society remain strong.[22]

History and Myth in Contemporary Lawyers' Discourse

History is everywhere in contemporary professional apologetics. It appears both as in-your-face, explicit appeals to "history" as a source of legitimacy for the status quo and, much more subtly, through a series of cultural codings that are so well understood as to register subconsciously only. But register they do.

History "in Your Face"

Explicit appeals to "history" as a source of authority are found in law society publications from coast to coast. The Law Society of British Columbia, for example, recounts a number of historical tales in a public "briefing" document. It asserts that the contemporary structure of professional regulation in the province is "in keeping with the centuries-old tradition in England" and that "historically" the profession has been "given self-governing status because of society's belief that a lawyer cannot serve two masters."[23] Lawyering, we are told, is "a profession," not a mere "trade," because "a profession has, over many years," developed an ethical code.[24]

The Alberta law society makes a similar appeal to history, claiming that despite its origins in an Alberta statute of 1907, the late-twentieth-century law society is a direct successor to mysterious "origins of an independent legal profession" that "can be traced to England in early times." Despite the long history of First Nations governance in the territory that is now Alberta, despite two centuries of nominal control by a private corporation, despite the origins of "western Canada" as a central Canadian colony, despite the fact that Alberta was created only in 1905, the Alberta legal profession is quite precise in asserting *its* origins far, far away and long, long ago: "Historically the profession developed as a self-governing entity before there was any legislation and although there has been a legislative framework in Alberta since 1907, it reflects that which had traditionally existed." One presumes here that the reference to what "traditionally existed" does not refer to Peigan or Cree professional structures.[25] A dusty prairie town in 1907 cannot provide pedigree adequate to match the needs of a proud Alberta law society.

The Manitoba law society takes pride in the independence of the legal profession manifest in "a long history and tradition of self-governance" that is "rooted in the English common law."[26] Saskatchewan modestly informs us only that "[h]istorically self government is rooted in the notion that a lawyer cannot serve two masters," and, therefore, that independence is "for the benefit of the client and the public, not the lawyers."[27] More modestly still, the New Brunswick and Prince Edward Island legal professions have produced no internal studies or public documents whatsoever that speak to matters of professional organization, independence of the legal profession, or self-governance. Despite a long, impressive, and relatively well-researched history, the Nova Scotia Barristers' Society has produced only a draft "objects clause" emphasizing that the "regulatory role of the Society ... has a long history and a mandate that has evolved over the years."[28] Newfoundland has produced an interesting document generally reiterating the argument that "lawyers have been viewed as standing between the government and private citizens" and, therefore, that lawyers must be "completely independent of government."[29]

Not the least modest or self-effacing, the Ontario law society has proved to be far and away the most important producer of lawyers' histories in common law Canada. Several of its texts have entered into the Canadian canon of professional apologetics, and a number of ideas first developed in Law Society of Upper Canada documents have popped up at various places in Canada with some frequency. In the November 1993 draft *Proposed Role Statement,* the Ontario law society invokes history frequently and powerfully.[30] The date 1797 appears twice on page 4, then on pages 8, 10, and 11 (note 12), and repeatedly in the three appendix pages where *An Act for the better Regulating the Practice of the Law* (U.K.), 37 Geo. III, c. 12 is "translated" into contemporary language and then reproduced in full (the translation itself is interesting, involving as it does the representation of a monarchical and committedly anti-democratic Imperial authority as the epitome of late-twentieth-century democratic constitutionalism). Overall three full pages of this seventeen-page document are dedicated to a 1797 colonial statute, while that date appears five times over fourteen pages of the principal text – suggesting greater antiquity and a much higher degree of commitment to it than any other Canadian jurisdiction.

In its *Presentation to the Standing Committee on the Ombudsman,* the Ontario law society dedicates fully two pages to the "History and Responsibilities of the Law Society."[31] "History" makes frequent reappearances thereafter.[32] An earlier document, the Ontario law society's *Submission to The Professional Organizations Committee,* is also replete with historical observations, some of which, in turn, have entered the professional canon. This document informs us that "law" reflects the "community" but is "essentially conservative,"[33] and that lawyers have an important and unique historical function (the "protection of rights").[34] It makes a powerful claim to ancient English tradition, fusing the colonial professional association with "its origins in England" and arguing that this history serves to "demonstrate the close association between the administration of justice and, not only lawyers, but their governing bodies as well." "This association," it is said, "has continued for centuries."[35] A collection of huts on a swampy colonial shore cannot, it seems, provide pedigree adequate to match the pretensions of the Law Society of Upper Canada.

A substantial portion of the first chapter of this report, headed "The Independence of the Legal Profession," addresses the history of the profession.[36] In addition to the above-cited remarks, this includes citation of Holdsworth on 250 years of (English) professional history,[37] an argument that the law society is not a "public" body despite its creation by statute,[38] and a genuinely astonishing argument for continuity of institutional order from the 1300s through 1797 to the present.[39] Again fusing the histories of an Imperial and a colonial legal profession, this portion of the report concludes that

> [t]his historical review has established that the Bar in England and in Ontario grew independently of government and exercises responsibility of its own making; that it requested and obtained from government recognition and a legal framework within which it continues to discharge its functions; that this independence of the Bar is necessary to the independence of the Bench and to the freedom for the individual citizens ... Unless there is strong reason for change a structure which has evolved over centuries and which is working well should not be interfered with.[40]

One intelligent and carefully balanced address by a treasurer of the Law Society of Upper Canada is also replete with historical reference, including several pages on "the origins of the modern legal profession in the European Renaissance,"[41] an invocation of the antiquity of lawyers' governing bodies in Canada – "The history of the governing bodies in Canada is a long one, stretching back two hundred years"[42] – and an appeal to the Canadian "tradition" of relying on "the self-governing status of the legal profession" to ensure "the independence of lawyers."[43]

In summary, then, it is not hard to find explicit appeals to "history" in the writings of Canadian law societies and their officers. I expect that a more thorough survey of professional literature in general would reveal a deep substrata of historical references. The point here is not to analyze or assess the content of these historical arguments but simply to note the frequency with which they appear. One suspects that there would be much less frequent appeals to either ancient English history or the continuity of Canadian tradition in other professions, such as nursing, teaching, engineering, or dental hygiene. The professional organizations of physicians, surgeons, psychiatrists, and psychologists are, of course, generally content to overlook the quack theories and brutal bodily assaults that have constituted their "respectable practice" in times past. Law celebrates, relishes, and revels in a vision of the past.

The past that lawyers celebrate, however, is richer, more subtle, and more pervasive than even this brief account of in-your-face professional histories would suggest. There is also a history "encoded" in professional rhetoric that contributes powerfully to our myths.

History Encoded

Every litigator, historian, literary critic, and legal historian knows well that language does not work in a simple, straightforward, or linear way. "[L]anguage is not," according to Mariana Valverde, "a transparent window giving access to the world but is rather itself a part of the world, a kind of object among objects."[44] Words can communicate meaning more or less directly ("literally") or by complex interplays of images, associations, or histories. Sometimes, perhaps invariably, the most simple statement communicates both sorts of meanings simultaneously.

Cultural context loads words with "slippages" whereby text apparently directed to one purpose simultaneously conveys meanings of quite another sort.[45] In all cultures, including our own, "certain images, words, or constellations of both [resonate] ... with pre-existing cosmologies."[46] Meaning is carried through multiple series of representations in which there is no "one-to-one correspondence of signifier and signified" but rather socially shared attributions of meaning working by means of "complex metaphors and chains of metonymies" – "complex relationships within each allegory and among different allegories/symbols."[47] Full understanding cannot be had at the surface level. "The meaning of texts is not contained within their boundaries; it can only be deciphered – and the power relations constituted by it exposed – through a thorough knowledge of the social context in which the texts were produced."[48]

Obvious and simple though it is, this insight has produced powerful new approaches to the understanding of English literature,[49] history,[50] contemporary culture,[51] geography,[52] and law.[53] Because, in this approach, understandings of text depend upon the appreciation of the reader or audience as well as the intent of an author or speaker, "real" meaning is elusive. Contextual understanding must be sought, however. There is no meaning more "real."

It is through such an appreciation of the ways in which language works that "encoded" histories can be identified throughout the literature of "professional apologetics." References to "liberty," personal freedom, or the "rule of law" infiltrate professional apologetics at every turn, producing linguistic slippages that lead the reader to quite wide-ranging associations – all of them, not surprisingly, tending towards reinforcement of the professional status quo. To illustrate the ways in which these slippages work, it may be helpful to consider some sample quotations, followed by an account of the sorts of historical readings that are likely to be brought to these texts. First, the examples:

> It may be trite to say that a free and independent legal system is a fundamental right in a free and democratic state. The dual components of any legal system are an independent judiciary and an independent bar. Without both, a legal system is not free, but is merely an agency designed to do the will of the state.[54]

> It is to an independent legal profession that a citizen must look to address his or her grievances against the state or to protect his or her interests from excessive, unlawful or improper interference by the state. Therefore it is surely a fundamental public right to have access to a truly independent bar for those purposes.[55]

> The legal profession has a unique position in the community. The distinguishing feature is that alone among the professions it is concerned with protecting the personal and property rights of citizens from whatever quarter they may be threatened and pre-eminently against the threat of encroachment by the state. The protection of rights has been an historic function of the law and it is the responsibility of lawyers to carry out that function.[56]

> Stress was rightly laid on the high value that free societies have placed historically on an independent judiciary, free of political influence on its decisions, and an independent bar, free to represent citizens without fear or favour in the protection of individual rights and civil liberties against incursion from any source, including the state.[57]

> The necessity of the independence of the judiciary is well recognized. The significance of the independence of the profession is often not fully understood. The profession is the source and training ground of the judiciary.[58]

> This historical review has established that ... independence of the Bar is necessary to the independence of the Bench and to the freedom for the individual citizens ... Unless there is strong reason for change a structure which has evolved over centuries and which is working well should not be interfered with.[59]

> Since in a free and democratic society the legal profession stands between the government and the individual, it is important that the governing body of the legal profession remain totally independent of government.[60]

> It is recognized that an independent legal profession is essential to a democratic society. The Chief Justice of the Trial Division of the Supreme Court of Newfoundland, in addressing newly admitted members of the Bar has stated that:
>
> > "Officers of the Court assume a very solemn obligation to defend the independence of the judiciary at all times and when appearing as barristers, to follow the standard of ethical conduct which prevails amongst practising lawyers in this Province. Hand in glove with the independence of the judiciary goes the independence of the Bar. It therefore follows that the constitutional protection which guarantees the independence of the judiciary applies with equal certainty to the independence of the legal profession."
>
> Lawyers have been viewed as standing between the government and private citizens who are directly impacted by the laws and regulations of government. Unless lawyers are completely independent of government, they cannot objectively interpret the laws and represent citizens in their interactions or conflicts with the laws and the government.[61]

> The legal profession has historically been given self-governing status because of society's belief that a lawyer cannot serve two masters. A lawyer who represents a client must have one allegiance and only one: the client's best interests. A lawyer who is accountable to government for his or her actions would inevitably let that relationship colour the handling of the client's affairs. It is a hopeless case of conflicting interests, and the loser is the client ... graphic examples from totalitarian countries ... Our legal system has always guaranteed the independence of the legal profession, not for the benefit of lawyers, but for the benefit of their clients ... the importance of the rule of law in a free and democratic society.[62]

Such passages will, of course, be understood in many different ways by different types of readers. Let us assume, however, that they are directed to a reader from the common law provinces of Canada who has had some direct or indirect exposure to British constitutional history *as that subject was popularly understood in early- to mid-twentieth-century Anglo-Canada* (I am thinking of individuals whose primary exposure to history would be through potted high school versions or their equivalent) and who is complacent about or reasonably content with the current state of social, political, and economic affairs in Canada – someone, in other words, very like Anglo-Canada's political and legal elite: white, Anglo-Saxon, Protestant or agnostic, middle-aged, middle-class, and, perhaps, male. The interpretive "grid" that overlies everything such a person reads involves a number of assumptions or working hypotheses about the way the world works and about what history has to say about human society.

His or her "pop" sociology and history might well be founded in the belief that there is no value greater than that of individual liberty (which might be valued either as a moral end in itself or because individual liberty is thought to promote economic, scientific, or moral advance). Happily, our hypothesized reader has concluded that no country is more "free" (or at least not substantially more free) than Canada. We are fortunate to have attained, through a lengthy historical process of evolution, a unique combination of liberty and political stability. Canadians, our reader concludes, are heirs to a *peculiarly* British tradition of liberties that can be traced back at least as far as the Magna Carta. Over the centuries, an evolving British constitutionalism has seen the displacement of monarchical power by "democracy." This has happened, our reader thinks, without descent into the "lawlessness" that so many other countries have experienced, when "mobs" have taken control through violent revolution (at this point, looking askance across the English Channel and recalling with horror 1789). The "magic key," the "genius of the English people" is found in the peculiarly British notion of the "rule of law" that has developed over centuries to protect us from the pretensions of monarchs and the excesses of mobs alike. Under the "rule of law," the courts have been crucially important forums for the protection of liberties. In order for them to fill this role, it has been of the utmost constitutional importance that English practice has established both the independence of the judiciary from the legislative and executive branches of government and the independence of the legal profession. As a result, Canadians are heirs and successors to a series of privileges and freedoms that together constitute the much celebrated "Englishman's birthright." These include security of property,

> freedom from foreign domination ... Freedom from absolutism (the constitutional monarchy), freedom from arbitrary arrest, trial by jury, equality before the law, the freedom of the home from arbitrary entrance and search, some limited liberty of thought, of speech, and of conscience, the vicarious

> participation in liberty ... afforded by the right of a parliamentary opposition and by elections ... as well as freedom to travel, trade, and sell one's own labour.[63]

Taken together, "the rule of law was the distinguishing inheritance of the 'freeborn Englishman', and was his defence against arbitrary power."[64] The bloodless "Glorious Revolution" of 1688 has an important place in this cultural tradition, not as a bold embrace of the future but as a restoration of ancient rights.[65]

If anything even vaguely resembling this sort of historic consciousness can be presumed on the part of the readership of Canadian professional apologetics, it is apparent that an encoded history is all-pervasive in the informational pamphlets, informal statements, and considered arguments produced by lawyers' organizations in Canada. While the "British liberties" theme occasionally touches down with concrete historical reference (to Magna Carta or to 1688), for the most part encoded histories register in popular consciousness only through knowledge that the heirs to British constitutionalism are the most free peoples in the world. The repeated references to England take on a heightened poignancy here. British tradition is invoked not merely as the imperial source of our institutions but also because England constitutes a conceptual apex of liberties – a sort of endpoint of history: more free, more stable, more developed, more pristine than any other human society at any other time or place (except, perhaps, us now). The tradition invoked is white, not red; occidental, not oriental; free, not absolutist; European, not African; and, importantly, English, not French.

In celebration of British achievement, multiple "others" are constructed as unenlightened, illogical, inferior, or simply dangerous. "British liberties" always evokes in the reader memories of a dangerous counter-example – the reader, however, being left to fill in the blank on his or her own, as it were. The genius of Alfred Hitchcock and professional apologists alike lies in consistently acting upon the knowledge that an audience can be more effectively terrorized by suggestion than by graphic, detailed, hysterical portrayal. Thus, for example, simple and seemingly straightforward assertions to the effect that without an "independent bar" the entire legal system is transformed into an instrument of the state[66] does not merely communicate a political belief but also conjures up ghosts of oppressive states throughout history. Depending on the reader, the image that moves to the foreground may be that of Stalin, Castro, Hitler, Mussolini, Idi Amin, the Pope, George III, Louis XIV, Saddam Hussein, Napoleon, Chairman Mao, Richard Nixon, Augusto Pinochet, or Charles II.[67]

All of these – and many more – lurk in the background for our supposed reader. Rather than appearing as weakness, the imprecision of encoded historical reference is a source of great power: presumed alternative histories are called to mind instantly and in infinite variation. Like Orwell's terrifying "room 101," professional myth intimidates through confident knowledge that "[t]he worst thing in the world varies from individual to individual."[68] But for an independent bar, Canada might not have escaped any number of unnamed horrors of despotism and revolution.

The implication that the present set of institutional arrangements in Canada is both the logical endpoint of developments within a long tradition of "British liberties" *and* that this tradition is better than any developed by lesser peoples, including those south of the forty-ninth parallel,[69] is irresistible. Many of the statements reproduced above encode historical narratives of just this sort, and several of these have entered into the emergent canon of professional utterances on these matters.[70] Inferentially, of course, critics of the status quo have chosen to side with Stalin, Hitler, and Charles II or else are simply too uninformed to know any better.

Although at least two law societies have explicitly raised the spectre of "graphic examples from totalitarian countries,"[71] it is, on the whole, unnecessary to do so. Simply reminding the reader that Canada is a "free and democratic society" and that the legal profession in this country is organized in a certain way is sufficient to call forth a whole range of such associations. When some, such as Mr. Justice Estey, imply that a free legal profession is the principal bulwark protecting us from unspeakable horrors ("in a free society ... [there is] no area more sensitive than the independence ... of the members of the bar"[72]), they render explicit only a portion of the meanings found in "history encoded."[73]

The Myth in Aggregate

It is, I hope, apparent from the above that "histories" of both the "in-your-face" and "encoded" varieties pervade professional apologetics in Canada. A very large portion of such literature is dedicated to one form or another of historical assertion rather than contemporary policy argumentation. Indeed, it can be said with very little fear of contradiction that such "policy" arguments as appear in these writings are so coloured by encoded histories as to amount to little more than historical myth in disguise.

Many features of the generalized historical "myth" as it appears in common law Canada will be apparent from the passages that have been quoted or described above. A sort of aggregate myth emerges that can be compared with what historians of the legal profession have been finding in Canada and elsewhere. In summary, the historical portrait that Canadian legal professions draw of themselves looks something like this:

1 A centuries-old English tradition requires that lawyers be governed by a body of other lawyers organized, as it happens, much in the fashion of any Canadian law society.[74] In this respect, Canadian lawyers are heirs to the amalgamated traditions of all English legal professions. In particular, we are heirs to the combined traditions of the English Bar and the solicitors' profession, there being no distinction of importance between these two traditions.
2 Despite the existence of statutes that *appear* to have created the possibility of self-governing legal professions (1885 or 1907 in Alberta; 1797 or 1822 in Ontario), the true origins of independent legal professions in Alberta and Ontario are to be found in private institutions in England in early times. There is a direct (though unexplained) continuity from ancient English institutions *that were not created by the state* through to modern Canadian law societies.[75]
3 The contemporary law society in British Columbia dates from 1884 and has since then enjoyed "full authority over lawyers and the practice of law in the province."[76] The Ontario law society, first recognized by Imperial statute in 1787, has had full power and authority to "discipline" lawyers in the jurisdiction since that time.[77] Canadian law societies routinely claim continuity of corporate existence since at least the time of their originating statute notwithstanding significant changes in the legislative framework of law society practice since that time.
4 Because the law societies originate not in statute but in private bodies in the distant past in England, they are not "public" bodies. They do not, therefore, exercise public power.[78]
5 Law societies have been given "self-governing status" in order to protect lawyers – and hence, their clients – from control by "the state."[79] The state is the most fundamental and pervasive threat to individual rights and liberties; the historic and unique responsibility of lawyers is to protect "rights" (principally, one presumes, against encroachment by the state).[80]
6 Freedom, democracy, and the "rule of law" rest on the independence of lawyers from state control.[81] In some formulations, the need for independence is not expressed in relation to the state only: "It has long been recognized that lawyers must be independent of external influence and pressure if they are to carry out their responsibilities properly."[82] In one formulation:

"It is the process of independent advocacy in individual cases ... that has raised us up from slavery."[83]

7 Constitutional governance *requires* the existence of a self-governing, organized legal profession.[84] A "lawyer's right to practice and to earn a living" must rest "in the hands of his or her professional association."[85] The source of authority for this constitutional arrangement is unclear but is variously associated with the Glorious Revolution,[86] mysterious developments in England in the fourteenth century,[87] or unnamed historical tradition.

8 An independent judiciary cannot exist without an independent bar.[88]

9 The independence of the legal profession is, for practical purposes, indistinguishable from the question of self-governance. "Self-governance" serves to ensure the independence of lawyers.[89]

10 The legal profession has, in the public interest, "over many years, developed a comprehensive code of ethical standards that its members must follow."[90]

11 The governing bodies of the legal profession have historically acted to protect the public interest.[91]

12 Professional rhetoric routinely elides the legal profession and the legal system as a whole, as in the Law Society of Alberta's assertion that "a mechanism or a policy for government interference or influence on the affairs of a self-governing legal system is an unjustified and unnecessary encroachment."[92]

We have here several of the key elements of myth identified earlier in this chapter. Lawyers' professional discourses provide an account of the "origins and identity ... of a group" (the legal profession originates in England in ancient time); the myth provides "the basis for claiming ... a superiority for the group" (the legal profession is unique in protecting the rights of subjects); the point of origin is rendered sacred, transcendent (the continuity between twentieth-century Canada and thirteenth-century England) beyond profane experience (which, knowing no better, would seek "origins" only in provincial originating statutes). The frequency with which mythic origins are invoked in contemporary professional discourses well illustrates that, for lawyers, myth provides "guidance and orientation to a reality which is perceived and lived through myth."

Policy Implications of Myth

Importantly, professional myth "sets the limits of the world, of what can be meant and done" in many ways and in all aspects of professional life. Any number of proposals with regard to the regulation of the legal profession have, in recent years, been said to contravene historically derived principles. These have included proposals for:

- any "transfer of regulation-making authority to the Lieutenant Governor in Council"[93] [including] "the authority of the Lieutenant Governor in Council to approve, amend, or enact regulations governing the day to day affairs of the legal profession"[94]
- an "increase of Lay Benchers to one-third of the total Benchers" [i.e., five] in Newfoundland[95] or any increase in the number of Lay Benchers above two in Alberta[96]
- the appointment of Lay Benchers by the Lieutenant-Governor-in-Council[97]
- "including Lay Benchers on discipline hearing panels"[98]
- abolishing the practice of naming "the Attorney-General [or the Registrar of the Supreme Court] as a bencher by virtue of Office"[99]
- allowing direct appeal of decisions of disciplinary adjudication panels to the Court of Appeal, rather than through intermediate internal appeal to the Benchers as a whole[100]
- granting complainants a right to appeal law society disciplinary decisions to the courts[101]
- enacting legislation to establish a structure of regulation respecting contingency fees[102]
- assigning responsibility for the oversight of the legal profession to any minister of the Crown other than the Attorney-General[103]
- holding counsel responsible for their undertakings regarding the allocation of court time (in this case a direction by the Court of Appeal of Alberta "that all counsel remain strictly within their estimated times for argument or face a personal penalty of costs associated with any resulting adjournments of any other appeals which had been set for consideration"[104])
- the adoption of a mechanism whereby the membership of the law society at large would participate directly in the approval of rules and regulations governing the profession[105]
- any narrowing of the protection of lawyers' economic monopoly provided under so-called "unauthorized practice" provisions[106]
- review of the law society by the provincial Ombudsman[107]
- the creation of a public defender system[108]
- an increase in court fees[109]
- the creation of any "central government bureaucracy, department or commission to oversee the legal profession and significantly alter the current form of self-government for lawyers"[110]

- the creation of "judicial conduct committees" or the development of a "written code of judicial conduct" – said to be an American "horror story."[111]

All of this is heavy duty for professional myth. Let us now probe the adequacy of our myths as measured against the standard of historical research.

Professional Historians' Fallacies

Unfortunately, the ways in which history is used in contemporary Canadian lawyers' apologetics fail miserably whether evaluated by the standards of logic governing historical research or by the substantive historical findings reported in published scholarship relating to the history of the legal professions.

One of the most striking features of professional myth in Canada is the way in which "historical" accounts of the origins of the contemporary structures of regulation in Canada are offered in place of rigorous policy analysis. David Hackett Fischer, author of the influential book *Historians' Fallacies,* explains this as one of several "fallacies of narration":

> The genetic fallacy mistakes the becoming of a thing for the thing which it has become. In other words, it is the erroneous idea that "an actual history of any science, art, or social institution can take the place of a [nontemporal] logical analysis of its structure."
>
> The most hateful forms of the genetic fallacy are those which convert a temporal sequence into an ethical system – history into morality. This pernicious error was embedded in a movement called historicism, which flourished in Germany during the period 1790–1930 ... Historicism was many things to many people, but in a general way its epistemology was idealist, its politics were antidemocratic, its aesthetics were romantic, and its ethics were organized around the nasty idea that whatever is becoming, is right.[112]

The "genetic fallacy" pervades Canadian lawyers' apologetics. It is perhaps the single most important failing of what passes for analysis in contemporary legal writing.

Beyond this, most of Fischer's "fallacies of narration" appear with some frequency in Canadian lawyers' apologetics. Time and space preclude a full development or illustration of these. For present purposes, suffice it to note that professional apologetics is chock-full of errors in historical logic, including *fallacies of anachronism*[113] and of *presentism*[114] in all its mutations[115] (including the very crudest form of "Whig" history),[116] the *antiquarian fallacy,*[117] the *fallacies of tunnel history*[118] and *false periodization,*[119] the *telescopic fallacy,*[120] the *interminable fallacy,*[121] the *fallacy of archetypes,*[122] the *static fallacy,*[123] the *fallacy of presumptive continuity,*[124] and, especially, the *didactic fallacy.*[125]

Being lawyers, professional apologists are peculiarly susceptible to the logical error of "argument *ad verecundiam,*"[126] which involves reliance on authority rather than logic to bludgeon into submission those who may hold opposing views. Argument *ad verecundiam* appears in most of its possible forms in contemporary professional apologetics: "never use a little word when a big one will do";[127] padding "a lean thesis with fat footnotes which are irrelevant, or superfluous";[128] "the use of quotations ... employed for forensic rather than empirical purposes";[129] and the excessive reliance on "the authority of the printed page," involving a tendency to believe anything found in written form.[130]

For fear of falling myself into the error of argument *ad verecundiam* – by sustaining "a thesis ... by the length of its exposition"[131] – I will decline the opportunity to engage in any detailed measurement of our apologetic literatures against the standards of historical logic. In general, canonical statements are most suspect in this regard – a coincidence that taints the entire project. These literatures lapse into teleological functionalism and perpetuate myths as to continuity with an ancient English tradition as well as myths as to what that tradition involves. They "translate" eighteenth-century statutes into a language of democracy and individual right. Though pleasing to contemporary sensibilities, this strategy is misleading in the extreme for the "translation" involves the major historical gaffe of conflating eighteenth-century constitutionalism with late-twentieth-century democracy.[132]

Canonical statements are also rife with the linking of ideas that obscure historical experience while purporting to reflect it. One example developed from a passage widely cited in professional apologetics will suffice for illustration and will also provide a point of connection with the next portion of this chapter, which provides a narrative of what historical research concerning the legal profession has to say to us.

> The independence of the Bar from the state in all its pervasive manifestations is one of the hallmarks of a free society. Consequently, regulation of these members of the law profession by the state must, so far as by human ingenuity it can be so designed, be free from state interference ... The public interest in a free society knows no area more sensitive than the independence, impartiality and availability to the general public of the members of the Bar and through these members, legal advice and services generally. The uniqueness of position of the barrister and solicitor in the community may well have led the province to select self-administration as the mode for administrative

> control over the supply of legal services throughout the community. Having said all that, it must be remembered that the assignment of administrative control to the field of self-administration by the profession is subject to such important protective restraints as the taxation officer, the appeal to the courts from action by the Benchers, the presence of the Attorney General as an ex-officio member of the Benchers and the legislative need of some or all of the authority granted to the Law Society.[133]

It is easy to allow a passage such as this to wash over us without much critical assessment. It sounds so fine, so logical, so necessary. In fact, however, the passage consists of one unexplained logical leap piled upon another. It deconstructs itself completely on what is called a "literal" reading of the text and disintegrates entirely when the actual historical record of the legal professions in the common law world is juxtaposed with assumed historical trajectories.

At the most elementary level, it should be jarring to any critical reader to be told in one sentence that "x" or "y" or "z" must, for tremendously important political reasons, be insulated from state interference, only to read, just three sentences later, a celebration of the direct participation of a member of cabinet (the Attorney-General) *and* of the legislature in that very sphere of activity. The fact that, as lawyers, we do not notice this should be a source of great embarrassment to us.

So too should the leaps of logic involved in simultaneously celebrating the virtues of an "independent" barristers' profession *and* the creation of a governing body with extensive powers of rule making and punishment. A bare dictionary definition reveals "independent" to mean "not depending on authority,"[134] yet the statutory creation of governing bodies that exist only to subject barristers to the authority of a political structure (albeit one not directly part of the "state") is celebrated as mysteriously enhancing rather than infringing upon the independence of barristers. The fact that it is probably very difficult for most modern Canadian lawyers to even perceive a logical flaw here only shows how entirely captive we are to a particular mentality. This was not always the case. In England throughout the nineteenth century, it was widely thought that in order for *barristers* to provide the political benefits associated with an independent legal profession, they would need to be independent *from the organized bar,* not just from the state.[135] That this is not widely known is testimony to the powerful silencing capability of "winners' history" in the professional realm.

My reference to English practice in the nineteenth century is not, in this context, merely the conditioned reflex of a colonial suffering a severe case of cultural cringe. *Our* legal professions widely celebrate the English inheritance without knowing what it is we supposedly inherited. In a third compression of historical experience, Estey J. confused the histories and functions of two quite distinct English legal professions, treating the barristers' and solicitors' professions as indistinguishable antecedents to the contemporary unified legal profession in Anglo-Canada. The leap in logic and in history is accomplished in a short space, only two sentences separating the idea that an independent *bar* is "one of the hallmarks of a free society" and the quite distinct emphasis on the "uniqueness of position of the barrister *and solicitor.*" Earlier generations of Canadian lawyers well understood that "the legal profession in Canada is made up of two distinct professions with different duties, different responsibilities and liabilities, different history and traditions, and subject to different rules."[136] But our real historical memory is short.

No student of the history of English lawyers would ever confuse the professions of barrister and solicitor in this way. To this day, those professions remain distinct. They perform different functions, are qualified through different professional structures, and have emerged through different historical trajectories. There may indeed be good reason to seek to enhance or to celebrate the "independence" of an advocates' profession. With the possible *exception* of the English profession,[137] it may be the case that an active advocates' profession has in fact done much to advance the development of political or economic liberalism[138] through speech and actions in the courtroom. It takes a peculiarly rose-tinted view of the world to find such heroism in the mundane world of solicitors' transactions, past or present. There is a tremendous leap of faith involved in arguing from the standpoint of a political appreciation of the independence of advocates for a regulatory regime that subjects both advocate and professional form-filler to the same regulatory regimen. In Canada, barristers and solicitors become one. That one, it seems, is the barrister.

The same sentence that produces this elision of distinct professions also provides us with a historical fiction that stands in place of historical inquiry. It is simply assumed that "the province" appreciated the "uniqueness" of our biune legal profession and therefore opted to create a system of "self-administration." This assumed history suppresses the reality of conflict, disagreement, and negotiation that has accompanied many changes in the structures of legal professionalism in Canada. It obliterates human agency or self-interest altogether, foreclosing rather than opening up historical inquiry. Like so much of professional apologetics, it denies history by assuming that what is has always been: it is presumed that nothing significant has happened in professional organization or structure or politics since long-gone days when "self-governance" emerged, fully formed. Such assumptions are the antithesis of the historical imagination.

Historians of Lawyers

Not all accounts of the legal profession in history are distorted to the same extent by the pressing day-to-day concerns of contemporary institutions. While it is regrettable that more primary historical research on the history of the organized legal profession is not under way, it is much more seriously a matter of regret that contemporary professional apologetics is produced in apparent ignorance of the scholarly work that is available. Many fine historians have addressed aspects of the history of the legal profession in Canada, the United States, Australia, and the United Kingdom.

It would be rash – indeed, ahistorical – to attempt to construct any singular storyline from these disparate literatures, dealing as they do with many professional bodies on three continents over four centuries. Nonetheless, at least three important points sit uneasily with history-as-Canadian-lawyers-would-like-it-to-be.

First, scholarly histories of common law legal professions point to the novelty rather than the antiquity of many contemporary professional structures, reflecting, as Eric Hobsbawm would have it, the fact that "'[t]raditions' which appear or claim to be old are often quite recent in origin and sometimes invented."[139] Because of the extraordinary reliance placed on appeals to "history" in (Anglo-Canadian) professional apologetics, this simple observation may have far-reaching implications. Far from having existed since time immemorial, each of the hallmarks of modern Canadian legal professionalism, as that concept is now understood by lawyers' governing bodies, is of relatively recent origin: monopoly, education, disciplinary powers, codes of ethics. What is more, the modern web of professionalism did not even emerge "naturally" from the irresistible though pure urges of colonial lawyers in British North America to emulate an Imperial model. It is rather the product of their deliberate attempt to create a new professionalism peculiarly suited to the needs of a twentieth-century North American state, and is heavily influenced from south of the border.[140] Leaders of the British legal professions all opposed the development of a professional ethical code when Winnipeg lawyers spearheaded that initiative in 1919.[141] The Law Society of England and Wales has never had the sorts of powers that Canadian law societies now take for granted,[142] while the English Bar, regardless of what the Law Society of Upper Canada may have said in 1833 or in 1979, did not even *begin* to develop into a disciplinary institution until the mid-nineteenth century![143]

A second point that emerges from the scholarly literature is that the legal profession has not always been as single-minded and pure of heart in the pursuit of the public interest as the law societies across Canada would have us believe. Very powerful arguments have been made to the effect that lawyers have used their professional organizations first and foremost to advance their own collective economic interest rather than the public interest at large.[144] For very many reasons, I think this is an unhelpful oversimplification, perhaps even an entirely misleading formulation.[145] Nonetheless, if one is committed to the workings of the free market (as most of the leaders of Canadian legal professions would claim to be), the institutions of the legal profession and the histories of many types of interference with free market principles, including freedom of contract, the suppression of economic competitors, restrictions on entry, and so on, do, to say the least, seem problematic. Certainly, Canadian legal professions have often been slow off the mark (generally responding only to great public pressure) to introduce many of the measures of public protection that contemporary law society leaders celebrate.[146]

Third, the history of the organized legal professions in Canada, England, and the United States reveals that lawyers have not always virtuously sought to advance the cause of liberty, democracy, and the Canadian way. Professional organizations would be pleased to project the image that they stand somehow apart from politics. They do not. All organizations have their own internal politics – "office politics," if you will. Moreover, the people who staff and set policy for organizations of all sorts have their own politics, values, opinions. These are not, cannot be, left outside the law society door. The politics that organized legal professions have in fact advanced has not always been liberative. In Canada, it is notorious that the British Columbia law society participated in a McCarthyite suppression of democratic communists after the Second World War,[147] while Auerbach has documented a pervasive racism, anti-Semitism, and class bias in the early "American Bar Association."[148] The early-nineteenth-century English Bar conspired to preclude the admission of individuals of democratic principle – and was roundly criticized for this in the first Reform Parliament.[149] In fact, there is no well-documented case of an exercise of disciplinary powers against a barrister by the English Inns of Court during at least the first two-thirds of the nineteenth century that is entirely free from the taint of political suppression.[150] Auerbach, Horwitz, and Foster have all described an American legal profession captive to large corporate interests.[151] Backhouse paints a rather unflattering picture of active opposition to equality for women within the Ontario legal profession.[152] We do not know exactly how or why a code of professional ethics was first developed in Canada, but we do know that it emerged from a professional culture that was xenophobic, elitist, and generally aligned with powerful interests.[153] Far from advancing a liberal notion of advocacy – now all the rage within our governing bodies – the original Canadian Bar Association code of ethics was heavy on duties to "the State" and *very* light on the theme of vigorous advocacy on behalf of the client.[154] It is distinctly possible that Canadian lawyers in the early twentieth century developed their profession wholly or partially in order to *constrain* a democracy that they found frightening.[155]

Lawyers' Histories: England, United States, Canada – Who Cares?

I do not offer these observations as an objective or complete "truth," only as a partial corrective to some of the worst excesses of professional myth as it is propagated in Canada.

Bridging the gap between historical research and professional rhetoric is essential if we are to develop a perspective on the legal profession, its history, and its role in contemporary Canadian society capable of transcending Frye's "cliché and prejudice and stock response."[156] All too often what is presented as "professional" history is merely a melange of assumptions or guesses as to what the history of the legal profession might look like in England or Canada or the United States, far too casually backed up even with reference to existing secondary literatures, much less by credible primary research.

There is reason for optimism, to be sure. Whatever the failings of comprehension made manifest in their writings, it is encouraging that professional organizations recognize the importance of the history of the legal profession to contemporary practice. Canadian legal professions have generally taken steps to preserve their written records for future generations. Many Canadian law schools now have at least one legal historian on faculty, as do a number of university history faculties. Still, the history of the legal profession lives most vibrantly in contemporary apologetics. It is crucially important that we constantly seek to produce better history and, in so doing, better "myth."

Notes

An earlier version of this chapter appeared as "In Pursuit of Better Myth: Lawyers' Histories and Histories of Lawyers" (1994-95) 33 Alta. L. Rev. 730. It has been revised and reprinted here with permission.

1 J. de P. Wright, "The Value of Tradition" (1991) 25 L. Soc. Gaz. 441 at 441.

2 E. Hobsbawm, "Introduction: Inventing Traditions" in E. Hobsbawm and T. Ranger, eds., *The Invention of Tradition* (Cambridge: Cambridge University Press, 1983) 1 at 13. On the problematic use of historical modes of arguments and justifications in legal practice, see R.W. Gordon "The Struggle over the Past" (1996) 44 Clev. St. L. Rev. 123, and "The Past as Authority and as Social Critic: Stabilizing and Destabilizing Functions of History in Legal

Argument" in T.J. McDonald, ed., *The Historic Turn in the Human Sciences* (Ann Arbor: University of Michigan Press, 1996). *Cf.* Bruce Granville Miller, *Oral History on Trial: Recognizing Aboriginal Narratives in the Courts* (Vancouver: UBC Press, 2011).

3 G. Santayana, *The Life of Reason; Reason in Common Sense* (New York: Charles Scribner's Sons, 1905) at 284: "Those who cannot remember the past are condemned to repeat it."

4 N. Frye, "The Rear-View Mirror: Notes Toward a Future" in N. Frye, *Divisions on a Ground: Essays on Canadian Culture* (Toronto: Anansi, 1982) 181 at 183 (edited, with a preface, by James Polk).

5 *Ibid.* at 185.

6 *Ibid.* Dworkin's much-celebrated account of how judges make law in common law systems shares much with Frye's account of literature. See R. Dworkin, *Law's Empire* (Cambridge, MA: Harvard University Press, 1986).

7 Frye, *ibid.*

8 P. Fitzpatrick, *The Mythology of Modern Law* (London: Routledge, 1992).

9 *Ibid.* at 13.

10 *Ibid.* at 15-16.

11 So as to avoid causing offence, I emphasize that I employ this term in a sense parallel to that in which one would speak of "Christian apologetics" – connoting "argumentative defence" or "justification" rather than "excuse."

12 Law Society of Yukon; Law Society of Northwest Territories; Federation of Law Societies of Canada; Law Society of British Columbia; Law Society of Alberta; Law Society of Saskatchewan; Law Society of Manitoba; Law Society of Upper Canada; Barreau du Québec; Chambre de Notaires du Québec; Law Society of New Brunswick; Nova Scotia Barrister's Society; Law Society of Prince Edward Island; Law Society of Newfoundland; Canadian Bar Association.

13 Law Society of Yukon; Law Society of Northwest Territories; Law Society of New Brunswick; Law Society of Prince Edward Island.

14 Letter of D.I. Pink to W.W. Pue (28 April 1994).

15 Law Society of Saskatchewan and Canadian Bar Association (Saskatchewan Branch), "The Self Governing Profession. An Introduction to the Functions and Responsibilities of The Law Society of Saskatchewan and the Canadian Bar Association" (pamphlet) ["The Self Governing Profession"]; Law Society of Saskatchewan, "Lawyer Referral Service" (pamphlet); Law Society of Saskatchewan, "Seniors Legal Assistance Service" (pamphlet); Law Society of Saskatchewan, "Understanding Your Lawyer's Fee" (pamphlet).

16 Law Society of Newfoundland, *Brief to the Minister of Justice The Honourable Mr. Edward Roberts, Q.C. Submitted by: The Law Society of Newfoundland Re: Bill 55 – An Act to Amend the Law Society Act* (May 1993) [*Brief to the Minister – Newfoundland*].

17 B.R. Ralph, "Law Societies – Can They Meet the Need of the Public? A Canadian Point of View" (April 1993) [unpublished]; Law Society of British Columbia, *Briefings: The Law Society of British Columbia* (March 1994) [*Briefings*].

18 Law Society of Manitoba, *Submission of the Law Society of Manitoba in Response to the Law Reform Commission of Manitoba Discussion Paper on the Future of Occupational Regulation in Manitoba* (March 1994) [*Manitoba Response*].

19 Law Society of Alberta, *Report of the Futures Committee* (Calgary).

20 T.F. McMahon, "The Importance of Self-Governance" (1991) 6 Benchers' Advisory 1.

21 Council on Professions and Occupations, Government of Alberta, *Principles and Policies Governing Professional Legislation in Alberta* (Edmonton: Queen's Printers, 1990) [*Professions and Occupations*]; Law Society of Alberta (D.G. Bishop), *Submission by the Law Society of Alberta to the Council on Professions and Occupations Regarding Discussion Paper: Principles and Policies Governing Professional Legislation in Alberta* (January 1990) [Bishop Submission].

22 See, for example, W.W. Pue, "Death Squads and 'Directions over Lunch': A Comparative Review of the Independence of the Bar" in Lorne Sossin, ed., *In the Public Interest: The Report and Research Papers of the Law Society's Task Force on the Rule of Law and the Independence of the Bar* (Toronto: Irwin Law, 2007).

23 *Briefings, supra* note 17 at 1.

24 *Ibid.* at 3.

25 Bishop Submission, *supra* note 21 at 8-9. Following this astonishing historical assertion, the document lapses into an entirely unintelligible discussion of differences between "self-regulatory" organizations and "delegated regulatory" organizations.

26 *Manitoba Response, supra* note 18 at 3.

27 "The Self Governing Profession," *supra* note 15 at 1.

28 Nova Scotia Barristers' Society, "The Objects of the Society" (Halifax: Nova Scotia Barristers' Society, 1993) 3 (draft "objects clause").

29 *Brief to the Minister – Newfoundland, supra* note 16 at 6.

30 Subcommittee on the Role of the Law Society, *Proposed Role Statement* (draft) (Toronto: Law Society of Upper Canada, November 1993).

31 Law Society of Upper Canada, *Presentation to the Standing Committee on the Ombudsman* (November 1992) [*Ombudsman*] at 2-3.

32 *Ibid.* at 8-9.

33 Law Society of Upper Canada, *Submission to the Professional Organizations Committee by the Law Society of Upper Canada* (Toronto: Law Society of Upper Canada, April 1979) [*Submission to Professional Organizations Committee*] at 1-2.

34 *Ibid.* at 3 (subsequently cited in *Ombudsman, supra* note 31, and *Proposed Role Statement, supra* note 30; and paraphrased without attribution in Bishop Submission, *supra* note 21).

35 *Submission to Professional Organizations Committee, ibid.* at 3 (subsequently cited in *Ombudsman, supra* note 31 at 12).

36 *Submission to Professional Organizations Committee, ibid.* at 3-8.

37 *Ibid.* at 3.

38 *Ibid.* at 4-5.

39 *Ibid.* at 5.

40 *Ibid.* at 7-8. It is noteworthy that the history of "the bar" is here misadapted to apply to a contemporary profession composed largely of individuals doing work of sorts not traditionally associated with the barrister's profession.

41 J.M. Spence, "Independence of the Legal System in Canada: The Judiciary and the Legal Profession" (Address to the Federation of Law Societies of Canada/Fédération des professions juridiques du Canada, 21 August 1992) [Spence Address] at 2-5.

42 *Ibid.* at 8.

43 *Ibid.* at 7 (the same point is made in different words, *ibid.* at 5).

44 M. Valverde, *The Age of Light, Soap, and Water: Moral Reform in English Canada, 1885-1925* (Toronto: McClelland and Stewart, 1991) at 10.

45 *Ibid.* at 13.

46 *Ibid.* at 34.

47 *Ibid.* at 41.

48 *Ibid.* at 43. For a recent defence and application of the hermeneutic tradition in another context, see S. Cornell, "Moving Beyond the Canon of Traditional Constitutional History: Anti-Federalists, the Bill of Rights, and the Promise of Post-Modern Historiography" (1994) 12 L. & Hist. Rev. 1.

49 *E.g.*, E.W. Said, *Orientalism* (New York: Vintage, 1978).

50 *E.g.*, Valverde, *supra* note 44.

51 L. Grossberg, C. Nelson, and P. Treichler, eds., *Cultural Studies* (New York: Routledge, 1992); S. During, ed., *The Cultural Studies Reader* (London: Routledge, 1993). A model study of

the interaction of text, image, and audience is found in J. D'Acci, *Defining Women: Television and the Case of Cagney & Lacey* (Charlotte: University of North Carolina Press, 1994), especially in c. 5, "Female/Feminine/Feminist Audiences, Spectators, and Readings," at 168-203.

52 R. Shields, *Places on the Margin: Alternative Geographies of Modernity* (London: Routledge, 1991). See also N.K. Blomley, *Law, Space, and the Geographies of Power* (New York: Guilford Press, 1994).

53 See, *e.g.*, H.L.A. Hart, *The Concept of Law* (Oxford: Clarendon Press, 1961); P. Fitzpatrick, "The Abstracts and Brief Chronicles of the Time: Supplementing Jurisprudence" in P. Fitzpatrick, ed., *Dangerous Supplements: Resistance and Renewal in Jurisprudence* (London: Pluto Press, 1991) 1; M.J. Frug, *Postmodern Legal Feminism* (London: Routledge; 1992); P. Fitzpatrick, *The Mythology of Modern Law* (London: Routledge, 1992).

54 Bishop Submission, *supra* note 21 at 2 (this passage appears almost verbatim in "The Importance of Self-Governance," *supra* note 20 at 1-2).

55 Bishop Submission, *ibid.* at 2-3 (this passage, too, appears almost verbatim in "The Importance of Self-Governance," *ibid.).*

56 *Submission to Professional Organizations Committee, supra* note 33 at 3 (cited in *Proposed Role Statement, supra* note 30, and *Ombudsman, supra* note 31 at 11, and substantially reproduced without attribution in Bishop Submission, *ibid.* at 5, and, again without attribution, in "The Importance of Self-Governance," *ibid.* at 1-2. These texts all closely follow words found in Royal Commission of Inquiry into Civil Rights, *Report Number One*, vol. 3 (Ottawa: Queen's Printer) [McRuer Commission].

57 Government of Ontario, *Report of the Professional Organizations Committee* (Ottawa: Queen's Printer, 1980) [*Report of the Professional Organizations Committee*] at 26 (cited by Iacobucci J., in *Pearlman v. Manitoba Law Society Judicial Committee* (1991), 84 D.L.R. (4th) at 118-19 [*Pearlman*]); *Brief to the Minister – Newfoundland, supra* note 16 at 8, cited in *Proposed Role Statement, ibid.* at 4, and *Ombudsman, ibid.* at 13.

58 *Submission to Professional Organizations Committee, supra* note 33 at 3 (also cited in *Ombudsman, ibid.* at 12).

59 Submission to *Professional Organizations Committee, ibid.* at 7-8.

60 *Brief to the Minister – Newfoundland, supra* note 16 at 3.

61 *Ibid.* at 6.

62 *Briefings, supra* note 17 at 1.

63 E.P. Thompson, *The Making of the English Working Class* (Harmondsworth, UK: Penguin, 1968) at 86.

64 *Ibid.* at 90. The "rule of law" is a persistent notion that should not be understood anachronistically as timelessly mapping onto the version articulated by Albert Venn Dicey in his *Introduction to the Study of the Law of the Constitution* (London: Macmillan, 1915).

65 Thompson, *The Making of the English Working Class, supra* note 63 at 94; see also G. Marquis, "In Defence of Liberty: 17th Century England and 19th Century Maritime Political Culture" (1993) 42 U.N.B.L.J. 69. See also David Dyzenhaus, "Judicial Independence, Transitional Justice and the Rule of Law" (2003) 10 Otago L. Rev. 345.

66 Bishop Submission, *supra* note 21 at 2.

67 A British Baptist's view on Charles II is provided in R.E. Cooper, *"From Stepney to St. Giles": The Story of Regent's Park College, 1810-1960* (London: Carey Kingsgate Press, 1960) at 11: "What happened became known as the Restoration. It was a restoration indeed; the restoration of a capricious monarchy, albeit at the invitation of Parliament, and a spirit of intolerance which put the clock back to the days of Charles I and Archbishop Laud. What his father lacked in wisdom, the new king supplied in cunning."

68 G. Orwell, *Nineteen Eighty-Four* (London: Penguin Books, 1975) at 227.

69 R.J. Scott, "Independence of the Legal System in Canada: the Judiciary and the Legal Profession" (Address to the Federation of Law Societies of Canada/Fédération des professions juridiques du Canada, 21 August 1992) [unpublished] [Scott Address] at 26.

70 Bishop Submission, *supra* note 21 at 2-3, 5; *Report of Professional Organizations Committee, supra* note 57 at 3, 7-8; *Brief to the Minister – Newfoundland, supra* note 16 at 3; *Briefings, supra* note 17 at 1.

71 *Briefings, ibid.* at 1. See the more subtle development of this theme by citation of international Human Rights work focusing on lawyers in *Brief to the Minister – Newfoundland, ibid.* at 9-10; see also B.F. Ralph, "Law Societies – Can They Meet the Need of the Public? A Canadian Point of View" (1993) at 12-13 [unpublished], explaining the need to educate the public as to "the importance of the independence of the legal profession" in light of "dramatic and tragic incidents" reported in Centre for the Independence of Judges and Lawyers of the International Commission of Jurists, *Attacks on Justice* (Geneva: International Commission of Jurists, 1992).

72 *British Columbia (A.-G.) v. Law Society of British Columbia,* [1982] 2 S.C.R. 307 at 336 [*A.-G. v. L.S.B.C.*].

73 A further development of these ideas would require an assessment of British views of the superiority of their structures by comparison with those across the Channel (particularly in France) or across the Atlantic in the revolutionary colonies and, inferentially, of Anglo-Canadian perceptions of Quebec. The ideas canvassed by R. Young, *White Mythologies: Writing History and the West* (London: Routledge, 1990), might well prove to be invaluable in accessing the embedded histories in professional apologetics as in other sorts of literature.

74 *Briefings, supra* note 17 at 1; *Submission to Professional Organizations Committee, supra* note 33 at 5-7.

75 Bishop Submission, *supra* note 21 at 8-9; *Submission to Professional Organizations Committee, ibid.* at 3, 5-6 (also cited in *Ombudsman, supra* note 31 at 12). James Spence partially defers to this position in asserting that "our governing bodies ... are recognized or created by statute" (Spence Address, *supra* note 41 at 8).

76 *Briefings, supra* note 17 at 1.

77 *Submission to Professional Organizations Committee, supra* note 33 at 6. Quoting the Law Society of Upper Canada's own minutes of 1833, involving the disciplinary process of "Doyle": "the power of degradation and expulsion as well as all other powers belonging to the Inns of Court in England are also by law vested in this Society." Although this in fact implies a limited and highly contested disciplinary power, this fact is not widely appreciated by Canadian law societies, which have assumed a long-standing continuity of almost unconstrained power over their members. The limited and contested disciplinary power vested in the English Inns and in nineteenth-century Canadian law societies is apparent (see Chapters 7, 8, 9, and 11 in this volume).

78 *Submission to Professional Organizations Committee, ibid.* at 4-7. This is contradicted in McRuer Commission, *supra* note 56, which asserted that "the granting of self-government is a delegation of legislative and judicial functions and can only be justified as a safeguard to the public interest" (quoted in *Proposed Role Statement, supra* note 30 at 8). See also *Regulating Professions and Occupations* (Winnipeg: Manitoba Law Reform Commission, Report No. 84, October 1994). For a historical study of the private and public dimensions of the Law Society of England and Wales, see D. Sugarman, "Bourgeois Collectivism, Professional Power and the Boundaries of the State: The Private and Public Life of the Law Society, 1825-1914" (1996) 3 International Journal of the Legal Profession 81.

Contra Bishop Submission, *supra* note 21 at 9, arguing that law societies are created by statute as "self-regulatory" organizations rather than bodies exercising "delegated" powers. No authority is cited for this proposition.

79 *Briefings, supra* note 17 at 1; Bishop Submission, *ibid.* at 2-3, 5; "The Self Governing Profession," *supra* note 15 at 1.

80 *Submission to Professional Organizations Committee, supra* note 33 at 3 (cited in turn in *Proposed Role Statement, supra* note 30, and *Ombudsman, supra* note 31 at 11; and paraphrased without attribution in Bishop Submission, *ibid.* at 5). See also *Brief to the Minister – Newfoundland, supra* note 15 at 3, 6; *Manitoba Response, supra* note 18 at 3-5.

81 *Briefings, supra* note 17 at 1; Bishop Submission, *ibid.* at 2; Estey J. in *A.-G. v. L.S.B.C., supra* note 72 (quoted in turn in Bishop Submission, *ibid.* at 40; Spence Address, *supra* note 41 at 6; *Brief to the Minister – Newfoundland, ibid.* at 6; *Report of the Professional Organizations Committee, supra* note 57 at 26, cited in turn by Iacobucci J., in *Pearlman, supra* note 57 at 118-19, and in *Brief to the Minister – Newfoundland, ibid.* at 8; and also cited in *Proposed Role Statement, ibid.* at 4; *Ombudsman, ibid.* at 13).

82 Spence Address, *ibid.* at 4. Arguing in defence of an expansive interpretation of lawyers' monopoly in the provision of "legal services," the Law Society of Upper Canada adopted the position that "an economically sound legal profession at all levels is necessary if the profession is to be in a position to retain its independence not only from government intrusion but from overreliance on a few clients and subservience to their demands" (*Submission to Professional Organizations Committee, supra* note 33 at 30).

To similar effect, Taylor argues, in M.R. Taylor, "The Independence of the Bar" (1981) 39 Advocate 209 at 216, that "[t]he bar must not only demand independence but must practice it. Members of the bar cannot afford to allow themselves to be dependent, whether on particular clients, or particular types of client, or a particular scale of remuneration. The bar must, of course, serve the public as a whole. It can do so only if individual members of the bar keep themselves free to discharge that obligation."

83 Taylor, *ibid.* at 209, as cited in Bishop Submission, *supra* note 21 at 10 [emphasis omitted].

84 Bishop Submission, *ibid.* at 8-9.

85 *Ibid.* at 2.

86 *Ibid.*; Taylor, *supra* note 82; see also W.R. Lederman, "The Independence of the Judiciary" (1956) 34 Can. Bar. Rev. 769.

87 *Submission to Professional Organizations Committee, supra* note 33 at 5: "The English Inns of Court which find their origins well back in the fourteenth century were transported from the old country to the new, with the adaptation required to meet local conditions."

88 Bishop Submission, *supra* note 21 at 2; Government of Ontario, *Report of the Professional Organizations Committee, supra* note 57 at 26. This canonical passage is cited in turn by Iacobucci J. in *Pearlman, supra* note 57 at 118-19, cited in turn in *Brief to the Minister – Newfoundland, supra* note 16 at 8; and is also cited in *Proposed Role Statement, supra* note 30 at 13; *Ombudsman, supra* note 31 at 12, 13; and *Submission to Professional Organizations Committee, supra* note 33 at 3.

89 Spence Address, *supra* note 41 at 12.

90 *Briefings, supra* note 17 at 3. In the Law Society of Saskatchewan formulation, "[t]he feature which distinguishes a profession from a trade is that a profession has, over many years, developed a comprehensive code of ethical standards to which its members ascribe" ("The Self Governing Profession," *supra* note 15 at 5).

91 Nova Scotia Barristers' Society, "The Objects of the Society," *supra* note 28 at 3.

92 Bishop Submission, *supra* note 21 at 22.

93 *Ibid.* at 12.

94 *Ibid.* at 22. It is interesting that the Ontario law society, on the other hand, expresses pride in the fact that it is "accountable" to the public through mechanisms including an arrangement in which "regulations made by the Law Society are subject to approval by the Lieutenant Governor in Council" (*Ombudsman, supra* note 31 at 18).

95 *Brief to the Minister – Newfoundland, supra* note 16 at 2, 13-14.

96 Bishop Submission, *supra* note 21 at 11.
97 *Brief to the Minister – Newfoundland, supra* note 16 at 3.
98 *Brief to the Minister – Newfoundland, Ibid.* at 16. In sharp contrast, however, the Ontario law society called for the creation of "the position of Complaints Commissioner to be appointed by a committee representative of the government, the Law Society and the public" (*Ombudsman, supra* note 31 at 21).
99 *Brief to the Minister – Newfoundland, ibid.* at 15.
100 *Ibid.* at 16-18.
101 Bishop Submission, *supra* note 21 at 12.
102 *Brief to the Minister – Newfoundland, supra* note 16 at 18-22. The logic of the Law Society of Newfoundland on this point is interesting: "To the extent that this legislation would dictate or have an effect on the conduct of litigation before the Courts, it may infringe upon the freedom of the legal profession to conduct litigation or not as appropriate. If it can be said that this legislation would so infringe upon the independence of the legal profession by virtue of the fact that lawyers are officers of the Court, it may be said to consequently infringe upon the independence of the judiciary" (*ibid.* at 21-22).
103 Bishop Submission, *supra* note 21 at 13.
104 C.B. Davison, "Letters to the Editor, Re: Court of Appeal Directive Concerning Time Estimates," Law Society of Alberta/Canadian Bar Association, Alberta Branch, Newsletter (January/February 1994) 10.
105 Bishop Submission, *supra* note 21 at 20.
106 *Ibid.* at 22.
107 *Ombudsman, supra* note 31 at 2; *Submission to Professional Organizations Committee, supra* note 33 at 10. This review mechanism is already in place in British Columbia.
108 Scott Address, *supra* note 69 at 20.
109 *Ibid.*
110 *Manitoba Response, supra* note 18 at 5.
111 Scott Address, *supra* note 69 at 22-27.
112 D.H. Fischer, *Historians' Fallacies: Toward a Logic of Historical Thought* (New York: Harper Colophon Books, 1970) at 155-56, quoting M.R. Cohen and E. Nagel, *An Introduction to Logic and the Scientific Method* (New York: Harcourt Brace, 1934) at 388-90.
113 "[T]he description, analysis, or judgment of an event as if it occurred at some point in time other than when it actually happened" (*ibid.* at 132-33).
114 "[A] complex anachronism, in which the antecedent in a narrative series is falsified by being defined or interpreted in terms of the consequent. Sometimes called the fallacy of nunc pro tunc, it is the mistaken idea that the proper way to do history is to prune away the dead branches of the past, and to preserve the green buds and twigs which have grown into the dark forest of our contemporary world" (*ibid.* at 135).
115 In one example cited by Fischer, "backward projections of present phenomena so grossly distorts the past that the reader receives an utterly erroneous idea of events in earlier periods, and of tendencies in his own as well" (*ibid.* at 136).
116 "No discussion of presentism in history can be complete without the classic example of the 'Whig interpretation of history,' which has been defined by Herbert Butterfield as the 'tendency in many historians to write on the side of Protestants and Whigs, to praise revolutions provided they have been successful, to emphasize certain principles of progress in the past and to produce a story which is the ratification if not the glorification of the present'" (*ibid.* at 139, quoting H. Butterfield, "Preface" in *The Whig Interpretation of History* [London: G. Bell and Sons, 1931]).
117 "An antiquarian is a collector of dead facts, which he stuffs full of sawdust and separately encloses in small glass cases. Often, he is a gentleman (or lady) of respectable origins who

is utterly alienated from the present. The past serves him as a sanctuary from a sordid world which he neither accepts nor understands" (Fischer, *ibid.* at 140).

118 "[I]dentified by J. H. Hexter, and so-named after the tendency of many historians to 'split the past into a series of tunnels, each continuous from the remote past to the present, but practically self-contained at every point and sealed off from contact with or contamination by anything that was going on in any of the other tunnels. At their entrances these tunnels bore signs saying diplomatic history, political history, institutional history, ecclesiastical history, intellectual history, military history, economic history, legal history, administrative history, art history, colonial history, social history, agricultural history, and so on, and so on'" (*ibid.* at 194-95).

119 "[A]ssigning inappropriate temporal limits to a historical problem" (*ibid.* at 144).

120 Which "makes a long story short. It appears in interpretations which reduce an extended trend to a momentary transformation" (*ibid.* at 147).

121 Which "makes a short story long, or a long story longer than it ought to be. It is a temporal form of a false extrapolation – a developmental trend stretched beyond the breaking point" (*ibid.* at 149-50).

122 "[C]onceptualizing change in terms of the re-enactment of primordial archetypes which exist outside of time. It is a method in which an event acquires meaning as a re-enactment of some aboriginal and atemporal model ... The myth of the return is an antithesis to time, change, and history itself. When it is used by a historian to conceptualize his subject, then it becomes a fallacy, for the myth implies that what is real does not change" (*ibid.* at 150-51).

123 "[A]ny attempt to conceptualize a dynamic problem in static terms. This form of error represents an intermediate stage of historical consciousness, in which change is perceived merely as the emergence of a nonchanging entity ... a good many liberal textbook historians of the American republic tend to conceptualize their dynamic subject in terms of the unfolding of a static idea of democratic society, which slowly reveals itself through three centuries, without ever really changing in the process. The result is a historiographical equivalent of the Dance of the Seven Veils" (*ibid.* at 153).

124 "[T]he fallacy of presumptive continuity and the fallacy of presumptive change are two fundamental forms of error which came to mind in a reading of Barrington Moore's *Social Origins of Dictatorship and Democracy.* Moore criticizes his colleagues for an assumption of social inertia in their work ... But I wonder if Moore has committed the counterfallacy of presumptive change. They are both equally indefensible" (*ibid.* at 154-55).

125 "[T]he attempt to extract specific 'lessons' from history, and to apply them literally as policies to present problems, without regard for intervening changes" (*ibid.* at 157).

126 *Ibid.* at 283.

127 *Ibid.* at 285.

128 *Ibid.* at 286.

129 *Ibid.* at 286-87.

130 *Ibid.* at 290.

131 *Ibid.* at 287.

132 For a parallel critique of a recent contribution to the history of crime in Canada, see P. Romney, Book Review of D.O. Carrigan, *Crime and Punishment in Canada – A History* (1993) 8 Can. J.L. & Soc.

133 Estey J. in *A.-G. v. L.S.B.C., supra* note 72 at 335-36 (quoted in full or in part in Bishop Submission, *supra* note 21 at 4; Spence Address, *supra* note 41 at 6; *Brief to the Minister – Newfoundland, supra* note 16 at 6-7; *Manitoba Response, supra* note 18 at 4; approved by Iacobucci J. in *Pearlman, supra* note 57 at 105).

134 H.W. Fowler and F.G. Fowler, *The Concise Oxford Dictionary of Current English,* 7th ed. (Oxford: Clarendon Press, 1983).

135 See Chapters 7, 8, and 11 in this volume; Inns of Court, *The Speech and Reply of D.W. Harvey Esq., MP, on the 14th of June, 1831, in the House of Commons* (London: James Ridgway, 1832).
136 C.J.M. Mathers, "Legal Ethics" (Address to Manitoba Bar Association, 19 May 1920) at 6 [Archive of Manitoba Legal History, Acc. No. 49.A222].
137 C. Robbins, *Eighteenth-Century Commonwealthman* (Cambridge, MA: Harvard University Press, 1959), argues that in George II's England, "Lawyers ... were protectors of tradition and contributed little to the development of liberalism in any way" (*ibid.* at 294-95). See also P. Lucas, "Collective Biography of Students and Barristers of Lincoln's Inn, 1680-1804: A Study in the 'Aristocratic Resurgence' of the Eighteenth Century" (1974) 46 J. Mod. Hist. 242.
138 L. Karpik and T. Halliday, eds., *Legal Professions and Political Liberalism* (Oxford: Oxford University Press, 1997); L. Karpik, "Lawyers and Politics in France, 1814-1950: The State, the Market, and the Public" (1988) 13 L. & Soc. lnq. 707.
139 Hobsbawm, "Introduction: Inventing Traditions," *supra* note 2 at 1.
140 For development of these arguments and a review of relevant literatures, see Chapters 5 and 9 in this volume.
141 See Chapter 9 in this volume.
142 R.L. Abel, *Legal Profession in England and Wales* (Oxford: Blackwell, 1988).
143 R. Cocks, *Foundations of the Modern Bar* (London: Sweet and Maxwell, 1983); Chapters 7, 8, and 11 in this volume. See also Abel, *ibid.*, and P. Polden, "Barristers," in W.R. Cornish et al., *The Oxford History of the Laws of England,* vol. 11, *1820-1914* (Oxford: Oxford University Press, 2010).
144 Abel, *ibid;* R.L. Abel, "The Rise of Professionalism" (1979) 6 Brit. J.L. & Soc. 82; R.L. Abel, *American Lawyers* (New York: Oxford University Press, 1989); H. Arthurs, R. Weisman, and F. Zemans, "Canadian Lawyers, a Peculiar Professionalism" in R. Abel and P. Lewis, eds., *Lawyers in Society: The Common Law World* (Berkeley: University of California Press, 1988) 123 at 124, arguing that the Canadian experience generally seems to confirm the "market control" thesis.
145 The arguments are developed in W.W. Pue, "Trajectories of Professionalism: Legal Professionalism after Abel" in A. Esau, ed., *Manitoba Law Annual, 1989-1990* (Winnipeg: Legal Research Institute, 1991) 57, reprinted from (1990) 19 Man. L.J. 384.
146 P.G. Giffen, "Social Control and Professional Self-Government: A Study in the Legal Profession in Canada" in S.D. Clark, ed., *Urbanism and the Changing Canadian Society* (Toronto: University of Toronto Press, 1961) 117.
147 See Chapter 10 in this volume.
148 J.S. Auerbach, *Unequal Justice: Lawyers and Social Change in Modern America* (New York: Oxford University Press, 1976).
149 Inns of Court, *supra* note 135.
150 See Chapters 7, 8, and 11 in this volume; W.W. Pue, "The Benchers' Suppression of an Independent Bar in Victorian England" (Paper presented to Victorian Studies Association of Western Canada Annual Conference, 1992) [unpublished].
151 J.S. Auerbach, *Unequal Justice: Lawyers and Social Change in Modern America, supra* note 148; M.J. Horwitz, *The Transformation of American Law, 1870-1960* (Cambridge, MA: Harvard University Press, 1977); J.C. Foster, *The Ideology of Apolitical Politics: The Elite Lawyer's Response to the Crisis in American Capitalism, 1870-1920* (New York: Associated Faculty Press, 1987).
152 C. Backhouse, "To Open the Way for Others of My Sex: Clara Brett Martin's Career as Canada's First Woman Lawyer" (1985) 1 C.J.W.L. 1; C. Backhouse, *Petticoats and Prejudice: Women and Law in Nineteenth-Century Canada* (Toronto: The Osgoode Society, 1991) at 293, c. 10, "Lawyering: Clara Brett Martin, Canada's First Woman Lawyer."

153 See Chapter 9 in this volume.
154 *Ibid.* at 274-77, 267, 267, 100n, 267, 102n.
155 See W.W. Pue, "Lawyers and the Constitution of Political Society: Containing Radicalism and Maintaining Order in Prairie Canada, 1900-1930," Canadian Legal History Project Working Paper 93-4 (1993).
156 Frye, *supra* note 4 at 185.

2

How "French" Was the English Bar?

BARRISTERS AND POLITICAL LIBERALISM IN THE EIGHTEENTH AND NINETEENTH CENTURIES

> It is a most important subject for the consideration of this House, whether any body of men, in their own private chamber, should have the power of determining whether any person shall be excluded for life from the practice of the higher branch of the Law.
>
> – A. Baring, Address to the House of Commons of the United Kingdom[1]

> The bar is public property.
>
> – D.W. Harvey[2]

English Barristers: Pillars of Stability?

Daniel Duman concluded his intriguing study of the English and colonial bars in the nineteenth century with the observation that despite rapid increases in admissions to the four Inns of Court between 1835 and 1885, "severe overcrowding at the English bar" was avoided by the fortuitous "emergence of new employment opportunities in the public service and in the law itself." Opportunities relating to "directing the economy and society," legal advice, colonial service, and business helped stave off the "threat of unemployment." According to Duman, this in turn had a significant political consequence in that the rosy career prospects for lawyers helped produce relative political stability in nineteenth-century England.

These employment opportunities prevented the emergence of a militant and powerful group of briefless barristers. Left idle, advocates tend to get into mischief. Briefless barristers could have posed a major problem for Britain and might have channelled social and political discontent, as other lawyers had done in the not-so-distant past. In fact, their role was just the opposite; the barristers were pillars of nineteenth-century stability.[3]

Lest anyone miss its unmistakable intent, the reference to "other lawyers in the not-so-distant past" is clarified in a footnote: the "English Civil War and the American and French Revolutions"[4] show the sorts of problems likely to flow from leaving too many lawyers underemployed for too long.[5]

Duman's observations reflect two important common assumptions about England, Englishness, and English lawyers. First, it is commonly believed that English barristers have been a politically quiescent lot since the troubled days of the English Civil War, the interregnum, and the Glorious Revolution. Second, a powerful assumption persists that this in turn has contributed immensely to English political stability and incrementalism, and to progressive political, economic, and social development, all uninterrupted by demagoguery, revolt, beheadings, or the disruptive actions of unruly mobs. Duman's passing reference to France is no gratuitous slight: that nation stands in English "common sense" as a dreadful warning of all that can go wrong, a sort of conceptual opposite to England's altogether more sensible ways.

Similar assumptions about the political conservatism of English barristers are commonplace. Historians and historical figures alike have not infrequently accused the English legal profession of being singularly uninvolved in the great liberating causes of the past two centuries. Caroline Robbins described lawyers of George II's reign as "protectors of tradition" who "contributed little to the development of liberalism in any way."[6] William Cobbett thought the lawyers of his time to be a reactionary force of "ruffians ... whose *business* it is to do injustice." He told Daniel Whittle Harvey in 1834 that the Benchers of the English Inns of Court were simply "corruption No. 2, doing the work of No. 1."[7] An early-nineteenth-century radical squib lumped "The Lawyers" in with other enemies of the people, including "The Dandy" (George IV), "The Irish Rat Catcher" (Castlereagh), "The Doctor" (Sidmouth), and "The Perjurers."[8]

Advocates and Liberalism: The European Standard

Questions relating to the role of English lawyers in the development of the liberal state gained prominence following a proliferation of research into the history of lawyers and politics on the European continent and in the United States. This work raised fundamental questions regarding the role of advocates in the construction of a liberal polity.[9] The work of T.C. Halliday and L. Karpik in developing a theoretical framework for understanding the general character of the relationship between lawyers and liberalism has been highly influential. Although they concede the necessary imprecision of any notion of political liberalism covering "several countries and several historical periods," and reflecting "a complex phenomenon with numerous streams and transformations," they nonetheless posit a necessary relationship between advocacy and the creation of "the liberal polity." For them, this "includes citizenship and the moderate state, and liberal political society, which includes civil society and the existence of independent publics."[10] In their view, professional advocates have played a central – perhaps even indispensable – role in relation to three essential components of political liberalism:

- judicial constraint on executive or sovereign power
- the creation of "publics"
- the enhancement of individual rights.

Conceptually, lawyers' activities within these areas relate to the constitution of the moderate state, civil society, and citizenship, respectively.[11] The creation of "publics" apart, each is familiar to common lawyers and students of British constitutionalism in the United Kingdom, Canada, the United States, and other former British colonies. Sophisticated scholarly research confirms, in effect, what less thoughtful professional apologists have asserted with monotonous regularity: lawyers emerge, apparently, as heroes in historical struggles for freedom, liberty, and democracy.[12]

This chapter demonstrates that eighteenth- and nineteenth-century English advocates, like their counterparts in other countries, were frequently drawn to political action. My range of reference is deliberately limited to barristers and to that portion of the attorneys' profession that specialized in advocacy. Notaries, solicitors, attorneys, and others whose workaday world involved large doses of bureaucratic work should not be confused with advocates. These latter are and have been culturally, socially, legally, and politically quite different sorts of professionals.[13] A further limitation should be noted. Although Paris *avocats* and English barristers (and, later, solicitors who specialized in litigation) engaged in analogous work, the professional context within which they operated was markedly different. It is arguable that this resulted in English barristers' playing a lesser role in establishing political liberalism than their cross-Channel peers.

Historical Trajectories of Lawyers' Liberalism in France

An examination of the role of advocates in the creation of a liberal society raises questions that cannot be resolved at the level of theory. The thoroughly historical issues raised for consideration within this *problematique* can be addressed only in particular contexts and in light of careful consideration of the best available historical evidence. There is powerful historical evidence from the United States and Europe that a strong, apparently causal relationship has existed in some countries at different times.[14] The French case is particularly intriguing, presenting the paradigm case against which all others are tested. It is of special interest precisely because of striking similarities – and at least one notable difference – between the conduct of Paris *avocats* and English barristers in a similar time period.

Paris *avocats* were actively engaged in most of France's great political battles throughout the eighteenth and nineteenth centuries, advancing the cause of political liberalism with remarkable consistency.[15] Despite immense transformations of French politics and society during the period, important features of the work of *avocats* seem to hold relatively constant. To put it crudely, lawyers intervened on the side of political liberalism in two modes. First, they sometimes challenged the state and ecclesiastical authority directly, unambiguously, *and collectively.* Second, *avocats* individually seized upon lawsuits to promote particular political causes and, *by the very process of representation,* advanced liberal notions of legality and citizens' rights.

The collective actions of Paris *avocats* in this period are noteworthy for they were both able and willing to stand together as a professional order in defence of political rights. The Paris *Ordre des avocats* (significantly, neither conceived of as, nor styled, a corporate body)[16] engaged in extraordinary collective action on a number of occasions. This included a dramatic August 1731 work stoppage in opposition to the Crown, arising from the political and religious difficulties surrounding Jansenism.[17] On that occasion, *avocats* paralyzed the courts, inconvenienced litigants,[18] and caused "grave material and symbolic difficulties for a state, the primary function of which, from time immemorial, had been to administer justice."[19] The success of this action simultaneously carved out a new role for the *Ordre des avocats* and chipped away at both royal and ecclesiastical power. Although work stoppages by and large gave way to other types of collective action in the 1730s, the strike remained a powerful reserve weapon that could, and did, reappear as occasion demanded. A failed strike a few years later gave the *Ordre des avocats* reason to pause but did not bring an end to

> their efforts on behalf of Jansenist-*parlementaire* constitutionalism ... the Order remained an *organisation de combat.* It simply functioned, so to speak, in a different key. It no longer expressed itself through collective action, but it still remained a tightly run, well-protected refuge from which [*avocats*] ... could produce pamphlets and *mémoires,* and formulate *parlementaire* strategy with impunity.[20]

Collective action by *avocats,* most dramatically made manifest in strikes against state or church authority, is certainly remarkable and without parallel in eighteenth- or nineteenth-century England. Equally important to the great political causes of the eighteenth and nineteenth centuries in France, however, was the accretion of a series of more modest actions by individual *avocats* in defence of individual clients. Paris *avocats* used their privileged location in the realms of public discourse to develop and promote political arguments. They developed a "no-holds-barred" strategy employing courtroom rhetoric and forensic skill as one component of a multifaceted political strategy. *Avocats* transformed themselves as necessary into constitutionalists, public speakers, authors of widely read political pamphlets, public figures, and demagogues. They "seized upon law suits, threats or decisions which they felt to be arbitrary,"[21] using the issues in litigation as raw material from which to develop multidimensioned juridical political argumentation. Moreover, they used the courtroom *politically:* it provided a rare forum of uncensored free expression from which *avocats* could speak to a larger public, disseminating their political views far beyond the parties involved in litigation. Knowing this, they spoke through and beyond the causes in which they acted. As representatives for litigants, they engaged in a form of "political pedagogy,"[22] which effectively turned "the public into a supreme court and thereby rival of the magistrates."[23] Individual accused were made to transcend localized reality as their cases entered the courtroom. Through the agency of lawyers, they were transmuted into "the site where superior forces came to terms: religion versus tolerance, order versus liberty, monarchy versus the republic."[24] Trials became momentous events: "avid crowds packed the courtroom, judicial chronicles sold out, pleadings were printed and sold: public passions crystallized around legal questions."[25] From the Restoration to the middle of the July Monarchy, "there was a succession of ... 'great trials'" that

> were often events of considerable importance. Among the thronging crowds, political and social celebrities mixed with youths and courthouse personalities. The public took sides, passions flared. And the audience was infinitely larger than the crowd in the courtroom; readers of the legal columns of newspapers, with their reports, commentaries, and portraits, passed on the accounts, some of which were to give rise to long-lived legends. A public passion had crystallized around judicial matters.[26]

In Old Regime France, *avocats* enjoyed a unique privilege in that their legal briefs could be published uncensored. As a result, "these documents – in theory, internal court memoranda – became an important means of appealing to, and speaking for, the new and nebulous creature called the 'Public.'"[27] According to David Bell, "the written arguments, or legal briefs (called either *mémoires judiciaires* or *factums* in French)" were important public documents. *Avocats* did not simply submit them to the judges in the rarefied confines of the courts but often had them printed and distributed to the public, sometimes along with auxiliary briefs called *consultations*, co-signed by a number of colleagues. Briefs could run from as few as three printed pages to as many as five hundred, and complicated cases produced scores of them, drafted by teams of barristers. Even the most inconsequential trial might easily generate three or four. In the course of the eighteenth century, barristers produced at least a hundred thousand, making legal briefs one of the most common forms of printed matter in early modern France. Jurists justified the practice by arguing that publicizing the facts of cases protected their clients from courtroom intrigue. In fact, however, the briefs had other uses as well. Because of their technical status as internal court documents, and the need to print them rapidly, royal legislation exempted them from preliminary censorship as long as they bore a barrister's signature. They were practically the only document published under the Old Regime that did not require preliminary censorship to circulate legally. Thus, they often served political as well as strictly legal purposes.[28] The *avocats*' brief developed into "a legal form of opposition journalism, and one of the most effective examples of it yet seen in France."[29]

Several key elements of liberalism were reproduced as the cumulative effect of representation in individual cases: regardless of the significant political differences separating them, monarchist, republican, and liberal *avocats* alike advanced notions concerning the rule of law and the protection of certain core liberties. By publishing *mémoires judiciaires* and *consultations* to a wide readership, they invoked a rational discourse of public life, and implicitly asserted the sovereignty of nation, not monarch. Notions of civil and political citizenship advanced by *avocats* in their professional work involved civil equality, property, personal security, and freedom of assembly, the press, and expression. In the years following the French Revolution, *avocats* repeatedly invoked the constitution in legal discourse.[30] On either side of the Revolution, they appealed to and purported to speak for the "public," an entity they simultaneously derived their strength from, empowered, *and* constituted.[31]

All things considered, Paris *avocats* appear to have been actively engaged, important, and dramatic political actors over two centuries of tremendous change in French social, economic, and political life. Indeed, liberal politics has historically been so important that Karpik concludes that lawyers' "relationship with the political sphere had become *the dominant organizing principle of the profession.*"[32]

The Political Agency of English Barristers

Looking across the Channel, English barristers of the eighteenth and nineteenth centuries seem a rather tame lot in comparison – merely a professional body concerned with bricks and mortar, wine cellars, dining, status, and jurisdiction, rather than with the pursuit of any coherent or even mildly significant political objectives.[33]

Neither the political quiescence of barristers nor the political stability of England in the period should be overstated, however. The relative paucity of research into the history of the English Bar[34] renders any comparison with the political activities of French *avocats* necessarily tentative. It is clear, nonetheless, that on a number of occasions throughout the eighteenth and nineteenth centuries, English advocates (usually barristers but also, albeit less visibly, attorneys or solicitors) stepped onto the political stage in ways analogous to *avocats*. At least some English lawyers were willing to use the courtroom, the printing press, the public meeting, and even the "mob" politically as occasion demanded. Often the political visions they articulated were, broadly speaking, "liberal." From the sophisticated and multifaceted politico-legal strategies of the Wilkites, through late-eighteenth-century moves towards the creation of a liberal (or at least a rationalist) mode of criminal trial, the various legal strategies that arose in response to the repressions of the 1790s, the defence of Queen Caroline's divorce, the working-class advocacy of W.P. Roberts (a solicitor), and mid- to late-nineteenth-century efforts by a number of barristers to expand citizenship in new directions, English advocates, like their French counterparts, used lawsuits instrumentally in order to score larger political points.

The special skill of the barrister was in rhetoric and persuasion: courtroom argument frequently traversed boundaries that have subsequently been erected between the legal and political spheres. Barristers, like *avocats*, employed their rhetorical powers in a highly public forum. Their words and actions were widely commented on, discussed, *and* reported (often nearly verbatim) in the press. Further, they not uncommonly published pamphlets or books arising from their cases, addressed public meetings, or otherwise sought to speak to (and constitute) a public considerably larger than that actually present in the courtroom. Moreover, the Bar (particularly, perhaps, the Criminal Defence Bar) provided a route to fame or notoriety that could create a public profile sufficient to secure election to local or national political office. Barristers travelled with England's itinerant assize courts, thereby becoming highly visible actors in the work of a centrally important seventeenth-century political institution.

> [W]hen the judges arrived on circuit in a county town, it was never purely a judicial affair: whether or not politics actually entered into the litigation ... the assize had its political dimension, for it was one of the ways in which government conveyed its views, through the mouths of the judges, to the locality; and conversely, it was an established means of expressing local political views which were meant to be heard by those at Westminster.[35]

The court circuits established networks connecting London and local elites, served as a propaganda machine and polling service for the central government, and provided means whereby radical or dissident barristers could maintain contacts with provincial allies. "This travelling train of justice," according to John Brewer, "linked the centre with the localities, enabling not only loyal servants of the Crown, but also radical dissidents, to publicize their views in the provinces."[36]

The social and political significance of courts is apparent. The criminal trial of late-eighteenth-century London has been described thus:

> The inherent drama of the courtroom when the confrontation between two versions of the truth took the form not of a squabble but of a game, a contest with rules, played by clever, skillful, and equally matched opponents, and a game that came quickly to a conclusion. The theatrical character of the trial was heightened in England by the provision of galleries for spectators in courtrooms open to the public ... A further dimension was added as the trial became more structured as a conflict between prosecuting and defense lawyers and as its adversarial capacities were developed, to the extent that the rules governing defense counsel allowed that to happen. For the trial came to have some of the characteristics of a sport, a contest with a winner and a loser – and, to heighten the drama, a loser whose client might be executed in another public arena. Theatre and sport made a perfect combination for a society in which spectator sports such as horse-racing and prize-fighting were developing rapidly and becoming commercialized. The gladiators in this judicial combat became known in part for their entertainment value.[37]

At a minimum, then, lawyers' work was *political* in the simple dictionary sense of unequivocally "belonging, or pertaining to ... the body of citizens" (*Oxford English Dictionary*).

If this was true of the central courts in London, it was arguably even more so in the provinces. Quarter sessions and assize courts provided intermittent spectacles unmatched in pageantry, ceremony, display, and drama. Doug Hay has provided a compelling portrait of the drama of the courtroom in eighteenth-century rural England:

> The antics surrounding the twice-yearly visits of the high-court judges had considerable psychic force. They were accorded far greater importance by contemporaries than by most historians, who have been concerned more with county government, particularly at Quarter Sessions, than with the majesty of the law. The assizes were a formidable spectacle in a country town, the most visible and elaborate manifestation of state power to be seen in the countryside, apart from the presence of a regiment. The town was crowded, not only with barristers and jurors, but with the cream of county society, attending the assize ball and county meetings, which were often held in the same week. Tradesmen and labourers journeyed in to enjoy the spectacle, meet friends, attend the court and watch the executions. And the court arrived in town with traditional, and calculated panoply ... Within this elaborate ritual of the irrational, judge and counsel displayed their learning with an eloquence that often rivalled that of leading statesmen. There was an acute consciousness that the courts were platforms for addressing "the multitude."[38]

In so doing, lawyers invoked the power of a public they themselves helped to constitute and reconstitute through their advocacy. The power of courtroom discourses was not lost on contemporaries.

It was a power to communicate freely though free communication might otherwise meet with criminal sanction; the power to speak what dare not be spoken, to challenge those one dared not challenge. It provided opportunities to attempt social engineering through manipulation of the languages of law, and provided a public platform unequalled by any other. The courtroom might be used either defensively to foil the aggressions of the state or proactively to advance social visions thought undesirable by rulers and class elites. Courtroom advocacy provided unique opportunities to advance one's own cause while embarrassing a rival. It simultaneously provided opportunity for crucial defences of dissident politics, assertion of individual rights, articulation of radically democratic political visions, and moments of significant class formation. Balanced on a knife edge between social control and "rule of law," the courtroom might at any moment be transformed into a significant arena for counter-hegemonic struggle.[39] Moreover, it provided a unique opportunity for the promotion of one's own career, whether in electoral or patronage politics:

the courtroom became a breeding ground for what was pejoratively called demagoguery.

Not surprisingly, English lawyers throughout the eighteenth and nineteenth centuries both sought out a political voice for themselves and were enlisted by others in aid of their political causes.

The Wilkites

The followers of John Wilkes (hence Wilkites) were one group of bourgeois radicals who consistently and effectively employed legal tactics as an indispensable part of their political strategy. The Wilkite "Society of the Supporters of the Bill of Rights" was dominated by lawyers, who made up fully 10 percent of its membership (the largest single group) and exerted disproportionate influence. The Wilkites "used the law itself as a political weapon, exploiting the highly ritualized theatre of the courts and the labyrinthine complexity of the criminal law to propagandize their cause, defend themselves and wreak vengeance on their enemies."[40] There is scarcely any imaginable legal/political strategy they did not employ. They exploited legal loopholes and also used the opportunities the law provided to promulgate their ideology, speaking through the courtroom to a wider public about grand political issues. Their activities were widely reported in the radical press as they took legal action against state officials or sought to "shame those in authority into reformation" by publicizing "abuses" as occasion demanded. Often they initiated litigation to redress their own injuries, as when two of Wilkes's supporters were killed in 1768 by government-hired thugs. On other occasions, they worked with ordinary victims of mundane elite manipulation to turn private grievance into *causes célèbres.*[41] Always, they presented their causes not as "matters of personal recrimination or vengeance, but [as] *class* actions which affected the rights and liberties of all subjects."[42] They engaged in extensive pamphleteering about the rule of law[43] and were not above using collusive actions to establish friendly legal-political precedent.[44] All of this took place as they pursued more orthodox parliamentary and extraparliamentary political activity.

Although not shy about using law as an instrument to achieve particular, limited ends, the legal vision of the Wilkites was at one with their political values. Law and politics collapsed "in one on another."[45] John Brewer explains that "political ideology and the law as ideology were intertwined," with the result that "legal bodies and processes (many of which had an overt political function anyway) were frequently the foci of political expression and political conflict."[46] Liberty, eighteenth-century England's foremost political value, was thought to be the product of law. Consequently, the making, administration, and execution of law constituted the very pith and substance of politics.[47] Wilkite views on these matters were, for our purposes, "liberal." Their political program, and hence their legal strategies, sought to ensure the public accountability of officials, effect equality before the law for all subjects regardless of rank, wealth, or personal association, advance legal due process, and minimize or eliminate official discretion. Generally, they hoped to create a state in which orderly government could be maintained by means of "the use of the civil power on behalf of the public rather than the deployment of military power on behalf of the Crown."[48] Government, in other words, was ultimately to rest upon the willing consent of the people, not upon the rule of force.[49]

The Transformation of Criminal Defence

There is no more important intersection of law and politics than the state trial and its next of kin, the criminal prosecution. Not surprisingly, then, the particular legal matters of concern to Wilkites often involved political offences or criminal prosecution. They attacked the legality of general warrants (which named no individual but authorized officials to seize *anyone's* papers and personal effects), more or less routinely prosecuted state officials for illegal conduct, defended "seditious libel" prosecutions, opposed the "corrupt" use of the Royal prerogative of mercy, objected to the imposition of court fees (which restricted access), insisted on strict compliance with procedural rules, strongly asserted the rights of the jury (including jury nullification of odious laws), insisted on public and open legal processes, and opposed summary procedures of all sorts.[50]

The Wilkite example focuses our attention on several important points. First, their many efforts illustrate that the administration of justice was of central importance in modern English politics. Eighteenth-century reformers believed that the legal system and the state at large had been captured by "oligarchy and corruption," to the detriment of "free-born Englishmen."[51] Legal processes were important in struggles of liberty, partly because the law was frequently used by "Corruption" as an instrument of oppression but also, more proactively, because rights could be asserted, defended, and won in the legal arena. More importantly still, law played a massive part in the discursive world of the English and was a central ingredient of true Englishness. Trials provided a highly public display of the status of English subjects *and* provided the raw material from which the languages of liberty were fashioned, adapted, and moulded. The Englishman's status as either a denuded subject, victimized by "privilege," or, alternatively, as free citizen fully clothed in robust individual rights was cast in stark relief in the courtroom. Immediate, often dire consequences for the individuals concerned captured and amplified much of importance in the invisible world of ideas, imagery, symbols, and myth that constitute the lived experience of citizenship.

Any trial seemingly contained within it the seeds from which a highly charged melodrama focused on hidden influence, the prerogatives of status or wealth, abuses of judicial discretion, corrupt process, or unfair substantive law might emerge unpredictably. Such matters lie especially near the surface in criminal prosecutions, and throughout the eighteenth and nineteenth centuries, lawyers' opinions regarding the appropriate conduct of criminal trials was strongly coloured by political conviction. Stephan Landsman asserts that English adversarial process originated in the eighteenth century:

> Criminal trials in Tudor and Stuart England were, according to J.S. Cockburn, "nasty, brutish, and essentially short." Counsel seldom participated, few, if any, rules of evidence constrained enquiry, judges routinely examined witnesses and defendants in the most vigorous, and at times ruthless, manner, only prosecution witnesses were allowed to swear testimonial oaths and thereby enhance the credibility of their statements, jurors were free to utilize private knowledge gained outside the confines of the courtroom, judges frequently introduced their political views into proceedings, and there was virtually no appellate procedure. By the early nineteenth-century, the traditional, non-contentious approach to adjudication had been supplanted in English felony trials by a system with the rudiments of an adversarial process. Party direction and control had replaced judicial enquiry, counsel's role had expanded dramatically, and sophisticated rules to regulate courtroom conduct had been developed.[52]

So dramatic a transformation over the course of a century is remarkable. It exaggerates only slightly to suggest that the common law's much-vaunted adversarial system was created in this period. The forces that produced this transformation played themselves out in reaction to diverse issues and in varied ways. The adversarial system emerged as advocates developed concrete responses to the exercise of state power. Their responses, conditioned by a discursive universe that included a mythologized historiography of English freedoms,[53] were broadly liberal or proto-liberal in character. Several central elements of what we came to think of as liberalism coalesced dramatically in many loosely scripted courtroom plays: a suspicion of state power, hostility to class prerogative, faith in rationality (especially, in rational processes of proof), and an overall inflation in the value attached to the individual.

Landsman has argued that "[t]he rise of contentious procedure undoubtedly was associated with the historical and intellectual changes that swept English society in the seventeenth and eighteenth centuries,"[54] and it is well to bear in mind that the causal relations between law, society, ideas, and economy were multidirectional and complex. The right to counsel, for example, though central to early-twenty-first-century liberal legal faith and professional myth alike, did not exist in early English criminal procedure. The enormous constitutional disruptions of the seventeenth century produced, in the *Treason Act* of 1696, however, an explicit parliamentary acknowledgment of "the value of counsel to those faced with serious charges and carefully orchestrated prosecutions. It was only natural in light of that legislation for the courts to allow defendants not only to press their cases with increased vigor, but to employ counsel to do it for them."[55] While the importance of this intellectual shift cannot be gauged with precision, it should not be underestimated. Any argument that might justify the presence of counsel in state trials *as such* slipped by inevitable analogy into a justification for the presence of lawyers in defence of nonpolitical criminal prosecutions. Although lacking state prosecutors, English state power was directly implicated in criminal law enforcement from 1692 onward through a system of bounties and rewards for the apprehension and prosecution of felons. This resulted in the "development of a cadre of professional thief catchers"[56] or bounty hunters who, not surprisingly, sometimes yielded to the temptation to fabricate accusations in order to gain easy convictions and quick financial reward. They did so even in capital cases ("it is not every day that one gets forty pounds for hanging a man"),[57] and during the 1720s and 1730s a growing awareness of these sorts of abuses led judges to concede a greater role to defence counsel in more or less routine criminal cases. This awareness and the participation of counsel in turn contributed incrementally to the development of a more liberal form of trial involving the testing of evidence, cross-examination, and all the panoply of a newly evolving adversarial system.[58]

A second strong influence on the character of criminal trials in eighteenth-century England grew more directly from the activities of liberal reformers. Wilkite legal battles provided a training ground in vigorous advocacy and also a highly visible display of new ways of conducting court cases. The lessons lawyers learned by observing or participating in those causes "were directly imported into the criminal process,"[59] where they took on a life of their own. Barristers constantly redefined, debated, and contested the meanings of citizenship, rights, and the rule of law in innumerable large and small courtroom battles. Many causes came before the courts and reformers of all colours participated in political legal strategies during the eighteenth century as, time and again, "courts were called upon to adjudicate social conflicts and modify the law."[60] Each had its impact on particular issues but also drew upon and contributed to wider discourses of liberal legalism and citizenship.[61]

The career of Thomas Erskine looms large. Many have accorded him pride of place in the struggle to promote what one hagiographer called "justice and liberty – the heritage of the Anglo Saxon!" Liberal notions of law and politics came into particularly sharp definition during the December 1792 prosecution of Thomas Paine for alleged seditious libel in publishing his *Rights of Man*. The lead prosecuting barrister, Attorney-General Sir Archibald Macdonald, began his opening address by asserting his personal conviction in the guilt of Paine and suggesting that he would consider it disgraceful for a barrister to represent a cause he did not believe in. Erskine responded with words that have been much repeated:

> I will forever, at all hazards, assert the dignity, independence, and integrity of the English bar, without which impartial justice, the most valuable part of the English constitution, can have no existence. From the moment that any advocate can be permitted to say that he will or will not stand between the Crown and the subject arraigned in the court where he daily sits to practice, from that moment the liberties of England are at an end. If the advocate refuses to defend from what he may think of the charge or of the defense, he assumes the character of the judge; nay, he assumes it before the hour of judgment; and in proportion to his rank and reputation, puts the heavy influence and perhaps mistaken opinion into the scale against the accused, in whose favor the benevolent principle of English law makes all presumptions, and which commands the very judge to be his counsel.[62]

David Mellinkoff's sensitive treatment of this exchange in *The Conscience of a Lawyer* cautions that Erskine (who has been "draped with sufficient worshipful nonsense to distort the image of a great lawyer") probably did not intend to advance a fully liberal notion of advocacy of the sort familiar to his readers in the late twentieth century.[63] Conceding entirely that the question of how to properly locate statements such as these in their appropriate historical context is complex and multifaceted, it is nonetheless reasonable to think of Erskine as having advanced a liberal notion of advocacy and citizenship, both as that term is used in this chapter and, indeed, as contemporaries and near-contemporaries perceived it. We need not, in so doing, slip unthinkingly to the conclusion that Erskine would have endorsed an adversarial ethic identical to the cynical disinterestedness that characterizes contemporary US legal professionalism or any other variant of "liberal" legal practice in our generation.

As the Erskine example suggests, wider changes in social and intellectual life that were taking place coloured many particular issues as they were litigated. These larger transformations too often tended to elevate the virtues of individualism and of "rationality." Both helped to generate new notions of proof and evidence in the courtroom. This has been brilliantly assessed in John Beattie's discussion of William Garrow's contributions to the development of adversarial justice (the liberal trial) in the late eighteenth century. Although the precise relations between lawyers, political liberalism, and particular forms of trial in this period have yet to be fully studied, Beattie's assessment of one moment in which the centre of gravity of criminal trials shifted markedly provides important evidence of a circumstantial nature:

> It is an interesting question, in light of a possible connection between the increase in the number of lawyers at the Old Bailey in the 1780s and contemporary concerns about the oppressive character of the government, whether Garrow's earlier [Whig] political views and connections had also shaped his career as a lawyer at the Old Bailey. For Garrow was not only the most active barrister in the ten years he practiced in that court. What is most striking was his apparent preference for the defense side: In fully 83 percent of the cases he appeared in during his first three years of practice at the Old Bailey (1784-86), he acted for the defendant, a preference he maintained until the year before he took silk. Does that betoken a political stance, a Whig view that a corrupt government threatened to overturn liberty at home as it had in America, and that the defense of the constitution could be carried on in the criminal courts as well as in Parliament? The connection did not need to be as clear as that for the Old Bailey to hold some attraction to a young Whig lawyer like Garrow as a place in which political views could be expressed during the American war and a distrust of the power and intentions of the administration registered. There is no evidence that such views lay behind Garrow's practice. But the possibility is clear, not only as an explanation of Garrow's career, but more generally as an explanation of the striking movement of lawyers into the criminal courts. That political context is at the least suggestive, especially because the greater participation of lawyers in criminal trials in the 1780s led not merely to more defendants being represented by counsel, but to a more committed advocacy of their cases in the courtroom and a new emphasis on their rights.[64]

Beattie has pointed out that during the American War of Independence many in England were concerned that the "rights and liberties of Englishmen" were not as secure as they should be. "There was widespread concern over corruption in the government, its unconstitutional behavior" and, correspondingly, a belief that "England was threatened by a tyrannical and oppressive regime." At the end of the war, various groups sought reform of Parliament or administration, and worked to establish "religious freedom and toleration" so that "the full rights of citizenship" could extend "to those outside the Anglican establishment."[65] Barristers could – and did – speak through the courts to a larger public about such matters. By so doing, they contributed to discourses about rights, citizenship, and liberty and simultaneously put themselves before the public in ways that could be useful to those intent on pursuing a political career. The political readings of criminal trials by late-eighteenth-century lawyers were quickly communicated to the larger public through the mass media of the day. The *Old Bailey Session Papers,* for example, reported criminal cases tried at that court for nearly 250 years from 1674. Unlike modern law reports, this was addressed to a lay readership, putting lawyers, their actions, and the criminal process before a reading public.

Nineteenth-Century Developments

The political visions of state, society, and citizenship that drew upon and reinforced the adversarial trial are thus found well before the beginning of the nineteenth century. Further, the use of trials for explicitly political purposes had advanced during the eighteenth century even though the development of a fully "liberal" form of criminal trial was not concluded by 1800. No point of stasis was then (or has since been) reached. Questions concerning state power, judicial discretion, individual right, and the rule of law continued to be important throughout the nineteenth century and down to the present.

During the nineteenth century, a number of *causes célèbres* focused public attention squarely on the rule of law and the evolving character of the state. Nineteenth-century English barristers frequently acted much like their counterparts across the Channel: engaging in vigorous advocacy on behalf of individual clients, framing their arguments in relation to issues of great national importance, translating individual grievance into constitutional cause, and employing the privileged sanctum of the courtroom as a podium from which to address a wider public, which, simultaneously, they invoked (and constituted) as a source of legitimacy. Like *avocats,* barristers knew that in the right circumstances their words and actions would be repeated, discussed, interpreted, reinterpreted, and sometimes celebrated well beyond the bounds of the courtroom. They were important and self-conscious contributors to public discourse. The press reported extensively on trials, the courtroom remained an important public forum, and barristers themselves engaged in active propaganda campaigns – writing to newspapers, addressing crowds at public meetings, and expressing their views with surprising regularity in privately printed pamphlets.[66] A high profile on circuit, at the Old Bailey, or in other London courts, could provide an excellent foundation for a political career of either an establishment or a radical sort.

A wide variety of issues were charged with political importance during the nineteenth century. State trials and criminal prosecutions, of course, continued to be important, as in the past. In the repression following the Napoleonic Wars, for example, political radicals embraced the opportunities presented by their prosecutions. According to one historian of London radicalism:

> All trials had educative potential, and the radicals knew this. For example, in the late autumn of 1819 Cartwright looked forward to his trial by a far from sympathetic Warwickshire jury as a chance "to meet and remove prejudices which are opposed to freedom and our country's future welfare". Some months later John Hunt prepared for his fifth prosecution for libels in the *Examiner* with thoroughness and the determination, as he told Place, to "say bold things when saying them may be useful to the cause we advocate". With the help of Place and Hone he collected materials for a defence based on "proof of the flagrant corruption of the House of Commons" and its constant offences against Justice and Humanity. Similarly, Carlile's trials for blasphemous libel served to advertise the very things that the government sought by prosecution to suppress.[67]

Radicals of this era made the fullest use of law to advance their goals, speaking through the courtroom when they were persecuted, defending themselves vigorously and with imagination, publicizing their cause through wide-circulation pamphlets, speaking of legal proceedings at public meetings, prosecuting their enemies, using the law proactively in their own interests, exposing the government's spy system, and illustrating, when appropriate, that it was "extremely difficult for humble persons to call the laws to their assistance in the hours of need when they are to be employed to punish powerful men."[68]

Nineteenth-century liberals thus continued to be concerned with oppressive state power exercised through politically motivated legal proceedings and criminal trials. They also became concerned, however, with matters arising from labour contracts, the privileges and duties of barristers, and inheritance and wills. The state writ large was sometimes the target of liberal political action through litigation, but on other occasions barristers turned their full rhetorical force on the lingering manifestations of "Old Corruption," or, simply, on the conduct of employers or the pretences and prerogatives of the wealthy, noble, or well connected. Victorian England's self-understanding was based on informal though clearly understood hierarchies of class, religion, and ethnicity. Not infrequently, social presumptions of entitlement originating from this terrain collided in the courtroom with alternative, more liberal notions of citizenship.[69]

One early-nineteenth-century case played at centre stage of English politics in highly charged circumstances. It generated understandings of advocacy, representation, and barristers' duties that have persisted, mutated, and provided the raw material from which others have fashioned many subsequent discussions of lawyers' professionalism. Oddly, this formative moment in the legal construction of liberal society centred on the lives of aristocrats.

On acceding to the throne at the height of the post-Napoleonic repression, George IV initiated divorce proceedings by trial before the House of Lords. He claimed that his wife, Caroline of Brunswick, had behaved in a scandalous fashion and committed adultery with one of her courtiers. The general political context, taken with widespread knowledge of George IV's notorious sexual indiscretions, transformed the entire matter into a politically charged morality tale. It was about double standards, public conduct, privilege, and equality of justice. In Dorothy Thompson's assessment, "the queen was seen not only, in Macaulay's phrase, as the victim of 'tyrant hatred' but also as the victim of male tyranny and sexual double standards."[70] Radicals from across England, but also many women and men who were not political radicals, petitioned on her behalf. Ultimately, the King's title to the throne was implicitly challenged[71] as the cause became transformed into a trial of an entire political system many thought to be corrupt and illegitimate.[72] Ironically, this aristocratic woman became "a symbol of many things, not the least of which were the struggles of an oppressed people against borough-mongering despotism."[73] Henry Brougham, one of Caroline's three principal barristers,[74] uttered his famous, unrestrainedly liberal dictum regarding the duties of an advocate:

> An advocate, by the sacred duty which he owes his client, knows in the discharge of that office but one person in the world, that client and none other. To save that client by all expedient means, to protect that client at all hazards and costs, to all others, and among others to himself, is the highest and most unquestioned of his duties; and he must not regard the alarm, the suffering, the torment, the destruction which he may bring upon any other. Nay, separating even the duties of a patriot from those of an advocate, and casting them, if need be to the wind, he must go on reckless of the consequences, if his fate it should unhappily be to involve his country in confusion for his client's protection.[75]

These words, much repeated since, were not merely empty rhetoric in the time and place in which they were uttered. The case combined issues relating to gender equity, transgression of class lines, political corruption, tyranny, and equality before the law. Nothing less than the throne itself was at stake, the public – indeed, the mob – was intensely interested in the matter, and Caroline's Whig barristers advanced her cause with unflinching nerve. Ultimately, Caroline prevailed, civil war – apparently a real possibility – was averted, and the monarchy sustained.

Caroline's advocates moved, through luck, persistence, connection, talent, and a change of administration, into positions of some prominence in the English legal system. Their vision of advocacy took root in a reforming nation and much of the nineteenth-century history of the English Bar is concerned with more precisely defining the ways in which barristers in liberal society should represent clients and present themselves and their causes to judges, juries, and the wider public. It is too early to enter any definitive assessment of the phases and stages of the processes creating liberalism. It is clear, however, that English barristers, like French *avocats,* were much involved in all aspects of the construction of a liberal polity in the nineteenth, as in the eighteenth, century. Chartist trials, defence of the rights of workers, and proceedings involving Tawell, Courvoisier, the Swinfen estate, and the Tichborne claimant (among others) reflect ongoing struggles of English barristers to carry a liberal vision of citizenship into the courtroom.

The "Frenchness" of the English Bar and the Peculiarities of the English?

How, then, does the English Bar compare with paradigm case of Paris *avocats* in terms of overall contribution to the development of political liberalism?

The question is not easy. While it is abundantly clear that English barristers have been actively involved in "liberal," "reform," or "radical" causes throughout the eighteenth and nineteenth centuries – and certainly before the eighteenth – the present state of research does not permit easy and accurate generalization. The sketch provided here demonstrates at least that some individual English barristers engaged in activities analogous to those of their French counterparts. They too challenged authority, used their privileged positions within the courtroom to address a larger public, engaged in carefully chosen strategic rights-oriented test-cases, published pamphlets, addressed crowds, and invoked, explicitly or implicitly, the unpredictable power of the mob.

A number of points distinguish Paris *avocats* from English barristers, just as significant differences distinguish the broader socio-political situations in the two countries. The English Bar, divided among Inner Temple, Middle Temple, Lincoln's Inn, Gray's Inn, and Serjeants' Inn in London, was also divided, along different lines, into "circuit messes" in the provinces. Beyond this, we simply have no idea how many barristers conducted professional work to one degree or another *without any reference whatsoever to the institutions or cultural life of the Bar*. Certainly, there was nothing to stop them from doing so. For its part, the organized Bar showed little inclination to political unity, much less towards cohesive political action, and less still towards disrupting the political or economic status quo of any given generation. The Inns were governed (to the extent that they were governed at all) by a self-perpetuating oligarchy of elite lawyers. Unaccountable to any professional electorate, organized on hierarchical lines, buffered by corporate status from any generalized mood of the profession, and dependent upon the solicitors of the rich and powerful for their briefs, the Benchers had little incentive to take bold or controversial action. Professional survivors to a man, the Benchers were beneficiaries, and potential future beneficiaries, of the distribution of lucrative legal offices. One English radical pointedly drew attention to this in his description of the Inner Temple Benchers who refused him admission to the Bar in the 1820s:

> WILLIAM WELCH, Esq., an independent country gentleman.
> FRANCIS MASERES, Esq., cursitor baron of the exchequer and judge of the sheriff's court.
> RICHARD BAKER, Esq. (This gentleman was one of the two who decided without hearing.)
> WILLIAM HOOD, Esq. a retired barrister formerly of considerable eminence at the chancery bar.
> JOSEPH JEKYLL, Esq.
> BARNE BARNE, Esq., a retired commissioner for the affairs of taxes, with a pension of 800L a year, and formerly M.P. for the rotten borough of Dunwich.
> H. C. LITCHFIELD, Esq., formerly solicitor to the Treasury, retired upon a pension of 3000L per annum. (Vide parliamentary grants of last year.)
> JAMES SCARLETT Esq.
> WILLIAM HARRISON, Esq., standing counsel to the Treasury, solicitor general to the duchy of Cornwall, and my professional opponent upon all occasions at Colchester.
> JOHN GURNEY, Esq., the avowed prosecutor.
> GILES TEMPLEMAN, Esq., an auditor of the public account.
> GIBBS WALKER JORDAN, Esq., colonial agent for the island of Barbadoes. (Vide Red Book.)

> SNOWDEN BARNE, Esq., chairman of the commissioners of the customs, and remembrancer of the lords treasurer's office with a deputy of 800L a year; and formerly M.P. for the rotten Borough of Dunwich; and one of the gentlemen who decided without hearing ...
> KEANE FITZGERALD, Esq., registrar of the Inrolment office, and clerk of the inrolments in the office of Custos Brevium, with a deputy.
> I. E. D. E. FINCH HATTON, Esq. ... this gentleman has as many sinecures as Christian names.[76]

Many elite barristers, in short, were thoroughly enmeshed in the formal and informal webs of political relationship, privilege, and office that reformers castigated as "Old Corruption." The Inns of Court were unlike the Paris *Ordre* in all essential respects.[77] English society was different too, and the tremendous upheavals of these two centuries did not simply replicate French developments. To the extent – which is only partly true – that English liberals confronted "corruption" rather than a despotic monarch, their target was different and both their public and professional politics might be expected to play out in different ways. "Corruption's" diffuse character, but also a generalized and genuinely held terror of the mob, fractured English professional guilds in ways that naked despotism could not.

By the nineteenth century, the English Inns of Court showed every sign of decay. Their traditional programs of education were in desuetude[78] and they had not yet assumed an important role in either qualification or discipline. Their minute books reveal preoccupation with the maintenance of buildings, collection of rents, and organization of dinners. The one marked exception to all of this – and it continued throughout the nineteenth century – is with regard to the Inns' attitudes towards "rebel," "liberal," "republican," or "reforming" barristers: there is a remarkable pattern of conduct in which the Inns of Court sought to exclude, silence, or expel any barrister whose politics – and particularly whose professional actions – exceeded the relatively narrow bounds of acceptability that circumscribed the political, social, and professional status quo. Although they sometimes came to this reluctantly, for these roles were not deeply embedded in their institutional culture, this is a crucially important point. It drives a wedge between the general association of lawyers with liberalism and the *formal associations* of lawyers. The latter not infrequently acted to suppress liberal legal practice.

Much is made in the common law world of the social, political, and economic importance of an independent legal profession. It is not uncommon to find both historians and officers of professional organizations asserting that an independent legal profession is crucial to the preservation of the liberties of citizens – a sort of keystone of civil rights, humane governance, and democracy itself. This position is traditionally defended by an interpretation that casts lawyers – since at least the time of England's century of revolution[79] – in the role of defenders of fundamental freedoms. This historiographic spin is employed to generate contemporary narratives asserting the political significance of a free and independent legal profession.[80] Typically, the absence of an independent bar is said to be a hallmark of totalitarianism. Traditional historical accounts portray the lawyer as a heroic figure who stands bravely between the citizen and a rapacious state, while the institutions of the legal profession are celebrated as providing the institutional and ideological structure necessary to insulate lawyers from state control, protecting individual advocates from the vindictiveness of those who may have been offended by their actions in protecting the "rights of the subject." Their professional organizations are variously portrayed as bulwarks of professional liberty[81] or, at worst, as inefficient but harmless associations.[82]

The Myth of Ineffectiveness

The four Inns of Court have been given a surprisingly easy go of it in this respect by historians. Despite a wealth of primary material documenting contemporary challenges to the exercise of disciplinary powers by the English Bar, the prevalent interpretation is that the organized Bar of the Victorian period was largely uninterested in policing either admissions or the activities of its members. In an outstanding study of the Victorian Bar, Raymond Cocks asserts that for a large part of the nineteenth century, the Inns failed "to have any significant effect upon professional life."[83] Similarly, Richard Abel concludes that "until the end of the nineteenth-century the Inns exercised little formal control over either entry into the profession or practice by barristers."[84] Not inspiring perhaps, this is at least a relatively benign interpretation of English forms of professional association.

Following Holdsworth,[85] Deborah Rhode describes the Victorian Bar as a sort of archetypal English institution: elitist, remarkably inefficient, blundering, disorganized, perhaps rumpled or frayed around the edges, a bit dusty, but ultimately charming, quaint, endearing, harmless:

> In the early nineteenth-century, the Inns began requiring applicants to obtain references from two barristers prior to admission, but there is no evidence that this mandate functioned other than to solidify the class bias of the admissions structure. Nor does it appear that barristers during this

> period were much interested in formally disciplining moral lapses, except where they affected the internal atmosphere of the Inns. Unbecoming behavior could trigger expulsion, but publicly sanctioned offenses typically involved breaches of etiquette rather than serious ethical lapses.[86]

The Benchers' minutes of the four English Inns of Court reveal, however, that the Inns were not *quite* as impotent as friend and foe alike would have it. The leaders of the Bar failed even to attempt to preserve the independence of the legal profession from repression. Worse, when forced to act, they consistently exercised their power to suppress those who offended powerful figures or whose legal practices challenged the status quo. Although individual barristers practised within an institutional structure that might plausibly have insulated them from patronage influences, state coercion, or private corruption, it was generally understood that this freedom existed within relatively narrow bounds. It took considerable fortitude for a barrister to step outside these limits. The organized legal profession could savagely punish barristers and would-be barristers whose beliefs or practices fell outside the political mainstream. There is a hidden history of professional repression that reveals the organized barristers' profession to have been antithetical to, rather than protective of, an independent Bar.

This seems entirely counterintuitive from our vantage point. A few preliminary comments are in order. First, it should be noted that, in celebrating the "independent" Bar, the question "Independence from whom?" is rarely raised. In *our* historical context (early-twentieth-first-century liberal democracies), it is often simply assumed that independence from direct state regulation is all that matters. Overlooking this basic question inadvertently reinforces that peculiar distortion of liberalism whereby it is only the abuse of public power that can be perceived. Once it is located exclusively in the private realm, the organized Bar is simply *assumed* to be unthreatening, harmless, devoid of disagreeable consequences for freedom, liberty, and political life.

This is, of course, a woefully inadequate conceptual framework. Private power can be as effective, intrusive, or harmful in its effects as public power. Because of this, its exercise needs to be at least as carefully scrutinized as the exercise of public power: neither can be *presumed* to be benign. This is perhaps especially so with regard to the regulation of the barristers' branch, a profession that, according to conventional analyses, must *in fact* be free from interference if constitutional liberty is to survive. Although easily lost sight of in the early twenty-first century, the point was readily apparent to Victorian observers. In introducing a bill to Parliament intended to effect major changes in the governance of the English Bar, Sir George Bowyer told the House of

Commons in 1862 that the Inns of Court were subject to "a system of absolute self-election, with an arbitrary power of exclusion, perfect irresponsibility, and perfect secrecy." These principles, he observed, "were repugnant to the doctrines of constitutional liberty recognized in this country, and *if the power of the Benchers extended, as it did, over a profession, it was a political power and ought not to be exercised in the dark, or without responsibility.*"[87]

To similar effect some three decades earlier, A. Baring had addressed the House of Commons and raised the question of whether the private power of the Benchers ought properly to be permitted to exclude an individual "for life from the practice of the higher branch of the Law."[88] In the same year, Daniel Whittle Harvey spoke of his own exclusion from the bar, telling the House of Commons that the law is "the people's patrimony," calling the Inns' monopoly over it "an entire and perfect despotism."[89]

A second problem making it difficult for contemporary observers to perceive the effectiveness of the exercise of bar power arises from an overly narrow focus. Many contemporary students of the legal profession begin from a perspective within liberal economics: hostility to economic monopolies and a belief that the bestowal of monopoly in any area of economic life must be offset by regulation if the public interest is to be served. Where, as in the case of lawyers, self-regulation is at issue, there is a natural suspicion that self-regulation might serve merely to mask the promotion of economic self-interest. These perspectives have produced a varied and extraordinarily rich secondary literature that critically addresses questions relating to how effectively the Bar "protects" the public from "bad" lawyers. Valuable though it is, this body of work has tended towards a surprisingly narrow focus on a few concerns: the apparent inability of the legal profession to guarantee the individual "moral character" of lawyers or their individual technical competence.

Wider questions that might arise from paying more attention to divisions within the profession (and the differences in outside constituencies to which those various factions wish to appeal) are too easily lost in the process of gathering statistics to assault the credibility of the legal profession as a guardian of the public interest, so conceived. When all incidents of professional discipline are treated as interchangeable for this limited purpose, the meaning of "ethics" is left unproblematized.

A third feature of much contemporary research that helps obscure the importance of nineteenth-century disciplinary actions of the Inns of Court also arises in the shadow of "market control" theory. Historians concerned primarily with the parameters of professional monopoly and its public-interest rationalizations concede too much to functionalist social sciences: mesmerized by an economic monopoly enjoyed by the profession *as a whole,* they find it difficult to perceive other, more important monopolies lurking in its shadow: discursive privilege, cultural monopoly, political monopoly, or ideological hegemony.[90] "Discipline," including proactive policing at the point of admission, is the foundation upon which these other monopolies rest.

One further point is important. A small number of documented discipline cases does not equate to an inconsequential authority. It is simultaneously possible that the nineteenth-century Inns failed to achieve the efficiency and regularity of a modern disciplinary apparatus *and* that they substantially inhibited the flourishing of liberal legal practices. Critics of the English Bar who argue that the barristers' profession failed to adequately "protect" the public from "bad" barristers imply that more rather than less discipline was rightly called for.[91] In itself, however, the absence of a large number of clear-cut disciplinary actions by the Benchers is poor evidence from which to fashion any argument relating to the character, purpose, or effect of professional association.

Because there was no formalized system for recording disciplinary incidents by any of the Inns of Court, all estimates of the reach and efficacy of the Bar's disciplinary power must be rough and tentative. Many are probably underestimates, if only because it seems likely that only the most hotly contested of cases have generated significant written record: the "gentlemanly" power of English elites has often been exercised subtly, shielded from the prying gaze of contemporary critic and historian alike. Innumerable interlocking webs of unspoken understanding had force. As Rhode observed:

> Of course, the absence of recorded disciplinary cases or formal character screening cannot be taken to imply an absence of moral oversight. The Inns constituted a small, homogeneous community, in which deviant behavior was unlikely to escape notice. The requirement that students eat a number of dinners at their Inn permitted some professional socialization, as well as *de facto* screening of potential clerks. And in many instances, collegial opprobrium undoubtedly proved as effective a disciplinary mechanism as formal sanctions. What is less clear is the extent to which character mandates had content apart from etiquette and social status.[92]

More crucially however, the effectiveness of bar discipline should not be confused with its quantum. The admonition, exclusion, or expulsion of individuals has striking symbolic importance: chilling effects ripple outward unpredictably, affecting the character of the legal profession far more than any simple numerical tally might indicate. This is especially so in cases of political repression, where, of necessity, the condemned activity is very much in the public eye, highly visible.[93] Mere deception of adjudicative tribunals or theft from clients is best done surreptitiously – ideally in the privacy of one's own chambers, where it is least likely to be deterred by even a fine-mesh disciplinary net. Unlike simple fraud, however, political advocacy cannot be done on the sly.

Trends in Discipline

A number of relatively well-documented cases of professional discipline are important, however. They serve as cultural showpieces and illustrate important issues surrounding the exercise of disciplinary powers by barristers' professional organizations during the first portion of the nineteenth century. The best-documented cases reveal certain striking shared features. In each case, the Inns of Court effectively used their powers over admission and discipline to demarcate the outer boundaries of liberal advocacy.

One noteworthy feature is that almost all of the individuals whose careers were at stake had some affiliation with parliamentary liberals or political radicals (Horne Tooke, Wooler, Harvey, James, Seymour, Kennedy, Kenealy, Claydon, Jones). The association was stronger in some cases than others in a period in which party factions were still taking shape. In some cases, a loose or strained alliance rather than party affiliation as such is the more accurate description. Nonetheless, the recurrence of some such association is noteworthy. Second, with the exception of Charles Claydon – a rather harmless local barrister caught in the cross-fire between powerful opposed forces – each of these individuals had achieved a considerable degree of national prominence either through political activity or through their conduct of famous cases. Third, it is noteworthy that the conduct for which several of these men were disciplined had taken place many years earlier or else involved continuing conduct that had been well known for some time before disciplinary proceedings were commenced (Harvey, James, Claydon, Seymour, Kennedy). Fourth, in most of these cases no complaint was made by any client of the individual involved. In several cases, disciplinary proceedings were taken in the face of evidence that the individuals alleged to have been injured felt no sense of grievance whatsoever (Jones, James, Claydon, Kenealy) or were widely acknowledged to have received exemplary professional services (Kennedy). In one case (Harvey), an individual was repeatedly denied admission to the Bar on character grounds notwithstanding a finding by the House of Commons that he had done nothing that should preclude admission.

These cases fall into two categories: refusals to admit (Harvey, Wooler, Horne Tooke) and the discipline of individuals who were already barristers (Jones, James, Claydon, Seymour, Kennedy, Kenealy). In most cases, some "provoking event" brought the individual barrister's conduct to the attention of the Bench of the relevant Inn of Court. This was, variously, the application for admission (Harvey, Wooler), appointment as Queen's Counsel (which would normally result in promotion to the Bench of his Inn – Seymour), or the conduct of highly public and controversial litigation (Jones, Kennedy, Kenealy). It also seems likely, although this was never unambiguously indicated in the Benchers' records, that the imminent rise of Edwin James to the office of Attorney-General of England was the provocation leading to his disbarment. With regard to the cases of refusal to admit (Harvey, Wooler, Horne Tooke), a more or less direct political blacklisting by the Benchers seems indisputable despite the rationalizations offered by the Inns of Court. This was the construction put on the Horne Tooke and Wooler cases during a House of Commons debate of the matter.

In other cases, however, it is less certain whether the Benchers took offence at professional practices *as such* or at the background political convictions that those practices reflected. Liberal free-traders were most likely to practise their profession in a way that turned barristers' etiquette upside down (Kennedy and, to a lesser extent, Seymour and Claydon). Liberal and radical alike could, in the proper case, be expected to assault class hierarchy, privilege, and the vestiges of Old Corruption with an uncommon virulence and lack of decorum (Jones, James, Seymour, Kennedy, Kenealy). In any case, the conduct of famous cases was clearly a significant political activity in itself, as trials ranging from Queen Caroline's divorce[94] through to Courvoisier,[95] Tawell,[96] Drury,[97] and Tichborne demonstrate.

Bar Discipline and the Rhetoric of Liberty

The case of D.W. Harvey is illustrative. Despite having been admitted as a student member of Inner Temple and fulfilling all of the normal prerequisites for call to the Bar, Harvey was repeatedly refused admission as a barrister. His exclusion is of special interest for several reasons.

First, he was a prominent democratic political activist. At the time of his exclusion from the Inner Temple, he was Member of Parliament for the radical borough of Colchester. His friends, allies, and supporters included many outstanding political radicals and reformers, such as William Cobbett, Daniel O'Connell, John Wilkes, J. Peel, George Sinclair, Edward Bulwer-Lytton, and Joseph Hume.[98]

Second, Harvey was peculiarly persistent in his desire to be admitted to the Bar. He pursued every avenue available to him in order to overcome the adverse decision of the Benchers, including appealing to the judges as Visitors of the Inns *and* causing a committee of the House of Commons to inquire into the matter. His attempts to fight his exclusion spanned a thirteen-year period from 1821 to 1834. Harvey published a number of pamphlets on the matter, and his efforts have left an extraordinarily full documentary record.

Third, the arguments that were developed in Harvey's case are revealing. In addition to specific responses to the Benchers' announced reasons for excluding him, Harvey and his allies developed a series of directly political arguments. They challenged the entire concept of independent professional regulation of Bar admissions. The organized profession's power was characterized as a manifestation of Old Corruption and it was asserted that any restrictions on the rights of citizens to practise as barristers seriously jeopardized the constitutional rights and liberties of the English people.[99]

Moreover, Harvey's challenges to the prerogatives of the Inns of Court were expressed as a matter of general principle. The discussions concerning his case involved an extensive review of the past admissions practices of the Inns of Court. The Harvey case, in short, captures much of the central concerns about the governance of the Inns of Court as these had developed during the period between the French Revolution and the decline of Chartism.

At a more general level, many commentators called into question the procedures and standards by which the Benchers of the Inns evaluated the appropriateness of individuals for practice at the Bar. This in turn shaded into critiques of the appropriateness of the exercise of such powers by private bodies operating without legislative sanction (the Inns), and into an extended criticism of the Benchers themselves. Critics of the Inns commonly identified the Bench with corruption, accusing the Benchers of having usurped an unconstitutional power to deny any Englishman his liberty or right to pursue the profession of barrister. Apologists for the Inns responded with the paternalistic argument. It was desirable, they said, to prevent the wrong sort of man from gaining admission to the Bar. They claimed that the Benchers had long exercised such a power, and, in any event, that any potential abuses of this power could be cured by the Visitorial jurisdiction of the twelve judges.

Harvey felt that his exclusion from the Bar had been "nothing less than a political and an inveterate party proceeding throughout," and claimed to have been "tried by a jury of Whigs and Tories, instead of by men acting in the character which they nevertheless assumed, of impartial judges of the moral and mental fitness of persons seeking to become members of the profession."[100] He offended the Benchers, he said, by his political career and not through long-finished civil actions of his youth, as his opponents claimed. Harvey told the House of Commons that he would have obtained a fair hearing "had I not been a politician as well as successful [*sic*] attorney, independent in my principles, belonging to neither party, and therefore the common prey of both, the sworn foe of corruption ... and always the bold, undaunted, and uncompromising enemy of the enemies of my country."[101]

William Cobbett concurred, writing on 10 January 1834 that Harvey would have been called to the bar without incident had not corruption been afraid "of your talents, and afraid, too, of her want of power to make those talents subservient to her purposes."[102] He chided Harvey:

> You should always have taken for *granted* that those who objected to you were corruption No. 2, doing the work of No. 1, and have spoken of them accordingly ... Hit corruption in her *soft places,* and hit *her hard;* and be delighted as I am, and laugh when she is in a rage.
>
> Come, come! it is time to lay upon the ruffians, and to waste no more of your precious time in efforts to obtain "justice" from men whose *business* it is to do injustice.[103]

Ireland's "Great Liberator," Daniel O'Connell, spoke to similar effect in support of Harvey's House of Commons motion regarding Bar admission. He too suggested that political malice motivated the professional gatekeeping of the Inns, going so far as to suggest that any individual of established reputation and untraditional political conviction would be denied the right to practise.[104]

Asserting that the practice of law was "the people's patrimony," Harvey argued that because the law "must be obeyed by all," its practice "should be open to all." Any restriction on this right was "odious," and the actual behaviour of the Inns of Court amounted to "an entire and perfect despotism."[105]

The clearest linkage of constitutional vision to questions of professional regulation was made during the House of Commons debate on Harvey's 1832 motion respecting the Inns of Court. Daniel O'Connell advanced a "free trade" vision of legal practice. Pointing out that Lincoln's Inn had once attempted to exclude reporters of parliamentary proceedings from admission to the Bar, he continued, pointedly citing developments in the United States as an appropriate model:

> And might not any other of these men make a similar rule to-morrow, if he chose, and exclude any other class of persons for any reason he chose to assign? Now, let us see how the law stands at present. In the case both of the attorney and the counsel, you must take the greatest care, and you must regard with the most rigid scrutiny, whoever you admit. Why, after you have admitted him, is anybody bound to employ him? There is no salary, no emolument whatever attached to a member of the profession. His only

> chance of reward is the confidence of the public; if he does not deserve it, he does not obtain it. Where, then, is the necessity of any tribunal to stand between the public and the practitioner? I take it to be altogether unnecessary; it has not been considered necessary in America, and its necessity does not seem to me very obvious ... It seems to me, therefore, that you have no necessity for this tribunal. What is done by admitting a man to the Bar? – You leave it open to the public to employ him.[106]

O'Connell, like Harvey, relied on principles of English constitutionalism to conclude "that no man's rights should be taken away capriciously – that no man's property should be disposed of without trial – that you should have no secret tribunal – no base inquisition – and every secret inquisition is base."[107]

Others expressed similar opinions. John Campbell, a Bencher of Lincoln's Inn, defended the character of Benchers and Judges but agreed that "I think it is an *arbitrary and irresponsible* power that ought not to attach to any tribunal." He admitted that the Inn's conduct of Wooler's case was "*highly objectionable*."[108] Hunt referred to the Inns as "this disgraceful Star Chamber Court,"[109] while Lennard asserted that they had usurped "a most unconstitutional power, and one which is contrary to the doctrines maintained in this country, that the road to professional honours is open, without distinction, to everyone."[110]

Harvey himself compared the Inns' censoring of admissions to the Bar with "the Star Chamber, or the Spanish Inquisition" in its arbitrariness, capriciousness, absurdity and unjustness.[111] The Inns had become, he said, "secret and self-created tribunals ... in the spirit of a pure and perfect despotism" that committed "a species of moral murder."[112]

Conclusion

The suppression of political and cultural unorthodoxy by the Benchers was possible even in times of apparent professional disintegration. Ultimately, no English barrister could practise law "at the edge" without fear of career-destroying reprisal by the professional establishment. The result is that a fully deliberate fettering of the independence of the English Bar by their own professional associations rendered English barristers a subservient profession in comparison to their French counterparts. One lesson might be that if professional independence is to be given meaning, barristers (and citizens) need independence *from* professional associations rather than the independence *of* those institutions.[113]

It is not necessary to celebrate those whose activities were questioned, investigated, or punished by the Benchers of the four Inns. It may be the case that many of them were arrogant, egotistical, deceptive, dishonest, selfish, untrustworthy, or otherwise thoroughly unpleasant individuals. They may have been wrong-headed, conspiratorial, politically wrong-headed. It cannot be presumed, however, that as a group these individuals were markedly more arrogant, egotistical, selfish, untrustworthy, or unpleasant than barristers at large. It is certainly quite remarkable that such a significant portion of disciplined individuals turned out to be of radical, liberal, democratic, or unorthodox political persuasion. Many, though not all, contemporary observers saw the hidden hand of political repression at work in the actions of the Inns of Court.

This raises some important questions with respect to those rationalizations of professional self-regulation. These commonly rest partly on the supposed ability of self-regulating bodies to shelter unorthodox individuals from political interference or suppression. If, however, professional organizations can themselves be employed as agents of political repression (Cobbett's "corruption No. 2, doing the work of No. 1"), this political underpinning for the maintenance of self-regulating professional structures is called into question. Despite long-standing and widespread assumptions about the historical roles of the English Bar vis-à-vis the rule of law and British liberty, one is left to wonder whether the cause of liberalism might not have been better served had English barristers, like Paris *avocats,* steadfastly refused to take on the characteristics of a corporate structure.

In 1750, Chancellor Henri-François d'Aguesseau expressed his repugnance at the very notion that the *avocats'* profession should organize as a corps. They could, he said, "have neither officers, nor leaders nor registers nor even a place of assembly." The reasoning behind this found expression in an anonymous 1782 pamphlet issued by the *Ordre des avocats* and quoted by Bell:

> "All corps are subject to a superior authority which makes them act as it pleases," the anonymous author declared. This reasoning runs counter to the assumptions made by some modern historians who (following Montesquieu) have assumed that corporate bodies, by providing a trade or profession with a unified voice, give its members greater autonomy than otherwise. [*Avocats*], however, clearly regarded themselves as an exception to this rule, and with some reason. Given the sensitivity of many of the cases that came before the *parlement,* it is reasonable to suppose that powerful magistrates or ministers would have used every instrument at their disposal – including the mechanisms of corporate discipline – to keep members of the bar under tight rein.[114]

Many liberal or radical English barristers of the eighteenth and nineteenth centuries would probably have agreed.

Notes

An earlier version of this chapter appeared as "Lawyers and Political Liberalism in Eighteenth- and Nineteenth-Century England" in Terence Halliday and Lucien Karpik, eds., *Lawyers and the Rise of Western Political Liberalism: Legal Professions and the Constitution of Modern Politics* (Oxford: Oxford University Press, 1997) 239. It has been revised and reprinted here with permission.

1 As quoted in D.W. Harvey, *A Letter to Lord John Russell, A.P. on the Benchers and the Bar* (London: Butterworth, 1852), frontispiece.

2 D.W. Harvey, as quoted in C. Fell Smith, "Daniel Whittle Harvey, 1786 1863" (1915) 24 Essex Review 24 at 29.

3 D. Duman, *The English and Colonial Bars in the Nineteenth Century* (London: Croom Helm, 1983) at 206-7.

4 *Ibid.* at 209, n. 29.

5 According to D.A. Bell, *Lawyers and Citizens: The Making of a Political Elite in Old Regime France* (New York: Oxford University Press, 1994) at 62. French *avocats* in the eighteenth century, by contrast, "could no longer expect many tangible rewards for their services to this monarchy. The idea of the bar as *pépinière des dignités,* leading to high office, had lost all relevance by the end of the seventeenth-century. Nor did barristers still serve as the most visible advisers to the great noble households."

6 C. Robbins, *The Eighteenth-Century Commonwealthman: Studies in the Transmission, Development, and Circumstance of English Liberal Thought from the Restoration of Charles II until the War with the Thirteen Colonies* (Cambridge, MA: Harvard University Press, 1959) at 294-95. See also P. Lucas, "Collective Biography of Students and Barristers of Lincoln's Inn, 1680-1804: A Study in the 'Aristocratic Resurgence' of the Eighteenth Century" (1974) 46 Journal of Modern History 227 at 242. I am grateful to Wilfrid Prest for bringing these sources to my attention.

7 As quoted in Harvey, *Letter to Lord John Russell, supra* note 1 at 7-8, note.

8 J.A. Hone, *For the Cause of Truth: Radicalism in London, 1796-1821* (Oxford: Clarendon Press, 1982) at 346.

9 T.C. Halliday and L. Karpik, "Politics Matter" in Terence Halliday and Lucien Karpik, eds., *Lawyers and the Rise of Western Political Liberalism: Legal Professions and the Constitution of Modern Politics* (Oxford: Oxford University Press, 1997); L. Karpik, "Builders of Liberal Society: French Lawyers and Politics" in Halliday and Karpik, *ibid.;* L. Karpik, "Lawyers and Politics in France, 1814-1950: The State, the Market, and the Public" (1988) 13 Law & Soc. Inquiry 707; L. Karpik, *French Lawyers: A Study of Collective Action, 1274-1994* (Oxford: Clarendon Press, 1999); Bell, *Lawyers and Citizens, supra* note 3; D.A. Bell, "Barristers, Politics, and the Failure of Civil Society in Old Regime France" in Halliday and Karpik, *ibid.*

10 Halliday and Karpik, "Politics Matter," *ibid.*

11 *Ibid.*

12 I have reviewed a substantial body of professional apologetics in Chapter 1 in this volume.

13 *Cf.* the burgeoning historical work on the interplay between law, lawyers, business, and politics in early modern and modern Britain. However, much of this scholarship focuses on attorneys, solicitors, and legal thought rather than the Bar. See, for example,

B. Abel-Smith and R. Stevens, *Lawyers and the Courts: A Sociological Study of the English Legal System, 1750-1965* (London: Hutchinson, 1967); R. Cocks, *Foundations of the Modern Bar* (London: Sweet and Maxwell, 1983); Duman, *supra* note 3; W.R. Prest, ed., *The Rise of the Barristers: A Social History of the English Bar, 1590-1640* (Oxford: Clarendon Press, 1986); J.S. Anderson, *Lawyers and the Making of English Land Law 1832-1940* (Oxford: Clarendon Press, 1992); G. Burgess, *The Politics of the Ancient Constitution* (Basingstoke, UK: Macmillan, 1992); D. Sugarman, "Simple Images and Complex Realities: English Lawyers and Their Relationship to Business and Politics, 1750-1950" (1993) 11 L.H.R. 257; D. Sugarman, *A Brief History of the Law Society* (London: The Law Society, 1995); D. Sugarman, "Who Colonised Whom? Reflections on the Intersection between Accountants, Lawyers and the Law" in Y. Dezalay and D. Sugarman, eds., *Professional Competition and Professional Power: Lawyers, Accountants and the Social Construction of Markets* (London: Routledge, 1995) 226; D. Sugarman, "Bourgeois Collectivism, Professional Power and the Boundaries of the State: The Private and Public Life of the Law Society, 1825-1914" (1996) 3 International Journal of the Legal Profession 81; R. Kostal, *Law and English Railway Capitalism, 1825-1875* (Oxford: Oxford University Press, 1994); C.W. Brooks, *Lawyers, Litigation and English Society since 1450* (London: Hambledon Press, 1998); D. Sugarman, *Law, Politics and Society in Early Modern England* (Cambridge: Cambridge University Press, 2009); D. Lemmings, "Lawyers" in I. McCalman, ed., *An Oxford Companion to the Romantic Age: British Culture, 1776-1832* (Oxford: Oxford University Press, 1999); D. Lemmings, *Professors of the Law: Barristers and English Legal Culture in the Eighteenth Century* (Oxford: Oxford University Press, 2000); P. Raffield, *Images and Cultures of Law in Early Modern England: Justice and Political Power, 1558-1660* (Cambridge: Cambridge University Press, 2004); P. Polden, "The Legal Professions" in W. Cornish et al., *The Oxford History of the Laws of England*, vol. 11 (Oxford: Oxford University Press, 2010) 959.

14 Terence Halliday and Lucien Karpik, eds., *Lawyers and the Rise of Western Political Liberalism: Legal Professions and the Constitution of Modern Politics* (Oxford: Oxford University Press, 1997).

15 Bell, *Lawyers and Citizens, supra* note 5; Karpik, *Les avocats, supra* note 9; Bell, "Barristers, Politics, and the Failure of Civil Society in Old Regime France," *supra* note 9; Karpik, "Lawyers and Politics," *supra* note 9; Karpik, "Builders of Liberal Society," *supra* note 9.

16 Bell, *Lawyers and Citizens, ibid.* at 51-52.

17 *Ibid.* at 98 ff.; Karpik, "Builders of Liberal Society," *supra* note 9.

18 Bell, *Lawyers and Citizens, ibid.* at 98.

19 Karpik, "Builders of Liberal Society," *supra* note 9.

20 Bell, *Lawyers and Citizens, supra* note 5 at 112.

21 Karpik, "Builders of Liberal Society," *supra* note 9.

22 *Ibid.*

23 *Ibid.*

24 Karpik, "Lawyers and Politics," *supra* note 9 at 724.

25 Karpik, "Builders of Liberal Society," *supra* note 9.

26 Karpik, "Lawyers and Politics," *supra* note 9 at 715.

27 Bell, *Lawyers and Citizens, supra* note 3 at 15.

28 *Ibid.* at 31.

29 *Ibid.* at 199.

30 Karpik, "Builders of Liberal Society," *supra* note 9.

31 "Central to lawyers' action was the public as an imaginary social construction, lawyers vested with the political legitimacy of the 'sovereign authority.' Symbolically constituted, this invisible entity was crafted by self-proclaimed prophets – like the lawyers – who seized upon a powerful counter-weight to the massive force of the Crown and state. This symbolic public became the new source of legitimation, the new last court of appeal ... a carefully

elaborated strategy largely built around a disinterestedness that demonstrated again and again the Bar's dedication to the public" (Halliday and Karpik, "Politics Matter," *supra* note 9). See also Karpik, "Builders of Liberal Society," *supra* note 9 (identifying the public as mandator of lawyers and noting that the "public" was constituted by lawyers in the act of representing).

32 Karpik, *ibid.*

33 M. Burrage, "Revolution as a Starting Point for the Comparative Analysis of the French, American and English Legal Professions" in R.L. Abel and P.S.C. Lewis, eds., *Lawyers in Society,* vol. 3 (Berkeley: University of California Press, 1989) 322 at 356-60.

34 David Lemmings, *Gentlemen and Barristers: The Inns of Court and the English Bar, 1680-1730* (Oxford: Clarendon Press, 1990); Lemmings, *Professors of the Law, supra* note 13; Prest, *Rise of the Barristers, supra* note 13; Suman Naresh, "Judah Philip Benjamin at the English Bar" (1996) 70 Tul. L. Rev. 2487.

35 J. Brewer, "The Wilkites and the Law, 1763-74: A Study in Radical Notions of Governance" in J. Brewer and J. Styles, eds., *An Ungovernable People: The English and Their Law in the Seventeenth and Eighteenth Centuries* (London: Hutchinson, 1980) 127 at 135.

36 *Ibid.* at 135.

37 J. Beattie, "Scales of Justice: Defence Counsel and the English Criminal Trial in the Eighteenth and Nineteenth Centuries" (1991) 9 Law & Hist. Rev. 221 at 247-48.

38 D. Hay, "Property, Authority and the Criminal Law" in D.P. Linebaugh Hay and E.P. Thompson, eds., *Albion's Fatal Tree: Crime and Society in Eighteenth Century England* (London: Allen Lane, 1975) 17 at 27-28.

39 See R. Challinor, *A Radical Lawyer in Victorian England: W.P. Roberts and the Struggle for Workers' Rights* (London: I.B. Tauris, 1990). It is the recognition of this that leads E.P. Thompson to describe the rule of law as an "unqualified human good" in *Whigs and Hunters* (London: Allen Lane, 1975). See also E.P. Thompson, "Custom, Law and Common Right" in E.P. Thompson, *Customs in Common: Studies in Traditional Popular Culture* (New York: New Press, 1993) 97 at 111ff., discussing John Lewis and the legal defence of customary rights in Richmond Park in the 1750s.

40 Brewer, "Wilkites," *supra* note 35 at 131. Brewer identifies a number of important lawyer-activists (a category encompassing barristers, solicitors, and attorneys): John Glynn, John Reynolds, William Ellis, George Bellas, Robert Morris, Arthur Lee, Watkin Lewes, Charles Martin, Sayer, and Dayrell.

41 *Ibid.* at 131-32, 135-36, 142, 148-50, 158.

42 *Ibid.* at 155, 163-64.

43 *Ibid.* at 156-57.

44 See *ibid.* at 140 for the case of Wheble, a printer summonsed before the House of Commons for printing its debates. Wheble was apprehended by his own servant and brought before John Wilkes, who, in his capacity as city alderman and magistrate for London, promptly released him on the "grounds that he was a London freeman, that Carpenter was not a City peace officer, and that the cause of arrest was neither a felony nor a breach of the peace. Wheble promptly counter-suited Carpenter and charged him with assault."

45 *Ibid.* at 132.

46 *Ibid.* at 133.

47 *Ibid.* at 132.

48 *Ibid.* at 136.

49 *Ibid.* at 165.

50 *Ibid.*

51 *Ibid.* at 145.

52 S. Landsman, "The Rise of the Contentious Spirit: Adversary Procedure in Eighteenth Century England" (1992) 75 Cornell L. Rev. 479 at 498-99 and 501-2. The quotation about

Tudor and Stuart trials is from J.S. Cockburn, *A History of the English Assizes 1558-1714* (Cambridge: Cambridge University Press, 1972) at 109, indicating that trials of that period almost never took longer than twenty minutes.

53 J. Beattie, *Crime and the Courts in England, 1660-1800* (Oxford: Clarendon Press, 1986) at 314, has put it thus: "*That Englishmen enjoyed* fundamental liberties beyond the reach of government was a commonplace in the eighteenth-century. It was a notion shared across society and across the political spectrum, celebrated by Whigs and Tories, by Hanoverian oligarchs and their country and radical opponents. There might be disagreements about whether those rights were being threatened and by whom, but no one questioned that Englishmen had inherited liberties won by their forefathers in the struggle against despotic governments" (emphasis in original).

54 Landsman, "Contentious Spirit," *supra* note 52 at 572.

55 7 and 8 Will. 3, c. 3, s. 1. (1696); Landsman, *ibid.* at 579.

56 Landsman, *ibid.* at 573.

57 So William Garrow charged in cross-examination of the victim of highway robbery during a trial in 1784. Quoted in Beattie, "Scales of Justice," *supra* note 37 at 240-41.

58 Landsman, "Contentious Spirit," *supra* note 52 at 534ff.

59 *Ibid.* at 589.

60 *Ibid.* at 590.

61 *Ibid.* at 589ff identifies a number of such individuals or causes, including Thomas Erskine, James Stephen, Granville Sharp, and other abolitionists.

62 L.P. Stryker, *For the Defense: Thomas Erskine, the Most Enlightened Liberal of His Times, 1750-1823* (New York: Doubleday, 1949) at vii, 212, 217. See also J.A. Lovat-Fraser, *Erskine* (Cambridge: Cambridge University Press, 1932).

63 D. Mellinkoff, *The Conscience of a Lawyer* (St. Paul, MN: West Publishing, 1973) at 240.

64 Beattie, "Scales of Justice," *supra* note 37 at 238.

65 *Ibid.* at 230.

66 The pamphlet collection of the Middle Temple Library is a huge, much underutilized resource. Rande Kostal made productive use of such sources in his book *Law and English Railway Capitalism, 1825-1875, supra* note 13. I have drawn somewhat unsystematically on such sources, in Chapters 4, 7, 8, and 11 in this volume.

67 Hone, *For the Cause of Truth, supra* note 8 at 337.

68 *Ibid.* at 337-54. The quotation is reproduced at 341. For a later period, see also J.M. Fellague Ariouat (formerly Sergent), *The Politics of Trial Procedure in the Chartist Trials in England and Wales, 1839-1848* (PhD Dissertation, University of Birmingham, 1995).

69 Challinor, *Radical Lawyer, supra* note 39, documents the extraordinary efforts of a radical barrister to give effect to workers' rights by means of vigorous advocacy before local, inferior courts. For a discussion of three highly politicized cases, see Bege Bowers Neel, *Lawyers on Trial: Attitudes toward the Lawyer's Use and Abuse of Rhetoric in Nineteenth-Century England* (PhD Dissertation, University of Tennessee, 1984), discussing Lord Brougham's defence of Queen Caroline (1820), Charles Phillips's defence of Courvoisier (1840), and Sir Fitzroy Kelly's defence of John Tawell (1845).

The cases that surrounded *Kennedy v. Broun* and *Swinfen v. Chelmsford* at mid-century were simultaneously about the privileges of barristers and about class and inheritance. I discuss these from various perspectives in Chapters 4, 7, 8, and 11 in this volume. Commercialized notions of legal practice represented a strongly "liberal" vision of lawyering, representation, and rights of citizens. They ran headlong into Bar "etiquette." See also J.R.S. Forbes, *The Divided Legal Profession in Australia: History, Rationalisation and Rationale* (Sydney: Law Book Company, 1979). Towards the century's end, an extraordinary case involving a contested inheritance was reinterpreted in popular discourse in terms of class and citizenship and raised stark questions regarding "liberal advocacy" before launching the important populist movement that became known as the "Kenealyites" or the "Magna Carta Association," which found expression through a newspaper called *The Englishman*. A massive literature on the "Tichborne cause" includes M. Roe, *Kenealy and the Tichborne Cause: A Study in Mid-Victorian Populism* (Melbourne: Melbourne University Press, 1974).

70 D. Thompson, "Queen Victoria, the Monarchy and Gender" in D. Thompson, ed., *Outsiders: Class, Gender and Nation* (London: Verso, 1993) 164 at 171.

71 D.L. Rhode, "An Adversarial Exchange on Adversarial Ethics: Text, Subtext, and Context" (1991) J. Legal Educ. 29 at 30.

72 H.J. Perkin, *The Origins of Modern English Society, 1780-1880* (London/Toronto: Routledge and Kegan Paul/University of Toronto Press, 1969) at 216-17, asserts that Queen Caroline's case in 1820 "ranked with Peterloo in crystallizing the working-class consciousness."

73 Hone, *For the Cause of Truth*, *supra* note 8 at 350.

74 The others were Thomas Denman and Dr. Lushington; Williams, Tindal, and Wild joined these three in representing the Queen. Brougham was variously a Whig politician, editor of the *Edinburgh Review*, and writer for the *Morning Chronicle*, the *Review*, and *The Times*. He had little love for the leaders of his profession. At one stage, his professional career was all but brought to an end by a form of professional blacklisting for, as T.H. Ford observes, "No solicitor in the Metropolis or on the Northern Circuit was willing to give him briefs because of his radical reputation. Brougham, consequently, devoted himself to promoting such radical change that the Whigs were forced to find a seat at Camelford, a pocket-borough in distant Cornwall" (at 110). He was involved in Hunt's seditious libel trial (for republication of an article by Cobbett), advertised professional services in the *Review*, reviewed Erskine's speeches as a barrister and Stockdale's libel actions, and worked in several liberal causes that came before the courts. He spoke against anti-Luddite measures in Parliament, and "[i]n November 1814 occurred Brougham's famous 'dressing down' of Ellenborough for confusing counsel with a client in a case of blasphemous libel" (at 119). Brougham was intensely disliked by Eldon but his career advanced through growing cooperation with Romilly (at 120) and he served as "Attorney-General" for Queen Caroline. See T.H. Ford, "Brougham as a Barrister: Courtroom Dilemmas of a Notorious Radical" (1984) 5 J. Legal Hist. 108.

75 Quoted in Rhode, "Adversarial Exchange," *supra* note 71 at 29.

76 D.W. Harvey, *A Letter to the Burgesses of Colchester, Containing a Plain Statement of the Proceedings before the Benchers of the Inner Temple, upon His Application to Be Called to the Bar, and upon His Appeal to the Judges* (London: R. and A. Taylor, 1832).

77 Bell, *Lawyers and Citizens*, *supra* note 5 at 53, notes that *avocats*, "unlike the procureurs, record-keepers, bailiffs, and nearly all other denizens of the *Palais de Justice*, not only never formed a *corps*, but never became venal officers." An eighteenth-century *bâtonnier*, unlike his eighteenth-century English equivalent, the Treasurer of an Inn, existed in a professional environment in which the very idea of an "officer," "leader," "register," or "even a place of assembly" was deemed illegitimate (*ibid.* at 52).

78 Prest, *supra* note 13; W.R. Prest, "Why the History of the Professions Is Not Written" in G. Rubin and D. Sugarman, eds., *Law, Economy and Society: Essays in the History of English Law 1750-1914* (London: Abingdon Books) 300. The state of mid-nineteenth-century English legal education is canvassed in Chapter 4 in this volume.

79 See J.E.C. Hill, *The Century of Revolution, 1603-1714* (Edinburgh: T. Nelson, 1961; New York: Norton, 1980).

80 See Chapter 1 in this volume.

81 See, *e.g.*, J.H. Cohen, *The Law: Business or Profession?* (New York: Banks Law Publishing, 1916), chs. 4, 5, and 6, which give accounts of the legal professions in China, Japan, and numerous European countries, illustrating the "need" for an independent legal profession. See also the literature reviewed in Chapter 1 in this volume.

82 R.L. Abel, *The Legal Profession in England and Wales* (Oxford: Blackwell, 1988), comes close to this second position.

83 Cocks, *supra* note 13. Cocks does argue that the circuit messes of the Bar had some significant regulatory role, although his only empirical evidence for this is derived from the Norfolk Circuit in the 1830s. While no thorough comparative study of the regulatory role of the nineteenth-century circuits has yet been undertaken, the Midland Circuit Mess at any rate did not assert a disciplinary function until the 1850s, by which time the authority of the circuits had, according to Cocks, been much eroded by the coming of the railways. In any event, given an absolute lack of power to prohibit barristers from practising, expulsion from a circuit Mess had the paradoxical effect of liberating the expelled individual from professional persuasion altogether: see Chapter 11 in this volume. Cocks reports later in the century that "the Inns were failing to provide anything like a vigorous disciplinary system and now, by the 1880s it was very difficult indeed to argue that the Circuit Messes provided adequate supervision of the whole profession" (at 214).

84 Abel, *The Legal Profession in England and Wales, supra* note 82 at 127.

85 W. Holdsworth, *A History of English Law,* vol. 12 (London: Methuen, 1938).

86 D.L. Rhode, "Moral Character as a Professional Credential" (1985) 94 Yale L.J. 491 at 495.

87 *The Times,* 26 June 1862, 10 (emphasis added).

88 Quoted in Harvey, *Letter to Lord John Russell,* frontispiece.

89 D.W. Harvey, *Inns of Court. The Speech and Reply of D.W. Harvey, Esq., M.P. on the 14th of June 1832, in the House of Commons, on Moving for Leave to Bring in a Bill to Empower the Court of King's Bench to Regulate the Admission of Students and Barristers* (London: James Ridgway, 1832) at 6-8.

90 Feminist scholars, for obvious reasons, are often better attuned to issues of cultural monopoly. See, *e.g.,* the insightful analysis of the "benchmark man" of the legal profession in relation to "others" in Australia in M. Thornton, *Dissonance and Distrust – Women in the Legal Profession* (Melbourne: Oxford University Press, 1996).

91 See, *e.g.,* Abel, *The Legal Profession in England and Wales, supra* note 82.

92 Rhode, "Moral Character," *supra* note 86 at 495. Rhode's reference to "clerks" here is confusing. She probably means apprentice barristers, not barristers' clerks.

93 *Cf.* Rhode's observations regarding the "moral fitness" requirement of American legal professions: "Throughout its history, the moral fitness requirement has functioned primarily as a cultural showpiece. In that role, it has excommunicated a diverse and changing community, variously defined to include not only former felons, but women, minorities, adulterers, radicals and bankrupts. Although the number of applicants formally denied admission has always been quite small, the number deterred, delayed, or harassed has been more substantial" *(ibid.* at 493-94).

94 E.P. Deutsch, "The Trial of Queen Caroline" (1971) 57 A.B.A. J. 1201; W.D. Bowman, *The Divorce Case of Queen Caroline* (New York: E.P. Dutton, 1930); Rhode, "Adversarial Exchange," *supra* note 71; and see also I. McCalman, *Radical Underworld: Prophets, Revolutionaries and Pornographers in London 1795-1840* (Cambridge: Cambridge University Press, 1988). Bowman suggests that the trial and Brougham's address had "shaken the aristocracy," and discusses the political dimensions of the case in relation to Brougham's zealous Whig partisanship (at 254-55, 259-61). The defeat of the King was seen by Erskine as a victory for the rule of law (at 281).

95 See Mellinkoff, *The Conscience of a Lawyer, supra* note 63.

96 "On the Principle of Advocacy as Developed in the Practice of the Bar" (1854) 20 n.s. *Law Magazine* 265 (reprinted from No. 84 of the *Law Magazine*). This article offers a defence of vigorous liberal advocacy through a discussion of the cases of Courvoisier, Tawell, and Queen Caroline and argues that "the writers who would uproot the profession of advocacy must seek the destruction of the Law itself."

97 In 1851, James acted as counsel for the defence in *The Queen v. Thomas Drury S.* His client, Dr. Simon Bernard, was accused of conspiring with Orsini to assassinate Napoleon III, a charge on which he was acquitted only by introducing evidence to show that Bernard had in fact intended to kill somebody else. Politically, James made it clear that he personally endorsed the views of Orsini and Bernard, for shortly after the defence was complete he appeared on a public platform to attack Napoleon III and endorse what were then radically democratic political views. The *Law Times* abhorred his politics and commented, after that speech, that "after the exhibition of Wednesday it will be impossible for any government, not Red Republican in its origin and objects, to give him place," and suggested that he should "resign the office of counsel to the Queen, as being altogether incompatible with the principles proclaimed upon the platform and to which he gave his public adhesion" (*Law Times,* 1 May 1858, 78).

98 Smith, "Daniel Whittle Harvey," *supra* note 2 at 69, describes him thus: "the novelist, father of the first Lord Lytton. He was at that time an ardent reformer in politics, and a few years previously had stood for Southwark and issued an address, but had retired on finding his prospects hopeless."

99 See, *e.g.*, Harvey, *Letter to Lord John Russell, supra* note 1 at 7.

100 Harvey, *Inns of Court, supra* note 89 at 55-56.

101 *Ibid.* at 75-76.

102 Quoted in Harvey, *Letter to Lord John Russell, supra* note 1 at 7-8, n.

103 *Ibid.*

104 "I say you should not shut out an individual who, instead of walking the Hall for six or seven years, and then being looked upon as a very promising young gentleman, would come to the bar with full-blown honours, with the knowledge and confidence of the public, with a steady independence, and who would make an unwilling Judge tremble on his seat. I am perfectly sure that if I had not been called to the Bar previous to my entering into political life, I should never have been permitted to come to the Bar at all" (O'Connell, quoted in Harvey, *Inns of Court, supra* note 89 at 43).

105 *Ibid.* at 6-8.

106 O'Connell, quoted in Harvey, *Inns of Court, supra* note 89 at 39-40.

107 O'Connell, quoted in *ibid.* at 43-44.

108 Campbell, quoted in *ibid.* at 44.

109 Hunt, quoted in *ibid.* at 44.

110 Lennard, quoted in *ibid.* at 45. He continued: "[A]rbitrary power should not be confided to any man, however respectable ... But we are told that there is an appeal to the Judges; but be it observed that it is not to the Judges, sitting in open Court and in public, but in private. In an action for the smallest amount of property, would the public bear that the trials should be behind closed doors? Yet it appears that in a matter of far greater importance than that of mere property – namely, in a question involving a man's character and his eligibility to a profession – this may be heard in private."

111 *Ibid.* at 91, 92, 93.

112 *Ibid.* at 88.

113 *Cf.* Bell, *Lawyers and Citizens, supra* note 5 at 51-53, 63-64.

114 *Cf. ibid.* at 52.

3

Law and Colony

MAKING THE CANADIAN LEGAL PROFESSION

A group of lawyers met in a small, dusty railway town in cattle country east of the Rocky Mountains in the spring of 1899. Their meeting established the Calgary Bar Association, reflecting their consensus "that the Bar of Calgary were sufficiently numerous to form an association for the purpose of cultivating a feeling of professional brotherhood, discussing various matters affecting the interests of the profession, and taking united action thereon."[1]

The matters most urgently in need of collective action, they thought, were the development of a conveyancing tariff, agreement on uniform office hours, and addressing the problem of "unlicensed conveyancers." From some viewpoints, this lawyers' project appears to provide inauspicious origins for organized professionalism, even in the cowboy capital of the British Empire. Whereas professional rhetoric makes much of public service – sometimes elevating professional self-governance to the status of an entrenched constitutional right[2] – the nitty-gritty of professional organization *seems* to have been self-interest. Their specific objectives were classic trade union stuff: money, workweek, and monopoly. From one viewpoint, this hints of professional conspiracy against clients, community, and the state.

Alluring though it may be, such interpretations dreadfully caricature the processes of professionalization. I wish to explore the history of the professionalization of Canadian lawyers in order to develop broader understandings of professionalism and lawyers alike. There is more here than meets the eye.

The Novelty of Lawyers' Professionalism

Lawyers west of Ontario spearheaded the movement that created modern professional forms in Canada. Although historical antecedents of some sort exist for every innovation, this is almost entirely a twentieth-century story. The forms and cultures of the professionalism we experience did not exist

Calgary was a dusty railway town in the early twentieth century. This photo shows First Nations riding in the Calgary Exhibition and Stampede parade in 1912, the year that the rodeo and festival was established. *Glenbow Museum, NA-335-5*

anywhere before the twentieth century.[3] The high-water mark of European imperialism, the spatial extension of both the United States and the Dominion of Canada, and the creation of modern professional structures occurred simultaneously. Each process affected the others.

In its paradigmatic expression, professionalism incorporates demanding admission standards, mandatory and extended formal education, examinations, admissions screening, state licensing, prohibitions on unauthorized practice, self-regulation, written codes of conduct, and technocratic or meritocratic culture. In its peculiar combinations and in its relationship to a culture that was being consumed by "galloping hegemony of instrumental reason," all this is very much part of the larger twentieth-century phenomenon.[4] The whole, distinctly greater than the sum of its parts, combined in our grandparents' and great-grandparents' generations to form the core structures or forms of contemporary professionalism.[5] North American professionalism was a new social technology for new times.

Noting this suggests the importance of several oft-overlooked themes. Most obviously, the *novelty* of contemporary professional form deserves greater emphasis than it is generally accorded. This is particularly so in the case of the legal profession. Because law is obviously an ancient profession, the suggestion that some essence of the existing profession might be of recent origin strikes many as very nearly heretical. Understandings of lawyers' professionalism in Canada and in other "British diaspora" lands (including the United States) characteristically assume that, although much changes in professional *culture*, the essential forms or structures have a timeless quality about them. The distilled essence of professionalism – corporate structures, codes of ethics, effective self-regulation, rigorous training programs, and admissions standards – are often assumed to have existed since time immemorial, only relatively inconsequential matters of detail changing over the generations. Not infrequently, key features are traced back through presumed genealogies to mysterious origins at the English Inns of Court in a time before recorded professional history. A heavy overlay of myth needs to be peeled back if the cultural origin of professionalism in our age is to be understood.[6]

Structures and Cultures of Legal Professionalism

The second theme is more complex. Broadly, it is that professional forms themselves need to be understood as cultural artifacts, that "culture" and "structure" are properly understood as mutually constitutive, not as distinct forces. There is no base, no bedrock professional core that is unmoved by the currents of time. The case study of Canadian legal professionalism lends support to the "general theoretical argument that conceptual distinctions between structure and culture have lost force and utility in providing compelling theoretical maps, accounts, and images of the social world."[7]

A cultural revolution of sorts transformed the structures of legal professionalism in the British Empire between 1867 and the Second World War. This was spurred, most dramatically, from Prairie Canada. The lawyers who led these efforts imagined that, in getting the structures of legal professionalism right, they would transform the country as a whole. They were remarkably successful in their professional project. Ironically, however, once their goals of structural transformation were attained, the larger cultural project they championed fell into disfavour. Subsequent changes were less perceptible, lacking in dramatic moment, but real and consequential nonetheless. In the result, the forms they created survived, but the meanings attributed to them were turned upside down by subsequent generations.

This chapter identifies changes in the first third of the twentieth century, illustrating how professional forms emerged from the cultural predispositions of reforming lawyers. Although subsequent metasomic processes cannot be explored here, they need to be noted so as to avoid leaving a misleading impression of the *effects* of the transformations described here. Often operating in directions *opposite* to those intended by the cultural revolutionaries of the earlier decades, a narrow and constrained technocratic pragmatism supplanted the essentially moral vision of modern professionalism's founding fathers.

Dominion and Empire

Before considering professional transformations in detail, it is useful to pause briefly to consider the social contexts from which they emerged. The bursts of Canadian professional reform between 1910 and 1939 occurred in heady times. For a brief period, Canadians fantasized that the world was theirs to lead, and believed that Canada's future lay in the west:

> Calculations of prairie greatness and celebrations of imperial power inevitably ran together; the west would have a population of 100 million; it would be the bread-basket of the world; it would become the centre of gravity for all Canada; and, if it ruled Canada, and Canada led the empire (as it soon would), then, as anyone could see, the west would lead the world.[8]

Not surprisingly, many reform initiatives originated in the Canadian west and especially in the Prairie provinces (Manitoba, Saskatchewan, and Alberta). The west was then an important place, simultaneously the object and the soul of Canadian imperialism. Conditions were ripe for social experimentation.

Numerically small and finding themselves in a new land, prairie legal professions lacked the inherited social capital of lawyers further east. They faced special difficulties in attempting to either assert cultural leadership or establish its prerequisite, a secure market niche. The political communities of the prairies were hostile to privilege, infused with an egalitarian and reform ethos. Even the structures of government itself could not be taken for granted. The mood was riotously democratic, consistent in both its rejection of hierarchy and its questioning of the authoritative voice. At the same time, extraordinarily rapid social change was under way. Outside forces perpetually destabilized the region economically, socially, and politically. The effects of a newly industrializing continent's "distended society"[9] were powerfully felt. Successive waves of populist politics threatened status, wealth, privilege, hierarchy, and order.

The region participated in a reforming culture that was shared with other parts of Anglo-Canada,[10] but less inhibited by the constraint of convention or the gravitational pull of congealed hierarchies. In Canada's new lands, relatively greater emphasis was placed on freedom and its prerequisite, the governance of the good and the deserving. Among the Anglo-elite, frontier egalitarianism combined creatively with pride in "Britishness" and a belief in pioneer virtue. They held out the hope that this new land "could re-create the individual just as it improved upon the social order."[11] A "militant view of British civilization" emerged and "the goal of prairie social leaders – a Protestant, law-respecting, English-speaking community in which democracy and social equality were fundamental assumptions – seemed within reach."[12] Proud of their Britishness, western leaders were nonetheless "not complacent about British social achievements" and they insisted on their "freedom to improve upon the parent culture."[13]

Yet, the first three decades of the twentieth century brought unusual challenges. The newness and social fluidity that promised so much also appeared in threatening guise. The Dominion seemed to totter on a knife edge between heaven on earth and a hell of human making. Massive urbanization, industrialization, recession, war, and growing xenophobia all took their toll. Economic dislocations corroded confidence in the future of governance. Class, ethnic, and rural/urban divisions were accentuated, culminating in a postwar burst of radicalism more pervasive than any other in North America. Winnipeg's crippling General Strike of 1919 was stunningly effective.[14] Anglo-elites experienced a rapid, discomforting erosion of confidence in their ability to assimilate newly "dangerous" others into proper British ways. Buffeted by temperance, women's suffrage, social gospel, labour radicalism, progressivism, the farmer's and cooperative movements, socialism, and maternal feminism, regional consciousness threatened to disintegrate under the pull of centrifugal forces.

Knowing that lasting social peace could not grow from the barrel of a gun, elites faced the conundrum of how best to contain radical urges in a society where deeply held commitment to an open, democratic, egalitarian social order coexisted with quite contrary cultural currents and with immense class and ethnic inequities. Lawyers kept all options under review as they contemplated their professional and civic futures. A degree of professional cohesion was attained through multiple professional and social connections, including those formed through the work of the Canadian Bar Association. Regional, Dominion-wide, and international webs of professional interconnection provided ideas, promoted consensus, and provided legitimation for novel professional projects.

Looking southward, lawyers discovered a social vision that held forth the promise of founding a better world on terrain midway between the Bolshevik abyss on the one hand and a sort of *Ancien Régime* repression on the other. The middle ground was professionalism.

Remaking Canadian Legal Professionalism

During the first half of the twentieth century, Canada was divided into nine provinces (Newfoundland not yet having joined the Dominion) and extensive, sparsely populated northern territories administered as colonies of the Dominion government. Quebec was – and remains – distinct from all the others, a civil law jurisdiction living in complex relationships to common law Canada. Its legal professions, cultures, and history are distinctive. Respecting that difference, I make no attempt to fold Quebec into the larger Canadian whole. This chapter focuses on legal professions in the rest of Canada.

Each of the eight common law provinces had its own structures of professional regulation, typically featuring a provincial "law society" or equivalent body established under provincial legislation.[15] All solicitors *and* barristers were required to be members of the law society of their province. Although Canadian federalism precludes any possibility of a pan-provincial regulatory body, reform-minded lawyers of the early twentieth century developed a national voluntary association through which to promote their professional visions. The Canadian Bar Association emerged as an important force in 1914. It was the creature of lawyers who had become frustrated to varying degrees by the inaction of provincial law societies (the formal regulatory bodies). Formed quite deliberately within the realm of culture, part of its purpose was to spur those bodies into action. It was backed up or egged on by an array of local bar associations, law student organizations, and similar voluntary bodies, organized with varying degrees of formality, ambition, and effectiveness.[16] Although Canada was a self-governing colony or British Dominion, it did not follow the English model of a "divided profession." In each of the common law provinces, barristers and solicitors, although *formally* distinct, were members of a single professional body. Most lawyers were both "barrister and solicitor" (a usage that continues to the present), and although some elite lawyers earnestly wished to create a distinctive and elite barristers' profession,[17] this never came about.

The Canadian Bar Association (confusingly, never restricted to barristers) provided a focal point for new initiatives. Its influence was felt across Canada and the patterns of professionalism that emerged were strongly shaped by it. Canadian professional reformers spearheaded a fundamental reshaping of their common law structures of legal professionalism. Significant reforms were implemented with regard to qualification, education and admission, professional ethics, the regulatory powers of professional organizations, and the assertion of a lawyers' monopoly over legal services.

Taken together, they radically reworked existing structures of professionalism to the point where something new and distinctive had emerged.

Qualification, Education, and Admission

The training, education, and socialization of aspiring lawyers were central to the reform agenda. During the early twentieth century, Canadian lawyers moved decisively away from their English inheritance. In place of almost exclusive reliance upon apprenticeship, they created ambitious blueprints for a new sort of legal education. The new model was explicitly cultural in content, university-focused, rigorous, and taught in novel ways. New law schools emerged in Winnipeg, Regina, Saskatoon, Calgary, Edmonton, Victoria, and Vancouver (later consolidated in Winnipeg, Saskatoon, Edmonton, and Vancouver). Most were affiliated with the provincial university. Moreover, there were significant developments in curriculum, staffing, and program delivery at the older law schools in Fredericton, Halifax, Montreal (where McGill uncomfortably straddled the cultures of the common law and the civil law world), and Toronto. Early-twentieth-century reformers sought to raise the prelaw educational requirements so that only university graduates would be admitted to legal education (a goal attained only after mid-century).

The founders of twentieth-century Canadian legal education sought nothing less than to impose a uniform cultural curriculum. Their objective involved more than producing better legal technicians. By restricting entry to the right persons and subjecting them to the right sort of legal education, they sought to achieve an enduring transformation of the law students' inner essence. They expected a new class of graduate lawyer to emerge: lawyers who were technically competent but also *better people,* permanently converted to a deep inner understanding of the virtues of British law. Inculcating the wisdom, judgment, and ethics of gentlemen was the central goal. It was hoped that an army of gentlemen lawyers would emerge, to be dispersed over Canada's enormous and varied territory, carrying within them the lifeblood of British civilization. Lawyers were to become missionaries in service of a secularized trinity: law, Britishness, and civilization.[18]

Law Societies

Reformers also sought to mutate existing provincial law societies into active agents of a new professionalism. They wished to do so in part to achieve particular instrumental goals, but symbolism was equally important. Law societies that played an active role in the project of professionalism would enjoy enhanced prestige *and* enhance the dignity of the profession as a whole. Lying below the field of vision of most twenty-first-century observers, such symbolic objectives were viewed as considerable and distinct goods in and of themselves. The dignity of the profession and the prestige of its collective leadership

This bronze statue of Moses holding the Ten Commandments is located to the right of the Speaker in the Manitoba Legislative Assembly Chamber. A statue of Solon, a famous lawmaker of ancient Athens (not pictured here) is located to the left of the Speaker. Both were sculpted by Georges Gardet. *Courtesy Legislative Reading Room*

were no small matters in an era when notions of honour, dignity, and gentlemanliness still carried considerable social weight.

In this respect, the reform of law societies was nestled within a larger vision of social ordering. Reformers wished to implant forms of social governance that were neither narrowly economic nor exclusively political. Law societies, like bar associations, gentlemen's clubs, and volunteer associations of all sorts, were thought to occupy an important space in civil society. They were to secure their niche in a realm that was neither fully public nor fully private, acting for the good of public and state alike – but distinctly *not* as agents of the state. A particular understanding of constitutional governance informed professional reform.[19]

This repositioning was most apparent in the revamped law society roles regarding ethics policing, admissions and qualification, discipline, and monopoly protection.

Law Societies' Roles

Ethics Policing

A radical remaking of approaches to policing the ethics of practising lawyers took place, the most tangible marker of which was the development of an ethics code. Undertaken at the initiative of the Canadian Bar Association, this appears in retrospect to have been a logical, perhaps necessary, development of modest proportions. The move was highly controversial at the time, however. It marked a striking deviation from British models of lawyers' professionalism.[20]

The Canadian Bar Association's cultural authority was powerfully felt, and most provincial law societies soon embraced the notion that a formal promulgation of professional ethical standards was desirable. They in turn sought changes in their statutory powers so as to expand their disciplinary reach into new territory. The *content* of Canada's first code of lawyerly ethics has provoked insightful scholarly commentary focused on its coverage, gaps, and omissions,[21] but for present purposes it is the novelty of this form of ethical regulation, rather than its particulars, that is most noteworthy.

Admission and Education

In and of themselves, the development of more formalized legal education for *some* aspiring lawyers (mandatory formal legal education for *all* came much later) and the promulgation of hortatory ethical codes operate only in the realm of culture. The matter was not left there, however. Further innovations gave force to the cultural aspirations of elite lawyers.

One area related to the "gatekeeping" function of law societies. Issues surrounding the eligibility of women for admission to the legal professions of Canada came to a head in some jurisdictions. There were also statutory changes relating to the enrollment of foreign, Aboriginal, or foreign-qualified lawyers. Both types of initiative clearly involved responses to centrally important questions concerning what sort of person from what sort of background could properly embody law in a new British Dominion, a question not yet adequately explored in Canadian historical writing.[22]

Other changes expanded the ambit of discretion exercisable by the governing boards of law societies (Benchers) in making decisions about admissions and qualifications. In some cases, statutory redefinitions of law society powers were passed (sometimes retroactively) in order to facilitate the creation of full-time professional law faculties.[23]

Such changes were important both in themselves and for their symbolic impact. The honour of the legal profession, and hence its cultural authority, was thought to be much bound up with its discretionary authority: the wider the discretion, the greater the honour, and hence the greater the cultural capital of the profession. A high point in this movement (in one way of seeing things) was the judgment of Hunter C.J. in *Re Hagel v. Law Society of British Columbia* holding that there "is no right of admission" to the law society.[24] Chief Justice Hunter explained that

> the discretion to call or to admit ought to be left exclusively to the Benchers ... it would not be in the public interest to permit any right of review. It must be evident that a judge is not in as good a position to pass on a matter of this kind as the Benchers ... There is a latitude and discretion in such a matter inherent in such a tribunal as the Benchers which is not available to a Court.[25]

The *ratio decidendi* (reason for decision) of the *Hagel* case could have been narrowly expressed as limited to circumstances in which a fully qualified lawyer who just happens to have been imprisoned for three years for aiding a jailbreak by smuggling a gun and rope in to one of his clients subsequently seeks admission to the legal profession in another province.[26] Chief Justice Hunter sought, however, to establish the broadest possible scope of cultural authority for the Benchers. In so doing, he imagined himself to be according the colonial law society a gentlemanly status and a role equivalent to that of England's ancient Inns of Court.[27] Similar cultural presuppositions also underlay the British Columbia courts' decisions in the late 1940s upholding the Law Society's rejection of a communist who, political belief apart, was fully qualified. The patterns of decision making in *Martin v. Law Society of British Columbia* have conventionally been understood as manifesting a sort of hysteria-driven conspiracy of the legal elite.[28] That interpretive frame, rendered plausible by the subsequent McCarthyite purges in the United States and by the fact that the judges undoubtedly shared the Benchers' opinion that communism was a "pernicious creed," obscures other aspects of the case. The Benchers' genuine commitment to an ideal of lawyering as a gentlemanly service and to visions of professional governance that were thought to advance this were shared by the judiciary. The assertion that "it is not for the Court to substitute its view for that of the Benchers"[29] (expressed by Coady J. at the Supreme Court of British Columbia and endorsed by the Court of Appeal) simultaneously reflects a constitutional commitment of sorts within "administrative law" *and* an understanding of the roles of Canadian legal professions that would have been unintelligible before the reforms spearheaded by the early Canadian Bar Association.[30]

Discipline

The historical antecedents of the contemporary legal professions' disciplinary powers are easily misunderstood. Many *assume* that such powers are somehow inherent in the idea of legal professionalism (they are not). Hence, it is commonly assumed that such bodies have always (or practically always) had full, unfettered discretion to discipline lawyers by means of censure, suspension, or expulsion. It also seems logical, from our vantage point, to assume that use of the power to expel a member necessarily has the consequence that that person is thereafter prohibited from earning a living from the practice of law. This in turn requires us to take for granted the effective policing of a monopoly on legal services.[31] Such assumptions, each of them false, are frequently reflected in hurriedly produced professional apologetics, but also underlie some of the more reflective writing on professional history.[32]

At least three further factors contribute to the confusion. First, the waters are muddied by a rather unreflective North American elision of the histories of the barristers' and solicitors' professions.[33] Second, confusion arises when the historical roles of courts and of lawyers' organizations are misunderstood. The inherent right of superior courts to limit *who* can appear before them and *how* those people (whether solicitors/attorneys or advocates) may conduct themselves has long been recognized. It should never be mistaken for the exercise of disciplinary powers by an organized professional body. These are quite distinct matters.[34] Finally, and most confusingly, the organized legal professions' long-standing exercise of the power to expel convicted criminals is too easily mistaken for a plenary disciplinary power. Although the former is of relatively ancient vintage within the Anglo-Canadian tradition, the latter has been asserted only in relatively recent times.[35]

Curiously, the writings of Justice William Renwick Riddell have added to the confusion. A prominent figure in the early-twentieth-century legal profession, Riddell J. was a Canadian legal historian and student of legal professionalism.[36] His conclusion that Ontario's law society (the Law Society of Upper Canada) had enjoyed full disciplinary powers over members of the bar, attorneys, solicitors, and articled clerks since 1876 (or 1881)[37] is easily misconstrued as having more expansive meaning than intended. It stands in apparent contradiction to his forceful argument against the adoption of codes of professional ethics by Canadian law societies. On *that* matter he argued vigorously that "[i]f it were proposed to make the Code a Penal Code violation of which would render the offender liable to disbarment, legislation would be necessary, and many considerations would arise ... which to my mind would be fatal to the proposition."[38]

The apparently glaring inconsistency is easily resolved by recalling that when one wrote *in 1926* of a law society having "full disciplinary powers," this in no way implied a plenary and exclusive jurisdiction over lawyers' conduct of the sort we now take for granted. Although the idea that law societies should be entirely sufficient *and* efficient in the control of their members' conduct was in the air in Riddell's day, no such plans had yet come to fruition. Existing powers were constrained by quasi-constitutional understandings regarding the autonomy of individual lawyers, by the jealousy of the courts in preserving their traditional authority over the legal profession, and by the terms of legislation in various provinces.

The idea that the organized legal professions should be the sole locus of disciplinary power over lawyers was boldly innovative. So too the related notion that powers of discipline and punishment should be enforced in a field as nebulous as professional ethics.[39] The hidden hand of the Canadian Bar Association was felt as a series of statutory changes transformed Canadian legal professions. The direction of movement was from rather loose gentlemanly guilds into something closer to a modern disciplinary apparatus. These changes more clearly defined law society powers over discipline, regularized or streamlined procedures, increased the ambit of that authority, and, over time, pushed the supervisory jurisdiction of the courts further and further into the background. None of this was part of common law Canada's English heritage, however. It was only in the first half of the last century that law societies were actively transformed into organizations with public regulatory roles that far surpassed those of earlier guild structures.[40]

Importantly, as their powers increased, so too did their "dignity." This mattered immensely to a generation less obsessed than our own with the efficacy of power and less exclusively focused on a narrow and pragmatical instrumentalism.

Asserting Monopoly

The final element of early-twentieth-century transformations in Canadian legal professions was the extension of the legal profession's monopoly beyond its traditional domain (rights of audience or agency before superior courts) and increased protection within the widening "competition-free" zone. The protected zone expanded consistently during the second and third decade of the twentieth century. Saskatchewan, for example, made it unlawful to act under false pretences by holding oneself "out to be a barrister and solicitor," whether or not the individual did so in appearing before the Court of King's Bench (1923). Manitoba extended lawyers' monopoly, first prohibiting unqualified individuals from threatening legal procedures or using documents simulating court forms (1932) and then protecting lawyers' monopolies over conveyancing (1933). Similar provisions were enacted in Alberta in 1936. In neighbouring Saskatchewan, nonlawyers were prohibited from threatening legal proceedings on behalf of a creditor (1933). In that province, the policing of monopoly by means of annual certification was strengthened in 1936. Manitoba again reinforced its unauthorized-practice prohibitions in 1943.[41]

Beneath the surface of legislative change, law societies invested considerable effort in enforcing prohibitions on "unauthorized practice."[42] Future research may reveal that this hidden terrain was where the action was.

Remaking the Legal Profession: Summary

All told, then, the contours of professionalism shifted significantly, even if we restrict our gaze to the most formal level. Less visible transformations were advanced by means of the delegated rule-making authority and less formal policies of law societies and, in part, through the creative interaction of all aspects of lawyering with wider social, cultural, and intellectual contexts.[43]

The more important questions, perhaps, are *why* these changes? *Why* in this place? *Why* at this time? We are taken partway to an answer by noting that this professional renewal was carefully planned in advance. Structural innovation, even in relatively narrow fields, takes time, labour, and energy. These are not tasks to be undertaken lightly, even where strong leaders find developed blueprints of change readily available for appropriation. Nor is it "rational" for individuals to undertake such projects – at least if rational behaviour is understood in terms of narrow self-interest. The time and energy demands are far in excess of any conceivable benefit individuals might derive from successful completion of such tasks. If we are to appreciate *why* leading lawyers invested so heavily in reforming their profession, it is necessary to look outward at their beliefs and at their larger social contexts. The founders of Canada's modern legal professions believed that developing a certain kind of lawyers' hegemony was essential to the preservation of constitutional monarchy, liberal governance, and Britishness. It is their deep and public-spirited commitment to these ideals that explains their actions. Professionalization was part of larger projects aimed at securing a safe future for all they held dear. Their parochial work in transforming their own profession was part of their contribution to a much larger cultural revolution.

The context in which these changes emerged is well behind us. Indeed, the culture of moral reform that spawned them invites ridicule. Nonetheless, their professional structures endure. This is so even though subsequent social changes have very nearly *inverted* the cultural ethos that originally gave them meaning. Subsequent processes have indeed transformed professionalism but have done so within inherited frames that sit oddly out of time in the twenty-first century.

Canada: An "American" Nation

Canada is an "American" nation.[44] Despite the widespread affection for the British Empire at the time, the dominant cultural influence on Canadian lawyers in this period arguably came from the United States. Long puzzled by the mystery of social order, North American social thought conceived of professionalism as the only acceptable bulwark capable of protecting ordered society from descent into "lawlessness and anarchy."[45] Although never fully implemented in the United States, a neatly packaged ideology of legal professionalism had been worked up there. Its form simultaneously advanced the cause of professional reform and deflected criticism, hostility, and anti-lawyer sentiment.

On both sides of the border, an intensely moral professionalism developed, designed to advance the rule of the righteous and the rule of law rather than the government of either the masses or of those who were merely knowledgeable. Lawyers commonly thought of their profession in such terms. Justice O'Halloran of the British Columbia Court of Appeal, for example, gave voice to such a view:

> Moreover, the law student's training is not manual training, but is training of the mind, not only in law, but if he wishes to be something more than a mere legal mechanic, he must study logic, history, in particular constitutional history, political science and economics, a certain amount of philosophy and acquire a reasonable familiarity with English literature, and know something at least of the literature of other countries. The job of a lawyer is basically to advise people upon all manner of things arising out of the complexities of life and the frailties of human nature. As such he cannot fail in time to acquire an influence upon others, impossible to reduce to purely material terms. It is not too much to say that the training and experience a lawyer undergoes fits him for leadership to a greater or less degree. Obviously such men should not be partial to political philosophies and movements that conflict with the interests of their own country.
>
> By reason of these things, all countries throughout the ages have given the lawyer a correspondingly high place in society – particularly so in the case of the lawyer who pleads in the higher Courts. The object of law training is to attract young men of high character, and to train them in a manner that they will be trustworthy, honourable and competent in the performance

> of their legal duties, and will use such influence as they may have to maintain and improve but not destroy our Canadian constitutional democracy. They are to be the defenders and not the destroyers of liberty. They are expected to be sufficiently well-informed and experienced to distinguish between liberty and licence.[46]

It mattered deeply, in other words, that lawyers be gentlemen, right-thinking, and politically sound. Such understandings provided a pervasive common language that gave direction to developing legal professionalism and rendered the projects of professional elites palatable – perhaps even attractive – to a wider public.

In developing a moral vision of professionalism, Canadians looked south for inspiration rather than home to Britain.[47] They did so for several reasons. Proximity as well as ease and density of social contact account for much. So too does social fit. The United States, like Canada, had suffered the disruptions associated with immigration, internal colonization, and the industrialization of an immense federation. It was also avowedly democratic; heterogeneous in ethnicity, language, and religion; regionally diverse; and its history heavily marked by a migrating frontier of European settlement. The United States experienced continuous change and was racked with uncertainty, at times overwhelmed by the sense of "the irrationality of life."[48] By the turn of the century, it had become a "distended" society marked by business and political disorganization, a widening "cultural gap between city and countryside," "[i]rresponsibility," and "ethical evasions."[49] "Respectable" citizens feared that "the true and simple America [was] in jeopardy from foes of extraordinary, raw strength – huge, devouring monopolies, swarms of sexually potent immigrants, and the like."[50] If Britain represented Canada's origins, it was easy to imagine the United States as foreshadowing its future.

Seeking ordered freedom, "science" stepped in to fill the governmental void left from the overthrow of traditional sources of authority.[51] A novel political and cultural project emerged, a "culture of professionalism" in which lay persons were required to trust the integrity and omnicompetence of an emergent educated class: "Science as a source for professional authority transcended the favoritism of politics, the corruption of personality, and the exclusiveness of partisanship."[52]

The political corollary of all this was the rise of progressivism in its various mutations, the development of the bureaucratic state, "reform," an abandonment of party loyalties, and a search for mechanisms whereby authority in discrete areas of social life might be entrusted to "experts" for the good of all.[53] Reformers of many stripes looked forward hopefully to a world made better by education, rational planning, proper procedures, regularity, and the creation of means by which to infuse ethics into the interstices of everyday life.[54] Religion transmuted into "social gospel" and the notion that ethical life could be segmented was eroded. Regulation seemed desirable to generations who perceived change as fundamental, inevitable, and rapid, but who had not yet forgotten the moral claims of a "public sphere."[55]

In this era, lawyers presented themselves not only as specialists in law but also as guardians of cultural knowledge – in effect, "universal experts."[56] Professional principles held forth the promise of containing social discontent and maintaining order.[57] One formulation had it that "if the down-pull of government by plebiscite is to be arrested, if the vortex movement of democracy is to be counter-balanced, it will be accomplished mainly by the grace of the professional spirit."[58] Curious combinations of conservatism, reverence for property, social elitism, community spiritedness, *laissez-faire*, "service," and "duty" resulted.

Obvious Unsuitability of Other Models

Whatever tugged on colonial heartstrings, it was clear to all that English models of legal professionalism could not practicably be sustained in North America. The fit was difficult enough in Ontario and Atlantic Canada, impossible in Quebec and the west. Key elements of English legal professionalism could not be transplanted. A strong egalitarian ethos combined with the small numbers of lawyers in the west to make a rigid demarcation of solicitors from barristers impracticable, in sharp contradistinction to the experience of some other British Dominions and colonies.[59] The legal professions in the western provinces were recent in origin, created by statute, and far removed in origin, structure, and governance from the English Inns of Court. Features central to the English barristers' profession were palpably absurd in the newest part of the New World at the dawn of "Canada's Century." Governance by a self-perpetuating oligarchy, qualification based on the number of meals eaten in Hall, expected (but largely unenforced) conformity to imprecise principles of "etiquette," and regulation by itinerant dining clubs, to pick only the most obvious examples, could not be transplanted into a new place.

Ontario's law society or its younger cousin, the Law Society of England and Wales, provided models more suited to transplantation, but American models proved even more compelling. A significant transboundary intercourse took place among professional leaders.[60]

The evolving culture wove six strands of a new professionalism together. The newly emerging model was founded on a confidence in professional meritocracy that, in turn, was to be constructed from stringent admission standards, formal education, examined expertise, and practical experience. It relied on an ongoing cleansing of the bar through the enforcement of ethical standards by professional governing bodies operating independently of state control. Minimum fee schedules and the creation of a secure monopoly over the right to provide legal services were seen as providing a necessary quid pro quo for such constraints on ordinary market principles. Of course, the suppression of all and any "unlicensed competition" was necessary if the new structures were to be effective.

First taking shape as a coherent, deliberate, and workable project in the early-twentieth-century United States, this web of professionalism had come to constitute a professional "common sense" by the time the Canadian Bar Association began to assert itself.[61] The individual components, moreover, were understood as constituting a unitary structure. It was a "whole cloth" of inseparable strands. A compelling logic bound the whole together. It was thought, for example, that individuals would not be willing to pursue an extensive professional education unless certain privileges (the dignity of self-governance) and financial benefits (mandatory fee schedules and protected monopoly) could be guaranteed. This in turn required statutory prohibition on unlicensed practice and the enforcement of codes of ethics. Without the latter, the privileges could not be justified and the benefits to society of the whole arrangement could not flow.[62] Because only practising lawyers could appreciate both the constitutional principles on which legality was based and the concrete problems that arose in day-to-day legal work, their own professional bodies, independent of state and lay interference alike, needed to be given charge of ethical and professional matters.[63]

Idealized traditions of the professional guild (emphasizing service orientation and anti-commercialism) were melded with the new ideology of regulation, bureaucratic regularity, scientific credentialling, and ethical policing to produce a distinctly twentieth-century, uniquely North American version of professionalism.[64] For example, Julius Cohen's remarkable book *The Law: Business or Profession?* is replete with self-conscious references to the ways in which a new "evolution of a new public opinion,"[65] a "new philosophy which is to be American democracy's great gift to the world,"[66] mandated professional reforms. It called for nothing less than an entire new formulation of professionalism, emphasizing "duty," "service rather than profit," rigorous educational standards, professional conscience, and enforcement of ethical codes so as to purge the dishonourable from the profession.[67] Of necessity, "unauthorized practice" would have to be prohibited and effectively punished.[68]

Canada's reform-minded lawyers similarly articulated their vision of professionalism as an immutable whole. This involved careful attention to defining the limits of acceptable society with an almost obsessive cultural emphasis on structured knowledge, rational education, and the virtues of science.[69] Finally, they shared the widespread notion that professionalism provided a magic key capable of maintaining authority in a society that would otherwise be rent by centrifugal forces.

The most articulate advocate of American-style professionalism was the intensely proud British Canadian lawyer Sir James Aikins. Variously a leading lawyer, Royal Commissioner, Manitoba Lieutenant-Governor, and founding president of the Canadian Bar Association, Aikins worked hard in the cause of professional reform. His address on "The Legal Profession in Relation to Ethics, Education and Emolument," delivered at the bar association meeting in Winnipeg in August 1919, makes clear the extent to which reforms of legal professionalism were implemented as part of an integrated plan.[70] Like those of Cohen, his remarks point to the absolute suffusion of the political, economic, cultural, and professional spheres.

Asserting that the lawyer's first duty is to the state, Aikins developed arguments against open admissions and in favour of both more rigorous educational requirements and more active moral policing:

> It is a false notion of democracy that the right to practice law should be free for all, that anyone can practice it, and without serious loss to the public, operate or help to operate the expensive and intricate machinery of justice which the State creates for its safety and well-being. *The administration of justice has always touched the nadir of its decline when the profession has been lowest in morals and least educated.* In such times there is seen a tendency on the part of practitioners to regard the work of the Bar as a trade and not a profession, a thing to be bartered and not a national service to be sought after; then also is found the pettifogger, the ambulance chaser, the fabricator of evidence and the trickster, and the man who is alien to the professional spirit and its traditions, destitute of *gentlemanly* instincts, *disrespectful* to his seniors, and a *slanderer* of Judges.[71]

Both tone and content echo contemporary professional apologetics in the United States.[72] His Majesty's representative was remarkably "American" in his professionalizing role.

One central feature of this new vision was to be the articulation of a code of professional conduct coupled with a new determination on the part of professional governing bodies to actively seek out and expunge "undesirable" practitioners. This was thought necessary for professional cohesion, utility, and security. As Aikins said on another occasion: "If the legal profession refuses to ruthlessly *rid itself of its barnacles and fungus,* how can the public be expected to extend to the profession, as a profession, the high honor, the dignity and revenue which that profession rightly deserves."[73] This project of defining the good practitioner turned towards explicit class bias or nativism, and wartime prohibitions on the admission of members of noncharter ethnic groups reflected a deep-seated fear of "foreigners."[74]

In proceeding to develop the case for a more thorough education of aspiring lawyers, Aikins acknowledged that this would require "adequate rewards for meritorious services" and hence, "Standard Solicitors' Tariffs."[75] This too was presented as being for the benefit of society as a whole for it would create "a higher type of barrister and advocate, well skilled in the law, gentlemanly in conduct, kindly disposed to his fellow practitioners and of a public spirit."[76] This was to be reinforced by "the frequent meetings of the members of each of the Provincial Bars."[77] These "official law and Bar societies" were, he said, invaluable "bulwarks protecting the people against incompetent and unscrupulous men posing as lawyers, and thus guarding the honour of the profession."[78]

Similarly, it was necessary to clearly demarcate lawyers from "unauthorized practitioners." The latter would not have the same education as lawyers, would not be subject to the same ethical codes, and therefore could not be trusted to provide competent service to their clientele. Aikins warned that those "without suitable qualifications would batten on a too credulous and unsuspecting people," and called upon the Benchers of the various law societies to adopt "the best methods and ways possible" to "fulfil the statutory and traditional obligations cast upon them and protect the profession from encroachment upon its sphere."[79]

There was a symmetry here as the various components blended together: a vision of professionalism cut of whole cloth.

Keystone of Social Cohesion

The rhetoric of service infused professional discourse during and after the Great War.[80] Lawyers were said to be qualified by training, experience, and commitment to service, as "natural leaders of the people in public affairs."[81] As such they could provide an antidote to various undesirable ideologies then in circulation:

> A special duty rests upon our profession both on the Bench and at the Bar, for we are the agents and ministers of the law ... Through a general neglect of that service in our country of popular suffrage our people are in imminent danger of the despotism not so much of individuals as of classes, organized on the principle of every one for himself.[82]

Two statues, *Veritas* (Truth) and *Justitia* (Justice), by Canadian sculptor Walter S. Allward, grace the front entrance of the Supreme Court of Canada. *Photographs by Colin Rose and D. Gordon E. Robertson*

The entire package of legal professionalism was thought to provide a bulwark against social unrest, despotism, and class warfare.[83] It was hoped that "greater unity of the profession would lead to the much needed and greater unity in the thought and action among the peoples of Canada and to like mindedness and singleness of heart and soul in the interest of our country."[84]

It was cultural revolution first and foremost that Canadian lawyers sought. The goal was to avert political disaster. More than anything else, the craving for national integration on such terms spurred lawyers towards modern professionalization. Seeking to avert radical social change, they discovered their profession.

Conclusion

This vision of professionalism resonated at many levels with popular conceptions of appropriate social organization. Ironically, it was thoroughly the product of the very modernity that, in other manifestations, its proponents resisted. This period, this time, and the peculiar circumstances relating to the opening of Canada's western empire provided the habitat from which emerged the forms of professionalism that Canadian lawyers now take for granted. The irony that the vision of social life it incorporates is anachronistic, however, is lost on contemporary lawyers.

Conclusions can be drawn along two axes. The first relates to theories of professionalization, the second to wider issues in cultural history.

Theories of Professionalization

The theories of professionalization that have enjoyed currency during the past fifty years have fallen into functionalist or "rational choice" camps (the latter assuming both "market control" and "work jurisdictions" variants). Two of the pre-eminent theorists of legal professionalism, Terence C. Halliday and Lucien Karpik, have described these approaches as focusing on (1) the achievement of "a service relationship," (2) "the monopolistic strategy of extracting market rent and thus social privilege," and (3) "the deployment of knowledge for the creation and defence of work jurisdictions as a way to define boundaries between work domains."[85] Each approach is inadequate, they assert, for each overlooks politics.[86]

Certainly, the history of lawyers' professionalization in Canada provides strong support for their critique of functionalist approaches premised on both "client-service" and narrowly economic interpretations of professionalism.[87] Even at their highest levels of sophistication, the "market control paradigm" and its cousins cannot adequately account for the very obvious nonmarket motivations of legal professionals who struggled to create their profession.[88] Nor can it account for the very important nonmarket effects of legal professionalism. More is at stake than who gets what portion of the economic pie. To the extent that Canada's legal professionals re-created their profession in an attempt to stave off political and social change by confining politics and civic life to "acceptable" channels, their project can appear almost conspiratorial and antidemocratic in intent. This is of greater significance than mere "market control."[89]

Canadian lawyers clearly had political objectives of sorts in mind as they went about this work. Their story might thus be taken as buttressing the thesis that there is a necessary and causal relationship between lawyering and the rise of western political liberalism.[90] There can be little doubt that "the politics of lawyers directly engage one of the great ideological and institutional movements of the past several centuries – the construction of political liberalism."[91] Equally, there can be little doubt that the lawyers who created twentieth-century Canadian common law legal professions were liberals in the broad sense. They were committed to private property (within limits), individual freedom (within limits), *laissez-faire* (within limits), a moderate state, civil society, and a rights-based form of citizenship that encompassed both British constitutionalism and the rule of law. By the same token, however, these lawyers appear Janus-faced in comparison with those who struggled to create political liberalism in more authoritarian places.[92] Their story points to an unseemly underside to liberalism. Not all lawyers have played key roles in the overthrow or containment of absolutist regimes, and it is dangerous to build theory on a few well-documented case studies addressing that theme. Theorists of state properly emphasize that successful liberal governance rests on the pre-adaptation of subjects to self-governance. It is dependent, at least in large nation states, on mechanisms of social control that contain difference. Theorists have detected cultural projects operating through temperance societies, welfare, state, education, policing, and professions. The modern organization of the legal profession, to be blunt, also originated in desires to contain political and social diversity. Where long-standing tradition or custom such as the dining rituals and complex rules of "etiquette" such as those of the English Inns of Court could not contain difference, substitutes were developed in order to exclude inappropriately socialized individuals from professional life. Legal professionalism, like other moral regulation movements, can be a manifestation of "an anxiety of freedom that haunts modern liberal forms of rule" where there "is no 'natural' system of order."[93] In assessing the history and social or political roles of legal professions, it is important to take this seemingly antidemocratic zone of professional activity into account along with the more obviously liberal contributions of individual lawyers and (less frequently) organized legal professions.

Lawyers' Histories and Cultural History

The second general conclusion that might be suggested by the example of legal professionalism in the early-twentieth-century Dominion of Canada concerns the relationships between professional forms and cultures. It is in this zone of liberal lawyers' "illiberal" activity that cultural projects come to the fore. They do so only in part to advance a political vision as such. We do well in this area to heed Alan Hunt's caution against taking conceptual categories too seriously:

> We conventionally make distinctions, such as those between social, economic and moral realms; such categories are useful, even necessary, so long as we do not fall into the trap of imagining that these terms create real separations as if there is some field, realm or space that is exclusively social,

> moral or economic ... Our conceptual distinctions are elaborated for analytical purposes only; in the real world they are always found in complex connection with other elements.[94]

The founding fathers of modern legal professionalism in Canada knew full well that their profession, personal ethics, religion, economic beliefs, and political convictions were bound together. It was not an absolutist binding together, however. For some purposes, Baptists or Jews or Catholics could be tolerated, just as in politics disagreements between Liberals and Conservatives were both legitimate and genuine. Nonetheless, a cultural web held the whole together. Leading lawyers would have understood the urges that led Michel Foucault to describe one project of western states as being to "constitute the populace as a moral subject."[95] This was no idle philosophy in their time and their place. In common cause with other prominent Canadians acting in many realms, it was their passion and their purpose. It was the essence of their commitment to public service.

What is interesting in the work of the legal profession is the extent to which lawyers combined an explicitly moral and reforming agenda with a profound restructuring of their profession. Their efforts to reform the curriculum of formal legal education, for example, was of a spirit with near-contemporaneous efforts to foster Sunday schools, introduce public schooling, reform private boys' schools, educate imperial civil servants, and fashion universities anew so as to meet the needs of a changing world.[96] Although it is perhaps less immediately obvious, their desire to attain self-regulation, enforce monopoly, assert professional independence, and develop plenary disciplinary powers was also directed towards cultural ends. The new professional structures were erected on cultural foundations, drawn to blueprints of moral origin.

This, of course, is a limited conclusion. First, and most obviously, to assert that Canadian legal professionalism originated in cultural projects is not to assert that *all* legal professions, *everywhere and always*, have originated in these ways.

Second, it cannot be assumed that professional structures have emerged from deliberate, self-conscious agency in all places and all times. Some professional structures may indeed have important origins that are lost in the mists of time, whereas others may accrete slowly in ad hoc response to periodic crises (the English Bar comes to mind in both categories). It is also undoubtedly the case that much cultural, economic, and political change takes place *within* frameworks provided by more or less durable structures. The legal profession of our day, for example, leaves little room for the rhetoric of moral reform. No contemporary lawyer can adopt the role of a "high priest" of law, just as no university law teacher could now seriously adopt as his or her mission the inculcation of the virtues of British gentlemanliness.

Third, it is not necessary to believe that the cultural project of these Dominion lawyers was effective in achieving their end goal. Certainly, their efforts resulted in a dramatically reworked notion of legal profession and in novel structures that persist to this day. It would be something else altogether, however, to argue that in doing so they succeeded in containing diversity and constraining politics within courses compatible with their larger objectives.

Modestly understood, however, the origins of modern legal professionalism in the Dominion of Canada direct our attention to questions of cultural agency and structural revolution that have been largely overlooked in the history of the professions. The connections between market control, political lawyering, culture, liberalism, and professionalism merit further exploration.

Notes

An earlier version of this chapter appeared as "Cowboy Jurists and the Making of Legal Professionalism" (2007-8) 45 Alta. L. Rev. 29. It has been revised and reprinted here with permission.

1 Minute Book of the Calgary Bar Association, 12 May 1899 (archived at the Glenbow-Alberta Institute, Calgary).

2 I review such arguments in Chapter 1 in this volume.

3 I do not wish to be taken as making the nonsense argument that "professionalism" or "professions" did not exist in earlier times; what I *am* saying is that twentieth-century Canadian professionalism is distinctive in its forms, manifestations, and cultures. Earlier forms of professionalism are also to be treated seriously in their own right: see Wilfrid R. Prest, ed., *The Professions in Early Modern England* (London: Croom Helm, 1987).

4 Charles Taylor, *The Malaise of Modernity* (Concord, ON: Anansi Press, 1991) at 112 (and on the nature of instrumental reason, see 5-6). *Cf.* the tracings out of professionalism provided by Harold Perkin, *The Rise of Professional Society: England since 1880* (London: Routledge, 1989); James C. Foster, *The Ideology of Apolitical Politics: Elite Lawyers' Response to the Legitimation Crisis of American Capitalism, 1870-1920* (New York: Garland, 1990); Jerold S. Auerbach, *Unequal Justice: Lawyers and Social Change in Modern America* (New York: Oxford University Press, 1976); Andrew Abbott, *The System of Professions: An Essay on the Division of Expert Labor* (Chicago: University of Chicago Press, 1988). *Cf.* Dorothy Ross, *The Origins of American Social Science* (New York: Cambridge University Press, 1990); John McLaren and Hamar Foster, "Hard Choices and Sharp Edges: The Legal History of British Columbia and the Yukon" in Hamar Foster and John McLaren, eds., *Essays in the History of Canadian Law*, vol. 6: *British Columbia and the Yukon* (Toronto: University of Toronto Press, 1995) 3.

5 I invoke this convenient and commonsensical understanding of professional "structures" in order to avoid the necessity of taking on the full-blown debate as to what, precisely, constitutes "structure" in social analysis. My workaday approach to professional structures in the twentieth century seems to fit William H. Sewell's definition that "[s]ets of schemas and resources may properly be said to constitute structures only when they mutually imply and sustain each other over time": William H. Sewell, Jr., "A Theory of Structure: Duality, Agency, and Transformation" (1992) 98 American Journal of Sociology 1 at 13.

6 See Chapter 1 in this volume; Sewell, *ibid.*, addresses the ways in which actors often falsely invoke history in order to effect transformation. See also Eric Hobsbawm and Terence Ranger, eds., *The Invention of Tradition* (Cambridge: Cambridge University Press, 1983).

7 Lyn Spillman, "How Are Structures Meaningful? Cultural Sociology and Theories of Social Structure" (1996) 22 Humboldt Journal of Social Relations 31 at 41; see also Pierre Bourdieu, *Outline of a Theory of Practice*, trans. by Richard Nice (Cambridge: Cambridge University Press, 1977).

8 Gerald Friesen, *The Canadian Prairies: A History* (Toronto: University of Toronto Press, 1987) at 342.

9 Robert H. Wiebe, *The Search for Order, 1877-1920* (New York: Hill and Wang, 1967) at 39.

10 Mariana Valverde, *The Age of Light, Soap, and Water: Moral Reform in English Canada, 1885-1925* (Toronto: McClelland and Stewart, 1991); Carl Berger, *The Sense of Power: Studies in the Ideas of Canadian Imperialism, 1867-1914* (Toronto: University of Toronto Press, 1970); Ramsay Cook, *The Regenerators: Social Criticism in Late Victorian English Canada* (Toronto: University of Toronto Press, 1985).

11 Friesen, *supra* note 8 at 304, discussing the novels of Ralph Connor.

12 *Ibid.* at 342-43.

13 *Ibid.* at 342.

14 *Ibid.* at 358, 361. The strike, which seemed to substitute government by strike committee for the ordinary organs of municipal government from 15 May to 21 June 1919, registered powerfully on elite consciousness. The establishment of a "proletarian dictatorship" was explicitly threatened. For a useful review of existing historiography and of previously unexplored archival records relating to the Winnipeg General Strike, see Ken Kehler and Alvin Esau, *Famous Manitoba Trials: The Winnipeg General Strike Trials – Research Resource* (Winnipeg: Legal Research Institute of the University of Manitoba, 1990); Craig Heron, ed., *The Workers' Revolt in Canada, 1917-1925* (Toronto: University Toronto Press, 1998); Tom Mitchell, "'To Reach the Leadership of This Revolutionary Movement': A.J. Andrews, the Canadian State and the Suppression of the Winnipeg General Strike" (1993) 18 Prairie Forum 239; Tom Mitchell, "'Repressive Measures': A.J. Andrews, the Committee of 1000 and the Campaign Against Radicalism after the Winnipeg General Strike" (1995-96) 3.2 and 4.1 *Left History* 133. The United States experienced similar concerns, which also motivated its "Bar Association Movement": see Foster, *supra* note 4 at 97ff.

15 A consequence of the division of powers under the Canadian constitution.

16 The Vancouver Law Students Association was a particularly important locus of professionalizing activity. It and the Vancouver Bar Association played key roles in the development of British Columbia legal education. See W. Wesley Pue, *Law School: The Story of Legal Education in British Columbia* (Vancouver: University of British Columbia, Faculty of Law, 1995) Pue, [*Law School*]. For writings on other similar bodies, see William C.V. Johnson, ed., *The First Century: Essays on the History of the County of Carleton Law Association by Various Hands on the Occasion of the Association's Centenary, 1888-1988* (Ottawa: Bonanza Press, 1988); Robert Crawford, "The New Westminster Bar Association, 1894-1994" (1994) 52 *The Advocate* 221. The story of the Calgary Bar Association is to be found in its own minutes, archived at the Glenbow-Alberta Institute, Calgary, and in twenty-three volumes of transcripts of oral history interviews pertaining to the legal history of southern Alberta circa 1900-82. Professionalizing movements in Manitoba, Ontario, and British Columbia are discussed respectively in Dale Gibson and Lee Gibson, *Substantial Justice: Law and Lawyers in Manitoba, 1670-1970* (Winnipeg: Peguis, 1972); Christopher Moore, *The Law Society of Upper Canada and Ontario's Lawyers, 1797-1997* (Toronto: University of Toronto Press, 1997); Alfred Watts, Q.C., *History of the Legal Profession in British Columbia, 1869-1984* (Vancouver: Law Society of British Columbia, 1984).

17 This was, for example, briefly considered within the Law Society of Manitoba during the 1920s. A short period of formal division was ended in Ontario in 1854: Moore, *ibid.* at 109.

18 See Chapter 12 in this volume.

19 The connections between professional organization and constitutional structures of governance in society at large are sketched out in Terence C. Halliday and Lucien Karpik, ["Politics Matter: A Comparative Theory of Lawyers in the Making of Political Liberalism" Halliday and Karpik, ["Politics Matter"] in Terence C. Halliday and Lucien Karpik, eds., *Lawyers and the Rise of Western Political Liberalism: Europe and North America from the Eighteenth to Twentieth Centuries* (New York: Oxford University Press, 1997) 15, *Lawyers and the Rise of Western Political Liberalism*], and in C. Moore, *The Law Society of Upper Canada and Ontario's Lawyers 1797-1997* (Toronto: University of Toronto Press, 1997).

20 An earlier attempt to create a code had been turned back in Ontario, and the Canadian Bar Association initiative was strongly resisted by prominent Ontario judge William Renwick Riddell on a number of grounds involving professional tradition and principle. See Chapter 9 in this volume.

21 Jonnette Watson Hamilton, "Metaphors of Lawyers' Professionalism" (1995) 33 Alta. L. Rev. 833.

22 See, however, Mary Kinnear, *In Subordination: Professional Women, 1870-1970* (Montreal and Kingston: McGill-Queen's University Press, 1995); Joan Brockman, "Exclusionary Tactics: The History of Women and Visible Minorities in the Legal Profession in British Columbia" in Foster and McLaren, *supra* note 4 at 508; Carol A. Aylward, *Canadian Critical Race Theory: Racism and the Law* (Halifax: Fernwood, 1999) at 44-45; Lois K. Yorke, "Mabel Penery French (1881-1955): A Life Re-Created" (1993) 42 U.N.B.L.J. 3; Constance Backhouse, *Petticoats and Prejudice: Women and Law in Nineteenth-Century Canada* (Toronto: Osgoode Society, 1991); Constance B. Backhouse, "'To Open the Way for Others of My Sex'; Clara Brett Martin's Career as Canada's First Woman Lawyer" (1985) 1 C.J.W.L. 1; Pue, *Law School, supra* note 16; Peter M. Sibenik, "Doorkeepers: Legal Education in the Territories and Alberta, 1885-1928" (1990) 13 Dal. L.J. 419; Watts, *supra* note 16; Dawna Tong, "A History of Exclusion: The Treatment of Racial and Ethnic Minorities by the Law Society of British Columbia in Admissions to the Legal Profession" (1998) 56 *The Advocate* 197; Chapter 12 in this volume. Further, Margaret Thornton, *Dissonance and Distrust: Women in the Legal Profession* (Melbourne: Oxford University Press, 1996), is, in part, an outstanding study of the embodiment of law in lawyers. See also Joan Brockman, *Racism and Legal Culture: Is There Room for Diversity in the Legal Profession?* (2007-8) 45 Alta. L. Rev. 75; Joan Brockman and Dorothy Chunn, "'A New Order of Things': Women's Entry into the Legal Profession in British Columbia" *The Advocate* 60 (May 2002) 385; Mary Jane Mossman, *The First Women Lawyers: A Comparative Study of Gender, Law and the Legal Professions* (Oxford: Hart Publishing, 2006).

23 See, *e.g.*, *An Act to Amend "The Law Society Act,"* S.M. 1909, c. 29, s. 54(d) (the admittance of attorneys not practising in the province rendered subject to rules framed by the Benchers); *An Act to Amend "The Law Society Act,"* S.M. 1911, c. 23 (increasing discretion of Benchers regarding the admission of members and students-at-law in special cases); *An Act to Amend "The Law Society Act,"* S.M. 1915, c. 37, s. 40 (powers of Benchers to make rules for improvement of legal education amended by specifically including the establishment and maintenance of a law school, permitting regulations respecting attendance at classes or instructions at law, and so on); *An Act to Amend the Motor Vehicle Act, the Unearned Increment Tax Act, and Certain Other Acts and Ordinances*, S.A. 1921, c. 5, amended the *Legal Profession Act* (new provision s. 35 [s. 32 in 1922 amendments] providing for the admission of University of Alberta graduates having completed degree in law and served articles); *An Act to Amend the Legal Profession Act*, S.A. 1947, c. 70 (adding s. 62[a] permitting Benchers to make

provision for enrollment of students from other universities than the University of Alberta under certain conditions). Some related developments are discussed in works such as Sibenik, *supra* note 22; Gibson and Gibson, *supra* note 16; Watts, *supra* note 16; Moore, *supra* note 16.

24 [1922] 31 B.C.R. 75 at 77 [*Hagel*].

25 *Ibid.*

26 See Gibson and Gibson, *supra* note 16 at 211.

27 *Hagel, supra* note 24 at 76-77.

28 See Chapter 10 in this volume.

29 *Hagel, supra* note 24.

30 See Chapter 10 in this volume.

31 Note, however, the recent case of Maurice Sychuk, disbarred by the Law Society of Alberta for murdering his wife, and denied reinstatement at the conclusion of his sentence: *Law Society of Alberta v. Sychuk*, [1999] L.S.D.D. No. 15 (QL). The press reported that Mr. Sychuk nonetheless earned a living from working in Calgary in the field of "oil and gas," an area within his established legal expertise. *Cf.* Fred Edge, *The Iron Rose: The Extraordinary Life of Charlotte Ross, M.D.* (Winnipeg: University of Manitoba Press, 1992), providing an account of a woman physician who was able to practise medicine despite being refused recognition by formal regulatory bodies.

32 See Chapter 1 in this volume.

33 *Ibid.*

34 This aspect, which raises a question of professional discipline in the context of a constitutional separation of powers, is ably dealt with in James Willard Hurst, *The Growth of American Law: The Law Makers* (Boston: Little Brown, 1950) at 278-79. The relationship between courts and professional bodies in the United States is complex and leads to some confusion between these quite different exercises of power. These matters are ably dealt with in William H. Hurlburt, *The Self-Regulation of the Legal Profession in Canada and in England and Wales* (Calgary/Edmonton: Law Society of Alberta/Alberta Law Reform Institute, 2000).

35 Robert Baldwin's fascinating report on the Law Society of Upper Canada's (LSUC) disciplinary powers, Law Society of Upper Canada, Minutes of Convocation, vol. 1: 476, *Report of the Committee on James Doyle* (29 June 1833), prepared in relation to the case of James Doyle, who had been removed from the Court of King's Bench list of attorneys for misconduct, merits further scrutiny. See Moore, *supra* note 16 at 70. Note, however, that in this case the primacy of the courts as the locus of discipline is taken entirely for granted.

36 See Law Society of Upper Canada, *The Riddell Collection in the Great Library at Osgoode Hall* (archived at LSUC), text from an exhibition prepared by the LSUC with financial support from the Law Foundation of Ontario.

37 William Renwick Riddell, *The Bar and Courts of the Province of Upper Canada, or Ontario* (Toronto: Macmillan, 1928) at 111-12. The legislative changes that Riddell addresses are ably explained in Curtis Cole, *"A Learned and Honorable Body": The Professionalization of the Ontario Bar, 1867-1929* (PhD Dissertation, University of Western Ontario, 1987) [unpublished], c. 5, "'To Purge the Profession of Those Who Bring Disgrace upon Their Brethren': The Bar's Assumption of Autonomous Professional Self-Discipline." See also Moore, *supra* note 16 at 149: "Discipline in the legal profession was also transformed. Though barristers had been disbarred for ungentlemanly behaviour as early as 1820, only in 1876 had the society's disciplinary power been made explicit in the Law Society Act, and judges had continued to assert a right to discipline the solicitors enrolled by their courts."

38 William Renwick Riddell, "A Code of Legal Ethics" (1919) 4 Reports of the Can. Bar Assn. 136 at 139.

39 Riddell's objections were cogent. See Chapter 9 in this volume. Peter M. Sibenik's research has traced out developments in relation to professional discipline in Alberta. See Peter M. Sibenik, "'The Black Sheep': The Disciplining of Territorial and Alberta Lawyers, 1885-1928" (1988) 3 C.J.L.S. 109 ["Black Sheep"].

40 This shift was reflected in a series of legislative changes to the framework of regulation by law societies, including: *An Act to Amend the Legal Profession Act,* S.A. 1911-12, c. 4, s. 29; *An Act to Amend "The Law Society Act,"* S.M. 1915, c. 37; *An Act to Amend the Legal Profession Act,* S.S. 1919-20, c. 44; *An Act to Amend the Legal Profession Act,* S.S. 1923, c. 49 [*An Act to Amend the Legal Profession Act* (Sask. 1923)]; *An Act to Amend the Legal Profession Act,* S.A. 1924, c. 19; *An Act to Amend the Legal Profession Act,* S.A. 1925, c. 13; *An Act to Amend the Legal Profession Act,* S.A. 1926, c. 18; *An Act to Amend "The Law Society Act,"* S.M. 1926, c. 26; *An Act to Amend the Legal Profession Act,* S.A. 1928, c. 19; *An Act to Amend the Legal Profession Act,* S.S. 1933, c. 54 [*An Act to Amend the Legal Profession Act* (Sask. 1933)]; *An Act to Amend the Legal Profession Act,* S.S. 1936, c. 85; *An Act to Amend the Legal Profession Act,* S.M. 1943, c. 29 [*An Act to Amend the Legal Profession Act* (Man. 1943)]. Generally, these provisions extended the powers of the Benchers to regulate the conduct of lawyers, limiting the authority of the courts in these matters. For accounts of law society disciplinary powers, see Watts, *supra* note 16, c. 10 at 117-32; Lee Gibson, "A Brief History of the Law Society of Manitoba" in Cameron Harvey, ed., *The Law Society of Manitoba, 1877-1977* (Winnipeg: Peguis, 1977) 28 at 50; Gibson and Gibson, *supra* note 16 at 128, 171-72, 240, 252, 257, 267, 305; Moore, *supra* note 16 at 61, 70, 125-26, 149-51, 300-2, 323-24, 326-29; Sibenik, "Black Sheep," *ibid.*, especially "The Locus of Disciplinary Power" at 113-20; Cole, *supra* note 37 (pointing out that the courts' exercise of disciplinary jurisdiction concurrent with that of the law society in Ontario continued well into the twentieth century).

41 *An Act to Amend the Legal Profession Act* (Sask. 1923), *ibid.*, s. 37(1); *An Act to Amend the Law Society Act,* S.M. 1932, c. 22, s. 53; *An Act to Amend the Law Society Act,* S.M. 1933, c. 20, s. 53A; *Act to Amend the Law Society Act,* S.M. 1937, c. 26 (added s. 53[a], specified that the prohibition extended to corporations as well as to natural persons; fines were imposed on unauthorized individuals preparing instruments for conveyancing of real and personal property); *An Act to Amend the Legal Profession Act,* S.A. 1936, c. 14, s. 59, amended by s. 59(a), imposing penalties for preparation of instruments (for reward) in relation to any real or personal estate or incorporation of joint stock proceedings; *An Act to Amend the Legal Profession Act* (Sask. 1933), *ibid.* (amending s. 64 of the *Legal Profession Act*); *An Act to Amend the Legal Profession Act* (Sask. 1936), *ibid.*, enacting that "[n]o person except those enrolled as barristers and solicitors of Saskatchewan and holding subsisting annual certificates issued to them pursuant to the rules and bylaws of the society shall practise at the bar of any court of civil or criminal jurisdiction in Saskatchewan," and making it an offence for anyone without a subsisting annual certificate to willfully pretend to be qualified to act as a barrister or solicitor; *An Act to Amend the Law Society Act* (Man. 1943), *ibid.*, ss. 53 and 54 repealed and replaced by a new, wider s. 53, expressly including the drawing of wills within the lawyers' monopoly, prohibiting simulating court procedures, and prohibiting employment of disbarred persons. The new legislation allowed for injunctions to be obtained against unauthorized persons. Statutory exceptions to the ambit of unauthorized practice prohibitions protected public officers, notaries, and persons acting for themselves. On similar developments in British Columbia during this time period, see Watts, *supra* note 16 at 119-20.

42 This is revealed in the records of the Law Society of Manitoba. See also Watts, *ibid.* at 120; Peter M. Sibenik, *The Doorkeepers: The Governance of Territorial and Alberta Lawyers, 1885-1928* (MA Thesis, University of Calgary, 1984) at 170-80, "The Protective Impulse."

43 The full cultural import of legal education, for example, cannot be discerned from statutory histories alone but needs to be understood in relation to universities, curriculum, and wider

cultural contexts. See Chapter 12 in this volume and sources cited therein. Further evidence of the sorts of changes that might be involved at this "hidden" level are documented in P.J. Giffen, "Social Control and Professional Self-Government: A Study of the Legal Profession in Canada" in S.D. Clark, *Urbanism and the Changing Canadian Society* (Toronto: University of Toronto Press, 1961) 117.

44 Allan Smith, *Canada – An American Nation? Essays on Continentalism, Identity, and the Canadian Frame of Mind* (Montreal and Kingston: McGill-Queen's University Press, 1994).

45 Julius Henry Cohen, *The Law: Business or Profession?* rev. ed. (New York: G.A. Jennings, 1924) at 109.

46 *Re Legal Professions Act*; *Re Martin*, [1949] 1 D.L.R. 105; *Re Legal Professions Act, Re Martin*, [1949] 2 D.L.R. 559 (B.C.S.C.); *Martin v. Law Society of British Columbia*, [1950] 3 D.L.R. 173 (B.C.C.A.) at 189 [*Martin*].

47 See also Philip Girard, "The Making of the Canadian Legal Profession: A Hybrid Heritage" (2014) 21 International Journal of the Legal Profession 145; Philip Girard, *Lawyers and Legal Culture in British North America: Beamish Murdoch of Halifax* (Toronto: University of Toronto Press, 2011).

48 Burton J. Bledstein, *Culture of Professionalism: The Middle Class and the Development of Higher Education in America* (New York: Norton, 1976) at 322 (discussing the 1860s and 1870s).

49 Wiebe, *supra* note 9 at 14, 19, 28.

50 *Ibid.* at 39, 52.

51 Bledstein, *supra* note 48 at 326.

52 *Ibid.* at 90. *Cf.* Wiebe, *supra* note 9 at 161. Science did not necessarily stand in opposition to religion in this period. For many, God, science, and cultural tradition for a time lived in mutually constitutive relations. See, *e.g.*, Cook, *supra* note 10.

53 The development of standardized testing was part of this process. A splendid account is found in Nicholas Lemann, *The Big Test: The Secret History of the American Meritocracy* (New York: Farrar, Straus and Giroux, 1999).

54 Wiebe, *supra* note 9 at 153-57, 164-69, 222.

55 Cohen, *supra* note 45 at 107: "Within two decades we have been whisked about and hurdled over Interstate Commerce Commissions, Public Service Commissions, Minimum Wage Laws, Industrial Boards, Workmen's Compensation Acts, Income Taxes, Inheritance Taxes ... Truth is, the conservatives have turned progressives, the progressives have turned socialists, and the socialists are looking about for new wearing apparel."

56 For development of this notion, see Peter L. Berger and Thomas Luckmann, *The Social Construction of Reality* (Garden City, NY: Doubleday, 1967) at 117. Berger and Luckmann's insight is deployed to good effect in relation to the US legal profession in Foster, *supra* note 4 at 12.

57 For example, Ontario Bar Association, "Address of Mr. Henry R. Rathbone, of Chicago, Delivered at the Last Annual Meeting" (1919) 55 Can. L.J. 168.

58 Robert N. Wilkin, *The Spirit of the Legal Profession* (New Haven, CT: Yale University Press, 1938) at 160.

59 Contrast, for example, the state of Victoria in Australia: Rob McQueen, "Together We Fall, Divided We Stand: The Victorian Legal Profession in Crisis 1890-1940" in W. Wesley Pue and David Sugarman, eds., *Lawyers and Vampires: Cultural Histories of Legal Professions* (Portland, OR: Hart, 2003) 293; J.R.S. Forbes, *The Divided Legal Profession in Australia: History, Rationalisation and Rationale* (Sydney: Law Book, 1979).

60 Reports of proceedings for both the "American Bar Association" and the "Canadian Bar Association" during the early decades of the century reveal patterns of elite interaction that have yet to be properly assessed. For one example, see Sir James Aikins, "Inaugural Address of the President. Sir James Aikins, K.C., Knt., Lieutenant-Governor of Manitoba" (1918)

54 Can. L.J. 344 at 348 (discussing the immense US influence on Canada) ["Inaugural Address"]. *Cf.* Bernard J. Hibbitts, "Our Arctic Brethren: Canadian Law and Lawyers as Portrayed in American Legal Periodicals, 1829-1911" in G. Blaine Baker and Jim Phillips, eds., *Essays in Canadian Law*, vol. 8: *In Honour of R.C.B. Risk* (Toronto: University of Toronto Press, 1999) 241.

61 This is broadly the agenda set forth by Cohen, *supra* note 45.

62 See, *e.g.*, Cohen, *ibid.*, c. 14, titled "'It Pays to Advertise.' Does It?" at 173.

63 According to Cohen, *ibid.*, at xvi, Dr. Felix Adler in 1908 "presented to the public his conviction that the further solution of problems of ethics, in industry, in business, and in the professions, must come from the definite assistance of men who live with these problems; that it is not enough for our day and generation to have a general philosophy of ethics, but that there must be daily application of the philosophy to the fact, and that this can be best done by the experts in the line."

64 An English version of "professional society" arose at a similar time period. See Perkin, *supra* note 4. In its English manifestation, however, "professionalism" never attained the fully "modern" character of its North American mutation. See, *e.g.*, Richard L. Abel, *The Legal Profession in England and Wales* (New York: Blackwell, 1988); David Howard Laycock, *Populism and Democratic Thought in the Canadian Prairies, 1910 to 1945* (Toronto: University of Toronto Press, 1990).

65 Cohen, *supra* note 45 at 144. Cohen observes that "[u]nless we grasp the meaning of these changes in American thought, we shall pass by an understanding of the momentous changes taking place in the practice of the law" (at 143).

66 *Ibid.* at 146.

67 *Ibid.* at 127, 143-44, 151, 155, 158, 159.

68 See *ibid.* at 173-200, 277-78. Ideas of this sort were commonplace. See also "Unauthorised Practice of Law" (1919) 55 Can. L.J. 375, reproducing an article from *Law Notes* (Northfield, US). The article establishes linkages between questions relating to lawyers' qualifications, ethical regulation, competition, bar organization, and the need to suppress competitors. Typical of the period, it amounts to a complete project of professionalization similar to that advanced in Cohen's work and implemented in Canada through the influence of the Canadian Bar Association.

69 See Laycock, *supra* note 64. On Canadian legal education, see Chapters 5, 6, and 12 in this volume.

70 Sir James Aikins, "The Legal Profession in Relation to Ethics, Education and Emolument" (1919) 55 Can. L.J. 335 [Aikins, "Ethics, Education and Emolument"].

71 *Ibid.* at 335 [emphasis added].

72 *Cf.*, *e.g.*, Cohen's extended comparative "history" of professional admission standards and the cause of "justice" (Cohen, *supra* note 45).

73 "Vancouver Benchers" *Vancouver Sun* (13 December 1927), 8 (reporting on Aikins's view of the general reputation of the legal profession) [emphasis added].

74 See, *e.g.*, Aikins, "Inaugural Address," *supra* note 60, arguing that the experience of 1914-18 demonstrated the desirability of careful immigration controls: "Even before the war that error was made manifest in industrial dissensions, in the ignorant, too often corrupt, use of the franchise and failure to understand the privileges and responsibilities of our free institutions ... Detached by distance from their own people they generally are all for self and none for the adopted nation" (at 354-55). Aikins indicates, however, that American, British, and French immigrants are not the subject of concern.

75 Aikins, "Ethics, Education and Emolument," *supra* note 70 at 336.

76 *Ibid.* at 338.

77 *Ibid.*

78 *Ibid.*

79 Archive of MB Legal-Judicial History (University of Manitoba), File #P1534, "Aikins Is Again Head of Governing Bodies" (28 August 1928) (Summary 2nd Annual Conference on Benchers) 2. In furtherance of this vision, the Manitoba Law Society's proactive "Committee on Encroachments" recommended investigating the areas in which the public should look to lawyers for service.
80 See, *e.g.*, Aikins, "Inaugural Address," *supra* note 60.
81 Canadian Bar Association, Proceedings at Fifth Annual Meeting, "The President's Address" (1920) 56 Can. L.J. 308 at 308.
82 *Ibid.* at 309.
83 A somewhat similar point is made with reference to US developments by James C. Foster, who argues that the "bar association" movement was a deliberately "ideological" response to the crises of US capitalism. See Foster, *supra* note 4.
84 Canadian Bar Association, *supra* note 81 at 308.
85 Halliday and Karpik, "Politics Matter," *supra* note 19 at 15.
86 *Ibid.*
87 *Cf.* Stuart A. Scheingold, "Taking Weber Seriously: Lawyers, Politics, and the Liberal State" (1999) 24 Law & Soc. Inquiry 1061; Michael Burrage, "Escaping the Dead Hand of Rational Choice: Karpik's Historical Sociology of French Advocates" (1999) 24 Law & Soc. Inquiry 1083.
88 Hurlburt, *supra* note 34, lends some support to what he calls the "honour" model of legal professionalism as developed by Michael Burrage, "From a Gentleman's to a Public Profession: Status and Politics in the History of English Solicitors" (1996) 3 International Journal of the Legal Profession 45.
89 *Cf.* Foster, *supra* note 4 at 47: "But the political importance of lawyers' trade association involves [*sic*] is considerably more than restricting competition ... The American bar's prerogatives are not simply occupational ... By insisting we see through all that lawyers professed, to the 'proprietary' motives behind their words, Auerbach directs our attention away from the very real imperative that both conservative and progressive lawyers perceived to shore up the hegemony of the liberal-capitalist steering principles underlying their power. What elite lawyers said is as significant as what they did."
90 Terence C. Halliday and Lucien Karpik, *Politics Matter: A Comparative Theory of Lawyers in the Making of Political Liberalism* (Chicago: American Bar Foundation, 1995); Scheingold, *supra* note 87.
91 Terence C. Halliday, "The Politics of Lawyers: An Emerging Agenda" (1999) 24 Law & Soc. Inquiry 1007 at 1010.
92 See the various contributions to Halliday and Karpik, *Lawyers and the Rise of Western Political Liberalism, supra* note 19.
93 Alan Hunt, *Governing Morals: A Social History of Moral Regulations* (New York: Cambridge University Press, 1999) at 215.
94 *Ibid.* at 7-8.
95 Michel Foucault, *Power/Knowledge: Selected Interview and Other Writings, 1972-1977,* ed. by Colin Gordon (Brighton, UK: Harvester Press, 1980) at 41.
96 See Chapter 12 in this volume.

PART 2

Shaping Minds and Souls: Legal Education

4

Professional Legal Education at Queen's College, Birmingham, in the 1850s

In the spring of 1850, Charles Rann Kennedy delivered his inaugural address as Professor of Law at Queen's College, Birmingham. This placed him in a unique position in the development of legal education in England. Had things gone better, he might well have been remembered as the pioneer of a new approach to legal qualification and legal education. What went right and what went wrong tell us a good deal about both the nature of the English legal profession and the character of higher education at the time. Tellingly, he began his inaugural lecture with a nod to Dr. Arnold's observation that "[t]he study of law is as wholesome to the human mind, as the practice of it is often injurious."[1] It was not an observation likely to be immediately endearing either to those who spent their days practising law or to those who wished to do so.

Kennedy assumed the professorship at a time when the nature and purpose of legal education – and indeed of higher education in colleges and universities – were up for grabs.[2] These matters had caught the attention of the reading public, lawyers, intellectuals, visionaries, and politicians. In the field of legal education, developments were driven to a large extent – as in so many matters affecting the legal profession – by the evolving relationship and divergent expectations of the barristers' and attorneys' professions.[3] Each profession's self-understanding and sense of its own needs as well as of its relations to the other were coloured by histories and historical myths, by differing traditions, social origins, and material needs, and by distinct claims to legitimacy.[4] Within each, an enormous gulf separated the men at the top from those in more humble practice. Despite the differences, however, attorneys and barristers were bound together as warring Siamese twins. The unseverable point of connection was the law: both groups were inescapably providers of legal services. Moreover, though often professional rivals, the two lived in a symbiotic relationship. Each relied upon the other.

The barristers claim to gentlemanly status rested in part on educational attainments that differed strongly from the more practical workaday concerns

Queen's College, Birmingham. *From* The Making of Birmingham: Being a History of the Rise and Growth of the Midland Metropolis, *by Robert K. Dent, published by J.L. Allday, 1894*

of solicitors. Their gentlemanly concern for classical education and erudition met a more narrowly utilitarian focus on the part of attorneys. This produced tension whenever legal education was considered. A synthesis of sorts emerged in 1846 in proposals for legal education outlined by the House of Commons' Select Committee on Legal Education.[5] Their proposals attempted to identify a common core of legal qualification that blended elements of practical training (emphasized by attorneys) with elements of the broader education lauded by barristers.

Though the committee's synthesis worked at the abstract level of ideas, it spoke insufficiently to the cultures and needs of the two professions in real life. However logical, appropriate, or right its report seemed as an intellectual exercise, its proposals failed to address adequately the living needs of either legal profession. Charles Rann Kennedy built England's first college-based program of professional legal education at Queen's College, Birmingham, in 1849, on the sand that was the committee's chimerical synthesis. The ultimate failure of his program had structural as well as idiosyncratic causes. It's somewhat more successful re-emergence under the direction of a quite different sort of professor was differently conceived and marketed. Kennedy's effort at professional education gave way to a reinvigorated and more limited version of guild training.

First, however, some background.

The Bar and Gentlemanly Legal Qualification

Barristers of the time justified their status, incomes, and special privileges in ways that startle the twenty-first century observer. Addressing the 1846 Select Committee on Legal Education, one barrister stressed the importance of barristers' being men "of a high tone of gentlemanly feeling," and stated that restricting entry to "men of liberal education" would go far towards ensuring this.[6] Another indicated that although there was "no test of legal competency" prior to a call to the bar, "as regards the Inner Temple, there is some test, on a young man's entering as a student, as to his classical attainments, but not at all regarding his legal attainments."[7] Charles Rann Kennedy argued that "a well-educated Barrister" was superior to attorneys ("an inferior class of men") because his mind was "enlightened by those liberal studies which make up the scholar and the gentleman – history, poetry, philosophy."[8] A writer in the *Law Times* in 1843 confidently asserted that the costs involved in establishing a successful practice as a barrister ensured that "necessary union of education and property" that was "a sufficiently accurate test that a man is a gentleman."[9] Yet another barrister denied any need for formal training or examination of barristers because "anyone of liberal education and good character who has the opportunity of acquiring the knowledge requisite for a Barrister will do so, if he really means to practice as a Barrister."[10] Dramatically, C.H. Whitehurst, QC, treasurer of the Middle Temple, proudly told the Inns of Court Commission in 1854 that "[s]ome of the very best and first advocates at the English Bar, were no lawyers, they were very ignorant of Law ... The Profession must be looked at, not as a mere profession of jurisconsult, to advise."[11]

Barristers as a class did not claim to derive status exclusively from legal knowledge, training, or demonstrable practical expertise. Rather, their claim to position, income, and authority was posited on ascribed characteristics and requirements respecting nonlegal learning. This approaches the portrait offered by M.S. Larson:

> The guarantees which they thought they offered the public were based on social privileges which pre-existed the entry into practice. A classical education certified beforehand as gentlemen those who were going to acquire, however, casually, specialization by apprenticeship with one of their social peers.

> Thus ennobled, those gentlemen could grace professional life with the virtues of aristocratic disinterestedness.[12]

Social groups, including professions, often define themselves by drawing exaggerated contrasts of their own virtues vis-à-vis the failings of others. The nineteenth-century barristers' self-image, not surprisingly, comes into clearest focus in comments about attorneys[13] who, variously, were accused of stirring up litigation,[14] encouraging abuse of the legal process, and deliberately derailing criminal prosecutions while charged with conducting the prosecution.[15] Attorneys were commonly portrayed as ill-bred, disreputable, lazy, selfish, ignorant, and disloyal. Characteristically, comments made by Kennedy about attorneys' appearance as advocates in the new County Courts makes the point in particularly harsh language:

> Gentlemen, scholars and men of honour [for this, read "barristers"] have been excluded from our provincial courts, and in lieu of them there has sprung up a tribe of a different character; the tribe of rascal pettifoggers; creatures that formerly crept not into the light of day, but now swarm like locusts over the country. The courts where such persons practise, having no respect for the advocate, lapse into a sort of easy indolence, which is fatal to the administration of justice. Some of these have been turned into bear-gardens, some into dens of thieves, where the suitors are betrayed, truth and honour derided, estates given up to wholesale pillage.[16]

Attorneys, in short, lacked the barrister's "gentlemanly" characteristics of classical education, disinterestedness, and honour. Consequently, they threatened both individuals and the administration of justice itself. They were simply people who could not be trusted.

Although such claims seem extravagant, anxiety about the attorney's profession extended beyond a few bad-tempered barristers and had deeper historical roots than the concerns of the day. W.J. Reader reports a "common prejudice" of the eighteenth century, when the "attorney was one of those stock figures of ridicule and contempt which every age seems to stand in need of: a convenient scapegoat, and at the same time giving just enough cause for offence to colour prejudice with a decent show of reason."[17] In response to petitions against attorneys by local justices, Parliament passed the *Attorney Act, 1729* (2 George II, c. 23), subjecting solicitors and attorneys

> to various mandatory regulations and to stiff penalties in case of infraction: clerks were theretofore to be articled for five years to an attorney who could

> not take more than two apprentices at a time; they had to be duly enrolled in the court where they intended to practice, and take their oath to be examined before admission by a judge.[18]

The Bar, however, remained unregulated, unpunished, and unexamined.[19] Although largely ineffective, the act was a significant symbolic statement.

Important plums of patronage were also denied attorneys, who were acutely aware of this differential treatment, and felt the grievance keenly. A member of the Metropolitan and Provincial Law Association complained that the barristers' branch consisted of "little more than one-fourth of the whole Profession" and yet enjoyed "almost every office of distinction and emolument connected with the Profession."[20] Conversely, he complained that attorneys ("who are required to have a general knowledge of every department of the law, and who directly communicate with and advise the client, and manage and conduct his entire legal business"[21]) "are excluded from almost every office of emolument or distinction"[22] connected with the legal profession.

Attorneys and Legal Qualification: Utilitarian Warrants

Self-interest drove the response of attorneys to these sorts of attacks, but the form their response took was much coloured by the pervasiveness of the barristers' ideology and its resonances with a wider culture. All of this was to some extent a moving target as the effects of industrial development and cultural transformation played out over the nineteenth century. There were both defensive and offensive skirmishes with the Bar, aggressive efforts to cleanse their own branch of "dishonourable practitioners," and a commitment to practical education.

Recurring turf wars between the upper and lower branches of the legal profession[23] often involved barristers' complaints about the type of work attorneys were undertaking or the ways in which they conducted their business. Conflicts arose over conveyancing,[24] the propriety of barristers' being engaged directly by clients (thereby assuming the role of *dominus litis*),[25] and rights of audience in lower-level courts.[26]

Solicitors and attorneys formed various professional associations during the eighteenth and nineteenth centuries. At the national level, these included the Society of Gentlemen Practicers in the Courts of Law and Equity (possibly formed directly in response to the *Attorney Act, 1729*), the Metropolitan and Provincial Law Association,[27] and the Law Society of England and Wales.[28] Attorneys could not directly compete with barristers' claims to status. In general, barristers were drawn from higher social strata, giving them the edge in claims grounded in gentlemanly status, classical learning, refinement, or social contacts. The Bar was dominated by men of "the urban professional and business classes supplemented by the greater and lesser gentry" from the late eighteenth century through the reign of Queen Victoria.[29] In contrast, the mid-nineteenth-century solicitor Sir George Stephen observed that "looking at the profession generally as a class, I would say that it consisted certainly of inferior men, both in point of station and of education."[30] In particular, he observed, "a very considerable number of our profession" were drawn from "a much lower stock" than others:

> They are young men who have probably been introduced in early days, at their early boyhood, at the age of 10 or 12 or 13, as soon as they could write, into an attorney's office, and employed as copying clerks. They pick up a great deal of practical knowledge, more especially a great deal of familiarity with the peculiar business and papers of the clients of their employer; they remain in his office for five or six years, or perhaps seven or eight years, and they become of extreme value to him; and then the attorney, with a view to retain them upon a very moderate salary, and probably with a view of ultimately making them partners, to take off the burthen of his business, will article them; and you may say with respect to a man of that sort, that he is suckled and cradled as an attorney.[31]

Stephen's comments speak to both the social origins of attorneys and the dominance of a world-view that privileged formal education over practically acquired knowledge. The triple fault lines of class origin, educational attainment, and practical knowledge would contour professional innovations throughout the nineteenth century. Attorneys engaged in their own professionalization projects could gain no traction by attempting to gloss over concerns about disreputable practitioners, just as they could not contradict the judgment that many were "inferior men" in both class and educational background, who might have been "suckled and cradled as an attorney." Similarly, the "broad," "liberal," and "refined" backgrounds of barristers could not be gainsaid. Attorneys could not reasonably hope to cast doubt even on the value of knowledge of poetry or of Ancient Greek and Latin literature to the practice of contemporary English law. Hence, for Sir George Stephen, the extensive "practical knowledge" developed during a long apprenticeship appears as a poor cousin to less practical education. Gentlemanliness trumps utility.

While attorneys could not make too much of the merits of on-the-job training, they were nonetheless forced to invoke the value of practical knowledge: it was all they had. Speaking to a meeting of the Metropolitan and Provincial Law Association in 1855, Mr. J. Bulmer of Leeds argued that the community needed "the services of men combining high intellect and extended education with *practical knowledge of business and the world.*"[32] The nod in the direction of "extended education" reaffirms the virtues of gentlemanliness as a professional aspiration, while the reference to "practical knowledge" asserts the unique value of attorneys' training. Bulmer, indeed, makes this the foundation for an explicit claim of attorney superiority as "it cannot be denied but that practical experience can only be obtained in the second branch of the Profession [i.e., attorneys], for they alone have communication with the client, and the management of his business, and are alone acquainted with his wants, his feelings, and his wishes."[33] To similar effect, W. Shaen, secretary of the Metropolitan and Provincial Law Association, observed in 1855 "that more than ninety per cent of the Law of this country is administered to the public in the private offices of Attorneys and Solicitors."[34] As a result of this work experience, Shaen claimed, attorneys became the paramount experts on matters of law and practice:

> It is we alone who see, without the interposition of any medium, the permanent effect of the Law, when declared, upon the thoughts and feelings, the acts and lives, of those who are affected by it. If that is our position with regard to law, properly so called, still more is it the case that ours is the most valuable experience with regard to that which is included under the term "practice."[35]

By contrast, barristers suffered from a constrained and partial practical experience of law, limited to the arena of litigation, Shaen claimed. Even here, there was limited exposure to the practical and contextual histories of suits: "of this history, Counsel only gather hints, partial and occasional, and producing partial and, for the most part, temporary impressions."[36] Attorneys, in short, were invaluable members of society, "members of an honourable Profession,"[37]and persons whose inimitable practical expertise made them essential participants in the process of law reform as well as in the day-to-day conduct of business affairs.[38]

Such claims had gained traction by the mid-nineteenth century among an increasingly important middle class, which embraced the virtues of practical knowledge. From the burial of "Old Corruption," through massive professionalization of middle-class occupations, to modernization and Benthamite-inspired projects of law reform, the direction of cultural drift was unmistakable.[39] Organizations such as the Society for the Promoting of Useful Knowledge[40] and the National Association for the Promotion of Social Science (which held its inaugural meeting at Queen's College, Birmingham, in 1857)[41] advocated the collection and promotion of useful, practical knowledge. The measure was utility and it powerfully influenced perceptions of professions and of professional education.[42]

Even those who emphasized the values of practical knowledge sometimes thought it might best be acquired through systematized training rather than through the asystematic and ad hoc learning experience of unstructured apprenticeships. The provision of practical education structured and directed by experienced practitioners could improve learning outcomes without traipsing too far into the territory of the gentleman's liberal education. Crudely, more knowledge could be crammed into student's heads in a classroom than by serendipity: "A student's education is a thing of shreds and patches. Their minds are a reflex of marginal notes, and a compendium of points of practice. Rarely do we find radical learning, enlarged powers of generalization, or a group of principles."[43] More pointedly, Lord Campbell criticized contemporary professional learning because "in the present want of system a great deal of time is wasted by the student, from his being left entirely without a guide to his own researches, discoveries and exertions."[44]

Professional associations stepped in to fill the gap. Robert Maugham, secretary of the Incorporated Law Society, reported in 1846 that his society offered a course of lectures on common law, conveyancing, equity, bankruptcy, and criminal law at its London premises each year, attended by some two hundred articled clerks and taught by three lecturers drawn from the Bar.[45] Other local law societies also offered courses of lectures, most of these apparently following a model established by the Manchester Law Society in 1844. That society offered lectures on Commercial Law, the Law of Evidence, Conveyancing, Criminal Law, and Legal and Moral Training, with lecturers drawn from the ranks of local attorneys assisted by one or two barristers. These lectures too were well attended.[46]

Such programs offered systematic exposure to important areas of practical knowledge taught by "practical men."[47] The lectures were modest in scope. Attendance was not compulsory for aspiring attorneys, and they did not conclude in examination. Nonetheless, contemporaries considered them to be significant and worthy innovations. Such programs appeared to validate the value of precise training in matters of practice as superior to apprenticeship alone (the traditional entry route for attorneys) and to the combination of classic liberal education with "dining" obligations and rudimentary apprenticeship requirements (the route to the Bar). The inclusion of barristers as well as attorneys as lecturers speaks, perhaps, to the hegemony of that profession, but also reflects respect for their own practice-derived knowledge.

Finally, although lectures of limited duration, attended voluntarily and unexamined, contained only the embryo of an educational system, these efforts meshed well with the emerging preference for systematized, cost-effective methods of education and evaluation. It was part of a larger "middle-class challenge in the first part of the nineteenth century [which] relied on a different, instrumental conception of education."[48]

Such developments on the attorneys' side tended to cast the Bar's qualification practices in bad light, however gentlemanly they might be. Lord Brougham and Vaux thought the legal education of barristers to be thoroughly inadequate:

> The inns of court have for ages past never affected to educate their members; and a person is called ... to the bar, merely because his name has been five years upon the books, or three if he has a degree of master of arts, and because he has what is called kept twelve terms, which means being present at the time grace is said, for a minute or two, a certain number of days in each term during those three years.[49]

The education provided for solicitors was, he thought, "less deficient, on this account, that a person cannot be a solicitor without having served a certain time as an articled clerk, and therefore he must needs obtain considerable practical knowledge."[50]

Both Magali Sarfatti Larson[51] and Raymond Cocks[52] have suggested that attorneys' moves toward formalized training was a source of embarrassment for barristers, and Cocks has pointed to a sustained debate as to the adequacy of barristers' education.[53] While there was little agreement among barristers as to whether or how the requirements for admission to the Bar should be changed, all "thought about the Bar in a defensive manner."[54] The *Law Times,* a journal highly critical of barristers' training, "sought to prepare defensive positions for the profession in an age that questioned the utility of the Bar; and it did so by attempting to justify the Bar in utilitarian terms – reform, not revolution, was what was needed."[55]

Combining Gentlemanly Education and Useful Training: The 1846 Report on Legal Education

The contradictory forces of gentlemanly and practical education clashed in public discussions for two reasons. A common-sense recognition that both barristers and attorneys applied legal knowledge in their professional work led commentators to draw the obvious comparisons. This was reinforced by a more general cultural drift towards a narrower utilitarianism that sat uncomfortably with the social warrants of the Bar. Nonetheless, there was currency and social capital in gentlemanliness. While barristers were increasingly attacked for their failure to justify themselves on utilitarian grounds, attorneys felt pressure to re-create their profession as more refined, more liberal, and more honourable than it had been.

A Select Committee appointed by the House of Commons to consider "the State, Improvement, and Extension of Legal Education in England"[56] and Ireland attempted to reconcile these various perspectives in 1846. The committee's assessment was dismal:

> The present state of Legal Education in England and Ireland, in reference to the classes professional and unprofessional concerned, to the extent and nature of the studies pursued, the time employed, and the facility with which instruction may be obtained, is extremely unsatisfactory and incomplete ... the student, professional and unprofessional, is left almost solely to his own individual exertions, industry and opportunities, and that no Legal Education, worthy of the name, is at this moment to be had in either country.[57]

In reaching its conclusion, the committee had reviewed the opportunities provided for legal education for barristers, attorneys, and general students. It found each deficient.

The committee criticized the haphazard, unsystematic training at the Bar: "This total absence of all provision for legal education in the Inns of Court, and the meagre amount, as already observed, provided in the Universities, had the natural effect of throwing the student on such chance instruction or studies as might fall in his way."[58] The committee quoted Lord Campbell's description of the requirements that he said had been in effect since the end of the seventeenth century:

> All that has been required has been, that the candidate to be called to the Bar should be of fair character; that he should have been a certain number of years upon the books of the Society; that he should have kept a certain number of terms, by eating a certain number of dinners in the Hall each term, and have gone through the form of performing what are still called Exercises, but which consist of a mere farce of a case being stated, and a debate on each side; but the parties being stopped by the time they have read three words of the case, or the argument on either side, the case and the argument being furnished to them by an officer of the Society.[59]

If one disregards the "farce" of the "Exercises," we are left with a system of qualification based on dining at the Inns. It may be that those seeking membership in the Bar only for social reasons slipped through on this basis alone. Young men intent on a life of practice as barristers, however, would have subjected themselves to a form of apprenticeship involving "at least a year," ordinarily two years, and occasionally three years "attending under special pleaders, draftsmen, or conveyancers."[60] Even this compared poorly with the statutory requirement of a minimum of five years' apprenticeship for attorneys. Lord Brougham observed:

> In attending his master, the pupil is not taught by interposition of the pleader or draftsman; generally speaking he is left entirely to himself; he sees the precedents; he may copy them or not as he chooses; he sees cases brought to be answered by the pleader, or draftsman, or conveyancer; he sees the answers, and he may obtain information by speaking to his master and discussing the subject; but, generally speaking, he is left very much to himself.[61]

At best, the education of barristers was ad hoc, unsystematic, and unstructured. The Select Committee on Legal Education viewed it as unsatisfactory because it was "in great measure technical and its acquisition must very much depend upon the individual intelligence and exertion of the pupil."[62]

The committee was equally critical of attorney training. Despite the mandated five-year apprenticeship, supplemented, for those who wished to attend, with lectures offered by local law societies and the Incorporated Law Society, the committee concluded:

> The future "solicitor" does not appear to have had even the same, or as good opportunities offered to him for legal education as the barrister. He has been treated more as a mechanical agent for carrying out the practical processes of the profession; and as the future chemist and apothecary is bound an apprentice, so is the future solicitor articled as a clerk, for the purpose of learning what has been too much considered in both cases matter of mere manual dexterity. Hence, whatever higher or more comprehensive instruction he has been able to acquire, he owes it almost exclusively to himself.[63]

The conclusion that this failed to provide "even ... as good opportunities ... for legal education as the barrister" seems jarring. Although the (compulsory) apprenticeship of attorneys suffered the same deficiencies of lack of structure as the (optional) apprenticeships of barristers, the attorneys' apprenticeship was at least two years longer and always concluded with a formal examination. Given the farcical and pro forma nature of barristers' exercises described by Lord Campbell, the committee's denigration of the more rigorous examination of intending attorneys seems jarring:

> This examination, either as to quantity or quality of knowledge required, mode in which it is insisted on, or precision with which it is tested, appears to be altogether inadequate to the purposes for which it is presumed it was designed. Six months previous application would, in the opinion of Mr. Payne, be quite sufficient to enable an ordinary student to pass. The questions refer to forms and principles, though the former considerably predominate. The examination is wholly written, and seldom lasts for more than a day. There is no inquiry made from the candidate as to previous study, beyond the mere qucry, unattended by any consequences, of "What books have you read, and what lectures have you attended?" nor is any notice taken of the more or less degree of application evinced during his apprenticeship. So far, then as the mass is concerned, no guarantee whatever exists for that competency which the public have a right to demand.[64]

This is not sheer hypocrisy, however. What concerned the committee was not so much lack of technical competence on the part of attorneys (forms) but their failure to attain a more refined sort of learning. The committee's concerns that "mere manual dexterity" was overemphasized at the cost of the study of principle and "higher or more comprehensive instruction" hint at concerns relating to gentlemanly deficiency rather than about task performance. Similarly, the lack of inquiry as to "previous study" is criticized. Elsewhere in the report, the committee expresses its disapproval of the profession's failure to require examination prior to admission to articles, and of the fact that "no particular amount of knowledge of any description is required."[65] The committee criticized the very inferior moral and intellectual education of some attorneys, and endorsed the opinion of Sir George Stephen:

> It is quite impossible to define, within a narrow compass, the nature of a solicitor's business; it extends to anything, it extends to everything; the fact is, that we are, as professional men, entrusted to a very great extent with the confidence of gentlemen; we are entrusted to a very great extent with the most sacred matters connected with the families of gentlemen. It often happens that the protection of their honour and their character, and of course, of their property, is left to our zeal and our integrity; and where we are brought into this confidential and habitual intercourse with men of every

> class in society, the highest as well as the lowest, I think that it is most important that the Profession should be so educated as to be qualified for carrying on that intercourse as gentlemen themselves; but I apprehend that that qualification cannot be attained except by educating them as gentlemen, with much greater attention to their general endowments and information than is at present the case.[66]

For the committee, this implied that all attorneys ought to have at least the equivalent of the distinctly elite education available at "the fifth form of a public school ["public school" in England means "private school"]."[67] The existing deficiencies were met only in part, in the committee's view, and then for only one-tenth of the profession, through rubbing of shoulders with gentlemen "by attendance at barristers' and conveyancers' chambers, for about one year of their apprenticeship."[68]

Taking the thing as a whole, the committee criticized barristers for lack of sufficient legal training and examination, while it criticized attorneys mostly for their failure in general education and schooling in principles. Its proposals were aimed at addressing these twinned deficiencies and at "rationalizing" legal education. In addition, they hoped to encourage "general" students to partake of legal studies in order to attain "a sufficient elementary knowledge, for all general purposes of Magistrates, Legislators, Diplomatists, and Officials."[69]

The committee offered a sketchy blueprint for legal education intended to address the needs of each of these constituencies. Unifying themes included the ideas of regularized education, gentlemanly virtues, and practical competence. The committee's ideal for legal education integrated the best of the available notions of what it was to be a professional lawyer. This involved a partial union of the worlds of the practitioner and the scholar in order to create a new type of thinker about law, "a class ... of Publicists and Professors, scientific jurists in the proper sense of the term, to whose consideration, undisturbed by local and temporary circumstances, great questions might be submitted, and adjudged on scientific principles as well as on practical grounds."[70] Scholarly learning and practical knowledge were thought to complement each other: "The scientific man will make but little way without practice and experience, but it is not less true that the practical man will find practice much surer when regulated by the guiding light of science."[71]

The committee had a clear vision of the "scientific jurist" as a person of broad reading and deep thought, not to be confused with the sort of empirical learning to be gleaned from law reports. By contrast, it said: "There is a remarkable deficiency in that higher class of scientific work, in those systematic developments of the history and philosophy of Law, which, arising from broader and deeper studies, also tends to render still broader and deeper its practice and administration."[72] In an era before modern university disciplines had hardened their boundaries, the committee thought of law as inextricably part of economics, geography, and statistics as well as of philosophy and history. The occupants of proposed "Chairs of Law" at "the New Irish Provincial Colleges" might accordingly teach "courses also of Political Geography, Statistics, and Political Economy, as subsidiary and supplementary to those of Jurisprudence."[73]

The committee thought the university to be the proper home for learned professors. Education of this sort would be valuable both for general students (who would become "country gentlemen," and therefore magistrates,[74] Members of Parliament,[75] peers,[76] or diplomatists and administrators[77]) and for aspiring barristers. University legal education was not perceived as an alternative to more practical training, however. While universities might offer the advantages of "scientific study" and "eligibility to lucrative and honourable situation, professional emolument, intellectual, moral, and social rank,"[78] they were distinctly flawed as reservoirs of practical knowledge:

> It would, indeed, be a total misapprehension of the purposes and character of this University Legal Education to consider it as a substitute for, or even appropriate to, the peculiar purposes of the professional student. For this, as in other departments, the special institution [read, "Inns of Court"] is absolutely essential. The province of the University is to teach the philosophy of the science, and to secure instruction in those branches for which it might be apprehended the more technical character of the special institution would inadequately provide.[79]

So, formal learning was valued, but not to the point where the "virtues of practical men"[80] were overlooked. This would have been inconceivable at the time, even if innumerable distinguished politicians, lawyers, and judges had not attained status, respect, and position on the basis of practical training. In working out the technical/science distinction, the committee identified subjects such as "Civil law" (meaning Canon or Ecclesiastical), Comparative "Constitutional and Parliamentary Law," "International Law," and "Administrative Law" ("in its connexion with magisterial and official duty") as appropriate to the university.[81] More generally, there was a notion that *ius gentium* might form the core of university legal education: "above all, the great and enduring principles on which all Law, whatever may be its local or temporary modifications, should rest, and which is no more than the highest morality, directed by the highest philosophy in action; this is the appropriate and honourable vocation of an University Law School or Faculty."[82]

The committee emphasized that university education of this character "in no way militates against or supersedes the peculiar province of the special professional institution."[83] Rather, they hoped that it would

> give a higher and more scientific tone to the entire study, and ... will go far to replace Law in its legitimate position; and from being, as it now is, an art depending, like others, on more or less experience, more or less dexterity in practice, will elevate it once more to a noble science; next to religion, the chief instrument for the civilization and happiness of mankind.[84]

The university would produce scientists of law who, in conjunction with "the most eminent of the Bench and Bar," would guide law reform and codification.[85]

The committee thought that after such an education the path to professional qualification should turn in different directions for aspiring barristers and attorneys, each pursuing distinct types of training suited to their distinctive practical needs. In contrast to the theoretical or comparative orientation proposed for university legal education, it was proposed that the Inns of Court should largely provide instruction in *ius civile:* Law of Real Property, Common Law, Criminal Law, Constitutional Law, Commercial Law, Medical Jurisprudence, and General Procedures.[86] In addition to these "practical" areas, however, the committee felt that the Inns should provide education in two distinctly more theoretical areas: Methods and History of Law and "General Jurisprudence, or the Philosophy of Law and Legislation,"[87] with chairs in these areas to be endowed by the Inns jointly. These would provide a "chart and compass" for the more specific legal studies offered, forming a "link ... between professional and non-professional studies."[88] It was also hoped that "this combination of the Inns amongst themselves, for one general purpose" would promote social cohesion and common socialization among barristers, judges, and legislators:

> The field of exertion and emulation, to both Professor and Student, is greatly enlarged, habits of intercourse and sympathy, so desireable [*sic*] amongst men whose future lives and labours lie so much together, are generated, and a harmony in instruction and action secure, the result of which cannot but be felt beneficially through the whole range of the Lawyer's afterpractice, and ultimately no doubt in the decisions of the Bench, and the Acts and other proceedings of the Legislature.[89]

The social cohesion of the Bar was to be further ensured by the imposition of an entrance examination. "[I]ncompetency and indolence" were to be eliminated by the imposition of a mandatory final examination on the lecture material.[90]

Taken as a whole these proposals sought to combine the traditional gentlemanly warrants of barristers with a sharpened focus on practical knowledge in a form demonstrably aligned with the temperament of the times.

Proposals for the professional education of attorneys followed a somewhat similar strategy, combining an enhanced focus on gentlemanliness with the provision of practical training. Attorneys needed education in both "mere practical details" and in "the higher and more undefinable duties and influences of the profession."[91] These twin concerns refracted into three distinct areas of educational programming: "mechanical" ability, practical knowledge, and bourgeois culture. The first was easily disposed of:

> For the mechanical and almost manual dexterity, which though inferior is still indispensable, sufficient care, it may be thought, is already taken by present practice and regulation. The system of apprenticing is in itself good inasmuch as it teaches in the most effectual way, that is by practice, this portion of the profession. The articled clerk not only learns what he is to do, but is gradually found doing it as he advances, and thus enters, in this particular usually well prepared, on the career of the Solicitor. But beyond this it does not appear its advantages extend.[92]

What lay "beyond this" was, presumably, the preparation of complex cases for litigation, the creative structuring of business arrangements, and intercourse with refined persons.

With respect to the "more important portion of the Solicitor's education, that which proposes to fit him for the higher duties of his profession,"[93] the committee endorsed Sir George Stephen's view of the desirability of increasing the educational requirements for beginning articling:

> [C]lerks should not be allowed to be articled till the age of 18, which, while it would not impair their efficiency, but the reverse, in their future profession, would allow an adequate period for the acquisition of most if not of all the branches, Latin, Mathematics, history, and one or more of the living languages.[94]

It was thought that demanding better prior education would produce clerks better able "to profit from such [professional] instruction as might be within their reach,"[95] although no direct connection was drawn between Latin or history or a living language and the tasks attorneys were called upon to perform. The committee was clearly aware that such proposals would introduce significant barriers to the profession, shifting its composition over time[96] and ensuring that future attorneys would reflect "gentlemanly principles and conduct."[97]

The suggestion that some formal instruction might be provided for aspiring attorneys through the Inns of Chancery, any local law society, or the Incorporated Law Society, was offered almost as an afterthought. Such arrangements could "provide class instruction on an efficient footing" and lead to examination of students in such a way as "to render much more useful, and, if it may be added, more vital, the almost technical or inappropriate examination now in use."[98] The committee briefly considered the possibility of having English articled clerks attend lectures at the Inns of Court alongside aspiring barristers, just as was done in Ireland. The idea was dismissed, however, because "such proposition would not be acceptable to the Bar collectively or individually."[99] In any event, "many of the lectures" to be provided at the Inns "would scarcely be appropriate and special enough for his wants, and in order to make them so, a considerable accession to the lectureships might be found necessary."[100]

In sum, the 1846 Select Committee on Legal Education provided a blueprint that blended a new emphasis on formal education with respect for inherited traditions of apprenticeship and the virtues of empirically derived knowledge. It called for both branches of the legal profession to become learned (in literature, languages, and abstract thought), but also skilled in the peculiar subject matters or technical competence needed by their clients. Heavy doses of utilitarian practicality and gentlemanly learning were prescribed all around. This was neither the outcome of some disinterested philosophical inquiry nor, though it is sometimes treated that way,[101] a timeless best model of legal education. The proposals emerged from a specific context. They were developed to meet the needs of the day, drew upon their era's conceptual toolbox, and were expressed in the respectable language of their time. Nonetheless, they were radical and innovative.

The committee's blueprint proved to be too bold for successful implementation. Although internally coherent and logical as far as they went, the proposals operated at the level of ideas only. For failing to adequately address the material circumstances of either of the two legal professions, much less the differences between them, the committee's work is best adjudged a failure.

It remains now to explore the earliest attempt to implement the committee's proposals for college-based legal education. Its failure, as well as the relative success of its successor, tells us much about the legal professions and their education at the time. It also marks a turning point in the career of Charles Rann Kennedy, putting him in place for his colourful career as a provincial barrister (see Chapters 7 and 12).

Queen's College, Birmingham

Birmingham provided fertile soil for innovation. This was as true in matters of education as of manufacturing. A newly developed urban centre, its institutions were new and more malleable than those in more ancient towns. It was a burgeoning industrial centre whose ethos was very much in step with the mood of the times: productive, practical, and utilitarian. Its middle class leaned radical in politics, and many saw their industry, politics, and nascent institutions as charting new courses for Britain.

Such a culture values practical education affordable for the children of middle-class parents,[102] and Queen's College developed from and served this constituency. It was founded in 1828 by a young surgeon, William Sands Cox, who had returned to his hometown after studies in London and on the Continent. What he found upon his return disappointed him, for "the greater number of country practitioners of that time were sadly deficient in medical and surgical knowledge; were lamentably ignorant of anatomy, pathology, and general science; and were greatly wanting in general culture."[103] The college was founded in order to ensure "that other men in Birmingham who wished to take up the medical profession should have an opportunity of training near their homes and at a moderate cost."[104] The approach to education was instrumental, its constituency middle class, its purpose service.

Supported by the wealthy clergyman and philanthropist Dr. S.W. Warneford, the college's mission expanded to include clerical training.[105] Incorporated by royal charter as "Queen's College, Birmingham" in 1843,[106] its objectives again broadened as dreams of a full-fledged Midlands university took hold. The creation of a Law Department was "specially advocated" by the Reverend Vaughan Thomas, Dr. Warneford, the Reverend Horace Gray, and Archdeacon Sandford. In 1850, the college appealed for public support in broadening the institution:

> Council clearly apprehend that although medical science from its own intrinsic excellence and its intimate bearing upon the good of the community must claim place in every University scheme ... yet there was no precedent for its exclusive establishment and but little hope that if exclusively established it would enjoy all the advantages of that philosophical and religious

> characterization and enlargement which it was their great object to confer. They aimed at a resort for general education, an academical body wherein all the faculties might be pursued ... an institution wherein youths preparing for any profession might be enlarged in their sentiment by the whole course of Learning placed before them and by associating with others more immediately dedicated to another pursuit in place of being narrowed and confined in one round of thought and expression perpetually recurring and thus mentally deteriorating into mere cant and technicality.
>
> It is therefore in accordance with the soundest principles of educational science and as well as with the precedents of our ancient universities to which we have so frequently referred already that the Departments for general literature, Law, Engineering and above all and chief of all for theology have been instituted in the College.[107]

Education as a route to upward mobility for the sons of the middle classes was important, and "the advantages which they offer to parents of moderate means of a liberal education generally for any profession in their Arts Department" were to be complemented by encouraging students to proceed to more specialized education within the same institution.[108] The college aspired to bridge the gentlemanly accoutrements of liberal education and the virtues of structured, career-minded, and practical training that resonated with the middle classes of the day. Warden Horace Gray delivered a lecture outlining a philosophy of legal education just a month before Kennedy was appointed as the first Professor of Law:

> The Department of Laws arises in some measure out of the General Department of Arts, inasmuch as the degree of Bachelor of Laws is taken one year after that of the Bachelor of Arts, and Doctor of Laws two years after that of the Bachelor in the same faculty. By this arrangement the foundation is laid of that classical, historical and mathematical knowledge without which eminence and even success in the profession of law is almost unattainable. In this department it is also to be observed that evening lectures will be delivered especially for the benefit of legal clerks and assistants in Birmingham who are engaged throughout the day, and desirous in their leisure hours of cultivating an acquaintance with the higher walks of their profession.[109]

Superbly suited to develop legal education as a project deeply connected to general arts, history, and mathematics, the first Professor's "fit" with legal clerks and assistants was another matter.

The Professorship of Charles Rann Kennedy

Charles Rann Kennedy was the son of a prominent Birmingham clergyman. Educated in classics at Cambridge, he won prizes in Latin and Greek and gained the presidency of the Union.[110] His abilities were exceptional, and he "had so far eclipsed all his competitors, that according to college tradition, the Examiners of his year hesitated to place anyone else in the first class of the Classical Tripos with him."[111] He was a published poet,[112] a respected translator of classical literature,[113] and author of a treatise defending classical education against displacement by "useful knowledge."[114] He was successively a fellow of Trinity College, Cambridge,[115] practising barrister, Master-elect of the school at Lichfield (a position that he declined),[116] and a candidate for the chair of Greek at the University of Edinburgh.[117]

Kennedy embodied the gentleman barrister almost to the point of caricature. He also brought to the post a background as a practical barrister. Called to the bar in 1835,[118] he served as a revising barrister,[119] and participated in the politically charged *Stockdale v. Hansard* litigation.[120] He was the author of legal works on annuities,[121] joint stock companies,[122] parliamentary privilege,[123] the rules of pleading,[124] and the role of revising barristers.[125] Other publications relating to the *Swinfen* litigation and bar etiquette were to follow.[126]

Kennedy's practical experience complemented a very high level of scholarly accomplishments suited to the college's objectives of ensuring that professional students did not deteriorate "into mere cant and technicality." There was little in his record or interests to suggest that he was well suited to training aspiring solicitors and attorneys in "the mechanical and almost manual dexterity" that was considered an indispensable element in an attorney's training by the 1846 Select Committee.[127]

In choosing Kennedy, the college hoped to develop a type of legal education that would appeal to the general student as well as to *both* aspiring barristers and aspiring solicitors. Their aspirations in this regard followed closely the 1846 committee's ideas about the purpose of university education. Distinct professional advantages would be enjoyed by those students who sought to join the legal profession following completion of a degree. For those intent on a career as an attorney, articling requirements would be reduced to three years from five,[128] while aspiring barristers would benefit from "shortening the number of terms to be kept in London ..."[129] Because the degree could be obtained at lower cost and more quickly (one year less) than at the "ancient Universities," the college hoped to provide a route by which a lower stratum of middle-class men could enter the higher branch of the legal profession. Upward class mobility was offered as "many persons of large families and small means ... may wish to bring up a son to the honourable profession of the Bar, and may be seriously hindered and distressed by the great expense hitherto attending on the carrying out of such a design."[130] There was also room to meet the educational needs of students wishing to become attorneys without first completing a degree, for the college hoped that "clerks and assistants in lawyers' offices in Birmingham and the neighbourhood" would register in evening courses for their own betterment: to "open to them the principles of their profession" rather than seeking instruction of a merely "technical character."[131] Kennedy's lectures would, it was promised, be open to "those who are articled to conveyancers and solicitors" and who thus could not "devote themselves to the regular studies of a College; but they may find time for attendance upon courses of law."[132]

In seeking to serve these multiple constituencies, the college sought to offer a program of lectures that would be all things to all men. Charles Rann Kennedy was heavily influenced by recent thinking about legal education. Unsurprisingly, he set a highly scholarly tone and probably developed a program that provided fine *professional* education. Its weakness was with regard to the perceived *training* needs of its largest potential student constituency. Kennedy's 1850 inaugural lecture was largely derivative of the 1846 committee's recommendations. Reflecting the approach shared by that committee and the college governors, he outlined an approach to formal legal education that would be relevant to the three student constituencies.

With regard to the general student, Kennedy observed that "[t]he Department of Law may ... fairly be said to arise out of the arts department, because it is to a certain extent a branch of general education."[133] The general student would benefit from the study of law, he thought, morally, practically, and as a cultured person. As a moral person, Kennedy concluded, "the philosopher and philanthropist" should give attention to legal studies because "the science of jurisprudence is intimately connected with ethical science" as "all positive law is founded on the moral law."[134] The practical person of affairs would, Kennedy thought, benefit from knowledge of the particular laws of his own country as this was "necessary to all who take an active part in public business, especially to the statesman and the legislator."[135] There was a clear need for individuals of influence to develop a systematic and coherent understanding of law, because "no one can be properly qualified to make laws, who knows nothing of the science of law; any more than a man can build a house, who knows nothing of architecture."[136] Finally, law was said to be an essential component of a gentleman's cultural repertoire. Kennedy believed that "it is impossible to understand the history of our country without some knowledge of law"[137] and that "some knowledge of legal phraseology is needful, if you desire fully to understand your own language" (the possibility that "Shakspeare" [*sic*] was a solicitor's clerk was duly noted).[138]

Gentlemanly legal education of this sort would transcend narrowly technical expertise, memorization of detailed rules, and rote learning of legal forms and documents. What was needed "for ordinary men" was to understand law's "general features and principles, and in particular those parts of it which concern our political constitution, the civil rights and franchises of the people, and their correlative duties and obligations."[139] More specifically:

> There is obviously a limit, beyond which a non-professional gentleman could never be expected to pursue legal studies. What that limit is, may be better understood than defined. He should apply himself to general principles, rather than to details. My meaning may be illustrated by an example – Every gentleman should understand the distinction between freehold and copyhold tenures, and something of the history of that subject; yet if he is not a lawyer, he need not be taught to draw a deed for the conveyance of real property.[140]

Although different considerations applied to students intending to become legal practitioners, this did not lead Kennedy to conclude that their college educational program should stray far from gentlemanly learning. He reasoned that,

> as every man is to be regarded not only in his professional character, but as a moral and social agent, and a member of a political community; it follows that a course of scientific study, which is desirable for an ordinary gentleman, must be peculiarly useful to the lawyer. It is important for him not only to study law as a professional acquirement, but as being an institution of his country; and also to comprehend its relation to the natural and the moral law; that is to study it ethically.[141]

Kennedy thought this would assist the lawyer in resolving ethical issues arising from "conflicting duties" owed to client and to society, as well as more generally in applying "a very cautious discretion ... to regulate the conduct of the lawyer in his practice."[142]

Coming closer to the sphere of the workaday world of practitioners, Kennedy believed that "a scientific course of study must be of the highest service to the lawyer" with regard to "professional acquirements."[143] Closely echoing the 1846 committee, he bemoaned the fact that "a systematic course of legal study, duly ordered and prescribed, is even yet nowhere to be found in this country. Law is learned at haphazard; and generally gleaned in scraps from professional practice."[144] In practical terms, this meant that "an enormous deal of time is wasted."[145] Worse, Kennedy felt that the entire profession was degraded:

> Few of our practical lawyers aim at anything more, than qualifying themselves to carry on their business with success. The result is, that even the ablest class of English lawyers very rarely distinguish themselves as scientific jurists, much less as philosophers or statesmen; even their eloquence has greatly degenerated; and there are few men among our successful advocates to be found of extensive accomplishments, or lofty aspirations.[146]

In short, the inaugural lecture hammered home the special role of college education in law as being about gentlemanly education, not about training in the work of lawyers. Ordinary students would become better public officials, educated in ethics and more cultured and literate than they otherwise would be. Likewise, legal professionals as "moral and social agent[s]" and "member[s] of a political community"[147] would derive similar benefits and for similar reasons. Finally, aspiring legal professionals would also benefit because they would acquire legal knowledge more efficiently, and become more learned, refined, and valued members of the political community. The argument constantly circles back on itself as every conceivable sort of student is said to be likely to benefit from a common approach to their education focused on the gentlemanly, not the practical, side of things.

The only clue that Kennedy provided regarding the exact nature of a curriculum suitable to meet these needs lies in a brief and approving mention of Cardinal Wolsey's plans to establish "a grand institution ... for the systematic study of all branches of the law."[148] Although Kennedy disparaged the existing paths to qualification for both branches of the legal profession, he was vague both as to the advantages a formal, structured education offered and as to desirable curricular content. Regarding attorneys, he observed: "A young man of sixteen, who has been imperfectly educated, is sent into a solicitor's office to commence the routine of business, before he knows anything of his subject, and when his mind is not sufficiently formed, to undertake the arduous task of teaching himself on right principles."[149] On the barrister's side, he felt that "nothing can be more absurd than the present system of calling to the bar,"[150] which lacked both structured education and examination of legal learning. The unreliability of a system in which "training for the bar is generally carried on in the chambers of a conveyancer, a special pleader, or equity draftsman" was unsatisfactory: "the student selects for his reading, generally by chance, such particular books, out of the multitude that are published, as appear most likely to assist his progress."[151]

Kennedy believed that formal college instruction would be cost-effective and that students destined for either branch of the profession would benefit from the courses to be offered.[152] In neither case did he advocate the abolition or replacement of apprenticeship. The inaugural lecture gave little hint of what exactly should be taught. For attorneys, he thought that "[t]he science should be studied, while the business of the office is carried on. Study and practice should go hand in hand together."[153] Aspiring attorneys would benefit from formal instruction running "concurrently with the routine of the office" because this would increase the likelihood that "the student may not only understand, but take an interest in what he is about. He should not only learn how to copy a precedent or get a deed engrossed, but to comprehend the principles of the deeds which he draws, and the foundations of the law which regulates the conveyance of real property."[154]

The inaugural lecture was sketched in broad strokes, impressionistically, and offered little detail about the program. Although he promoted formalized instruction of law as a science and focused on principle, these notions are not fully fleshed out. A certain circularity of reasoning emerges with regard to the presumed acquisition of professional, as distinct from "gentlemanly," learning. Even in speaking to the advantages of attorneys being examined on their knowledge, he failed to offer a unique rationale for college legal education: attorneys would "not only ... reap the benefit of higher intellectual improvement, but their clients will feel themselves safer in entrusting their cases to men, who have passed the ordeal of sound education."[155] Even this falls far short endorsing practical professional training at the college. Likewise, the graduate of any rigorous program of study would have "passed the ordeal of sound education." In general, he thought it unnecessary to distinguish between cultural knowledge and professional legal knowledge: whatever form and content of formal legal education at an institution of higher learning was good for nonprofessional "gentlemen" was also good for aspiring practitioners.

The course of lectures that Kennedy developed was entirely consistent. *Aris's Birmingham Gazette* carried an advertisement announcing that the lectures would take place over three terms, each comprising forty lectures, "with examinations."[156] An accompanying news item explained:

> Mr. K. proposes to follow the plan indicated by Blackstone, having reference also to those books which the University of London has prescribed as subjects of examination; namely, Kents' Commentaries, Bentham's Treatise

> on Morals and Legislation, and Rutherford's Institute of Natural Laws. He will commence with the foundation of all positive laws, showing that their basis is the moral nature of man implanted in him by God. He will then proceed to the history of the Common Law of England, and give a general review of its principles and characters; after which he will take up each particular department in the same order, generally speaking, as they occur in Blackstone's Commentaries. The first series of lectures will embrace those parts of our law which concern the Crown and the Executive Government, the Revenues, the Parliament, and the Church, all those subjects, in short, which are usually comprised under the name of Constitutional Law; next the various laws which concern the private relations and commercial usages of society; the law of real and personal property, the nature of civil remedies, the practice of the Common Law Courts, and the principles of pleading. Criminal Jurisprudence will be next in order; and lastly, a general view will be given of the principles of Equity Law, and the practice of the Court of Chancery.[157]

The item concluded with a reminder of the reduced period of articles (apprenticeship) required of degree holders, noting also that "in order to facilitate attendance on this important course, Mr. Kennedy has consented to deliver the lectures in the evening."[158]

The alignment of the educational program with gentlemanly knowledge is striking. Of the program's three components, the first ("the foundation of all positive laws" and "history of the Common Law") and second (Constitutional Law) fall solidly on the gentlemanly side. Although "legal," each was in the domain of classics, philosophy, history, or political theory more than the law of legal practice. Only the third component ("private relations and commercial usages") comes at all close to the day-to-day work of attorneys or barristers. Even here, however, lectures would be most attractive to apprenticing attorneys if closely aligned with their qualifying examinations. Kennedy's lecture notes have not survived, but everything we know about him makes this seem unlikely. The attorneys' examination consisted largely of questions concerning "forms,"[159] an area in which barristers would have little experience and precisely the sort of thing that Kennedy dismissed as "the routine of business,"[160] more appropriate to on-the-job acquisition during apprenticeship than to the academy. Kennedy's life commitments, classical education, poetic writings, legal work, and, frankly, arrogance point in other directions. The heavy emphasis on philosophically sound, "scientific" learning in his inaugural lecture did not leave much room for teaching to qualifying examinations. Finally, a hint of criticism of Kennedy for failing to address the practical needs of articled clerks is found in the selection of George James Johnson, a solicitor, as his successor (see below).

The program so developed was "cutting edge" for its day. It was scholarly, interdisciplinary, and grounded solidly in liberal education. It failed miserably. Only nine students attended Kennedy's lectures during his first term,[161] leading him to complain about both the articled students and their profession, which would not make attendance at his lectures compulsory.[162] It is tempting to conclude that the antagonism that developed between Kennedy and leading Birmingham attorneys as well as Midland Circuit barristers probably did not help. This should not be overemphasized, however. Open conflict with the leadership of the Birmingham Law Society came about only in 1852, well after it was clear that the law program had failed. Spectacular conflict with Midland Circuit barristers in 1850, almost immediately upon Kennedy's move to Birmingham, may or may not have troubled local attorneys or their apprentices.[163] His friend and ally John Pym Yeatman observed that "the great bulk of the attorneys, who are fearless and honest enough, and sufficiently independent of the Bar to act as they think right, supported Mr. Kennedy, and he rose rapidly into good practice."[164]

Rather, the program he offered was simply too far removed from the practical needs of prospective students to capture their attention. Changes in the governance structures established by the college did not bring an immediate turnaround. The *Birmingham Journal and Commercial Advertiser* of 24 January 1852 reported:

> It is also "her Majesty's further will and pleasure," in order to carry forward the statutes 6th and 7th Vic., c.73, s.7, enacted to improve the education of students intended for the profession of the law, "that two members of the Law Society established in Birmingham, to be elected by the said society ... shall be members of the Council of the said College."[165]

This may well have been too little too late. It seems unlikely in any event that Kennedy would take kindly to direction by local attorneys, whether on or off the college council.

The Professorship of George James Johnson

The Law Department was left in disarray when Kennedy eventually resigned from the professorship. His failure was so dismal that the council spoke not of continuing but of reviving the law program.[166] The new Professor of Law more or less inverted Kennedy's program. He differed from Kennedy in almost every respect.

George James Johnson was a local attorney with significant professional contacts.[167] His selection broke new terrain for solicitors, as the *Law Times* observed:

> A solicitor has been appointed to a Law Professorship. This is creditable alike to appointers and appointee. We could never understand why barristers only should be looked upon as competent to teach or write law books. It seems not to be at all understood by the public and but dimly understood by the profession, that there are two distinct branches of the law to be learned by the lawyer – its principles and its practice, a knowledge of what the law is, and also knowledge of the norms and rules by which the law is administered. From the nature of their education, though the barrister would probably be the better expounder of the law, an intelligent and industrious solicitor must be the best teacher of its practice, and it is at least as important that the law student should be versed in practice as in law. Therefore do we congratulate all parties on the appointment of Mr. Johnson.[168]

The appointment marked a turn for the college and also signalled a new approach to education in law, outreach to local attorneys, and a strong assertion of the value of practical knowledge. The appointment of a solicitor to such a role was highly unusual.[169] The Queen's College Department of Law was about to change.[170]

The college council reinforced its message at every opportunity. An announcement in August 1857 indicated that the resurrected department was specifically conceived as a place for training legal professionals, and would focus directly on preparing students for the attorneys' examination.[171] A stronger contrast with Kennedy's efforts to fold the needs of aspiring attorneys and barristers into those of gentlemanly learning would be hard to imagine. A College announcement emphasized its commitment to service of local professionals, while unmistakably renouncing the program developed by its first Professor of Law:

> The Professorship of Law having become vacant by the retirement from the town of Professor Kennedy, Mr. George James Johnson has been elected on the recommendation of the Law Society and on a strong testimonial in his favour from a large number of solicitors who had formerly been members of the Law Students Society. In that testimonial it is stated "that the Department of Law in the College in the hands of a competent Professor is calculated to obviate to a great extent an acknowledged deficiency in legal education, and as Mr. Johnson is fully alive to this deficiency and the causes

> occasioning the same, we do not doubt but that the department will in his hands become what its founders intended it to be, "a school for *sound practical legal education*."[172]

The point was underlined in the announcement of Johnson's appointment, which explicitly assigned a professional support role to the Department of Law:

> Bearing in mind that the Law Department is intended to facilitate the professional training of attorneys and solicitors, we are glad to find that the Council have appointed a member of that branch of the profession to fill the vacant chair, because an attorney must necessarily have a more accurate knowledge of the wants of his professional brethren than could be possessed by a barrister.[173]

Consistently, the revived department emphasized professional training in place of the wider gentlemanly education advocated by Johnson's predecessor. Student recruiting efforts proceeded in the same vein. Although the Queen's College calendar for 1858 advertised the relevance of education in "Classics, Mathematics and General Science," "scientific details," and "the Latin and French languages" to a constituency of general students seeking the Bachelor of Arts or Bachelor of Laws degree, the appeal of the program was mostly for "another class of Law Students."[174] It was understood that students "who are articled to Conveyancers and Solicitors" would be too busy at work to engage in the "regular studies of a College" but might find time to attend "Courses of Law."[175]

The calendar description of the course of study Johnson developed was crafted to emphasize its relevance to students taking professional examinations, clarifying that although more scholarly, interdisciplinary education was possible, this would cause no discomfort to those who sought only professional training. The calendar stated that "the course of Study pursued in this department has especial reference to the three branches of Real Property law, Equity, and Common Law, *in which all articled Clerks must be examined previous to their admission as Attorneys and Solicitors*."[176] The only required textbook was Stephen's *Commentaries,* though anybody aspiring to the Bachelor of Laws degree would also be required to read Kent's *Commentaries* and Bentham's *Treatise on Morals and Legislation*. Lest this provoke fear of an overly scholarly orientation, the calendar concluded by reasserting the program's practical utility: "Whilst the instruction given in this department is intended to be thoroughly systematic, every effort is made to base it upon, and illustrate it by means of, the ordinary routine of a Solicitor's practice."[177]

The new Professor of Law was the perfect vehicle for this reorientation. His close ties to the local attorney's profession conditioned his views on the role of the Department of Law as outlined in his inaugural lecture.[178] It set out "the peculiar difficulties which beset the study of law," made a case for the role of formal education, and sketched out a course of education of immediate value to students preparing for professional examinations. The contrast with Kennedy's inaugural lecture, delivered only seven and a half years earlier, could not be greater. Johnson's workaday approach left no room for grand statements of the value of classical education, or of knowledge of poetry and living languages. There is no desire to develop a course of lectures equally suitable for "non-professional gentlemen," barristers, and attorneys, and certainly no hint that aspiring attorneys should be required to engage in learning intended to make them better "gentlemen."

Johnson sought the transmission of practical skills rather than the pursuit of profound understanding. He believed that the peculiar difficulties of the study of law arose from "the great extent and detail of the subject; secondly, in its historical complications, and thirdly, in its obscure and absurd terminology."[179] The first and last would justify the development of systematized formal education but raised no questions relating to philosophy, morality, or political or social theory. In principle the "historical complications" opened up exactly those sorts of questions. In other hands, it would have opened the door to wider inquiry. Johnson, however, did not wish to go that route. The "historical complications" suggested only the value of formal education in transmitting practical knowledge: "Without thoroughly acquainting themselves with the origin and historical basis of our laws," he said, students could never understand the laws

> in their integrity. Without such previous preparation the effect would be analogous to viewing a picture out of distance, or out of the proper light in which it was painted; they would only perceive a blurred and undefined object ... In short it was necessary that every system of legal procedure now existing or that ever took root in this country should be understood, not only for practice, but for the settlement of all recondite or intricate points; and *no decision of the Courts or efforts of the Legislature could be properly apprehended by any one ignorant of the gradual historical progress of the law.*[180]

Even at his least practical, then, Johnson formulated his blueprint of legal education so as to appeal to the perceived needs of practising attorneys. The contrast could not be greater with Kennedy's insistence that attorneys study law as "an institution of his country; and also to comprehend its relation to natural and the moral law; that is to study it ethically."[181]

The idea that formal instruction in the law was a useful addition to private reading was still novel and Johnson defended it. He knew that he had to persuade "the legal profession that much solid good might be effected by a careful and systematic course of oral instruction."[182] The main advantages were that a professor could aid the student by directing attention to those books that it would be most profitable to read, and also by presenting and interpreting book-derived knowledge in a fashion sensitive to the realities of practice. Conceding that much could be gained by private study, Johnson nevertheless felt that a good teacher enhanced the value of reading even the best texts:

> In the course he proposed to adopt he should avoid ground that had been gone over before. It was impossible to give a synthetical view of the profession equal to that contained in Stephen's text book; but no text book, nevertheless, could yet supply the place of a teacher in explaining difficulties of the character he had before referred to. Work of this kind, indeed, was the *especial office of the teacher who understood the practical necessities of the profession,* and he added that such a method of instruction had been adopted with the best results by the Inns of Court and the Incorporated Law Society.[183]

The role of the man of practical experience (an attorney) in bridging book knowledge to apprenticing students comes to the fore. Johnson's preferred precedents were the Inns of Court and the Incorporated Law Society, not the great institutions of learning, Oxford and the University of London, to which Kennedy had looked in developing his model. The 1846 Select Committee's belief, shared by Kennedy, was that college-based legal education supplemented professional training at a gentlemanly distance. There is no echo of this in Johnson's inaugural lecture, and his approach allows for no gap between the pedagogical objectives of the college and those of professional organizations.

This academy's role in service to the professional guild suffused Johnson's vision. His lectures would be of immediate value to students preparing for professional examinations, and he had no qualms about "teaching to the examination." "[T]he examination had to be passed," he said, "and it would be his endeavour to fit them for it by imparting sound, reliable, and practical information upon the law of real property, common law, and equity, in an unconventional and familiar manner. [Loud cheering.]"[184]

Queen's College's somewhat haughty law program was thus transformed into something of an adjunct to the local law society. This was Johnson's purpose, the intent of the college council, and an approach endorsed by contemporary observers in Birmingham. The Law Department, in effect, would relieve the local law society of the need to prepare students for professional examinations. The college subsequently confirmed the new relationship and constrained educational vision in announcing that its own examinations were to be prepared and administered by a professional association. Its annual report for 1858 expressed the hope that "next year the Birmingham Law Society will appoint examiners to conduct terminal examinations [for the law courses], and that the College will be thus enabled to distinguish its meritorious students in this as in other departments."[185]

The program was more successful than Kennedy's had been. Thirteen students attended lectures in Johnson's first term, fourteen in his second and third terms. Of these, eleven were articled clerks, one was "keeping terms" for his call to the bar and another was preparing for the LL.B. degree. The college's annual report for 1858 described this as a promising start, especially given that "attendance on law lectures is not at present made a necessary condition to examination by the Incorporated Law Society" and because "much prejudice on this subject has yet to be overcome."[186] At the opening of the winter session in October 1858, the Reverend J.G. Cumming observed that the value of the Law Department "was rightly understood ... in this town." Proof was provided by "the large numbers of students who, during the past year, in which the department was in its infancy, attended the able lectures of the Professor of English law."[187] The Law Department made satisfactory progress the following year,[188] and Johnson continued as professor for five more years before "his increasing practice compelled him to resign."[189] By that time, the college was facing serious financial difficulties.[190] The Law Department closed with Johnson's resignation and an attempt to revive it in 1867-69 was unsuccessful.[191]

Conclusion

Under Charles Rann Kennedy, the Law Department of Queen's College, Birmingham, was one of England's earliest efforts to provide professional legal education in an academic setting. It came at a time of tension between barristers' traditions – rooted in history, status, and gentlemanliness – and a growing demand for the certified practical knowledge that a new economy demanded. The attorney's profession, more than the bar, was able to speak in the language of the day, offering the concrete promise of precise, practical, useful workaday expertise of immediate instrumental value.

The practical needs of aspiring barristers and solicitors also differed from each other. Attorneys often came from distinctly lower social origins than barristers, and few had the luxury of searching out an education solely for the sake of personal betterment or greater refinement. In professional terms, articled clerks could benefit more from the sponsorship of a senior attorney than from proof of attendance at lectures.[192] Clients, for their part, were likely focused on obtaining cost-effective service and on the sort of "recipe-knowledge"[193] needed to get a job done. Barristers traded on their "respectability," but there were limits. They depended on the patronage of solicitors to steer business to them; this, in turn, rested on their individual record of success in the courtroom and in performing other professional functions. Deep legal learning was not essential to success at the bar.

Charles Rann Kennedy's program – premised on the idea that all aspiring legal practitioners ought to become both learned gentlemen of wide education and masters of the detailed, precise knowledge required for the practical work of their branch of the profession – failed precisely because it was inadequately anchored in the circumstances of the only possible student constituency and their needs for training, status, and credentialling. No professional organization or qualifying body required aspiring barristers or solicitors to be university-educated, much less to hold a degree in law. At the time, the status, autonomy, prestige, and income potential of professional groups was not tied as closely to university-based credentials as they were to become. Simply, the student constituency that Kennedy envisaged did not exist in the Birmingham of his day. True, the upwardly mobile would benefit from the certification of "gentlemanliness" that came with a degree, but the *law* degree added nothing. Anyone intent on pursuing class certification by acquiring a degree would have been better advised to pursue studies at Oxford, Cambridge, or even London rather than at an upstart college in a provincial industrial town. For the bulk of students seeking to enter legal practice in Birmingham, there was little to be gained from attending lectures on anything more ambitious than the contents of the solicitor's examinations.

It is tempting to view this as evidence that "the reform of legal education is hopeless,"[194] with the story of Queen's College providing a new footnote in support of Robert Stevens's assertion that legal education can never escape the deadening hand of lawyers.[195] George James Johnson's program corrected Kennedy's mistakes. He developed a modified form of guild training distinguished by close ties to a professional guild (the Birmingham Law Society), emphasizing practical training rather than broad education, teaching to professional qualifying examinations, and catering to the needs of a constituency of students destined for careers as attorneys. Whatever it lacked in educational breadth, it made up for in being useful for aspiring attorneys, and thus more marketable.

Notes

An earlier version of this chapter appeared as "Guild Training vs. Professional Education: The Committee on Legal Education and the Law Department of Queen's College, Birmingham in the 1850s" (1989) 33 Am. J. Legal Hist. 241. It has been revised and reprinted here with permission.

1 Charles Rann Kennedy, *An Inaugural Address, Delivered in the Theatre of the Queen's College, Birmingham* (Birmingham: John Tanks, 1850) at 9 [*An Inaugural Address*] (quoting Dr. Arnold).

2 See Christopher W. Brooks and Michael Lobban, "Apprenticeship or Academy? The Idea of a Law University, 1830-1860" in Jonathan A. Bush and Alain Wijffels, eds., *Learning the Law: Teaching and the Transmission of English Law, 1150-1900* (London: Hambledon Press, 1999) at 353-82; William Twining, *Blackstone's Tower: The English Law School* (London: Stevens and Sons, 1994); William Twining, "1836 and All That: Laws in the University of London, 1836 -1986" (1987) 40 Curr. Legal Probs. 26; J.H. Baker, *Legal Education in London 1250-1850: Selden Society Lecture Delivered at University College London, July 4th, 2005* (London: Selden Society, 2007).

3 Technically, "attorney" referred to members of the lower branch of the legal profession who worked on legal matters, while "solicitor" referred to members of the lower branch of the legal profession who worked on the equity side. Both denoted "solicitors" since the *Judicature Act,* 1873, s. 87; the more common generic term in the earlier part of the century was "attorney," a usage I follow here.

4 On the distinct traditions and social origins of the two branches, see Magali Sarfatti Larson, *Rise of Professionalism: A Sociological Analysis* (Berkeley/Los Angeles: University of California Press, 1977); Harry Kirk, *Portrait of a Profession: A History of the Solicitor's Profession, 1100 to the Present Day* (London: Oye, 1976); Raymond Cocks, *Foundations of the Modern Bar* (London: Sweet and Maxwell, 1983); Brian Abel-Smith and Robert Stevens, *Lawyers and the Courts: A Sociological Study of the English Legal System, 1750-1965* (London: Heinemann Educational Books, 1967); A.H. Manchester, *Modern Legal History* (London: Butterworths, 1980); Daniel Duman, *The English and Colonial Bars in the Nineteenth Century* (London: Croom Helm, 1983); W.J. Reader, *Professional Men: The Rise of the Professional Classes in Nineteenth-Century England* (London: Weidenfeld and Nicolson, 1966); and Robert Robson, *The Attorney in Eighteenth-Century England* (Cambridge: Cambridge University Press, 1959).

5 United Kingdom, *Report of the Select Committee on Legal Education* (25 August 1846) [*Select Committee on Legal Education*].

6 Evidence of E.S. Creasy, *ibid.* at 36.

7 Evidence of T. Starkie, *ibid.* at 6.

8 Charles Rann Kennedy, *Address to the Mutual Law Association* (Birmingham: John Tonks, 1852) at 4.

9 *Law Times* 1 (1843) 42, quoted in Cocks, *supra* note 4 at 70.

10 Evidence of Sir Fitzroy Kelly, QC, MP, Treasurer of Lincoln's Inn, Inns of Court Commission 1854 at 18, quoted in Reader, *supra* note 4 at 56. It should be noted that many nineteenth-century barristers did not in fact practise their profession. See Duman, *supra* note 4 at 4-9.

11 Evidence before the Inns of Court Commission, 524, quoted in Reader, *supra* note 4 at 56.

12 Larson, *supra* note 4 at 90. From at least 1762, the Bar consistently passed regulations aimed at ensuring its own continuing social homogeneity. See Duman, *supra* note 4 at 20-21.

13 See, for example, the evidence given by witnesses before England's criminal law commissioners in the *Eighth Report of Her Majesty's Commissioners on Criminal Law* (London: HMSO, 1845).

14 *E.g.,* W. Wesley Pue, "'The Criminal Twilight Zone': Pre-Trial Procedures in the 1840s" (1983) 21 Alta. L. Rev. 344 at 350-51.

15 *Ibid.* at 344.
16 Kennedy, *Address to the Mutual Law Association, supra* note 8.
17 Reader, *supra* note 4 at 25.
18 Larson, *supra* note 4 at 85.
19 Abel-Smith and Stevens, *supra* note 4 at 54.
20 J. Bulmer, "Upon the Present State of the Legal Profession in England" *Metropolitan and Provincial Law Association,* Circular No. VIII (1855) 25.
21 *Ibid.*
22 *Ibid.* at 26.
23 As well as turf wars between those professions and other groups seeking to provide similar services. See Reader, *supra* note 4 at 30 (attorneys versus scriveners); Abel-Smith and Stevens, *supra* note 4 at 58 (competition with solicitors by banks, patent agents, house agents, brokers, and accountants); Robson, *supra* note 4 at 25-30 (scriveners).
24 See the various discussions of this in Abel-Smith and Stevens, *ibid.*
25 See Charles Rann Kennedy, *Mr. Kennedy's Argument in the Common Pleas against the Rule Obtained by the Defendants in Kennedy v. Broun and Wife* (Birmingham: S.B. Howell, 1862) at 56-61 [*Mr. Kennedy's Argument*]. Compare the 1852 agitation by London barristers to work in a direct relationship with clients. On this point, see *Legal Observer* 43 (1847) at 1-2, 12, 29-30, 47-48, 61-62, 211-13, 311-12, 348-50; *Legal Observer* 44 (1848) at 114-16, 129-31, 149-50, 172, 209-11, 271-73, 309-10. See also the discussion of Kennedy's efforts with regard to a "Mutual Law Association" in Chapter 11 in this volume.
26 See Chapter 7 in this volume.
27 *Metropolitan and Provincial Law Association* Circulars (1852-73); Metropolitan and Provincial Law Association, *Report of the Committee of Management Made to the Annual General Meeting. 1848-1874.* The MPLA is discussed in Abel-Smith and Stevens, *supra* note 4 at 54, 58, 62, 72.
28 See Abel-Smith and Stevens, *ibid.;* Kirk, *supra* note 4; Reader, *supra* note 4; V.R. Parrott, *Pettyfogging to Respectability: A History of the Development of Solicitors in the Manchester Area, 1800-1914* (PhD Dissertation, University of Salford, 1992); D. Sugarman, "Bourgeois Collectivism, Professional Power and the Boundaries of the State: The Private and Public Life of the Law Society, 1825-1914" (1996) 3 International Journal of the Legal Profession 81.
29 Duman, *supra* note 4 at 19.
30 Evidence of Sir George Stephen, solicitor, *Select Committee on Legal Education, supra* note 5 at 144.
31 *Ibid.* at 145.
32 J. Bulmer, "Upon the Present State of the Legal Profession in England" *Metropolitan and Provincial Law Association,* Circular No. VIII (1855) 31 [emphasis in original].
33 *Ibid.* at 31-32.
34 W. Shaen, "On the Organization of the Profession, as It Ought to Be, and as It Is" *Metropolitan and Provincial Law Association,* Circular No. VIII (1855) 45-46.
35 *Ibid.* at 46.
36 *Ibid.*
37 *Ibid.* at 40.
38 *Ibid.* at 47.
39 See ch. 5, "Planting the Liberty Tree," in E.P. Thompson, *The Making of the English Working Class* (London: Penguin, 1968); W.D. Rubenstein, "The End of 'Old Corruption' in Britain, 1780-1860" (1983) 101 Past and Present 55. See Larson, *supra* note 4; Burton J. Bledstein, "The Culture of Professionalism: The Middle Class and the Development of Higher Education in America" (New York: W.W. Norton, 1978). See A.H. Manchester, *A Modern Legal History of England and Wales, 1750-1950* (London: Butterworths, 1980) at 10-20;

J.R. Dinwiddy, "Bentham and the Early Nineteenth Century" *Bentham Newsletter* (8 June 1984) 15-33.

40 The preface of Kennedy's *A Treatise on Annuities* (London: W. Berning, 1846) indicates that the work was inspired by the "Society for Promoting Useful Knowledge." A "Society for the Diffusion of Useful Knowledge" (founded by Lord Brougham and others) functioned in London from 1826 to 1848, although there were earlier American antecedents, including one founded by Benjamin Franklin and others in 1743. See Jonathan Lyons, *The Society for Useful Knowledge: How Benjamin Franklin and Friends Brought the Enlightenment to America* (London: Bloomsbury Press, 2013).

41 *Aris's Birmingham Gazette* (12 October 1857) 2. For a discussion of the wider context, see Lawrence Goldman, *Science, Reform, and Politics in Victorian Britain: The Social Science Association 1857-1886* (Cambridge: Cambridge University Press, 2007).

42 See Peter Stein, "Legal Theory and the Reform of Legal Education in Mid-Nineteenth Century England" in A. Giuliani and N. Picarda, eds., *L'Educazione Giuridica* (Perugia, 1979) at 185. The notion of utility was routinely invoked in discussions of professionalism, including, for example, Shaen, *supra* note 34.

43 "Legal Education" (NSG 1847) 37 Law Magazine or Quarterly Review of Jurisprudence 189, quoted in Stein, "Legal Theory," *supra* note 42 at 188.

44 *Ibid.* at 189.

45 Evidence of Robert Maugham, solicitor, *Select Committee on Legal Education, supra* note 5 at 160-61.

46 Evidence of Thomas Taylor, Honorary Secretary, Manchester Law Association, *ibid.* at 74.

47 On the perceived virtues of "practical men" at the Bar, see ch. 8, "The Virtues of Practical Men" in Cocks, *supra* note 4.

48 Larson, *supra* note 4 at 89.

49 Evidence of Lord Brougham and Vaux, *Select Committee on Legal Education, supra* note 5 at 274.

50 *Ibid.* at 277.

51 Larson, *supra* note 4 at 89-90.

52 Cocks, *supra* note 4 at 79.

53 *Ibid.* at 69-77.

54 *Ibid.* at 77.

55 *Ibid.*

56 *Select Committee on Legal Education, supra* note 5 at ii.

57 *Ibid.* at lvi.

58 *Ibid.* at xi.

59 Lord Campbell, quoted in *ibid.* at xi.

60 Lord Brougham and Vaux, quoted in *ibid.* at xii.

61 *Ibid.*

62 *Ibid.*

63 *Ibid.* at xiii.

64 *Ibid.* at xiv-xv.

65 *Ibid.* at xiv.

66 Sir George Stephen, quoted in *ibid.* at xxxv-xxxvi.

67 *Ibid.* at xxxvi.

68 *Ibid.* at xv.

69 *Ibid.* at xlvi.

70 *Ibid.* at xxxix.

71 *Ibid.*

72 *Ibid.* at xi. Legal writings changed in important ways from the eighteenth century onward. The modern legal treatise – primarily designed for undergraduate law students as well as

would-be practitioners and practitioners – was largely the product of the period c. 1850-1907: A.W.B. Simpson, "Rise and Fall of the Legal Treatise: Legal Principles and the Forms of Legal Literature" (1981) 48 U. Chicago L. Rev. 632; D. Sugarman, "Legal Theory, the Common Law Mind and the Making of the Textbook Tradition" in W. Twining, ed., *Legal Theory and Common Law* (Oxford: Basil Blackwell, 1986) 26.

73 *Select Committee on Legal Education, supra* note 5 at xlvii.
74 *Ibid.* at xxxvii.
75 *Ibid.* at xxxviii.
76 *Ibid.*
77 *Ibid.* at xxxix.
78 *Ibid.* at xlvii.
79 *Ibid.*
80 Cocks, *supra* note 4 at 177.
81 *Select Committee on Legal Education, supra* note 5 at xlvii-xlviii.
82 *Ibid.* at xlviii.
83 *Ibid.*
84 *Ibid.*
85 *Ibid.*
86 *Ibid.* at xlix.
87 *Ibid.*
88 *Ibid.*
89 *Ibid.*
90 *Ibid.* at l.
91 *Ibid.* at lii.
92 *Ibid.*
93 *Ibid.*
94 *Ibid.* at liii.
95 *Ibid.*
96 *Ibid.* at lii-liii: "If the acquirements which he [Sir George Stephen] demands as qualification appear to be somewhat higher than what might be expected from opportunities at present within the reach of the generality of young clerks, they assuredly are not higher ... than what are found to be indispensable in after life, for even a decent discharge of his professional duties."
97 *Ibid.* at liii.
98 *Ibid.*
99 *Ibid.*
100 *Ibid.*
101 See "The Ormrod Report" (1972-73) 12 Journal of the Society of Public Teachers of Law, New Series, 39; Manchester, *supra* note 4; Stein, *supra* note 42.
102 For a United States comparison, see Bledstein, *supra* note 39.
103 E. Edwards, *Personal Recollections of Birmingham and Birmingham Men* (Birmingham: Midland Educational Trading Company, 1877) at 134.
104 Conrad Gill, *History of Birmingham*, vol. 1 (London: Oxford University Press, 1952) at 37. For further discussions of Queen's College, see Robert K. Dent, *Old and New Birmingham* (Birmingham: Houghton and Hammond, 1880); Walter Showell, *Dictionary of Birmingham* (Oldbury: Walter Showell and Sons, 1885); J.T.J. Morrison, *William Sands Cox and the Birmingham Medical School* (Birmingham: Cornish Brothers, 1926); William Sands Cox, ed., *Annals of the Queen's College, Birmingham Reprint of Addresses*, 4 vols. (1873); John Thomas Law, *Materials for a Brief History of the Advance and Decline of the Queen's College, Birmingham* (Lichfield, 1869); Queen's College, *Official Report of the Charity Commissioners* (Birmingham, 1863).

105 Gill, *ibid.* at 37.
106 *Ibid.*
107 Untitled document regarding the Law Department of Queen's College, Birmingham, signed by George William Lyttleton, James Thomas Law, Horace F. Gray, and William Sands Cox [n.d.], 1-3; document lodged with the Birmingham Reference Library. This appeal is also recorded in *Aris's Birmingham Gazette* (25 February 1850).
108 Untitled document, *ibid.* at 3.
109 *Aris's Birmingham Gazette* (8 October 1849) 2.
110 See *Dictionary of National Biography, s.v.* "Charles Rann Kennedy."
111 John Pym Yeatman, *The Professorship of the Law Department of the Queen's College. Birmingham: A Letter to the Council and Governors* (Birmingham: M. Maher and Son, 1869) at 5.
112 Charles Rann Kennedy, *Poems: Original and Translated* (London: William Walker, 1857); Charles Rann Kennedy, *Ode on the Birth of the Prince* (London: Brettell, 1842); Charles Rann Kennedy, *Hannibal: A Poem*, pt. 1 (London: Simpkin, Marshall).
113 Charles Rann Kennedy, trans., *The Orations of Demosthenes on the Croll'n and on the Embassy* (New York: Harper and Brothers, 1859); Rann Kennedy and Charles Rann Kennedy, *The Works of Virgil: Translated* (London: Stevens and Company, 1849); Charles Rann Kennedy, trans., *The Olynthiac and Other Public Orations of Demosthenes* (London: H.G. Bohn, 1852); Charles Rann Kennedy, *Translation of Select Speeches of Demosthenes* (London: Deighton and Parker, 1841); Charles Rann Kennedy, trans., *The Orations of Demosthenes against Timocrates, Aritogiton, etc.* (London: H.G. Bohn, 1861); Charles Rann Kennedy, trans., *The Orations of Demosthenes against Leptines, Midias, Androtion and Aristocrates* (London: H.G. Bohn 1856); Charles Rann Kennedy, *Specimens of Greek and Latin Verse: Chiefly Translations* (London: H.G. Bohn, 1853).
114 Charles Rann Kennedy, *Classical Education Reformed* (London: Longman, Rees, Orme, Brown, Green and Longman, 1837).
115 See *Dictionary of National Biography, s.v.* "Charles Rann Kennedy."
116 "Testimonial to the Rev. Rann Kennedy, M.A." *Aris's Birmingham Gazette* (26 November 1849) 1.
117 "Mr. Kennedy's Testimonials for the Vacant Chair of Greek at the University of Edinburgh" in Papers Relating to Professorships, Etc., British Museum, Department of Printed Books, Shelfmark 8366, bb 33 (1851).
118 *Dictionary of National Biography, s.v.* "Charles Rann Kennedy."
119 Charles Rann Kennedy, *A Letter to the Lord Chancellor on the Subject of Revising Barristers* (London: Butterworth, ca. 1840) [*Revising Barristers*].
120 *Stockdale v. Hansard*, 9 Ad. & E. I (1839), discussed in Charles Rann Kennedy, *The Privileges of the House of Commons* (London: Stevens and Norton, 1840) [*Privileges of the House of Commons*]; Charles Rann Kennedy, *A Report of the Sheriff's Application to the Queen's Bench in the Case of Stockdale v. Hansard* (London: William Stevens, 1840) [*Report of the Sheriff's Application*].
121 Kennedy, *Treatise on Annuities, supra* note 40.
122 James Burchell and Charles Rann Kennedy, *The Joint Stock Companies Registration Act* (London: Henry Butterworth, 1844).
123 See Kennedy, *Privileges of the House of Commons, supra* note 120; Kennedy, *Report of the Sheriff's Application, supra* note 120.
124 Charles Rann Kennedy, *A Treatise on the New Rules of Pleading* (London: Henry Butterworth, 1841).
125 Kennedy, *Revising Barristers, supra* note 119.
126 Charles Rann Kennedy, *A Letter to the Lord Chancellor on the Subject of Circuit Leagues* (Birmingham: Josiah Allen and Son, 1850); Kennedy, *Address to the Mutual Law Association, supra* note 8; Charles Rann Kennedy, *Swinfen v. Swinfen. Report of the Argument in the*

Common Pleas, in Michaelmas Term, 1856 (London: Richard Hatton, 1856); Kennedy, *Mr. Kennedy's Argument, supra* note 25; Charles Rann Kennedy, *The Great Swinfen Case. Report of the Extraordinary Trial at Warwick in the Matter of Kennedy v. Broun and Wife* (London: Hatton and Son, 1862); Charles Rann Kennedy, "To the Legal Profession and the Public Bar Unionists" (1867), reproduced in Yeatman, *supra* note 111 at 23-26.

127 *Select Committee on Legal Education, supra* note 5 at lii.

128 *Aris's Birmingham Gazette* (8 April 1850; 10 November 1851); *Queen's College Calendar 1858,* City of Birmingham, Reference Library, Local Studies Department.

129 *Aris's Birmingham Gazette* (25 February 1850).

130 *Ibid.*

131 *Ibid.*

132 *Aris's Birmingham Gazette* (10 November 1850).

133 Kennedy, *An Inaugural Address, supra* note 1 at 9.

134 *Ibid.*

135 *Ibid.* at 9-10.

136 *Ibid.* at 10.

137 *Ibid.* at 11.

138 *Ibid.* at 12.

139 *Ibid.* at 10.

140 *Ibid.* at 12-13.

141 *Ibid.* at 13.

142 *Ibid.* at 14.

143 *Ibid.*

144 *Ibid.* at 15.

145 *Ibid.*

146 *Ibid.*

147 *Ibid.* at 13.

148 *Ibid.* at 15.

149 *Ibid.* at 17.

150 *Ibid.* at 19.

151 *Ibid.* at 18.

152 *Ibid.* at 17, 18.

153 *Ibid.* at 17.

154 *Ibid.* at 16.

155 *Ibid.* at 18.

156 *Aris's Birmingham Gazette* (8 April 1850) 3, col. 6.

157 *Ibid.* at 3, col. 2. An identical course description is to be found in *Aris's Birmingham Gazette* (10 November 1851) 3, col. 2.

158 *Ibid.*

159 *Select Committee on Legal Education, supra* note 5 at xiv. For contemporary sources that indicate the nature of examined expertise for attorneys, see *The Leguleian* (August 1850 – October 1851); *Examination of Articled Clerks* (December 1850 – Easter 1865); *Law Clerk's Magazine* (October 1842 – September 1843); *Law Student's Magazine* (August 1844 – December 1854); *Law Chronicle* (June 1854 – December 1858); *Law Chronicle and Law Student's Magazine* (January 1859 – December 1860); *Law Students' Examination Chronicle* (January 1861 – December 1868); *Law Examination Journal and Law Students' Magazine* (Michaelmas 1869 – Hilary 1885); *Law Examination Reporter* (Hilary 1866 – Trinity 1869). These and other journals are briefly discussed in Donald Daintree, *The Legal Periodical: A Study in the Communication of Information* (MA Thesis, University of Sheffield, 1975).

160 Kennedy, *An Inaugural Address, supra* note 1 at 16.

161 *Aris's Birmingham Gazette* (13 October 1851) 1 (reporting on Joseph Webster's report of the council).

162 See Kennedy, *Address to the Mutual Law Association, supra* note 8 at 9: "My inaugural address gave universal satisfaction. It was printed at public request. But it produced little fruits – nine pupils, at two guineas apiece, made the year's profits of the Professorship. I do not complain, it might have been foreseen that lectures would never answer, unless the attendance were compulsory. The want which they undertook to supply was not felt by the parties concerned."

163 This is briefly sketched out in Chapters 7 and 11.

164 Yeatman, *supra* note 111 at 8.

165 "Supplementary Charter of the Queen's College" *Birmingham Journal and Commercial Advertiser* (24 January 1852) 5. The undated document of Lyttleton *et al., supra* note 107 at 1, reports: "In order to promote the formation of the Law Department the supplemental charter of the date 1847 contains a clause 'that two members of the Law Society established in Birmingham' to be elected by the society previously to the annual general meeting of the Governors of the College shall be members of the Council." 6 and 7 Victoria, c. 73, s.7, mentioned in the *Birmingham Journal* item, re-enacted and extended the provisions of 2 and 2 Geo. IV, c. 48, s.1, which reduced the period of articles for university students from five to three years.

166 See *Aris's Birmingham Gazette* (23 March 1857) 2; (12 October 1857) 4.

167 *Ibid.* (26 January 1857) 2 reports Mr. Johnson's election to the committee of the Birmingham Law Student's Society.

168 As quoted in *ibid.* (5 October 1857) 1.

169 Johnson knew that his appointment "infringed the rule ordinarily observed." See reports of his inaugural lecture in *Supplement to the Birmingham Journal* (10 October 1857) 2; *Aris's Birmingham Gazette* (12 October 1857) 4.

170 See also "Law Department of Queen's College. Professor Johnson's Lectures" *Supplement to the Birmingham Journal* (10 October 1857) 2, where the Reverend J. Bates, Classical Tutor of the College, is quoted as referring "to the desire entertained by the Council of that institution to place the Law department on a more satisfactory footing, as indicated by the election of Professor Johnson, whose talents and well-known acquirements as a solicitor eminently qualified him for the discharge of the important duties appertaining to the office."

171 *Aris's Birmingham Gazette* (17 August 1857) 2, under the heading "Local. The Queen's College," reports: "The College will prepare students in a Department of Law for entering upon the study of the legal profession and the examinations of the legal bodies." *Aris's Birmingham Gazette* also makes clear that the program nested within larger aspirations for improvement of the middle classes: "The chief Continental States, wisely alive to the value of science in the development of national resources, justly boast of their numerous scientific Universities for the middle classes." The Bar at this time did not have an entrance examination: "The Proposed Law University, Legal Education of the Several Branches of the Profession" *Legal Observer* 52 (15 November 1856) at 473-74.

172 *Aris's Birmingham Gazette* (5 October 1857) 1 [emphasis added].

173 *Aris's Birmingham Gazette* (7 September 1857) 3; *Birmingham Journal* (9 September 1857) 3 (the two sources are identical).

174 *Queen's College Calendar 1858* at 131, 132, City of Birmingham, Reference Library, Local Studies Department.

175 *Ibid.*

176 *Ibid.* at 132-33 [emphasis added].

177 *Ibid.* at 133.
178 Reported in *Supplement to the Birmingham Journal* (10 October 1857) 2; *Aris's Birmingham Gazette* (12 October 1857) 4.
179 *Ibid.*
180 *Ibid.* [emphasis added]. Johnson, a future mayor of Birmingham (1893), had a serious interest in history. His publications include: George James Johnson, *The Natural History of Law* (Birmingham: Birmingham Speculative Club, 1870); George James Johnson, *On the Conflict in English History between Private Ownership of Land and the Ownership of the State and the Community; a Paper Read before the Birmingham Historical Society, May 9th, 1882* (Birmingham: Watson and Hall, 1882); George James Johnson, *Books on Law and Jurisprudence* (Birmingham: Free Libraries, 1885); George James Johnson, *Books on Legal and Constitutional History* (Birmingham: Free Libraries, 1885); William Wright Wilson, *The Life of George Dawson, M.A., Being an Account of His Parentage and His Career as a Preacher, Lecturer, Municipal and Social Reformer, Politician and Journalist ... With Two Chapters [and a prefatory note] Written by G. J. Johnson ... Second Edition* (Birmingham: Percival Jones, 1905).
181 Kennedy, *An Inaugural Address, supra* note 1 at 13.
182 *Supplement to the Birmingham Journal* (10 October 1857) 2.
183 *Ibid.* [emphasis added].
184 *Ibid.* Other evidence as to Johnson's general orientation is to be found in G.J. Johnson, "On the Relation between the Profession, Their Clients, and the Public" *Metropolitan and Provincial Law Association,* Circular No. XXII (Proceedings of the Annual Provincial Meeting, Birmingham, 7-9 October 1862) 19-28.
185 *Queen's College Annual Report* (26 August 1858) 8, City of Birmingham, Reference Library, Local Studies Department. The college's 1863 prospectus indicated a further shift in the way the Law Department was marketed, although again the emphasis remained on the needs of would-be lawyers: "The judges have ordered that every person before entering into articles of clerkship shall pass an examination in general knowledge, and that all persons articled after the 1st of January, 1861, shall be examined ... [approximately] ... after one-half of his term of service, in elementary works on the Laws of England and in Bookkeeping. The Council of Queen's College undertake to prepare students for the examinations now required before and during articles of clerkship." *Queen's College Prospectus 1863* at 115, City of Birmingham, Reference Library, Local Studies Department.
186 *Queen's College Annual Report, ibid.* at 7-8.
187 "The Queen's College" *Aris's Birmingham Gazette* (11 October 1858) 4.
188 *Ibid.* (3 October 1859) 4.
189 "Mr. Councillor George James Johnson" *Edgbastonia* (15 December 1882) 189 (with photograph). There is some uncertainty as Johnson continued to be described as Professor of Law in "Law Student's Society" *Aris's Birmingham Gazette* (23 January 1864) 7.
190 See *Aris's Birmingham Gazette* throughout 1859-62, especially 20 April 1861 at 7, which reports arrangements with creditors and discusses the medical and theological departments but not the Law Department or junior department; *Official Report to the Charity Commissioners, 1863* (on Queen's College). A good account of the financial crisis of the late 1850s and the 1860s is to be found in Morrison, *supra* note 104 at 114.
191 See Yeatman, *supra* note 111.
192 Testimony of Sir George Stephen, *Select Committee on Legal Education,* supra note 5 at 145.
193 "Recipe-knowledge is held by regular participants in legal processes who not only know the rules in abstract, but they also know the contexts of rule application so that the rules can be used to enable and justify particular actions in particular circumstances." R. Ericson and P. Baranek, *The Ordering of Justice* (Toronto: University of Toronto Press, 1982).

194 D. Sugarman, "Is the Reform of Legal Education Hopeless? or, Seeing the Hole instead of the Doughnut" (1985) 48 Mod. L. Rev. 728.

195 Robert Stevens, *Law School: Legal Education in America from the 1850s to the 1980s* (Chapel Hill: University of North Carolina Press, 1983).

5

Common Law Legal Education in the Dominion of Canada's Moral Project

Three storylines reappear persistently in accounts of the development of legal education. The first is a tale of progressive development. From tiny acorns, great oaks do grow: from small, infrequent, voluntary, and ad hoc lectures offered by busy practitioners grew patterns of experimentation, a trial-and-error approach that culminated in the post–Second World War adoption of mandatory, postgraduate (in effect), three-year Bachelor of Laws programs, now rebranded as "Juris Doctor" degrees.

The second presents a story of heroic struggles by great (academic) men to establish a scholarly university education in law as the necessary prerequisite for admission to the legal profession. In most accounts, heroic and learned individuals were opposed in their worthy endeavours by hostile and small-minded legal practitioners. Despite setbacks and humiliations, good prevailed. The great scholars prevailed to lay the foundations of present-day legal education.

A third storyline is largely of US origins. In this account, the move towards formalized university legal education forms but one component of a self-seeking project of lawyers to secure an extensive economic monopoly for themselves, reduce competition, exclude ethnic minorities, or otherwise advance their own economic and social status. Frequently referenced only to show its wrong-headedness, it is often invoked in order to lay the groundwork for one of the more orthodox accounts.

The three are not mutually exclusive. They can be mixed and matched in a variety of creative ways. Naturally, there is more subtlety and nuance in the historiography of Canadian legal education than this summary overview allows. No one piece of writing fits precisely within any category and, for the most part, historians of common law Canadian legal education are first-rate scholars whose thoughtfulness and scholarship are more sophisticated than a quick summary can capture. Nonetheless, these themes will be recognizable to any reader familiar with the field. Each contains elements of truth just as none captures its wholeness. My taxonomy represents caricature, not fabrication; ideal types, not the messiness of raw data.

The power of these frameworks is such that they can obscure many themes that might otherwise be developed. One shortcoming is a failure to sufficiently locate developments in legal education within their appropriate "cultural and regional milieux."[1] The failure to place legal education within a larger cultural history distorts in at least five directions:

- The false impression develops of historical processes moving in one direction only, that of "progress."
- Disagreements between some legal practitioners and some academics can take on exaggerated importance.
- The importance of the early twentieth century as a formative moment is easily missed as attention focuses elsewhere.
- The educational leadership of lawyers in Canada's western provinces (and Manitoba in particular) is overlooked.
- We are led to overemphasize legal education as training for lawyers' tasks at the expense of understanding its cultural import.

The March of Progress

The notion of "the university as merely an ivory tower, somehow levitating above the hard realities of Canadian society" enjoys little currency among historians. The notion that "the world" has always "directly and powerfully ... impinged upon university life" passes for common sense.[2] It has no power to startle and does not pass for fresh insight.

Surprisingly, however, "the world" remains a shadowy presence in histories of legal education. Much remains to be done in developing the "internal" history of legal education by identifying the constituencies and individuals who played key roles in particular developments. Even outstanding contributions to the literature necessarily focus mostly on "internal accounts": a world in which changes in legal education are accounted for by reference to the actions and ideas of judges, practitioners, law students, academic lawyers, Benchers, and bar associations.[3] Valuable though it is, "within-the-box" legal history has inherent limitations:

> The internal legal historian stays as much as possible within the box of distinctive-appearing legal things; his or her sources are legal, and so are the basic matters s/he wants to describe or explain, such as changes in

> pleading rules, in the jurisdiction of a court, the text assigned to beginning law students, or the doctrine of contributory negligence. The external historian writes about the interaction between the boxful of legal things and the wider society of which they are a part, in particular to explore the social context of law and its social effects, and s/he is usually looking for conclusions about those effects.[4]

"Inside-the-box" legal histories need to be written, if only because we need to know much more about the law box. Those inclined to observe from without would do well to be attentive to perspectives from within if they are to avoid going seriously off-track. Much is gained by locating accounts of common law legal education in the social, intellectual, cultural, and political histories of the diverse provinces and territories of Canada. "Internal" and "external" do not represent neatly bounded spaces. The "legal" and "social" are interpenetrating, mutually constituting, inseparable. It would mislead if we think of the history of legal education as occurring within a box into which "causes" flow and from which "effects" emerge.[5]

Amputating legal education from its cultural context forces us to succumb to the logic of chronology, and the logic of chronology can imply a dubious theory of historical causation. The idea of "progress" can quickly overtake any chronology not deliberately cast within other interpretive frameworks. The richness and fullness of the past can be lost.

Pedants, Practitioners, and Prophets

Histories of common law legal education frequently focus on past struggles between seemingly irreconcilable ideas of professional training held by legal practitioners on one side and academics on the other. Fierce debates, long periods of frustration, negotiation, manoeuvres, confrontations, and great tribulation suffered by academic lawyers precede the happy moment when the objections of narrow-minded practitioners are overcome. "Academic" legal education is established, the world is put right, and the stage is set for future progress. In many accounts, the tale is rendered only somewhat more complex by the interjection of an early "golden age" or "false dawn" that subsequently faded, slipping again into a narrow practitioner's training that succeeding generations of heroic academics in their turn struggled to transform.

The interpretive framework of a pioneering article on legal education in Ontario remains influential. "Pedants, Practitioners and Prophets: Legal Education at Osgoode Hall to 1957" reports on Ontario tensions between practitioners and the more academically inclined educators, developing this as its main interpretive framework. There is an undeniable truth to this storyline in much of Ontario's history. While "[s]poradic attempts were made to supplement practical training in law with formal and academic lectures from 1848 on,"[6] the authors show that the Law Society and the practising lawyers who composed it simply failed to appreciate the necessity of academic education (it is a given in the article that the practitioners were wrong and the academics right). Repeated failures to establish an Ontario law school during the nineteenth century are attributed to the antiquated beliefs of "the Law Society and its out-dated view of training in the practice of law"[7] ("progress" slips in here too). Their failings derived from many factors, most importantly "the fact that the profession, having itself been trained in legal practice, found it difficult to appreciate the claims that Law had to being an academic discipline."[8] Even when a law school was properly established in Toronto, its scholarly principal, William Albert Reeve, was repeatedly constrained by the Law Society of Upper Canada's Legal Education Committee. So too was his rather less imaginative successor, Principal Hoyles.[9] While some practising lawyers were clearly on the side of the gods,[10] the larger number, who were unable to transcend their "Victorian ideas on training in law,"[11] prevailed. Fortunately, they were eventually more or less beaten into submission by the fiery Dean "Caesar" Wright.[12]

Kyer and Bickenbach's more recent study of legal education in Ontario from 1923 through 1957 is developed more fully. It describes confrontation between "an uncompromising Law Society of Upper Canada" and a body of full-time legal educators who "stressed the 'learned' nature of the profession and the need for the educational process to be developed and controlled by professional educators."[13] Even the work of the Canadian Bar Association's unabashedly academic Committee on Legal Education is presented as a practitioners' body captured and "used"[14] by academic law teachers such as McGill's Dean Robert Warden Lee, Dalhousie's Dean Donald A. McRae, or Saskatchewan's Dean T.D. Brown.[15]

Similarly, John Willis's *History of Dalhousie Law School* emphasizes the contrast between "cultural" or academic legal education and mere technical training.[16] Dalhousie has a long and strong tradition of "cultural" education in law. Over the course of its history, Willis attributes developments such as Dean Weldon's early pursuit of a liberal legal education[17] or its replacement by a more narrowly professionally oriented curriculum in 1915[18] to the periodic ascendance of academic or practitioner influence, as the case may be. Jack London's account of legal education in Manitoba similarly has as its central theme an ongoing war between champions of "law as a science" and apologists for training in mere "technique and mechanics."[19] An important overview piece by John McLaren follows the established pattern.[20]

The academic/practitioner distinction provides a sort of quick shorthand referring to a bundle of diverse pedagogical assumptions, cultural orientations, and curricular structures. Some awareness of these polarities has persisted at least since the launch of legal education at Queen's College, Birmingham, in the mid-nineteenth century.[21] In historical practice, however, casual shorthand can misdirect. Its terminology insinuates a monocausal theory of historical change. It reduces the history of legal education to a story about the interplay between an unchanging practitioner preference for instruction in only the most mechanical of law office tasks and a countervailing academic desire to establish a genuinely cultural, interdisciplinary, or scholarly education. This can degenerate too quickly into assumptions that all developments emerge from a bad guys–versus–good guys scenario.

History is much more ambivalent, less saturated with heroes and villains than this. The academic/practitioner dichotomy fails to capture either the practical utility of an academic legal education or the academic relevance of practical knowledge. Philosophical positivism and an appreciation of the virtues of "practical knowledge" pervaded middle-class English Canadian culture during Victoria's reign and the early twentieth century to such an extent that the perception of a fundamental incompatibility between practical and academic as *the* defining feature of the period seems unlikely.[22] Over-reliance on the opposed ideal-types downplays the very substantial record of a spirited advocacy of "cultural" university legal education by practitioners. Lost too is any possibility that there may be a relationship between the forms of legal education and developing visions of either legal professionalism or the needs of the Dominion of Canada itself.

Western Canada's Formative Era?

The decades on either side of the First World War have been accorded less attention than they deserve. One result is that innovations in legal education that originated in the Prairie provinces and British Columbia have not been as widely noted as they deserve. Researchers focused on Ontario have often been most interested in the nineteenth century and the years following the Second World War. The early twentieth century, and with it western Canada, has received relatively less attention.

Three university-affiliated schools for professional legal education were launched during the second decade of the twentieth century, bringing the Canadian common law total from two (Dalhousie and the University of New Brunswick) to five. A burst of educational innovation in the new Prairie provinces resulted in the founding of university-affiliated law schools in Alberta, Saskatchewan, and Manitoba. In overlooking this period, we are likely to underestimate the enthusiasm shown for educational reform by the early Canadian Bar Association, its Committee on Legal Education, and similar committees of various provincial and local bar associations at the time. There were, in addition, significant changes taking place at both Dalhousie and Osgoode Hall. Each experienced important curricular reform and each reached new staffing levels during the 1910s and1920s. Beyond this, these decades saw scholarly activity, debate, and publication blossom and congeal in new ways. Even the New Brunswick Law School, which David Bell says was becoming "an increasingly remote backwater of Canadian legal education," shifted its affiliation from King's College to the University of New Brunswick and raised its admissions standards. It did so in response both to Canadian Bar Association urgings and to local concerns about "spectacular ethical lapses."[23] New law schools were established by the Law Society of British Columbia in both Victoria and Vancouver.[24]

Only a distorted and partial impression of the trajectory of legal education in Canada is possible if developments such as these are neglected. The result can be either an overemphasis on continuity and progressive development from nineteenth-century origins to the present, or the opposite, an exaggeration of post–Second World War discontinuity. The temptation arises to portray the tale of Canadian legal education as one of dozy inertia, unmarked by noteworthy innovation from the 1880s until Dean Wright's mythologized "shoot out at Osgoode Hall"[25] in 1949. Reclaiming the early twentieth century compels interpretations of a different character. These missing years reveal that common law education has been shaped by its own internal logic, including the parochial concerns of the legal profession. They also reveal varying degrees of responsiveness to the surrounding social, political, and intellectual environments. The decades that bookend the Great War laid new cultural foundations for modern common law legal education. The result melded new ideas imported from the United States with long-standing British middle-class traditions of practical knowledge, honour, and authority. Both were refracted through English Canada's peculiar cultural ethos as they were put into play. The character of the emerging west put its stamp on all of this. Industrialization combined with rapid population growth in the region to create a new Canadian territory characterized by relative social fluidity, astonishing ethnic and linguistic diversity, and a smorgasbord of utopian visions. An absence of established institutions made it an exciting, volatile place. Challenged by a world of social diversity that held no tradition sacrosanct, English elites were freed and forced to reconsider their own futures. The problem of determining which institutional arrangements best suited the peculiarities of this new, northern, British, and free people had to be squarely confronted.

Canada's Western Empire

Only a century ago, many of English Canada's aspirations focused on the prairie region. The National Policy had made Canadian territorial expansion into the west the key element of the new Dominion's developing state idea. "Canada's empire" represented the hope of an English Canadian nation. In Gerald Friesen's appraisal, during the "boom of the early twentieth-century, the confidence inspired by the western frontier and the social impulse of a new outlook in the Protestant churches was assimilated to the British-Canadian inheritance to create a powerful new regional image that transcended earlier definitions of the national mission: the promise of the west became the promise of Canada."[26] Importantly, this "promise of the west" was a cultural promise. It held forth hope for a new vision of social ordering, a new and unique prairie culture that would showcase the way of the future:

> [A] militant view of British civilization was a crucial aspect of the western Canadian image. But, if western Canadian leaders were proud of their British heritage, they were not complacent about British social achievements. They insisted that they lived on a frontier and had the freedom to improve upon the parent culture. What better way to create a perfect society than to build it on virgin land, to employ the finest raw material of a dozen lands, and to work to plans inherited from the world's greatest civilization? The frontier, in western Canada as in the United States, was a land of new beginnings. Where all citizens started as social equals, merit and value rather than class would be rewarded. Where farms and rural life, rather than factories and cities, were the foundations of the economy, true wealth would be created. Where life was lived close to nature, individuals learned the lessons of God at first hand. Calculations of prairie greatness and celebrations of imperial power inevitably ran together; the west would have a population of 100 million; it would be the bread-basket of the world; it would become the centre of gravity of all Canada; and, if it ruled Canada, and Canada led the empire (as it soon would), then, as anyone could see, the west would lead the world.[27]

The "militant" new view of British civilization required a new idea of the legal profession, and new ways of educating lawyers.

Saskatchewan and Alberta

Scholarship on the history of legal education in Saskatchewan and Alberta reveals that the idea of formal instruction in law had been in the air from the earliest years of provincial status.

From its creation in 1909, the University of Saskatchewan's president, Walter C. Murray, planned to establish a law faculty. Two of the initial five teaching staff, Arthur Moxon (a classicist and lawyer) and Ira MacKay (a lawyer and political scientist), were fully qualified to provide double service as instructors in arts and law. It was not long before their legal talents were put to use. In 1913, two law schools were established in the province. The law society established Wetmore Hall in Regina as a professional law school, and the University of Saskatchewan in Saskatoon opened a College of Law. Although the programs were similar, nothing like an integrated system of legal education was initially established. Graduates of the College of Law initially earned an LL.B. degree without gaining exemption from professional examinations, while students at Wetmore Hall became fully qualified lawyers without any credit towards a law degree. A limited reciprocity arrangement was entered into in 1919, foreshadowing closure of Wetmore Hall in 1922. Legal education thereafter was centralized in Saskatoon.[28] The earliest deans established a tradition of scholarship, and the College of Law came under Harvard influences in both pedagogy and in its ways of thinking about law.[29]

Similarly, the University of Alberta expressed early interest in establishing a faculty of law. In 1909, his first full year as president of the university, Dr. Henry Marshall Tory laid plans for future development before the University Senate, "including provision for applied science and education in the Faculty of Arts and Science, and the establishment of new Faculties of Agriculture, Medicine, and Law." A Senate committee was mandated "to consult with the Supreme Court Justices and the Law Society about holding joint examinations in Law."[30] A committee of the Law Society of Alberta soon produced a blueprint for university legal education, and in 1912 the University of Alberta approved the creation of a Department of Law within its Faculty of Arts and Sciences.[31] Under the initial arrangement, Edmonton lawyers provided lectures and examinations were administered by the university under close supervision by the Law Society. Not to be outdone, Calgary lawyers made their own arrangements for a lecture series in collaboration with the Law Society and Calgary College.[32] In 1914, under financial pressure, the Law Society accepted Dr. Tory's invitation to cede its responsibility for the arrangement of lectures in both cities to the University of Alberta.[33] Calgary College closed in 1915 and structured legal education became centralized at the university.[34]

Although the university now arranged lectures for all Alberta law students, there were effectively two programs in place. The LL.B. program remained distinct from a somewhat narrower range of offerings directed only towards professional qualification.[35] Degree students were required to complete additional lecture courses on subjects perceived to be of limited practical relevance.

Moreover, many law students continued to earn professional qualifications without attending lectures and without earning the LL.B. degree.[36] The university program adopted a case method of teaching from the start, declaring its intention to follow the state-of-the-art method of instruction championed in the United States by Harvard's Law School.[37]

Alberta's early enthusiasm for radical innovation in legal education is apparent too in its eager adoption of a 1919 recommendation by the Canadian Bar Association's Committee on Legal Education that full-time legal education should replace part-time programs. In 1921 the Law Society of Alberta reached agreement in principle with the university by which "prospective students of the Society would undertake three years of full-time studies leading to the LL.B. and a year of articling, and then write the Society's examination on provincial statutes."[38] The society continued to advise the faculty, and the full-time LL.B. quickly became the normal route to qualification.[39] Sibenik has concluded that the Faculty of Law was cast entirely in Harvard's image by the mid-1920s: a full-time three-year program, entrance standards set at two years of college work, stiff examinations, and instruction by means of "large, well organized casebooks containing leading English and American decisions."[40] All of this was complemented by a "Socratic" classroom experience: "Students were given assignments and cases were discussed in class, under the direction of the instructor, with a view to determining their reasoning and correctness. The instructors sought to instill in the students' minds a capacity for independent thinking which is absolutely lacking under the text book system."[41]

By the end of the 1920s, Sibenik concludes, "modern" legal education had arrived in Alberta: the university, "the syllabus, the case method, law as science and precedent, and three years of urban life in Edmonton."[42]

Manitoba

Ideas about university legal education had also been in the air from Manitoba's earliest years. The eventual establishment of a law school in 1914 was the product of work by law students, elite lawyers, university officials, and royal commissioners during the first years of the twentieth century. Their ideas jelled and gained currency with surprising speed during the century's second decade.

Developments in Manitoba have been well documented.[43] The years from the founding of the Manitoba Law School in 1914 to 1931 were bold, exciting, and formative. And a massive failure. While the University of Manitoba had formally established an LL.B. degree as a reading course in 1885,[44] aspiring lawyers rarely took the degree before its 1914 merger with the professional courses of the Manitoba Law Society.[45]

It was the legal profession, not the academy, which led the movement to establish university legal education in Manitoba. During the late nineteenth and early twentieth centuries, apprenticing lawyers frequently petitioned the Law Society to establish a course of lectures for their benefit.[46] Without instruction, they struggled on their own to acquire the knowledge their profession demanded. Lectures were delivered in 1877 by Chief Justice Wood,[47] and a tradition of some form of more or less unstructured expository teaching developed in the following years. Law Society lectures lapsed in 1905 (and probably at other times) but were revived by James Aikins and Isaac Pitblado acting together as a committee of the Law Society.[48] By the end of the first decade of the twentieth century, a more or less regular pattern of lectures had been established.[49] The Law Society pressed to formalize legal education in the province,[50] while the university's more or less irrelevant LL.B. program continued independently as a reading course, unaffected by these professional initiatives.

A call for the creation of a university school of law was put forward in 1909 by two members of the Royal Commission on Manitoba University Education. The omnipresent James Aikins and the Reverend A.A. Chevrier suggested that "a law school [should] be established in connection with the University of Manitoba."[51] Building on the precedent of existing arrangements for university training in other professions, such as medicine, engineering, and theology, they called for the creation of a university-affiliated college of law:

> We believe it would not be difficult for the University to make an arrangement with the Law Society whereby a regular course of instruction would be given to those studying, the University establishing Chairs in some subjects such as Constitutional, Municipal, Commercial and Criminal Law, and the Law Society providing Lectures in the other subjects. If the University has the funds available to do so, we recommend such a course ...
>
> If the University has not the funds to do so after providing for the teaching of those subjects which we have previously recommended as University subjects, then we recommend that State aid be granted so as to place the Students of these Professions on a somewhat equal footing in respect of a regular course of instruction in their intended vocations, and that when regular teaching in Law is undertaken by the Law Society with the aid of the State or of the University, then the Law Society should be affiliated with the University in respect of such teaching or of the School or College it may establish for such purpose.[52]

Although he chaired the Royal Commission, Aikins failed to carry the other commissioners. In the end, the commission's widely divergent reports were largely ignored by the Roblin government. Nonetheless, their views marked an important point in the developing "common sense" about legal education. Pitblado was emboldened a few months later to prod his fellow Benchers on the matter of creating a Manitoba Law School.[53]

Pressed by student demands,[54] the Benchers acknowledged the value of systematic legal instruction in 1910, agreeing "to allow up to a year's leave of absence to a student wishing to study law at a law school in Canada, the United States of America, or England."[55] Between 1910 and 1914, aspiring lawyers voted with their feet, as at least a dozen Manitobans took advantage of such opportunities.[56] In 1910, a Winnipeg newspaper reported that law students, perhaps egged on by elite practitioners, had expressed a need for a "less indirect, more controlled education" and were giving serious consideration to petitioning the university to hold their examinations under its auspices.[57] Students repeated the demand for a course of lectures in 1911. They asked that a law school be created, and threatened a student exodus to Saskatchewan if nothing was done.[58] The Manitoba Bar Association joined in the call for university legal education at its inaugural banquet in November 1911.[59] The hand of J.A.M. Aikins, founder of both the Winnipeg Bar Association and its successor, the Manitoba Bar Association, was most certainly at work here.

Inertia held, however. It was only when the Benchers were put in fear of the development of a commercial provider of legal instruction that they moved decisively to occupy the field. When education-for-profit appeared as a real possibility, they responded with surprising speed. In March 1912, the Manitoba Legislature considered a *University Extension Bill* that would have conferred powers upon a private business to give degrees by correspondence or instruction in the fields of law and business. Although (perhaps, because) private "crammers" of one sort or another had long been in existence in England and the United States, the prospect was not well received by Manitoba lawyers.[60] Objections were raised in the legislature by George R. Coldwell, who objected that any such development would infringe on the provisions of the *Law Society Act*. He expressed the fear that it would "cause many to shirk the more thorough training in law demanded under the terms of the *Law Society Act*," objected to the granting of degrees by a correspondence school,[61] and raised the spectre of a private law school throwing "the province open to professional men without training."[62]

This all seems unduly alarmist when it is recalled that the Law Society failed entirely to provide anything even remotely approaching a program of systematic legal education. Why the idea seemed so disturbing is somewhat opaque. Direct evidence is both sparse and ambiguous. It seems unlikely that any private system of education could have possibly been less thorough or rigorous than the Law Society's disorganized lectures. These, it will be recalled, were sporadically offered, irregularly attended, and complemented only with a dose of unregulated law office employment and undemanding examinations. The introduction of a proprietary law school in Manitoba would, to a degree, have diminished the Law Society's role as the sole authoritative voice in such matters and detracted from its cultural authority. If US experience is any guide, a privately operated law school would also almost certainly have opened the door to legal careers for much larger numbers of young men (and women?) of working class or minority ethnic background.[63] This prospect would not have been viewed with equanimity by Manitoba's Anglo elite, embedded as they were in a culture that was fiercely pro-British and hierarchical, nativist, even xenophobic.[64]

It may be too that elite lawyers shared a transboundary vision of professional culture. Relying on University of Michigan Law Dean Henry M. Bates's report for the US Bureau of Education,[65] Julius Cohen complained in 1916:

> [T]here are still proprietary schools run for profit, which do not take into account the larger interests of the State, the profession, and the requirements of justice and which grant diplomas on low standards of admission and of work. Unless this tendency is checked, much of the good that the better university schools are attempting to accomplish, at the expense of loss in students and money to themselves, will be offset by the schools run mainly for revenue only.[66]

Over twenty years after the defeat of the *University Extension Bill*, E.H. Coleman (then dean of the Manitoba Law School) observed that US commercial law schools admitted students ill equipped "by education, character or temperament" for legal practice, producing graduates with "little conception of ethical standards and who enter on practice without any idea that the profession has any other end or duty than the making of money by the practitioner."[67] Relieved that Manitoba had been spared these evils, Coleman expressed his satisfaction with Manitoba's "advantage" of "having the control of legal education lodged in our official society." He observed:

> Had the Law School not been established, I think I may say quite safely that you would have in Winnipeg a commercial law school, probably a branch of one of the institutions in Chicago or Minneapolis, the only aim of which would be the profit of the owner with the result that there would be pumped out each year an army of graduates, whose chief qualifications, so far as the Law School would be concerned, would be the payment of fees.[68]

With the defeat of the 1912 initiative,[69] Manitoba was spared from free enterprise in legal education. A university-affiliated law school was quickly created to occupy the field.

Other developments continued apace. From 1911 to 1913, the Law Society organized lectures for students[70] and H.A. Robson continued his personal quest for the creation of a provincial law school. He prodded apprenticing lawyers to "keep hammering at the question,"[71] and kept hammering at it himself. Even so, as late as September1913, a Manitoba law school seemed a distant prospect. Correspondence between Robson and James Alexander MacLean, the University of Manitoba's new president, indicates that despite their shared enthusiasm, the "Law School idea" was only "developing slowly."[72]

The cause gathered further momentum following the opening of Saskatchewan's two law schools in October 1913. Robson was authorized by the Benchers to "lay plans for the establishment ... of a permanent law school modelled after Osgoode Hall," a project in which he was assisted by a recent Osgoode Hall graduate, E.K. Williams.[73] Taking some liberty in interpreting the Osgoode Hall model, he persuaded the Law Society to move toward creation of a law school in collaboration with the university. Isaac Pitblado asserted confidently that "the Law society was determined to establish a law school, and that it would be a great mistake if the university did not take it under its wing."[74] Things had turned around fast. An innovative arrangement for a professional law school emerged. It was to be run as a sort of joint enterprise governed by a board of trustees appointed equally by the university and the Law Society.[75] In June 1914, the University of Manitoba approved the plan.[76] The first board of trustees took office with Robson as chair.[77] Academic matters were to be subject to Law Society review.[78] The Benchers also exercised considerable informal and formal control through their appointees to the board of trustees, their ability to make rules for admission to practise in the province,[79] and, no doubt, general habits of deference to them.

On this basis, formal legal education commenced. The first classes were taught in Winnipeg's YMCA building on 5 October 1914. It was not a particularly auspicious start: part-time, no dean, no declared pedagogy or intellectual agenda, no teaching staff other than a "recorder," R.P. Hills, "assisted by seven practising lawyers as part-time lecturers."[80] The school offered two distinct three-year programs, taken concurrently by most students. Different courses and examinations were required for each of admission as an attorney, call to the bar, and for award of the LL.B. degree. It remained possible to qualify for practice by service of articles and examination alone.[81] Even law school students were required to provide law office service concurrently throughout the three-year program. Nonetheless, "[t]he seeds of didactic legal education as a basic component of training had," according to London, "been firmly sown."[82]

Despite its modest resources and humble beginning, the board of trustees sought to be at the forefront of North American legal education. Their vision incorporated all that was thought to be state-of-the-art among elite US lawyers at the time: wholesale embrace of the case method,[83] a desire to make attendance at law school the necessary and sufficient method of qualification for the legal profession,[84] an ambition to create a full-time staff of professional law teachers,[85] and a pedagogical vision that encompassed both "cultural" legal education and "practical" training.[86] There were also early indications of a desire to raise admission standards,[87] perhaps to the point of requiring that only degree holders be permitted to begin legal education.

These ideas were highly innovative in their time and place, and outright radical by Ontario standards. No doubt, many Manitoba lawyers were less enthusiastic for these changes than the leaders of innovation. Nonetheless, the model that emerged incorporated each of these elements. The first dean took office in May 1921. J.T. Thorson, a graduate of Manitoba College, Rhodes Scholar, and Manitoba lawyer, presided over a brief golden age. Following recommendations of the Canadian Bar Association's Committee on Legal Education,[88] the system of concurrent articles was all but abolished in 1921, supplanted by an arrangement under which "students were required to serve only one year in law offices; simultaneously with the Law School programme in the case of university graduates, and after completion of the programme in the case of nongraduates."[89] Conceived as a full-time educational program, teaching hours for the first time extended "throughout the business day," from Monday to Friday.[90] Manitoba's law school became the first in Canada to adopt the new model curriculum proposed by the Canadian Bar Association.[91] Two further full-time law professors were hired, bringing the school's staff to the same level as Dalhousie Law School's at the beginning of its own golden age[92] and surpassing Osgoode Hall's solitary full-time instructor.[93] The law school raised its minimum admission standards to completion of second-year arts or equivalent.[94]

The newly structured school quickly established a reputation for excellence. It was hailed as a worthy model by the chair of the Canadian Bar Association's Committee on Legal Education in 1923,[95] and was rated Canada's best law school by the Carnegie Foundation in both 1926 and 1927.[96]

These developments were a natural outcome of the forces at play in Manitoba since some time before the school's inception. The Canadian Bar Association and its Committee on Legal Education were themselves very largely

Manitoba creations. It is much nearer to the truth to think of the educational initiatives of the Canadian Bar Association as embodying the thinking of elite Manitoba lawyers rather than as an outside force prodding sleepy prairie lawyers to wakefulness. Canada's great academic project of legal education was initiated in the offices of elite Winnipeg lawyers.

This remarkable experiment in legal education was, however, entirely expunged in short order. Though the reasons remain opaque, the sequence of events is clear. Between 1927 and 1931, the Manitoba Law School purged itself of all traces of full-time legal education, delivering a serious blow to the academic study of law from which the institution long struggled to recover. Nonetheless, its brief moment at centre stage left its imprint on Canada at large. Manitoba's common sense was translated to the national stage, and the culture that produced the Manitoba experiment continued to speak to a larger Canadian constituency, even as it faded in the province. The post–Second World War model of legal education that took hold across common law Canada was on all fours with Manitoba's initiative of the 1920s.

Canadian Bar Association as a Prairie Cultural Expression

The early Canadian Bar Association was pre-eminently an embodiment of prairie thought, political vision, and legal culture. Founded in the west, directed by Manitobans, it was an important vehicle through which elite prairie lawyers sought to develop and articulate their visions of professionalism. Sir James Aikins of Winnipeg founded the association, serving as president from 1914 to 1927.[97] Manitoba's H.A. Robson headed its first committee on legal education, laying the foundation on which the association's "Lee committee" built its crucial 1918 report.[98] A distinct but related CBA committee on legal ethics was chaired by Manitoba's Chief Justice Mathers.[99] Manitoba Law Society president Isaac Pitblado, who served as chair of the University of Manitoba's first board of governors[100] and had earlier been involved in the establishment of the Manitoba Law School,[101] enthusiastically endorsed the Lee committee's 1918 report.[102] Robson was subsequently appointed to a CBA subcommittee on curriculum,[103] joining McGill's Dean R.W. Lee, Dalhousie's Dean D.A. MacRae, Wetmore Hall's Dean T.D. Brown, and W.E Kerr of the Law Society of Upper Canada.

The recommendation for a standard curriculum modelled on the Dalhousie program was adopted by the Canadian Bar Association in 1920.[104] Although Kyer and Bickenbach assess this as only "a minor victory for the university-minded members of the committee,"[105] it was much more. The CBA reports established the terrain over which all subsequent battles about common law legal education in Canada have been fought. Their proposal to combine

H.A. Robson. *Archives of Manitoba, Personalities Collection, Robson H.A. #1*

knowledge of legal doctrine with some exposure to what we now think of as the sociology and history of law remained a powerful aspirational statement, which echoes in curriculum discussions at Canadian law schools to this day. Beyond curriculum, there is little in current structures of legal education that was not contemplated, developed, and advocated during these years of Canadian Bar Association activity.

Regenerating Law

It is unhelpful to attempt to force the story of educational developments during this period into any of the three conventional storylines. Although some prominent Ontario lawyers opposed these developments, it makes little sense to speak of a practitioner/academic divide as the defining fault-line. The individuals directly involved were aware of no such polarity.[106] On the contrary, the most vigorous proponents of what might be called a cultural agenda in legal education were prominent, energetic, busy, and successful practising lawyers. All were born into the Anglo elite or thoroughly integrated into it. All were active in matters of law society governance or in the activities of bar associations. Most played on both stages. Their cultural assumptions tell us a great deal about the history of common law legal education. Theirs was an elite British and Protestant world. While some of their core ideas may have been most frequently and elegantly expressed by law teachers, lofty ideals were not the domain of academics alone.

Early-twentieth-century commentators did bear a dichotomy in mind as they contemplated legal education. They appreciated the divergence but not divorce between a purely practice-oriented training and a more rounded legal education. Words can mislead: although they disparaged training limited to the mechanics of legal practice, they appreciated the importance of "practical" training. Their objective was to forge a body of learned practitioners working to serve the larger society, knowledgeable in law, and sensitive to community needs. Theirs was a holistic vision that could not be parsed. All of legal education, even the "cultural" parts, was to inform the day-to-day work of the future practitioner, and all practical work was to advance a cultural agenda: lawyers carried a "great commission" of sorts. Their legal mission is sketched in the writings of the three early-twentieth-century lawyers.

Ira MacKay

Ira MacKay's comments to a general meeting of the Law Society of Alberta in 1913 are illustrative:

> So long as students are allowed to gather their legal knowledge scrap by scrap in the hundred different offices in which they serve their time, no consensus of legal opinion and honor is possible. The clerks in the offices spend most of their time doing clerical work which they will not do for themselves but which they will require their own clerks to do for them when they themselves begin to practise. The result is a profession of apprentices without principals. These clerks receive absolutely no instruction and scarcely any assistance in their work. If once and again they are delegated to gather law on some matter in litigation they only succeed in gathering information which is wholly one-sided and misleading for purposes of impartial and effective legal advice. The only studying they do is during tired afterhours by reading legal text books or hand books, most of which are so condensed and the number of authorities so great and so confusing that thorough study is wholly out of the question. This system may possibly produce collectors, conveyancers, money lenders and real estate dealers but it cannot produce lawyers. Clearly this system is only designed to degrade the profession into the position of a mere stepping stone for purely mercenary ends.[107]

MacKay was partly concerned with finding an efficient way of teaching positive law. His principal concern was greater, however. Legal education was to help to develop a "consensus of legal opinion and honor," including preparing aspiring lawyers to give "impartial and effective legal advice" *not distorted by the desires of their clients*. Insofar as possible, legal education aspired to create lawyers of honour and integrity, dedicated to the public good and disinterested enough in their own "mercenary end" to pursue it. The lawyer was no mere sum of the mechanical tasks performed as legal work (e.g., debt collection, conveyancing, etc.).

MacKay saw the rapid development of university legal education as a precondition of science, progress, reform, community integration, social peace, order, good government, and human welfare. His 1913 speech reflected the approach – and perhaps the mentality – of a modern-day televangelist: a litany of great changes (in transportation, economics, and social organization) is put forward to disrupt the complacency of the audience (the word "reform" appears four times in the second paragraph, the words "advance" or "progress" five times). There follows an alarming observation that "English Law" had become "the least learned of all the noble professions,"[108] and, finally, the combination of social change and legal unpreparedness is presented as a formula for catastrophe. MacKay thought of law as foundational: "the most far-reaching, fundamental and vital of all branches of knowledge." Law had become fragmented and unintelligible, however. The very success of the Empire had led to a situation in which common law threatened to implode. Courts in "nearly one hundred distinct and separate jurisdictions" were, in theory, "making law for all the others."[109] The problem was especially severe in western Canada, where lawyers had fallen "into the habit of consulting ... not only our own local authorities but also the authorities of the other Canadian provinces, of Ireland, of England and even of the more than 40 separate states in the American Union."[110] An explosive increase in the production of "law" threatened lawlessness.

The difficulties posed by so daunting a search for authority were amplified by social conditions in Prairie Canada. MacKay adopted the surprisingly radical "realist" position that "[t]he law is what the consensus of legal opinion in the community believes it to be, first the judges, next the lawyers, and finally the mass of intelligent laymen who direct the organized activities of the state."[111] Without professional consensus, both case law and statute were mere chimera ("statute law is as much a creation of the judiciary and the lawyers as case law"[112]). Disturbingly, prevailing conditions impeded the development of any such consensus of professional opinion. Overwhelmed by myriad authorities, geographically dispersed across a vast region, western Canadian practitioners lacked the opportunity English lawyers enjoyed of forming professional consensus through regular meetings "in chambers, in court, in the inns of court, in the clubs and on the circuit."[113] The problem was compounded by the social and legal pluralism that characterized the western legal professions:

> [T]his task of maintaining a consensus of legal opinion is made doubly difficult in Western Canada by the fact that we have lawyers practising from every part of the English speaking world. English lawyers, Irish lawyers, Scottish lawyers, lawyers from Quebec, lawyers from Ontario, lawyers from the Maritime Provinces, lawyers from the United States. I even know one lawyer from New Zealand and another from Natal.[114]

MacKay saw risk in this state of affairs. If centrifugal social forces could not be corralled, anarchy threatened. The disintegration of the state and failure of western Canada's promise was possible. Fortunately, the road to salvation was clear: "Create this consensus of legal opinion and you create the state; allow it to perish and peace, good order, and good government must perish with it."[115] Conditions in the prairies amplified more general concerns, yet also permitted unconstrained utopian visions because "in the new western land ... we are laying the foundations of a system of law and government upon which the peace, happiness and welfare of all those who come after us will largely depend."[116] The effective pursuit of collective ends rested, in MacKay's view, on the micro-politics of lawyers' work. Community social progress and the state itself emerged from the aggregation of many mundane tasks:

> The lawyer's office is unquestionably the most important office in the community, and that for the obvious reason that the lawyer is really the only man in the community who really makes it his business to understand the delicate and complex organization of government and law by which the community directs its activities for common ends. I have already mentioned some of the advances which have been made in recent years in practical economics and government. Even the lay mind can see at a glance that these advances are almost wholly creations of the legal profession. All the projects, hopes, fears and plans of financiers, captains of industry and statesmen are only so much raw material until legal machinery is devised and set up by which they may be turned to account for human uses. All our institutions depend implicitly upon their solicitors to guide them in every new venture, and upon counsel to deliver them from any dangers which they may encounter. In the last analysis every simple contract made between private individuals is wholly a matter of law. The state itself is an edifice constructed solely out of legal material. It is literally made of law.[117]

Reduced to its barest essentials, MacKay's thinking ran along these lines: the British people have created the highest civilization known to humankind. Science, technology, and British government have advanced human welfare. All such achievements rest on law. Law, however, turns out to rest entirely upon professional consensus. Hence, in the absence of professional consensus, there will be anarchy. The state will crumble, progress will be reversed, community goals will be incapable of attainment, humans will suffer. The attainment of professional consensus is daily more difficult, especially in the conditions of western Canada. Hence, the preservation of British Canadian civilization requires the development of some mechanism by which professional consensus can be formed, anarchy avoided, and the path of progress followed.

Fortunately, in MacKay's view, such a mechanism was available. One of the great innovations of the age was at hand: formal university education in practical subjects. In the local environment, only the creation of proper university law schools could ensure a "uniform standard of legal opinion," a "professional consensus of opinion and a professional élite de corps." Unnecessary litigation would be avoided, professional honour advanced, and social integration ensured.[118] Crudely, the options were law school or chaos. It is easy to dismiss MacKay's apocalyptic forebodings and aspirations. The temptation is strong to ignore the utopian vision, moral reform aspirations, and rhetoric as embarrassing or as mere padding, meaningless colour, empty phrases, and overly dramatic flourish. If we carefully excise such elements from our reading of his speech, it can be turned into a simple and straightforward appeal to replace "irrational" apprenticing mechanisms with systematic instruction through university-based education. But that is not what he said. Skipping over the bits we find strange in order to find the element we expect does damage to the integrity of MacKay's thought. The urge to reform was central to social thought in middle-class English Canada at the time, and that ethos motivated educational reform. MacKay's thoughts about his profession and its education would have had reasonably wide currency among thoughtful lawyers of his time. It amounted to a sort of common sense shared by much of the profession's elite.

James A.M. Aikins

Sir James Aikins was an imaginative, influential, and energetic reformer of things legal. He was, perhaps, the prime mover in reforming the early-twentieth-century Canadian legal professions. Founder, in rapid succession, of the Winnipeg Bar Association, the Manitoba Bar Association, and the

Canadian Bar Association, he aspired to create conditions under which lawyers would play a pivotal role in the preservation of British virtues. Like MacKay, he knew that Canadian society was enveloped in enormous social, economic, and political transformations and felt that these threatened the vitality of British civilization. In the face of crisis, law provided a panacea. Legal education would shore up law, British legality, and civilization itself.

In his presidential address to the Canadian Bar Association's first annual meeting in 1915, Aikins spoke to "The Advancement of the Science of Jurisprudence in Canada." He laid heavy emphasis on the key role of lawyers in popular governance. Lawyers, he said, were

> not only with the people, but of the people, working among men, advising in their personal affairs, sympathising in their efforts, guiding in their business, aiding in their social movements for reform, taking share in all the departments of public government, yet, withal, maintaining the professional ideals of the past, their intellectual attainments, dignity, strength of honour and independence of character, which will not cringe before courts or be carried away by popular emotions or a hostile press.[119]

Aikins shared Canadian imperialists' puffed-up vision of future Canadian greatness[120] and MacKay's concern that only committed public leadership by the legal profession could prevent disruption under centrifugal forces. Canada's diversity was at once a source of strength and of great weakness:

> However excellent the *British North America Act* as constitution of our country, however wise its distribution of legislative powers, it cannot create or assure a real united Canada unless the spirit of union and co-operation is pervasive among the people. Our provinces are far-flung, and feelings of mistrust, lack of sympathy or cordiality, asperities which may have happened between the respective bodies of citizens in the different provinces arises very largely from the fact that the separated communities do not know or understand each other or their aims and ideals or the various steps which may have been taken toward the development of those ideals and the accomplishment of those aims. Yet every true Canadian in his heart purposes a strong, united Canada, founded upon that spirit of freedom, justice and honour inherited from our great ancestors.
>
> True it is that, owing to our historic beginnings, there will be diversity in our population, but that will not prevent oneness. That very diversity in our unity may make for our safety and ennoblement. Different grafts on the

> one national stem, nourished by the same soil, refreshened by the same showers, gladdened by the same sunshine, bringing forth blossoms of various hues, the people of Canada should produce the one rich fruit – one true and virile Canadianism. In this our profession has an important and essential part to play.[121]

The legal profession was poised to tip the balance from possible disintegration to the flourishing of a "virile Canadianism." Aikins identified lawyers as "children of Light"[122] who, when united in the cause of good, would "confer a benefit upon the country more general and lasting than that of statesmen and politicians."[123] This was crucial to the fulfillment of Canada's destiny: "This youngest of the nations, heir of all the ages, was not born for a position of insignificance but of greatness. It needs the leadership of our best jurists and lawyers."[124] In1916, as the Great War was being fought in Europe, Aikins called upon lawyers to become "an influence for the good ... for the people and the nation." His meaning was augmented and clarified by Isaac Campbell, with whom he shared the podium: lawyers were to work in the resolution of postwar dislocations, "withstanding the remedies for these problems which would be suggested by demagogues and anarchists."[125]

Aikins, like MacKay, emphasized that the work of lawyers in private practice had a public dimension "far beyond those resting upon persons in other employments." It followed that an "élite de corps"[126] needed to be developed. Pointing to the overwhelming volume and confusion of case law, he called for codification, asking Canadian lawyers to imitate Roman jurisconsults, gathering "knowledge in the secret places of wisdom and [giving] it to the people among whom they dwelt."[127] The law that lawyers would give to the people was to be a "responsive expression of its social and business life" and would, over time, come to approximate "the inherent laws of human nature which are as constant as matter and its universal laws."[128]

Aikins's proposals were developed from this baseline. In the midst of the social upheavals that rocked Canada following the Great War, his rhetoric, like that of many respectable Canadians, became more alarmist, his social vision less tolerant. Noting the "intellectual, temperamental and spiritual ferment" of the age, he expressed distaste for the social gospel, contempt for "anarchistic uprisings," and alarm at political movements advocating "collectivism and enslavement to system," "class control," and "Bolshevism."[129] In times of change, he thought, new laws should be developed, but only under the guidance of a legal profession working in a "co-operative spirit."[130] Lawyers were called to a great public duty:

> The leaven of law-making is working among the Canadian people just as it did among the English in that distant period where the common law grew up. Those to whom the privilege has come of knowing our jurisprudence and laws and their efficacy, and who understand the principles of responsible self government must unite in so wisely and patiently guiding the law-making multitude that there may be sane and steady national progress and no set-back, and that the noblest purposes and best impulses and finest ideals of the people may be expressed in the rules of conduct or laws which they are making for themselves. Thus will our profession do its essential part in the realizing by Canada of that larger nationhood to which, by the worthy aspirations, energy and sacrifice of its people, it has been admitted by the great world powers.[131]

As "agents and ministers of the law," lawyers had a special duty to serve as "safe and constructive advisers and leaders in national activities," holding fast always to "laws and customs which have been of value in the past." Lawyerly wisdom needed to intervene between the people in this new democracy and the reform of their law, in this view. Otherwise, Aikins believed, popular suffrage threatened an "imminent danger of the despotism not so much of individuals as of classes, organized on the principle of every one for himself and the de'il take the hindermost, which results as the de'il would have it in his taking all."[132]

A revitalized program of legal education emerged, nested within a larger strategy of placing lawyers on the front lines of social intercourse. The profession was to be reconstructed from the bottom up and legal education was to play a key role in defining lawyers' professionalism. Aikins argued that only those "who possess the qualifications of mind and character"[133] that could be formed into true lawyers should be permitted to begin legal studies. In the postwar period, this would effectively exclude many so-called ethnic Canadians,[134] as well as British Canadians of lower class origins and, probably, women. His long-time ally in educational reform, H.A. Robson, had secretly recorded approval of a "pious fraud" employed by one US institution which deterred men of "an undesirable class" from entering the profession under the guise of increased educational requirements.[135] Aikins's comments for public consumption are somewhat more subtle but leave little doubt that he shared this sentiment.

Student lawyers selected according to appropriate ethnic, class, and gender criteria were to be taught so as to become "masters in their calling," "happy in their work ... and helpful to the community."[136] Whatever else might be necessary, legal education should not be confined to merely imparting legal knowledge but should aspire to develop "the right spirit," a "professional spirit," and "gentlemanly instincts," and to inculcate the "ethics of the Bar." The objective was to form a highly public-spirited profession: "As we are ministers or agents of the law, the habit of our thought in all our professional and public activities should be, Does this serve the State?"[137] Aikins's address at the formal opening of the Manitoba Law School in 1914 is notable for its virtual disregard for technocratic knowledge and obsession with "gentlemanly" values: legal education as finishing school for boys. The speech occupies only seven full pages in the *Canadian Law Times*. Two of the seven advise students to apply themselves fully to the study of law, to "control" themselves, and to avoid any "excesses," including especially the evils of alcohol.[138] The next two pages emphasize the importance of "integrity," "moral fibre," "character," "honour," and the "habit of industry."[139] The address concludes with a plea for law students "not only to aspire to be the thorough lawyer, but to be the best Canadian." Characteristically, Aikins implored them to use wisely the "wide-spread influence" that lawyers enjoyed in order

> to create a sentiment and ideals among the people with whom you come into contact which will place them upon a higher level and justify your influence. You should aim to be leaders in thought, promoters of the intellectual and moral development of our young nation, so that it may become a strong and forceful leader in the Empire.[140]

His vision for the law school was thus sandwiched between a lecture on personal "moral fibre" and a resounding commission. There, too, he developed themes of self-improvement, responsibility, and morality.

The purpose of the law school was said to involve teaching "law in a big way," promoting "profound knowledge," and creating "an inextinguishable desire to become perfect as students, ambitious to know thoroughly the law."[141] It is plain that the new institution was only incidentally concerned with developing more efficient ways of communicating information to students. Its principal purpose was not the effective teaching of legal rules, though that would be one of its characteristics. More ambitiously, law school was intended to make better men. Aikins dismissed the notion that "smartness" unencumbered "by any other knowledge than the latest edition of the Digest, the last Consolidated Statutes, and a text book on some particular branch of the law" was adequate.[142] "Bigness" implied "that culture which can come from a broad study of subjects which are more or less connected with the law," but also a concern with "the highest interests of man in practical affairs." Importantly, it involved the development of "dignity of moral feeling and profound knowledge."[143] Aikins's cultural context and personal values resonated with the sentiment expressed by a New York lawyer who sought to establish "a method of education which educates jurists rather than mere lawyers, having in mind the thought that a jurist seeks to conform law to current ideas of moral rectitude, while a lawyer is too prone to perpetrate existing monstrosities of artificial wrong."[144] Presumably too, proper education through the case method[145] would lead students to adopt those (liberal) political values that Aikins felt to be obvious, uncontroversial, and the natural outgrowths of deep legal understanding.

In short, law schools were to develop character. They were intended to transform individuals who in turn might transform Canada, the Empire, and the world. Aikins, like MacKay, thought his generation was poised on a historic knife edge between misery and a splendid future. His conception of legal education transcended the more trivial dichotomy between practical training and academic education.

Robert W. Lee

McGill's Law Dean, R.W. Lee, succeeded Robson as chair of the Canadian Bar Association's Committee on Legal Education. He too subscribed to the common-sense view that university legal education would create an altogether new and superior sort of legal practitioner. Its product would be graduates who were learned, reflective, ethical, and public-spirited: men entirely suited to the leadership roles the new world demanded.

Lee had modest expectations of the role of university legal education in producing more skillful lawyers: "You cannot teach a man in your class-rooms to practise law, any more than you can teach him to play the fiddle by lecturing to him on fiddling." While he thought it was appropriate for the modern university "to impart the theoretical knowledge which is necessary to the mastery of a profession," his advocacy on behalf of university legal education was not motivated by a desire to find a more efficient way of cramming rules or procedures into student heads. The narrowness of learning under such an approach would fall short of the ideal and could even be harmful. The university's forté was in relation to the "scientific study of law," meaning a comparative and historical study of the legal systems of the world. Properly understood, legal studies approached theological studies in usefulness. Lee sought to instill "the vision of a divine justice transcending the imperfections of human justice, a vision which has seemed to many to be reflected in the classical definition of jurisprudence" as the knowledge of things divine and human, the science of the just and the unjust.[146]

A scientific approach to legal education emphasizing comparative law, legal history, jurisprudence, constitutional law, and public international law[147] would enlarge "the mental horizon" while simultaneously quickening the understanding.[148] The object was to make citizens capable of leadership, not merely to turn out "complete lawyers."[149] Lee hoped that this plan, modelled on programs at Oxford and Cambridge, would instill "into the student a sense of professional honour and of civic duty; ... legal education should be directed to producing not only competent practitioners, but men who by their wise and sympathetic handling of the problems of our national life, will add to the dignity and influence of the great profession of the Law."[150]

American Influences on Canadian Thought

The writings of Aikins, Lee, and MacKay align in their understanding of lawyers as critical players in social governance. In their world a renewed and structured legal education was thought necessary to preserve the purity of the profession, to channel social diversity, and ultimately to save the state from disintegration.

In thinking such thoughts and planning such plans, they were not bravely sallying forth into uncharted territory. Their perception of social crisis and of the legal profession's role drew upon both the thinking of elite US lawyers and the wider Canadian intellectual climate. Aikins, for example, rehashes similar ideas worked out by American lawyers,[151] and Alfred Z. Reed's 1921 Carnegie Foundation report on *Training for the Public Profession of Law* could as easily have been generated by elite Canadian lawyers. MacKay, Aikins, or Lee, as easily as Reed, might have penned words such as these:

> [P]ractising lawyers do not merely render to the community a social service, which the community is interested in having them render well. They are part of the governing mechanism of the state. Their functions are in a broad sense political. This is not primarily due to the circumstance that a large portion of our legislative and administrative officials, and virtually all of our judges, are chosen from among this practically ruling class ... It springs even more fundamentally from the fact, early discovered, that private individuals cannot secure justice without the aid of a special professional order to represent and advise them.[152]

Such views constituted a kind of common sense.

Taking Civilization's Survival Seriously

All of this reveals that the attainment of university legal education in common law Canada represents neither the inevitable working out of "progress" nor the outcome of a struggle in which great men with demonstrably superior ideas overcame the petty objections of lesser beings. It is, rather, the product of a very specific cultural vision suited to the felt needs of a particular place and time. On the evidence of those most closely involved, the primary motivation for the rapid development of university education in law during this period had little to do with dissatisfaction concerning the technical abilities or general competence of lawyers trained by apprenticeship. Recall, for example, that MacKay had expressly denied that university education would make better lawyers in this sense. Rather, university legal education was to be moral education. Its object was to turn out better individuals charged with the task of ensuring the integration of a pluralistic society and state.

This vision seems very nearly unintelligible in our day. It is much more natural for us to either overlook the moral reform and national survival components of speeches, reports, or articles from the period. If we do not overlook them entirely, it is easy to dismiss all declarations of altruistic motivation as empty rhetoric. If not that, perhaps it is a ploy, a verbal Trojan horse crudely employed by lawyers intent on sneaking a monopolistic professional strategy past public defences. And yet, the notion that individual and national regeneration could be achieved through the university education of aspiring lawyers provided a neat fit with the culture of English Canada's middle class during this period. The rhetoric, program, plans, and social vision of men such as MacKay, Aikins, Robson, and Lee nested within a culture dominated by moral and social reformers. Mariana Valverde's brilliant treatment of the era argues that middle-class English Canada's cultural lodestar was found in the linked metaphors of "light, soap, and water": although originating in the temperance movement, "[t]he image of reform as illuminating society while purifying or cleansing it" enjoyed wider currency.[153] The projects of elite lawyers regarding legal education and their hopes of saving Canada from disintegration by producing more upright lawyers, seemed neither naïve nor preposterous within their discursive world. Lawyers were, in their work, perfectly situated both to constrain evil and to positively advance the good. The professional programs that have been reviewed here emerged within a context in which

> [t]he building of a nation was rightly equated with the organization of assent, not just outward conformity to legal and administrative rules. This is one reason why the outright punishment of political and moral deviants came to be seen as a last resort and as an admission of failure ... While the

> criminal, the fallen, and the destitute were being increasingly seen as subjects of treatment, through the medicalization of crime, sexuality, and poverty, non-criminal populations and in particular youth were being seen as requiring a process of character-building, the individual equivalent of ... nation-building ... An individual without character ... was a miniature mob: disorganized, immoral, and unhealthy as well as an inefficient member of the collectivity. Character was not to be acquired bureaucratically, by learning information or following rules. What Clark called the production of self and others called character-building was an inner, subjective task. It involved learning to lead a morally and physically pure life, not only for the sake of individual health and salvation but for the sake of the nation.[154]

It is crucial both to Valverde's assessment of the period and to the understanding of legal education in this chapter that "language is not a transparent window giving access to the world but is rather itself a part of the world, a kind of object among objects"; that "practical social relations are always mediated and articulated through linguistic and non-linguistic signifying practices."[155] In studies of legal education, just as in other areas of social or intellectual history, it is important to take seriously patterns of discourse that might be too readily "dismissed as the flowery rhetoric of the time."[156] Moral reform discourse, according to Valverde, entirely obliterated dichotomies such as those between theory and practice or science and charity, displacing these with "a holistic image of a knowledge that would be simultaneously scientific and charitable, true and useful."[157] This general cultural displacement screams through the rhetoric of reformers of legal education. Moreover, just as the prevalent discourses of moral and social reform were characterized by "slippages," whereby words apparently directed towards one problem might contain a "strong and complex subtext" on another aspect of social life,[158] so too cultural context rendered pronouncements on superficially narrow issues of legal education simultaneously powerful commentaries on race, gender, or class hierarchy.

The prevailing cultural logic was one in which some vision of professionalism seemed to offer a panacea to the problems of democracy, authority, and social integration in a society tugged at by powerful centrifugal forces. England's developing "professional ideal"[159] and the United States' "culture of professionalism"[160] provided a pervasive cultural ethos, the logic of which could be, and was, worked out in all social interstices. It should not be surprising that the same culture that contributed Durkheim's *Professional Ethics and Civic Morals*[161] to the world of ideas also produced "on the ground" new professional visions implemented through new educational schemes.

The origins of modern Canadian legal education are to be found neither in a natural evolution of ever more rational training structures nor in a crude conspiracy of a profession to advance its own financial well-being by the suppression of potential competitors. It misses the mark to reduce the interaction of so many and diverse social forces to a mere self-interested urge for market control.[162] Such analyses paint with far too broad a brush, substituting economic or ideological principle for historical understanding.

Professional projects, including those relating to education, are much more significant – and perhaps more disturbing[163] – than that.

Notes

An earlier version of this chapter appeared as "Common Law Legal Education in Canada's Age of Light, Soap and Water" (1995) 23 Man. L.J. 654. It has been revised and reprinted here with permission.

1 Paul Axelrod and John G. Reid, eds., *Youth, University and Canadian Society: Essays in the Social History of Higher Education* (Montreal and Kingston: McGill-Queen's University Press, 1989) at xii. Three very important exceptions to this pattern are G. Blaine Baker's excellent study of early Ontario, "Legal Education in Upper Canada 1785-1889: The Law Society as Educator" in David H. Flaherty, ed., *Essays in the History of Canadian Law*, vol. 2 (Toronto: Osgoode Society for Canadian Legal History, 1983) at 49; Philip Girard's fine study, "The Roots of a Professional Renaissance: Lawyers in Nova Scotia 1850-1910" in Dale Gibson and W. Wesley Pue, eds., *Glimpses of Canadian Legal History* (Winnipeg: Legal Research Institute, 1991) at 155; and David G. Bell, *Legal Education in New Brunswick: A History* (Fredericton: University of New Brunswick, 1992). Work on Canada's civil law legal history is often less insensitive to culture and place. In the area of legal education, see, for example, David Howes, "The Origin and Demise of Legal Education in Quebec (or Hercules Bound)" (1989) 38 U.N.B.L.J. 127; Roderick Macdonald, "The National Law Programme at McGill: Origins, Evolution, Prospects" (1990) 13 Dal. L.J. 211.

2 Axelrod and Reid, *ibid.* at xiii.

3 C. Ian Kyer and Jerome E. Bickenbach, *The Fiercest Debate: Cecil A. Wright, the Benchers, and Legal Education in Ontario, 1923-1957* (Toronto: University of Toronto Press, 1987); Peter M. Sibenik, "Doorkeepers: Legal Education in the Territories and Alberta, 1885-1928" (1990) 13 Dal. L.J. 419; Dale Gibson and Lee Gibson, *Substantial Justice: Law and Lawyers in Manitoba, 1670-1970* (Winnipeg: Peguis Publishers, 1972); a pamphlet prepared for the opening of Robson Hall in1970 covers much of the same ground [Robson Hall Pamphlet]. See also Jack R. London, "The Admissions and Education Committee: A Perspective on Legal Education and Admission to Practice in the Province of Manitoba – Past, Present and Future" in Cameron Harvey, ed., *The Law Society of Manitoba, 1877-1977* (Winnipeg: Peguis Publishers, 1977) at 74; Lee Gibson, "A Brief History of the Law Society of Manitoba" in Harvey, *ibid.* at 28; Harold Buchwald, "The Law School's Fortieth Anniversary" (1954) 26 Man. Bar N. 77; E.K. Williams, "Legal Education in Manitoba: 1913-1950" (1950) 28 Can. Bar Rev. 759 at 759-79 and 880-92; W.H. McConnell, *Prairie Justice* (Calgary: Burroughs, 1980); Brian D. Bucknell, Thomas C.H. Baldwin, and J. David Lakin, "Pedants, Practitioners and Prophets: Legal Education at Osgoode Hall to 1957" (1968) 6 Osgoode Hall L.J. 137; Alfred Watts, *History of the Legal Profession in British Columbia, 1869-1984*, rev. ed. (Vancouver: Law Society of British Columbia, 1984); John Willis, *A History of Dalhousie Law School* (Toronto: University of Toronto Press, 1979).

4 Robert W. Gordon, "J. Willard Hurst and the Common Law Tradition in American Legal Historiography" (1976) 10 Law & Soc'y Rev 9 at 11 ["J. Willard Hurst"]. David Hackett Fischer would call this the "fallacy of tunnel history": David Hackett Fischer, *Historians' Fallacies: Toward a Logic of Historical Thought* (New York: Harper Colophon Books, 1970) at 142. I have taken the liberty of rendering Robert Gordon's words gender-inclusive without otherwise changing the sense.

5 A point very much like this is made in Gordon's later article, "Critical Legal Histories" (1984) 36 Stan. L. Rev. 57 at 102-9 ["Critical Legal Histories"] ("Blurring the 'Law/Society' Distinction").

6 Bucknell *et al.*, *supra* note 3 at 149.

7 *Ibid.* at 160.

8 *Ibid.* at 162.

9 *Ibid.* at 169ff; Newman Wright Hoyles served from 1894 to 1923.

10 *Ibid.* at 182 and 187 (the Canadian Bar Association and the Lawyer's Club of Toronto are mentioned).

11 *Ibid.* at 188; this was the era of Dean John D. Falconbridge, 1923-48.

12 *Ibid.* at 207ff.

13 Kyer and Bickenbach, *supra* note 3 at 4-5. The governing body for the Ontario legal profession continues to be called by this title despite the disappearance of "Upper Canada" in 1867.

14 *Ibid.* at 69 (discussing McRae's use of the Canadian Bar Association committee).

15 *Ibid.*, ch. 2, "The Bar Associations and Legal Education," at 60-79.

16 Willis, *supra* note 3.

17 *Ibid.* at 21. Also *ibid.*, Appendix I, "Weldon," at 249-54; Appendix II, "The Weldon Tradition," at 255-58; Appendix III, "What Dalhousie Law School Says about Itself When It Is on Parade," at 259-69.

18 *Ibid.* at 68-69, 74, 78-80.

19 London, *supra* note 3 at 74-120, esp. 75.

20 John P.S. McLaren, "The History of Legal Education in Common Law Canada" in Roy J. Matas and Deborah J. McCawley, eds., *Legal Education in Canada: Reports and Background Papers of a National Conference on Legal Education Held in Winnipeg, Manitoba, 23-26 October, 1985* (Montreal: Federation of Law Societies of Canada, 1987) at 111-45.

21 See Chapter 4 in this volume. Certainly, this short-hand is familiar to many scholars who find their intellectual lives constrained by contemporary law school culture.

22 David Howes has developed a similar argument with respect to legal education in nineteenth-century Quebec, arguing that "philosophy, history and politics used to be internal to law ... While it is not difficult for us moderns to imagine a lawyer with no grounding in philosophy, to the legal imagination of the 1880s such a creature was unthinkable; i.e., that professional ideology included philosophy. As for history and politics, the main reason they were internal to law is that they had not yet been departmentalized as autonomous branches of knowledge. Law was political history" (*supra* note 1 at 128). See also Macdonald, *supra* note 1.

23 Bell, *supra* note 1 at 130, 118-20, 124-25.

24 See Watts, *supra* note 3; W. Wesley Pue, *Law School: The Story of Legal Education in British Columbia* (Vancouver: Continuing Legal Education Society of British Columbia, 1995) [*Law School*], available in a fully documented version as W. Wesley Pue, "A History of British Columbia Legal Education" (2000), online: <http://papers.ssrn.com/sol3/papers.cfm?abstract_id=897084>.

25 So characterized by McLaren, *supra* note 20 at 111-45.

26 Gerald Friesen, *The Canadian Prairies: A History* (Toronto: University of Toronto Press, 1987), ch. 8, "Canada's Empire 1870-1900: The Region and the National Policy," at 340.

27 *Ibid.* at 342.
28 McConnell, *supra* note 3, ch. 4, "Legal Education in Saskatchewan," at 103-53.
29 McLaren, *supra* note 20 at 125; McConnell, *ibid.*
30 Walter H. Johns, *A History of the University of Alberta, 1908-1969* (Edmonton: University of Alberta Press, 1981) at 30. Johns has also discussed the history of the University of Alberta law faculty in his "History of the Faculty of Law" (1980) 25 Alta. L. Rev. 1.
31 Sibenik, *supra* note 3 at 439, 440.
32 *Ibid.* at 440-43.
33 *Ibid.* at 441.
34 *Ibid.* at 445.
35 *Ibid.* at 445-46.
36 *Ibid.* at 454, reporting that one-third of the students in 1915, mostly in rural locations, were in this situation.
37 *Ibid.* at 447.
38 *Ibid.* at 457.
39 *Ibid.* at 459-60.
40 *Ibid.* at 458, 461, 462. This form of reliance on case law was apparently designed to facilitate the career mobility of lawyers among common law jurisdictions. See *ibid.* at 461, n. 175, citing correspondence from W.A.R. Kerr to Howe, n.d.
41 *Ibid.* at 461-62. The quotation is from correspondence between William A.R. Kerr, Dean of Arts and Sciences, and Howe, n.d.
42 *Ibid.* at 464.
43 The extraordinary work of Dale Gibson and Lee Gibson, *supra* note 3, holds pride of place in this as in many other aspects of Manitoba legal history. A pamphlet prepared on the opening of Robson Hall in 1970 covers much of the same ground. See also London, *supra* note 3 at 74; Lee Gibson, *supra* note 3 at 28; Buchwald, *supra* note 3 at 77-82; and Williams, *supra* note 3 at 759-79, 880-92.
44 London, *supra* note 3 at 77.
45 Lee Gibson, *supra* note 3 at 33.
46 Report of Law Society of Manitoba Examining Committee (establishing a course of lectures pursuant to student petition), 12 January 1903, Archive of Manitoba Legal History, Faculty of Law [AMLH]; Law Society of Manitoba Minutes, 7 December 1906 (petition from the Law Students' Society asking for a course of lectures, referred to a special committee of the President, Mr. Wilson, and Mr. Cameron).
47 Gibson and Gibson, *supra* note 3 at 129.
48 Law Society of Manitoba Minutes, 7 February 1905.
49 Letter to L.G. McPhillips of Vancouver, author unknown, 29 May 1909, AMLH file A225. A limited range of lectures were approved by the Law Society at various times prior to and after the date of this letter; see, for example, Law Society of Manitoba Minutes, 7 January 1907, 9 October 1907, 28 October 1907, 14 October 1907, 11 November 1908, and 28 October 1909.
50 Law Society of Manitoba Minutes, 29 September 1908: "in response to a letter from Mr. W.H. Trueman, secretary to write and say no idea of establishing a Law School at the present time." Trueman also appeared frequently as a lecturer in the early courses, and in 1915 was briefly named head of the teaching staff of the new Manitoba Law School: *ibid.*, 19 February 1915.
51 Report by J.A.M. Aikins and Rev. A.A. Chevrier on the university and professional training (commission appointed 26 September 1907; report delivered in the fall of 1909) at 73, University of Manitoba Archives, UA 20, Box 7, Folder 5, P378.7127 W B MS. This recommendation is similar to one made by Ontario's 1906 Royal Commission on the University of Toronto, chaired by Joseph Flavelle, which recommended "that a Faculty of Law should

be established in the University, and that, if possible, arrangements should be made with the Law Society by which the duplication of the work which is common to both in the courses of instruction may be avoided." The Law Society of Upper Canada rejected this notion altogether (quoted in Kyer and Bickenbach, *supra* note 3 at 36).

52 Kyer and Bickenbach, *ibid.* at 73-74. The analogies provided by the constitutive colleges of the University of Manitoba would have been particularly influential in the thinking of Aikins and Chevrier. Their report has been characterized by W.L. Morton, *One University: A History of the University of Manitoba, 1877-1952* (Toronto: McClelland and Stewart, 1957), as follows: "a full, historical defence of the founding colleges and of the autonomy of the university as organized in 1877... proposed a reorganization which would have kept the colleges constituent parts of the university while effecting a separation of financial and academic administration" (at 77). Elsewhere, Morton describes Aikins and Chevrier as "traditionalists" who "accepted the original organization of the university with its denominational control through the constituent colleges supported by the churches and private benefactors, but coupled with a modicum of state aid for the maintenance of an examining body and a teaching faculty limited to the natural sciences" (at 65).

53 Law Society of Manitoba Minutes, 15 February 1910: "Mr. Pitblado gave notice that he would move at the next meeting that the time has come when a Law School should be established either by the Law Society, or in connection with the University of Manitoba and that a Committee of the Benchers be appointed to consider the matter and report."

54 Law Society of Manitoba Minutes, 17 December 1909 ("Letters from Adamson, Baker and Martin re attending a law school; request denied but should ask for legislation to amend *The Law Society Act*").

55 Lee Gibson, *supra* note 3 at 33. See Law Society of Manitoba Minutes, 6 May 1910; AMLH, Newspaper Clippings file, 6 June 1910.

56 Law Society Manitoba Minutes, 14 June 1910 (*e.g.*, P. Balser, W. Martin, and A.E. Dilts); 27 September 1910 ("four students"); 7 June 1912 (G.C. Lindsay); 14 May 1913 (L.P. Napier); 10 June 1913 (William Nasore[?]); 30 September 1913 (C.D. Roblin; F.C.S. Davision).

57 "Desire University Control," 15 December 1910, AMLH, Newspaper Clippings file, 1889-1963, 12: "The law students of the city have been for some time considering some improvements which they think might be made in their course of study and examinations. A hint dropped at one of their moot courts by the attorney-general who was acting as judge, has given an encouragement to their purpose, and it is probable that they may petition the university regarding the holding of their examinations under its auspices."

58 Letter to the Benchers from Mr. E.D. Honeyman, 20 February 1911, AMLH, A225.The Benchers' minutes for 21 February record receipt of a letter from the Law Students' Association requesting lectures, and authorizes lectures to be given at remuneration of $25 per lecture. Again, the Law Society of Manitoba Minutes for 28 November 1911 record that a series of lectures was to be arranged in response to a request from the Winnipeg Law Students' Society.

59 "Manitoba Bar Association Born at Banquet" *Winnipeg Telegram*, 10 November, AMLII Newspaper Clippings file, 1911; see also "Aikins Entertains Local Barristers," n.d., AMLH Newspaper Clippings file, 1911.

60 The Law Society of Manitoba Minutes for 8 March 1912 record that a *Bill for An Act to Incorporate the University Extension Society of Canada* was opposed by the Benchers.

61 "Would Give Women Right to Practice Law in Province" *Winnipeg Telegram*, 7 March 1912, AMLH Newspaper Clippings file, 1912, 24.

62 AMLH Newspaper Clippings file, 1912, 21.

63 See Robert Stevens, *Law School: Legal Education in America from the 1850s to the 1980s* (Chapel Hill: University of North Carolina Press, 1983) at 99, 112-13, 176; Jerold S. Auerbach, *Unequal Justice: Lawyers and Social Change in Modern America* (New York:

Oxford University Press, 1977), ch. 3, "Scientific Expertise: The Triumph of the New Professoriat."

64 See discussion *infra*, notes 131-33 and accompanying text.

65 Henry M. Bates, Dean of the Law School, University of Michigan, "Recent Progress in Legal Education," ch. 10, US Bureau of Education Report 1914, 227.

66 Julius Henry Cohen, *The Law: Business or Profession?* (New York: Banks Law Publishing, 1916) at 138-39. Interestingly, Cohen concludes this chapter with the comment that "[e]ducation for the Bar must include moral training – if it is to be education for *the Bar*" (at 141; emphasis in original). It should be noted that although couched in the language of public interest and objective standards, the attempts of the "better university schools" to raise their standards may have been the result of discriminatory and exclusionary motivations. See Auerbach, *supra* note 63 at 94-101.

67 E.H. Coleman, "Legal Education" (1933) 5 Man. Bar N. 1 at 2. Coleman's comments are entirely derivative of the cultural web that permitted Josef Redlich, *The Common Law and the Case Method in American University Law Schools* (New York, 1914), to comment that proprietary schools "supply the needs primarily of those social strata whose sons are not thinking of university education in either the American or the continental sense. They consider the legal profession as a trade like any other, and regard legal education in the same light as commercial education in a commercial school" (as quoted in Robert Stevens, *supra* note 63 at 113).

68 Coleman, *ibid.* at 2.

69 The Law Society of Manitoba Minutes for 26 April 1912 indicate that the *University Extension Society Bill* was withdrawn.

70 Lee Gibson, *supra* note 3 at 33.

71 A newspaper article of 23 November 1912 under the heading "Annual Banquet of Law Students" reports that in an address to law students, Robson commented: "The modern tendency to over much reform must be checked. Remember the ethics and the etiquette of your profession so that you may maintain the high standards. You must keep off all trespassers for the benefit of the profession and the community. A very necessary reform, however, is the establishment of a law school" (AMLH, Newspaper Clippings file, 1912, 71).

72 Letter to J.A. MacLean from H.A. Robson, 19 September 1913, University of Manitoba Archives, UA 20, Box 10, Folder 5.

73 Robson Hall Pamphlet, *supra* note 3 at 6; Gibson and Gibson, *supra* note 3 at 216.

74 Unidentified newspaper clipping (probably from the *Tribune* of 15 or 16 May 1914), University of Manitoba Archives, UA 20, Box 8, Folder 2. The arrangement would, Pitblado said, be similar to that between the university and the school of medicine.

75 Lee Gibson, *supra* note 3 at 33-34; Gibson and Gibson, *supra* note 3 at 216.

76 By a motion of 14 June moved by President MacLean and seconded by C.K. Newcombe. Letter from W.J. Spence, Registrar of University of Manitoba, to Benchers, Law Society, 25 June 1914, AMLH, A440.

77 The Law Society of Manitoba Minutes for 17 July 1914 indicate that the first board of trustees consisted of Edwin Loftus and the Reverend Dr. G.B. Wilson (university representatives), and I. Campbell and J.H. Munson (Law Society representatives). The Law Society suggested that Robson chair the board.

78 *Ibid.;* also see 1914, AMLH, A440.

79 Lee Gibson, *supra* note 3 at 34.

80 *Ibid.* The recorder was "R. P. Hills, LL.D." (Robson Hall Pamphlet, *supra* note 3 at 6).

81 Curriculum of the Manitoba Law School under the University of Manitoba and the Manitoba Law Society, Winnipeg, June 1915, AMLH, A100, 1-2.

82 London, *supra* note 3 at 77-78. In 1915, the *Law Society Act* was amended in order to retroactively authorize the arrangements.

83 See Chapter 6. Over and above any assigned treatises or casebooks, the school in its early years produced pamphlets listing cases that were recommended for reading in various courses.

84 H.A. Robson to J.A. MacLean, 3 April 1914, University of Manitoba Archives, UA20, Box 10, Folder 5 (also appears in AMLH, A440, Board of Trustees Minutes); Robson to Pitblado, 18 May1915, AMLH, A369.

85 University of Manitoba Archives, UA20, Box 10, Folder 5 (also appears in AMLH, A440, Board of Trustees Minutes) (memorandum recording view that the teachers should be professional, full-time instructors) and also A205/2.

86 The Manitoba Law School curriculum from 1914 to 1920 was notable for its inclusion of a wide range of courses that advanced a general "cultural" education rather than merely providing training in the mundane tasks of workaday legal practice. University president Dr. J.A. MacLean, a classicist who came to Manitoba from the presidency of the University of Idaho, took an early active interest in the business of the law school, and apparently did what he could to prevent slippage into a narrowly practical curriculum, a task that he shared with Robson. See: Letter to J.A. MacLean from H.A. Robson, 30 April 1915; Letter from H.A. Robson to J.A. MacLean, President of the University, 31 December 1915; Letter from MacLean to H.A. Robson, 7 January 1916, University of Manitoba Archives, UA20, Box 10, Folder 5.

87 Curriculum of the Manitoba Law School, Session 1919-20, AMLH, A100, indicates that by 1919-20, admission standards had been raised to completion of "First Year in Arts of the University of Manitoba or its equivalent."

88 See discussion in Kyer and Bickenbach, *supra* note 3 at 64-70.

89 Gibson and Gibson, *supra* note 3 at 248; Robson Hall Pamphlet, *supra* note 3 at 8.

90 Curriculum of the Manitoba Law School, Session 1921-22, AMLH, A100/6.

91 Minutes of a Meeting of the Board of Trustees, 28 February 1921, AMLH A440, 123 (motion to move curriculum as close as possible to that proposed by the Canadian Bar Association; motion for a permanent teaching staff of two).

92 Willis, *supra* note 3 at 81.

93 Kyer and Bickenbach, *supra* note 3 at 42.

94 Gibson and Gibson, *supra* note 3 at 248; Robson Hall Pamphlet, *supra* note 3 at 8; Curriculum of the Manitoba Law School, Session 1921-22, AMLH, A100/6; Buchwald, *supra* note 3 at 80.

95 (1923) 8 Proceedings: Canadian Bar Association 387; quoted in Gibson and Gibson, *supra* note 3 at 48; Robson Hall Pamphlet, *supra* note 3 at 9.

96 Gibson and Gibson, *ibid.* at 249; Robson Hall Pamphlet, *ibid.* at 9; Carnegie Foundation for the Advancement of Teaching, *Annual Review of Legal Education* (Princeton, NJ: Carnegie Foundation, 1926, 1927).

97 Harvey, *supra* note 3 at 222-72, 225-26. An earlier attempt to found a Canadian Bar Association had not produced enduring results.

98 This report called for an arrangement in which articles would follow completion of law school. It endorsed Langdell's methods of legal education. E.K. Williams described the process as moving from first draft report – (1918) 38 Can. L.T. 2571 – to final report (published in the *Canadian Bar Association Year Book* for 1918), with final changes being adopted at the 1919 CBA meeting (Williams, *supra* note 3 at 762). See R.W. Lee, "Legal Education: A Symposium" (1919) 39 Can. L.T. 138 ["Legal Education: A Symposium"]; (1918) 38 Can. L.T. Lee's report on legal education also appeared in *Proceedings of the 4th Annual Meeting of the Canadian Bar Association*, 1919 (published 1920) at 150-52; "Committee on

Legal Education – Standard Curriculum" in *Report and Notes on the Proceedings of the 5th Annual Meeting of the Canadian Bar Association,* 1920 (published 1920).

99 "Legal Ethics: An Address by Chief Justice Mathers," *ibid.* at 269-301; Chapter 9 in this volume (also published in Gibson and Pue, *supra* note 1 at 337-77).

100 Harvey, *supra* note 3 at 231-34.

101 On 7 February 1905, Aikins and Pitblado formed a committee to discuss with the University of Manitoba a course of lectures in connection with the LL.B. course (Law Society of Manitoba Minutes). Pitblado's subsequent interventions in favour of university legal education are recorded in Law Society of Manitoba Minutes, 15 February 1910; and University of Manitoba Archives, UA20, Box 8, Folder 2 (unidentified newspaper article).

102 Minutes of the Proceedings of Canadian Bar Association (1919) at 150 (as cited in Kyer and Bickenbach, *supra* note 3 at 66).

103 However, he found himself unable to participate. The result was that Brown represented both the Saskatchewan and Manitoba law societies. Brown consulted "with Judge Robson, with the head of the Manitoba Law School, and with some of the benchers of the Law Society" (Proceedings, CBA, 1920, "Committee on Legal Education, Standard Curriculum," 250 at 252).

104 *Ibid.* at 250-57.

105 Kyer and Bickenbach, *supra* note 3 at 69.

106 Such is conceded in *Report to the Social Sciences and Humanities Research Council of Canada by the Consultative Group on Research and Education in Law, Law and Learning* (Ottawa: Social Sciences and Humanities Research Council of Canada, 1983), generally identified as (Harry) Arthur's Report, at 13: "In principle, the university law schools and the professional schools ought to have provided dramatic contrasts, reflecting the ethos and objectives of their parent bodies. However, in practice no such clear-cut opposition of styles seems to have developed ... The two traditions, in fact, coexisted without undue overt conflict." The report notes that "[o]nly in 1948-49 did a clear polarization of positions occur" (at Osgoode Hall). It is important that the Ontario trauma of 1948-49 not be read backward and forward into the history of legal education in Canada.

107 I.A. MacKay, "The Education of a Lawyer" (speech delivered in December 1913 to the Third Annual Meeting of the Law Society of Alberta), published in (1940-42) Alta. L. Q. 103 at 110.

108 *Ibid.* at 105. In referring to "English law," MacKay meant to include the laws of the United Kingdom, the British Empire, and the United States.

109 *Ibid.* at 107.

110 *Ibid.*

111 *Ibid.* at 108.

112 *Ibid.*

113 *Ibid.* at 107. This account of the English legal profession has little application to the vast majority of English lawyers who worked on the solicitor's side of the profession. Even with regard to the Bar, the portrait of some happy professional consensus generated through work and social institutions was a highly distorted, idealized impression. For a brief discussion and reference to further literature, see W. Wesley Pue, "Trajectories of Professionalism: Legal Professionalism after Abel" in Alvin Esau, ed., *Manitoba Law Annual, 1989-90* (Winnipeg: Legal Research Institute, 1991) 57 ["Trajectories of Professionalism"], esp. "The Peculiarities of the Yanks" at 67-76.

114 I.A. MacKay, *supra* note 107 at 108.

115 *Ibid.*

116 *Ibid.* at 115.

117 *Ibid.*

118 *Ibid.*

119 James Aikins, "The Advancement of the Science of Jurisprudence in Canada" (1915) 51 Can. L.J. 161 at 163-64 ["Advancement"].
120 Carl Berger, *The Sense of Power: Studies in the Ideas of Canadian Imperialism, 1867-1914* (Toronto: University of Toronto Press, 1970).
121 Aikins, "Advancement," *supra* note 119 at 165-66.
122 *Ibid.* at 165. On the rhetorical devices of reform – and the need to take these seriously – see Mariana Valverde, *The Age of Light, Soap, and Water: Moral Reform in English Canada, 1885-1925* (Toronto: McClelland and Stewart, 1991), esp. ch. 2, "The Work of Allegories," at 34-43.
123 Aikins, "Advancement," *supra* note 119 at 177.
124 *Ibid.* at 175. Three years later, Aikins wrote: "Canada has this faith that it was born for a great world purpose, to help in maintaining peace and to aid other nations toward the attainment of the same freedom of self-government, and similar elevated ideals it possesses." James Aikins, "Inaugural Address of the President, Sir James Aikins, K.C., KIL, Lieutenant-Governor of Manitoba" (1918) 54 Can. L.J. 344 at 354 ["Inaugural Address"].
125 "Sir James Aiken Host of Bar Association Banquet" *Calgary Albertan,* 20 May 1916.
126 Aikins, "Advancement," *supra* note 119 at 165.
127 *Ibid.* at 177.
128 *Ibid.* at 176.
129 James Aikins, "[Presidential] Address to the Canadian Bar Association" (1919) 39 Can. L.T. 537 at 539-40 ["Presidential Address"].
130 *Ibid.* at 548.
131 *Ibid.*
132 James Aikins, "The President's Address" (1920) 56 Can. L.J. 308 at 309.
133 Aikins, "Presidential Address," *supra* note 129 at 546.
134 Given Canada's predestined greatness in world affairs, Aikins argued, "it should religiously guard against the introduction of strangers from other countries who may hinder in the performance of that duty to itself and to its citizens, and in the attainment of that world purpose ... Even before the war that error was made manifest in industrial dissensions, in the ignorant, too often corrupt, use of the franchise and failure to understand the privileges and responsibilities of our free institutions and government, in the denationalizing and too frequently demoralizing force of undesirable foreigners. Detached by distance from their own people they are generally all for self and none for adopted nation. If then, larger numbers are admitted to asylum in Canada from foreign lands, of different race, traditions, language and spirit than it can quickly and quietly absorb, Canada will be a sick nation with a long period of convalescing weakness": Aikins, "Inaugural Address," *supra* note 124 at 354-55. Fear of the foreigner pervaded early debates concerning the development of a Canadian Bar Association Ethical Code. See Chapter 9 in this volume. For further discussion of the extent to which concerns about race pervaded English Canada's middle-class consciousness at this time, see Valverde, *supra* note 122; Angus McLaren, *Our Own Master Race: Eugenics in Canada, 1885-1945* (Toronto: McClelland and Stewart, 1990).
135 Memo, Robson to MacLean, 22 April 1914, University of Manitoba Archives, UA20, Box 10, Folder 5.
136 Aikins, "Presidential Address," *supra* note 129 at 546.
137 *Ibid.* at 545.
138 Sir James Aikins, "Formal Opening of the Manitoba Law School. Inaugural Address to the Students by Sir James Aikins, K.C., M.P." (1914) 34 Can. L.T. 1183 at 1183-85 ["Formal Opening"].
139 *Ibid.* at 1186-87.
140 *Ibid.* at 1190.
141 *Ibid.* at 1188-89.

142 *Ibid.* at 1188.
143 *Ibid.* at 1187, 1188.
144 Charles A. Boston, "Some Neglected Fields in Legal Education. Address of Chairman. Delivered before the Section of Legal Education of the American Bar Association at Washington, D.C., October 20, 1914" (1914) 34 Can. L.T. 1081 at 1091.
145 Aikins, "Formal Opening," *supra* note 138 at 1183-90, 1188-89.
146 R.W. Lee, "Legal Education, Old and New, III" (1916) 36 Can. L.T. 109 at 114.
147 *Ibid.* at 115.
148 *Ibid.* at 114.
149 *Ibid.* at 115.
150 Lee, "Legal Education: A Symposium," *supra* note 98 at 141. For further assessment of Lee's contribution, including the cultural urgings underlying his attempt to establish common law education in Quebec, see Macdonald, *supra* note 1.
151 See, for example, Julius Henry Cohen, *The Law: Business or Profession?* (New York: Banks Law Publishing, 1916); David J. Brewer, "Protection to Private Property from Public Attack" (1891)10 Railway and Corporation Law Journal 281; David J. Brewer, "The Nation's Safeguard" (1893) 16 Proceedings of the New York State Bar Association 37 at 39. See generally James C. Foster, *The Ideology of Apolitical Politics: Elite Lawyers' Response to the Legitimation Crisis of American Capitalism, 1870-1920* (New York: Garland Publishing, 1990) and the following discussions of Brewer, as cited therein: Arnold M. Paul, *Conservative Crisis and the Rule of Law* (New York: Harper and Row, 1969); Benjamin Rollins Twiss, *Lawyers and the Constitution* (New York: Russell and Russell, 1962); Lynford A. Lardner, *The Constitutional Doctrines of Justice David Josiah Brewer* (PhD Dissertation, Princeton University, 1938).
152 Alfred Z. Reed, *Training for the Public Profession of the Law: Historical Development and Principal Contemporary Problems of Legal Education in the United States, with Some Account of Conditions in England and Canada* (New York: Carnegie Foundation, 1921) at 3 (as quoted in Stevens, *supra* note 63 at 113).
153 Valverde, *supra* note 122 at 17-18.
154 *Ibid.* at 26-27.
155 *Ibid.* at 10, 11.
156 *Ibid.* at 34.
157 *Ibid.* at 35.
158 *Ibid.* at 14.
159 Harold Perkin, *The Rise of Professional Society: England since 1880* (London: Routledge, 1989).
160 Burton Bledstein, *The Culture of Professionalism: The Middle Class and the Development of Higher Education in America* (New York: W.W. Norton, 1978).
161 Emile Durkheim, *Professional Ethics and Civic Morals* (London: Routledge and Kegan Paul, 1957).
162 For a fuller critique of this line of interpretation, see Pue, "Trajectories," *supra* note 113 at 57-92. The writings of Weber have been relied upon in turn by (the early) Magali Larson and by Richard Abel to develop a model of professionalism as being essentially concerned with the collective pursuit of market control. Magali Sarfatti Larson, *The Rise of Professionalism: A Sociological Analysis* (Berkeley: University of California Press, 1977). Among the many writings of Richard Abel on the legal profession, see especially "The Rise of Professionalism" (1976) 6 British Journal of Law and Society 82, a review of Larson's book of same title; *The Legal Profession in England and Wales* (Oxford: B.H. Blackwell, 1988); *American Lawyers* (New York: Oxford University Press, 1989).
163 Foster, *supra* note 151.

6

British Empire Perspectives on the Case Method of Legal Education

CANADA, 1885-1931

> It behooves you not only to aspire to be the thorough lawyer, but to be the best Canadian, and to create a sentiment and ideals among the people with whom you come into contact which will place them upon a higher level and justify your influence. You should aim to be leaders in thought, promoters of the intellectual and moral development of our young nation, so that it may become a strong and forceful leader in the Empire.
>
> – James Aikins, Address on Opening of Manitoba Law School, 1914[1]

When the history of lawyers' education in common law Canada comes to be written, it will probably be noted that Manitoba has often marched to its own drummer – sometimes at the forefront of national developments, often not. Paradoxically, the home of one of common law Canada's first university-affiliated schools was also the last Canadian province to adopt a system of full-time university legal education.[2]

This chapter explores the rise and fall of Manitoban legal education from 1885 to 1931. For much of this period Canada's "keystone province" held a central place in the aspirations and plans of English Canadian nationalism. In this new territory on which the virtues of British Canadianness were yet to be securely inscribed, some influential lawyers worked hard to protect the culture of English Canadian law. Some, as the epigraph of this chapter suggests, thought they could best do this by nurturing an appropriately educated, socialized, and structured legal profession. This cultural project of certain elite lawyers was one force propelling extraordinary changes in professional legal education during the second and third decades of the twentieth century.

It was not the only force, however. Although the story of Manitoban legal education is partly about forceful, visionary men and their work, it is also a tale of professional inertia, borrowing from abroad, happenstance, and an unstable accommodation between competing visions of professionalism and pedagogy. Visionaries (to describe them thus is not to endorse their views) were certainly a minority within the profession. Most lawyers probably viewed their work prosaically, as being primarily about earning a living, serving their clients, and surviving another month, rather than as a public calling directed to the mission of implanting British law in a new land. For such individuals, law was their trade, something best learned by doing, and for which training by apprenticeship made both good business sense and good practical education.[3]

A third important factor was the dissatisfaction apprenticing lawyers felt with turn-of-the-century systems of professional qualification. In the nature of things, the leadership of student organizations turns over rapidly and there were inevitably ebbs and flows in both the positions and energy of Manitoba's law students (the sparseness of the historical record makes it impossible to sketch this out in any detail). It is also important not to lose sight of the fact that apprenticing lawyers' views on legal education probably spanned the entire range of opinion held by their professional elders. As with their elders, only outspoken student leaders produced records that leave a historical trace. Nonetheless, it was always the case that apprenticing lawyers more than anyone else benefited from or suffered under prevailing forms of professional qualification. For most of the period before 1914, many apprenticing lawyers felt the need for some form of regular instruction in law. While it is less clear that they shared fully in the cultural vision of senior professional reformers, the overlap of interest was sufficient to make the two groups allies of sorts. Whatever potential there was for cleavage to develop between a "cultural" vision of legal education and one directed more narrowly towards ensuring regularity of technical instruction would not have been fully apparent in a time and a place where neither was available.

Legal education in Manitoba has always been primarily about training aspiring lawyers for careers. In 1872, the first rules of the Law Society of Manitoba established a structure whereby aspiring lawyers earned professional qualification by examination and service of an extended apprenticeship as an "articled clerk" or "a student at law."[4] Neither category of apprentice was provided with any systematic instruction.[5] The quality of on-the-job training probably varied enormously from one law office to another.[6]

Although the University of Manitoba offered an LL.B. degree as early as 1885, the degree was not an important part of professional education in this period.[7] "[M]erely a question of reading the books and passing the examinations,"[8] the law degree provided no professional qualification or exemption other than entitling graduates to a slightly shortened period of apprenticeship – a benefit to which any other university graduate was also entitled. Not surprisingly, few aspiring lawyers took the university program until its transmogrification and effective merger with Law Society courses in 1914.

Before then, there were repeated efforts to establish regular lectures under the auspices of the Law Society (often at the urging of apprenticing lawyers).[9] The province's method of professional credentialling in law was also the subject of occasional investigations or reports. Apprenticing lawyers actively sought out systematic legal education both to prepare them better for their chosen careers and, more immediately, to help them pass the Law Society's professional examinations. Their motivations may have been self-interested and pragmatic, but in articulating their demands, students both drew upon and contributed to evolving discourses of professionalism.[10] By 1908, a more or less regular series of lectures had been established under the auspices of the Law Society of Manitoba. In the winter of 1908-09, the Law Society organized and paid for lectures on five subjects in central Winnipeg on Tuesdays and Fridays. The lectures were scheduled to avoid conflict with office duties, but attendance was entirely voluntary. Although "some students attended very regularly indeed, others never took the trouble to go to a single lecture."[11] Despite these inadequacies, the achievement of more or less regular lecture series was a significant accomplishment in their time and place. No script ordained this: the subsequent development of university-based professional education as the North American norm was not in any sense a necessary end towards which all turn-of-the-century developments inevitably pointed.

Such an arrangement was not, however, satisfactory to ardent professional reformers who sought the establishment of a full law school, either on the model of the Toronto profession's trade school at Osgoode Hall[12] or in affiliation with the provincial university.[13] For their part, students appreciated the lectures but felt they were still left to "blind preparation" for their qualifying examinations. The general lectures provided by interested practitioners were, they pointed out, not intended to address the texts upon which professional examinations were based.[14] Student pressure to create either a professional school of law or a university program suited to their needs was unrelenting. A choreographed performance developed, involving repeated demands by law students,[15] supported or encouraged by elite lawyers, and cautious, usually minimal responses from the Benchers. The influence of a few elite lawyers, including James Aikins, Isaac Pitblado,[16] and H.A. Robson, is usually discernible; they appear sometimes in highly visible roles, while on other occasions they are found behind the scenes. Aikins was omnipresent. Energetic, smart, and influential, he was a key figure in the Winnipeg Bar Association (founded in 1906), and a founding father of both the Manitoba Bar Association (as the Winnipeg Bar Association renamed itself in 1911) and the Canadian Bar Association (effectively founded in 1914).[17] Each of these professional organizations supported the cause of cultural training for lawyers championed by their creator.

At its inaugural banquet in 1911, the Manitoba Bar Association called for the creation of university legal education,[18] passing a motion asking that the University of Manitoba create "two chairs to the Faculty of law, or that provision be made for one professor to lecture in the department of law in connection with the university" in coordination with the Law Society of Manitoba.[19] The importance of individual agency in all of this is apparent in the fact that one newspaper account of these events appeared under the heading "Aikins Entertains Local Barristers."

There are hints that this particular motion was part of a larger campaign orchestrated by apprenticing lawyers in concert with elite lawyers. A 15 December 1910 newspaper article reported:

> The law students of the city have been for some time considering some improvements which they think might be made in their course of study and examinations. A hint dropped at one of their moot courts by the attorney-general who was acting as judge, has given an encouragement to their purpose, and it is probable that they may petition the university regarding the holding of their examinations under its auspices ... It is hoped that some means may be devised for holding a course of lectures upon the authorized texts as well as upon the general subjects and the students feel that this could be done to more advantage under the tutelage of the university. Though nothing definite has been attempted so far, it is possible that some steps may be taken shortly towards securing the desired lectures, and having a university control of examinations.[20]

In addition to pressures from apprenticing lawyers, individual lawyers, and the Manitoba Bar Association, an official inquiry reported on legal education in 1909. The Royal Commission on Manitoba University Education (established in 1907) was not centred on legal education, and the commissioners' widely divergent reports were largely ignored by the government on all issues. One of the commissioners was none other than James Aikins, who, along with the Reverend A.A. Chevrier, addressed legal education. Building on the precedent of existing arrangements for university training in medicine and engineering,[21] the report called for the creation of a college of law affiliated with the university. Theological training could not have been far from their minds, for they proposed a model of administration for the college of law analogous to that governing the constituent denominational colleges of the University of Manitoba:[22]

> We believe it would not be difficult for the University to make an arrangement with the Law Society whereby a regular course of instruction would be given to those studying, the University establishing Chairs in some subjects such as Constitutional, Municipal, Commercial and Criminal Law, and the Law Society providing Lectures in the other subjects. If the University has the funds available to do so, we recommend such a course
>
> ...
>
> If the University has not the funds to do so after providing for the teaching of those subjects which we have previously recommended as University subjects, then we recommend that State aid be granted so as to place the Students of these Professions on a somewhat equal footing in respect of a regular course of instruction in their intended vocations, and that when regular teaching in Law is undertaken by the Law Society with the aid of the State or of the University, then the Law Society should be affiliated with the University in respect of such teaching or of the School or College it may establish for such purpose.[23]

Aikins and Chevrier's report, like those of the other commissioners, was ignored by the government. Although it had no immediate practical consequence, the report did give voice to a developing notion of practical university education in law. It became, in effect, a blueprint for what developed only a half-decade later.

Force of logic or personality, imagination, coordination of efforts, and the power of persistence are not always sufficient to overcome the weight of inertia. Major reforms need all of these, but significant change rarely comes about unless such forces coincide with a precipitating event that focuses attention on the need for reform and points to the inevitability of change. The precipitating event here was a development that, though modest, illustrated that the status quo could not persist indefinitely. Forces beyond the control of the provincial law society were in play.

The Spectre: Legal Education for Profit

Law societies and universities are not the only conceivable providers of structured legal education. Private "crammers" of one sort or another had long been in existence in both England and the United States.[24] In March 1912, the Manitoba legislature gave consideration to a "University Extension Bill." This would have permitted a private business to grant degrees by correspondence or instruction in the fields of law and business. The Benchers immediately objected.[25] Speaking with his authority both as a member of the legislature and as a long-term Bencher, G.R. Coldwell[26] told the legislature that such an institution would infringe the provisions of the *Law Society Act*. He feared it would "cause many to shirk the more thorough training in law demanded under the terms of the Law Society Act." He objected also to the granting of degrees by a correspondence school. Interestingly, although the gender composition of the legal profession is nowhere mentioned in the body of the article, the Winnipeg *Telegram*'s account of the matter was headed, "Would Give Women Right to Practice Law in Province."[27] On another occasion, Coldwell expressed concern that a private law school would throw "the province open to professional men without training."[28]

It is not entirely clear why private education so disturbed the Benchers. Direct evidence is sparse. It seems unlikely that anyone could possibly have thought that *any* private system of education might have been less thorough or rigorous than the Law Society's amalgam of voluntary attendance at sporadically offered lectures, unregulated service in a law office, and undemanding examinations. On the other hand, the introduction of a proprietary law school would have challenged the Law Society's role as the sole authoritative voice and diminished its cultural authority. Coldwell's comments also serve as a reminder that Canadian law societies were relatively insecure in their monopoly. Graduates of a private law school would likely have assumed the right to practise law as they saw fit, with or without Law Society blessing. Manitoba lawyers would have known that Dr. Charlotte Ross had practised medicine in both Quebec and Manitoba for thirty-seven years after her graduation from the Women's Medical College of Pennsylvania in 1875, despite opposition from the organized medical profession and lack of any formal recognition by qualifying associations.[29] There was no reason to assume that locally graduated lawyers would have proved any more amenable to the Law Society's jurisdiction than Dr. Ross had been to that of Manitoba's College of Physicians and Surgeons.

Another factor also probably came into play, although this remains speculative. Experience in the United States had shown that private law schools provided access to legal careers for a broader and more diverse group of individuals than other means of qualification. The result, from one point of view, was to open a key social role to much larger numbers of inadequately socialized young men *and women* – particularly those of working-class or ethnic minority background. Not everyone thought this desirable. The prospect would not have appealed to Manitoba's Anglo legal elite, whose culture was British, hierarchical, nativist, and sometimes even xenophobic.[30] Their professional counterparts in the United States had by this time reached a consensus about the dangers of proprietary law schools. Julius Cohen's 1916 book on the legal profession drew heavily on a report prepared by University of Michigan Law Dean Henry M. Bates[31] to observe that, in the United States, "there are still proprietary schools run for profit, which do not take into account the larger interests of the State, the profession, and the requirements of justice" and which grant diplomas on low standards of admission and of work. "Unless this tendency is checked, much of the good that the better university schools are attempting to accomplish, at the expense of loss in students and money to themselves, will be offset by the schools run mainly for revenue only."[32] Reflecting on such matters many years later, E.H. Coleman (then dean of the Manitoba Law School), asserted that US commercial law schools took students ill equipped "by education, character or temperament" for legal practice, producing graduates with "little conception of ethical standards and who enter on practice without any idea that the profession has any other end or duty than the making of money by the practitioner."[33] The Manitoba dean celebrated the "advantage" Manitoba enjoyed of "having the control of legal education lodged in our official society." In apparent reference to the 1912 *University Extension Bill,* he observed that "[h]ad the Law School not been established, I think I may say quite safely that you would have in Winnipeg a commercial law school, probably a branch of one of the institutions in Chicago or Minneapolis, the only aim of which would be the profit of the owner with the result that there would be pumped out each year an army of graduates, whose chief qualifications, so far as the Law School would be concerned, would be the payment of fees."[34]

Manitoba was spared both education-for-profit and the increasingly open and diverse legal profession it promised. A university-affiliated law school soon emerged to occupy the field.[35]

Creation of the Manitoba Law School, 1911-13

From 1911 to 1913, the Law Society organized lectures for students, much as it had in the past.[36] Robson continued his work to create a law school and prodded apprenticing lawyers to "keep hammering at the question" of legal education.[37] Despite all efforts, however, a provincial law school seemed a distant prospect at best. As late as autumn 1913, Robson told the University of Manitoba's new president, James Alexander MacLean:[38] "The Law School idea is developing slowly but I think surely." Encouraged by the fact that "lectures are taking more formal shape this year,"[39] Robson sought to have Law

Society lectures held in a university building so as to "bring us into the desirable atmosphere of higher education." Dr. MacLean himself sought the creation of a university law school and Robson told him that this would "in a small way be a start in the direction you have in mind."[40]

The opening of two new law schools in Saskatchewan in October 1913[41] provided another sort of incentive for Manitoba's Law Society to review the matter. Robson, assisted by recent Osgoode Hall graduate E.K. Williams, was authorized by the Benchers to "lay plans for the establishment ... of a permanent law school modelled after Osgoode Hall."[42] Fearful of private crammers, pressured by law students and professional leaders alike, shamed by the example of other prairie legal professions, the Law Society finally acted.

An innovative arrangement for a school of law run as a sort of joint enterprise of the university and the Law Society under the governance of a board of trustees emerged.[43] This was much as Aikins and Chevrier had recommended in their 1909 report. In June 1914, the University of Manitoba approved a "plan for legal institution."[44] The composition of the board of trustees suggested equal control and influence by the university and the Law Society, but in fact the university was careful to ensure that its appointees were acceptable to the Law Society. Winnipeg lawyer Edwin Loftus served with the Reverend Doctor G.B. Wilson as university appointees on the first board. With Robson as chair and two lawyers (I. Campbell and J.H. Munson) serving as Law Society appointees,[45] the dominance of elite lawyers was ensured. Underlining the point, the early board took the view that even the academic decisions of the school should be subject to Law Society review,[46] and the outcomes of their deliberations were routinely brought to the Law Society for approval. Moreover, the Law Society retained in full its power to make rules for admission to practice in the province.[47] Informally and behind the scenes, the influence of the Benchers was no doubt pervasive.

The law school's first classes were taught in the YMCA building on 5 October 1914. There was initially no developed pedagogy, no dean, and no teaching staff other than a "recorder," R.P. Hills, "assisted by seven practising lawyers as part-time lecturers."[48] The school offered two programs, an "academic" bachelor of laws and a practice-oriented program of qualification for solicitor's practice. Carefully structured incentives made the academic program attractive, and most students near Winnipeg in fact took both programs. The law school at first operated as a supplement to the pre-existing apprenticeship structure, courses running concurrently with articles and taught outside of normal office hours. An early curriculum explained that the course would cover "work necessary for Bachelor of Laws degree from the University or for admission as an Attorney at Law by the Law Society. It does not include the special reading for the Call to the Bar, but Call examinations will be conducted by the Law School ... Graduates in Arts must serve a period of four years as clerks and students in articles; non-graduates must serve five years. Those who complete Manitoba Law School will have this period reduced by one year."[49] Modest though it was, this was a significant turning point. One historian has observed that "[t]he seeds of didactic legal education as a basic component of training had now been firmly sown."[50]

Further development stalled during the Great War, but the law school survived. Apart from some change in personnel,[51] it entered the postwar period more or less as it had begun, as a three-year, part-time program. Radical change was to come. Despite the disruptions of war, Manitoba lawyers and the Canadian Bar Association (which Manitobans dominated) had been giving careful consideration to the reform of legal education. One indicator of pending changes was the gradual increase in admission requirements. By 1919-20, admission to the law school was restricted to those who had completed "First Year in Arts of the University of Manitoba or its equivalent,"[52] a requirement clearly signalling a conviction that lawyers should be both learned and cultured. Further changes followed with surprising speed.

Professional Education in Manitoba: The Early Vision, 1914-21

The changes that created the law school's golden age (1921-27) had been anticipated and planned from the start. Probably influenced by progressive ideas about legal education in the United States,[53] the new arrangements of the 1920s were more or less fully formed in the heads of James Aikins, H.A. Robson, and others ten or even twenty years before they were implemented. Despite the misfortune of being launched just as Canada was drawn into total war, the law school's first six years provided a crucial testing ground for new ideas about training for lawyering. Lacking both the staff and facilities one might think necessary to implement any program whatsoever, the early board of trustees nonetheless sought to create a program of legal education that would be a continental leader. They endorsed all that was considered state-of-the-art at the time: the case method, the goal of making attendance at law school the necessary and sufficient method of qualification for the legal profession, an ambition to create a full-time staff of professional law teachers, and a pedagogical vision embracing both "cultural" and "practical" legal education. From the beginning, there was a desire to raise admission standards, perhaps even to the point of requiring that all law students be university graduates.

Although everything the board of trustees sought would become established throughout common law Canada in the coming decades, these were radical ideas for their time and place.[54] Many Manitoba lawyers probably did not endorse these visions – if they thought about them at all – and there were probably differences of opinion on particulars even among the law school's lecturers and trustees. Nonetheless, the early board moved consistently in these directions.

Displacing Apprenticeship

The clearest articulation of Manitoba legal educators' ambitions is found in the writings and correspondence of H.A. Robson. In 1914, he told the board of trustees that "[t]he ultimate aim" was to establish "attendance at the Law School and passing the examinations thereof" as "the exclusive method of call to the bar or admission as a solicitor," and expressed his view that teaching should be done by professional, full-time instructors.[55] Manitoba's large geographic area and substantial rural population made it practically impossible to actually *require* attendance, but Robson proposed shortening the period of articles for those who did attend and that the lecturers should also serve as examiners for all student lawyers in the province. His intent was to do indirectly that which could not be done directly: to create a system "practically equivalent to making law school attendance compulsory."[56] Robson hoped that formal legal education would, in time, displace apprenticeship altogether.[57] He told his fellow trustees: "If we follow the pure Law School method there would be no office attendance requirement for students taking that method except in the 'Barrister's year,' and a substitute method of student enrollment would be adopted by the Law Society."[58]

Although he quickly retreated from his objective of making "University examination and degree the only means of obtaining admission as a Solicitor or Call to the Bar,"[59] Robson viewed this as only a temporary concession in the battle to drag Manitoba "out of the backward state in which it now is in respect of the important subject of legal education."[60] Frustrated by the *realpolitik* surrounding professional innovation, he felt that the "idea will ultimately come, but it is too big a step to take at once."[61]

"Scientific" Legal Education: The Case Method

In early-twentieth-century Canada, science and technocratic thought were commonly thought to provide the means to peaceful resolution of social and economic problems.[62] It should not be surprising that many thoughtful Canadian lawyers saw the creation of a "scientific" legal education as their contribution to this larger project. Fortunately, a "science" was readily available in the form of the case method of legal instruction developed by the Harvard Law School's innovative dean, Christopher Columbus Langdell.[63] Langdell's "case teaching" had come to be considered state-of-the-art. In 1914, the Carnegie Foundation for the Advancement of Teaching released an influential report endorsing the approach.[64] By that time, Langdell's method had already achieved almost complete dominance at leading US centres of legal instruction:[65] "The spirit of scientific expertise inspired the generation of law teachers who spanned the Progressive era after the turn of the century."[66] "Scientific," "practical," somewhat Darwinian, the case method resonated well with the dominant cultural ethos of early-twentieth-century North America.[67] It also reflected and reinforced the political status quo.[68]

In the introduction to his groundbreaking 1891 *Cases on Contracts*, Langdell explained that the science of law consisted of principles found in the decided cases:

> To have such a mastery of these as to be able to apply them with constant facility and certainty to the ever-tangled skein of human affairs, is what constitutes a true lawyer; and hence to acquire that mastery should be the business of every earnest student of law ... [M]uch the shortest and best, if not the only way of mastering the doctrine effectively is by studying the cases in which it is embodied ... It seems to me, therefore, to be possible to take such a branch of the law as Contracts, for example, and without exceeding comparatively moderate limits, to select, classify, and arrange all the cases which had contributed in any important degree to the growth, development, or establishment of any of its essential doctrines; and that such a work could not fail to be of material service to all who desire to study that branch of law systematically and in its original sources.[69]

Law was a science, the library its laboratory, case analysis its method.

In practice, the study of appellate decisions "became entangled with the question-and-answer technique, similar in purpose and form to the traditional law school 'quiz.'"[70] The method sought to displace podium-down lectures delivered to passive student note takers. Instead, instructor-interrogators would pepper students with questions, leading or bullying them to discover fundamental principles of law for themselves. It aimed not to convey information but to teach students to teach themselves, to "think like lawyers." "The law teacher's task," Kyer and Bickenbach argue, "was changed from that of setting out the principles and practices of the law to the considerably more challenging one of selecting and presenting cases that embodied or exemplified legal principles and, through a process of careful questioning, drawing out these principles from the responses of his students."[71] This task was enthusiastically taken up by a new breed of full-time American law teachers who "happily made the change from treatise-reading clerk to flamboyant actor in a drama."[72]

The outstanding early Canadian master of the method was the University of Saskatchewan's Thaddeaus Hébert. He assigned

> specific cases from the law reports for students to read and study with care. They had to be prepared to state in class the essential facts of a case, the precise decision made by the judges on the facts, and the legal reasoning given for the decision. The student (or perhaps I should say the victim) who reported on a particular case was then questioned by the instructor and by such of his fellow students as found some defect in his report. Did he think the decision right or wrong by law? Why? What facts had been decisive in the opinion of the judges? How did he distinguish this decision from that in other cases on similar facts where the decision had been different?
>
> Then, if the distinction could not be made clearly other, often suppositious, cases would be put to the student – or to the class as a whole. What was the right answer in these cases? Could he reconcile his views on these hypothetical cases with the judgment in the principle [*sic*] case as he had reported it? If there were strong differences of view within the class as a whole, there might be a torrent of suppositious cases to be analysed.
>
> The immediate purpose was to shake the student in the view he had adopted, entice him into adopting indefensible positions, and trap him into contradicting himself. Any other student who had expressed firm views would be given the same treatment. It was a great victory to get most of the class confused. The longer-run purpose, of course, was to rouse the student's critical faculties, sharpen his mind, compel him to think clearly and consistently, and make him wary of pitfalls. In short, the objective was to make him think, as a lawyer must, about all sides of the facts and to anticipate opposing legal arguments which would almost certainly be raised in a courtroom.[73]

Advocates of the Socratic method considered it to be a significant advance over the formal lecture method "inherited from English universities." The latter approach to teaching, developed in a period before books were readily available, offered the advantage of clarity of exposition. It tended, however, "to degenerate into dictation of notes by the lecturer, written down at breakneck speed by the students," as C.R. Smith noted in 1935. Even at its best, "the formal lecture ... does very little to develop the power of analysis and gives little practice in expression and argument."[74] It was not always at its best: Cecil Wright said that his student experience at Osgoode Hall involved entirely uninspired lectures, dogmatic presentation, furious note taking, and the assignment of a solitary textbook, slavishly followed by students and lecturer alike.[75] The Socratic method should not be confused with other teaching styles that attempt to draw students into discussion:[76] there is a world of difference between the sort of education students experienced at Hébert's hands and less combative classroom discussions. Few students exposed to "discussional" teaching think of themselves as victims. Non-Socratic teachers do not relish leaving a class confused, nor do they seek to generate "perplexity, frustration, and anger."[77]

Willis has observed that "the case method is something more" than discussional teaching "and more rigorous and more demanding both of teacher and of student."[78] Because of the peculiar demands it imposed, the case method became associated both with the view that legal education should take place within a university setting (the appropriate place for study of a science rather than a craft) and with an emphasis on the need for a full-time teaching staff, who alone would be able to take on the rigorous preparation that such teaching required.[79]

It is not surprising that the case method became the focus of pedagogical innovation in Manitoba. Dalhousie,[80] Saskatchewan,[81] and Osgoode Hall Law School[82] each claim the first Canadian adoption of the case method. The Manitoba Law School made the approach integral to its mission at least five years earlier, however. As early as 1914, Manitoba legal educators invested considerable effort in developing teaching materials and a curriculum that would Canadianize this leading-edge teaching strategy imported from south of the border. None of them had experienced the approach first-hand and it may be that their efforts to emulate it were imperfect. Nonetheless, the earliest Manitoba Law School curriculum demonstrates their commitment and enthusiasm.

Two commercially published casebooks developed by Manitoba law teachers appeared in 1916. Both were compiled jointly by H.A. Robson and J.B. Hugg. Unfortunately, the editors were parsimonious with introductory or prefatory material and the volumes consequently lack any clear statement of educational philosophy. The preface to *Leading Cases on Public Corporations* explains simply that the "collection of cases" in the area of municipal law brought together numerous "judicial discussions of important topics." The editors provide little insight into the principles of selection that motivated them, promising only that the book offered an "interesting ... opportunity" to examine "side by side the considered work of the representative English and Canadian Judges." Despite the volume's title, the editors declared their intent to present cases of educational value rather than leading status as such: "Clear expositions of principles have been sought for rather than cases in which the principles have been first laid down."[83]

The preface to *Cases on Company Law* explained only that "[t]he desirability of placing actual cases on Company Law before law students was the motive for this collection."[84] No doubt this points in part to a desire to provide students with miniature portable law libraries at a time when access to extensive legal materials could be difficult.[85] This was only part of their motivation, however. Robson and Hugg provided a somewhat fuller explanation of their jurisprudential assumptions in that volume's introduction. Despite variations in the statutory schemes governing companies from one place to another, the editors included cases from several jurisdictions. They justified this approach on the grounds that each statutory scheme was undergirded by "the same solid body of general principles as expressed in a thoroughly matured jurisprudence." As in "many other branches of our law," they thought "[t]he differences in the organic provisions and in the details of regulation" were "easy to grasp."[86]

The introduction concluded with a testimonial to the superiority of a legal education focused on reading judicial decisions over one organized around assigned textbooks. The editors explained that, although the cases were arranged under headings and subheadings, "a perusal of the selected judgments will expose a view broader in comprehension than would be indicated merely by the topic under which the case is usually cited. The disquisitions of learned Judges are more illuminating than a text writer's epitomes." The excerpted cases were said to "faithfully state the principle and indicate its origin, that is to say, the leading case ... the student by means of the cases used will get the leading cases. It is not merely the selected cases that he is to learn, but the cases referred to in them, and which form their foundation."[87]

Turning from the expressed philosophy (such as it is) to substance of these volumes, it is notable that the table of contents for *Leading Cases on Public Corporations* has only one substantive heading, and that – "Leading Cases" – is not very helpful. The editors expended little effort in creative taxonomy and, as the following excerpt illustrates, the cases are unadorned, explained only by a brief parenthetical note indicating the principle of law addressed.

Atty.-Gen v. London County Council.
(Powers of Statutory Corporations) 1
Ashbury v. Riche.
(Doctrine of Ultra Vires Explained) 6
Westminster v. London & N. W. Ry.
(Bad Faith in Exercise of Statutory Powers) 8
Bell Telephone Co. v. Owen Sound.
(Bad Faith in Refusing Permission to Telephone
Company to use Streets) 11

Only one case is presented in support of each principle and the excerpts are brief. Much of what later came to be thought of as part and parcel of the case method is missing. There is, for example, no critical engagement of point and counterpoint, no preference for the difficult, confusing, or brilliantly misleading judicial analysis. There are no excerpts from secondary literature, no editorial notes, comments, critiques, or recommended further readings. The volume makes no attempt to encourage policy critique by exposing students to divergent streams of judicial opinion. The only user's guide is a lengthy Table of Cases indexing cases cited in the volume ("Leading Cases" are italicized).

Cases on Company Law appeared several months later. It is similar in form though somewhat more developed in arrangement. Cases are classified by subject and the volume is divided into twenty-five chapters, most of which reproduce portions of several cases. Chapter 2 is divided into two parts:

An editors' note in the volume (a single paragraph) provides further references on the "Effect of Local Laws upon International Comity" in relation to recognition of foreign corporations. Although more sophisticated than its sister volume, *Cases on Company Law* remains a rudimentary first effort. From our post-realist vantage point, it is easy to dismiss the work as a failure, the smallest possible deviation from the black letter tradition, amounting at best to a crude and oversimplified digest. The editors, had they wished, might as easily have written a "nutshell" pamphlet of ten or twenty pages listing a series of propositions, each supported by citation of a single case.

These books have been overlooked by historians of legal education. From one point of view, the oversight may be insignificant. The volumes might simply fail to qualify either as casebooks properly understood or as a significant contribution to Canadian legal education. Kyer and Bickenbach's brilliant assessment of Toronto legal education, for example, defines "a Langdellian casebook" as a volume "intended to be not merely a compendium of current decisions, but a tool for leading students through a line of legal argument." In such a volume, "cases are selected more as examples of legal reasoning than as 'leading cases' setting out current law."[88] Their disqualification of two other early volumes seems to establish standards by which Robson and Hugg's efforts also fail. Cockle's *Cases on Evidence* does not qualify, they say, because "selected cases, heavily edited, were set out with the aim of presenting the 'textbook' rules."[89] A.H.F. Lefroy's *Leading Cases in Canadian Constitutional Law*[90] is similarly dismissed as too English, too black letter, mechanically reproducing cases reflecting current law. Lefroy, "instead of offering for discussion cases that might not state current law, but were there to show the evolution of leading principles ... collected cases that stated the law applicable at the date of publication."[91] Robson and Hugg's work is clearly closer to Lefroy's effort than to the idealized Langdellian casebook that Kyer and Bickenbach prefer.

We need to be careful, however, not to overlook one historical achievement on the grounds that it is not identical to another. In the history of legal thought and legal education, it is important not to conflate either cultural legal education or the case method with the forms of American legal realism and rule skepticism that subsequently affected Canadian academic law teaching. At a minimum, the two Manitoba volumes demonstrate a conviction that law is to be found in the decisions of the courts and that a study of the primary sources of law provided the best possible education in both substantive legal knowledge *and* in habits of legal thought. The editors clearly thought their work marked a significant departure from the more traditional study of "text writer's epitomes." They certainly had good reason to think that their materials contributed to establishing a new method of legal education in Canada. The significance of a new Canadian approach to legal education premised on the notions that "[t]he common law was a set of internally consistent and coherent general rules, which expressed important moral and social standards, but which were autonomous or independent from their immediate context"[92] should not be overlooked merely because it is the opposite of later approaches.

Moreover, Robson had frequently expressed his desire to push Manitoba into compliance with the "modern ideas of law teaching" of US university law schools.[93] The two co-editors would have endorsed J.T. Hébert's classic argument that the case method provided an altogether superior training in legal reasoning: "it makes him study the opinions of the great lawyers of the past, and it compels him to reach his own conclusions on the same or similar legal problems. It teaches him the law as it is, in a manner which, interesting if not easy, indelibly fixes it in his mind, and gives him a just appreciation of its application to the specific questions which are going to come before him as a practising lawyer, and where the law is uncertain or unsatisfactory, it offers him the opportunity and the means to find out what it ought to be."[94] Manitoba's earliest casebooks exposed students to "the opinions of great lawyers," forcing them to seek out principles for themselves in order to discern the "law as it is" *and* to absorb the method by which uncertainty can be approached. Near in both space and time to Hébert, it is reasonable to infer that Robson and Hugg inhabited a similar discursive universe and shared something of his educational vision. All told, these books marked a significant departure from past practice. Given the leadership – indeed, dominance – of Manitoba lawyers in the work of the early Canadian Bar Association, this prairie experiment provides something of a benchmark in the history of Canadian legal education.[95]

Commitment to the case method at the early Manitoba Law School is also manifest in other ways. In 1914, the board of trustees had established a committee (Robson and Hugg) to consider the utility of the "case system,"[96] and Robson wrote to prominent Winnipeg lawyer Isaac Pitblado early in 1915 indicating that his draft curriculum incorporated "a number of 'Case Books.'" This, he said, was to be "a growing feature but I think we are going as far as possible just now in that direction."[97] One early draft curriculum emphasized an intended reliance on teaching through the cases:

> *First Year.*
> Contracts: Caporn's *Leading Cases on Contracts*
> English Constitutional Law and History: *Thomas Leading Cases*
>
> *Second Year.*
> Evidence: *Cockles' Leading Cases*
> Canadian Constitutional Law: *Lefroy's Leading Cases*
>
> *Third Year.*
> Equity: *Randall's Leading Cases*
> Torts: *Radcliffe and Miles Cases illustrating the Law of Torts*
>
> *Fourth Year (barrister's examinations).*
> International Law: *Bentwick Leading Cases and Statutes*[98]

Ultimately, the curriculum adopted for the 1914-15 academic year was more conventional than this suggested.[99] The case method was in the air, however, and certainly would have been implemented to some extent in the teaching of Robson, Hugg, and other members of the early faculty (another Manitoba law teacher of the same period, R.F. McWilliams, edited the second edition of Lefroy's *Leading Cases in Canadian Constitutional Law*).[100] In addition to assigning treatises and casebooks, the school also produced pamphlets listing cases that were recommended reading in various courses.

Speeches delivered at the opening ceremonies for the new school also underlined its founders' intentions. The ubiquitous James Aikins (by now founding president of the Canadian Bar Association) delivered an inaugural address emphasizing the expectation that the case method would make students "enthusiastic lawyers, interested and absorbed in their profession":[101]

> It is not the purpose of the school simply to instruct in text books, but rather in cases which decide principles and which system has to some extent changed the teaching of law in some parts of Canada and in the United States, and is being adopted in England ... There is an advantage in teaching case law for when once the student has vividly before him a concrete instance he will remember the principle decided much more readily than by reading the principle alone. The tendency will be for the students to examine with greater accuracy any question submitted, having studied decided cases, than they will from simply reading a text book which states only general principles.
>
> In the study of case law, the student is really teaching himself and will become more thoroughly conversant with the law in that way than if he was simply a docile listener to a dry lecture. The purpose of this school is to make the students know the law not superficially, but to take them to the very fundamentals of what they seek to know, and thus create in them an inextinguishable desire to become perfect as students, ambitious to know thoroughly the law.[102]

For Aikins the case method was central to the law school's educational mission. It would make its students superior lawyers, more competent advisers, more learned professionals and – importantly – better men.

Unfortunately, little evidence survives to tell us how the case method was embodied in its teachers, lived by its students. We cannot know precisely in what form the method flourished in the early Manitoba Law School, nor even whether its teachers were competent in Socratic instruction. Such matters will, unfortunately, remain mysteries unless student notebooks, teachers' lecture notes, diaries, or reminiscences speaking to these matters turn up.

"Scientific" Legal Education: Curriculum

More evidence is available with respect to another educational innovation of the early Manitoba Law School. This was the attempt to create an education that would simultaneously provide "guild training" in law practice and the "professional education"[103] required of a new breed of cultured gentleman lawyers.[104] The school's curriculum from 1914 to 1920 incorporated relatively heavy doses of cultural education.

In order to appreciate the significance of these developments, it must be remembered that "the really distinctive characteristic" of Dalhousie's celebrated law school (founded three decades earlier) had been its focus on the "'cultural" or "public law" subjects of Constitutional History, International Law, and Conflict of Laws. Courses such as these were lacking at Harvard, for example, where legal education was limited "to subjects which would be of immediate use to the hard-shell practitioner."[105] These were still controversial components of professional education when Manitoba's law school was launched. Well into the twentieth century, such offerings stood beyond the pale of practitioners' training. When W.P.M. Kennedy founded an academic program in law at the University of Toronto in 1926, its commitment to "law as a science" and distancing from practical training was marked out by a singularly unpractical curriculum "focused on Roman law, the history of English law, English and Canadian constitutional law, jurisprudence, international law, and – rare in Canada – Canadian administrative and municipal law." Such courses "were viewed by lawyers as being of limited practical importance, and indeed as having little to do with the law."[106] Kennedy's program brought its students no qualification that Ontario's Law Society would recognize. This unlawyerly "scientific" legal education of the 1920s, however, reproduced to a large extent courses that Manitoba lawyers had been forced to study *as part of qualification for practice* throughout the previous decade.

The following list excludes readings required for the barrister's examinations, which were set by the Law Society and not part of the Law School curriculum as such. It includes courses that were part of the basic professional curriculum as well as those required of students taking the LL.B. degree. The imposition of a cultural curriculum on non-degree students speaks powerfully to the educational vision of Manitoba's early legal educators.[107] The Manitoba Law Society's embrace of the "intellectual" or "cultural" agenda was remarkable.

Constitutional History of Canada with special reference to BNA Act (Bourinot's Manual) [first year, 1914-15]
Canadian Constitutional Law [second year, 1915-16, 1916-17, 1917-18, 1918-19]
Canadian Constitutional Law and History [second year, 1919-20]
English Constitution Law and History [first year, 1915-16]
History of English Law [third year, 1915-16, 1916-17, 1917-18, 1918-19, 1919-20, 1920-21]
Roman Law [second year, 1915-16, 1916-17, 1917-18, 1918-19, 1919-20, 1920-21]
Jurisprudence [first year, 1918-19, 1919-20, 1920-21]
International Law [third year, 1915-16, 1916-17, 1917-18, 1918-19, 1919-20, 1920-21]

Dicey's Conflict of Laws [second year, 1914-15]
Municipal Law [third year, 1915-16, 1916-17, 1917-18, 1918-19, 1919-20, 1920-21]

One reason why the Manitoba Law School went so far so fast may simply have been the practical necessity of justifying itself to the university. The curriculum was jointly negotiated and involved nominally distinct programs for professional qualification and the LL.B. degree. Furthermore, university president Dr. J.A. MacLean, a classicist by training,[108] took an early active interest in the business of the law school and opposed the development of a narrowly practical curriculum.[109] The Law Society of Upper Canada's proprietary law school at Osgoode Hall, by comparison, suffered no such constraint.

One must be careful, however, of making too much of institutional structures. The structures in Manitoba were not imposed on a reluctant Law Society by politicians or university administrators. They had been actively sought out by leading legal practitioners. Influential working lawyers subscribed to a vision of professional education every bit as "intellectual" or "cultural" or "scholarly" as that of any academic of the period. There is no evidence of conflict in Manitoba between the profession and legal educators even remotely similar to that which characterized the story of legal education in twentieth-century Ontario. On the contrary, Manitoba's leading lawyers believed that changing legal education from a merely mechanical to a scholarly undertaking would transform the profession for the good, making it useful to the state and preserving Canada from the centrifugal forces that threatened it.[110]

Manitoba's Golden Age, 1921-27

Manitoba's law school consolidated its past achievements and advanced rapidly during a brief golden age, quickly responding to recommendations of the Canadian Bar Association's Committee on Legal Education.[111] The system of concurrent articles was virtually abolished in 1921 and replaced with an arrangement whereby "students were required to serve only one year in law offices; simultaneously with the Law School program in the case of university graduates, and after completion of the program in the case of nongraduates."[112] In a bold move unequivocally establishing the full-time character of the new program, teaching hours were extended "throughout the business day" daily except for Saturday and holidays.[113] Manitoba also became the first Canadian law school to adopt the new model curriculum of the Canadian Bar Association[114] (see table below) and to increase entrance requirements to "second year Arts standing commencing in the 1921-1922 session."[115]

Comparison of Manitoba Law School curriculum, 1922-23, and Canadian Bar Association, "Standard Curriculum," 1920[116]

Manitoba Law School	"Standard Curriculum"
First Year	
Contracts	Contracts
Torts	Torts
Real Property	Property (Real and Personal) 1
Personal Property	
English Constitutional Law and History	Constitutional History
Criminal Law	Criminal Law
Civil Procedure	Practice and Procedure (Civil and Criminal) Elementary
Criminal Procedure	
History of English Law	History of English Law
Roman Law	Jurisprudence*
Second Year	
Equity	Equity 1
Wills	Wills and Administration
Evidence	Evidence 1
Sale of Goods	Sale of Goods
Bills and Notes	Bills and Notes
Agency	Agency
Corporations	Corporations and Partnership
Partnerships	Insurance
	Practice and Procedure (including instructions as to the use of law reports, digests, and textbooks)
Real Property	Property (Real and Personal) 2
Personal Property	
Landlord and Tenant Law	Landlord and Tenant
Ancient Law	
Third Year	
Constitutional Law and History (Canadian)	Constitutional Law
Equity – Trusts and Trustees	Equity 2
	Evidence
Practice and Procedure (Civil and Criminal)	Practice and Procedure (including criminal procedure)
Conflict of Laws	Conflict of Laws
Mortgages	Mortgages
Suretyship	Suretyship
Practical Statutes	Practical Statutes

Manitoba Law School	"Standard Curriculum"
Rules of Interpretation and Drafting	Shipping and/or Railway Law
Domestic Relations	Domestic Relations
Public International Law	Public International Law†
Jurisprudence	Jurisprudence†‡
Legal Ethics	Legal Ethics†

* if not taken in the third year
† recommended if in accordance with the needs of the province or school
‡ if not taken in the first year

Manitoba's curriculum was more cultural than either Dalhousie's or the CBA's model. Advances were quick in other respects, too. J.T. Thorson,[117] a graduate of Manitoba College, Rhodes Scholar, and Manitoba lawyer, was appointed the faculty's first dean in May 1921. Two further full-time law professors were hired (H.W.H. Knott and Frederick Read) in 1922, bringing the school's staff up to the level attained by Dalhousie Law School at the beginning of its own golden age[118] – and well surpassing the Law Society of Upper Canada's single full-time instructor at Osgoode Hall.[119] When Knott was sacked by the board of trustees in 1925, he was replaced by the formidable C. Rhodes Smith.

Anyone familiar with Canadian scholarship on the history of legal education will be puzzled by how it came about that Manitoba's profession-dominated school went further in scholarly directions than even the Canadian Bar Association Committee on Legal Education had recommended. This question reverses the order of things, however. Historians have not generally realized that the most influential and creative force propelling cultural legal education *for the profession* in this period was in fact Manitoba's working profession. Both the Canadian Bar Association and its Committee on Legal Education were very largely Manitoba creations: Sir James Aikins was founding father, *éminence grise,* and president of the Canadian Bar Association; H.A. Robson headed the first CBA Committee on Legal Education, laying the foundation on which the 1918 Lee committee report was built.[120] The related committee on legal ethics was chaired by Manitoba's Chief Justice Mathers.[121] When the education subcommittee ultimately recommended a curriculum similar to that of Dalhousie, Isaac Pitblado, a powerful Manitoba lawyer, spoke in its defence at the association's annual meeting.[122] Pitblado spoke with both authority and commitment: then in his seventeenth year as a Bencher, third year as president of the Law Society, *and* chair of the University of Manitoba's first board of governors, he had consistently worked for the establishment of a Manitoba Law School.[123]

Both the active involvement of Manitobans in the development of the Lee report and their immediate embrace of its program are clear. R.W. Lee, fortunately, was an articulate spokesperson for the arrangement who left a more substantial written record of his assumptions than his practitioner or judicial allies. It was, he thought, absurd to confine legal education to cramming students' heads with rules or, more narrowly still, teaching students how to practise law. These were not the purposes of the classroom. He considered the project of legal education to be primarily about developing and imparting a science of law for the good of the larger political community.[124] In endorsing a wide vision of the purposes and functions of legal education, Lee's committee tapped a deep cultural current among elite Canadian lawyers,[125] one that had professional antecedents both in mid-nineteenth-century England[126] and in early Ontario (Upper Canada). Distinct continuities of thought link the proposals of Aikins, Lee, Robson, and others with Toronto's Archdeacon John Strachan's oft-cited observations of 1826:

> Lawyers must, from the very nature of our political institutions – from there being no great landed proprietors – no privileged orders – become the most powerful profession and must in time possess more influence and authority than any other ... [they should] acquire similar views and modes of thinking, and be taught by precept and example to love and venerate our parent state. It is surely of great consequence that a class of intelligent men belonging to a profession which offers the highest inducements of reputation, wealth, influence, and authority, should be actuated by sentiments and feelings of attachment to the British Empire.[127]

Not surprisingly, the newly structured law school quickly gained a reputation for excellence. It was hailed as a model for the rest of Canada by the chair of the Canadian Bar Association's Committee on Legal Education in 1923,[128] and, in both 1926 and 1927, was found by the Carnegie Foundation to be the best law school in Canada.[129]

Decline, 1927-31

The glory was short-lived, however. Dean Thorson was elected to Parliament, departing to take his seat in the House of Commons in September 1926.[130] H.A. Robson (assisted by Edwin Loftus) assumed duties as acting dean without pay and on a part-time basis. Although it was probably not immediately apparent, momentous change was around the corner. No full-time dean was again appointed for over a decade. Within two months of Thorson's departure, the board of trustees approved a resolution requiring students to serve a full year in actual service under articles in the case of graduates, or a full two years for nongraduates.[131] The resolution never took effect, however, for it was supplanted by another that effectively sounded the death knell for academic legal education. Dale and Lee Gibson have reported a "decision in 1927 to lengthen the Law School course to four years, and to re-institute concurrent articling in the third and fourth years."[132] Under the new rules, all students were required to provide service in a law office during the last two years of their law school course. An additional year of apprenticeship was required of students who held no prior university degree.[133] Surprisingly, Robson, who had struggled so long and effectively to create full-time academic legal education, presided over its demise. It has been suggested that there may have been a perception that the full-time program was "too theoretical in nature,"[134] but it is unclear what precisely this denotes.

Demise of Professional Education, 1931

In July 1929, E.H. Coleman assumed duties as dean under a part-time arrangement that left him free to practise law in the afternoons.[135] Although he had been secretary to James Aikins in an unusually close and sustained relationship,[136] Coleman apparently shared little of his mentor's vision for the legal profession or legal education. Trained exclusively within Manitoba and uncontaminated by exposure to the leading educational institutions of the world, Coleman's tenure saw the last vestiges of a full-time program abolished. In 1931, the Benchers established a requirement that "all students should serve under articles for the entire four year period (5 years in the case of non-graduates) except for the time they were actually required to be in the classroom."[137]

In barely a decade, the school had come full circle. Its most daring innovations expunged entirely by 1931, the Manitoba Law School turned decisively away from full-time legal education for the next three decades. It was only in 1965, then well behind the rest of Canada, that Manitoba again launched full-time university legal education.[138]

It is curious that a small province with a tiny legal elite should have witnessed such rapid and contradictory changes in so short a period. What cultural symbolism these changes may have carried for the key players is unclear. The Canadian Bar Association Committee on Legal Education explained:

> In Manitoba a modification of the concurrent system was tried whereby the student was required to serve in an office only during the last two years of

his four years' course – the course there having been extended from three to four years. But this system proved unsatisfactory, apparently because the student was not required to be articled before being admitted to the Law School. The result was that many students found, at the end of their first two years in the Law School, that they could not get into offices, and so were blocked in the midst of their course. To remedy this situation, Manitoba reverted to the old system.[139]

Two decades later, E.K. Williams explained:

We found that the students who passed through the school during the 1921-1931 period almost without exception felt that they had lost something by not having had any office training during their academic years. Although they had passed all the examinations entitling them to be called and admitted, they realized that they were not yet ready to practise law. They found, too, that the members of the profession generally preferred students who combined their academic work with practical experience in an office. There was, too, a very practical matter that entered into their consideration, and that was the salary they could earn as law students in an office.[140]

Jack London has asserted that "one of the inarticulate premises of the opposition of the lawyers to a full-time study programme might have been the deprivation of low-paid legal assistants for the practising law offices of the period."[141]

Both Williams's account and London's explanation seem to offer partial explanation at best. Disentangling the various threads of principle, interest, ideology, and bluster surrounding legal education is a virtually hopeless task, as anyone who has ever been near a law faculty knows. The explanation for the decline and fall of the Manitoba Law School is likely to be found in some combination of economic viability, the practical demands of students and lawyers, and competing visions of what it meant to be a lawyer. The mental image one holds of the "good lawyer" profoundly affects the forms of legal education deemed necessary, the limits of acceptable compromise, and how excellence itself is defined and understood. The ascendancy of a vision that portrayed lawyering as a noble public calling was marked by the creation of the Canadian Bar Association and its initial flurry of activity. The notion that the legal profession had important obligations to community and state motivated professional reformers of this period. Their vision took institutional form in Thorson's School of Law. How far it was absorbed by the profession at large is another question.

A counter-vision was persistent. Its more workaday view saw law as a business, legal work as enterprise, lawyer as white-collar worker, and law student as drudge. It is difficult to discern where virtue lies or which of the alternative professional visions is more clearly antisocial in its tendency. The broad tradition encompassing Strachan, Aikins, and the Arthurs Committee[142] has emphasized learning, scholarship, and the need for socially located understandings of the legal profession and its duties. Opponents of such visions have often seemed inarticulate, short-sighted, unthinking – sometimes incapable of thought. Paradoxically, however, the better-articulated professional visions have often worked to create class, gender, and racial or ethnic barriers to admission to the legal profession.[143] "Liberal advocacy" and all its contributions to democracy and human freedom[144] have often emerged from lawyers whose practices lay outside the pale of "respectable" professionalism. In short, the intellectual ambition, public spiritedness, and integrity of the Aikins tradition seem admirable, but its social exclusivity, narrow definition of the public good, and elitism are not endearing features.

The question remains: why did Manitoba lawyers allow their state-of-the-art law school to die? Thorson's resignation from the deanship and James Aikins's death were undoubtedly significant. The more interesting question is not so much about force of personality but how and why the vision of powerful and influential professional reformers failed to take root within the leadership of the profession at large. Surviving accounts suggest only four possible reasons. These relate to cost, the public interest, lawyers' interests, and law students' interests. A fifth possible reason relates to the cultural project itself.

The possibility that the cost of providing a quality legal education was simply too great for the Law Society to bear should be taken seriously. Law Society finances in this period have not been studied and the direct effect of financial considerations on legal education remains a matter of speculation. It is distinctly possible that Manitoba simply could not afford state-of-the-art legal education during the Depression years.[145] There are, however, two reasons for thinking that other considerations were in play. Most directly, this is not the reason cited by those few Manitoba lawyers of the era who explained or commented upon the decision to downgrade their law school.

Second, even in difficult financial times, available funds are allocated according to the decision maker's priorities. Except in the most extreme circumstances – apparently not the situation of the Manitoba Law Society at the time[146] – an economic rationale can provide only partial explanation for cultural and institutional changes. Everything about how one perceives or understands legal education is coloured by personal inclinations with respect to the two very different visions of lawyering. In the midst of the Great

Depression, for example, members of the Canadian Bar Association Committee on Legal Education were surveyed on the question "In your opinion wherein does the lawyer, when admitted, fall short?" One member responded that "times have so altered that the lawyer must lay less stress on the purely academical and become a practical everyday business adviser of his client." Another responded in a quite different vein: "I must say that what I think it lacks most is scholarly interest in law. The lawyer seems to me to acquire quickly enough the technical tricks of his trade, and a knowledge of those business methods which are really tending to destroy the liberal character of the profession. Law is far too much regarded by law students as an avenue to eminence in big business. Where I think our legal education breaks down worst is in its failure to inculcate a love of law and the lawyer's work as a liberal mode of life." The intellectual and professional commitments of these two unidentified gentlemen are clearly worlds apart.[147] Their perceptions, offered in the same period of social, economic, and political disruption, serve as a useful reminder that economic constraint rarely dictates educational policy: choices remain to be made and budget concerns are articulated against a backdrop of cultural assumptions and values.

E.K. Williams's assertion, quoted above, that law school graduates who had not served law office apprenticeships "were not yet ready to practise law" speaks to a public interest. Exactly what he meant by this is unclear. It certainly seems likely that graduates of the full-time program would have known little about law office procedures, solicitor's form filling, or the procedural niceties of a barrister's practice. Even a very good graduate might have had little or none of the local "recipe knowledge" that makes effective legal work possible.[148] Defects such as these might have been met (as they generally are now) by a relatively brief stint of supervised work in a law office. Law school graduates seeking their first professional employment, however, found themselves in competition with less educated but nonetheless fully qualified new lawyers who had accumulated as much as five years of law office experience: the law school of the 1920s had never entirely displaced qualification by apprenticeship.

In such circumstances, it is possible that the market may have spoken rather directly. Understandably, lawyers who employed newly qualified lawyers were more concerned with their own incomes than any public interest attached to mentoring a degreed profession. The market does not typically reward time invested in mentoring – at least not when there is an available pool of lowly paid workers who, though not "learned gentlemen," are familiar with the mechanical side of law office work and immediately able to generate profit. The public interest in having lawyers who could actually do law jobs overlapped with the private interest of established lawyers. London's point that apprenticeship provided established lawyers with a pool of useful, inexpensive labour is certainly valid and need not be cynically understood. Sir George Stephen observed of the English profession in 1846 that, by performing repeated mundane tasks, articled clerks "pick up a great deal of practical knowledge, more especially a great deal of familiarity with the peculiar business and papers of the clients of their employer; ... and they become of extreme value to him." They were kept by their employers "upon a very moderate salary," Stephen said, "probably with a view to ultimately making them partners, to take off the burthen of his business."[149] In short, the business and personal reasons why established lawyers would approve of the apprenticeship system are simple: the system worked to their personal pecuniary advantage. Only the wealthiest lawyers and the most saintly would not feel its attraction.

The law students' interests in matters of professional education are reasonably clear, too. The intangible though not inconsiderable benefit of "gentlemanly education" lay in the conferral of status on those who did not inherit it. For most people most of the time, however, the pursuit of status was secondary to the search for food, shelter, and material comfort. Some law students voted with their feet, preferring office work, a modest salary, and the development of personal connections to three years out of the job market in pursuit of a degree. Students in Manitoba, as elsewhere, sought out systematic legal education, regularity of instruction, and predictability in examination. An ambitious full-time program of cultural legal education might be nice but was unnecessary in relation to their most basic needs.[150]

A cultural education of the sort Aikins, Robson, Lee, and Thorson sought to establish was clearly propelled by a transformative vision of professionalism subscribed to by an elite fraction of the early-twentieth-century Canadian legal professions. Aimed explicitly at securing Anglo ascendancy and at inculcating values of Britishness in lawyers regardless of their ethnic background, it was patently elitist. It is not clear, however, that opposition to structured legal education necessarily arose from any levelling instinct. Whereas apprenticeship systems of professional qualification can sustain illegitimate hierarchy by hiding its operation in the private sphere, the university's meritocratic warrants hold forth the promise of opening professions to talented individuals from even the most discriminated-against groups. Articling certainly can serve as "a kind of social screening device; undesirables – women, racial minorities, and Jews – knew that they would have to struggle to find and keep suitable articling employment."[151] It is possible that Manitoba's cutting-edge law school caused offence to some precisely because it provided a route to upward social mobility and legal influence for "undesirables" in Canada's most multiethnic, polyglot province. More research would be needed on the composition of the legal profession and professional reactions to it before reaching a firm conclusion on these matters.

Conclusion

The failure of Manitoba's bold experiment in legal education was certainly noticed and talked about by lawyers in other provinces. Word that full-time academic education in law was undesirable spread, communicated privately, by word of mouth. Professional culture was (and is) formed less in formal correspondence and earnest publication than in conversation at bars and cafes, gentlemen's clubs, bar association dinners, golf games, and railway cars.[152] What lawyers told each other in such moments is shielded from the prying gaze of the historian. We can to some extent infer what they chatted about from two traces left behind.

When the Ontario Law Society's Special Committee on legal education reported to Convocation in early 1935, it followed Manitoba's most recent lead, recommending lower admission standards, placing emphasis on law office training, and criticizing the case method.[153] A decade later, when the University of British Columbia's Faculty of Law was being created, Canada's westernmost province also felt the ripple effects of Manitoba's earlier battles. The memory of Manitoba's experience haunted the new initiative and apparently caused some influential lawyers to resist it. C.H. Locke, treasurer (*i.e.*, president) of the Law Society of British Columbia, told Dean George Curtis in 1945 that he had opposed the creation of university legal education because he had "been through all this in Manitoba" and was aware of "the controversy there."[154]

The Manitoba Law School's moment of glory was not unimportant in its day and not without consequence elsewhere. The story is worthy of study for its own sake. It also stands as a reminder that historical significance cannot be geographically ascribed or "read back" from the present. Metropolitan legal history is partial legal history.[155] Failed institutions can tell us as much about cultural evolution as accounts of institutional survivors. The curious question is perhaps not why the Manitoba Law School "failed." The greater mystery, rather, relates to why and how the sort of university law faculty we now take for granted could ever have become successfully established as the exclusive route to professional qualification in common law Canada. Although the outline history of events leading to this result is reasonably well known,[156] the shifting cultural terrain that made possible so remarkable a transformation only three decades after Manitoba's failed experiment has yet to be fully explored.

The hope remains, as Dick Risk observed, that the study of our legal past will "give understanding and perspective"[157] as we confront the future. Many puzzles remain to be solved in pursuit of that mission. Canada's peripheral places need to be part of the mix.

Notes

An earlier version of this chapter originally appeared as "'The Disquisitions of Learned Judges': Making Manitoba Lawyers, 1885-1931" in Jim Phillips and G. Blaine Baker, eds., *Essays in the History of Canadian Law: In Honour of R.C.B. Risk* (Toronto: Osgoode Society for Canadian Legal History, 1999) 825. It has been revised and reprinted here with permission.

1 Sir J. Aikins, "Formal Opening of the Manitoba Law School. Inaugural Address to the Students by Sir James Aikins, K.C., M.P." *Canadian Law Times* 34 (1914) 1183 at 1189.

2 D. Gibson and L. Gibson, *Substantial Justice: Law and Lawyers in Manitoba, 1670-1970* (Winnipeg: Peguis Publishers 1972) at 302.

3 This diversity of opinion as to the purposes and functions of a legal education has a long lineage and was reflected in debates in mid-nineteenth-century England, which, like early-twentieth-century Manitoba, also produced an innovative educational program that failed. See Chapter 4 in this volume and works cited therein.

4 Manitoba lawyers at this time were well attuned to the different histories and functions of solicitors and barristers, and the use of different terms for individuals intent on work as barristers or solicitors characterized Law Society discussions in this period. See, for example, Law Society of Manitoba Minutes, 6 May 1910, varying the educational requirements of "any student at law or articled clerk" [LSMM].

5 Gibson and Gibson, *supra* note 2 at 128.

6 *Cf.* ch. 2, "Indentured Labour," in W. Wesley Pue, *Law School: The Story of Legal Education in British Columbia* (Vancouver: Continuing Legal Education Society of British Columbia, 1995) [*Law School*].

7 J.R. London, "The Admissions and Education Committee: A Perspective on Legal Education and Admission to Practice in the Province of Manitoba – Past, Present and Future" in C. Harvey, ed., *The Law Society of Manitoba, 1877-1977* (Winnipeg: Peguis Publishers, 1977) 74 at 77. The attempt to create law degrees as part of a liberal education rather than as part of professional training has antecedents in nineteenth-century Ontario. See R.D. Gidney and W.P.J. Millar, *Professional Gentlemen: The Professions in Nineteenth-Century Ontario* (Toronto: University of Toronto Press, 1994) at 172; C. Moore, *The Law Society of Upper Canada and Ontario's Lawyers 1797-1997* (Toronto: University of Toronto Press, 1997) at 114.

8 Letter to L.G. McPhillips of Vancouver (author unknown, 29 May 1909), Archive of Manitoba Legal-Judicial History [AMLJH], Public Archives of Manitoba (File A225).

9 See Gibson and Gibson, *supra* note 2 at 129 (Chief Justice Wood's 1877 lectures and subsequent Law Society lectures). See also AMLJH (File A225); LSMM, 12 January 1903 (Report of Law Society of Manitoba Examining Committee, establishing a course of lectures pursuant to student petition); LSMM, 7 February 1905 (complaint by D.R. White, "Secretary of the Law Students' Society," resulted in appointment of James Aikins and Isaac Pitblado "to discuss with the University of Manitoba a course of lectures in connection with the LL.B. course"); LSMM, 7 December 1906 (petition from the Law Students' Society asking for a course of lectures, referred to a special committee of the president, Mr. Wilson, and Mr. Cameron); LSMM, 7 January 1907, 9 October 1907, 14 October 1907, 28 October 1907, 11 November 1908, 28 October 1909.

10 The mixture of interests and discursive strategies is well reflected in "Quill," "Correspondence" Vancouver Law Students' Annual (1911) 17 (and see discussion of this piece in Pue, *Law School, supra* note 6 at 36-38).

11 *Supra* note 8.

12 LSMM, 29 September 1908, record, for example, that "in response to a letter from Mr. W.H. Trueman, secretary to write and say no idea of establishing a Law School at the present time." Trueman was a frequent lecturer in the early courses of lectures and in 1915 was briefly named head of the teaching staff of the new Manitoba Law School. LSMM, 19 February 1915. Gibson and Gibson, *supra* note 2 at 216, argue (mistakenly, I believe) that Toronto's Osgoode Hall Law School provided the blueprint from which the Manitoba Law School was developed.

13 The *Report by J.A.M. Aikins and Rev. A.A. Chevrier on the University and Professional training. Commission appointed 26 Sept. 1907. Report delivered in the fall of 1909,* University of Manitoba Archives [UMA] (RBR [oversize], LE 3, .M32877, M36, 1910) [*Report by J.A.M. Aikins and Rev. A.A. Chevrier*], records a petition received from apprenticing lawyers: "That it is the desire of many of the Manitoba Students-at-Law, owing to the obvious disadvantages under which we as a student body are labouring in our study of the principles of law, that a law school be established in connection with the University of Manitoba."

A similar recommendation was made by Ontario's 1906 Royal Commission on the University of Toronto, chaired by J. Flavelle, "that a Faculty of Law should be established in the University" under arrangements agreed between the university and the provincial Law Society. Ontario's Law Society rejected this notion altogether: see C.I. Kyer and J.E. Bickenbach, *The Fiercest Debate: Cecil A. Wright, the Benchers and Legal Education in Ontario 1923-1957* (Toronto: Osgoode Society for Canadian Legal History, 1987) at 36.

14 "Desire University Control" (15 December 1910), AMLJH (Law Society of Manitoba Newspaper Clipping Scrapbooks, unidentified 1910 newspaper clipping).

15 For example, LSMM, 17 December 1909, record that three law students (identified as "Adamson, Baker and Martin") sought the Benchers' permission to count time in attendance in a law school in another jurisdiction as part of their apprenticeship. Although their request was initially denied on the grounds that the *Law Society Act* did not permit it, the Benchers agreed to seek the necessary changes in their governing statute. A few months later, they agreed to allow up to a year's leave of absence to nongraduate apprenticing lawyers (and up to six months for university graduates) for a student wishing to study law at a law school in Canada, the United States, or England. LSMM, 6 May 1910, and the account provided in a newspaper clipping of 6 June 1910, "Rules for Law Students"; AMLJH (Law Society of Manitoba Newspaper Clipping Scrapbooks, unidentified newspaper clipping). These events are discussed by L. Gibson, "A Brief History of the Law Society of Manitoba" in Harvey, *supra* note 7, 28 at 33, and by Gibson and Gibson, *supra* note 2 at 216, who point to this as the first explicit acknowledgment by the Benchers that systematic legal instruction was of value in training for the legal profession. In fact, during the next four years, at least a dozen students attended law schools outside of the province with the approval of the Law Society. LSMM record their approvals as follows: 14 June 1910 (E.G.P. Balser, W. Martin, A.E. Dilts); 27 September 1910 ("four students ... to attend Osgoode Hall Law School"); 7 June 1912 (G.C. Lindsay "to attend the Law School at the University of Chicago"); 14 May 1913 (L.P. Napier credited with "two terms at the Inner Temple"); 10 June 1913 (William Nasore – illegible – to attend Oriel College, Oxford, for six months); 30 September 1913 (C.D. Roblin to attend Osgoode Hall; F.C.S. Davision to attend law lectures at England's University of London). Other indicators of student calls to create a law school include: Letter to the Benchers from Mr. E.D. Honeyman (20 February 1911), AMLJH (File A225); LSMM, 21 February 1911 (recording receipt of a letter from "the Law Students' Association"); LSMM, 28 November 1911 (response to request from the "Winnipeg Law Students' Society").

16 See LSMM, 7 February 1905 (Aikins and Pitblado formed a committee to discuss with the University of Manitoba a course of lectures in connection with the LL.B. course); 15 February 1910 (Pitblado's notice of motion re establishment of a law school either by the Law Society or in connection with the University of Manitoba); *Tribune* (16 May 1914) (Pitblado reported as saying that "the Law society was determined to establish a law school, and that it would be a great mistake if the university did not take it under its wing") UMA (20, Box 8, Folder 2).

17 Gibson and Gibson, *supra* note 2 at 219-20.

18 "Manitoba Bar Association Born at Banquet" *Winnipeg Telegram* (10 November 1911), AMLJH (Law Society of Manitoba Newspaper Clipping Scrapbooks).

19 "Aikins Entertains Local Barristers" (1911), AMLJH (Law Society of Manitoba Newspaper Clipping Scrapbooks, unidentified newspaper clipping).

20 "Desire University Control," *supra* note 14. The attorney general at this time was Colin Campbell.

21 *Report by J.A.M. Aikins and Rev. A.A. Chevrier, supra* note 13.

22 W.L. Morton, *One University: A History of the University of Manitoba, 1877-1952* (Toronto: McClelland and Stewart, 1957) at 65, describes Aikins and Chevrier as "traditionalists" who "accepted the original organization of the university with its denominational control through the constituent colleges supported by the churches and private benefactors, but coupled with a modicum of state aid for the maintenance of an examining body and a teaching faculty limited to the natural sciences."

23 *Report by J.A.M. Aikins and Rev. A.A. Chevrier, supra* note 13.

24 See R.H. Kersley, *Gibson's 1876-1962: A Chapter in Legal Education* (London: Law Notes Lending Library, 1973); W.R. Johnson, *Schooled Lawyers: A Study in the Clash of Professional Cultures* (New York: New York University Press, 1978); R. Stevens, *Law School: Legal Education in America from the 1850s to the 1980s* (Chapel Hill: University of North Carolina Press, 1983).

25 LSMM, 8 March 1912.

26 Brandon's G.R. Coldwell was a Bencher of the Law Society of Manitoba from 1898 to 1916. Harvey, *supra* note 7 at 278. Coldwell is an important figure in C. Backhouse, "The Legal Prohibition of Aboriginal Dance on the Canadian Prairies: The 1902 Trial of Wanduta" (Paper presented at Canadian Legal History Conference, "Exploring Canada's Legal Past," University of Toronto, 7-9 May 1998). I am grateful to Professor Backhouse for sharing her information about Coldwell with me. There are notes on Coldwell in the Index Cards of the AMLJH citing M. Baker, *Symbol in Stone: The Art and Politics of a Public Building* (Winnipeg: Hyperion Press, 1986), as a principal source. Coldwell is also discussed in G.F. Barker, *Brandon: A City 1881-1961* (Altona, MB: G.F. Barker, 1977); "Coldwell, Hon. Geo. Robson, K.C." in Major E.J. Chambers, ed., *The Canadian Parliamentary Guide 1915* (Ottawa: Gazette Printing, 1915) at 428; W. Leland Clark, *Brandon's Politics and Politicians* (Altona, MB: D.W. Friesen and Sons, 1981) at 51-55, 71-75, 85; C.W. Parker, ed., *Who's Who and Why: A Biographical Dictionary of Men & Women of Canada and Newfoundland* (Vancouver: International Press, 1914) at 5:220; and "Brandon" *Western Sun* (15 January 1903).

27 "Would Give Women Right to Practice Law in Province" *Winnipeg Telegram* (7 March 1912).

28 Unidentified newspaper clipping (1912), AMLJH (Law Society of Manitoba Newspaper Clipping Scrapbooks, Clip 83-69, 21).

29 F. Edge, *The Iron Rose – The Extraordinary Life of Charlotte Ross, M.D.* (Winnipeg: University of Manitoba Press, 1992). (James Aikins had been Ross's lawyer in some of her struggles with the Manitoba medical profession.) Gidney and Millar, *supra* note 7 at 39, point to the lack of conceptual clarity around the idea of "irregular practice" that characterized nineteenth-century thought, and their point applies equally to law and medicine. Effective

policing of professional monopoly became established only during the middle half of the twentieth century.

30 See J.W. Hamilton, "Metaphors of Lawyers' Professionalism" (1995) 33 Alta. L. Rev. 833; Chapters 5 and 9 in this volume.

31 H.M. Bates, Dean of the Law School, University of Michigan, "Chapter 10: Recent Progress in Legal Education" in *US Bureau of Education Report* (1914) 227.

32 J.H. Cohen, *The Law: Business or Profession?* (New York: Banks Law Publishing, 1916) 138. Cohen concludes with the observation that "[e]ducation for the Bar must include moral training – if it is to be education for the Bar" (at 141). Although couched in the language of public interest and objective standards, the attempts of the "better university schools" to raise their standards may itself have been the result of discriminatory and exclusionary motivations. See ch. 4 in J.S. Auerbach, *Unequal Justice: Lawyers and Social Change in Modern America* (New York: Oxford University Press, 1976) 102. This interpretation is strongly corroborated by H.A. Robson's impressions of Columbia University's law program. Robson reported, favourably, that Columbia University's project of raising educational standards was a "pious fraud." See notes enclosed in a memo, H.A. Robson to President MacLean (22 April 1914), UMA (20, Box 10, Folder 5).

33 E.H. Coleman, "Legal Education" (1933) Man. Bar N. 1 at 2.

34 *Ibid.*

35 LSMM, 26 April 1912, indicates that the *University Extension Society Bill* was withdrawn.

36 Gibson, *supra* note 15 at 33.

37 "Annual Banquet of Law Students" (23 November 1912), AMLJH (Law Society of Manitoba Newspaper Clipping Scrapbooks, unidentified newspaper clipping) at 71.

38 Dr. J.A. MacLean, a University of Toronto–trained classicist, came to Winnipeg from the presidency of the University of Idaho as the first president of the University of Manitoba (which had earlier been governed by a different administrative structure). Morton, *supra* note 22 at 93.

39 Letter to J.A. MacLean from H.A. Robson (19 September 1913), UMA (20, Box 10, Folder 5). The shape things were taking at this time are reflected in a letter from H.A. Robson to W.A. Taylor, 26 September 1913, discussing the arrangements for a course of lectures for law students for the coming year. There were to be two or three lecturers and they would cover almost all aspects of common law. A room was to be provided at the university at cost. The proposed lecturers asked that the lectures commence at 8:00 p.m. and that they be compulsory for the students. AMLJH (File A925).

40 See Robson to MacLean (19 September 1913). It is possible that the university's new president may have been an important behind-the-scenes player in initiating structured legal education in the province.

41 See Notice of the Law Society of Saskatchewan (10 September 1913), AMLJH (File A931), regarding the Law Society of Saskatchewan's law school (later named Wetmore Hall) in Regina. The University of Saskatchewan's College of Law started in Saskatoon at the same time. On legal education in Saskatchewan, see W.H. McConnell, *Prairie Justice* (Calgary: Burroughs, 1980); B. Bilson, "'Prudence Rather than Valor': Legal Education in Saskatchewan 1908-1923" (1998) 61:2 Sask. L. Rev. 341. Professor Bilson's account shows that the University of Saskatchewan's President Murray played central roles. On Walter Murray's role, see also D.R. Murray and R.A. Murray, *The Prairie Builder: Walter Murray of Saskatchewan* (Edmonton: NeWest Publishers, 1984).

42 *Robson Hall: Faculty of Law, University of Manitoba* (Pamphlet published on official opening of Robson Hall, 15 September 1969) (Winnipeg: Faculty of Law, University of Manitoba, 1969) at 6; Gibson and Gibson, *supra* note 2 at 216. Prominent Winnipeg lawyer Isaac Pitblado was quoted in a local newspaper in May 1914 as saying that "the Law Society was determined to establish a law school, and that it would be a great mistake if the university

did not take it under its wing." The arrangement would, he said, be similar to that between the university and the school of medicine. UMA (20, Box 8, Folder 2).

43 Gibson, *supra* note 15 at 33-34; Gibson and Gibson, *supra* note 2 at 216.

44 Letter from W.J. Spence, Registrar of University of Manitoba, to Benchers, Law Society (25 June 1914), AMLJH (File A440) (on 14 June, moved by President McLean, seconded by C.K. Newcombe).

45 LSMM, 17 July 1914 (recording letter from registrar of the University of Manitoba).

46 1914, AMLJH (File A440).

47 Gibson, *supra* note 15 at 34.

48 *Ibid.* The recorder was "R. P. Hills, LL.D." *Robson Hall, supra* note 42 at 6.

49 Curriculum of the Manitoba Law School under the University of Manitoba and the Manitoba Law Society, Winnipeg (June 1915), AMLJH (File A100) at 1-2 [Curriculum of the Manitoba Law School].

50 London, *supra* note 7 at 77-78. In 1915, the *Law Society Act* was amended to retroactively authorize the Benchers to make arrangements with the university regarding education.

51 Hills resigned as recorder in 1918. He was succeeded by a nonlawyer administrator, R.J. Russell, overseen in "the administration of academic matters" by "a three-man 'Board of Supervisors,' consisting of D.H. Laird, J.B. Hugg and A.T. Hawley." Gibson and Gibson, *supra* note 2 at 247; *Robson Hall, supra* note 42 at 7-8.

52 Curriculum of the Manitoba Law School, Session 1919-20, AMLJH (File A100).

53 Discussed in passing in Auerbach, *supra* note 32 at 76-80, and in W.P. LaPiana, *Logic and Experience: The Origin of Modern American Legal Education* (New York: Oxford University Press, 1994) at 152-53.

54 Concurrent apprenticeship, for example, did not yield to full-time formal instruction in British Columbia until 1945 or in Ontario until 1957. See Pue, *Law School, supra* note 6, ch. 5; Moore, *supra* note 7 at 258-64.

55 UMA (20, Box 10, Folder 5); also appears in "Board of Trustees Minutes," AMLJH (File A440). See also a memo of 1914 recording discussions on the proposed law school: AMLJH (File A205/2).

56 UMA (20, Box 10, Folder 5); also appears in "Board of Trustees Minutes," *ibid.*

57 This result had not been attained anywhere in common law Canada. Dalhousie's law school contributed to professional qualification by means of a system that "interpolated" apprenticeship and classroom attendance even after law school examinations were accepted by the Barristers' Society in lieu of their own. See J. Willis, *A History of Dalhousie Law School* (Toronto: University of Toronto Press 1979) at 42, 131-32.

58 UMA (20, Box 10, Folder 5); also appears in "Board of Trustees Minutes," *supra* note 55. This idea was also pursued in a letter from H.A. Robson to Isaac Pitblado, 18 May 1915, indicating that three years of attendance at the law school should make "a person an LLB or an Attorney." It would take six to twelve months more to be called as a barrister, however. AMLJH (File A369).

59 Letter from H.A. Robson to J.A. MacLean (3 April 1914), UMA (20, Box 10, Folder 5).

60 *Ibid.*

61 *Ibid.*

62 For a discussion of the effects of science and technology on western Canadian thought, see D. Laycock's extraordinary *Populism and Democratic Thought in the Canadian Prairies 1910-1945* (Toronto: University of Toronto Press, 1990).

63 Langdell is generally credited with the development of the case method, although, as Kyer and Bickenbach, *supra* note 13 at 15, observe, there is reason to suspect Harvard president Charles W. Elliot's hand in this. Elliot had, they say, earlier argued for a case method in science education that "involved the replacement of lectures by an 'inductive' analysis of concrete cases with the aim of identifying general principles." Stevens, *supra* note 24 at 53,

argues that Langdell was extraordinarily confused between "science as an empirical and as a rational activity." See also A.E. Sutherland, *The Law at Harvard: A History of Ideas and Men, 1817-1967* (Cambridge, MA: Belknap Press, 1967); A. Chase, "Birth of the Modern Law School" (1979) 23 Am. J. Legal Hist. 329; Auerbach, *supra* note 32 at 74-101; LaPiana, *supra* note 53; R.W. Gordon, "The Case for (and against) Harvard" (1995) 93 Mich. L. Rev. 1231.

64 Josef Redlich, *The Common Law and the Case Method in American University Law Schools* (New York: Carnegie Foundation for the Advancement of Teaching, 1914).

65 Kyer and Bickenbach, *supra* note 13 at 84-85. The Redlich report was evaluated in J.H. Beale, "The Law School as Professor Redlich Sees It" *Harvard Graduates' Magazine* 23 (1915) 617; Albert Kocourek, "The Redlich Report and the Case Method" (1915) 10 Ill. L. Rev. 321; Cohen, *supra* note 32 at 137, 140-41.

66 Auerbach, *supra* note 32 at 76.

67 Stevens, *supra* note 24 at 55. In a passage ripe with implications for the study of legal education in twentieth-century Canada, Auerbach, *ibid.* at 79, observes: "Without the particular rhythms characteristic of early twentieth-century life, law teachers might have remained merely the 'expounders, systematizers, and historians' described by Eliot ... Such, indeed, was the experience in England ... The delayed birth of university legal education in the United States, and its coincidence with national reform, was fortuitously decisive. Had it emerged before 1890, or after 1915, the profession of law teaching probably would have been conspicuously different."

68 Gordon, *supra* note 63. For a transatlantic comparison, see D. Sugarman, "'A Hatred of Disorder': Legal Science, Liberalism, and Imperialism" in P. Fitzpatrick, ed., *Dangerous Supplements* (London: Pluto, 1991) 34.

69 C.C. Langdell, *Record of the Commemoration, November Fifth to Eighth, 1886, on the Two Hundred and Fiftieth Anniversary of the Founding of Harvard College* (1887) at 97, 98, as quoted in Sutherland, *supra* note 63 at 174-75.

70 Stevens, *supra* note 24 at 53.

71 Kyer and Bickenbach, *supra* note 13 at 15.

72 Stevens, *supra* note 24 at 63.

73 J.A. Corry, *My Life and Work: A Happy Partnership (Memoirs of J. A. Corry)* (Kingston, ON: Queen's University, 1981). Corry's own contributions to Canadian legal thought are discussed in R.C.B. Risk, "Lawyers, Courts, and the Rise of the Regulatory State" (1984) 9 Dal. L.J. 31. The process of education Corry describes is remarkably similar to the "endless class of competitive evaluation" by means of "verbal clashes" that characterized the core of male youth culture in young men's societies. E.A. Rotundo *American Manhood: Transformations in Masculinity from the Revolution to the Modern Era* (New York: Basic Books, 1993) at 68.

74 C.R. Smith, "Legal Education: A Manitoba View" (1935) Can. Bar Rev. 404 at 408. Smith was a lecturer at the Manitoba Law School at the time.

75 "Memorandum by Cecil A. Wright Concerning Matters Discussed at the Legal Education Committee, Law Society of Upper Canada Meeting Dec. 1 1933," cited in Kyer and Bickenbach, *supra* note 13 at 82. A senior legal academic with whom I once worked consistently presented lectures that were thoughtful, well organized, informative, and erudite: an effect achieved by reading word-for-word the text that, selected on the advice of other professors, he had assigned to his students! For a discussion of Cecil Wright's jurisprudence, see R.C.B. Risk, "Volume 1 of the Journal: A Tribute and Belated Review" (1987) 37 U.T.L.J. 193 ["Volume 1 of the Journal"]. See also J.E. Bickenbach and C.I. Kyer, "The Harvardization of Caesar Wright" (1983) 33 U.T.L.J.162.

76 The antebellum Harvard Law School itself had been characterized by both "interactive discussion and lectures." Gordon, *supra* note 63 at 1233.

77 Willis, *supra* note 57 at 83.

78 *Ibid.*

79 Stevens, *supra* note 24, esp. ch. 4, "Harvard Sets the Style"; Kyer and Bickenbach, *supra* note 13 at 16, summarize Langdell's subsequent celebration of the case method thus: "Since the law is a science, and since cases are the experimental data of the science, legal education must be limited to the university; he boldly rejected the notion that law was 'a species of handicraft ... best learned by serving an apprenticeship to one who practices it.'"

80 Willis, *supra* note 47 at 82, asserts that in 1920 no teacher at any Canadian law school had yet used the case method, and thus accords pride of place to either Sidney Earle Smith, who "sprang" the case method on the Dalhousie graduating class in contracts and trusts in 1921-22 (at 84, 97), or to John Read, who used it in his conflict of laws class in the same year and who was "in 1924 or 1925 the author of the first case book ever compiled in Canada, a mimeographed one on Constitutional Law" (at 97). In support of this latter assessment, Willis cites C. Morse, "The Teaching of Law" (1926) 4 Can. Bar Rev. 483 at 487.

81 Kyer and Bickenbach, *supra* note 13 at 76, suggest that J.T. Hébert, who resigned from the University of Saskatchewan Law Faculty in 1924, "may have been the first legal educator in Canada to adopt the casebook method in his teaching." The case method in Saskatchewan is briefly discussed in Bilson, *supra* note 41 at 344.

82 Kyer and Bickenbach, *ibid.*, suggest that Falconbridge's 1924 mimeographed casebook on the sale of goods – subsequently published as J.D. Falconbridge, *A Selection of Cases on the Sale of Goods* (Toronto: Canada Law Book, 1927) – "may be counted as the first Harvard-inspired casebook compiled and published in Canada" (at 43). The Falconbridge volume was reviewed by V.C. MacDonald in (1928) 6 Can. Bar. Rev. 173.

83 H.A. Robson, KC, and J.B. Hugg, *Leading Cases on Public Corporations* (Toronto: Carswell, 1916), Preface [*Public Corporations*].

84 H.A. Robson and J.B. Hugg, *Cases on Company Law* (Toronto: Carswell, 1916), Preface [*Company Law*].

85 Casebooks continued to serve as a valuable source of basic legal information for lawyers even many years later, as in British Columbia thirty years later (Pue, *Law School, supra* note 6 at 261-63).

86 Robson and Hugg, *Company Law, supra* note 84, "Introduction" at 8.

87 *Ibid.* at 9.

88 Kyer and Bickenbach, *supra* note 13 at 52.

89 *Ibid.*

90 (Toronto: Carswell, 1914). Lefroy's juristic thought is ably described in R.C.B. Risk, "A.H.F. Lefroy: Common Law Thought in Late Nineteenth-Century Canada: On Burying One's Grandfather" (1991) 41 U.T.L.J. 307 ["A.H.F. Lefroy"]; R. Risk, "The Scholars and the Constitution: P.O.G.G. and the Privy Council" in *Canada's Legal Inheritances* (1996) 23 Man. L. Rev. 496 at 497-500 (symposium issue edited by W. Pue and D. Guth) ["Scholars and the Constitution"].

91 Kyer and Bickenbach, *supra* note 13 at 43.

92 Risk, "A.H.F. Lefroy," *supra* note 90 at 312.

93 Letter from H.A. Robson to Isaac Pitblado (30 April 1915), AMLJH (File A369); Letter from H.A. Robson to Pitblado (20 April 1915), AMLJH (File A369).

94 J.T. Hébert, "An Unsolicited Report on Legal Education in Canada" *Canadian Law Times* 41 (1921) 593 at 611.

95 Western leadership in the history of legal professionalism in Canada is often underestimated. Kyer and Bickenbach argue, for example, that "Falconbridge's initial steps ... count not as the beginning but as the climax of the first important country-wide campaign to bring legal education in Canada into line with the standard advocated by legal academics in the United States in the first two decades of the twentieth century. The Canadian movement was led by Falconbridge, MacRae, R.W. Lee, and H.A. Smith, the last two of whom were

English scholars sojourning in Canada at McGill University Law School" (*supra* note 13 at 51). Leaders of the movement whose contributions are missed in this assessment include J.A.M. Aikins, founder of the Canadian Bar Association and president from 1914 to 1927; H.A. Robson, founder of Manitoba legal education and early chair of the CBA Committee on Legal Education; Manitoba's Thorson, a member of the Committee on Legal Education and first Canadian law dean to implement the CBA's curriculum proposals; Saskatchewan's Hébert, likely the first wholeheartedly "Socratic" teacher in Canada, and others. I have sketched out prairie contributions in this period in Chapter 5 in this volume, while British Columbia's role in the development of Canadian legal education is recorded in Pue, *Law School, supra* note 6.

96 E.K. Williams, "Legal Education in Manitoba: 1913-1950" (1950) 28 Can. Bar Rev. 759 at 771-72.

97 Letter from H.A. Robson to Isaac Pitblado (18 May 1915), AMLJH (File A369).

98 "Second Draft of Proposed Curriculum, Manitoba Law School," AMLJH (File A369). The emphasis on a casebook approach stands in contrast to the curriculum at Osgoode Hall in 1923, where the first-year curriculum emphasized assigned treatises, statutes, or forms, with a lesser emphasis on direct exposure to case law. Contracts: C.S. Kenny, *A Selection of Cases Illustrative of the Law of Contracts* (published in England in 1922), and *Anson on Contracts.* Real property: E.D. Armour, *A Treatise on the Law of Real Property.* Jurisprudence: Thomas Erskind Holland, *The Elements of Jurisprudence.* Common Law: John Indermaur, *Principles of the Common Law.* Constitutional law and history: Sir J.G. Bourinot, *A Manual of the Constitutional History of Canada,* and A.H.F. Lefroy, *Leading Cases in Canadian Constitutional Law* (1914). The remainder of the "first year curriculum – criminal law, practice, and procedure and statute law – concentrated on statutory material and forms." Kyer and Bickenbach, *supra* note 13 at 42, 43.

99 "Board of Trustees Minutes" (14 September 1914), *supra* note 55, indicate acceptance of the following curriculum for 1914-15 (only the first two years were taught in law school in the initial period):

> First Year: *Williams on Real Property, Snell's Equity* (Part I and Part II, to end of Cap. XIX), *Smith's Common Law, Anson on Contracts.* Statutes: Manitoba Wills, Devolution of Estates, Bills of Exchange, Constitutional History of Canada with special reference to BNA Act (*Bourinot's Manual*).
>
> Second Year: *Armour on Titles* (L.S.) and *Challis on Real Property* (U.), *Stephen's Digest of Evidence* (L.S.) and *Best on Evidence* (U.), *Underhill on Torts* (L.S.) *and Radcliffe on Torts* (U.), *Snell's Equity* (L.S.) and *Strachan's Leading Cases in Equity* (U.). Possible offerings were *William's Personal Property* (L.S.) and Dicey's *Conflict of Laws* (U.).

100 Gibson and Gibson, *supra* note 2 at 251. McWilliams was selected as a teacher by the board of trustees at the law school at its 9 June 1915 meeting ("Board of Trustees Minutes," *supra* note 55).

101 Aikins, *supra* note 1 at 1188.

102 *Ibid.* at 1188-89.

103 An early English attempt to establish professional education for lawyers in Birmingham floundered. See Chapter 4 in this volume.

104 Despite the presence of women lawyers in Manitoba at this time, professional leaders persisted in thinking of their profession as "manly" work and aspired to create a profession of gentlemen. *Cf.* Gidney and Millar, *supra* note 7. On women lawyers in Manitoba, see M. Kinnear, *In Subordination: Professional Women, 1870-1970* (Montreal and Kingston: McGill-Queen's University Press, 1995) at 78-97.

105 Willis, *supra* note 57 at 31. On Harvard's late-nineteenth-century law program, see, among many others, Sutherland, *supra* note 63; LaPiana, *supra* note 53; Gordon, *supra* note 63.

106 Kyer and Bickenbach, *supra* note 13 at 58. The program imitated "the general outlines of BA courses in jurisprudence offered at Oxford, Cambridge, and Dublin" (at 58). A useful general description of Kennedy's program and the jurisprudential school that informed it is to be found in R.C.B. Risk, "The Many Minds of W.P.M. Kennedy" (1998) 48 U.T.L.J. 353; R.C.B. Risk, "W.P.M. Kennedy and Canadian Constitutional Thought" (Paper presented at Canadian Legal History Conference, "Exploring Canada's Legal Past," University of Toronto, 7-9 May 1998); and Risk, "Volume 1 of the Journal," *supra* note 75. See also Risk, "Scholars and the Constitution," *supra* note 90 at 497-500; R.C.B. Risk, "Lawyers, Courts, and the Rise of the Regulatory State" (1984) 9 Dal. L.J. 31.

The University of Toronto's curriculum under W.P.M. Kennedy in fact covered territory that overlapped considerably with general arts education at the University of British Columbia in this period. Pue, *Law School, supra* note 6 at 65-94.

107 Compiled from the following sources: "Board of Trustees Minutes" (14 September 1914, 15 September 1916, 25 September 1918), *supra* note 55; Curriculum of the Manitoba Law School (June 1915, June 1917), *supra* note 49; Curriculum of the Manitoba Law School, Session 1919-20, Curriculum of the Manitoba Law School, Session 1920-22, AMLJH (File A100).

108 Morton, *supra* note 22.

109 See Letter, H.A. Robson to J.A. MacLean (30 April 1915) (enclosing a draft curriculum and indicating that the Law Society had broadened its own curriculum to match the university's more closely); Letter, H.A. Robson to J.A. MacLean (31 December 1915) (explaining that the university lectures on international law and the history of English law are considered "unprofitable"); Letter, J.A. MacLean to H.A. Robson (7 January 1916) (indicating that, while the selection of courses is completely within the purview of the board of trustees, he would be sorry to see the courses in international law and history of English law disappear from the curriculum or the course of instruction permanently), UMA (20, Box 10, Folder 5). MacLean made the strength of his commitment to cultural education in law clear, indicating that "it would be a mistake to confine the lectures of the School to the subjects which the lawyer needs in his daily practice. I suppose it is not necessary to enlarge on this point because I think I know that you and the members of the Board are doing everything in your power to make the course broader as well as more intensive, and am writing this only because I wanted you to know that I am regarding the discontinuance of the lectures in International Law and the History of English Law as a temporary and not a permanent disposition in respect of these subjects."

110 This is not the place to develop these themes at length. See, however, Chapter 5 in this volume. Although Ontario's path to legal education seems to be very different, Manitoba's early-twentieth-century path to law school is similar to that of British Columbia. See B.D. Bucknall, T.C.H. Baldwin, and J.D. Lakin, "Pedants, Practitioners and Prophets: Legal Education at Osgoode Hall to 1957" (1968) 6 Osgoode Hall L.J. 137; *cf.* Pue, *Law School, supra* note 6.

111 See discussion in Kyer and Bickenbach, *supra* note 13 at 64-70.

112 Gibson and Gibson, *supra* note 2 at 248; *Robson Hall, supra* note 42 at 8.

113 Curriculum of the Manitoba Law School, Session 1921-22, AMLJH (File A100/6).

114 "Board of Trustees Minutes" (28 February 1921), *supra* note 55 at 123, motion to move curriculum as close as possible to that proposed by the Canadian Bar Association, motion for a permanent teaching staff of two.

115 H. Buchwald, "The Manitoba Law School – 40 Years" (1954) 26 Man. Bar N. 77 at 80; Gibson and Gibson, *supra* note 2 at 248; *Robson Hall, supra* note 42 at 8; Curriculum of the Manitoba Law School, Session 1921-22, *supra* note 113.

116 Curriculum Book for 1921-22, AMLJH (File A100), and "Board of Trustees Minutes" (31 May 1922), *supra* note 55.

117 Thorson (although not his role as a legal educator) is discussed in I. Bushnell, *The Federal Court of Canada: A History, 1875-1992* (Toronto: Osgoode Society for Canadian Legal History, 1997) at 124-37, and in Gibson and Gibson, *supra* note 2 at 247-48, 274, 299, 314.

118 Willis, *supra* note 57 at 81.

119 Kyer and Bickenbach, *supra* note 13 at 42.

120 When the Canadian Bar Association Committee on Legal Education struck a subcommittee to consider curriculum, Robson was appointed alongside McGill's Dean R.W. Lee, Dalhousie's Dean MacRae, the University of Saskatchewan's Dean T.D. Brown, and the Law Society of Upper Canada's W.F. Kerr. When Robson found himself unable to participate, Brown represented both the Saskatchewan and Manitoba law societies. Brown consulted "with Judge Robson, with the head of the Manitoba Law School, and with some of the benchers of the Law Society." Committee on Legal Education, "Standard Curriculum" (1920) Proceedings of the Canadian Bar Association 250 at 252. The committee's "first draft report was printed in Canadian Law Times 38 (1918) 257, and the final report in the Canadian Bar Association Year Book for 1918. Changes were made and adopted at the 1919 CBA meeting": Williams, *supra* note 96 at 762.

See R.W. Lee, "Legal Education: A Symposium" *Canadian Law Times* 39 (1919) 13 ["Legal Education: A Symposium"]. Lee's report on legal education also appeared in *Proceedings of the 4th Annual Meeting of the Canadian Bar Association, 1919* (published 1920) at 150-52; "Committee on Legal Education – Standard Curriculum – Report and Notes on Report" in *Proceedings of 5th Annual Meeting of the Canadian Bar Association, 1920* (published 1920) at 250-57.

121 See Chapter 9 in this volume; "Legal Ethics: An Address by Chief Justice Mathers" in *Proceedings of the 5th Annual Meeting of the Canadian Bar Association, 1920* (published 1920) at 268-301.

122 Minutes of the *Proceedings of the Canadian Bar Association* (1919) at 150, as cited in Kyer and Bickenbach, *supra* note 13 at 66.

123 C. Harvey, "Some Benchers and Secretaries, Benchers 1877-1920's, Isaac Pitblado" in Harvey, *supra* note 7, 222 at 231-34.

124 R.W. Lee, "Legal Education Old and New (Part III)" *Canadian Law Times* 36 (1916) 109; Lee, "Legal Education: A Symposium," *supra* note 120. See Roderick Macdonald, "The National Law Programme at McGill: Origins, Evolution, Prospects" (1990) 13 Dal. L.J. 211.

125 See, for example, *Canada Law Journal* 51 (1915) 161; report on the proceedings of the CBA, including speeches of Sir J. Aikins, KC, president of the CBA, on "The Advancement of the Science of Jurisprudence in Canada." For discussions of the cultural ethos surrounding legal education at this time, see Chapter 5 in this volume and Pue, "Revolution by Legal Means," *supra* note 30.

126 For a discussion of the "gentlemanly" aspirations and cultural objectives of Victorian English professional reformers, see Sugarman, *supra* note 68; Chapter 4 in this volume.

127 J.G. Hodgins, comp., *Documentary History of Education in Upper Canada*, 28 vols. (Toronto: Warwick Bros. and Rutter, 1894-1910) at 1:213. The passage is cited in Moore, *supra* note 7 at 78, and in G.B. Baker, "Legal Education in Upper Canada 1785-1889: The Law Society as Educator" in D.H. Flaherty, ed., *Essays in the History of Canadian Law*, vol. 2 (Toronto: Osgoode Society for Canadian Legal History, 1983).

128 (1923) 8 Proceedings of the Canadian Bar Association 387; quoted in Gibson and Gibson, *supra* note 2 at 248; *Robson Hall, supra* note 42 at 9.

129 Gibson and Gibson, *ibid.* at 249; *Robson Hall, ibid.* at 9; Carnegie Foundation, *Review of Legal Education in the United States and Canada for the Years 1926 and 1927* (New York: Carnegie Foundation for the Advancement of Teaching, 1928).

130 Gibson and Gibson, *ibid.*

131 "Board of Trustees Minutes" (12 November 1926), *supra* note 55 at 187.

132 Gibson and Gibson, *supra* note 2 at 249; *Robson Hall, supra* note 42 at 9-12; "Board of Trustees Minutes" (7 July 1927), *ibid.* at 195, approved the proposal for a four-year course of study with lectures during the third and fourth year outside of office hours, recommended nongraduates' three years' articles, graduates' two years' articles, to be completed after first two years of law school.

133 Gibson and Gibson, *ibid.* at 249; *Robson Hall, ibid.* at 12.

134 Gibson and Gibson, *ibid.*; *supra* note 2 at 249; London, *supra* note 7 at 79.

135 Gibson and Gibson, *ibid.*; *supra* note 2 at 249; *Robson Hall, supra* note 42 at 12.

136 The unconventional living arrangements of James Aikins, his de facto separation from his wife, and his apparent intimacy with Coleman are described briefly in L. Gibson and D. Gibson, "Sir James Aikins' Seamless Web: Finding Fortune and Fame as a Lawyer in the Adolescent Canadian West" (1992) 21 Man. L.J. 161.

137 *Robson Hall, supra* note 42 at 12; see also Gibson and Gibson, *supra* note 2 at 250-51.

138 Gibson and Gibson, *ibid.* at 303, 304.

139 Committee on Legal Education, (1931) Proceedings of the Canadian Bar Association 206.

140 Williams, *supra* note 96 at 779. A Bencher by 1931, Williams had earlier assisted Robson in creating the 1914 law school.

141 London, *supra* note 7 at 80.

142 Consultative Group on Legal Education, Law and Learning, *Report to the Social Sciences and Humanities Research Council of Canada by the Consultative Group on Research and Education in Law* (Ottawa: Social Sciences and Humanities Research Council of Canada, 1983). See also Ron Saunders's book review: "Law and Learning: Report of the Social Sciences and Humanities Research Council of Canada" (1984) 23 Ottawa L. Rev. 218.

143 See J. Brockman, "Exclusionary Tactics: The History of Women and Minorities in the Legal Profession in British Columbia" in H. Foster and J. McLaren, eds., *Essays in the History of Canadian Law*, vol. 6, *British Columbia and the Yukon* (Toronto: Osgoode Society for Canadian Legal History, 1995) 508; D. Tong, "A History of Exclusion: The Treatment of Racial and Ethnic Minorities by the Law Society of British Columbia in Admissions to the Legal Profession" *The Advocate* 56:2 (March 1998) 197; M. Thornton, *Dissonance and Distrust: Women in the Legal Profession* (Melbourne: Oxford University Press, 1996); Auerbach, *supra* note 32; Gordon, *supra* note 63; M.J. Powell, *From Patrician to Professional Elite: The Transformation of the New York City Bar Association* (New York: Russell Sage Foundation, 1988). A long-sustained backlash against scholarly legal education over the late twentieth century and focused on Ontario is documented in W.W. Pue and Annie Rochette, "Back to Basics? University Legal Education and 21st Century Professionalism" (2001) 20 Windsor Y.B. Access Just. 167.

144 See L. Karpik and T. Halliday, eds., *Legal Professions and Political Liberalism* (Oxford: Oxford University Press, 1997).

145 See Gibson and Gibson, *supra* note 2 at 256, 267.

146 *Ibid.* at 256 (indicating that even in 1931 the Law Society was reasonably well-off).

147 Letter to H.A. Robson from Cronkite at University of Saskatchewan in relation to the Canadian Bar Association Committee on Legal Education (5 February 1934), AMLJH (File A224).

148 On the notion of "recipe knowledge," see R. Ericson and P. Baranek, *The Ordering of Justice: A Study of Accused Persons as Dependents in the Criminal Process* (Toronto: University of Toronto Press, 1982).

149 Evidence of Sir George Stephen, solicitor, in United Kingdom, *Report of the Select Committee on Legal Education* (25 August 1846) 144 at para. 1965.

150 There are striking similarities in these respects to the meteoric rise and fall of a cutting-edge program of legal education at Queen's College, Birmingham, in the previous century. See Chapter 4 in this volume.

151 Kyer and Bickenbach, *supra* note 13 at 75. M. Kinnear, *supra* note 104 at 85, makes a similar point in her observation that, once a full-time law faculty was re-established in Manitoba in the 1960s, "when training switched to an academic system, it was 'a door opener for women. You didn't need to find an office at the start.' Even then, the reluctance of firms to take on women for their subsequent articling persisted."

152 Rotundo, *supra* note 73 at 199, reminds us that much important business was concluded in "informal talks" that "happened within the context of male sociability. They took place in train cars, on station platforms, in hotel lobbies; often they happened at formal social occasions."

153 Kyer and Bickenbach, *supra* note 13 at 125-33; the committee report was published in (1935) 13 Can. Bar Rev. 347.

154 As quoted in Pue, *Law School, supra* note 6 at 148.

155 Risk pointed to the need for a geographically informed legal history in R.C.B. Risk, "A Prospectus for Canadian Legal History" (1973) 1 Dal. L.J. 227 at 230-31 ["A Prospectus"]. See also G. Parker, "Canadian Legal Culture" in L. Knafla, ed., *Law and Justice in a New Land: Essays in Western Canadian Legal History* (Toronto: Carswell, 1986) 3; I. Duncanson, "Close Your Eyes and Think of England" (1997) 3:2 Canberra L. Rev. 123; I. Duncanson, "Finding a History for the Common Law" (1996) Australian Journal of Legal History 1; Ian Duncanson, "The Politics of Common Law in History and Theory" (1989) 27 Osgoode Hall L.J. 687.

156 Bucknall *et al., supra* note 110; Kyer and Bickenbach, *supra* note 13; Gibson and Gibson, *supra* note 2; J.P.S. McLaren, "The History of Legal Education in Common Law Canada" in R.J. Matas and D. McCawley, eds., *Legal Education in Canada* (Montreal: Federation of Law Societies of Canada, 1987) 111; J.P.S. McLaren, "Book Review: Kyer and Bickenbach, *The Fiercest Debate: Cecil A. Wright, the Benchers and Legal Education in Ontario 1923-1957*" (1989) 68 Can. Bar Rev. 193; Moore, *supra* note 7; Pue, *Law School, supra* note 6.

157 Risk, "A Prospectus," *supra* note 155 at 245.

PART 3

Ethics, Regulation, and the Business of Law

7

Free Trade in Law

ENGLISH BARRISTERS, COUNTY COURTS, AND PROVINCIAL PRACTICE IN THE 1850s

Tensions arose in the English legal system during the nineteenth century as reform initiatives began to bring ancient institutions into alignment with evolving economic conditions and the rising cultural ethos of the age. The experience was unsettling for many and profoundly disruptive for some. In such circumstances, new ideas, some radical, were mooted and taken seriously. Traditional leadership was challenged in matters of state, church, society, and law. The limits of existing social relations were probed and the reality of power sharply defined.

Instability affected the English Bar in the middle years of the nineteenth century. The immediate cause was an "overcrowding" of the barristers' branch of the legal profession, at least in relation to barristers' expectations and at a time of shrinking professional monopoly. Daniel Duman has calculated that the total number of barristers increased from 2,500 in 1835 to 7,250 in 1885. Not all men admitted to the bar practiced law. Astonishingly, the total number of *practising* barristers increased by 800 percent.[1] Asymmetrical opportunity exacerbated the resulting stresses. Duman has concluded that professional opportunity diminished for rank-and-file barristers and that the situation worsened as "changes in the distribution of work between the two branches of the profession, beginning in 1846, worked almost entirely at the expense of junior barristers, and this considerably reduced the ability of new men to gain a foothold."[2] An overtly anti-commercial conception of barristers' practice exaggerated the effects of overcrowding, forcing some to adopt innovative approaches if they were to survive.

Their purpose was simply to establish market positioning sufficient to achieve their economic aspirations and to maintain status as "gentlemen." In doing so, they had to articulate new understandings of barristers' professionalism. At the end of the day, some of their innovations threatened the very structures of the legal profession.

These efforts, though arising from simple need and defined by ambient conditions, had a transforming power that might well have changed the very shape of the arena defining their profession and the market within which they worked. That it did not do so is a tribute to the power of inertia, the resilience of their opponents, and, to some degree, the unpredictability of circumstance. The defeat of the rebel barristers was in the end a double-edged sword. Although established institutions, habits, and structures came out victorious, they were not unscarred, emerging with a character transformed from where they had begun. The unpredictable outcomes gave shape to significantly altered modes of practice and notions of professionalism. Although rebel barristers failed to achieve their particular goals, their efforts effected significant alterations in the economic and ideological fortresses around which subsequent professional struggles would take place. The effect on the bar was one of metasomatic change: its composition was pervasively transformed beneath a form and structure that seemed unaltered.

The Economy of Barristers' Practice in the 1850s

Magali Larson has emphasized that in a market economy professions need to persuade potential customers both of the need for particular services and of the desirability of purchasing specified services only from particular "professional" producers.[3] Economic success rests upon the ability to create a secure market by persuasion.

Mid-nineteenth-century English barristers enjoyed an enviable advantage in the marketplace for professional services as they enjoyed a monopoly over advocacy in the superior courts. Monopolies of all sorts were falling out of favour, however, and law reform was threatening. Always, the presence of solicitors and attorneys[4] as parallel professions providing complementary services, feeding barristers legal work, or competing with them gave rise to challenges to be managed.

Attorneys (or solicitors) also engaged in legal practice. Apart from the barrister's acknowledged monopoly on the right to speak in superior courts, the dividing line between the two professions was fluid. Barristers generally lived and worked mostly in London, travelling to the provinces only to attend circuit courts. For the most part, the day-to-day legal work of the provinces was conducted exclusively by attorneys in local practice. Even in London, almost all legal work short of superior court litigation was undertaken by attorneys.[5] One attorney estimated that in 1855 "more than ninety per cent of the Law in this country is administered to the public in the private offices of Attorneys and Solicitors."[6] To the extent that the two legal professions might come into direct competition, attorneys enjoyed the distinct advantages of living and working near their clients, being better known, and generally charging lower fees. Theirs was the more nimble of the two professions.

Attorneys, unlike barristers, practised a sort of "holistic" law, in contrast to the sporadic surgical intervention in litigation. Attorneys knew of their advantage and pressed it home whenever they could. It was attorneys, they said, who had "practical knowledge of business and the world ... for they alone have communication with the client, and the management of his business, and are alone acquainted with his wants, his feelings, and his wishes."[7] The developing spatial economy of industrial Britain also conferred advantages upon attorneys, who, unlike barristers, were located in the great new industrial towns of the provinces where much legal business was generated.

These competitive advantages vis-à-vis the Bar were amplified considerably in 1846 when the introduction of County Courts warped both the geographies and structures of legal practice. County Courts sat in approximately five hundred locations grouped into sixty circuits. Each court initially had jurisdiction over almost all personal suits involving amounts in dispute up to twenty pounds, increased to fifty pounds in 1850.[8] Significantly, the legislation of 1846 granted attorneys a right of audience and prohibited barristers from taking briefs directly from clients (i.e., without the intervention of an instructing attorney).[9] In an earlier debate on the creation of County Courts (1833), Lord Lyndhurst had warned of the dangers that a provincial bar might develop around provincial courts and that the removal of small business from young barristers would hurt the Bar as a whole: "Such barristers would be inferior in learning, would be inferior in talent, would be inferior in intelligence, would be inferior in all those great and glorious qualifications which had so long distinguished the bar of England." His Lordship feared that such courts "would take two-thirds of the ordinary business from the Assizes, where young men recently called to the bar went to learn experience ... The business done at the Assizes would be so small in consequence, that young men would cease to go the circuits, and the little business that was left would be absorbed and monopolized by the provincial counsel."

The effects of these changes on the legal professions were dramatic. Five years later, the *Legal Observer* commented that "[t]he whole economy of the profession was deranged."[10] The new County Courts saw an average of well over 400,000 proceedings begun each year from 1846 to 1851,[11] reallocating substantial legal work from London to the provinces.[12] A reduction in High Court business may have hurt some attorneys,[13] but that branch of the legal profession was also able to take advantage of new professional opportunities. The large volume of County Court litigation gave attorneys opportunities to offer preliminary advice to parties to actions, draft pleadings, deal with preparation of evidentiary matters, *and* act as advocates in the proceedings.

The *County Courts Act* reinforced every advantage that attorneys had previously enjoyed in their competition with barristers for dominance in the market for legal services, and added some. The addition of a local judicial forum reinforced their competitive advantages as resident legal practitioners. Attorneys lived locally, saw many of their clients frequently, and could provide services at relatively low cost, partly because they enjoyed lower overhead than barristers travelling out from London. The conferral of rights of audience upon attorneys removed the necessity of hiring a barrister for routine cases. Further, the statutory prohibition on barristers' appearing in County Court cases without having been briefed by an attorney ensured that clients wishing to retain a barrister would face punishing costs, paying two legal fees where one – to an attorney – would do.

To these natural and legislative advantages of the attorney's branch were added a number of disadvantages suffered by barristers by their own profession's rules of "etiquette." However lucrative successful barristers' practices might be, the ideology of the Bar was intensely anticommercial. Founded on the notion that the best men would always come out well, it was considered "ungentlemanly" to actively seek out legal work. While the Bar's etiquette was not directly enforceable by any professional disciplinary tribunals,[14] its understandings operated as powerful normative constraints. Moreover, informal sanctions tantamount to blacklisting could be relied upon to punish offenders.[15] In competing for County Court work, barristers were hampered by rules of etiquette constraining changing of circuits, discouraging the establishment of provincial practices,[16] discouraging or prohibiting direct contact with clients (that is, without using an attorney intermediary), and setting minimum fee levels beyond what was reasonable within the County Court's jurisdiction.[17] In addition:

> The most important class of rules of etiquette are unquestionably those that regulate the relations between Barristers and Attorneys. They are more precise and better defined than most of the rules ... and can be summed up under two heads:
>
> 1. A barrister must not take upon himself any of the functions of an attorney: he must not collect evidence, nor even, except in peculiar cases, see the

witnesses; he must not serve process, nor perform any of the practical business of a cause.

2. A barrister must be instructed by an attorney, and receive no fees but from an attorney's hand.[18]

The deck was stacked heavily against the Junior Bar in its efforts to win County Court briefs. They simply could not compete with attorneys. And, of course, the creation of County Courts diverted many actions from the superior court forums where the Bar enjoyed an undisputed monopoly. The Junior Bar chafed.

Perhaps the only argument barristers could offer to persuade potential clients that their services should be retained in preference to those of attorneys was that they provided services of superior quality. While tradition might suggest as much, pragmatic judgment often did not. Despite their higher fees and gentlemanly status, barristers sometimes failed to provide exemplary service. They frequently appeared with only a very superficial knowledge of the matter being litigated or, because of multiple scheduling of cases, failed to appear at all in cases for which they had been briefed and paid.[19] Even with regard to education, where their gentlemanly status might seem most likely to have given barristers a claim to preference by consumers of legal services, it was generally the solicitors' branch that could best substantiate claims to possession of practically useful expertise certified after instruction and examination.[20]

The results were predictable: barristers' career opportunities were diminished, precipitating a very real crisis for the Bar. The impact was compounded by the effects of law reform,[21] increased admissions to the Bar, and important economic transformations.

In *The English and Colonial Bars in the Nineteenth Century*,[22] Daniel Duman argues that the issue of "overcrowding" can be understood properly only if we appreciate that qualifying as a barrister did not necessarily indicate an intent to practise law. The status of barrister was considered desirable as certifying gentlemanly status (much as a university degree did), and Victorians did not entirely view the degrees of either the universities or the Inns of Court entirely instrumentally. Excluding retired and inactive barristers, Duman concludes that the Bar grew by 250 percent in the first half of the nineteenth century (while the general population grew at a rate of 80 percent), slowing to a 50 percent increase in the second half of the century (when population growth continued at 80 percent).[23]

This suffices to make a *prima facie* case that barristers would have felt the effects of overcrowding relative to work opportunities by the middle years of the nineteenth century. Duman concludes, however, that new career opportunities in public service at home and in the Empire, as well as new opportunities in business, prevented a crisis in unemployment from developing.[24] Such job opportunities "prevented the emergence of a militant and powerful group of briefless barristers who could have posed a major problem for Britain."[25]

Careers are made or broken over periods shorter than a century, however, and Duman's century-long perspective obscures shorter-term imbalances.[26] These proved quite capable of disrupting the lives of large numbers of aspiring practitioners, for whom success had to be established in a relatively short period of time if it was to be established at all. Timing was everything.[27] The most significant period of stress occurred in the late 1840s and the 1850s. By any measure, the Bar had grown enormously in the previous half-century, while employment opportunities outside of legal practice were relatively few.[28] To this was added the disruption of the *County Courts Act*, 1846.

The disruption was severe. In 1857, H. Byerley Thomson estimated that the usual income for an ordinary junior barrister fell within the range of between five hundred and twelve hundred pounds per annum,[29] and Duman estimates that this is likely two or three times more than the earnings of the lowest quartile.[30] The *Law Times* of 1847 reported that "[t]he prospects of the Bar are, indeed very gloomy,"[31] and in 1849 asserted that the Bar was "virtually annihilated,"[32] there being sufficient work for fewer than one-fiftieth of the profession.[33] Lord Denman spoke of the "destitution of the Bar," blaming it on the creation of County Courts where attorneys had a right of audience,[34] while a correspondent of the *Legal Observer* in 1852 similarly blamed the County Courts for the "degradation of the Bar."[35] The *Law Times* was blunt. In May 1852, an article titled "What's to Be Done?" offered this advice to junior barristers: "*Quit the Profession.* It does not, it cannot, and it will not, give you a maintenance. It is vain to wait and hope. *There is no hope.* The fact is palpable, that there is an enormous superabundance of Barristers."[36]

To similar effect, the plight of a young barrister was said to be "not called to honour and profit, but to idleness, poverty, and hopelessness."[37] Charles Rann Kennedy described the day-to-day work life of junior barristers:

> [S]cores of junior barristers – innocent mortals – are sitting in their chambers, reading "Coke upon Littleton," and volumes of reports, that will never be of the slightest use to one-sixth of them, each anxiously expecting that some clerk will soon be calling with a paper marked – "Case for the opinion of Mr. ..., ... one guinea." and astonished that no such person makes his appearance.[38]

Books offering career advice warned that only the well connected would succeed at the Bar.[39]

Many individual barristers, then, had to either graciously accept a life of deprivation and professional failure or actively seek to increase their own share of such market as existed for legal services. Not surprisingly, many junior barristers thought it best not to surrender their career ambitions without a struggle. Their grievance that a legitimate barristers' monopoly had been unfairly taken away from them was genuine. It combined with a belief that a public interest was adversely affected when the inferior branch of the legal profession engaged in advocacy on a large scale. In seeking to adjust to their circumstances, however, they ran head-on into an inherited professional ideology.

The Ideology of Advocacy

In order to survive, the bulk of junior barristers needed to engage in a businesslike practice, actively seeking out clients, advertising their services, offering to do legal work at fees competitive with those charged by attorneys, taking steps to cut down on business overhead, and generally working to stimulate the market, increase income, and decrease expenses. Such practices, however, violated generally accepted standards of behaviour at the Bar. While every barrister or attorney knew that there were "rules" of professional "etiquette," that is almost the only point on which there was general consensus. Professional etiquette did not operate like a code of conduct. Rather, it was "*lex non scripta* ... somewhat vague and difficult to define" so that even "the highest authorities differ on points of constant recurrence."[40]

Uncertainty attached to the content of the rules of etiquette, the source of their authority, the appropriate arbiters when questions arose, and even fundamental questions as to whether "etiquette" was in any way enforceable in the courts, the Inns, or the circuit messes (the informal organization of barristers as they travelled on circuit), or elsewhere – and, if so, by whom and by what means.[41] To recognize its nebulous quality is not to deny etiquette's effects, however. This ideology of barristering was pervasive, ever-felt. Most often unquestioned, it operated as an assumed "common sense" and was generally followed. Etiquette had the power of tradition, backed by the expectations, assumptions, and practices of established actors within and without the legal professions. Although neither fixed nor bureaucratically enforced, it had power to condition behaviour. Dicey aptly observed "that the laws of the Bar are so uncertain and indefinite that it is almost impossible that any one should be punished for their breach. It has also been urged, and with perfect truth, that they are constantly undergoing a silent change."[42]

The world-view of the Inns of Court placed heavy emphasis on the qualities of "gentlemen," importing a strikingly anti-commercial conception of legal practice.[43] For our purposes, eleven main rules, or conventions of practice, are significant:

- Barristers were prohibited from changing circuits after two or three years at the bar.[44]
- Barristers were prohibited from dealing directly with clients in civil cases and were expected to rely upon attorney intermediaries.[45]
- Barristers were prohibited from entering assize towns in advance of the court.[46]
- Barristers were discouraged from establishing permanent practices in provincial centres.[47]
- Barristers were prohibited from undertaking legal work for any fee less than one guinea (£1/1/- or £1.05).[48]
- Barristers were prohibited from undertaking legal work on any circuit other than the one they had joined, except upon payment of a special fee.[49]
- Barristers who were members of a particular circuit were discouraged from holding briefs before the courts of that circuit with anyone who was not a member of the circuit mess unless they charged a special fee.[50]
- Barristers were prohibited from advertising their services.[51]
- Barristers were prohibited from practising law in partnership with attorneys.[52]
- Barristers were prohibited from soliciting business directly by fraternizing with or currying the favour of attorneys.[53]
- Barristers were prohibited from entering into what would now be known as a contingency fee arrangement.[54]

Taken together, this constituted a starkly anti-commercial ideology of legal practice. Although it reflected long-established notions of gentlemanliness, it was increasingly in tension with the temper of the times, where "free trade is the all but universal rule in all careers."[55] Moreover, its impact was disparately felt. To take just one example, "the prohibition against counsel entering into direct consultations with lay clients and his resulting dependence upon the lower branch undoubtedly served to depress the earnings of fledgling barristers, while at the same time inflating the emoluments of the leaders whose services were most in demand."[56]

Contemporaries knew well that younger barristers bore the brunt of restrictions on competitive practices. They also knew that certain types of competitive advantage – such as family ties and connections – were left unhindered by the etiquette of the profession.[57] It was common knowledge that barristers "often owe their first start in life to the zeal with which relations or friends or acquaintances have solicited employment for them."[58] *The Times* asserted that "barristers can only expect to get into good practice through the interest of attorneys, and thence that the office becomes one of hereditary succession."[59] The effects were apparent:

> Legal etiquette, again, tends, on the whole, to lessen the rapidity with which any given barrister can obtain a pecuniary award for his labours ... It is a further and by no means desirable result of legal etiquette, to make the success of a young lawyer depend, far more than it naturally should do, upon connection. In fact, the rules of the Bar, while on the one hand attempting to make barristers assume an attitude of conventional independence towards attorneys, on the other hand render success, to a great extent, dependent upon the friendship of solicitors.[60]

This was a volatile mix. A dominant ideology within the profession hindered the careers of the majority of barristers while preserving the status, wealth, and privileges of the few. The profession's emphasis on its inherited etiquette enjoyed little credibility in the larger society.[61] This gave unsuccessful barristers reason to conclude that their lack of success was not attributable to their lack of ability or effort but to the artificial restrictions of professional etiquette.

A crucial third element was added at mid-century: the breakdown of traditional means of informal socialization and social control. Informal inducements and coercion diminished in effectiveness as it became apparent that the established bar could do little to sanction deviant behaviour. Significantly, even informal socialization suffered in the middle years of the nineteenth century, in part on account of increasing numbers[62] and in part because of technological advances. Raymond Cocks has shown that "the failure of the Inns to have any significant effect upon professional life" meant that the only significant locus of professional socialization in the second third of the nineteenth century was the circuit mess.[63] However, the development of rail communications radiating out from London drastically cut travel time and severely disrupted the messes.[64] Sir John Coleridge observed that

> many things – railways especially – have materially changed the circuit since I first joined the Western Circuit. Then we assembled usually in nearly our full number, at Winchester and continued together till the close in

> Somersetshire ... [Now,] ... the facilities that railways afforded made the attendance somewhat less regular, and in consequence the moral influence of the body on its members is much diminished.[65]

The disruptions caused by the creation of the County Courts took place at a time when self-interest, a reformist temperament of the times, a growing number of barristers, and the diminished moral influence of professional leaders had already fostered a rebellious mood among less successful barristers.

The Barristers' Revolt

The stage was set for a revolt of sorts as barristers sought to establish as legitimate certain forms of professional practice that would enable them to succeed. Some chose to work in unorthodox ways. They fought their battles, as necessary, in the marketplace, the legislature, the press, and the courts, and within the institutions that served as the custodians of professional etiquette. They had powerful allies and powerful foes. The revolt was less the result of coordinated insurrection than the product of a series of individual business activities. Professional innovators won a series of important victories in the legislature and in the courts. For a moment, they seemed likely to succeed in transforming professional practice. Ultimately, however, the force of inertia overcame their momentum.

Every good rebellion needs emotive appeal, identifiable opponents, specific short-term objectives, powerful supporters, a degree of external support, and bold martyr figures. The barristers' revolt of the 1850s had each of these.

Emotive Appeal

The twin issues that gave emotive appeal to the barristers' revolt drew elements from both the traditional ideology of the Bar and, incoherently, from prevailing notions of free trade. Pushed far enough, the one would have entirely destroyed the other, including the Bar's protected monopoly.[66] The revolt did not go so far, of course. Rebel barristers positioned themselves as gentlemen, albeit less fusty ones than their seniors. Their self-image was as "men of honour" whose services were uniquely valuable to their clients and essential to the proper functioning of justice. It coexisted with a willingness to shake things up within the Bar. Theirs was a limited free trade commitment, informed by a belief that their work should be free from some artificial restrictions: they should be able to perform legal services as they wished, whenever they wished, for whomever they wished, and at whatever fee might be negotiated.

The seemingly inconsistent threads reinforced one another in powerful combination. The creation by the *County Courts Act* of what was effectively a monopoly for attorneys generated criticism such as the following:

> Gentlemen, scholars and men of honour have been excluded from our provincial courts, and in lieu of them there has sprung up a tribe of a different character; the tribe of rascal pettifoggers; creatures that formerly crept not into the light of day, but now swarm like locusts over the country. The courts where such persons practise, having no respect for the advocate, lapse into a sort of easy indolence, which is fatal to the administration of justice. Some of these have been turned into beargardens, some into dens of thieves, where the suitors are betrayed, truth and honour derided, estates given up to wholesale pillage.[67]

Specific Short-Term Objectives

The particular objectives of the barristers' revolt took shape from the contradictory claims of status and commitment to free market principles. Barristers took pride in their status as men of superior capabilities and refinement. Gentlemen and barristers foremost, they were not inclined to abolish the formal distinction between the two branches of the legal profession, to restructure fundamentally the method of qualifying for the Bar, or otherwise change the legal world too much.[68]

The limits of their mission are indicted in the 1852 reflections of "A Junior."[69] The writer thought that the important problems with the recent reforms to the legal system lay in their adverse impact on the career prospects of junior barristers. This was a public, not just a private, problem because it affected "the public at large, to whom the due administration of justice is most important," by cutting off the sorts of opportunities constituting "that class of business by which the most eminent men were first brought into notice."[70] Blame was laid at the feet of a legislature that, by creating the County Courts, had diminished the role of the superior courts and effectively transferred work from junior barristers to the attorneys' profession.

"A Junior" considered three contemporary proposals for improving the condition of the Junior Bar. These were: (1) extending the jurisdiction of the County Courts into matters of equity as well as law;[71] (2) permitting advocates and attorneys to work in partnership, "adopting the system pursued in America"; and (3) abolishing "the existing system of etiquette" so as to permit "the barrister and his client to meet together professionally." "A Junior" thought the first absurdly impracticable as it would upset theories of law that were "the work of the most clearheaded, sagacious, and profound men for centuries past." He rejected the second on the basis that it would create a monopoly, have the effect of "destroying the independence of the Bar,"[72] and "gradually abolish all the distinctions which, at present, subsist" between barristers and attorneys, reducing "both branches of the Legal Profession to a mere trade."[73]

On this analysis, the only viable option was to free barristers from anti-competitive constraints imposed on them by legislation or etiquette. They would preserve their distinct professional status, monopoly of audience in superior courts, and exclusive eligibility for appointment to judicial and government positions.[74] Specifically, "A Junior" proposed that rules of etiquette prohibiting barristers from meeting clients other than through an attorney should be abolished, that barristers and attorneys should charge fees according to a statutory scale and *at the same rates,* and that "local 'Bars'" should be formed "throughout the country."[75]

While from one perspective all of this may have seemed quite radical, the proposals were, in context, modest. Knowing this, "A Junior" did not consider them to be farfetched, at least with regard to changes in bar etiquette. He assumed that the rule requiring an attorney intermediary would soon be gone "by consent of the Bar."[76] His concerns were widely felt within the Junior Bar and proposals such as these, no doubt, resonated within that constituency.

The most urgent needs were to respond somehow to the disruptions wrought by the *County Courts Act,* and abolishing (or simply ignoring) restrictions on direct client contact was the most obvious first step. Around this nucleus swirled initiatives relating to fee competition, advertising, the creation of "friendly societies" for the provision of legal services, change of circuits, prohibition of attorney advocacy, and the establishment of provincially based barristers' practices. The central focus of the rebellious junior barristers, however, was to open up possibilities to practise in the County Courts and to facilitate direct client contact: these gave logic, shape, and direction to everything else.

Reform of the County Courts Act

The problem that the original *County Courts Act* posed for junior barristers lay in a seemingly innocuous clause intended to preserve the monopolies of the two professions by preventing nonprofessional lay advocates from appearing on behalf of parties. Section 91 of the act provided that "no person shall be entitled to appear for any other party to any proceedings in any of the said Courts, unless he be an attorney of one of her Majesty's Superior Courts of Record, or a barrister at law instructed by such attorney, on behalf of the party."[77] On its face, this clause did little more than preserve the existing arrangements, while adding a right of audience for attorneys in the new court. It was not a radical innovation and barristers were specifically accorded a right of audience, subject only to a restriction that had long been generally recognized as part of professional etiquette: that they be instructed by an attorney and avoid direct client contact.[78] Enshrining etiquette in legislation fundamentally changed its character, however. It ceased to be fluid and contestable, and took on all the rigidity of a legal *rule.*

The new courts had transferred professional work from the superior courts, where barristers had a state-protected monopoly, to a new forum where, for the first time, they faced competition from attorney advocates. This came at a time when the Bar was already under pressure because of its growing size. Moreover, in this new forum, the old constraint of etiquette, now turned into law, meant that barristers' services would be prohibitively expensive. A client's decision to employ a barrister rather than an attorney advocate became in fact a decision to employ two lawyers, not one. This seemed to offend principles of political economy:

> To employ two men to do what can be better done by one, is as little expedient in law as in manufactures. Such an arrangement is not a division but a multiplication of labour, and therefore of expense. Nine tenths of the money spent in obtaining an opinion are spent in removing artificial difficulties interposed between the client and the barrister – the other tenth is for the opinion itself.[79]

The Bar's competitive disadvantage was aggravated by the combined effects of the *County Courts Act*'s scale of fees[80] and a rule of etiquette prohibiting barristers from charging fees less than one guinea.[81] The Junior Bar was squeezed further in 1850 when the monetary jurisdiction of the County Courts increased from twenty to fifty pounds.[82]

Acting at the behest of junior barristers in 1851, the Attorney-General attempted to move three related amendments through the House of Commons. One would have preserved the Bar's historical monopoly in cases above twenty pounds, another clarified expectations concerning attorneys acting as advocates, and the third sought to soften the 1846 legislative hardening of the constraints on direct client contact by barristers. Although no one of these was particularly radical, their combined effect would have turned the clock back. The *Legal Observer,* a vociferous defender of the attorneys' branch, introduced its discussion of the bill as follows:

> We think it is much to be regretted on the part of the Bar, that a few of its members have induced the Attorney-General to claim – 1st, exclusive audience in the County Courts in cases above £20; secondly, to prevent one attorney to act as the agent for another; and thirdly to enable a barrister to receive his instructions personally from the suitors, without the intervention of an attorney.[83]

The proposals sought to ameliorate the condition of junior barristers *at the expense of* attorneys. Coming after the increase in the County Courts' monetary jurisdiction, these changes might compel an attorney "to choose, between abandoning his client, or accompanying him to the county court and conducting the case without the assistance of counsel."[84] The Attorney-General's first two measures in a sense would have eliminated the professional impact of County Courts for cases where the matter in dispute was between £20 and £50: only barristers would have been able to appear and, for them, the only difference would have been that the cases would be heard in County Courts. The forum would change and little else. The convenience of County Courts would be considerably diminished if litigants were forced to wait until counsel were available in town to litigate their disputes. Both the affordability and relative cost-effectiveness of the forum would be compromised. A manifestly popular tribunal was threatened. These proposals were clearly protectionist in character and collided head-on with prevailing notions of free trade, the undesirability of monopoly, and utilitarian principle. Not surprisingly, the first two proposals failed to obtain the support of a majority of the House.[85]

The third proposal was a different matter, however. Removing a *legislated* prohibition on direct contact between barrister and client was consistent with free trade principles and did not directly subvert the etiquette of the Bar or its institutions. Although such a move would affect attorneys adversely,[86] it was difficult to maintain the position that a legislative barrier should be maintained solely to preserve their monopoly. The change would not *require* clients to retain barristers, and it seemed to open rather than restrict competition. Much more palatable than its companion measures, it made its way successfully through the House of Commons. The House of Lords was another matter, however. There it met a hostile reception from the Law Lords, most notably Lords Truro and Campbell.[87] Rejected by the upper chamber, the result was said to have "afforded very general satisfaction"[88] according to the *Legal Observer*.

Any satisfaction on the part of attorneys and established barristers was short-lived, however. An impressive campaign quickly emerged seeking amendment of the *County Courts Act* to permit direct client contact by barristers. Parliament was petitioned, pamphlets were circulated, and articles were published in the press. The Committee of Management for the Metropolitan and Provincial Law Association commented that this new phase in public debate about the County Courts continued to consume "a large share" of their "time and labour":

> The struggle on the part of the Bar, to obtain exclusive audience or pre-audience in those Courts – a struggle which, were it successful, would entirely subvert the whole principle and object of the institution of the Courts – having become evidently hopeless, has been turned into an agitation for the repeal of the restriction which prevents barristers appearing in the Courts, unless instructed by an attorney.[89]

Powerful Supporters

The external alliances and support enjoyed by the junior barristers was impressive. *The Times* of 1, 7, and 8 November 1851 criticized the prohibition on barristers' taking of instructions directly from clients as illogical, costly, and objectionable for making the Bar too dependent on the patronage of attorneys:

> Attorneys, and those, too, occupying the most respectable places in the profession, have sons, brothers, and sons-in-law in abundance, among whom to divide the money instructed to them by their clients for procuring the ablest legal advice ... The public have a right to get the best men for their money, and this *they certainly do not get under the present system.*[90]

The discussion focused attention on less-than-reputable practices by attorneys in their role as gatekeepers to the Bar. Both *The Times* and the *Law Review* suggested that attorneys frequently retained barristers, charged for a barrister's services, and then kept the money for themselves, safe in the knowledge that the barrister was unlikely to sue for fees.[91] Such a suit would appear ungentlemanly and contribute little to the cause of persuading other attorneys to bring work his way.

In December 1851, William D. Lewis at Gray's Inn advocated direct client contact for barristers in a lecture delivered at Gray's Inn.[92] A few months later, Serjeant Gaselee chaired a meeting of barristers interested in "breaking through the long-established Etiquette of the Bar, under which 'Instructions' can alone be received through the medium of an attorney."[93] A pamphlet campaign advanced the cause both before and after the failure of the Attorney-General's bill.[94] One pamphleteer, James Stephen, called for revolution within the Bar:

> [W]e would suggest that, without waiting for the decision of the leaders of the Bar, who having everything to lose and nothing to gain by any change, cannot fairly be expected to be very energetic in the cause of reform, and without calling a general meeting of the Bar, where much talk would be had without any result, a number of barristers sufficiently numerous to command attention, and to produce a *revolution* not a rebellion, should, by manifesto or otherwise, pledge themselves to see and transact business for clients desirous of their assistance, without the intervention of an attorney in all cases not inconsistent with the provisions of 6 & 7 Vict. c.73.[95]

A committee of the Law Amendment Society advocated the abolition of both the statutory requirement of attorney intermediaries in County Court actions *and* the rule of etiquette that discouraged direct client contact in other sorts of cases.[96]

The *Legal Observer* considered these sorts of ideas as being promoted on behalf of less competent barristers and thought the legislature inadequately informed as to the state of professional opinion.[97] The *Law Times* noted that the call for direct client contact was "unfortunately advocated by a considerable section of the Junior Bar."[98]

In June 1852, "Lord Brougham presented a petition from 130 members of the Inner Bar, to whose high position his Lordship bore testimony, in favour of the clause introduced into the County Courts Further Extension Bill, to enable barristers to practice in those courts without the intervention of an attorney."[99] How representative the petitioners were is, of course, a matter of conjecture. As barristers were entirely dependent on the patronage of attorneys, some would be reluctant to sign a petition likely to aggravate their patrons. At least one signatory withdrew his name when attorneys threatened to stop sending him business.[100] A separate account of the petition, which has not survived, has it that there were 150, not 130, petitioners, as well as a further 100 barristers who highly approved but did not sign.[101] The *Legal Observer* thought this to be unrepresentative of Bar opinion. Assuming that there were 3,500 barristers in total,[102] the inference that 3,250 disapproved was possible. It is difficult to know whether this calculation reflects wishful thinking or mere ineptitude. The number is wildly out of line with contemporary estimates of the number of working barristers. The *Legal Observer*'s estimate of the overall population of barristers could only have been a tally of the names included in the Law List or some similar source, with no effort to discern how many of the total number were practising. In fact, the 130 or 150 signatories, and perhaps a further 100 who supported but did not sign, represented a very significant proportion of the working bar. Even if it were true that no accomplished barristers favoured direct client contact,[103] there was considerable grassroots support.

In 1852, Lord Brougham presented a draft amendment to the *County Courts Act* to the House of Lords. It would have permitted the party himself or herself, an attorney or a barrister, *but not* an attorney instructed by another attorney, to appear as advocates.[104] The bill was amended in the House of Lords to read as follows: "It shall be competent for the party to appear personally, or by his wife, or by a clerk or servant *bona fide* in his actual employ, or by an Attorney properly concerned therein, and retained and instructed by the party, or by a Counsel instructed by such Attorney, but by no other person."[105] An expanded scope for lay advocacy within the confines of a household or business was to be permitted, but neither specialist attorney advocacy nor direct engagement of barristers was to be allowed.

The House of Commons took a different view, altering the right of audience so as to introduce complete *laissez-faire* in lawyering before the County Courts.[106] The reworded clause stated: "It shall be lawful for the party, or for an Attorney retained by or on behalf of the party, or for a Barrister retained by or on behalf of the party, or by leave of the Judge for any other person ..."[107] Thus stated, barristers and attorneys and – subject to judicial discretion – anyone else would have had equal right of audience in the County Courts under whatever arrangements client and representative might choose to make. Both direct client contact and attorney advocacy would have been permitted, and the County Courts would have opened up to competition between the two professions and, perhaps, between both and non-lawyer advocates.

Not surprisingly, the Commons' formulation did not meet with the approval of the House of Lords. They further amended the clause as follows:

> It shall be lawful for the party to the suit, or for an attorney of one of her Majesty's Superior Courts of Record, being an attorney acting generally in the action for such party, but not an attorney retained as an advocate by such first mentioned attorney, or for a barrister retained by or on behalf of the party on either side, but without any right of exclusive or pre-audience, or by leave of the Judge for any other person allowed by the Judge to appear instead of the party to address the Court, but subject to such regulations as the Judge may from time to time prescribe for the orderly transaction of the business of the Court.[108]

It was in this form that the clause ultimately became part of the 1852 *County Courts Act*. It gave barristers a distinct advantage.

The Junior Bar had won a significant victory. Or so it seemed. Specialist attorney advocacy was prohibited, and barristers were freed of the *statutory* prohibition on appearing in County Court cases without involvement of an attorney. Parliamentary blessing had been given to having some barristers focus on the County Courts and represent clients who engaged their services directly.[109] Only the Bar's etiquette blocked that path. It seemed to be a weak barrier. The *Law Times* observed that "[i]t rested entirely on usage and professional etiquette, and there was no provision of common or statute law against the practice of receiving instructions directly from the client."[110] Only two years earlier, the Court of Queen's Bench had ruled that it could not enforce a rule of etiquette preventing barristers from accepting briefs directly from clients in civil cases.[111] Moreover, it was at least arguable that *neither the circuit messes nor the Inns of Court* had the power to enforce their rules of etiquette against recalcitrant barristers.[112]

Significant statutory reform having been achieved, the conditions were now ripe for serious innovations in day-to-day practice. It was here that the "barristers' revolt" came into its own. On 3 July 1852, the *Legal Examiner* encouraged barristers to take advantage of the new permissive legislation by practising in County Courts for such fees as they might command: "[S]hall we take halfguinea fees or throw away a *great opportunity?*"[113]

From "Etiquette" to "Free Trade"

Barristers soon took advantage of the new opportunities. One highly publicized initiative involved a "Mutual Law Association," founded by Charles Rann Kennedy in Birmingham in July 1852 in association with John Raymond Grace (as counsel), Morton Jones (secretary), and Dr. Eccles and John Boucher (honorary directors).[114] Under the scheme, Kennedy and Grace would provide legal services at low cost to subscribers paying an annual fee of five shillings. Solicitors would work under the instruction of the two barristers, but it was emphasized "that members may have personal access to Counsel for advice." The legal services that were to have been provided by the barristers extended beyond litigation, to include "legal advice, instruction, assistance."[115] Advertisements indicated that the barristers would work on "Wills, Leases, Agreements, all kinds of Conveyancing, besides Court business," and that all work would "be charged for on a system intelligible to the Client, whereby the cost will be greatly diminished."[116] They also promised to settle "disputes by Arbitration, at small expense."[117]

The Mutual Law Association was fast off the mark in responding to the new situation. It massively flouted barristers' etiquette with respect to advertising, fee competition, direct client contact, and partnerships between barristers or with attorneys. It abutted common law prohibitions on champerty and maintenance.[118] The association relied upon solid, middle-class utilitarianism in defence of its turn from fusty traditions:

> Let us have done then with fustian and balderdash!
> Let us sweep away the dust and rubbish of antiquated ideas; let us do that which is right and honest, and adapt ourselves to the exigencies of society.[119]
>
> Oh, but the Inns of Court! Well! They are governed by gentlemen entitled to your respect; but they are not legislators, nor keepers of consciences. Do nothing but what is lawful and right, and you need fear no human being. The Benchers have plenty of work on their hands, without impeding useful reforms. They have much to do which their predecessors have left undone, in regard to legal education. I believe they are disposed to do their duty.[120]
>
> John Doe and Richard Roe were this year consigned to the grave, without a single person to lament their loss, or sing a dirge over their funeral. We have seen strange things. We have tolerated many absurdities; but there will be an end to them all. The abuses of centuries must be rectified.[121]
>
> That is the free-trade principle. The people of England have declared they will have it for corn. Lord Campbell declares in its favour for books. We will extend it to law.[122]

In short, an unapologetically commercial endeavour openly declared an intent to violate professional convention. Unsurprisingly, the Mutual Law Association was soon attacked in solicitors' journals,[123] blacklisted by local attorneys,[124] and scrutinized by both the Midland Circuit Mess[125] and the Inns of Court.[126]

The path of the Bar's processes, responses to them, and eventual outcomes are revealing. Although they must have known of Kennedy's Mutual Law Association at least from 10 July 1852, when it was reported in the *Law Observer*,[127] Inner Temple's Benchers took no action until November. They did not do so of their own initiative, but responded cautiously only in response to a letter of complaint from Thomas S. James, secretary of the Birmingham Law Society.[128] Received on 3 September 1852, the complaint was first brought forward at a Benchers' meeting on 5 November. At that occasion and throughout the month (9, 12, and 17 November), consideration was postponed. Finally, a specially convened meeting of the Benchers on 1 December took notice of Kennedy's address to the Mutual Law Association, concluding that it was "necessary to institute an investigation thereon." Although dealing with flagrant and admitted breach of barristers' etiquette, the Benchers were addressing unfamiliar questions and were hesitant about how to proceed. The *Bench Table Orders* recorded: "Committee of this House appointed to confer with the other Inns of Court on the same matter."[129] The questions referred to the other Inns for advice were fundamental:

> 1st. Whether Barristers may do business with Clients and without the intervention of Attornies.
> 2nd. Whether they may take fees on a rate of their own without reference to the usual rule as at present established in the profession.
> 3rd. Whether they may be disbarred for doing so in either case, or whether any and what order should be taken in the matter of such conduct.[130]

Kennedy seemingly felt little urgency about the investigation by his Inn. He neither retained counsel[131] nor made a personal appearance. His only response was to send to the Benchers copies of his address to the Mutual Law Association, inaugural lecture as Professor of Law at Queen's College, and letter to the Lord Chancellor on "Circuit Leagues." These were sent under cover of a letter stating that the documents would provide a "sufficiently full explanation of the plan and objects of the Society."[132]

The enclosures hammered away at the idea that barristers' etiquette was outdated, the product of "vanity," impracticable, un-English,[133] and unenforceable. Even if the Benchers were inclined to take a different view, Kennedy's perspective undoubtedly enjoyed a certain social licence. The Benchers had good reason to respond cautiously. Only two years earlier, Kennedy had forced the Midland Circuit Mess to withdraw a prohibition on its members' holding briefs with him (a form of blacklisting) in a dispute about etiquette.[134] The Inn confronted a formidable rebel.

Moreover, although disapproved by attorneys and by many senior barristers, the scheme *did* appear to have Parliament's blessing in the recent amendments to the *County Courts Act*. It was compatible with the general middle-class ethos favouring free trade and with recommendations of the Law Amendment Society. This constrained the Bar's institutions, themselves under public scrutiny at this time.[135] Nor could Benchers opposed to Kennedy's practices assume the uniform support of leading barristers. Lord Brougham's efforts on behalf of the junior barristers has been noted, and Lord Denman, who had previously gone on record regarding his concern for the Junior Bar,[136] waded into the etiquette debate with a lengthy letter to *The Times* in November 1852 calling for an overturn of the rules of etiquette and endorsing innovation.[137]

The Benchers clearly did not have a free hand. On the other hand, the attorneys had to be dealt with and not provoked. They passed a carefully worded resolution on 17 December:

> Resolved that ... Mr. Kennedy in projecting and carrying on the Scheme of the Mutual Law Association and by advertizing his name as that of the Counsel thereof and by otherwise advertizing himself as Counsel in manner appearing in the printed papers above referred to, has violated the practical rules (sanctioned by usage and public convenience) which govern the relations of Members of the Bar with each other, with the Attornies, and with the public.
>
> That Mr. Kennedy be admonished to withdraw himself from the promotion of the said Society and from advertizing himself as the Counsel thereof, or as Counsel generally.[138]

The Inn's modest rebuke and cautious wording reveal much about the state of Bar discipline and etiquette.[139] The assertion that the Bar's "practical rules" were "sanctioned by usage and public convenience" grounds authority in a fashion but also serves to signal that no greater foundation could be claimed. Moreover, they lacked the confidence even to specify most of the rules of etiquette breached by the Mutual Law Association. In focusing only on advertising and promotion, they let much else go by. Their caution suggests that they did not want another test case to emerge.

Kennedy responded that he would comply with the Benchers' request, but protested "against the whole proceeding" and threatened to seek legal redress.[140] He seems never to have followed through with this threat, but outlined his grounds of complaint in his response. These touched upon the inchoate nature of rules of etiquette, their unenforceability, the public interest, and the illegitimacy of any disciplinary proceedings by the Benchers:

> Mr K. gives notices that he will seek to obtain such redress as the laws of this country may afford on the following grounds.
>
> Because the proceedings of the Benchers though it may be founded on some precedents is unconstitutional.
>
> Because the Acts which the Benchers have censured are not an offence against any law of God or man or culpable in any point of view.
>
> Because if Mr K. has committed any offence at all it is one that should be cognizable by public opinion only.
>
> Because public opinion does not condemn Mr K., except perhaps that portion of it which is represented by his Rivals and their supporters.

> Because the facts which Mr K. has stated are true and his arguments have been unanswered.
>
> Because the practical rules which Mr K. is alleged to have violated are in no way defined or intelligible nor do the Benchers give any exposition of them except by reference to Mr Kennedy's acts.
>
> Because an inquisitorial body empowered to interpret such rules and to punish for their alleged violation of them is contrary to the spirit of English law, dangerous to the rights of the subject, and wholly unnecessary.
>
> Because the practical rules which have hitherto prevailed in regard to the profession of the Bar have not been found conducive to their advantage or to that of the public.
>
> Because the very sitting of an inquisitorial tribunal to judge of his conduct (independently of the result) is calculated to injure Mr K.'s character and his only protection against it is publicity.
>
> Because Mr K. is labouring to introduce reforms which he believes will elevate the Character and improve the condition of the Bar, which are in accordance with recent legislative enactments and are generally needed by the people of England but which the proceeding of the Benchers is calculated to impede.[141]

Kennedy clearly saw himself as a pioneer, leading the course of history. In any event, he managed to work without further interference by either Inn or circuit mess for the next decade. Despite the demise of the Mutual Law Association, he continued to engage in direct contact with his clients, working sometimes with an attorney or sharing a brief with another barrister, and sometimes working alone. Local newspaper reports reveal that he was a frequent advocate in County Court cases, usually representing smaller businesses and tradesmen.[142]

While Kennedy was one of the more flamboyant rebels at the bar, others also engaged in innovative practices that appeared likely to transform the work of the Bar. In the decade preceding the Mutual Law Association, no fewer than ten barristers had attempted to establish a local practice in Birmingham. All except Serjeant Allen (who was made standing counsel of the Licensed Victuallers' Association) failed and left the town.[143] Charles Broadbelt Claydon left Birmingham after fifteen months in which he "scarcely got a brief,"[144] eventually settling in Wolverhampton. There he engaged in direct client contact and maintained a successful practice in insolvency and County Court cases until 1862.[145]

In May 1853, a barrister advertised his services in the *Carlisle Patriot* as follows:

> To the public. Solomon Atkinson, Barrister-at-Law, may be consulted personally at his Offices, No. 8, Crescent, Carlisle, by all persons having business in the County Courts or Magistrates' Courts, in cases of Insolvency or Bankruptcy, or on all matters relating to the sale, purchase, or mortgage of landed or other property. Conveyances, Mortgages, Leases, Assignments, for the benefit of Creditors, Wills, Agreements, and other legal documents, prepared at one-third the usual charge.[146]

All of the main features of the Mutual Law Association are here – direct client contact, multifaceted legal services, litigation focused on inferior tribunals, local practice, and fee cutting. Predictably, Atkinson encountered resistance. The Metropolitan and Provincial Law Association viewed his initiatives as a "case of encroachment, being an offence, not against the law of the land, but against the well-understood etiquette of the Profession," and complained to the Benchers of Lincoln's Inn, where, they believed, the matter had been concluded.[147]

In London, a group of seven barristers announced their intention to regularly practise at the Westminster County Court forming, in effect, a metropolitan version of a "local" bar. This group too thumbed their noses at professional etiquette, announcing that "they intend to hold themselves at liberty, upon proper occasions, to exercise their common right of direct communication with the client."[148] They would, moreover, represent clients at a fee that was only one-half the usual minimum of one guinea prescribed by etiquette.[149]

Although there had been earlier calls for competitive pricing[150] and precedents permitting fee cutting,[151] the new Westminster County Court bar met considerable hostility. Lord St. Leonard, LC, speaking in the House of Lords, criticized barristers who attempted to compete with attorneys and who engaged in direct contact with clients.[152] The attorneys' periodical press mixed regular appeals to the Benchers to "do something" about flagrant breaches of etiquette[153] with threats to proceed against deviant barristers on their own, including for unauthorized practice as a solicitor.[154] In the event, the Westminster County Court bar was left to its natural fate – quite possibly because its practice signified little new and little of consequence. Early in 1853 it was reported to "have had few clients, we believe, and no followers."[155]

Support for such innovations soon faded. In February 1853, the Law Amendment Society issued "an authoritative announcement" disclaiming "all consent or concurrence with those members of the Junior Bar, who sought to make the repeal of the 9 & 10 Vict. c. 95, s. 91, a pretext for abandoning the established usage of the profession, and uniting in their own persons the separate functions of barrister and attorney."[156] By May 1853, attorneys viewed the upcoming Parliament with equanimity, assured that "*the worst has past*"[157] and pleased with their success in stymieing innovation: "[E]xperience has shown that the timely interference of the Law Societies, and even of individual members of the Legal Profession, has been frequently efficacious in preventing or mitigating the operation of objectionable provisions."[158]

The attorneys' victory was greatly exaggerated, however. In the decade after 1853, a sort of stand-off emerged and a period of quiet ensued. There were no further mass petitions to Parliament, no large meetings of disaffected barristers, no headline-grabbing experiments in legal practice. The established leaders of the Bar stayed their hand. They avoided any moves likely to provoke further public inquiry or a more determined rebellion within their profession. While Benchers and the leaders of circuit messes continued to frown upon the establishment of local practices, fee cutting, and direct client contact, they did little to interfere with barristers who practised in these ways.

Two documented cases illustrate this. Although Kennedy dissolved his Mutual Law Association, he continued to work in the County Courts, taking instructions directly from his clients for such fees as might be arranged between them, accepting briefs referred from attorneys, *and* sharing briefs with other barristers, for the rest of his life.[159] Charles Broadbelt Claydon earned a living as a local barrister engaging in County Court work in Wolverhampton, taking instructions directly from clients until 1862, when he was disbarred.[160] Neither sparked formal protest by attorneys during the stand-off period. The editors of legal periodicals remained silent, and the exploits of the barristers were reported only in local newspapers, if at all. It seems likely that other barristers engaged in similar low-profile local practices throughout the country.[161]

Stand-off

In sum, rebel junior barristers gained considerable momentum in their quest to commercialize the barristers' profession during the 1850s. Their opponents, however, were both well placed and well organized, and included most of the recognized leadership of both the barristers' and the attorneys' branches of the legal profession.

Nonetheless, neither Benchers nor law society leaders had much in the way of practical response once collegial suasion and then blacklisting were exhausted. The barristers' rebellion was provoked in part precisely because established attorneys did not control sufficient patronage to make – and therefore break – barristers' careers: there was little to fear from threats of blacklisting by those who would never employ you anyway. Attorneys could bluster about unauthorized practice as an attorney, but threats to bring charges were largely idle. One reason may have been the difficulty in articulating a clear and judicable dividing line between the privileges and duties of two professions whose relations to each other were defined by etiquette, not by law.[162] Lacking effective economic or legal leverage, the attorneys' profession could act against rebel barristers only by pressing Benchers and circuit leaders – individuals whose success *was* attributable to attorney patronage – to use such power as they had against renegades at the bar.

Astute observers knew they had no power to speak of.[163] The Inns were simply not in the habit of punishing barristers and had no legal authority to do so. Similarly, the circuit messes had little real power beyond peer pressure. This was least effective against impecunious or genuine rebel barristers who expected to gain little from the good feelings of their peers. Kennedy's case provides well-documented illustration: the Midland Circuit Mess's earlier refusal to admit him had the effect of liberating him of any future constraint. There were some notable attempts within the Bar to enforce the rules of etiquette, but even these reveal hesitancy, uncertainty, and, in truth, the impotence of their institutions. At a time when the entire legal system was under intensely skeptical public scrutiny, the Benchers could not allow the Inns to appear as private clubs pursuing their own interest. The informed public was aware that decisions of the elite patriarchy that formed the Bench of each Inn could affect both the livelihood of individual barristers and the administration of justice at large. The self-regulation of the Bar was not then conceived of as it is for twenty-first-century regulatory bodies. And even the continuation of its more limited traditional roles could not be taken for granted. There was a real risk that missteps by the Benchers might well provoke legislative intervention, possibly of a fundamental nature.

The Bar had no tradition of exercising disciplinary power in the way opponents of free market barristers wished. The word "disbar" was in currency, but did not generally connote the culmination of disciplinary proceedings. Individuals who could not afford the expenses of bar membership, who wished to become attorneys, or who were leaving England would ask to be "disbarred."[164] No shame was implied. In other cases, the Benchers of an Inn might disbar a barrister on account of some offence,[165] but there was no established routine for disciplinary disbarment as such. In 1850, the Lincoln's Inn Benchers were uncertain how to proceed when Robert French Burnett asked to be disbarred. A report produced by the committee struck to look into the matter reveals that the notion of "disbarring" was unfamiliar.[166]

The pressures of the 1840s and 1850s did lead to some continuing attention to such matters. Consultation among the Inns arising from Thomas James's complaint about the Mutual Law Association indicates uncertainty as to the character of etiquette, its boundaries, and the Inns' authority. The Benchers' lack of confidence resurfaced nearly a decade later, when the Inner Temple Bench sought a committee report "as to the expediency of establishing some authority to which all questions connected with the practice of the Bar may be referred," directing the under-treasurer to inquire of the other Inns "for which crime or misconduct a Barrister has at any time been disbarred."[167] Similarly, in 1863, the Lincoln's Inn Benchers "[o]rdered that precedents be searched for, in the Books of this Society, and obtained from the Other Inns" in order to support their defence to a court challenge of a disbarment.[168] The novelty of the idea of punitive disbarment was confirmed by the treasurer's subsequent report that the Inn had only once previously punished a barrister by disbarment – and that over twenty years earlier.[169]

In sum, the Inns were exploring the idea of enforcing professional etiquette, but doing so cautiously, unsure of their own past and uncertain of where they wished to end up. Nonetheless, the Inns presented the only plausible locus from which to constitute a disciplinary apparatus. Though circuit messes might influence behaviour, they lacked systematic enforcement procedures and were incapable of dealing with determined deviants.[170]

When the Inns did take action against rebels against etiquette, it was under pressure from attorneys objecting to new competition. A failure to police etiquette might provoke increasing commercial competition with the attorneys' branch.[171] That the fusion of the two professions was one possible longer-term consequence was well recognized.[172] The Benchers, however, had little freedom of movement. As leaders of archaic institutions subjected to intense public scrutiny in an age of reform, they lacked precedential, utilitarian, or democratic legitimation for the routine exercise of disciplinary powers.

Nonetheless, institutions are typically more durable than those who seek to change them. The sense that the Bar establishment was powerless was soon to shift. Generational die-off and a smaller rate of growth worked to strengthen the hand of more conservative elements of the Bar. The Inns learned from the missteps of the previous decade and grew in their experience of disciplinary matters, and the terrain shifted rapidly again in the early 1860s.

Conclusion

The barristers' revolt of the 1850s did not have apocalyptic effect. A quiet stand-off followed the noise and fury: the petitions to Parliament, mass meetings of the reform-minded barristers, disruptive legislative changes, public letters of distinguished jurists, recommendations of "expert" bodies, dramatic innovations by individuals or groups of barristers, press debate, attorney protests, commentary in professional journals, and threats and counter-threats fell away. The Inns were not swept aside, the attorneys' branch was not decimated. "Justice" was not compromised, and fusion of the two legal professions soon seemed as unlikely as it had ever been.

For the most part, barristers continued to practise law wherever they saw fit and in whatever manner they wished. While the hostility of attorneys, circuit messes, and Benchers would have been daunting to most, the junior barristers' revolt of the early 1850s concluded in a quiet period of largely unfettered *laissez-faire*.

The very success of the junior barristers' revolt provoked their opponents to more aggressive response. The idea of transforming the Inns from private clubs or bare qualifying associations into disciplinary jurisdictions capable of seeking out and punishing law-abiding but socially deviant individuals began to take shape. Within the Inns, the practice of conferring with one another about etiquette developed, demonstrating the desirability of establishing an authoritative code of etiquette and identifying means of enforcement. Local law societies had learned to watch what barristers were doing in their localities and to express any concerns they had to the formal organs of the Bar. In the result, a disruptive *laissez-faire* ideology of legal practice provoked responses that were authoritarian, centrist, and monopolistic in character.

Although their opponents would ultimately prevail, the rebel barristers of the 1850s had good reason to act as they did. They achieved a considerable degree of success, and had every reason to believe that historical forces were unalterably aligned on their side.

Notes

An earlier version of this chapter appeared as "Rebels at the Bar: English Barristers and the County Courts in the 1850s" (1987) 16 Anglo-Am. L. Rev. 303. It has been revised and reprinted here with permission.

1 Daniel Duman, *The English and Colonial Bars in the Nineteenth Century* (London: Croom Helm, 1983) [*English and Colonial Bars*].

2 *Ibid.* at 9.

3 Magali Sarfatti Larson, *The Rise of Professionalism: A Sociological Analysis* (Berkeley: University of California Press, 1977) at 9, 14.

4 By the mid-nineteenth century, the functions and regulation of solicitors and attorneys had become identical. Later, the common title "solicitor" was sanctioned by statute: the *Supreme Court of Judicature Act,* 36 & 37 Vict., c. 66, 1873. See B. Abel-Smith and R.B. Stevens, *Lawyers and the Courts: A Sociological Study of the English Legal System, 1750-1965* (London: Heinemann, 1967) at 15, 53n. The term "attorney" was commonly used in the 1850s, however, and that usage is adopted here.

5 For an overview of relations between the attorneys' and barristers' branches of the legal profession, see Harry Kirk, *Portrait of a Profession: A History of the Solicitor's Profession,*

1100 to the Present Day (London: Oycz Publishing, 1976) at 168-87; Richard L. Abel, *Legal Profession in England and Wales* (Oxford: Oxford University Press, 1988).

6 W. Shaen, Secretary of the Metropolitan and Provincial Law Association, "On the Organization of the Profession, as It Ought to Be, and as It Is" *Metropolitan and Provincial Law Association, Circular 8* (1855) 39 at 45-46.

7 J. Bulmer, "Upon the Present State of the Legal Profession in England" *Metropolitan and Provincial Law Association, Circular 8* (1855) 24 at 31-32.

8 *County Courts Act, 1846,* 9 & 10 Vict., c. 95; *County Courts Act, 1850,* 13 & 14 Vict., c. 61; Abel-Smith and Stevens, *supra* note 4 at 35. See also Patrick Polden, *A History of the County Court, 1846-1971* (Cambridge: Cambridge University Press, 1999).

9 Abel-Smith and Stevens, *supra* note 4 at 35. Lord Lyndhurst, *Hansard,* 3d series (H of L), 18 (17 June 1833) at col. 880, as quoted in Abel-Smith and Stevens, *ibid.* at 33, n. 9.

10 "Relations between the Bar and Attorneys. Report of the Law Amendment Society" *Legal Observer* 43 (20 December 1851) 125 at 125 ["Relations between the Bar and Attorneys"].

11 Abel-Smith and Stevens, *supra* note 4 at 35, quoting figures of Sir Geoffrey Cross and G.D.G. Hall, eds., *Radcliffe and Cross: The English Legal System,* 4th ed. (London: Butterworths, 1964) at 282.

12 Kirk, *supra* note 5 at 157; A.H. Manchester, *Modern Legal History of England and Wales, 1750-1950* (London: Butterworths, 1980) at 72 reports that Henry Mayhew published "a table showing the distribution of the professional classes throughout London, a map of the Inns of Court and their descriptions."

13 Kirk, *ibid.* at 156-57.

14 See A.V. Dicey, "Legal Etiquette" *Fortnightly Review* 8 (1 August 1867) 169 at 173; Raymond Cocks, *Foundations of the Modern Bar* (London: Sweet and Maxwell, 1983); Duman, *English and Colonial Bars, supra* note 1.

15 See Charles Rann Kennedy, *A Letter to the Lord Chancellor on the Subject of Circuit Leagues* (Birmingham: Josiah Allen and Son, 1850) [*Circuit Leagues*]. The unenforceable character of bar etiquette was recognized by the courts in *Bennett (Doe d.) v. Hale* (1850), 15 QB 171; 117 ER 423 [*Bennett v. Hale*].

16 See "County Courts Further Extension Bill" *Legal Observer* 44 (19 June 1852) 121, expressing the fear (albeit in an attorney's organ) that County Courts resulted in the appearance of "a race of barristers ... who would not be altogether influenced by the prevalent feeling of the heads of the Profession."

17 See "Etiquette of the Bar" *Law Times* 17 (30 August 1851) 209. On the etiquette of the Bar, see P. Polden, "The Courts of Law" in W. Cornish et al., *The Oxford History of the Laws of England,* vol. 11 (Oxford: Oxford University Press, 2010) at 1096-1107.

18 "The Etiquette of the Bar" *Law Magazine* (1857) 236 at 240.

19 See Abel-Smith and Stevens, *supra* note 4 at 231-32 and the sources cited therein (failure to appear). Also "Counsel Practising in Several Courts" *Solicitors Journal* 2 (20 February 1858) 329 (letter complaining of barristers failing to appear); "Relations between the Bar and Attorneys," *supra* note 10. General complaints about "cavalier" treatment of briefs or of "negligence" were common. See, for example, a letter from "A Managing Clerk" headed "The Status of Counsel" *Solicitor's Journal* (20 June 1863) 625; a letter from "B" headed "Remuneration of Barristers" *Solicitor's Journal* (4 July 1863) 661.

20 See Chapter 4 in this volume.

21 See Abel-Smith and Stevens, *supra* note 4 at chs. 2 and 3; Manchester, *supra* note 12 at chs. 6 and 7; Cocks, *Foundations of the Modern Bar, supra* note 14 at ch. 3. Cocks, *ibid.* at 93, describes the Bar as being "trapped in a situation in which legislative reform, professional mismanagement, and public indignation continually reinforced each other."

22 Duman, *English and Colonial Bars, supra* note 1.

23 *Ibid.* at 8.

24 *Ibid.* at 207.
25 *Ibid.*
26 See, further, R. Cocks, "The Middle Temple in the 19th Century" in R.O. Havery, ed., *History of the Middle Temple* (Oxford: Hart, 2011) 287 ["The Middle Temple"]; and D. Woolley, "Article: The Inn as a Disciplinary Body" in Havery, *ibid.* at 337-72.
27 See E.P. Thompson, *The Making of the English Working Class* (Harmondsworth: Penguin Books, 1968) at ch. 10 (partially qualified in "Postscript" at 916) for an analogous discussion of the "standard of living" debate in the history of industrialization.
28 Duman, *English and Colonial Bars, supra* note 1 at 96-98, discusses bankruptcy commissioners (abolished in London in 1831), revising barristerships ("two or three hundred men," according to Charles Rann Kennedy, *A Letter to the Lord Chancellor on the Subject of the Revising Barristers* [London: Butterworth, n.d.]), and recorderships (approximately one hundred in England and Wales in the last quarter of the century). Only the revising barristerships offered any significant amelioration to bar underemployment in the middle portion of the century, while other opportunities that Duman discusses did not, by his own account, become significant until the later decades of the century. See *supra* note 23 and accompanying text. The County Court judgeships provided alternative careers for only sixty barristers in total, and even these positions were not open to barristers in general upon the creation of the new courts, judges of the Courts of Request being given first claim (Duman, *English and Colonial Bars, supra* note 1 at 97 and 119, n. 94).
29 Thompson, *supra* note 27 at 94, 97-98.
30 Duman, *English and Colonial Bars, supra* note 1 at 146. See also Daniel Duman, *The Judicial Bench in England, 1727-1875* (London: Royal Historical Society, 1982) at ch. 5 [*Judicial Bench*]. For evidence of a more anecdotal nature concerning barristers' incomes, see J.R. Lewis, *The Victorian Bar* (London: Robert Hale, 1982) at 38-41.
31 *Law Times* 8 (27 March 1847) 563.
32 *Law Times* 13 (15 September 1849) 583.
33 *Law Times* 13 (11 August 1849) 438.
34 Reported in "Lord Denman, the Bar, and the County Courts" *Legal Observer* 42 (28 June 1851) 149.
35 "Selections from Correspondence," "County Courts – Degradation of the Bar" *Legal Observer* 43 (24 January 1852) 237.
36 "What's to Be Done?" *Law Times* 19 (29 May 1852) 65 [emphasis in original].
37 "Professional Prospects" *Law Times* 19 (12 June 1852) 82.
38 Charles Rann Kennedy, *Address to the Mutual Law Association* (Birmingham: John Tonks, 1852) at 5 [*Address to the Mutual Law Association*].
39 Samuel Warren, *A Popular and Practical Introduction to Law Studies,* 2d ed./3d ed. (London, 1844/1863).
40 "The Etiquette of the Bar" *Law Magazine* (1857) 236 at 237.
41 For example, "Etiquette of the Bar" *Law Times* 17 (1851) 209; *Advocacy in the County Courts. A Letter to Sir Alexander Cockburn, MP, Her Majesty's Attorney General, by a Barrister of the Inner Temple* (London, 1851); "Societies and Institutions. The Law Amendment Society" *Solicitor's Journal and Reporter* (7 February 1863) 265. See also Kennedy, *Circuit Leagues, supra* note 15; *Address to the Mutual Law Association, supra* note 38; *Mr. Kennedy's Argument in the Common Pleas against the Rule Obtained by the Defendants in Kennedy v. Brown and Wife* (Birmingham: S.B. Howell, 1863 [?]).
42 Dicey, *supra* note 14 at 179. Dicey was weighing in on a contemporary discussion of the trades union analogy. His immediate foils were an article by a journeyman engineer in the *Pall Mall Gazette* of 15 May 1867 and a reply by a "Barrister" within a day or two (*ibid.* at 169). That debate may, in turn, have been sparked by the March 1867 publication of Charles Rann Kennedy's "To the Legal Profession and the Public. Bar Unionists" ["Bar Unionists"],

reproduced in John Pym Yeatman's *The Professorship of the Law Department of the Queen's College, Birmingham. A Letter to the Council and Governors* (Birmingham: M. Maher and Son, 1869) at 23-26 [*Professorship of the Law Department*].

43 Duman, *Judicial Bench, supra* note 30 at 178-79, offers a somewhat different perspective in contrasting the mid-nineteenth century with the eighteenth. In fact, most of the distinctions between eighteenth- and nineteenth-century professionalism that he points to were still in contention in the 1850s.

44 See Yeatman, *Professorship of the Law Department, supra* note 42 at 6-7.

45 See *Bennett v. Hale, supra* note 15; speeches of the Lord Chancellor and Lord Campbell regarding 15 & 16 Vict., c. 54, *An Act to Facilitate and Arrange Proceedings in the County Courts,* as cited in *Metropolitan and Provincial Law Association, Circular 2* (1852) 11 at 13. "County Courts Further Extension Bill" *Legal Observer* 44 (26 June 1852) 144 reports that all the Law Lords hoped that this rule of etiquette would be adhered to notwithstanding the passage of the *County Courts Further Extension Bill.*

46 Anthony Harwood, QC, *A Hundred Years of the Midland Circuit* (unpublished manuscript lodged with the Bodleian Library) records that at a Midland Circuit Mess meeting, at Leicester on 26 March 1850, "Mr. Humfrey, QC, wanted to know if there was any rule preventing members of the circuit entering an assize town during the assize before commission day ... it appeared to be the *unanimous* feeling of the members of the circuit court not to enter Coventry or any other assize town during the assize before commission day."

47 "The Profession in the County Courts" *Law Times* 19 (26 June 1852) 101.

48 See Kennedy, *Address to the Mutual Law Association, supra* note 38 at 5; Dicey, *supra* note 14 at 171, 172.

49 For scathing criticisms of this rule, see Charles Rann Kennedy's pamphlets: *Circuit Leagues, supra* note 15; *Address to the Mutual Law Association, ibid.*

50 See John Pym Yeatman, *The Humble Petition of John Pym Yeatman* (1907), privately printed, copy in Chesterfield Local Studies Library, Derbyshire, UK; Kennedy, "Bar Unionists," *supra* note 44.

51 Inner Temple, *Bench Table Orders,* 17 December 1852. See also Dicey, *supra* note 14 at 175.

52 Dicey, *ibid.* at 172.

53 Dicey, *ibid.* at 173, says that "[a]ll the rules which have the first aim (*i.e.,* promoting 'honourable conduct') may be summed up under the one law – thou shalt not hug attorneys. Under this head may be brought many minor regulations, such as rules against frequenting public coffee-rooms, or unduly cultivating the society of attorneys during circuit."

54 Such arrangements were frowned upon by the legal establishment, as the *Kennedy v. Brown* litigation reveals, even when they did not cross the line into the legally prohibited territory of champerty or maintenance.

55 Dicey, *supra* note 14 at 178.

56 Duman, *English and Colonial Bars, supra* note 1 at 146-47.

57 A pattern also observed elsewhere. See, for example, J.S. Auerbach, *Unequal Justice: Lawyers and Social Change in Modern America* (New York: Oxford University Press, 1976), on the United States forty to seventy years later.

58 Dicey, *supra* note 14 at 175.

59 *The Times* (1 November 1851).

60 Dicey, *supra* note 14 at 177.

61 In addition to Duman and Dicey, see Cocks, *Foundations of the Modern Bar, supra* note 14; Abel-Smith and Stevens, *supra* note 4. *The Times* frequently criticized the Bar from the perspective of utilitarian and "free trade" ideology: see Cocks, *ibid.* at 89ff., and discussion below.

62 Lord Denman, *The Times* (1 November 1852) 5 (as cited in Cocks, *ibid.* at 88-89).

63 Cocks, *ibid.* at 22 and generally ch. 1.

64 Abel-Smith and Stevens, *supra* note 4 at 84-86; Cocks, *ibid.* at 126.
65 Sir John Coleridge, "Address to Exeter Library Society" *Law Times* 34 (1859) 28 (as cited in Cocks, *ibid.*).
66 A letter to the editor published as "The Bar and the Attorneys" *Legal Observer* 45 (20 November 1852) 45 complains about "the junior barrister of 7 years standing, whose lamentation appeared in *The Times* of the 2nd inst ... If barristers think fit thus to repudiate one old-established rule of their Profession, they should be content to submit the entire code of their protecting and *productive* rules to a searching revision, and which would afford more relief to a suitor than the severest taxation of his attorney's bill."
67 Kennedy, *Address to the Mutual Law Association, supra* note 38 at 8. To similar effect, see "County Courts – The Degradation of the Bar," a letter published in *Legal Observer* 43 (24 January 1852) 237: "The dignity and majesty of the law seems almost forgotten in the sort of free trade in law occasioned by the County Courts." The writer called for "a reasonable consideration of the effect occasioned by the establishment of these petty local courts upon the Bar ... to which this country owes no small proportion of its solid grandeur and useful greatness."
68 Many attorneys, on the other hand, particularly members of the Metropolitan and Provincial Law Association, saw no reason for not carrying their utilitarian critiques of the status quo through to such conclusions. See, for example, the speech of J. Bulmer to the Metropolitan and Provincial Law Association at Birmingham in 1855 advocating the fusion of the two professions: *Supplement to the Birmingham Journal and Commercial Advertiser* (27 October 1855) at 3, col. 1-5; Mr. Field, (1856) "Economical Considerations on the Autocracy of the Bar, and on the System of Prescribed Tariffs for Legal Wages, and on the Connection of these Two Subjects" *Metropolitan and Provincial Law Association, Circular 10* (1856). In December 1855, the *Daily News* advocated fusion on the grounds that "as regards the barrister, it at once gets rid of the favourite grievance of Mr Phillimore – the hardship, namely, of not being put in direct communication with the public ... As regards the attorneys, it raises them at once in the social scale, does away for ever with an invidious and now groundless distinction, throws open to them the official prizes of the law," as quoted in "Opinions of the Press on the Proposed Law University" *Legal Observer* 51 (22 December 1855) 146.
69 "A Junior," *Thoughts of a Junior on His Position and Prospects: With a Few Hints to Reformers* (London: Simpkin, Marshall, 1852). This pamphlet was quoted extensively and critiqued in "Prospects of the Junior Bar" *Legal Observer* 44 (12 June 1852)114 ["Prospects of the Junior Bar"]; "Position and Prospects of the Bar" *Law Times* 19 (22 May 1852) 7. It appeared just months before Charles Kennedy began his Mutual Law Association.
70 "Prospects of the Junior Bar," *ibid.* at 114.
71 This idea came up again in evidence given to the County Court Commission on 26 May 1854. See *Legal Observer* 49 (11 November 1854) 21, reaching the conclusion that "there is no subject, Civil or Criminal, that ought not to be brought within the jurisdiction of the County Courts, though limited as they were expressly on their creation to 'small debts and demands'" (at 24).
72 "Prospects of the Junior Bar," *supra* note 69. The "monopoly" he referred to was the exclusive relationship between attorney and barrister such that the attorney would not likely engage other barristers on behalf of his clients. The barrister's independent judgment would be clouded by his exclusive arrangement with a particular attorney, making him less likely to give advice or pursue strategies that were not to the attorney's liking.
73 *Ibid.* at 115.
74 The Bar's monopoly and special entitlements were much resented by some attorneys. See Bulmer, *supra* note 7.
75 "A Junior," *supra* note 69 at 115.

76 *Ibid.* When the Benchers of Inner Temple subsequently intervened against Kennedy's Mutual Law Association, they did so only on the grounds that it involved advertising – even though it was well known that Kennedy engaged in direct client contact. See Inner Temple, *supra* note 51. Compare the disbarment of Charles Broadbelt Claydon a decade later, regarding which the *Morning Star* observed that "the reason is not, as is supposed, that Mr Claydon has taken briefs from clients without the intervention of an attorney. Such a ground would be entirely unwarranted in law" (as quoted in *Aris's Birmingham Gazette* [1 March 1862] at 7, col. 2).

77 *County Courts Act, 1846,* 9 & 10 Vict., c. 95. To similar effect, the *Bankrupt Law Consolidation Act, 1849,* 12 & 13 Vict., c. 106, s. 247, provided that solicitors admitted in the Court of Bankruptcy "may appear and plead in any proceedings in that Court without being required to employ counsel."

78 The *Legal Observer* published an article critical of proposals for direct contact between barristers and clients. In "The County Court's Extension Bill. The Bar and the Attorneys" *Legal Observer* 42 (19 July 1851) 216, the importance of work undertaken by attorneys is emphasized: "[T]he permission to communicate directly with suitors, is both a dangerous and inconvenient privilege. Is the barrister or his clerk, or some other unqualified person to 'get up the case?' Is he to take the instructions, investigate the facts, serve the notices, see the witnesses, and issue and serve subpoenas; or is the bailiff of the Court to perform all or any of these services?"

79 *The Times* (7 November 1851). The perspective offered by *The Times* was objected to on the basis that "*The Times* has evidently been deceived by some ill-informed, prejudiced, or interested law reformers of the Junior Bar, who desire some mighty change by which their brieflessness may be relieved ... We have heard the name of the writer who has been permitted to pour forth his ignorant slander before the public, but defer the notice we have been called upon to take of his further misrepresentations": "The Bar and the Attorneys. Remarks on Assertions in *The Times*" *Legal Observer* 43 (15 November 1851) 39 at 39 ["The Bar and the Attorneys"].

80 Both branches of the legal profession complained of the scale of fees in County Court cases. See Abel-Smith and Stevens, *supra* note 4 at 34-36.

81 The rule of etiquette was referred to the Attorney-General as an arbiter of etiquette by Special Pleaders in response to a series of procedural law reforms in 1852. See *Legal Observer* 45 (6 November 1852) 1 at 2. It should be noted that various minimum fees were prescribed for barristers, of which the one-guinea fee was the rock bottom. See the Northern Circuit ruling on County Court practice reported in "Etiquette of the Bar" *Law Times* 17 (30 August 1851) 209. Rules of etiquette regarding fees were rejected by Charles Rann Kennedy as "contrary to every maxim of political economy and common sense"; see *Address to the Mutual Law Association, supra* note 38 at 5.

82 *County Courts Act, 1850,* 13 & 14 Vict., c. 61.

83 "The County Courts Extension Bill. The Bar and the Attorneys" *Legal Observer* 42 (19 July 1851) 216.

84 "Relations between the Bar and Attorneys," *supra* note 10 at 126.

85 *Ibid.*

86 See the discussion of the proposal in *Legal Observer* 42 (7 June 1851) 89.

87 See the *Annual Report of the Metropolitan and Provincial Law Association* (1852) at 15.

88 "County Courts Further Extension Bill. Bar Etiquette" *Legal Observer* 42 (23 August 1851) 311.

89 *Annual Report of the Metropolitan and Provincial Law Association, supra* note 87 at 12.

90 *The Times* (8 November 1851). See the discussion in "The Bar and the Attorneys," *supra* note 79 at 39-40. Specific assertions contained in *The Times* on 1 November were contradicted

in a letter to the *Legal Observer* titled "'The Bar and the Attorneys. Remarks on Assertions in *The Times*," *supra* note 79 at 40-41.

91 The *Times* and *Law Review* articles are discussed critically in "Non-payment by Attorneys of Counsels' Fees" *Legal Observer* 43 (22 November 1851) 56.

92 See "County Courts – The Bar and the Attorneys – Professional Remuneration" *Legal Observer* 43 (13 December 1852) 107. The *Legal Observer* thought this amounted to a proposal to abolish all distinction between the two legal professions.

93 "The County Court Bar Meeting" *Legal Observer* 43 (6 March 1852) 348.

94 *E.g.*, "A Junior," *supra* note 69; James Stephen, *Bar Etiquette, in Reference to the Rule Requiring the Intermediary Agency of an Attorney between Counsel and Client* (London: Butterworths, 1851); John Warrington Rogers, *County Courts. A Letter to Lord Campbell, Lord Chief Justice of England, on the Bill now before Parliament ...* (London: Benning and Co., 1850); "A Barrister of the Inner Temple," *Advocacy in the County Courts. A Letter to Sir A. Cockburn, M.P. Her Majesty's Attorney-General* (London: Sweet, 1851).

95 Stephen, *supra* note 94 at 30-31 [emphasis in original].

96 See discussion in *Legal Observer* 43 (20 December 1851) 125. The proposal was one of a package of recommendations regarding the legal profession made by the Law Amendment Society committee.

97 See, *e.g.*, "County Courts Further Extension Bill," *supra* note 45, which stated, following passage of the 1852 *County Courts Act* (discussed *infra*), that "[t]he agitation set on foot by a portion of the Junior Bar, and which was zealously supported and promoted by *The Times* newspaper, has been for the present to a degree successful."

98 "The Profession in the County Courts" *Law Times* 19 (26 June 1852) 101.

99 "House of Lords. The County Court Practice" *Law Times* 19 (26 June 1852) 102.

100 *Ibid.*

101 "The Junior Bar and the Attorneys. County Court Practitioners" *Legal Observer* 44 (7 August 1852) 271.

102 *Ibid.*

103 For example, the *Legal Observer* commented on the efforts of "a small portion of the Junior Bar" (42 [7 June 1851] 89), "a small section of the Junior Bar" (42 [23 August 1851] 311), "a small minority of the Juniors" (44 [12 June 1852] 114), or "a section of the Junior Bar" (44 [19 June 1852] 129 at 130); suggested that "a few of its [the Bar's] members" induced the Attorney-General to pursue the *County Courts Extension Bill* (42 [19 July 1851] 216); asserted that "those men who give distinction to our profession in both its branches – the men of business, with their sound sense and practical experience – the men whose characters inspire respect and engender confidence – are unanimously opposed to the proposition of confounding the functions of advocate and attorney" (43 [20 December 1851] 125 at 126); referred to "some ill-informed, prejudiced, or interested law reformers of the Junior Bar, who desire some mighty change by which their brieflessness may be relieved" (43 [15 November 1851] 39 at 40). To similar effect, "it is understood to be the private opinion of nearly every man of standing and position in the Profession, that the interests of the Junior Bar and of the Attorneys – and what is still more important, the interests of the Public – will be best promoted by Barristers and Attorneys continuing to confine themselves strictly to their legitimate and distinct province" (44 [21 August 1852] 309 at 310). Regarding the petition to Parliament, the journal referred to "this minority of the Bar" (44 [7 August 1852] 271 at 272) and asserted that "the great majority of that distinguished body, the Bar of England, repudiate altogether this miserable contention" (*ibid.* at 273). This theme was picked up also by the *Law Times* 19 (26 June 1852) 102, which reported that "The heads of the Profession [*i.e.*, the barristers' profession], however, discountenanced barristers receiving instructions, except through the intervention of an attorney or solicitor."

104 The draft legislation read: "The party to the Suit or other proceeding, or any Attorney employed by virtue of the retainer in writing of the party, or any Barrister retained by or on behalf of the party on either side, may address the Court without any right of exclusive or preaudience, but subject to such regulations, ... etc."; quoted in "Another Act Has Been Passed, 'To Facilitate and Arrange Proceedings in the County Courts'" *Metropolitan and Provincial Law Association, Circular 2* (1852) 11 at 12 ["Another Act Has Been Passed"].

105 *Ibid.*

106 Competition from persons who were not members of either legal profession was a fact of life. Commenting on amendments to the *County Court Act* passed in 1852, the Metropolitan and Provincial Law Association referred to "all those irregular classes of Agents, whose practice in the Courts has been a growing evil, and it is to be feared will now extend to getting up cases and preparing Briefs for the less scrupulous Members of the Bar." See "Another Act Has Been Passed," *supra* note 104 at 13. To similar effect, a letter, "Encroachments on the Profession" *Legal Observer* 47 (21 January 1854) 214 at 214, complained of "the operations of inferior grades, such as agents and accountants."

107 As quoted in "Another Act Has Been Passed," *supra* note 104 at 12.

108 *County Courts Act, 1852,* 15 & 16 Vict., c. 54, s. 10. Lord Campbell had apparently insisted upon the amendment to restrict attorney advocacy: Abel-Smith and Stevens, *supra* note 4 at 57n.

109 In the House of Lords, two Law Lords had expressly attempted to put an alternative gloss on the Act of Parliament. In reference to barristers taking instructions directly from clients, the Lord Chancellor said that "no one disapproved of such practice more than he did, and no one would be more anxious to prevent Members of the Bar from resorting to such a practice. He would not, however, have consented to stigmatize the Bar, by providing that they should not do that which it was discreditable to do, according to the general feeling of the Profession." Lord Campbell stated that he "had been apprehensive that the withdrawal of the Prohibition which had been imposed by Parliament, would seem like giving a sort of Parliamentary sanction to the encroachment of the Barrister upon the province of the Attorney; but after the authoritative declaration of his noble and learned friend, he thought the honour of the Bar and the interests of the Public would be as safe in the County Courts, as in the Superior Courts at Westminster Hall, or upon Circuit" (both as quoted in "Another Act Has Been Passed," *supra* note 104 at 13.

110 "County Courts Extension Bill" *Law Times* 19 (26 June 1852) 102 at 102.

111 *Bennett v. Hale, supra* note 15, per Lord Campbell.

112 See Kennedy, *Circuit Leagues, supra* note 15 at 5. Kennedy's view that matters of etiquette were *legally* unenforceable was considered accurate by at least some of the Benchers, judges, Attorney-General, and Lord Chancellor. See Yeatman, *Professorship of the Law Department, supra* note 42 at 20. See also Inner Temple, *Bench Table Orders,* 11 January 1853 (in which Kennedy protests another matter); and Kennedy, "Bar Unionists," *supra* note 42. Even as late as 1867, Dicey considered "[t]he jurisdiction of the Inns of Court ... [to be] ... scarcely more than nominal, and the Circuit Court ... little more than a sham" (*supra* note 14 at 170).

113 Emphasis in original; as quoted in *Legal Observer* 44 (17 July 1852) 209.

114 See "Something New" *Law Times* 19 (10 July 1852) 117.

115 A brief description of how the society was to work is also found in Kennedy, *Address to the Mutual Law Association, supra* note 38 at 3, 12.

116 Prospectus of the Mutual Law Association as quoted in a letter of 3 September 1852 from Thomas S. James, Secretary of the Birmingham Law Association, to the Benchers of Inner Temple (Inner Temple, *Bench Table Orders,* 5 November 1852).

117 As quoted in "Something New," *supra* note 114.

118 "Mutual Law Association" *Legal Observer* 44 (16 October 1852) 473, put the association in context and explained this notion of its illegality: "Our readers are aware that various cheap Law Societies have been formed or attempted in several parts of the country, for the purpose of supplying the suitors of the County Courts and other persons with advice and assistance to be paid to some legal functionary out of the fund derived from the subscriptions received. Such associations are clearly illegal if the expense of proceedings in Courts of Justice are defrayed out of a common fund of the members. These establishments have, for the most part, been promoted by some attorney 'in search of practice'. It seems we are now to witness the experiment of 'A Society of Barristers in search of Briefs.'"
119 Kennedy, *Address to the Mutual Law Association, supra* note 38 at 6.
120 *Ibid.* at 7.
121 *Ibid.* at 1.
122 *Ibid.* at 9.
123 "Something New," *supra* note 114; "The Attack on the Attorneys" *Law Times* 20 (9 October 1852) 25; "Mr Kennedy's Manifesto" *Law Times* 20 (30 October 1852) 58; "Mutual Law Association" *Legal Observer* 44 (16 October 1852) 473; "The Bar and the Attorneys. Mr Rann Kennedy's Speech at Birmingham" *Legal Observer* 44 (23 October 1852) 501; "The Bar and the Attorneys. Mr Rann Kennedy's Birmingham Speech" (letter) *Legal Observer* 45 (6 November 1852) 12. See also Shaen, *supra* note 6 at 44-45.
124 Kennedy, *Address to the Mutual Law Association, supra* note 38 at 10: "There is a systematic and organized conspiracy among the pettifoggers to deter or dissuade all independent solicitors from employing us, and it has succeeded to a very great extent. They have tried to tamper in this way with divers of my clients. For example – Mr Harrison was thus accosted by an attorney, ... – 'What do you employ that prating fellow, Kennedy, for?' Of this Mr Harrison informed me. Mr Walters, clerk to Mr Edmonds, tells me, he has repeatedly been remonstrated with for retaining me. The same miscreant whom I last alluded to, deprived me of an important case, which I had been requested to conduct for a public body in this town. He effected this purpose thus – He went privately to a member of the Board, and begged of him as a personal favour, to dissuade the Board from employing me: he abused barristers in general, and me in particular, and by some means or other he accomplished his malignant purpose, for which, if he had his deserts, he would be sent to the treadmill."
125 In "The Attack on the Attorneys," *supra* note 123 at 25, it is reported that the Mutual Law Association "came under the consideration of the Bar mess of the Midland Circuit, and that one of the gentlemen, Mr Grace, solemnly repudiated all knowledge of the document, and declared that his name had been passed there without his concurrence, upon which assurance he was acquitted by his peers." Kennedy was not subject to mess discipline as he was not a member.
126 See Inner Temple, *Bench Table Orders*, 5, 9, 12, 17 November 1852; 1, 8, 17, December 1852; 11 January 1853.
127 "Mutual Law Association," *supra* note 118.
128 In English usage, "law society" denotes a professional association of the attorneys/solicitors' branch of the profession. What has come to be known as *the* Law Society of England and Wales was, in 1852, merely one of many such local professional associations. An account of the activities of some law societies is to be found in United Kingdom, *Report of the Select Committee on Legal Education* (25 August 1846).
129 Inner Temple, *Bench Table Orders,* 1 December 1852.
130 Lincoln's Inn, *The Black Books,* Adjourned Council of 15 December 1852, at 50.
131 As he did when further disciplinary proceedings were begun a decade later. See Yeatman, *Professorship of the Law Department, supra* note 42 at 22.

132 Inner Temple, *Bench Table Orders,* 8 December 1852.

133 In this respect, he commented that barristers were "bound hand and foot by a ridiculous etiquette – (I am obliged to use the French word; England has no name for such an absurdity)" (*Address to the Mutual Law Association, supra* note 38 at 6).

134 In *Professorship of Law Department, supra* note 42 at 20, John Pym Yeatman records that when the mess blacklisted him, Kennedy "appealed to the Benchers, to the Judges, to the Attorney-General, to the Lord Chancellor. The nature of the proceedings will probably never be known. Such scandals, involving the great men of the day, are best buried in oblivion. But the result was soon known; the Circuit was advised of the illegality of its proceedings, and Charles Kennedy for the time triumphed. They resumed the practice of holding briefs with him, and he continued the tenor of his ways. Baron Alderson wrote most kindly, expressing entire concurrence in the views which I have adopted as my guide in this matter, and which have, I believe, never been seriously disputed by any independent person."

135 See generally, Cocks, *Foundations of the Modern Bar, supra* note 14.

136 In June 1851, he had written a letter to the Law Amendment Society about the "destitution of the bar," which he blamed on the wholesale transfer of jurisdiction to inferior tribunals where attorneys had a right of audience. See *supra* note 34 and accompanying text.

137 *The Times* (1 November 1852) 5, discussed in Cocks, *Foundations of the Modern Bar, supra* note 14 at 88-89. This letter provoked a flurry of discussion in the popular and professional press. See *The Times* (2 November 1852) 3 (letter from a junior of seven years' standing); "Lord Denman's Letter – The Bar and the Attorney" *Law Times* 20 (6 November 1852) 73 (which expressly links Denman's letter to Kennedy's practices, suggesting that such forms of practice would lead to fusion of the two legal professions); "The Bar and the Attorney" *Law Times* 20 (27 November 1852) 109 (letter in response to both Lord Denman's letter and the Mutual Law Association); "Commencement of Michaelmas Term. Pts of the Profession" *Legal Observer* 45 (6 November 1852) 1 (critical account of Denman's letter and discussion of the Attorney-General's approval of a half-guinea bar); "The Bar and the Attorneys" *Legal Observer* 45 (20 November 1852) 45 (complaining about the letter in *The Times* from a junior of seven years' standing: "If barristers think fit thus to repudiate one old-established rule of their Profession, they should be content to submit the entire code of their protecting and productive rules to a searching revision, and which would afford more relief to the suitor than the severest taxation of his attorney's bill").

138 Inner Temple, *Bench Table Orders,* 17 December 1852. Present were the Treasurer, Sir Frederick Thesiger (Attorney-General), Mr. Evans, Sir David Dundas, Messrs. Whateley, Lee, Rolt, Bliss, Ingham, Mellor, Warren, Atherton, and Headlam, Dr. Lushington, Messrs. Harrison and Adolphus, and Sir John Harding. The participation of Sir Frederick Thesiger (later Lord Chelmsford) in it may lend credence to subsequent allegations that Kennedy's later conduct of a suit against Chelmsford for legal malpractice in the *Swinfen* litigation was motivated by hostility towards Thesiger.

139 See, further, Cocks, "The Middle Temple," *supra* note 26; D. Woolley, *supra* note 26.

140 Inner Temple, *Bench Table Orders,* 11 January 1853.

141 *Ibid.*

142 See *Aris's Birmingham Gazette* and the *Birmingham Journal and Advertiser* reports on County Court cases, especially for the period 1852 to 1858. His involvement in the *Swinfen* litigation resulted in his abandoning his County Court practice for work on that case in London, returning to Birmingham only in 1862. See Kennedy, "Bar Unionists," *supra* note 42 at 24.

143 Kennedy, *Address to the Mutual Law Association, supra* note 38 at 8.

144 *Ibid.* at 9.

145 "The Etiquette of the Bar" *Aris's Birmingham Gazette* (8 February 1862) at 5, col. 4; "The Etiquette of the Bar" *Aris's Birmingham Gazette* (15 February 1862) at 5, col. 4; *Aris's Birmingham Gazette* (1 March 1862) at 7, col. 2 (quoting at length from an article in the *Morning Star*).

146 As quoted in Shaen, *supra* note 6 at 45n. The advertisement is also reproduced in Lincoln's Inn, *The Black Books,* 1853, at 106.

147 Metropolitan and Provincial Law Association, *Report of the Committee of Management Made to the Fifth Annual General Meeting, Held April 21, 1852* (London: Miall and Cockshaw, 1852) at 5. The Benchers' minutes of Lincoln's Inn report that "[t]he Treasurer was requested to write to Mr Solomon Atkinson, who is a Barrister of this Society, to ask whether the advertisement referred to was published by him, or by his authority, or whether he has any explanation to offer with respect to it." The Benchers were considering Atkinson's membership of Lincoln's Inn and whether he "[o]ught to remain so?" Lincoln's Inn, *The Black Books,* summer 1853, at 106.

148 As quoted in "Etiquette at the Bar. Westminster County Court" *Legal Observer* 45 (6 November 1852) 12, referencing an item published in the *Legal Examiner,* described as "the organ of the junior Bar" in "County Courts Advocacy. Etiquette of the Bar" *Legal Observer* 44 (17 July 1852) 209.

149 "A New Movement at the Bar" *Law Times* 20 (13 November 1852) 96.

150 The *Law Review* of August 1852 had endorsed the 1852 amendments to the *County Courts Act,* proposing half-guinea fees. See criticisms in "The Junior Bar and the Attorneys," *supra* note 101 at 272-73.

151 The Northern Circuit Mess ruled in 1851 that it did *not* breach etiquette for barristers to work for one-guinea fees in County Court cases. "County Courts Further Extension Bill," *supra* note 88 at 311 commented: "Whether these resolutions will produce any practical change in the County Courts in the North of England, we are not prepared to state, but in the neighbourhood of the metropolis, the County Courts, we have reason to think, have been constantly attended by barristers, and we are apprehensive that some well-authenticated instances might be adduced in which the *quidam honorarium* has fallen short of one guinea."

152 "The Movement of the Junior Bar" *Law Times* 20 (20 November 1852) 98.

153 *E.g.,* "Prospects of the Junior Bar" *Legal Observer* 44 (12 June 1852) 114 at 116 (asking whether, if County Court amendments are passed, breaches of professional etiquette might nonetheless be met "with the punishment of disbarring?"); "The Junior Bar and the Attorneys," *supra* note 101 at 272 ("We yet hope the higher authorities of the Bar will interpose and prevent any attempts to *compel* the delivery of briefs"); *Legal Observer* 44 (21 August 1852) 309 at 310 (calling for an express statement by "every man of standing and position in the Profession" of the desirability of strict adherence to traditional etiquette); "Encroachments on the Profession," *supra* note 106 at 215 ("Surely the Inns of Court can and will, if appealed to, rectify the evil").

154 "The Junior Bar and the Attorneys" *Law Times* 20 (27 November 1852) 110; before the 1852 amendments, see *Legal Observer* 40 (25 May 1850) 63 (complaining about Mr. Bird, a local barrister in Exeter, taking County Court cases without the intervention of an attorney). Both types of threat were, apparently, made good before the 1852 amendments, as "The County Court Bar Meeting" *Legal Observer* 43 (1852) 348, makes clear: "Persons who should so act [*i.e.,* take instructions directly from clients] may either be indicted and convicted, as was done by the Kent Law Society, or may be subjected to an application in a summary way for contempt of Court, or may be disbarred as lately happened to a member of Gray's Inn."

155 "Relation between the Bar and Attorneys" *Legal Observer* 45 (19 February 1853) 311.

156 As quoted in *ibid.*

157 "Proposed Law Reforms. Prospects of the Profession" *Legal Observer* 46 (7 May 1853) 1 at 3 [emphasis in original].

158 *Ibid.* at 1. "Law Societies" here refers to local law societies as well as the Law Society in London.

159 See Chapter 11 in this volume.

160 *Aris's Birmingham Gazette* (1 March 1862) at 7, col. 2, quoted at length from a lead article in the *Morning Star* asserting that "[o]f one thing we are assured – namely, that the reason for the decision is not, as is supposed, that Mr Claydon has taken briefs from clients without the intervention of an attorney. Such a ground would be entirely unwarranted by law." See discussion in Chapter 8 in this volume.

161 In "Relations between the Bar and Attorneys. Report of the Law Amendment Society," *supra* note 10 at 127, the *Legal Observer* reported that "[n]o one who glances through the newspaper reports of the proceedings of the Criminal Courts and the Police Offices, can doubt, that the moment it was announced that the Bar no longer required the intervention of an attorney, the quiet precincts of Old Court and Harcourt Buildings would be beset with *touters,* diligently pursuing their calling, in humble imitation of their fellows in the neighbouring locality of Holywell Street." (Holywell Street had a reputation for the sale of pornography. *Punch* reported that "Holywell Street still stands, a proud monument of the vested rights of every sort of physical and moral filth and foulness." *Punch* (19 January 19 1856), online: <http://www.victorianlondon.org/districts/holywellstreet.htm>.

162 See *supra* note 18 and accompanying text.

163 "County Courts Further Extension Bill," *supra* note 45, referred to the Law Lords' expressed hope that etiquette would be followed in any event, commenting that the "seniors of Bar" were powerless to enforce it.

164 For example, Lincoln's Inn, *The Black Books,* Council of 3 January 1850; Adjourned Council of 20 February 1850.

165 Lincoln's Inn, *The Black Books,* Council of 25 November 1851 (reporting that Henry William Hemsworth was disbarred from Inner Temple for unspecified misconduct); Council of 15 April 1852 (reporting that William Vesey Langdale was disbarred from Gray's Inn for having been an attorney at the time of call). Hemsworth had been imprisoned for contempt of court for nonpayment of a judgment in *R. v. Henry William Hemsworth* (1846) 3 Manning, Granger & Scott, reproduced in Thomas Sergeant and Thomas McKean Pettit, *Reports of Cases Argued and Determined in the English Courts of Common Law,* vol. 54 (Philadelphia: T. & J.W. Johnson, 1871), 745-53.

166 Lincoln's Inn, *The Black Books,* Adjourned Special Council of 20 February 1850 (report of committee composed of M.D. Hill, W. Mathews, and William Loftus Lowndes).

167 Inner Temple, *Bench Table Orders,* 16 April 1861.

168 Lincoln's Inn, The *Black Books,* Adjourned Council of 15 January 1863 (disbarment of Claydon).

169 *Ibid.,* Special Council of 19 January 1863. The unfortunate barrister was William Cheek Bonsfield.

170 See Chapter 11 in this volume.

171 In "Meeting of the Legal Profession" *Birmingham Journal and Commercial Advertiser* (16 October 1852) at 7, col. 6, Edwin Field had suggested that the traditional division of labour between the two professions was hard to justify: "Before a suitor could approach the seat of justice sufficiently near to obtain a hearing, he had to make as many obeisances as a Chinese courtier, and with every obeisance there was a delay, and with each delay there was a payment of a fee ... the solicitors desire all these things abolished as obstructions in the administration of justice; and if it were asked why were these abuses maintained, the true answer would be, 'because the bar must be maintained.' This was a secret motive for much of the obstruction to law reform."

172 The fear of fusion was discussed in the *Legal Observer* on a number of occasions, including 13 December 1851, 17 January 1852, 20 November 1852, 19 February 1853, 21 January 1854, 22 and 29 December, 12 and 19 January 1856, and 1 March 1856. See, generally, Cocks, *Foundations of the Modern Bar, supra* note 17.

8

The End of Free Trade in Law

DISCIPLINE AT THE INNS IN THE 1860S

For about half a decade from 1859, several high-profile cases focused critical scrutiny on the senior branch of the legal profession. A Lord Chancellor was accused of unlawful conspiracy against his client, a Queen's Counsel and Attorney-General designate was disbarred, and a more humble provincial barrister was disbarred for engaging in long-standing practices. In turn, another Member of Parliament and Queen's Counsel was investigated by a professional tribunal. Finally, amid much sound and fury, the flamboyant Charles Rann Kennedy was called to account for his conduct over a range of matters, including his pursuit of litigation against a Lord Chancellor for malpractice as a barrister.

Each case was widely publicized. Each briefly focused middle-class attention on the conduct of barristers. Individual reputations were tarnished and careers diverted. The prominence of some of these men made things all the more unsettling. The uneven responses of the Bar's governing bodies did little to reassure. As one case followed another in quick succession, their import was magnified. Together they seemed to reveal deep problems within the barristers' branch, which threatened British justice itself. The cases conjured up established scripts of a legal profession detrimental to the social good, and long-simmering concerns about the Bar came to a head. This brief period produced important changes in the way in which barristerial practice was conceived. The Bar itself was changed as the profession slipped from being a relatively open, nonregulatory status group – G. Shaw Lefevre described the Bar as lacking any rules whatsoever[1] – into a disciplinary regime of sorts. The door to reimaging professional bodies as rule-enforcing punitive regimes of the sort we now take for granted had been opened.[2]

Moral Panics

It is important to acknowledge that the social purposes of punishing deviance within professions are not only about public protection or the punishment of wrongdoing in the cause of "justice" or deterrence. Defining and punishing deviants also serves to establish and define the acceptable mainstream. Professions, like the larger societies of which they are part, come to understand themselves in opposition to those they identify and punish as deviant:

> *[S]ocial groups create deviance by making the rules whose infraction constitutes deviance* and by applying those rules to particular persons and labelling them as outsiders ... [D]eviance is not a quality of the act the person commits, but rather a consequence of the application by others of rules and sanctions to an "offender." The deviant is one to whom the label has been successfully applied; deviant behavior is behavior that people so label.[3]

Significant social, legal, or normative changes can take place quickly when there is heightened public anxiety about people or their behaviour.[4] Socially available metanarratives combine unpredictably with enduring beliefs, values, and fears. When pent-up forces are released abruptly in such moments, shifts in unlikely directions can occur. Novel definitions of deviance emerge.

One surprising result of the confluence of events affecting the mid-nineteenth-century Bar was that practices previously considered acceptable, perhaps even commendable, to the public at large were successfully branded as "deviant" by the Bar's leadership.

Background

"British Justice"[5] was then a central value in English self-image. This, in turn, put lawyers, courts, and the law in pivotal roles. One journal asserted that "writers who would uproot the profession of advocacy must seek the destruction of the Law itself."[6] The sentiment was widely shared.

The role of advocates in the drama of the courtroom loomed large against an otherwise relatively sparse Victorian state. The work of barristers, their conduct of trials, and the law itself were much discussed by the literate public. When the conduct of barristers was in question, concerns over deep social insecurities were easily aroused. Three cases had loomed large in earlier decades. The representation of Queen Caroline in divorce proceedings (1820) and the criminal defences of Courvoisier (executed in 1840) and Tawell (executed in 1845) had brought issues relating to morality and the public duty of counsel into sharp focus.[7] Although it was entirely clear that a barrister's foremost duty was to represent his client, what this meant in real life was less certain, as these cases illustrated. What limitations on that principle of representation, if any, were imposed by good taste, ethics, or concern for the public good? Henry (later Lord) Brougham adopted a strong position in his defence of Queen Caroline from King George IV's attempt to divorce her:

> An advocate, by the sacred duty which he owes his client, knows in the discharge of that office but one person in the world, that client and none other. To save the client by all expedient means, to protect the client at all hazards and cost to all others, and among others to himself, is the highest and most unquestioned of his duties. He must not regard the alarm, the suffering, the torment, the destruction which he may bring upon any other.[8]

The particular context was explosive. Brougham was signalling steely determination to proceed without regard to personal risk. It was also a blunt warning both that the King was bound by the law and that he could not expect to be treated gingerly. But there was much more. Brougham's coded language threatened constitutional crisis. The statement amounted to

> a message to George IV and his ministers that the advocate for the Queen consort would reveal the secret marriage of George IV as heir apparent to Mrs. Fitzherbert, a Roman Catholic, if the ministers did not withdraw the divorce bill. Since he was prohibited by the Act of Settlement from marrying a person of the Roman Catholic faith, the revelation of George's indiscretion would have created a constitutional crisis and possibly deprived him of his crown.[9]

Although not all acts of legal representation deal this directly with matters of state, a barrister's role in the court is inevitably connected to the rule of law. The courts have played a central role in English constitutionalism from the time of Magna Carta, through Lord Coke's celebrated seventeenth-century rulings, to the *Act of Settlement* and much beyond.[10] Even in the most mundane of cases, an advocate's fidelity to his client carries constitutional significance. It is the foundation on which independent courts, equality before the law, and freedom from repression rest.

Not all cases are mundane. Mid-nineteenth century cases involving defence of Chartists and the freedom of the press, among others, carried a celebrated tradition forward in very public ways.[11] If we overlook the practical matter that not everyone can afford barristers' fees, it is clear that equality before the law hinges on their services being available if the constitutional promise of impartial and independent courts is to hold. Representation by a barrister ensured "an approximation to equality between those who, by talent, education, fortune, sex, or age, are unequal." This alone could ground the earnest belief that "even a pauper's cause [is] ... as earnestly maintained as if it were that of a nobleman or of the Crown."[12] A radical conception of equality before the law formed part of British identity and, with it, the mythology of the Bar. Barristers were to protect freedom when political issues were involved,[13] but also, even in the most ordinary of cases, whenever power was exercised improperly. Then, as now, barristers took great pride in celebrated cases where their co-professionals had disregarded personal risk to stand bravely in defence of cherished liberties. At its best, the delicate balance attained by the Bar's system of etiquette sought to immunize the profession from the corrupting influence of "the powerful class by whom the success of its members is determined."[14] By happy coincidence, the Bar's collective bravery and good judgment, buttressed by its rules of etiquette, also produced opportunities for those of "personal worth and intellectual power" to prosper. Recent decades had produced cause for celebration:

> When Lord Erskine withstood Mr. Justice Buller, with propriety and taste equal to his courage, and began the exposure of the monstrous doctrine that, in prosecutions for libel, the fact of publishing was all the jury could investigate, to which the Press is indebted for that statute which deserves to be considered as the charter of its freedom – he set an example of independence of mind, not of class, of which any profession might be proud. Still nobler was the sacrifice which he made to the claim of professional duty, – and that a duty he would gladly have avoided for its own hardships, – when he resigned his office of attorney-general to the Prince of Wales, rather than abandon the defence of the prosecution instituted against Paine's Rights of Man. So the independence of party feeling has been nobly manifested by the generous defence of persons charged with political offences, when the accused were of political sentiments the most opposite to those of their advocates; – as in Erskine's defence of Stockdale; in Wetherell's defence of Watson; and in the defence, sustained with admirable spirit and power, of Frost by Pollock and Kelly – who, not compromising in the least in their opinions, devoted the same energy to their client's service as though he had been a Conservative prosecuted by Whigs, instead of an insurrectionary Chartist.[15]

Professional ideology celebrated those who embraced the role of barristers as partisans, fearlessly protecting their clients at all cost. There were limits, however. Although partisans, they were nonetheless expected to be "ministers of justice ... [acting] zealously for their clients, but fairly by the Court,"[16] never creating a false impression of evidence, hiding an adverse authority, or pressing an unfair point.[17] A barrister was not a hired assassin. Where was the line, and what would happen to barristers who crossed it?

Public perception of the Bar was not uniformly positive. Any high-profile case could attract negative attention to the work of barristers depending on the cause they represented and how they pursued it. The cost of barristers' services, prohibitive to individuals of modest means, was obvious and the artificial monopolies of the legal professions were incongruent with the spirit of the time. The organized barristers' profession seemed to operate both in constraint of free trade and ineffectually when deviance deserved sanction. A paralysis of sorts infected the Inns of Court when unwelcome professional innovations took hold. If "professional opinion" proved insufficient to ensure conformity to established etiquette, the institutions of the Bar were uncertain how to develop new and effective ways of ensuring compliance. Doing so would fundamentally change their institutional character.

The nineteenth-century Inns had little sense of themselves as disciplinary bodies. The four venerable bodies had been mostly reactive in matters of discipline prior to the 1860s. Only ten barristers were disbarred during the first sixty years of the century, generally following conviction on a criminal charge. Some knowledgeable individuals believed that disbarment "could only be inflicted for conviction of Crime."[18] The few exceptions prior to 1860 involved blatant dishonesty in matters of personal debt or attorneys who continued to work in that capacity after their call to the Bar or while "keeping terms" (*i.e.*, qualifying for the barristers' profession). Only one barrister was disbarred between 1851 and 1861.[19] That this was so despite many deliberate and well-publicized breaches of professional etiquette underlines both the limited cultural force and lack of lawful authority of the organized Bar.

Outside forces threatened change. Law reform discomfited barristers,[20] not least when parliamentary committees conducted inquiries touching on their own educational requirements and governance.[21] One journal spoke of "growing symptoms of dissatisfaction with the whole system which regulates the profession of the Bar," noting that some "irreverent minds ... assert that bodies invested with large privileges, and richly endowed, had a public trust to perform."[22] Parliamentary committees focused on other matters would also hear complaints about the Bar;[23] the London satirical magazine *Punch* ridiculed the profession;[24] *The Times* thundered its criticisms;[25] and Dickens's *Bleak*

House, published in installments between March 1852 and September 1853, famously laid the blame for many absurdities of English law at the feet of legal practitioners.[26]

Of the two branches of the profession, the Bar seemed particularly anachronistic. Attorneys seemed more nimble, plausibly aligned with the needs of modern times.[27] Edwin Field told attorneys in Birmingham in 1852 that their interests were identical with those of suitors:

> He stated that now, before a suitor could approach the seat of justice sufficiently near to obtain a hearing, he had to make as many obeisances as a Chinese courtier, and with every obeisance there was delay, and with each delay there was a payment of a fee. What the solicitors had attempted to procure was an unobstructed path to every court, so that every one with a wrong might straightway go to the proper tribunal for a remedy: as it was, they had to get counsel's signatures to mere matters of form ... the solicitors desire all these things abolished as obstructions in the administration of justice; and if it were asked why were these abuses maintained, the true answer would be, "because the bar must be maintained." This was a secret motive for much of the obstruction to law reform.[28]

Barristers who ignored established bar etiquette as they plied their trade defended their deviance from the informal norms of their profession by appeal to utilitarianism, public interest, and free-trade ideology.[29] Their arguments resonated widely. The spirit of the age, said G. Shaw-Lefevre, ran contrary to the ideology of advocacy. The logical outcome, if free-trade practices took hold would be the destruction of the traditional Bar:

> Let it be remembered that there are wanting those who consider that the organization of the bar is, in itself, abnormal and unwarranted by true economical principles. It is urged that there is no good reason why the Bar should be separated as it now is from other professions, whether cognate to it, as that of attorneys, or not, protected by immunities, endowed with privileges, and entrusted with duties. They would advocate throwing open to any person whatever the right of addressing the courts, either on his own or on any other person's behalf. That the feeling of the age, and the legislation with regard to other professions and trades are in favour of such a course ...
>
> [T]hose whose views are thus baldly stated ... [rely] on the soundness of the general principles of political economy, [and] are averse to all artificial restrictions on professional employments.[30]

Spirit of the age notwithstanding, attacks on the Bar establishment were unfocused and, thus, ineffective. A general sense that "something ought to be done" led in contradictory directions. One commentator attacked the whole "system of Etiquette" as "inexpedient for ourselves, and injurious to the public," and unenforceable. Nonetheless, he believed the remedy was more effective bar discipline, not its elimination.[31] Greater enforcement was also called for by solicitors' journals.[32] Some, however, advocated following the model of the United States and fusing the two legal professions. This would have amounted to the destruction of the Bar.[33] Still others objected to particular rules of etiquette or practices.[34] Meanwhile, dissident barristers,[35] sections of the press,[36] and even judicial members of the House of Lords argued that the Bar's etiquette had outlived its usefulness and should be abolished or simply ignored.

In short, the Bar was attacked from without, divided within, and incapable of reforming itself. It had considerable assets, however. The Inns were truly ancient institutions and past members had played distinguished roles in shaping English public life. Many contemporary great barristers, judges, and officers of state had been nurtured by its culture and within its institutions. It was said that no other profession could match the Bar in producing individuals "more truthful, more generous, more gentle; whose minds were more free from perversion; and whose hearts had been kept more purely 'unspotted from the world.'"[37] Even allowing for hyperbole, the Bar was protected by a significant defensive berm. These were important cultural assets.

When events threatened to diminish the honour of leaders of the profession, however, things took a different turn.

Scandalous Judicial Behaviour

In 1859, a highly publicized wills case went off track, effectively putting the entire barristers' profession on trial.

The will of Samuel Swinfen left his substantial Staffordshire estate to Patience Swinfen, wife of his deceased son. It was challenged by Samuel's heir-at-law, Frederick Hay Swinfen, on grounds amounting to undue influence. If the will could be set aside, Frederick would inherit. The case was, so far, a rather ordinary inheritance dispute. It came before a special jury empanelled at Staffordshire in March 1856. A talented legal lineup appeared on both sides. Sir Frederick Thesiger, QC, served as counsel for Patience Swinfen, assisted by M. Alexander, QC, Mr. Whitmore, QC, and Mr. Gray. Opposing them on behalf of the heir-at-law were Sir Alexander Cockburn (then the Attorney-General), Mr. Whatley, QC, Mr. Keating, QC, and Mr. Vaughan Richards.

Historical photos of Swinfen Hall: exterior, interior, and boathouse. *Reproduced with the permission of the Library of Birmingham, MS 3196, Box 81, Print 4, 5, and 8*

Portrait of a youthful looking Patience Swinfen. *Reproduced with the permission of the Library of Birmingham, MS 3196, Box 81, Print 6*

This more or less ordinary wills case resulted in a more or less ordinary compromise, entered into between barristers for the parties at the end of the first day's testimony. "Ordinary" ceased soon enough, however, and high drama ensued. Patience Swinfen alleged that Thesiger, her lead counsel, had compromised the case in violation of her explicit instructions and on terms she had unambiguously rejected. Against considerable odds, the validity of the will was reopened on her behalf by Charles Rann Kennedy, who succeeded in overturning the compromise, proving the will, and winning the inheritance for her.[38] This was a highly satisfactory outcome and in the normal course of events one might have expected the matter to end there. Kennedy, however, launched proceedings against Sir Frederick Thesiger, in effect alleging professional negligence or worse. The status of the lawyers involved immediately made the case a matter of public interest and the Bar itself appeared in a bad light.

In the interim, Thesiger had become Baron Chelmsford, Lord Chancellor in 1858, during the second short-lived administration of the Earl of Derby (Edward Smith-Stanley, Lord Stanley from 1834 to 1851). Sir Alexander Cockburn had succeeded John Jervis as Chief Justice of the Common Pleas in 1856. The judge in the original case, Sir Cresswell Cresswell, had assumed an important role as the first judge of the newly created probate and divorce court in January 1858.[39] Consequently, Kennedy's allegations of impropriety tainted three important judicial figures. *Bell's Life in London and Sporting Chronicle* noted the importance of the case:

> *The Times* truly says that "the questions involved in this case were among the most important which affect the interests of the community." In a country of which it was asserted that "the purpose of our fleets and armies was to preserve a judge on the bench, and twelve jurymen in the box," it could not be otherwise. In fact, our freedom is essentially and inseparably bound up with our legal system, and it is of every day interest to all that the system should be the means of good, and should give universal satisfaction. Though a defeated party to a suit may think the result totally wrong, we require that he should attribute this result to human fallibility and liability to error, and not to defects in the system itself.[40]

In a sense, the law itself was on trial. The question of when and how a barrister might bind his client to a settlement arrangement made the case a sort of "political" trial. Diverging views about the ideology and practice of adversarial justice were at play, as were ideas related to class status, femininity, the rule of law, and equality. It was also a more directly party-political

Sir Frederick Thesiger, as he was drawn in an article titled "The Ministerial Challenge to the Country," published on 20 March 1852. © *Illustrated London News Ltd/Mary Evans, 11070619*

event, however. Chelmsford had been a Conservative minister and Cresswell a Conservative Member of Parliament. Sir Fitzroy Kelly, William Bovill, and Montague Smith, appearing for Chelmsford, had all been Conservative MPs. Opposing them, Kennedy appeared with a Liberal Member of Parliament, George Denman (son of the great law reformer Thomas Denman),[41] for Patience Swinfen. Although Kennedy was less politically involved than the others, he too lined up as Liberal by association, had considered launching a parliamentary career, and expected to be named Queen's Counsel by a future Liberal administration.[42]

At trial, the defence emphasized the paternalist obligations of barristers and bench working together through litigation to ensure suitable outcomes. Often, the flexibility that was available only through a compromise would produce a more substantively just result than the winner-take-all choice that judge and jury were forced to make. Lay clients could not fully appreciate this as experienced legal professionals did. The barristers' expert knowledge, experience, wisdom, and professional distance removed them from the emotion of the moment. Kennedy, however, emphasized the barrister's role as agent for the client. This too had resonance in the history of the profession and was a logical extension of a "free trade" approach to practice. In lieu of a balanced paternalism, this view emphasized the barrister's duty to fight fearlessly and without compromise on behalf of his client. The courtroom was not a place where compromises were worked out by the most knowledgeable, but a forum where a titanic contest for truth played out before an uninvolved, neutral, and passive judge and jury. Both approaches were grounded in the history and culture of bar and courts, with the result that the proceedings revealed a fundamental incoherence embedded within the law. A dangerous fissure opened up.

Swinfen v. Lord Chelmsford was high drama acted out by well-known advocates on a very public stage. A sympathetic widow forced to struggle tenaciously for the simple justice of securing her proper inheritance now sought recompense from the powerful and well-connected men who had betrayed her. A Lord Chancellor was called upon to defend himself from charges of legal malpractice, and one of the most distinguished judges of the day, Sir Cresswell Cresswell, was implicated. The sitting Chief Justice of England was called to testify, and thus was tainted by association.

In the custom of the day, judges invited distinguished guests to sit beside them on the bench – a sort of legal equivalent of being invited to the royal box at the theatre. On this occasion "the Earl of Shrewsbury and Talbot, and Mr. Justice Haliburton, the celebrated author of 'Sam Slick,' occupied seats on the bench."[43] The courtroom was quickly filled to capacity by those keen to view the spectacle. Had tickets been sold, it would have been a scalper's dream. Barristers crowded to gain entry.[44] Contemporaries described the trial as if it were a theatre performance. The liberal *Daily News* (a London newspaper founded by Joseph Paxton) observed "at the end of the proceedings that '[t]he last act of the great Swinfen case has just closed ... It is seldom indeed that the sightseers in the London season have the chance of beholding ex-Chancellors, Judges in Ordinary, and even Chief Justices, in their robes put upon their defence in a witness-box.'" Despite the humiliating circumstances, a degree of stage management worked to preserve somewhat the dignity of sitting judges. Justice Cresswell Cresswell "gave his evidence from the bench." The Lord Chief Justice made a dramatic entrance in full judicial garb, and he too gave evidence from the bench.[45]

The spectacle focused attention at the very heart of barristers' practice. It was alleged that the defendant, Lord Chelmsford (then Sir Frederick Thesiger),

> well knowing that he had no authority from the plaintiff to enter into ... any terms of compromise on her behalf, without the authority and against the will of the plaintiff, and contrary to her instructions ... *wrongfully and fraudulently,* and in neglect and violation of his duty to the plaintiff, entered into what purported to be an arrangement ... to compromise the said cause.[46]

The second allegation was even more inflammatory:

> Sir Cresswell Cresswell, Knight, one of the Justices of Her Majesty's Court of Common Pleas ... *privately, clandestinely, and illegally* ... communicated with the defendant ... and gave him to understand that he, Sir Cresswell Cresswell, had formed an unfavourable opinion of the plaintiff's case, and that she would probably lose the verdict, for the purpose of intimidating the defendant, and inducing him to compromise the said cause ... [T]he defendant ... *being unduly and improperly influenced* by the communication from the said judge and in *collusion with him, wrongfully and fraudulently* ... became a party to the said *illegal and improper purpose of the judge* to put an end to and compromise the said cause, and *wrongfully, illegally, and in violation of his duty* ... entered into an arrangement.[47]

The actual conduct of the case did nothing to smooth troubled waters. Kennedy accused Lord Chelmsford of committing "an act of spoliation," of suppressing the truth, and of "shuffling and prevaricating."[48] Cresswell's behaviour was described as being of a "highly criminal nature," "a fraud,"[49] and a "misdemeanour."[50] Directed at some of the leading judicial figures of the day, this was pyrotechnic stuff. Of the key figures involved in the original *Swinfen* trial, only Sir Alexander Cockburn's behaviour (interestingly, the only Liberal of the three) appeared to Kennedy to be "in all respects proper."[51]

The matter was not to be resolved on a technical legal basis, and Kennedy was unremitting in keeping it a contest of principle. Behind the human wrongdoing, professional paternalism and the Bar's anti-commercial pretensions were on trial. The establishment view was that barristers' public duties required that they enjoy authority to act without being subject to their clients' command. Swinfen's counsel accorded greater importance to the self-determination of lay clients and emphasized barristers' contractual duties to clients. Both positions claimed justification in professional tradition and in the name of justice. As positions took shape, Swinfen's side evoked compelling social scripts: an oppressed widow of humble class origins had been done out of her rightful inheritance through the manipulations of her father-in-law's better-bred distant relatives. The mechanism of this theft was nothing less than betrayal by those whose duty was to protect her.

Kennedy argued that if Lord Chelmsford was not punished, a precedent "inimical to the interests of the law and of justice" would be created. He claimed that "[i]f these things were to be tolerated there would be an end of justice, for its very fountains would be dried up." Continuing in like vein, he asserted that "if such an act could be successfully upheld and justified in the administration of the law; if, indeed, it could, then the law of England would for all time to come be stigmatised as rotten to the core." "Happily," he believed, "it was not so." His client had confidence in the "rectitude of English law and justice," the "majesty of the law." Patience Swinfen "felt that she was fighting the battle of the law itself, and that however powerful her antagonist might be the law was too pure and strong to sanction an act of gross injustice."[52]

> It was her earnest desire, shared by millions of Englishmen, that punishment should be dealt to one who had betrayed so sacred a duty and had lent himself to the perversion of justice. Until that was done there could be neither security for the client nor respect for the profession to which the defendant belonged. His client would by their verdict accomplish her high and noble purpose. She would arrest the progress of a growing abuse, and would defend the insulted majesty of the law.[53]

The case quickly reduced itself to a test case between different visions of advocacy as the evidence of what had actually happened was overwhelming. Kennedy's previous successes established that Thesiger's compromise had been entered into without Patience Swinfen's authority. It was on this basis that the arrangement had been overturned and the will upheld.[54] Moreover, Kennedy was able to provide solid evidence that there was no rational basis on which Sir Frederick Thesiger might have suffered *bona fide* error regarding his client's instructions. There was contradictory evidence on this matter, however, and the trier of fact was left to decide.[55]

The fact of a private communication between judge and barrister was not denied. Chelmsford was unabashed:

> [W]hen the court was adjourned I had a communication with the judge. My impression is that I went to shake hands with him; he was a very old friend of mine. I do not think he beckoned to me, or called me over to him. I do not recollect exactly what he said: but I can say that the impression it left on my mind was that he had formed an unfavourable impression as to our case. I think he made that communication as between friends, not as between judge and counsel ... I certainly told Mr. Alexander and Mr. Whitmore that the judge was unfavourably disposed towards our case.[56]

Cresswell freely admitted to having told Thesiger that "Cockburn's examination had rather damaged his lady witnesses."[57] The ribald connotation was deliberate, to the amusement of those in the courtroom. It did not occur to him that a judge should withhold such opinions in the midst of a trial or that any such remarks should be made only in the presence of both parties. Sir Cresswell admitted that "[i]f any gentleman had asked me a question about it [the trial] I should have answered him," and would "no doubt" have "expressed an opinion adverse to the plaintiff's case."[58]

No one on Lord Chelmsford's side viewed any of this as improper. It was simply *assumed* that old friends would continue to discuss matters freely despite the different roles assigned to them, that judges would share their private thoughts about the merit of cases before them with gentlemen, and that litigation might best be "arranged" among counsel. This was routine for them. The ideology of adversarial justice also held, however, that barristers were to be their client's champions, fiercely and without compromise advancing her position before an impartial judge. Being impartial required the judge to withhold judgment until he had heard all the evidence and argument. The matter was very simple for Swinfen's legal team: "The judge ought to give no hint during the progress of the cause of the opinion he had formed in his own mind."[59] It was bad enough in this view that judges and counsel arranged cases by means of "private whisperings" if they thought they were acting in the best interests of the parties.[60] It would be much worse, however, if arrangements were foisted on unwilling parties in order to suit the convenience or biases of the arrangers themselves. Precisely this was alleged.

Successful barristers commonly undertook more than they could handle. Attorneys frequently complained that barristers would accept briefs knowing that they would probably not be able to appear at the trial.[61] This set up potential conflicts of commitment. Kennedy aggressively asserted that Chelmsford had compromised the Swinfen case *against his client's best interest* so that he could attend to another matter elsewhere.[62] If true, Mrs. Swinfen's rights had been sacrificed for the convenience of a greedy elite barrister who double-booked his time without concern for his clients' needs. Worse still, Kennedy claimed that naked class bias had steered the arrangement. Cresswell and Thesiger, he said, had false confidence in their ability to foist the arrangement on Patience Swinfen because they assumed "that as a person of humble origin, and somewhat unprotected," she "would have been glad to have accepted a handsome income, and retire into obscurity."[63] If that was their thought, they severely underestimated her. The implication that the heir-at-law's superior class origins had worked to his advantage was clear.

These allegations were based on inference only. Solid evidence to that effect would have made Chelmsford's defence all but impossible. He could not have defended the position that outcomes should be driven by class bias, that barristers should abandon winnable suits for personal convenience, or that it was legitimate to trade off one client's interest in order to obtain favour from a judge on another. Lord Chelmsford rested his defence almost entirely on reputation: he was respectable and so was Cresswell Cresswell. It also rested on their opposite assumptions about advocacy. Sir Fitzroy Kelly's defence emphasized that no fair-minded person could doubt the integrity of a distinguished man such as Chelmsford and that barristers were required to exercise superior judgment on behalf of their clients. Men of integrity needed to be trusted with the widest possible discretion if they were to truly serve lay clients who were ill-equipped to understand their own best interests.

Status was played shamelessly in defence. The *presumption* that senior barristers and judges were men of integrity permeated Kelly's remarks. Lord Chelmsford, he said, "had passed through a brilliant career," and on his "honour, and zeal for his client, the shadow of a shade of suspicion had never been cast." He was "one of the most distinguished advocates the English bar had ever produced," and a man who had borne a "spotless character ... through a long, an active, and an honourable career." The respectability of barristers as a professional group was incontestable. Speaking from his own extensive experience, he asserted that "from the moment when a counsel is retained in the cause, that object which is paramount to all others for the time – before which politics give way, and to which private friendships are sometimes sacrificed, the great object above all others was to obtain a verdict."[64]

He tied the constitutional liberties of the English inseparably to the integrity of the Bar, and the integrity of the Bar inseparably to the honour of his client:

> This case embraces the most important element in the administration of justice, for ... next to the responsibility of the jurors stands in the order of safeguards of the people the independence of the members of the bar ... [I]f the day should ever come when the bar of England shall fail in their duty lest they should be liable to legal consequences, the severest blow will be inflicted on the liberties of England that can be inflicted by human means. Let me call your attention to the real circumstances of the case. The defendant, my Lord Chelmsford ... is charged with having betrayed his duty to his client, with having dishonoured his profession, and that fraudulently and from unworthy motives, and for base purposes he entered into an agreement prejudicial to his client ... If he be guilty of this charge so is the learned judge, Sir Cresswell Cresswell, guilty of like offence – so are all the counsel, Mr. Alexander, Mr. Whitmore, and Mr. Gray, equally involved in this criminal charge – in this grave offence – for all united with him though he alone has been selected to answer for the offence in a court of justice.[65]

It was, in other words, an argument for innocence by association, and such an argument had emotive force. English jurors would have taken it as axiomatic that their England enjoyed the finest system of justice humans could devise, the greatest of liberty, and the best "safeguards of the people" that there had ever been. Obviously, the system of justice rested on the integrity of jurors and barristers. As England *in fact* enjoyed liberty, it could not be the case that barristers in general failed in their duties. It remained only to note the high professional status of the impugned barristers to complete the circle of reasoning: because each of Chelmsford, Cresswell, Alexander, Whitmore, and Gray shared responsibility for the Swinfen compromise and each was a prominent barrister or judge, it strained credulity to believe that that they had acted improperly.[66] Baldly, Lord Chelmsford's status was offered as a formidable defensive barrier.

Chelmsford's counsel argued that the honourable men who served as barristers should be afforded the widest possible latitude. Theirs was a peculiarly difficult task not susceptible to second-guessing. Montague Smith, appearing for Chelmsford in subsequent proceedings, asserted that "[t]he relation between the counsel and his client is unlike any other relation; the very nature of his position as counsel makes his authority necessarily indefinite."[67] "Infinite" might have been a better word. Kelly argued that recognizing any limitation on counsel's discretion regarding the conduct, compromise, or abandonment of a client's case would make it "utterly impossible ... to discharge his duty in that fearless, impartial, and intelligent way" that characterized the Bar of England. Bizarrely, the liberties of the English people were made to depend on counsel's absolute lack of accountability to clients:

> If the Court looked to the effect of making a barrister personally liable in an action, when he had perfectly, bona fide, and according to the best of his skill, learning, and ability, conducted his client's cause, and done that which appeared to him, exercising all due care and caution, for the good and advancement of his client's interests, then there was an end to that independent and upright spirit which up to the present day had actuated the advocates in the English courts.[68]

This brashly elitist and paternalistic view was opposite in all respects to that advanced for Patience Swinfen. The two sides shared the view that barristers were champions of English liberty and concurred in the need for counsel to be "independent." Their disagreement was over what independence meant and how "liberty" was best defended. "Large words were used," Kennedy said, "by Sir Fitzroy Kelly about the independence of the bar and the benefit arising from it; and I go along with him in a great measure; but that independence is not secured by giving them an unconditional power over cases in which they are engaged."[69] Kennedy countered Chelmsford's sweeping claims of authority with very ordinary, very modern contract law: "[A] counsel has no inherent authority, but requires a special one, and like everyone else, he only undertakes to do that which he has power to do."[70] In Mrs. Swinfen's argument, the client was a self-determining and competent *employer* of counsel whose relationship with her barrister derived from the ordinary laws of contract and agency: there was no room for any "necessarily indefinite" authority.

The judge had little sympathy for Swinfen's cause or theory of advocacy. At the close of the plaintiff's case, the Lord Chief Baron Pollock tried to persuade her to withdraw the charge of conspiracy between Thesiger (Chelmsford) and Cresswell. Failing in this, he encouraged the defendant to raise a motion to strike.[71] When that too failed, he simply directed a verdict for Chelmsford on that count.[72] On other matters, his charge to the jury was in complete alignment with the arguments of Lord Chelmsford's counsel. Echoing Kelly, he said that Swinfen's barristers had outraged "public decorum and decency ... by putting on the records of the court such a charge as this." He followed Kelly too in asserting that "the independence ... of the bar was one of the greatest safeguards to constitutional rights, and therefore, of their social happiness." The law, he said, only "required a barrister to discharge his duty towards his client as best he could. He might be utterly wrong or mistaken – he might be ... under the influence of fear; but if he intended to act honestly by his client he was not responsible."

This was a boldly innovative assertion of barrister's irresponsibility. His instructions to the jury would excuse incompetence, ineffectiveness, and insubordination provided only that a barrister's *bona fides* was not in doubt. Of course, Chelmsford's *bona fides* had been called into doubt. Quite apart from Kennedy's unprovable allegations, only a weak notion of good faith was consistent with deliberate violation of explicit instructions. Unsurprisingly, the jury found for Lord Chelmsford. It was all they could do, especially as the allegations of conspiracy had been removed from their purview. Barristers who crowded the courtroom greeted the verdict for Chelmsford "with loud applause."[73]

The outcome set the stage for further legal wrangling, the results of which were to have long-term effects on the contours of the English and colonial legal professions and the law of professional responsibility. The sentiment provoking applause by the barristers present was not universally shared. Reactions outside the courtroom aligned loosely with the diverse opinions of a reforming age. The spectacle of two junior barristers, a Queen's Counsel, a senior judge, the Lord Chief Justice of England, and a Lord Chancellor being cross-examined for obvious professional failings did little to enhance the majesty of the law or the dignity of the Bar. Contemporary commentary accorded little weight to the jury's verdict. Chelmsford's claimed belief that he had authority to enter into the compromise was greeted skeptically,[74] and middle-class unease about barristers' ethics, their relationships with clients, and the forces steering adversarial justice was stoked. Kennedy's "intemperance"[75] or vindictiveness[76] cast him in a poor light but did not obscure the possibility that he had brought serious problems in the English justice system to light. Three issues had become linked: the impropriety of the "great men," the corruption of English justice, and reform of the barristers' profession. The verdict did little to calm anxieties. Some mud stuck to the "great men" of law, regardless of the legal outcome.

The *Daily News* went on the attack. It said that only a senior barrister would try such a thing and, further, that Chelmsford's behaviour was typical of the leaders of the Bar. In deliberately violating his client's instructions, Thesiger, it said, "acted in a manner in which only the *irresponsible chiefs of the Bar* would venture to act."[77] *The Times* was less inclined to assume general rot, but it too rejected the notion that a barrister's special wisdom, intuition, or insider knowledge could justify such behaviour: "Sir F. Thesiger over-stepped the bounds of sound judgment, nor can we think that such compromises are within the just authority of any body of men, however learned or honourable."[78] The *Daily News* claimed that the practice of "counsel betraying his client by a compromise ... is a growing one."[79] It believed that "until this case of Mrs. Swinfen the great leaders were too much in the habit of adopting an arbitrary tone of dictation which was becoming intolerable."[80] Kennedy himself could have said it no more directly.

In a sense, the truthfulness of such observations is of secondary importance. They had currency. A widely shared belief that justice was threatened by the activities of precisely that segment of the Bar that should most fully embody achievement, learning, honour, and ethical professionalism was profoundly unsettling. This group of elite barristers, in their guise as Benchers and circuit leaders, were expected to "protect" the public through the mechanisms of ethical or "etiquette" regulation available to them. This was the group, too, from whom Her Majesty's judges were selected. An unseemly intimacy among the entire group had been revealed, causing them to act in apparent disregard of their courtroom roles. The failings of such a group went to the core of barristers' professionalism. Precisely because of their high status, this could not be casually discounted as the activities of a few "bad men." If the Bar's elite was untrustworthy, it was but a short step to questioning the autonomy of the Inns, the self-governance of the Bar, and the Bar's monopoly. Lord Chelmsford's defence rested upon an arrogant paternalism that was hard to reconcile with then-current notions of individual autonomy, adversarial justice, and the principles of free trade political economy. It required litigants to accept that the barrister whose fees they paid might act in utter disregard for their wishes and in violation of their direct instructions. *The Times* said the real question was whether counsel are "supreme and irresponsible in dealing with the interests of their clients," and whether "when we bring a cause into court ... we abrogate all control over it?"[81] That, indeed, was the gist of the Lord Chief Baron's summing up. A lead article in the *Morning Star* (a politically radical London daily established by George Hardy) emphasized what was at stake:

> By this trial the veil has been lifted from an obliquity in our legal system which, when examined, can hardly bear the light of day. The theory that

> justice is administered, and that the rights of litigants are determined in open Court, should not be lightly exposed to suspicion. Suitors should not be allowed to think that their interests may be compromised in deference to the private whisperings of judges, or that their counsel may be constrained by an unworthy fear to abandon the cause which they were instructed and paid to defend. The suitor who at great expense and labour has marshalled the evidence, on the strength and truth of which he appeals to a jury for a verdict, must not be baulked of the decision of that jury through the ill concealed impatience of a judge. The suitor has his rights, and they must be respected.[82]

The *Daily News* took comfort from the thought that both counsel and judiciary had learned "a useful lesson." Cresswell's "indecorous" behaviour was believed to be common. The *Daily News* noted that "[a]rrangements and references are favourite themes of judicial eloquence; nor is it unusual to find suitors driven to accept suggestions from the Bench which their better judgment opposes." The newspaper endorsed Kennedy's view of how adversarial justice should work:

> There is no need to depreciate the immense importance of that good understanding which happily exists in this country between the Bench and the Bar. But the issue which is being tried ought to be a forbidden topic. And a judge ought to refrain with the most scrupulous care from expressing any opinion in favour of one side or the other; above all he should refrain, during any friendly intercourse with either counsel or suitor, from indulging in any such indiscretion.[83]

The *Morning Star* agreed that "[p]rivate feelings, or personal ease and convenience, should never be permitted to disturb the calm stoicism of the judicial mind."[84] The more professionally invested *Solicitors' Journal and Reporter* (founded as an offshoot of the Metropolitan and Provincial Law Association in 1857 to promote the interests of solicitors[85]) rejected any suggestion of bias, concluding that Cresswell had simply wished to be done with the case and move on: "The judges and the bar pass on to other scenes and fresh business." This, it said, was likely to infuriate litigants and more generally provoke belief "that no reliance can be placed on assize justice. If lawyers are wise they will look into these things in time."[86]

Kennedy's poem "The Reference (A Law Case of the Last Century)" offered his insight into judicial behaviour:

> 'Twas on the last day of assize
>   All in a circuit town,...
>
> A Serjeant rose with stately mien,
>   His voice was clear and strong,
> And launch'd into an opening speech
>   Which threaten'd to be long:
> ...
>   Defendant quaked with fear:
>
> But all this while the learned Judge
>   Unto himself did say,
> "Sure at the Bishop's I'm engaged
>   To dine this very day;
>
> A Marquis and a royal Duke
>   And Duchess will be there;
> I cannot really stop away
>   From such a grand affair:
> ...
>
> No sooner him it flash'd across
>   Then up his mind he made:
> "No, Brother, to your statement I
>   Have close attention paid;
>
> And turning all things in my mind,
>   It hath to me occurr'd,
> A case like this – 'twere not amiss
>   That it should be referr'd."[87]

Swinfen v. Lord Chelmsford had fixed public attention on the conduct of bench and bar at a time when ancient institutions were vulnerable to reforming urges. The previous decade had revealed sustained support for reform or abolition of customary Bar etiquette in Parliament and among a wider public, as well as a drift toward continued erosion of the Bar's monopoly in favour of the attorneys'/solicitors' branch. It was in this context that embarrassing failures of propriety or judgment by establishment leaders was revealed. Despite a narrow legal outcome exonerating Lord Chelmsford, its reverberations were unsettling. *It* served as a morality tale about the Bar's failings. Informed commentators believed that important issues had been raised, and many sided with Kennedy's and Denman's understanding of how barrister/client relationships should be.[88] Most believed the conduct of Chelmsford and

Cresswell to be both commonplace and improper. Contemporary observers might well have imagined that the logical next steps would be reforms aimed at democratizing and commercializing the Bar, opening up new types of professional competition, and loosening the grip of the self-replicating oligarchy that governed the Inns.

It was not to be. The power of inertia, resilience of the Bar leadership, influence, opportunism, and fortuitous circumstances allowed focus to shift in other directions. New morality plays took centre stage, shifting attention elsewhere. The Bar's leadership developed other sorts of parables from events that suggested moral conclusions quite contrary to those of *Swinfen v. Lord Chelmsford.* These revolved around four individuals: Edwin James, Digby Seymour, Charles Claydon, and – again – Charles Rann Kennedy.

Disbarment of Edwin James, QC

The Chelmsford case dragged on, proceeding through motion for a new trial (November 1859)[89] and legal argument[90] to judgment of the Exchequer Court on 9 June 1860.[91] The case kept alive public anxieties over the Bar's "best men." The status of the defendants helped but could not guarantee an outcome, leaving room for "the widest field for speculation, as to whether the rule would be discharged or made absolute."[92] Some speculated that the court's unanimous decision for Chelmsford masked judicial division.[93]

Edwin James as he appeared in the *Illustrated London News,* 13 October 1860. © *Illustrated London News Ltd/ Mary Evans, 10161691*

Court of Exchequer (tax court). *Artist: Rudolf Ackermann, 1808; Boston College Law Library, Daniel R. Coquillette Rare Book Room*

As Chelmsford's conduct faded from public view, the Inns of Court worked behind the scenes to develop a more coherent approach to the exercise of their powers. They were all too aware that this and other recent episodes had caught them on the back foot. The Pension (governing body) of Gray's Inn invited their counterparts to join with them in forming "a Committee of the four Inns of Court for the purpose of inquiry into and reporting upon instances of improper professional conduct on the part of Members of the Bar."[94] Discussions proceeded quietly, invisible to the public. Solicitors continued to be upset with barristers' etiquette[95] but, briefly, quiet set in. It was not to be so for long.

The next scandal began mysteriously. On 9 April 1861, Edwin James abruptly announced his resignation from all public offices.[96] A Queen's Counsel and well-known Member of Parliament, he was poised to assume the role of law officer of the Crown at the time. (In an odd twist of circumstances, he had appeared as counsel for the heirs-at-law in the case brought by Kennedy to restore the Swinfen estate to Patience Swinfen.[97]) His explanation that he was leaving public life in order to focus fully on his professional career seemed implausible. The moderately conservative *Saturday Review* (a

London middle-class weekly featuring Liberal and Conservative writers) noted that he had resigned lawyers' sinecures along with demanding and less lucrative offices. Something darker was suggested.[98]

Personal scandal was revealed in due course and the personal became professional soon enough. The Inner Temple Benchers first discussed rumours about James in April 1861.[99] On the same day, coincidentally, they received a report from their committee assessing "the expediency of [establishing] some authority to which all questions connected with the practice of the Bar may be referred." The under-treasurer asked the other Inns of Court "for which crime or misconduct a Barr., has at any time been disbarred,"[100] and also "whether any proceedings with a view to disbarring a Queen's Counsel for crime or misconduct of any kind have ever been taken against him?"[101] A committee struck to consider Edwin James's conduct[102] led to his disbarment on 18 June 1861. James became one of the earliest disciplinary disbarments and the first Queen's Counsel to suffer this punishment.

New ground had been broken. James's disbarment was followed by a modest Benchers' offensive against barristers of whom they disapproved. This too was unprecedented. There had previously been no formal process of disbarment and no established convention regarding communication of either the outcomes or the reasons for disciplinary decisions. It was the infancy of modern professional discipline. In James's case, the disbarment was announced[103] but all else remained mysterious. The Benchers' June decision was confirmed by the Parliament of the Inner Temple in November. Only in February 1862 was any public explanation offered.[104] Rumour commonly fills the void left by the failure of direct communication, and so it proved. The *Solicitors' Journal and Reporter* considered it unsatisfactory "that the entire proceedings were conducted in secret, and that even the very charges against Mr. James were not officially made known." The *Journal* reported that "not only the profession but the general public were of course acquainted with them in all their details."[105]

Secrecy breeds suspicion. In October 1861, Edwin James crossed the Atlantic as a sort of refugee from professional persecution. Seeking to establish legal practice in New York, he was greeted as "one of the most eminent leaders of the English bar and one of her Majesty's counsel," and reputed to be "a frequenter at the receptions of the 'White House.'"[106] Back in England, the Benchers could only be displeased that "he was received with fraternization and rejoicing by the bar and Supreme Court of New York; and this was done with full knowledge that he had been disbarred."[107] The Yanks apparently had little confidence in the fairness of British ways or the integrity of the Inns.

Even at home, the Benchers' silence raised doubts. The *Spectator* published a caustic piece regretting that James had not "remained – what he deserved to become – obscure":

> The Old World knows nothing of its greatest men and half of Mr. Edwin James's achievements in this country have never become known till *The New York Times* pointed them out. In the first place, we learn that he was impeded in his rise by all those aristocratic influences that are an obstacle to mere talent at the bar. This is what, alas! is too often seen with us. Many barristers find that his humble rank is a barrier between himself and the attorney of gentle blood. We have no doubt that this was the case with Mr. Edwin James. Young sprigs of fashionable solicitors gave all the work to the younger sons of dukes and earls, and the humble Mr. James was trampled under foot by the haughty attorney's clerk. *The New York Times* is right in scourging what is the crying sin of all attorneys ... namely, too great disposition to frequent the men of rank, and to throw hindrances in the way of plebeian genius.[108]

James wrote, "I have been *sacrificed* by *my rivals* from feelings of *political* jealousy and professional *rivalry*," and Mr. H.H. Pyke ("the champion of Mr. Edwin James in this country") called on Lord Westbury, Lord Chancellor, as a "Bible Christian," to restore James to his position. Pyke believed that the "Inns have no legal power for what they have done."[109]

The fuss eventually flushed the Benchers out. They explained that "[i]n America he has been received as a political exile, and he has had a few defenders and sympathizers at home as really the victim of professional jealousy!"[110] The Benchers presented a damning case. They had investigated three transactions. Two were purely financial, while the third seemed akin to a protection racket. James had run into serious debt despite earning professional fees of £7,000 per year, quite likely on account of the expenses of a high-profile public career.[111] Upon attaining the age of twenty-one (in 1857), Lord Worsley, the son of Lord Yarborough, agreed to assume co-responsibility for over £30,000 of James's debts. Yarborough, for obvious reasons, was displeased and began looking into James's financial status.[112] When another creditor obtained execution against James's Berkeley Square house, Yarborough took action. He forced James's resignation from all public offices and compelled him to devote himself fully to his legal practice, "to enable Mr. James to reduce his debts."[113] He also insisted that James resign from Brooks's ("Lord Yarborough having introduced him to Brooks's and Lord Worsley being a member"[114]).

James also owed some £20,000 to Mr. Fryer, a West Country solicitor from Wimborne who had financed his election costs and "went so far as to press unto Mr. James the necessity, for purposes of political advancement, of a more splendid style of living, and to take for him a large home in Berkeley Square that he might gather round him such a following as judicious dinner-giving can provide."[115] This debt, too, appeared unlikely to be repaid.

The final transaction of concern to the Benchers arose directly from advocacy. In 1859, James had cross-examined a Mr. Ingram so aggressively as to leave him "in a state of totally shattered nerves and utterly broken down." In an interval between two trials in the same matter, Ingram loaned James either £1,000 or £1,250 (the exact figure was disputed), telling a friend that he was motivated by fear. Ingram's executor reported:

> I then went to Mr._____, who was very intimate with Mr. Ingram ... Mr._____ told me that in the interval between the first and the second trials of the case of *Scully v. Ingram,* Mr. Ingram came to him and said, in a state of great excitement, "I must lend Mr. James some money." Mr._____ replied that he did not see that he must. Mr. Ingram answered, "I must – I am so afraid of him; I must do anything he asks, and you must lend him the money for me."[116]

James promised Ingram that "you should not repent your kindness to me." He apparently made good on his promise as "a compromise was effected"[117] at the second trial without Ingram having to give testimony. In a "Statement of Explanations," James asserted that he would "ever regret the *indiscretion* of *accepting* the loan." Nonetheless, he said that the money was intended to assist with election expenses and that there was nothing dishonourable about it.[118] The Inn's investigating committee found the arrangement to be improper and "unprofessional," and concluded that the financial transaction did in fact influence James's handling of the case.[119] This debt, like the others, went unpaid.[120]

Although the arrangement sounds like extortion, contemporaries viewed it as merely dishonourable rather than scandalous. The *Solicitors' Journal and Reporter* doubted "whether the benchers on this disreputable transaction alone would have done more than reprimand the unscrupulous debtor."[121] The journal agreed, however, that the three incidents together called for disbarment.

From one point of view, it was impressive that a Queen's Counsel, leader of the Bar, Member of Parliament, and Attorney-General designate had been forced to account for his actions, and even punished with the ultimate sanction. The Benchers seemed to demonstrate determination and commitment in protecting the public from even the most prominent and powerful barristers. Only five days before their decision, an editorial in the *Solicitors' Journal and Reporter* had accused the Benchers of shirking their duty by failing to protect the public from barristers, "some of whom," the journal asserted, "have the slenderest pretensions to assume the guardianship of public morals." The editorial continued:

> [I]t is by no means impossible for members of the Bar to pursue for many years an unimpeached and successful course of practice, while it is a matter of common notoriety that they have rendered themselves obnoxious to imputations which, so long as they remain unexplained, ought to be sufficient to place them outside the pale of respectable society. Yet so strangely inert are the governing bodies of the profession that nothing short of the greatest public scandal appears to have the least effect in putting them in motion against wrong-doers. This is no doubt partly owing to the jealousy in favour of personal independence which exists among all bodies of Englishmen; but in the case of the Bar it is to be attributed much more to the exceptional and inefficient character of the self-constituted tribunals for the determination of questions affecting the honour of its members, and also to the mysterious secrecy with which such proceedings are conducted. The time seems to have come, however, for the Bar to contrive some more active and efficient means than it now possesses for this purpose.[122]

James's case seemed to provide convincing evidence otherwise, for the Inn had acted in advance of any public scandal and shown neither fear nor favour.

Aware that their leniency or inactivity had "been of late years the subject of private and public animadversion,"[123] the Benchers proudly proclaimed their boldness and impartiality:

> Mr. James's antecedents were patent – the benchers more or less having been personally acquainted with him, and his general professional habits, conduct, and private character. Several of the benchers were members of both Houses of Parliament, and a few may be designated as once his social friends; some were members of the same clubs – all of course were his associates for years at the hall dinners of the inn. Such a body was a special jury.[124]

But this exaggerates any affection felt for James. In disbarring him, the Benchers simultaneously rid themselves of an irritant *and* made public display of their diligent supervision of the profession. The case deflected criticism that the Inns shied away from the exercise of disciplinary powers. It contradicted the assumption that senior barristers were immune from sanction. If some thought the existing apparatus ineffective in protecting the public from predatory barristers, the case of Edwin James proved otherwise. Through their bold action, the ancient autonomy of the Inns was shown to operate in the public interest.

Yet questions remain.[125] Indebtedness alone seemed an unlikely ground for disbarment. If it was, the amount of debt or stage of defalcation necessary to trigger professional sanction was left uncertain. Disbarment did nothing to resolve the debt and could not have been pleasing to James's creditors. It was very much in their interests that he continue to earn large professional fees. Moreover, it surely was not the case that James was the only barrister with debt problems. The most obvious trigger of the Benchers' attention, the curious arrangement with Ingram, is denied by the record of their investigation. It is easy from our point of view to assume that accepting money from your client's opponent in the expectation of going easy on him in the course of litigation would be viewed as a fundamental betrayal warranting disbarment. In the early 1860s, however, neither Benchers nor outside observers were terribly fussed.

What was it about James that provoked professional discipline, then? A clue may be found in an incident some nine years earlier. Appointed Queen's Counsel then, he would normally have automatically become a Bencher of his Inn. The Benchers, however, "unusually but not discriminately,"[126] refused to elect him to join their number. The *Annual Register* concluded that the decision not to elect him to the Bench was "a circumstance significant of the estimation in which the learned gentleman's character was held by his legal brethren."[127] It may be that they objected to the unsavory sort of legal business that had given him prominence[128] as "leader in all actions for seduction, breach of promise of marriage, assault, and false imprisonment, and in all cases which involved the reputation of an actress or a horse."[129] Alternatively, it may be that his genuinely radical political convictions or something different altogether, or a combination of things, caused offence. Regardless, the snub was noteworthy.

A radical democrat, James was elected to Parliament as a Liberal in 1859, the year a "Liberal party" as such emerged. In 1847, he had helped John Jervis Jr. (son of Attorney-General Sir John Jervis) win election to Parliament for the borough of Horsham. James was a democrat before democracy was respectable. He conducted both politics and law flamboyantly. He was said to have engaged in "the most unblushing bribery" on behalf of John Jervis Jr.,[130] and he gained notoriety or fame for his conduct of politically charged cases as well as those involving the reputation of actresses or horses. In 1851, he acted as defence counsel in *The Queen v. Thomas Drury.* His client, Dr. Simon François Bernard, was a French socialist accused of conspiring with Felice Orsini to assassinate Napoleon III. The assassination failed but the conspirators managed to kill eight people and wound as many as a hundred and fifty in the attempt. James won Bernard's acquittal through the seemingly improper tactic of introducing evidence that Bernard had in fact intended to kill somebody else. He crossed the line from representation to partisanship in making it clear that he agreed with Orsini's and Bernard's political views. After the trial, he gave a speech attacking Napoleon III and endorsing radically democratic political views (this at a time not long after the Chartist disturbances in England). The *Law Times* (a weekly solicitors' and attorneys' journal[131]) abhorred his politics, saying that this speech made it "impossible for any government, not Red Republican in its origin and objects, to give him place." It suggested that he "resign the office of counsel to that Queen, as being altogether incompatible with the principles proclaimed upon the platform and to which he gave his public adhesion."[132]

James was consistent in his radical politics. In 1859, he travelled to Italy to demonstrate his support of Italian unification and to visit the camp of the colourful nationalist warrior Giuseppe Garibaldi. The *Illustrated London News* (a "respectable" working-class periodical) reported on the trip. The *Saturday Review* sniffed that "he imparted an air of vulgarity to the whole history of the last year by visiting Italy in the character of an English politician during the Neapolitan revolution. He wrote to the *Times* about Neapolitan prisons, and made writing to the *Times* ridiculous."[133] In Parliament, he "shouted like the rest for Reform."[134] Some Benchers probably shared the *Saturday Review*'s anxieties:

> It would have been as reputable to have had [Baptist Minister] MR. SPURGEON for the new Dean of Exeter as to have seen MR. EDWIN JAMES made Attorney-General ... Had he been more sensitive, he would not have been the man for Marylebone. Nothing but the conviction of the truth of Liberal principles can possibly console Liberals for the many disappointments incidental to the progress of their cause. Ultimately, perhaps, a Marylebone mob will rise to some superior state of intelligence and moral being, which may enable them to distinguish a good candidate from a bad one. At present, it must be confessed that, were it not for the sake of theory and consistency, many British electors would have been better off by having their representatives chosen for them without the disastrous expedient of an election ... It needs a considerable emotion to affect rapidly and thoroughly a very large constituency ... For the present, intelligence and respectability

> in our metropolitan boroughs must be content to take whatever goods the gods in the gallery provide for them. But it is something to have got rid of MR. EDWIN JAMES.[135]

From such a perspective, the timing of the Benchers' move against James was fortuitous. It cut a rising political career just as he was to assume the role of law officer of the Crown.

James claimed the deck had been stacked against him. The inchoate character of bar etiquette and the novelty of using disbarment in this way suggests that something deeper than objective application of professional standards was in motion. After all, the Bar establishment had little to say about the conduct of Lord Chelmsford and Cresswell Cresswell, and expressed no concern about the treatment of clients by leaders of the Bar more generally. James's supporters believed that he had been victimized for his political views. It is not hard to imagine the antipathy of the Benchers for his radical politics and the scent of scandal surrounding his legal practice. As important, perhaps, he may have crossed an invisible line in reputation or honour. Those notions were taken seriously, earnestly discussed, and policed by gentlemen's clubs as well as less formal social arrangements.

Be that as it may, the case served the institutional interests of the Inns rather well. It demonstrated to the public at large that the Benchers were willing and able to ensure the honourable conduct of barristers. That they did so by purging their ranks of one who had achieved prominence without ingratiating himself to the professional establishment also sent a message that could not be lost on others. By proving that they could act boldly, they deflected public criticism of the Inns and their guild structures. For those who questioned the Bar's monopoly, here was proof of its public utility.[136] It showed solicitors that the Inns could enforce bar etiquette. Junior barristers learned that the Benchers were powerful, and those inclined towards either unorthodox practices or radical politics were given something to think about. It is unlikely that the Benchers would have acted without external pressure – the Inns had no tradition of acting punitively. But if they were forced to act, the matter could be put to good use.

Attention, hitherto focused steadfastly on the leaders of the Bar, began to shift towards the profession's fringe-dwellers. The pattern repeated itself on three further occasions.

Charles B. Claydon, Barrister for the "Oppressed"

On the day that Inner Temple's Parliament affirmed James's disbarment, the Benchers of Lincoln's Inn met to determine the punishment of a less prominent barrister. In November 1861, a special council considered alleged breach of etiquette by Charles Broadbelt Claydon, a local barrister "residing at Handsworth near Birmingham but having Chambers at Wolverhampton."[137] His case is a near-perfect counterpoise to the drama and high profile of Edwin James, for it took the Benchers deep into the diurnal work practices of a very ordinary junior barrister. Where one case signalled a novel assertion of Benchers' discipline, the other provided early warning that practices established for over a decade or more were not unassailable.[138] If the punishment of Edwin James was important for the exceptional circumstances and flamboyant personality of the barrister involved, Charles Claydon's case was significant because of its very ordinary character.

As he often had before, Claydon appeared in the Staffordshire County Court on 12 July 1861. On this occasion, he appeared as counsel for Francis Plimley, the debtor in an insolvency matter. In cross-examination, attorneys for the creditors questioned Plimley extensively about his relationship with Claydon. Their questions had little to do with the merits of the action but served to create a public record of Claydon's professional practices. Engaged directly by Plimley without the intervention of an attorney, Claydon or his clerk (Mr. Bridgewater) did almost all the work in preparing the case. Plimley paid no fees in advance. The attorney whose name appeared on court documents (William Ward) was never engaged by Plimley. Ward "only acted as attesting witness at the request of Mr. Bridgewater ... which he said he did without payment, and at the request of, and to oblige Mr. Bridgewater."[139]

Each aspect of these arrangements could be said to breach professional etiquette. This was clear with regard to both direct client contact and failure to obtain prepayment of fees. Moreover, some of the work done by Bridgewater and Claydon might be construed as unauthorized practice as an attorney, while engaging Ward as an attesting witness seemed designed to camouflage the arrangement's true nature. At a minimum, they inverted the order prescribed by etiquette, wherein attorneys were to "instruct" barristers, not vice versa. Finally, Bridgewater's function in negotiating fees directly with the client (barristers' clerks generally negotiated fees with attorneys) arguably amounted to "touting" for business. The violations were clear enough, though the consequences, if any, attaching to mere breaches of etiquette were uncertain.

On the other hand, it was only just such arrangements that made it possible for less well-off clients to be represented by a barrister in County Court proceedings. Clients in smaller cases could not normally pay for the services of both an attorney *and* a barrister. The employment of an attorney as intermediary between client and barrister would have to be dispensed with and one professional, not two, hired. Finally, in many cases, including insolvency proceedings, most individuals would simply be unable to pay fees in advance. Each impugned aspect of the relationship between Claydon and Plimley was necessary if barristers were to represent individuals such as Plimley in a County Court case.

Claydon made no attempt to conceal the nature of his practice. County Court Judge A.M. Skinner reported that:

> I said ... we can neither of us forget the fact that I am a Bencher of your Inn. On which he said, I know that, and am glad of this opportunity, this charge has been going on so long, that I am quite anxious to have it settled one way or the other; – I avow that I receive Clients without the intervention of an Attorney, and I will continue to do so. – I then said that is a challenge to me, to send an account of this Case to Lincoln's Inn – Mr. Claydon replied that he wished I would do so as he desired to have the question settled.[140]

Knowing the outcome, Claydon's challenge seems rash or even self-destructive. It was, however, a rationally calculated risk. Skinner could not be avoided as he held the position of County Court judge where Claydon practised. His hostility had to be contained and an authoritative ruling of the Inn in Claydon's favour would have been of great assistance. Claydon in fact had reason to believe that his conduct was both lawful *and* accepted as such by the professions' governing bodies. The *County Courts Act* expressly made provision for counsel to be instructed by clients directly and, as we have seen, many barristers had taken advantage of this provision during the previous decade.[141] Moreover, a previous court ruling had established that "[t]here is no positive rule of law or practice of the courts which prevents a defendant from having in the conduct of a cause the assistance of counsel instructed by himself instead of an attorney."[142] Finally, neither circuit messes nor Inns had previously been able to put a stop to such practices. All signs were that public opinion would weigh in Claydon's favour.

The *Staffordshire Advertiser* went to bat for Claydon. In an article that was quickly reprinted in the *Worcestershire Chronicle*, another Midlands weekly newspaper, the rules of etiquette were portrayed as blatantly protectionist, equivalent to "the laws of a Trades Union." The newspaper condemned them as contrary to both fundamental principles of political economy and the best traditions of the Bar. It was confident in the outcome:

> [W]hat we contend for is free trade, and that Barristers shall be free Agents; that if they please they shall be at liberty to do as the great Romans did;

> to do as Lord Brougham thinks they might advantageously and without any sacrifice of position do; to do as Mr. Claydon is doing at Wolverhampton, thereby shewing his spirit and superiority to vulgar prejudice. We have no apprehension of any penalty the Benchers of Lincolns Inn can impose on him; they will have against them public opinion, common sense, ancient practice, and the views of the most eminent Law reformers the Country has produced; and if they venture on any tyrannical measures for suppressing the freedom of practice claimed by Mr. Claydon for the benefit of the public, they will bring a hornet's nest about their ears.[143]

Claydon in fact had developed a successful County Court practice over the previous decade. Having failed to establish a successful practice in London[144] and Birmingham,[145] he moved to Wolverhampton in 1856,[146] where he established a "practice in the county courts of South Staffordshire."[147] Arriving there, he found that many attorneys were accustomed to acting as advocates in County Court matters. Attorneys could appear in the County Courts as well as do "all that is necessary for the client out of court, such as collecting evidence, writing letters, serving notices, etc."[148] Unsurprisingly, local attorneys saw no reason to brief a barrister. It was an uncomfortable position for Claydon. Superior courts were only occasional visitors in the provinces and local barristers had to focus their work on the County Courts if they were to make a go of it. Although the law allowed direct client contact for barristers in County Court proceedings, etiquette required the involvement of attorneys who had little reason to share work with barristers. Strict compliance with etiquette would force local barristers to forgo business opportunities available under statute, leaving them with little hope of successful practice. It was only the unenforceability of the rules of etiquette that allowed for professional survival. On discovering that provincial attorneys preferred "to act as Advocates in the Local Courts rather than incur the expense of retaining Counsel," Claydon eventually took advantage of "the undoubted privilege of every Barrister" to "receive instructions without the intervention of an Attorney."[149]

He knew both that the *County Courts Act* allowed this, and that "the same course had been pursued by other Provincial Barristers."[150] Claydon's approach to practice had initially been supported by County Court judge Mr. Serjeant Clarke,[151] and he practised without any problem until Skinner's arrival to replace Clarke. By that time he had, he said, "become somewhat popular as an Advocate and am now able to take business on my own terms, so that my profession now yields me an income of 300 or 400 pounds per annum clear of all outgoings for Clerk and Chamber expenses."[152]

Claydon served legal needs that would otherwise have been unmet. He took some cases "without any hope of remuneration," and felt that "it is mainly owing to my sympathy with the poor and oppressed that I have attained the position I now occupy."[153] In this marginal niche, he avoided direct competition with either established barristers or successful attorneys. Although he must have brought cases against the *clients* of well-established lawyers, there is no reason to suspect that this in itself would have poisoned them against him. Lawyers are used to having opposing counsel. He competed directly, however, with less well-off attorneys, generating the hostility of what he called "a certain class of attornies."[154] His opponents seized the opportunity presented by the arrival of a new County Court judge. Claydon believed that Skinner had become his "accuser to the Honourable Society of Lincoln's Inn" under pressure from attorneys.[155] In November 1861, the Benchers received a report from a committee of the Oxford Circuit[156] investigating charges first communicated to a committee of the "Staffordshire Sessions Bar early in 1861."[157] There were four "complaints and charges against Mr. Claydon":[158]

1 He "practised habitually, both before Justices and in the County Courts without the intervention of an Attorney, and for fees which no Barrister should accept" (*i.e.*, his fees were too low).
2 He took cases on the understanding that no fee would be paid if the case was lost.
3 He "acted as an Attorney, by collecting and taking down evidence, by taking out Summonses to appear before Magistrates, and giving notices to produce, either in person or through the medium of his Clerk, named Bridgwater."
4 Bridgewater had "got up" a case so that some of the parties involved "believed Bridgewater to be the Attorney."[159]

Claydon responded that Skinner had a personal bias against him[160] and had given in to pressure from local attorneys. He again freely admitted working without the intervention of an attorney and asserted his legal right to do so. Although he admitted accepting low fees at an earlier time, he reported that this was no longer so: "I am however happy to be able to say, I can now command an amount of honorarium in all cases in which I am engaged which would be deemed respectable by any Barrister attending the Stafford Sessions."[161] Although he had sometimes acted without fee, he denied having ever entered into arrangements making payment contingent upon success.[162] He admitted to having "occasionally selected Attornies to act for Clients" who consulted him, and to having once written a letter on behalf of a client,[163] but denied ever having "acted as an Attorney."[164]

The Benchers passed a resolution disbarring and expelling him on 24 January 1862.[165] Surprisingly, their resolution did not clearly specify the offences deserving this punishment. The evidence they had considered related to taking instructions without the intervention of an attorney, entering into contingency fee arrangements, fee cutting, touting, and acting as an attorney. Which of these were taken as proved, and which or which combination constituted ground for disbarment, are unclear. This ambiguity may have been deliberate and designed to mask divergences of opinion as to evidence or policy.

Outsiders assumed that Claydon's punishment was for taking instructions directly from clients. Although Skinner's complaint covered more ground, their courtroom exchange focused on that issue[166] and the other charges necessarily followed from that starting point. Nearly a year later (December 1862), Claydon petitioned Lord Justices Cockburn, Pollock, and Erle as Visitors of Lincoln's Inn:

> That your petitioner being thus situated as a Local Barrister, and finding himself called upon to encounter such formidable opposition, was compelled to have recourse to such means as were open to him by strict legal right to enable him to procure a livelihood; and *as the County Court Act enables Counsel to conduct cases without a retainer by an* Attorney, *he supposed* it *was competent for him to perform all the preliminary duties which were necessary to bring a Case into Court.* The irregularities charged against your Petitioner were chiefly proceedings of this nature, he having frequently advised instructed and assisted his Clients in the commencement and progress of their causes from the beginning to the end, including the examination of Witnesses and the drawing of plaints, pleas, Etc.[167]

The logic seemed irrefutable.

Public reaction was critical of the Benchers.[168] A letter in the *Morning Star and Dial* asserted that barristers had a clear legal right to deal directly with their clients in the County Courts. In any event, the writer believed that the "legitimate tribunal by which such questions should always be decided" was not the Bench table of an Inn, but "one of the superior courts of law."[169] The *Morning Star and Dial* declared that "[i]n the case of Mr. Claydon ... we should think the vast majority of the public would ... give their sympathies to the individual thus condemned."[170] Others criticized the infringement of freedom of contract and condemned the Bar's etiquette as violating generally accepted notions of "free trade" political economy.[171] Some newspapers published verbatim a letter from Claydon to Lord Chancellor Westbury accusing the Benchers of treating him "harshly and cruelly" and asking Westbury to "take such steps as may be necessary to bring the whole of the recent proceedings against me under review, in order that if possible some remedy may be applied to the injury I have sustained."[172] Even the *Solicitor's Journal and Reporter* – hardly a friend of barristers tilling solicitors' fields – criticized the Benchers' secrecy and doubted their explanation: "It is not easy to believe that the benchers would have been so eager to punish a mere breach of professional propriety with so severe a sentence."[173]

The *Morning Star and Dial* criticized the Inns for imposing "a host of absurd restrictions" and acting "without reference to the wants of the public" in imposing constraints on "the free exercise by the advocate of his talents, and the free use of his legal experience in the way most beneficial to himself and the world."[174] It also criticized the secrecy of the process and doubted that the punishment could have been imposed simply for maintaining direct contact with clients. Such action, the editorialist asserted, "would be entirely unwarranted by law."

> By the County Court Act ... not only a barrister or an attorney, but, by leave of the judge, any other person may appear in the conduct of the cause. Before magistrates the intervention of an attorney is equally unnecessary, and at the Old Bailey and other criminal courts the advocates practising there are held bound in honour to take briefs offered them from the dock, if accompanied by a fee, and such is the continual practice. In the matter of advising, also, barristers enjoy a monopoly; and judges have given it as their opinion that a barrister is as much bound to advise upon a written case, when submitted by a client in person, as when the brief is conveyed to him by more learned hands. In the superior courts the complicated system of procedure almost forbids a layman, however skilled, from being his own lawyer; but still, even there, it is not an unheard of circumstance for a counsel to be briefed at the trial by the party himself.[175]

One is left wondering not so much how Claydon could risk exposing himself to "trial" by the Bench but why the Benchers would risk exposing themselves to condemnation for imposing an unprecedented and draconian punishment on an obscure provincial barrister who was doing something that *seemed* to be authorized by legislation.

The accident that Skinner rather than someone else had arrived in South Staffordshire as County Court judge was fateful. Another newly appointed judge might well have followed Serjeant Clarke's earlier endorsement of Claydon's practice. Claydon's misfortune was amplified by the coincidence that Skinner was a Bencher of his own Inn. He had deep connections with other Benchers and the lines between judge and Inn may have been blurred.

The larger structures of legal professions were tilted against Claydon's sort. Most successful barristers had reached their eminence within a system that frowned upon direct client contact, and probably believed that it should be discouraged. Attorney patronage mattered too. Successful barristers built their careers mostly on briefs fed by attorneys, giving them every reason to be attentive to the needs of the "junior" branch of the legal profession. The Inns were in a double bind here. Attorneys' professional journals wanted them to stop the practice and more or less dared the Bar to justify its monopolies by showing it could act decisively. The Inns were not well positioned to confront attorneys directly about the monopolies of either profession. Attorneys could plausibly assert their practical experience, educational requirements, rigorous examinations, and more effective regulation in an open challenge to the continued privileges of the Bar.[176] Better on the whole to avoid alienating a powerful allied profession.

Attorneys made it hard for Benchers to overlook transgressions of etiquette. Claydon's case reveals their persistence. Although he prevailed during Serjeant Clarke's term as County Court judge, their sense of grievance persisted as long as he took work from them. Forced to bide their time, they could weather setbacks, even over an extended period. For a local barrister, however, even a short-term loss of business could be ruinous and disbarment would take him out of play altogether. Time was on the attorneys' side, as it turned out.

Digby Seymour, QC – People's MP

As these matters unfolded in Lincoln's Inn, the Middle Temple focused its attention on Digby Seymour. Their interest was triggered in the spring of 1861 by his appointment as Queen's Counsel,[177] and the Benchers' judgment was published on 21 February 1862.[178] Like Edwin James, he had risen fast. The *Spectator* described him as "no obscure person. He is still a member of Parliament and a Queen's counsel. He holds a judicial post, if not of very great emolument, yet of great dignity and importance. He is in the class from which even judges are selected."[179]

Seymour had gained prominence without endearing himself to the establishment. He knew better than to seek election to the bench of his Inn, which normally followed appointment as QC.[180] Seymour, like James, was a Liberal[181] MP. As in Claydon's case, the events reviewed by the Benchers were of long standing. The *Saturday Review* commented that "the mere accident of professional promotion" had occasioned "an inquiry which, if called for at all, was imperatively called for ten years since."[182]

Although it formed no part of the matters before the Benchers, they would have been aware of Seymour's scandalous conduct of a murder case some years earlier. In 1847, he represented Patrick Reid, one of two men accused of the murder of James Wraith, his wife, and a young servant. Although Seymour believed his client to be solely responsible for the murders (it was rumoured that Reid had confessed to Seymour before the trial), he attempted to lay blame on one Michael M'Cabe, whom he believed to be entirely innocent. *The Times* remarked that knowingly sending an innocent man to the gallows was not acceptable:

> [T]to save a client by the sacrifice of an innocent man, whom counsel know to be innocent, is a direct violation of honour, of morality, and of the laws of God and man. If such were – as it is not – the general feeling of the bar, no man of common honesty – not to say, no gentleman – would submit to the degradation of being enrolled in its ranks.[183]

In early 1861, Seymour applied for appointment to the order of the coif (*i.e.*, admission to Serjeants' Inn). Lord Chancellor Campbell refused his appointment as a Serjeant at Law because "some doubts were entertained as to the fitness of the applicant to become a Member of Serjeants Inn."[184] That Inn's treasurer, Serjeant Manning, told the Middle Temple treasurer that the benchers might wish to investigate.[185] They duly struck a committee[186] that identified four charges for investigation. Three involved business transactions unrelated to Seymour's practice. At least some of the Benchers concurred with

> the opinion frankly and honorably expressed by your Counsel Mr. Lush that you have tried the unfortunate enterprize of mixing yourself up with speculations which he would not hesitate to say in your presence no gentleman, no Barrister especially, would engage in – because though they have for their object the getting rich by a short road, they involve a risk of a man's morals as well as of his means. The assurance that was given us by your Counsel, that you have long ceased to be connected with such transactions, we accept as a pledge of the uprightness of your conduct in the future.[187]

Apparently unable to reach consensus, the Benchers concluded that the improprieties imputed to Seymour were unproven but deserved censure. Their ambiguity and inconsistency were apparent.[188]

The fourth charge arose from legal practice. Seymour had agreed to work off debt by holding "briefs for an Attorney, in a liquidation of his costs payable by you."[189] Seymour admitted this, explaining that he had been put "in the difficult position in which honesty pointed one way and etiquette another."[190] The Benchers scolded him for acting in a "most improper" fashion. This arrangement, they said,

> invited a breach of duty on the part of the Attorney ... a Client would never be likely to suspect that his Attorney, from secret motives of interest was selecting an Advocate for him whom otherwise he might not have chosen. It was therefore, promoting deception, and likely to generate suspicion where confidence should prevail. If such a practice were tolerated it would lower the character and honor of both branches of the profession and would be injurious to the public, not only by reason of such debasement, but also its tendency to introduce into, or maintain in the practice of their profession, men more distinguished for the pliancy of their principles than by the gifts of nature improved by industrious and honest pursuit of eminence by honorable means.[191]

Despite their disapproval, the Benchers took no steps to expel Seymour. The matter spawned efforts to obstruct him at the Northern Circuit and the Midland Circuit Messes[192] and blocked him from becoming a Bencher.[193] Nonetheless, he developed a practice on the Midland circuit, going on to appointment as a County Court judge.[194]

It is not clear that the Inn's inquiries were politically motivated, but some Benchers happily put their work as governors of the profession to work in aid of the Conservative cause. In a postscript to a letter of 3 February 1862 "To the Honourable the Treasurer and Masters of the Bench of the Middle Temple," Seymour complained:

> I went down to address my constituents at Southampton, on Tuesday evening last ... I was then, for the first time, informed that the walls of the town were posted with a handbill, of which I beg to enclose a copy.
>
> I ask the Bench whether the peculiar wording of these four questions, and that so as to convey the most unfavourable construction, does not evidence the hand of some one who has been acting on information derived not very far from their parliamentary chamber. This, however, is not all. A prominent member of the Tory party in Southampton has been going from place to place exhibiting a written document, giving in minute detail

> the result of the voting in your chamber on the various charges, the numbers for a verdict of "Not guilty," or of "not proved," &c.
>
> Whence has this person been furnished with this information? By what right, and by whom, are the facts made known to him which have not been communicated to me?[195]

The coincidence that Seymour, Kennedy, and James were all aligned, to varying degrees, with the Liberal Party is noteworthy. That alone cannot explain their fate, however.

Seymour believed that the Benchers' actions arose from "professional jealousy" and "that his brother barristers who had been less successful than himself had entered into a conspiracy to ruin him for that reason."[196] This too seems implausible, if only because Benchers are necessarily among the most successful of their profession. They enjoyed high professional status and many had made service as Members of Parliament part of their career path. A letter to the *Morning Star and Dial* suggested a slightly modified version of Seymour's conspiracy theory. It asked whether his case was "part of an organized plot between benchers, special pleaders, and leaders of the circuits, to keep down and oppress – aye, and to destroy, if need be – any men of mark and genius who cannot be kept down in their profession by the ordinary contrivances?"[197]

John Bull (a London conservative and patriotic journal founded by Samuel Carter) found even this modified conspiracy theory implausible, saying that it took "audacity and bad taste" to suggest such a thing.[198] The rhetorical question raised in the letter to the *Morning Star and Dial* hints, however, at something more plausible than ordinary jealousy. Its focus on "the ordinary contrivances" that operated to suppress "men of mark and genius" invites us into the realm of the Bar's etiquette. Seymour, like James and Kennedy, had achieved prominence by unorthodox means. Barristers who rose to the status of Queen's Counsel (or, in James's case, Attorney-General) in disregard of the Inns, the circuit messes, and bar etiquette and without accumulating obligations to patrons within either of the legal professions, threatened the entire edifice. Their example could only encourage others to follow similar paths.

The one charge against Seymour that stuck was his admitted barter of barristerial services as a way of paying off debt. Seymour's exclusive arrangement with an attorney was agreed to by both lawyers as a convenient way of paying off a debt. In that sense, it was an ordinary commercial arrangement. It was of a cloth with other commercializing innovations undertaken by barristers over the previous decade or so: direct client contact, fee cutting, conditional fee arrangements, special commercial arrangements with clients or attorneys, and so on. Non-elite barristers asserted principles of free trade against the professional establishment's anti-commercialism, all defended by credible interpretations of the traditions of the Bar and the limits of etiquette. The interests and commitments of commercially inclined barristers aligned loosely with those of the Liberal party as the party of free trade (*laissez-faire*). While the Benchers thought that Seymour's agreement with a solicitor tended towards "debasement" of the profession,[199] the *Morning Star and Dial* commented simply that "[t]here may be offences against the rules of the profession which the public would not judge very harshly."[200] The arcane rules of ancient institutions clashed with a reforming spirit. Even the Benchers' defenders acknowledged that Seymour had been singled out for punishment.[201]

Charles Rann Kennedy and the Inner Temple

As details of Seymour's case were emerging, a fourth matter came before the Benchers of an Inn. This was none other than Lord Chelmsford's nemesis. Lacking the prominence of Digby Seymour or Edwin James, Charles Rann Kennedy had nonetheless gained national profile through the Swinfen wills case and subsequent proceedings against Lord Chelmsford. His trademarks were boldness, pyrotechnics, and strong language. These were backed by an enviable intellect and diverse talents. Kennedy was a published poet, translator of Greek literature, professor of law, and legal writer. Drama followed wherever he went.

Patience Swinfen had promised Kennedy a sizable fee (£20,000) for his extraordinary work in recovering her inheritance against all odds. Lines blurred as the two became lovers. Although they spoke of marriage, Kennedy's wife was still alive and they could not formalize their relationship. This intrinsically difficult situation changed in 1861 when Mrs. Swinfen returned from a holiday engaged to one Charles Broun.[202] They married in due course and Patience refused to honour her fees agreement with Kennedy. Stung by the financial hurt coming on top of emotional rejection, Kennedy was doubly outraged. Insult was added to injury when she subsequently alleged that he had fraudulently obtained a deed given as security for fees. Kennedy began proceedings, seeking payment for both professional and nonprofessional services provided by him during the long-drawn-out litigation. This made both the nature of work done by him and the character of their fee arrangements matters for judicial decision making.[203]

On its face, the case was straightforward. Kennedy asserted that they had entered into a valid contract and that she should not now be permitted to enjoy its benefit without paying the agreed-upon fees. The significant benefit she won from his efforts was beyond doubt as the Swinfen estate she inherited was a very substantial property. Undoubtedly, work had been done and benefit conferred. Payment for the services rendered would normally be expected. That he had thrown mud at distinguished men of law, including the Lord Chancellor of England, in obtaining victory was not strictly relevant. The case against Mrs. Broun became a contest between competing visions of advocacy and lawyering. The contract, though simple enough, violated conventional bar etiquette. Kennedy's success depended upon judicial acceptance of barristers' taking instructions directly from their clients and negotiating fees without the intervention of an attorney. It required treating barristers' fees as contractual in nature, enforceable through contract law, and not mere professional honoraria, as etiquette's fiction had it. The case progressed into a sort of judicial inquiry into "alternate" forms of law practice. The possibility that an adulterer had taken advantage of a vulnerable woman certainly tainted perceptions. And none could forget that the adulterer in question had used the forum the courtroom provided to besmirch the reputation of the Lord Chancellor and other distinguished barristers and judges.

It came to light that Kennedy's high fee was to be paid only if he won the case. It was akin to what would now be called a contingency fee arrangement. Etiquette, however, required advance payment of barristers' fees. The need to deviate from accepted practice was obvious if a disinherited widow of no independent means was to pursue legal redress. There was good reason on both sides for an agreement by which Kennedy would receive very large fees (an amount equal to one-third of the estate's £60,000 value) but *only if* he won the property for her. Nonetheless, the amount was large, etiquette had been breached, and the possibility of undue influence could not be overlooked. The agreement may also have violated long-standing legal prohibitions on champerty and maintenance.

Commencing professional employment on unorthodox terms, Kennedy provided extraordinary service. Barrister, friend, public relations specialist, and lover, he devoted himself entirely to working for her. He assumed complete control of the cause, and inverted the usual order of professional relationships by instructing Mrs. Swinfen's attorneys (rather than taking instructions from them). Much of the work he did encroached upon things attorneys considered to be their exclusive preserve. A case that in form was about nothing more than a breach of contract became a trial of whether barristers' work could be treated like any ordinary commercial arrangement. Entirely comfortable with this, Kennedy used the courtroom as a stage from which to denounce the disutility or hypocrisy of the establishment Bar's interpretation of professional etiquette. The case, like *Swinfen v. Lord Chelmsford* before it, became a contest between opposing visions of legal practice.

Kennedy's modern ideology of contract clashed with the inherited anti-commercial ethos of his professional guild. Eccentric and volatile but a brilliant lawyer, Kennedy offered an extended historical and legal argument contradicting the assertion that barristers' fees had long been mere honoraria.[204] That notion, he said, was attributable to the "vanity and pedantry"[205] of barristers and the monopolistic interests of attorneys[206] and leading barristers.[207] The alleged rule requiring prepayment of fees was mischievous, he said, simultaneously protecting elite barristers from the competition of their juniors and operating as a barrier to impecunious litigants.[208] The question, he said, was "whether a suitor with small means shall have his case taken up by the lawyers, or whether he shall fall into the hands of the money-lenders, or whether he shall be denied justice altogether."[209] In any event, he argued, it was hypocritical to insist on prepayment when the practice was only sometimes followed:

> A long experience of the present system has proved, not that counsel (as a rule) get ready money with their briefs, but that they are at the mercy of the attorneys ...
>
> It is idle to shut our eyes to what is going on around us ... We must look at the mode in which an ordinary counsel ascends the ladder. He begins by being an attorney's drudge, depending on his patronage for preferment, if not for daily bread. The attorney selects him for employment for pretty much the same reason that he selects his law-stationer. It is a matter of arrangement or convenience; perhaps a family affair, or what is vulgarly called a job ... Look at some of the great London firms; huge mills for the manufacture of law proceedings; establishments of permanent value, transmissible as a heritage from father to son. With what feelings does a young barrister regard the lord of one of these establishments? He could make his fortune, or raise him to the bench! Demand a fee beforehand of such a person! He would as soon pull the beard of the great Sultan! ... That the great firms generally discharge their accounts with counsel, I don't deny; but there are exceptions to this rule, and the settlement is often slow, irregular, and unsatisfactory ... The evil is not lessened by the absence of express bargain. Understandings are soon established, and, instead of occasional measures of liberty to distressed clients, you get compulsory sacrifices and perpetual servitude.[210]

In sum: divisions within the Bar, subordination of junior barristers, hypocrisy, and ineffective rules of etiquette.

Similarly, Kennedy believed the accusation of champerty or maintenance to be inaccurate in fact, wrong in principle, and hypocritical. He denied that he had technically engaged in champerty, however defined.[211] The hypocrisy of his opponents' position was clear because it was widely known that the "promises inscribed on briefs [by attorneys] are not always performed,"[212] or were performed late or in part. If this constituted an offence, most barristers violated the rules against champerty and maintenance. The argument of principle was simply that restrictions on contractual freedom violated modern principles of political economy. If an ancient rule was bad policy, it "should be limited rather than extended by legal construction."[213] Further, any doctrine making it illegal for a lawyer to take on a case where there would be no possibility of payment if a suit failed "would be a denial of justice to the poor."[214] Mrs. Swinfen's case illustrated this. As a devisee whose "whole property was contested," she could not have obtained legal assistance except under some such arrangement. The only alternative would have been to have lawyers "tak[e] the cause for nothing; which would be practically a denial of justice to persons situated like the defendant."[215]

His arguments about a barrister's proper role were also derived from a commercialized conception of legal practice. Kennedy sought to demonstrate that there had been continuous acceptance of freedom of contract between barristers and clients from Roman times to the seventeenth century.[216] While forced to concede that "modern practice precludes any implied contract for payment,"[217] Kennedy maintained that the "old common law right" of counsel and client to enter into *express* contracts regarding barristers' services had "not been abolished."[218] In other words, a presumption against relations between barrister and client contractual in nature was overcome by an express agreement.

For Kennedy, two key points followed logically. First, the fact of a contractual arrangement put the lie to any suggestion that a barrister should be "a perfectly indifferent person, an assistant of the court, or a minister of justice, rather than a partisan of his client."[219] Counsel might be expected to act "temperately and discreetly,"[220] but his work was properly partisan (oddly, Kennedy may have thought he demonstrated discretion in the conduct of litigation). This followed from the employment relationship:

> An advocate is the client's representative before the court, and the exponent of his case; an assistant of the court thus far, that he brings before it all that may be urged on his client's behalf, but not an assistant of the court in any other sense. If he were a minister of justice, as the Judge is, he should be paid by the public, not by his client.[221]

For Kennedy, the role of the barrister was derived directly from nothing more pretentious than private obligation founded on the principle that who pays the piper calls the tune.

The second conclusion flowing from the contractual basis of the relationship was that a barrister might arrange work for the client on *any* mutually agreed terms. It did not matter that the arrangement deviated markedly from the general pattern. He freely admitted having done work "collateral" to his professional duties[222] and, more significantly, assuming a degree of control over the action that infringed bar etiquette and caused affront to the attorneys' profession. He denied having done anything that formed part of the attorney's statutory monopoly under the *Attorney's Act*,[223] but admitted to having taken full management of the case:

> With respect to the charges of illegality, that is soon disposed of. Had I done anything which can be done by an attorney only, such as taking out a writ, entering an appearance, or the like, it would be an offence against the Attorney's Act, and, if part of my bargain, it would have vitiated the contract. As nothing of this sort however was proved, or could have been proved, the matter is reduced to this, that I inverted the usual order of things, and became what the attorney commonly is, the *dominus litis*. I did so; and what then? The law allows it. The courts do not interfere in matters of etiquette ... It is enough for me to stand upon the law.[224]

Kennedy conceded that the rule of etiquette was appropriate in run-of-the-mill cases but argued that there was no reason why clients should not be permitted to enter into exceptional contractual arrangements. It was especially appropriate that "great causes" should be managed by barristers "to whom that department of the law peculiarly belongs" because such cases clearly exceeded the abilities of attorneys, whose role was confined to that of an "inferior functionary."[225] In effect, he had to assume the role of *dominus litis* in Swinfen's case because attorneys had proved incompetent: "out of confusion, panic, despair, I organised discipline, battle, and final victory!"[226]

An argument presented in terms of legal right, public policy, and fairness to clients in difficult circumstances might sound compelling. What stood against this were only the customs of the legal professions – and Kennedy's scandalous behaviour. He weighed in heavily on the Bar's institutions:

> When it is so clearly beneficial to the client to make his counsel dictator in a cause, ought the counsel to refuse that trust on account of some silly rule, established, not by the legislature, but by the Lord-knows-who, at some

> convivial mess perchance, amid drunken songs and revels? Ought he therefore to abdicate a function, which the greatest ornaments of our law have exercised century after century, to the great advantage of the public, and without complaint from any human being? For it is remarkable, that the modern custom has been a change of fashion only, not the reform of an abuse, or the removal of a grievance. You can no more compel a counsel to submit to it, than you can force a lady to wear crinoline. The right to do what I did is, in fact, the right of the subject, which nothing but the statute can take away: but you would take it away, if you decided that a client could not lawfully contract to remunerate his counsel.[227]

Thus, the circle was completed. The charge of acting as an attorney was defended on the grounds that no statute or common law rule had been breached, that public policy demanded deviation from etiquette, and that the alleged rule of etiquette was an unjustifiable interference with the foundational right of freedom of contract – *laissez-faire* should prevail unless the law said otherwise. The authority of the Bar's institutions was denied: their etiquette was not law and the Inns were not law-making bodies.

On the other hand, Kennedy *had* sued the Lord Chancellor. And committed adultery with his client. Rejecting his arguments, the courts gave judicial effect to the rules of etiquette for the first time. Kennedy was outcast, branded as a wicked and threatening renegade. The courts' judgments were to have long-lasting effects on English and Commonwealth law, including, among other things, the continuance of a divided legal profession. *Kennedy v. Broun* capped a decade or more of public anxiety about the Bar, providing added impetus to subsequent transformations of the Bar's institutions.

The responses of barristers, attorneys, and the general public were complex and multifaceted. Many attorneys reacted negatively to Kennedy's attack on their profession and encroachment on terrain they viewed as exclusively theirs. The newspapers and periodical press, often supporters of both Kennedy and the principle of free trade within the professions, took a more distanced stance upon learning of Kennedy's adultery with his client. Observers were as appalled that he would bring the matter into public view to advance his own interests as by the sexual indiscretion itself. Leaders of the Bar must have been angered by the actions of a barrister who had flouted professional etiquette, viciously attacked their own (in *Swinfen v. Lord Chelmsford*), embarrassed their profession, and launched an attack on both professional governance institutions and operational practices demarcating the two branches of the legal profession (in *Kennedy v. Broun*).

Nonetheless, there was no certainty as to how things would end. As details of Kennedy's affair with Mrs. Swinfen became public, the press muttered disapproval – they could scarcely do otherwise. It was often assumed that the moral lapse had arisen at least partly from the unorthodox professional relationship. The *Saturday Review* was strident in linking personal improprieties to breach of professional etiquette. A brilliant barrister, it said Kennedy had displayed "an ability which was equal to his want of taste and propriety." It feared a slippery slope that ended in the United States of America: "[I]f the point raised by Mr. Kennedy had been conceded [*i.e.,* that barristers should have the right to contract for their fees], it would have been impossible to resist the course of innovation, until advocacy had become, as it is in some countries, open to all the world, without any of the restraints which the traditions of an honourable profession have thrown around it." In this the newspaper may well have been right. Kennedy's unforgivable behaviour and failings by the standards expected of the "high tone of the Bar" and the "purity of justice" illustrated the importance of the "traditions and usages of the Bar":[228]

> [I]t is easy to see how a legalized system of bargaining with clients would tend to degrade the status and character of what should be the most honourable of all professions. Even those who, on theoretical grounds, think they see some reason in the arguments for free trade in advocacy ought to be cured of their delusion by looking at the facts of the great Kennedy case. Who would desire to see the peculiar relations between this gentleman and his client, culminating as they did in the monstrous bargain for £20,000, established as the normal and recognised footing on which litigants and their counsel should stand? That the judgment of Chief Justice Erle has vindicated the honour of the Bar and made future Kennedys impossible, is in itself sufficient to command the warm approbation of all who would see English justice flow, as of old, in unpolluted channels.[229]

The Times accused Kennedy of "pecuniary meanness" and "unmanly behaviour." Apparently persuaded that the peculiar characteristics of the barristers' profession justified carving out an exception from full application of the ordinary principles of free trade, it too had come around to the view that the rules of etiquette should be followed. Kennedy's failure to have his remuneration fixed by an attorney meant that the only means of removing "the suspicion of extortion or undue influence" and providing "proper professional supervision and taxation" of barristers' fees had been circumvented.[230] *The Times* urged the governing bodies of the Bar to do something to purge their profession:

> The Bar would be a curse to society if such things were tolerated in its members, and the public have a right to appeal to the Benchers of the Inns of Court for protection against practices which, if recognized by the inaction of these bodies, must deprive litigants of all confidence in members of the Bar ...
>
> ... We see by the *Law List* that Mr. Kennedy is a member of Lincoln's Inn and the Home Circuit. We wait to hear what these bodies say to the facts now made public.[231]

Similar calls for punishment appeared in the *Daily News*, the *Birmingham Daily Post* (a newspaper of Liberal orientation), the *Solicitors' Journal and Reporter*, and *Aris's Birmingham Gazette* (the leading Birmingham newspaper of the day, known for middle-of-the-road editorial policies).[232]

Others understood things differently. Even before the Inn launched disciplinary proceedings, the *Birmingham Daily Gazette* said that Kennedy had suffered out of all proportion to his wrongdoing. When Mrs. Broun seized his business assets against costs, the *Gazette* concluded that "there are few of us who would not be sorry to see our own mistakes visited with such terrible punishment." The paper thought that his efforts leading up to *Swinfen v. Lord Chelmsford* had "effected a great reform, and that to this extent the public are his debtors."[233] The *Gazette* thought "that stipulated pay for honest work does not degrade any man," and noted, aptly, that the "beau ideal" of a bar working without expectation of payment "is not carried out, and is probably impracticable." Further, full compliance with the Bar's etiquette could effectively deny justice to "a man or woman without immediate funds."[234] The *Spectator* disapproved Kennedy's deviation from "wholesome professional rules" and "repulsive spirit" but believed that Christian charity should be exercised in his favour: he should be judged "as fellow-sinners should judge a man of violent passions sorely tried."[235] The *Birmingham Journal* commented simply that, as between Kennedy and Broun, "so far as the public is concerned, little sympathy is manifested for either side."[236]

Other newspapers were more sympathetic to Kennedy. A lead article in the *Morning Star and Dial* supported Kennedy and criticized both the Bar's etiquette and Patience Broun.[237] *John Bull* believed Kennedy was entitled to the fees promised to him and that other papers had used "a great deal of claptrap available" to attack him.[238] Although it had condemned Kennedy's practices, *Aris's Birmingham Gazette* reproduced an editorial from *The Times* arguing that professional discipline was unnecessary given his court loss:

> The body of advocates are not in such high and palmy state that they can desire to drive from among them a scholar and an eloquent man of great purpose and courage, unless these qualities are counterbalanced by some moral derelictions too serious to be ignored. This is not alleged in the present instance ... [E]nough has been said about it, and enough has been done.[239]

Unfortunately for Kennedy, neither the Midlands Circuit Mess nor the Inner Temple Benchers agreed. Both began proceedings leading to sanctions.

Although there was no love lost between Kennedy and the Benchers, it was not a foregone conclusion that "disciplinary" proceedings would be initiated. Notwithstanding the recent cases involving Claydon, Seymour, and James, the Benchers' moral and legal authority was insecure. Kennedy's case was a matter of notorious public record, however, and important voices called for disciplinary action. Some virtually dared the Inn. The Bar's institutions would be criticized whether they took punitive action or failed to act. In the circumstances, inaction would send a dangerous signal that the Inns lacked disciplinary authority. That in turn would invite further chipping away at the invisible boundaries preserving distinct barristers' and attorneys' professions. Failure to act might even lead to attempts at legislative intervention.

In the event, the Inn's investigation was sparked by the Midland Circuit Mess, which "cited Mr. Kennedy before the Benchers of the Inner Temple" in 1864.[240] Three charges emerged. The first was against the contract's provision that fees were to be paid only if the litigation succeeded. The second was that "by means of the influence he had acquired over Mrs. Broun through his relation as such Counsel," Kennedy had "induced her to convey a deed for a reversionary interest in the Estate."[241] Finally, he was charged with having made threats to publish his allegations of adultery and to publish a pamphlet titled "The Serpent of Swynfen" if his fees were not paid.[242] John Pym Yeatman (who described himself as the most successful junior on the Midland Circuit) represented Kennedy in the proceedings.[243]

A defence based largely on arguments in favour of free trade at the Bar[244] was partially successful. The Benchers found that "the conduct of Mr. Kennedy has been highly disgraceful and unworthy of a member of an honourable profession" and ordered their opinion to be posted ("screened") "in the Hall of this Society."[245] Symbolic punishment was added, which the *Solicitors' Journal and Reporter* reported sarcastically:

> The Benchers of the Middle Temple, who some time ago decided that they would not disbar Mr. William Digby Seymour, may take a lesson from the

> terrific sentence lately fulminated against Mr. Charles Rann Kennedy, by their brethren of the Inner Temple. That unhappy gentleman is, we understand, "suspended for two years from attendance in the hall, library, and gardens" of the house.[246]

This stopped far short of disbarment. Exclusion from the Inn's buildings and grounds would have little practical consequence. It simply underlined the Benchers' public statement condemning his practices. This moderate response underlines the Benchers' insecurity regarding the limits of their lawful authority and the character of etiquette. Kennedy's counsel was pleased to have held off the worst, commenting that "I had the gratification to defend him successfully, and to spare his honoured name from the reproach of disgrace. The Circuit failed in their miserable attempt to disbar him, and he returned to Birmingham."[247]

The mess passed a resolution "[t]hat it be not competent for members of this Circuit to hold Briefs with Gentlemen not members of this Circuit unless they come with Special Retainers."[248] This effectively froze Kennedy out and matters appear to have ended there. Two members of the circuit, a Mr. Gibbons[249] and Mr. Yeatman, were subsequently presented before the circuit court for holding briefs with Kennedy. Gibbons was let off with a fine upon promising never to do so again, while Yeatman retired rather than submit to a disciplinary process that he viewed as arbitrary and illegitimate.[250] Kennedy continued to practise in the region and seemed about to resume in earnest his campaign against the Bar's institutions when he died in December 1867.[251]

Outcomes of the Moral Panic of the 1860s

Kennedy's death marks an end point of sorts. The heightened public anxiety over the legal professions since the early 1850s waned. To be sure, substantive issues remained controversial and the Bar and courts were never far from the public eye. Issues regarding advocacy, the governance of the Inns, and the privileges and duties of barristers were neither dislodged nor entirely resolved. Nonetheless, the contours of a divided profession were preserved as a result of the double whammy of *Swinfen v. Lord Chelmsford* and *Kennedy v. Broun*, accompanied by the stirring of disciplinary powers by the Inns and circuit messes. The organized Bar nudged towards a novel, more regularized, and modern form of "professionalism." Both legacies shaped the development of legal professionalism in England and throughout the English-speaking world.

The sequence of events affecting Seymour, Claydon, James, Chelmsford, and Kennedy, and the public, professional, and political reactions to them, formed important elements in the history of the legal profession. Beneath each particular issue lurked tensions between utilitarianism's free trade ideology and the Inns' paternalistic inheritance.

It was obvious in the nineteenth-century era of law reform that a public sufficiently aroused might turn the professional world of barristers, attorneys, and solicitors upside down.[252] The cases of Edwin James, Charles Claydon, Digby Seymour, and Charles Rann Kennedy turned a public focus, initially skeptical about the organized Bar's pretensions and its leaders, in a different direction. A new reading of events was possible, laying the blame for failings of English justice on those who ignored the profession's inherited etiquette as much as on the irresponsibility of the profession's leaders. If this was "the problem," then it seemed reasonable to hope that "the solution" lay in the enforcement of professional etiquette through the exercise of wide disciplinary power by the Inns.[253]

A translation and inversion of public concerns about the state of law, legal practice, and justice had come about. Prior to about 1860, public enthusiasm for free trade had focused critical attention on the paternalistic leaders of the bar – epitomized by the Chelmsford/Cresswell scandal – while supporting commercialized innovations in legal practice by junior barristers. In the 1860s, however, new challenges were issued, daring the Inns to justify their monopoly by showing that they were capable of policing themselves. The organized Bar was called upon to show that it could enforce the ideals of its own ideology by stamping out the immoral and unvirtuous among their number. Clubbish and ineffective professional guilds were called upon to develop efficient disciplinary professional machinery. A move in that direction began to reshape the notion of barristers' professionalism.

A turning point was reached when the Inns came to focus attention on the conduct of a miscellaneous collection of marginalized though usually prominent individuals. The political radicalism of Edwin James – a Liberal and supporter of Garibaldi and other revolutionary movements – was paralleled by the professional radicalism of Charles Rann Kennedy and the merger of eccentric professional practices with demagogic Liberal politics in the person of Digby Seymour. Two of these men were sitting Liberal Members of Parliament, while the third, Kennedy, had previously indicated his desire to seek election as a Liberal. He had been expected to rise to Queen's Counsel when Lord Cairns became Lord Chancellor.[254] Sir Frederick Thesiger, his counsel, and others implicated in the Swinfen compromise were all Conservative party supporters or Conservative Members of Parliament.[255]

The final barrister to suffer in the disciplinary purges of the early 1860s, Charles Claydon, was the least politically active. However, he too engaged in a *laissez-faire* approach to legal practice that paid little heed to the Bar's inherited etiquette. In so doing, he carved out a practice niche that he claimed served individuals exploited by local businesses. He provoked the enmity of local solicitors, circuit barristers, and the Benchers of his Inn.

It was fortuitous from the Benchers' perspective that Kennedy's conduct generated negative attention. He was a particularly outspoken critic of bar etiquette and an especially egregious flouter of professional norms. In turning on his own client and exposing her as a fornicator as he attempted to recover apparently unconscionable professional fees, a case for more, not less, rigorous enforcement of professional discipline became compelling. If violation of conventional etiquette produced scandalous behaviour, better enforcement might provide a remedy. Kennedy became, as one contemporary newspaper put it, "a scarecrow by which younger members of his profession may be warned off dangerous ground."[256]

One enduring image of professional problems in the 1860s is of Kennedy's great genius destroyed by avarice and lust, each unleashed by his deviation from rules of professional etiquette. Another is of Edwin James portrayed in the media as a bandit chief.[257] These images, linked with the less dramatic events touching on Digby Seymour and the pathetically swift destruction of Charles Claydon, deflected the heterogeneous and often more radically reformist public impulses of only a few years earlier. Attention shifted from the dubious activities of the leaders of the Bar towards the activities of fringe barristers – a pattern replicated several decades later in the United States.[258] The sense of disquiet that had prevailed for the better part of two decades resulted in fundamental change in the character of the Inns of Court as they began to transform from little more than dining societies into disciplinary institutions.

The events of the 1860s played out against a background of longer-standing concerns about the morality of advocacy. The question of the degree to which a barrister should be single-mindedly partisan or constrained by higher moral duties was recurrent and troubling. The logic of the market pulled in one direction while the logic of morality seemed to pull in the other. And the contradictory impulses were both deeply embedded in the history, practice, and ethos of advocacy. There was nothing irrational in concerns about the barristers' profession in the 1860s, and the forces that came to a head in the cases of Kennedy, James, Claydon, and Seymour had long been in play. There is irony, perhaps, in the particular outcome: a stronger role for Benchers and the shift to more energetic and extensive exercise of penal powers against individual barristers were the opposite of the bundle of ideas that had appeared to have the initiative. Momentum, which seemed to lie with free traders, Liberal reformers, utilitarians, and rebel barristers, shifted abruptly in a different direction.

The large questions relating to the ideology of advocacy were not definitively resolved. Indeed, they are live issues to this day.[259] What happened in the 1860s was an important shift in the terrain. The ideological and institutional arenas in which discussions and advocacy took place had been perceptibly altered, the Inns strengthened, and their roles transformed. The possibility of "free trade in law" was extinguished. England's ancient guilds would survive and England would not follow the American path towards fusion of its two legal professions or open competition in the market for legal services.

Notes

An earlier version of this chapter appeared as "Moral Panic at the English Bar: Paternal vs. Commercial Ideologies of Legal Practice in the 1860s" (1990) 15 Law & Soc. Inquiry 49. It has been revised and reprinted here with permission.

1 "The Discipline of the Bar" (1863) 15 Law Magazine and Review: Quarterly Journal of Jurisprudence 1.

2 On the etiquette of the Bar, see P. Polden, "The Courts of Law" in W. Cornish et al., *The Oxford History of the Laws of England*, vol. 11 (Oxford: Oxford University Press, 2010) at 1096-1107. See also D. Woolley, "Article: The Inn as a Disciplinary Body" in R.O. Havery, ed., *History of the Middle Temple* (Oxford: Hart, 2011) 337.

3 H. Becker, *Outsiders: Studies in the Sociology of Deviance* (New York: Free Press, 1963) at 9 [emphasis in original].

4 Contemporary understandings of "moral panic" and public policy have been powerfully influenced by Stanley Cohen, *Folk Devils and Moral Panics* (London: Routledge Classics, 2011), first published in 1972. The term has a longer lineage, however. See Mike Sutton, "The British Moral Panic Creation Myth Is Bust" (2012) Best Thinking, online: <http://www.bestthinking.com/articles/science/social_sciences/sociology/the-british-moral-panic-creation-myth-is-bust>.

5 Provocatively treated in Greg Marquis, "Doing Justice to 'British Justice': Law, Ideology and Canadian Historiography" in W. Wesley Pue and Barry Wright, *Canadian Perspectives on Law and Society: Issues in Legal History* (Ottawa: Carleton University Press, 1988) 43.

6 "On the Principle of Advocacy as Developed in the Practice of the Bar" (February-May 1854) 20 (n.s.) Law Magazine; or Quarterly Review of Jurisprudence 265 (vol. 51 of Old Series, no. 103; reprinted from no. 84 of *Law Magazine*) ["On the Principle of Advocacy"].

7 *Ibid.* On Courvoisier's defence by Charles Phillips, see David Mellinkoff, *The Conscience of a Lawyer* (St. Paul, MN: West Publishing, 1973); Michael Diamond, *Victorian Sensation* (London: Anthem Press, 2003).

8 Lord Brougham, as quoted in "The Defence of Courvoisier, and the Plea for It" (February-May 1850) 12 (n.s.) Law Magazine; or Quarterly Review of Jurisprudence 26 (vol. 43 of Old Series) ["Defence of Courvoisier"]. Brougham's words are some of the most quoted in literature on the duties of lawyers and have resonated particularly strongly with American lawyers and legal scholars. See, for example, L. Ray Patterson, "Legal Ethics and the Lawyer's Duty of Loyalty" (1980) 29 Emory L.J. 909; Monroe H. Freeman, "Henry Brougham and Zeal" (2006) 34 Hofstra L. Rev. 1319, online: <http://law.hofstra.edu/pdf/academics/journals/lawreview/lrv_issues_v34n04_bb1_freedman_final.pdf >.

9 Patterson, *ibid.* at 909-10.

10 See, for example, Chapter 2 in this volume and works cited therein.

11 "On the Principle of Advocacy," *supra* note 6 at 284, celebrating Erskine, Wetherell, Pollock, and Kelly. Although both controversial and un-British at its core, the twentieth century's classic is Monroe Freedman, "The Professional Responsibility of the Criminal Defense Lawyer: The Three Hardest Questions" (1966) 64 Mich. L. Rev. 1469.

12 "On the Principle of Advocacy," *ibid.* at 283 and 281, respectively.

13 Barry Wright's scholarship in collaboration with F. Murray Greenwood, Susan Binnie, and others has probed the state trial genre thoroughly. See Barry Wright and Susan Binnie, eds., *Canadian State Trials,* vol. 3, *Political Trials and Security Measures, 1840-1914* (Toronto: University of Toronto Press/Osgoode Society for Canadian Legal History, 2009); Barry Wright and F.M. Greenwood, *Canadian State Trials,* vol. 2, *Rebellion and Invasion in the Canadas, 1837-39* (Toronto: University of Toronto Press/Osgoode Society for Canadian Legal History, 2002); Barry Wright and F.M. Greenwood, *Canadian State Trials,* vol. 1, *Law, Politics, and Security Measures, 1608-1836* (Toronto: University of Toronto Press/Osgoode Society for Canadian Legal History, 1996).

14 "On the Principle of Advocacy," *supra* note 6.

15 *Ibid.* at 284-85.

16 *Ibid.* at 270-71.

17 *Ibid.* See also "Defence of Courvoisier," *supra* note 8 at 35: "The advocate is merely bound to screen his client from a conviction on insufficient evidence. He ought to deal with the whole of the data, exposing the weak parts of the evidence against him, and enlarging on those which are for him. It is also his duty to exhibit, as fully and forcibly as he can, any hypothesis consistent alike with the evidence and the possible innocence of his client: and he is bound to do this, however strongly he may suspect, nay although he may *know* his guilt."

18 Mr. Hill, as quoted in Gray's Inn, *Book of Orders* 20 (20 January 1847) at 381.

19 The unfortunates prior to 1861 were Edward William Roberts (Lincoln's Inn, 1809); Robert Cook and John Richard Cook (Gray's Inn, 1841); William Cheek Bonsfield (Lincoln's Inn, 1838-39); Henry Hugh Pyke (Gray's Inn, 1845); John Angus Homes (Middle Temple, 1846); Augustus Newton (Middle Temple, 1850); Edward Power (Middle Temple, 1851; subsequently reinstated); Henry William Hemsworth (Inner Temple, 1851); Wilmot Parker (Lincoln's Inn, 1857).

20 See ch. 4, "The Problems of the 1850's," in Raymond Cocks, *Foundations of the Modern Bar* (London: Sweet and Maxwell, 1983) 85.

21 United Kingdom, *Report of the Select Committee on Legal Education* (25 August 1846); United Kingdom, *Report of the Commissioners Appointed to Inquire into Arrangements in the Inns of Court and the Inns of Chancery for Promoting the Stud y of Law and Jurisprudence,* 1855 (HMSO, 1854-55).

22 "Art. IV – The Etiquette of the Bar" (1857) 3 (First Series) Law Magazine; or Quarterly Review of Jurisprudence 236 at 236 ["Art. IV"].

23 See, for example, *Eighth Report of Her Majesty's Commissioners on Criminal Law* (HMSO, 1845), which includes many comments critical of contemporary practitioners and contemporary legal practice.

24 See Cocks, *supra* note 20 at 90.

25 *Ibid.* at 88-90, 123-24.

26 Charles Dickens, *Bleak House* (Harmondsworth: Penguin Books, 1971). See discussion in William Searle Holdsworth, *Charles Dickens as a Legal Historian* (Storrs Lectures) (New Haven, CT: Yale University Press, 1928).

27 As debates about legal education (above) show.

28 "Meeting of the Legal Profession" *Birmingham Journal and Commercial Advertiser* (16 October 1852) 7.

29 See discussion above. *Cf.* "A Barrister of the Inner Temple," *Advocacy in the County Courts. A Letter to Sir Alexander Cockburn, M.P., Her Majesty's Attorney General by a Barrister of the Inner Temple* (London: S. Sweet, 1851) at 6: arguing against the position "that all class privileges whatsoever savour of monopoly, and monopolies are proverbially odious and injurious."

30 G. Shaw Lefevre, "Discipline of the Bar" (Paper presented to the Law Amendment Society), as reported in "Societies and Institutions: The Law Amendment Society" *Solicitors' Journal and Reporter* (7 February 1863) at 265-66. A similar argument in response to generally accepted norms of "political economy" was made in "A Barrister," *Advocacy in the County Courts: A Letter to Sir Alexander Cockburn, M.P. (by a Barrister of the Inner Temple)* (London: Sweet, 1851).

31 "Art. IV," *supra* note 22.

32 See *Legal Observer* 40 (1850) at 32; "Bar Etiquette and Advocacy by Attorneys" *Legal Observer* 42 (9 August 1851) at 269-72; "Relations between the Bar and Attorneys" *Legal Observer* 43 (20 December 1851) at 125-27; "The County Court Bar Meeting" *Legal Observer* 43 (6 March 1852) at 348-50; "Prospects of the Junior Bar" *Legal Observer* 44 (12 June 1852) at 114-16; "The Junior Bar and the Attorneys. County Court Practitioners" *Legal Observer* 44 (7 August 1852) at 271-73; "Relation between the Bar and Attorneys. Law Amendment Society's Report" *Legal Observer* 44 (21 August 1852) at 309-10; "Mutual Law Association" *Legal Observer* 44 (16 October 1852) at 473-75; "Etiquette at the Bar, Westminster County Court" *Legal Observer* 45 (6 November 1852) at 12; "The Bar and the Attorneys" *Legal Observer* 45 (20 November 1852); "The Junior Bar and the Attorneys" *Legal Observer* 45 (27 November 1852); "Encroachments on the Profession" *Legal Observer* 47 (21 January 1854); *Proceedings of the Metropolitan & Provincial Law Association* (1854); "Bar University and Attorneys' College" *Legal Observer* 51 (29 December 1855) at 157-60; *Legal Observer* 52 (29 November 1856) at 506-8.

33 Speech of J. Bulmer to the Metropolitan and Provincial Law Association, as reported in *Birmingham Journal and Commercial Advertiser* (25 October 1855) at 3, col. 4, and in the *Supplement to Birmingham Journal and Commercial Advertiser* (27 October 1855); "Opinions of the Press on the Proposed Law University" *Legal Observer* 51 (22 December 1855) at 146-47.

34 "The Bar and the Attorneys," *supra* note 32 at 45-46; "Economical Considerations on the Autocracy of the Bar, and on the System of Prescribed Tariffs for Legal Wages, and on the Connection of These Two Subjects" *Metropolitan and Provincial Law Association, Circular 10* (1856) at 34-59; "Counsel Practising in Several Courts" *Solicitors' Journal and Reporter* (20 February 1858) at 584; "Fees and Duties of Leading Counsel" *Solicitors' Journal and Reporter* (5 June 1858) at 642; "Bar Etiquette" *Solicitors' Journal and Reporter* (8 December 1860) at 90-91; "Meeting of the Provincial Law Association" *Aris's Birmingham Gazette* (13 October 1860) at 5, col. 4 (report of an address by Mr. Shaen on the "Etiquette of the Bar").

35 "A Junior," "Thoughts of a Junior on His Position and Prospects: With a Few Hints to Reformers" (Pamphlet), discussed in "Prospects of the Junior Bar" *Legal Observer* 44 (12 June 1852) at 114-16; *Legal Examiner* 44 (3 July 1852).

36 *E.g., The Times* of 1, 7, and 8 November 1851 attacked the rule requiring an attorney intermediary. See "The Attorneys and the Times" *Legal Observer* 43 (15 November 1852) at 39-40.

37 "On the Principle of Advocacy," *supra* note 6 at 273.

38 See "Mrs. Patience Swinfen versus Barristers" (1974) 2 Queensland Lawyer at 40-45; Howard Clayton, *The Great Swinfen Case* (London and New York: Regency Press, 1980).

39 *The Dictionary of National Biography,* 22 vols. (London: Oxford University Press, 1885-1921) [DNB].

40 *Bell's Life in London and Sporting Chronicle* (10 July 1859).

41 DNB, *supra* note 39, entries for Sir Fitzroy Kelly, William Bovill, Montague Smith, George Denman, and Thomas Denman.

42 See Charles Rann Kennedy, *The Great Swinfen Case: Report of the Extraordinary Trial at Warwick in the Matter of Kennedy v. Broun and Wife* (London: Hatton and Son, 1862). Lord Denman had supported Kennedy's role as a reformer of the bar, for which Kennedy rewarded him with the poetic tribute "The Late Lord Denman" in Charles Rann Kennedy, *Poems, Original and Translated* (London: William Walker, 1857) [*Poems*].

43 "Swinfen v. Lord Chelmsford – Extraordinary Case" *Daily News* (5 July 1859) at 6. See also "Swinfen v. Lord Chelmsford" *Morning Star* (5 July 1859) at 6. Thomas Chandler Haliburton was a Nova Scotia judge and author who retired to England in 1856 and was elected as MP for Launceston, Cornwall, for the Conservatives in 1859 (DNB, *supra* note 39). Henry John Chetwynd-Talbot was the 18th Earl of Shrewsbury and Waterford, and 3rd Earl Talbot of Hensol. Before his claim to the Earldom of Shrewsbury was established by the Committee for Privileges in 1858 (http://www.library.georgetown.edu/dept/speccoll/shrews.htm) he had served as a Conservative Member of Parliament. Macaulay called him "a violent Tory" (http://www.historyofparliamentonline.org/volume/1820-1832/member/chetwynd-talbot-henry-1803-1868).

44 *Daily News* (5 July 1859) at 6.

45 "Swinfen v. Lord Chelmsford" *Morning Star* (6 July 1859) at 6.

46 "Patience Swinfen v. The Right Hon. Lord Chelmsford" *The Times* (5 July 1859) at 11 [emphasis added].

47 *Ibid.* [emphasis added].

48 "Swinfen v. Lord Chelmsford – Extraordinary Case" *Staffordshire Advertiser* (9 July 1859) at 6.

49 "Swinfen v. Lord Chelmsford – Extraordinary Case" *Daily News* (5 July 1859) at 6.

50 "Patience Swinfen v. The Right Hon. Lord Chelmsford" *The Times* (15 July 1859) at 11.

51 "Swinfen v. Lord Chelmsford – Extraordinary Case" *Daily News* (5 July 1859) at 6.

52 *Ibid.*

53 "Swinfen v. Lord Chelmsford – Extraordinary Case" *Staffordshire Advertiser* (9 July 1859) at 6.

54 See *Swinfen v. Swinfen,* 24 Beav. 549, 53 E.R. 470 (before the Master of the Rolls, Sir John Romilly); *Swinfen v. Swinfen,* 1 F. & F. 584, 175 E.R. (Staffordshire Summer Assizes, coram Byles, J.). Romilly had been a political Liberal. Byles, a "protectionist Conservative," was appointed to the bench "by Lord Cranworth, a Whig" (DNB, *supra* note 39).

55 Accounts of the evidence are to be found in *The Times* (5 July 1859) at 11; *Daily News* (5 July 1859) at 6; *Morning Star* (5 July 1859) at 6; *The Times* (6 July 1859) at 11; *Daily News* (6 July 1859) at 6-7; *Morning Star* (6 July 1859) at 6; *Staffordshire Advertiser* (9 July 1859) at 4; *Supplement to the Birmingham Journal* (9 July 1859) at 4.

56 "Swinfen v. Lord Chelmsford – Extraordinary Case" *Daily News* (6 July 1859) at 6-7.

57 "Swinfen v. The Right Hon. Lord Chelmsford" *The Times* (6 July 1859) 11 at 12; "Swinfen v. Lord Chelmsford" *Monthly Law Reporter* 22 (1860) at 421; "The Metropolis" *The Spectator* 32 (9 July 1859) at 707.

58 "Swinfen v. Lord Chelmsford" *Morning Star* (6 July 1859) at 6.

59 Kennedy, quoted in "Swinfen v. Lord Chelmsford" *The Times* (9 November 1859) at 11.

60 Lead article, *Morning Star* (7 July 1859) at 4.

61 See, for example, "The Status of Counsel" *Solicitors' Journal and Reporter* (20 June 1863) at 625-26; "Etiquette at the Bar" *Solicitors' Journal and Reporter* (21 March 1863) at 380-81. A lead article in *Solicitors' Journal and Reporter* (11 August 1866) at 977-78 complained of "front rank" barristers "taking business with a deliberate intention of not attending to it."

62 "Swinfen v. Lord Chelmsford" *Morning Star* (5 July 1859) at 6.

63 *Ibid.*

64 "Swinfen v. Lord Chelmsford – Extraordinary Case" *Daily News* (6 July 1859) 6 at 6.
65 *Ibid.*
66 Kennedy shared much of this world-view. He could not conceive of a world in which England was unjust or barristers as a class were corrupt. Chelmsford's actions were presented as aberrational, corrupting an otherwise pristine system of justice.
67 "Swinfen v. Lord Chelmsford" *The Times* (25 November 1859) at 9. The position here is expanded somewhat from the original trial. The change in emphasis is explained by the nature of the proceedings. Here, on a motion for a new trial, Kennedy asserted that the judge had erred in charging the jury "that a counsel might do anything if he did it honestly, and if what he did was for the benefit of his client": "Swinfen v. Lord Chelmsford" *The Times* (9 November 1859) at 11. *Cf.* "Swinfen v. Lord Chelmsford – Extraordinary Case" *Daily News* (5 July 1859) at 6.
68 "Swinfen v. Lord Chelmsford" *The Times* (25 November 1859) at 9.
69 *Ibid.*
70 "Swinfen v. Lord Chelmsford" *The Times* (9 November 1859) at 11.
71 "Swinfen v. Lord Chelmsford – Extraordinary Case" *Daily News* (6 July 1859) at 6-7.
72 "Swinfen v. Lord Chelmsford – Extraordinary Case" *Staffordshire Advertiser* (9 July 1859) at 6.
73 *Ibid.* What Lord Chief Baron Pollock did not say but intended in his instructions to the jury is that independence from the client – *i.e.*, not being bound by contract – is critical, not just the independence from the state that we usually think of when we consider independence of barristers. This in turn leads to the position that barristers' fees are honoraria only: the *ratio decidendi* of *Kennedy v. Broun.*
74 *E.g., Daily News* (7 July 1859) at 4; *The Times* (7 July 1859), quoted in *Staffordshire Advertiser* (9 July 1859) at 4); "Current Topics" *Solicitors' Journal and Reporter* (9 July 1859) at 673. For a contrary opinion, see "History of the Week" *John Bull and Britannia* (9 July 1859) at 440.
75 Lead article, *Daily News* (7 July 1859) at 4, cols. 3-4.
76 "Current Topics" *Solicitors' Journal and Reporter* (9 July 1859) at 673.
77 Lead article, *Daily News* (7 July 1859) at 4 [emphasis added].
78 *The Times* (7 July 1859); also reported in *Staffordshire Advertiser* (9 July 1859) at 4.
79 C.R. Kennedy, *Swinfen v. Swinfen: Report of the Argument in the Common Pleas, in Michaelmas Term, 1856* (London: Richard Hatton, 1857) at 19.
80 Lead article, *Daily News* (7 July 1859) at 4.
81 *The Times* (7 July 1859); also reported in *Staffordshire Advertiser* (9 July 1859) at 4.
82 Lead article, *Morning Star* (7 July 1859) at 4.
83 Lead article, *Daily News* (7 July 1859) at 4.
84 Lead article, *Morning Star* (7 July 1859) at 4.
85 See Donald Daintree, *The Legal Periodical: A Study in the Communication of Information* (MA Thesis, University of Sheffield, 1975) esp. at 201-2.
86 "Current Topics" *Solicitors' Journal and Reporter* (9 July 1859) at 673.
87 Kennedy, *Poems, supra* note 42 at 107-12. This poem is discussed in Clayton, *supra* note 38 at 68ff.
88 See, however, "History of the Week" *John Bull and Britannia* (9 July 1859) at 440.
89 See "Swinfen v. Lord Chelmsford" *The Times* (7 November 1859) at 11; "Swinfen v. Lord Chelmsford" *The Times* (9 November 1859) at 11; "Swinfen v. Lord Chelmsford" *The Times* (12 November 1859) at 11 (granting rule *nisi* on Kennedy's motion).
90 "Swinfen v. Lord Chelmsford" *The Times* (24 November 1859) at 11; "Swinfen v. Lord Chelmsford" *The Times* (25 November 1859) at 9; "Swinfen v. Lord Chelmsford" *The Times* (26 November 1859) at 11; "Swinfen v. Lord Chelmsford" *The Times* (12 January 1860) at 11.

91 "Swinfen v. Lord Chelmsford" *The Times* (11 June 1860) at 11. Also reported or discussed, *Daily News* (15 June 1860) at 4-5; "Law Intelligence. Swinfen v. Lord Chelmsford" *Staffordshire Advertiser* (16 June 1860) at 7; "The Case of Swinfen v. Lord Chelmsford" *Solicitors' Journal and Reporter* (16 June 1860) at 638-39; "Law Intelligence. Court of Exchequer. Mrs. Swinfen's Action against Lord Chelmsford" *Wolverhampton Journal and Herald* (16 June 1860) at 6; *John Bull and Britannia* (16 June 1860) at 381.

92 "Responsibility of Counsel" *Solicitors' Journal and Reporter* (30 June 1860) at 679-80.

93 "Law Intelligence. Court of Exchequer. Mrs. Swinfen's Action against Lord Chelmsford" *Staffordshire Advertiser* (16 June 1860) at 7.

94 Gray's Inn, *Book of Orders, 1855-1861* 12 (6 June 1860) at 540, and (11 June 1860) at 542-43.

95 *E.g.*, "Meeting of the Provincial Law Association," *supra* note 34; "Bar Etiquette" *Solicitors' Journal and Reporter* (8 December 1860) at 90-91 (complaint of B. Blundell, FSA, that "[t]he whole system of 'tail briefs' and needless fees is, however, based on wrong, since courts are constituted to redress the grievances of suitors, and not to swell the money bags of counsel").

96 "Retirement of Mr. Edwin James" *The Times* (10 April 1861) at 9; *Manchester Guardian* (11 April 1861) at 5; "The Fall of Mr. Edwin James" *Saturday Review* 11 (13 April 1861) at 358.

97 Clayton, *supra* note 38 at 109: "The plaintiff, Mrs. Swinfen, was represented by Mr. Kennedy (specially retained), Mr. Gray, Mr. Cripps (specially retained), and Mr. McNamara. Mr. Edwin James, Q.C., (specially retained), Mr. Huddlestone, Q.C., and Mr. Henry James appeared for the defendant, Captain Swinfen."

98 "The Fall of Mr. Edwin James" *Saturday Review* (13 April 1861) at 358.

99 Inner Temple, *Bench Table Orders,* 16 April 1861.

100 *Ibid.*

101 Lincoln's Inn, *The Black Books,* no. 29, Special Council of 22 April 1861, at 141-47. The minutes of this date also record an extensive discussion of the problems of etiquette, including how to determine what etiquette required and how it was to be enforced.

102 Inner Temple, *Bench Table Orders,* 26 April 1861. Further discussions of James are to be found in the *Bench Table Orders* for 7, 24, 28, 31 May; 4, 7, 11, 18, 20, 26 June; 4, 11, 18 July (disbarred this date); 5, 31 November 1861; 12 February, 22 April, 9 May, 13 and 17 June 1862.

103 "Current Topics" *Solicitors' Journal and Reporter* (20 July 1861) at 643.

104 "The Disbarment of Edwin James, Esq. Q.C." *Solicitors' Journal and Reporter* (8 February 1862) at 253; "The Inner Temple Benchers – Disbarment of Edwin James, Q.C." (1862) 12 Law Magazine and Review: Quarterly Journal of Jurisprudence 266. The *Solicitors' Journal and Reporter* believed that the *Law Magazine* article had likely been written by a Bencher: "Disbarment of Mr. Edwin James, Q.C." *Solicitors' Journal and Reporter* (15 February 1862) at 275.

105 "Disbarment of Mr. Edwin James, Q.C.," *ibid.*

106 "The Disbarment of Edwin James, Esq. Q.C.," *supra* note 104 at 253.

107 "Edwin James on the Trent Affair" *Solicitors' Journal and Reporter* (14 December 1861) at 103.

108 "Mr. Edwin James in His Place" *Spectator* (23 November 1861) at 1283.

109 *Solicitors' Journal and Reporter* (22 February 1862) at 285-86. Pyke had also had his own run-ins with the establishment legal profession. See: *Ex parte Pyke,* 15 June 1865, in William Mawdesley Best and George James Philip Smith, eds., *Reports of Cases Argued and Determined in the Court of Queen's Bench, and the Court of Exchequer Chamber on Appeal from the Court of Queen's Bench,* vol. 6 (London: H. Sweet, 1867) 703. Pyke, who had previously been an attorney, had been disbarred in 1845 for blurring the attorney/bar line.

110 "Art. V. – The Inner Temple Benchers – Disbarment of Edwin J. James, Q.C." (1862) 13 Law Magazine and Review: Quarterly Review of Jurisprudence 263; "The Disbarment of Edwin James, Esq. Q.C.," *supra* note 104 at 258.
111 "The Disbarment of Edwin James, Esq. Q.C.," *ibid.* at 255. See also "Disbarment" *Monthly Law Reporter* (April 1862) 323 (discussing the James, Claydon, and Seymour cases).
112 "Disbarment of Mr. Edwin James, Q.C.," *supra* note 104 at 276.
113 Agreement between Lord Yarborough and Edwin James, dated 8 April 1861, as reproduced in *ibid.* See also "The Career of a Q.C." *Spectator* (8 February 1862) 151.
114 "Disbarment of Mr. Edwin James, Q.C.," *supra* note 104.
115 "Mr. Edwin James" *Saturday Review* (15 February 1862) at 185.
116 Testimony of Mr. Edwin Watkins before the Benchers of Inner Temple, as reported in "Disbarment of Mr. Edwin James, Q.C.," *supra* note 104 at 277.
117 "The Career of a Q.C.," *supra* note 113 at 151.
118 *Ibid.* [emphasis in original].
119 The Inner Temple's *Bench Table Orders,* 24 May 1861, includes an inserted printed copy of the "Report of the Committee appointed to inquire into the Charges against Mr. Edwin James, Q.C."
120 Testimony of Watkins, as reported in "Disbarment of Mr. Edwin James, Q.C.," *supra* note 104 at 277. It was not uncommon at the time for Members of Parliament to incur debts they could never repay, and even the distinguished Conservative two-time prime minister Benjamin Disraeli famously feared being imprisoned for debt when he was briefly between parliamentary seats.
121 *Ibid.*
122 Untitled article, *Solicitors' Journal and Reporter* (13 July 1861) at 626.
123 "The Disbarment of Edwin James, Esq. Q.C.," *supra* note 104 at 254.
124 *Ibid.* at 255.
125 Chelmsford's was much clearer, the allegation against James being either conjectural or unrelated to professional practice.
126 "The Disbarment of Edwin James, Esq. Q.C.," *supra* note 104 at 254.
127 "Case of Mr. Edwin James" *The Annual Register, or a View of the History and Politics of the Year 1862* 104 (July 1862) at 140.
128 "The Disbarment of Edwin James, Esq. Q.C.," *supra* note 104.
129 "The Career of a Q.C.," *supra* note 113 at 150-51. In 1852, Charles Eicke had complained to the Benchers about James's conduct, including, among other things, taking a transfer of a prisoner's property for the purpose of making an arrangement with the prosecutor: Inner Temple, *Bench Table Orders,* 20 April 1852, 9 November 1852.
130 *The Times* (23 March 1849) at 6.
131 See Daintree, *supra* note 85, esp. at 123-28, 151-57.
132 *Law Times* 20 (1 May 1858) at 78.
133 "The Fall of Mr. Edwin James," *supra* note 96 at 359.
134 *Ibid.*
135 *Ibid.* at 358-59.
136 See, for example, "Societies and Institutions" *Solicitors' Journal and Reporter* (7 February 1863) at 265-66, reporting a lecture to the Law Amendment Society by G. Shaw Lefevre on the "Discipline of the Bar" in 1863, in which he argued that the barristers' monopoly and immunities ran contrary to sound principles of political economy and "the feeling of the age," and were justifiable only if "it can be shown that there is within the Bar itself a power of enforcing that discipline of its members, and carrying out those rules, sufficient to prevent it from relaxing into the state of absolute freedom so much dreaded, and to supply the place of the legal consequences which would follow in other professions which have no such privileges and immunities" (at 266).

137 Letter of Allan Maclean Skinner, Judge of the County Court of Staffordshire, to the Treasurer, Lincoln's Inn, 12 July 1861 (recorded in Lincoln's Inn, *The Black Books,* no. 29, Special Council of 7 November 1861, at 231) ["Skinner Letter"].

138 The relative lack of restraint of junior barristers during the preceding decade is documented in Chapter 7 in this volume.

139 "Skinner Letter," *supra* note 137 at 229-30.

140 *Ibid.* at 230. Except where otherwise indicated, the account of Claydon's run-in is taken from the "Skinner Letter," *ibid.* at 229-30. Further accounts of the proceedings are found in Lincoln's Inn, *The Black Books,* no. 29, as follows: Special Council of 14 November 1861, at 241-45; Special Council of 3 December 1861, at 269-85; Special Council of 6 December 1861, at 286; Special Council of 12 December 1861, at 297; Special Council of 13 December 1861, at 298; Council of 13 January 1862, at 319-20; Special Council of 14 January 1862, at 323-24; Special Council of 24 January 1862, at 336-37; Adjourned Council of 19 February 1862, at 359; Council of 25 November 1862, at 492-94; and in Lincoln's Inn, *The Black Books,* no. 30, Adjourned Council of 15 January 1863, at 26-29; Special Council of 19 January 1863, at 35-37.

141 15 & 16 Vict., c. 54, s. 10. See discussion in Chapter 7 in this volume.

142 *Doe d. Bennett v. Hale,* 15 Q.B. Rep. 171.

143 *Worcestershire Chronicle* (17 July 1861).

144 Claydon, who joined Lincoln's Inn in 1835, reported: "Having no attorney patronage ... the profession proved ruinously expensive to me; for eighteen years I struggled on, assisted by the benevolence of my family and friends, until at last my own resources expended, and the patience and forbearance of my friends exhausted, I was driven to seek a livelihood as a provincial barrister." Letter to Lord Westbury, Lord Chancellor, dated 22 February 1862, as quoted in "The Disbarment of Mr. Claydon" *Wolverhampton Spirit of Times* (15 February 1862) at 105 ["Claydon to Westbury"].

145 See C.R. Kennedy, *Address to the Mutual Law Association* (Birmingham: John Tonks, 1852) at 8-9.

146 Letter of Claydon "To the Masters of the Bench of the Honourable Society of Lincoln's Inn," dated November 1861, as recorded in Lincoln's Inn, *The Black Books,* no. 29, Special Council of 3 December 1861, at 270 ["Claydon Letter"].

147 "Claydon to Westbury," *supra* note 144; "Disbarring a Barrister" *Morning Star and Dial* (18 February 1862) at 8.

148 Petition of C.B. Claydon to Sir Alexander Cockburn, Lord Chief Justice of England; Sir Frederick Pollock, Lord Chief Baron of the Court of Exchequer; Sir William Erle, Lord Chief Justice of the Court of Common Pleas, dated 27 December 1862 and recorded in Lincoln's Inn, *The Black Books,* no. 30, Adjourned Council of 15 January 1863, at 28 ["Claydon Petition"].

149 "Claydon Letter," *supra* note 146.

150 *Ibid.* at 272.

151 "Claydon to Westbury," *supra* note 144 at 105; "Disbarring a Barrister," *supra* note 147 at 8.

152 "Claydon Letter," *supra* note 146 at 270.

153 *Ibid.* at 275.

154 *Ibid.* at 270.

155 "Claydon to Westbury," *supra* note 144.

156 Letter of Henry Matthews to J. Walker, QC, Treasurer of Lincoln's Inn, as recorded in Lincoln's Inn, *The Black Books,* no. 29, Special Council of 7 November 1861, at 233-34; Lincoln's Inn, *The Black Books,* no. 29, Special Council of 14 November 1861, at 241-45.

157 "Statement of the Oxford Circuit Committee," as recorded in Lincoln's Inn, *The Black Books,* no. 29, Special Council of 14 November 1861, at 243.

158 *Ibid.* at 241.

159 *Ibid.* at 241-42.
160 "Claydon Letter," *supra* note 146 at 271.
161 *Ibid.* at 274.
162 *Ibid.* at 275.
163 *Ibid.* at 276.
164 *Ibid.* at 275.
165 Lincoln's Inn, *The Black Books*, no. 29, Special Council of 24 January 1862, at 336-37.
166 See "Etiquette and Morality of the Bar" *Worcestershire Chronicle* (17 July 1861), reprinted from *Staffordshire Advertiser;* "Skinner Letter," *supra* note 137.
167 "Claydon Petition," *supra* note 148 at 28 [emphasis added].
168 Lead article, *Solicitors' Journal and Reporter* (15 February 1862) at 265; "Claydon to Westbury," *supra* note 144 at 105; "Disbarring a Barrister," *supra* note 147 at 8; "A Barrister Disbarred. – The Law and Practice of County and Magisterial Courts" *Morning Star and Dial* (10 February 1862) at 5 [Letter from "Labeo"]. In a lead article on 27 February 1862, the *Morning Star and Dial* states (at 4) that this is the general impression of the case while expressing disbelief that direct client contact alone could have been the reason for such strong disciplinary action. The *Wolverhampton Journal* (15 February 1862) at 1 reports the publication of Claydon's pamphlet on the matter and identifies six "charges" against Claydon without specifying which combination determined the result.
169 Letter from "Labeo," *ibid.* at 5.
170 Lead article, *Morning Star and Dial* (25 February 1862) at 4.
171 "Etiquette and Morality of the Bar," *supra* note 166.
172 "Claydon to Westbury," *supra* note 144 at 105; "Disbarring a Barrister," *supra* note 147 at 8.
173 Lead article, *Solicitors' Journal and Reporter* (15 February 1862) at 265.
174 Lead article, *Morning Star and Dial* (27 February 1862) at 4.
175 *Ibid.*
176 On the educational attainments of the attorneys' branch, see Chapter 4 in this volume.
177 *Parliament of the Middle Temple*, 26 April 1861, records receipt of letter from Serjt. Manning (Treasurer of Serjeants Inn) alerting the Benchers to concerns should Seymour apply for election to the Middle Temple bench. One law journal reported that Seymour's elevation to Queen's Counsel emerged from the parliamentary patronage politics of the day: "Lord Palmerston's present administration has probably never numbered a working majority ... It probably became necessary to secure every doubtful adherent, and this consideration may palliate, but cannot excuse, the promotion of Mr. Digby Seymour to the rank of Queen's Counsel ... [W]e have heard that Lord Campbell, shortly before his death, expressed his deep regret that he had ever been led by political pressure to promise a silk gown to the member for Southampton": "Case of W. Digby Seymour, Q.C., M.P." (1862) 13 Law Magazine and Review: Quarterly Journal of Jurisprudence at 166.
178 The judgment was "screened" (posted) in the hall of Middle Temple and copies were circulated to the other Inns. See *Parliament of the Middle Temple*, 15 January 1862 (ff. 152-57), 17 January 1862 (f. 163), 21 February 1862 (ff. 187-90). While the Benchers declined to release the text of the judgment to *The Times*, it appeared in the *Morning Star and Dial* within a week of their 21 February 1862 meeting.
179 *Spectator* (6 December 1862) at 1351.
180 "Mr. Digby Seymour's Case" *The Times* (27 June 1862) at 2 (letter).
181 Party boundaries were more flexible at the time than they have become since. The *Oxford Dictionary of National Biography* reports that William Digby Seymour had been elected for Sunderland in 1852 and was rewarded by the Liberal Party with appointment as recorder for Newcastle in 1854. He apparently secured Conservative support in Southampton on a promise to support Lord Derby's government. He claimed his election had been won "by

a clear majority of the Liberal votes." "Court of Queen's Bench. The Late Division in the House of Commons. *The Queen v. Johnstone*. – June 16" *Solicitors' Journal and Reporter* (25 June 1859) 638. *Cf.* "William Digby Seymour" in *Oxford Dictionary of National Biography*, online: <http://www.oxforddnb.com.ezproxy.library.ubc.ca/view/article/25183>.

182 "Mr. Digby Seymour and the Middle Temple Benchers" *Saturday Review* (1 March 1862) at 226.

183 *The Times* (29 December 1847) at 4, as quoted in Mellinkoff, *supra* note 7 at 198. The case is discussed at 184-98.

184 *Parliament of the Middle Temple*, 26 April 1861, letter from Serjt. Manning (Treasurer of Serjeants Inn).

185 Letter dated 16 April 1861 from Serjeant Manning to the treasurer of Middle Temple, as recorded in minute books for the *Parliament of the Middle Temple*, 26 April 1861 ["Manning Letter"].

186 *Parliament of the Middle Temple*, 3 May 1861 (committee consisting of the treasurer, Sir Wm. Alexander, as well as White, Rodwell, Sir F. Slade, Bagshaw, and Bovill, any three constituting a quorum).

187 This passage appears in the Inn's original committee report but was not approved by the full Bench table: *Parliament of the Middle Temple*, 15 January 1862.

188 Lead article, *Morning Star and Dial* (25 February 1862) at 4. Seymour subsequently published a full account of the proceedings in *William Digby Seymour: The Middle Temple Benchers, and the Northern Circuit Committee* (London: W.H. Cox, 1862).

189 Judgment of the Middle Temple Bench as recorded in *Parliament of the Middle Temple*, 15 January 1862 (ff. 152-57).

190 Letter of Seymour "To the Honourable the Treasurer and Masters of the Bench of the Middle Temple," dated 3 February 1862 and printed in "Mr. Digby Seymour and the Benchers" *Morning Star and Dial* (26 February 1862) at 8 ["Seymour Letter"].

191 Judgment of the Bench of the Middle Temple in the case of Digby Seymour, *Parliament of the Middle Temple*, 15 January 1862 (ff. 152-57). Also recorded in Lincoln's Inn, *The Black Books*, no. 29, Adjourned Council of 12 March 1862, at 375-77, 377.

192 George Clement Boase, "William Digby Seymour" in *Dictionary of National Biography, 1885-1900*, vol. 51 (London: Oxford University Press, 1897); John Pym Yeatman, *To the King's Most Excellent Majesty, 17 March 1907. The High Court of Justice Chancery Division. Mr. Justice Kekewich. Derbyshire to Wit. The Humble Petition of John Pym Yeatman of Lincoln's Inn* ... at 5-6 [*Humble Petition*]: "Mr. Price at once endeavoured to prevent Mr. Seymour from publishing his name on the Midland Bar List, and Mr. Macaulay, the then Leader, struck it out, but an immediate appeal to the Judges, brought these gentlemen to their senses, and they were compelled to restore it."

193 Unusually, Seymour declined to seek election to the bench of his Inn when it was first possible because, he said, of financial insecurity. See "Mr. Digby Seymour's Case," *supra* note 180 at 9.

194 *Humble Petition*, *supra* note 192 at 5; Boase, *supra* note 192.

195 "Seymour Letter," *supra* note 190. The parliament referred to is the Parliament of the Middle Temple, *i.e.*, the Benchers. The voting patterns of the Benchers do not line up consistently with a simple split along party lines, however. Masters Karslake (a Conservative MP) and William Bovill (a Conservative MP) consistently sided with Seymour, while Masters Monk (a Liberal MP) and (especially) Wyndham Slade voted against him. See *Parliament of the Middle Temple*, 10 January 1862 (evening) (ff. 148-51).

196 "Legal Courts of Honour" *John Bull* (15 February 1862) at 105. See also lead article, *Solicitors' Journal and Reporter* (15 February 1862) at 265 (Mr. Seymour "did not hesitate to impute the entire proceeding against him to professional rivalry"); Yeatman, *Humble Petition*, *supra*

note 192 at 5 (Seymour is described as "an orator of great power, and his intellectual superiority [just as in Mr. Kennedy's case] had excited the envy and hatred of his mediocre fellows").

197 A. Newton, "The 'Star Chamber' of the Middle Temple" *Morning Star and Dial* (27 February 1862) at 3.

198 "Legal Courts of Honour," *supra* note 196 at 105.

199 *Parliament of the Middle Temple,* 15 January 1862 (ff. 152-57).

200 Lead article, Morning *Star and Dial* (25 February 1862) at 4.

201 "Mr. Digby Seymour and the Middle Temple Benchers," *supra* note 182 at 226; "Legal Courts of Honour," *supra* note 196 at 105.

202 For more information, see Clayton, *supra* note 38.

203 See Chapter 11 in this volume.

204 C.R. Kennedy, *Mr. Kennedy's Argument in the Common Pleas against the Rule Obtained by the Defendants in Kennedy v. Broun and Wife* (Birmingham: S.B. Howell, 1862) [*Mr. Kennedy's Argument*].

205 *Ibid.* at 37 (side note).

206 *Ibid.* at 38-43.

207 *Ibid.* at 43-45.

208 *Ibid.* at 44.

209 *Ibid.* at 56.

210 *Ibid.* at 52-53.

211 *Ibid.* at 13.

212 *Ibid.* at 53.

213 *Ibid.* at 17. Kennedy at 17-18 quoted Lord Mansfield that strict adherence to the law of maintenance would deprive the poor of their rights: *Goodright v. Forester,* 1 Taunt. 613.

214 *Ibid.* at 15 (side note).

215 *Ibid.*

216 *Ibid.* at 32. Indeed, in the course of a discussion of Roman practice, Kennedy asserted that any inhibition of contractual freedom between counsel and client was "contrary to natural justice and opposed to the exigencies of society." *Ibid.* at 28.

217 *Ibid.* at 45.

218 *Ibid.* Only three years earlier, during the *Swinfen v. Lord Chelmsford* litigation, Chief Baron Pollock had admitted the legality of express contracts between client and barrister. *Ibid.* at 46.

219 *Ibid.* at 55.

220 *Ibid.*

221 *Ibid.*

222 *Ibid.* at 3, 26.

223 *Ibid.* at 56. The *Legal Observer* (25 May 1850) at 63-64, had complained about "Bird," a local barrister in Exeter, taking County Court cases without the intervention of an attorney, and threatened such barristers with suit for unauthorized practice. Similarly, a letter titled "The Junior Bar and the Attorneys" *Law Times* 20 (27 November 1852) at 110, threatened the prosecution of barristers for unauthorized practice if they conducted the whole cause in their cases. The threat was made good on at least one occasion. See "The County Court Bar Meeting" *Legal Observer* 43 (6 March 1852) at 348-50: "Persons who should so act [*i.e.,* take instructions directly from clients] may either be indicted and convicted, as was done by the Kent Law Society or may be subjected to an application in a summary way for contempt of Court, or may be disbarred, as lately happened to a member of Gray's Inn."

224 Kennedy, *Mr. Kennedy's Argument, supra* note 204 at 56.

225 *Ibid.* at 56-57.

226 *Ibid.* at 59.

227 *Ibid.*

228 "The Status of the Bar" *Saturday Review* (24 January 1863) at 105.

229 *Ibid.* This article was responded to by Charles Kennedy's son Edmund, who, in the course of defending his father, accused the *Saturday Review* writer of animus. See *Daily Telegraph* (28 January 1863), reprinted in *Birmingham Daily Gazette* (29 January 1863) at 3.

230 Lead article, *The Times* (2 April 1862) at 9.

231 *Ibid.* Kennedy responded in a letter published as "Kennedy v. Broun" *The Times* (5 April 1862) at 5.

232 Lead article, *Daily News* (1 April 1862) at 4; "News of the Day" *Birmingham Daily Post* (3 April 1862) at 2; "Counsel and Client. Kennedy v. Broun and Wife" *Solicitors' Journal and Reporter* (5 April 1862) at 410-12; Lead article, *Solicitors' Journal and Reporter* (12 April 1862) at 427; "The Swinfen Case" *Aris's Birmingham Gazette* (5 April 1862) at 4. More general support for vigorous bar discipline was recorded in "Societies and Institutions" *Solicitors' Journal and Reporter* (7 February 1863) at 265-66.

233 Lead article, *Birmingham Daily Gazette* (25 February 1863) at 2.

234 Lead article, *Birmingham Daily Gazette* (19 January 1863) at 2. Although not generally as supportive of Kennedy in this phase of his career, *The Times* and *Law Times* viewed the idea that barristers' fees were an honorarium as absurd. See "Law Summary" *Birmingham Journal* (31 January 1863) at 7. To similar effect: Lead article, *Aris's Birmingham Gazette* (21 June 1862) at 5 (a barrister should be paid like a "shopkeeper"!); Lead article, *Birmingham Daily Gazette* (19 January 1863) at 2 (critical of noncommercial rules of etiquette).

235 "Mr. Kennedy and His Judges" *Spectator* (12 April 1862) at 402-3.

236 "Private Correspondence" *Birmingham Journal* (24 January 1863) at 6. Similarly, in "The Case of Broun v. Kennedy," the *Solicitors' Journal and Reporter* (13 February 1864) at 281-82, commented: "We are unable to applaud the success of one party, and a true fidelity to our profession forbids us to sympathize with the discomfiture of the other."

237 Lead article, *Morning Star and Dial* (1 April 1862) at 4.

238 "The Lady and the Lawyer" *John Bull* (5 April 1862) at 216-17.

239 "The End of the Broun-Kennedy Case (from Times)" *Aris's Birmingham Gazette* (6 February 1864) at 7.

240 John Pym Yeatman, *The Professorship of the Law Department of the Queen's College, Birmingham: A Letter to the Council and Governors* (Birmingham: M. Maher and Son, 1869) [*The Professorship*]. The Midland Circuit Mess was active in policing barristers' conduct in this period. See Yeatman, *Humble Petition, supra* note 192. See also "The Rearrangement of the Circuits" *Solicitors' Journal and Reporter* (2 January 1864) at 157, observing that "[o]ne who knew the Midland Circuit well, and has since, in another capacity, gone to the Northern, describes the Midland as equal to the Northern, minus York and Liverpool – in other words, deducting five weeks' work." There may have been economic reasons for restrictive practices on the Midland Circuit.

241 Inner Temple, *Bench Table Orders,* 15 April 1864.

242 The three charges are recorded in Inner Temple, *Bench Table Orders,* 20 May 1864. See also Clayton, *supra* note 38 for more information on the "Serpent of Swynfen."

243 Yeatman, *Humble Petition, supra* note 192 at 6.

244 See generally the Inner Temple, *Bench Table Orders* for 10 June 1864 (letter of Kennedy referring to "Analysis of My Refutation of the Common Pleas Judgment") and 28 June 1864 (including "Mr. Kennedy's Further Explanations").

245 Inner Temple, *Bench Table Orders,* 28 June 1864.

246 "The Discipline of the Bar" *Solicitors' Journal and Reporter* (3 December 1864) at 109.

247 Yeatman, *The Professorship, supra* note 240 at 22.

248 Anthony Harwood, QC, "A Hundred Years of the Midland Circuit" (Manuscript lodged with the Bodleian Library; pages are unnumbered), Adjourned Circuit Court, Warwick,

24 March 1863. Correspondence between the Midland Circuit Mess and the Northern Circuit on 13 March 1862 set special fees in the amount of 300 guineas for QCs, 100 guineas for leading juniors, and 50 guineas for others (*Minutes of the Midland Circuit Mess,* 13 March 1862).

249 Quite possibly the "Henry Frederick Gibbons, LL.B. Cantab., Barrister-at-Law, Midland Circuit" indicated as author of *Equity in the County Court* (as advertised in the *Law Times'* list of "New Law Books for Office Use," 6 October 1866, online: <https://books.google.ca/books?id=Wo8DAAAAQAAJ&pg=PA195&lpg=PA195&dq=%22henry+frederick+gibbons%22+LL.B.+barrister&source=bl&ots=d5g9HPf16P&sig=qHwvbX1hxkptwjmJ-BWZ4yOTUuE&hl=en&sa=X&ved=0CCEQ6AEwAmoVChMIl-z65pWUyQIVkJaICh29mAcb#v=onepage&q=gibbons&f=false>.

250 Harwood, *supra* note 248 at Derby, 17 July 1865 (Gibbons); Derby, 7 March 1867 (Yeatman). General accounts of Kennedy's professional struggles are to be found in Yeatman, *The Professorship, supra* note 240 at 22-23; Charles Rann Kennedy, *To the Legal Profession and the Public. Bar Unionists* (this pamphlet does not seem to have survived as published but is reproduced in Yeatman, *The Professorship, ibid.* at 23-26); Yeatman, *Humble Petition, supra* note 192 at 7.

251 Yeatman, *Humble Petition, ibid.* at 7. Obituaries of Kennedy were carried in *Solicitors' Journal and Reporter* (28 December 1867) at 182; *Aris's Birmingham Gazette* (21 December 1867) at 6; *Birmingham Journal* (21 December 1867) at 7; *Law Journal* (20 December 1867) at 557; *Staffordshire Advertiser* (21 December 1867) at 5; and *Wolverhampton Journal* (28 December 1867) at 2.

252 James Stephen, *Bar Etiquette (In Reference to the Rule Requiring the Intermediary Agency of an Attorney between Counsel and Client)* (London: Butterworths, 1851) at 25, offered a perspective on the politics of professional reform: "And this leads us to make some remarks upon the general aspect of the Bar at the present crisis, assailed as it is by country gentlemen in the House of Commons, mischievous generally in proportion to the grossness of their ignorance upon this subject, vituperated or 'damned with faint praise,' in articles, often written by barristers, who, having failed in the pursuit of their profession, not unnaturally undervalue its importance, and intrenched on, as it has been of late, in its own peculiar province of advocacy, by a new body of men known as attorney *advocates*" [emphasis in original].

253 Radical solicitors in nineteenth-century England probably fared better than their barrister brothers. The activities of W.P. Roberts, the nineteenth-century "miners' attorney-general" is a case in point: see R. Challinor, *A Radical Lawyer in Victorian England: W.P. Roberts and the Struggle for Workers' Rights* (London: I.B. Tauris, 1990); C. Frank, *Master and Servant Law: Chartists, Trade Unions, Radical Lawyers and the Magistracy in England, 1840-1865* (Farnham, UK: Ashgate, 2010).

254 Yeatman, *The Professorship, supra* note 240 at 26.

255 See *Aris's Birmingham Gazette* (11 and 13 July 1859).

256 "The Swinfen Case" *Aris's Birmingham Gazette* (5 April 1862) at 4.

257 So was the interpretation of the *Solicitors' Journal and Reporter* (29 December 1860) at 142, of an illustration published in the *Illustrated London News* showing James at Garibaldi's camp.

258 J. Auerbach, *Unequal Justice: Lawyers and Social Change in Modern America* (New York: Oxford University Press, 1976).

259 Carol Rice Andrews, "Ethical Limits on Civil Litigation Advocacy: A Historical Perspective" (2012) 63 Case W. Res. L. Rev. 381.

9

Regulating Lawyers' Ethics in Early-Twentieth-Century Canada

Why do legal professions promulgate codes of ethics? Why, the better to be ethical, of course!

This unadorned explanation is routine. In his 1916 address to the American Bar Association, Elihu Root explained:

> To the student of the law there come from all the glorious history of the profession of advocacy, great traditions and ethical ideals and lofty conceptions of the honor and dignity of the profession, of courage and loyalty for the maintenance of the law and the liberty that it guards. It is to a Bar inspired by these traditions, imbued with this spirit, not commercialized, not playing a sordid game, not cunning and subtle and technical, or seeking unfair advantage – a Bar jealous of the honor of the profession and proud of its high calling for the maintenance of justice – that we must look for the effective administration of the law.[1]

Such words resonate in professional history: Root's views were endorsed by a Canadian Bar Association Committee on Legal Education and Ethics in 1918.[2]

And yet this rationale seems too pat, too convenient. Why would a profession that had gotten along without ethics codes for a thousand years or more come to need such a thing in the twentieth century?

Scholars from a range of disciplines have long been intrigued by the historical forces that motivate the development of "professional ethics." A diverse body of literature generally repudiates claims that codes of ethics arise exclusively (or even primarily) from altruistic impulses. While the range of inquiries, methodologies, and perspectives are too scattered to permit the extraction of any single explanation, it seems fair to say that many have viewed codes of ethics as self-serving. The projection of an "ethical" image is sometimes portrayed as necessary in order to legitimate self-interested market control strategies, including state enforcement of a professional monopoly over the provision of services. Alternatively, the "ethical" project might be conceived as a means by which the cultural authority of the profession as a whole is enhanced. Alternatively, again, it can serve as a device by which elites within the profession repress those of whom they disapprove.

Visions of Professionalism

As Elihu Root's 1916 address illustrates, one of the core notions of professional ethics is the idea that a legal career should not be pursued as any ordinary business. The sense that values are at stake that are too important to be left to the vagaries of the free market is pervasive.

Harvard Law Dean Roscoe Pound, for example, asserted that the concept of profession involves three ideas: "organization, learning, and the spirit of public service. The remaining idea, that of gaining a livelihood, is incidental."[3] The spirit of public service is, according to Pound, the most important. Even at its worst, he thought professional activity to be "restrained and guided by something better than the desire for money rewards."[4] Pound's ideal of professionalism stood as a sort of polar opposite to the "extreme regime of competitive individual self-assertion" that characterized many areas of social life. Through its traditions "of organization, of learning, and of a spirit of service," he hoped that the US legal professions of the 1940s might foster the development of a wider spirit of cooperation in place of American capitalism's otherwise unfettered competition.[5]

While all of this may seem somewhat quaint – perhaps even naïve – the linkage of professionalism with a rejection of market principles is powerful and continuing. Osgoode Hall Law School Dean H.W. Arthurs wrote in 1975 that "[t]he existence of a code of ethics is often thought to be the very essence of professionalism," to so great a degree that the terms "ethical" and "professional" are sometimes used interchangeably.[6] Sociologists treat the existence of a code of ethics as the hallmark of professions (in contradistinction to mere occupations), historians have increasingly come to focus their attention on how notions of appropriate practice have operated in the development of the modern legal profession, and legal academics have viewed professional ethics as a means of effecting progressive social change.[7] Courses in professional ethics (or "professional responsibility") are mandatory at many law schools and bar admission courses.[8] One of the more onerous tasks undertaken by organized legal professions is the enforcement of ethical standards. The Canadian Bar Association, provincial bar associations, and provincial law societies, like their US counterparts, continue to promulgate and refine statements of professional ethics. While the content of these codes of ethics is more or less subject to constant renegotiation, the idea that the legal profession should generate, publicize, and enforce ethical standards of conduct is largely taken to be commonsensical.

It was not always so. While the legal profession in common law countries has frequently held itself out as being in some sense bound by special standards of conduct and customs, the idea that a professional body equipped with coercive powers should presume to dictate to individual practitioners how they should go about their work is of recent vintage. This is not only the case in the United States (where Jacksonian democracy in the nineteenth century largely destroyed professional organizations, challenged professional monopolies, and thus effectively precluded the development of enforceable standards of ethical conduct)[9] but also – contrary to a persistent myth – in England, where the transformation of the Inns of Court into disciplinary organs began only in the 1860s, and only after heated contest.[10]

Moreover, the development of professional ethics has generally not been confined to prohibiting "obviously" harmful or undesirable conduct. Much else gets swept into the category when "ethics" become a focus of attention. Legal professions in both the United States and England have sometimes revealed a pattern whereby the "ethical codes" promulgated by elite lawyers tend to prohibit practices helpful to non-elite practitioners and their clients while condoning virtually any conduct that is actually engaged in by elite practitioners. The idea of a traditional, timeless, consensual, or revealed "ethics" proves elusive. This, of course, should not be a shocking conclusion.[11] In the result, professional codes have often been, in varying degrees, class-biased, disempowering of ordinary citizens, antidemocratic, racist, anti-Semitic, patriarchal, and xenophobic or nativist.[12]

It is unclear, however, to what degree any such findings apply in Canada. Kyer and Bickenbach suggest that there is no evidence of this,[13] and Arthurs points to an indeterminate pattern of similarity and difference.[14] In truth, however, we simply know too little about what motivated Canadian lawyers to first develop codes of professional ethics, who took on the task, what they hoped to achieve, or what the effects were. An adequate consideration of professional ethics among lawyers in Canada would require simultaneous consideration of developments in each of the provinces and territories from at least the time the first informal association of "lawyers" was formed. It would require a careful consideration of the various policies developed in relation to admission to the profession, unauthorized practice, the exercise of disciplinary powers (which probably, as in England, preceded the articulation of codes of ethics), legal education, and professional "custom," "tradition," "etiquette," and "ethics." The relative importance of local concerns and external influences from Europe, England, and the United States would have to be taken into account, and the study would have to concurrently investigate principle, interest, and the social construction of knowledge. Cognate fields of learning such as philosophy and political theory would have to be accessed. The internal dynamics of the profession as well as its complex interwoven relationships with the larger society would have to be probed.[15] An adequate study of the origins of professional ethics among lawyers in Canada would problematize the very notion of "lawyer"[16] and would take seriously ethnicity as well as regional, class, linguistic, racial, and gender diversities of legal practice in times past.[17] This chapter has the more modest objectives of sketching out the ways in which the Canadian Bar Association first moved towards the adoption of a Code of Professional Ethics, and of sketching the contours of a debate among eminent lawyers as to the desirability of adopting any such code at all.

Professional Organization

As a preliminary matter, it is important to appreciate that certain features relating to the organization and structure of Canadian legal professions in the first quarter of the twentieth century produced lawyers' self-conceptions distinct from our own. The legal professions then differed in four essential respects from those that we take for granted today:[18]

1. The idea of a national professional organization was novel, the Canadian Bar Association having become successfully established only in 1915.[19]
2. Provincial law societies (by whatever name) generally lacked the powers now assumed to be essential to self-governance (and hence lacked the *sine qua non* of modern professionalism).
3. Forms of professional education and qualification were relatively loose, varying widely from province to province.[20]
4. The idea of a unified profession had not yet fully taken hold. Formal distinctions between barrister and solicitor mattered still in the common law provinces, just as that between *avocat* and *notaire* mattered (and matters today) in Quebec.

For present purposes two points in particular merit further exploration: (1) the absence of full powers of professional self-governance, and (2) the formal division of the legal professions (outside of Quebec) into barristers' and solicitors' branches.

Self-Governance

Taking first the matter of professional governance, it is important to note that while professional organization in Canada can lay claim to a relatively ancient lineage,[21] it has been only within the last century that full privileges of self-governance have been conferred upon law societies by the various provincial governments in Canada. In all cases, the common law professional organizations bore some resemblance to the English Bar, with the important qualification that their powers originated in "statute instead of by prescriptive right."[22] In other respects, they resembled English solicitors' organizations. In England, as in Canada, professional organizations evolved considerably during the course of the nineteenth century.

The Benchers of Ontario's Law Society (the Law Society of Upper Canada) had long exercised powers of suspension or disbarment of barristers and, from 1876, had the right to discipline attorneys. Only in 1880, however, was legislation passed to unequivocally empower the Benchers to suspend, disbar, expel (or, in the case of attorneys, move to strike) barristers, attorneys, or clerks guilty of "professional misconduct or of conduct unbecoming."[23] Even this stopped short of full-fledged disciplinary powers.

In 1919, Mr. Justice William Renwick Riddell of the Supreme Court of Ontario indicated that while the law society in that province had "ample power to disbar in a proper case," in fact "the power has been exercised only in the case of a crime." Any attempt to develop a code of ethics backed by significant punishment would, he thought, be *ultra vires* the law society as then constituted.[24] The next year, Manitoba Chief Justice T.G. Mathers[25] noted that Canada lacked "agencies clothed with express authority to punish breaches of an ethical code, adopted for the whole Dominion. The incorporated Law Associations in the several provinces possess by statute certain control over their members but the disciplinary power of their Associations is by no means uniform."[26] Quebec's Bar Council had extensive disciplinary powers.[27] Manitoba's, New Brunswick's, and Nova Scotia's Benchers held disciplinary powers similar to those of their counterparts in Ontario,[28] while disciplinary powers were "possessed by the Superior Courts or the Judges" in Saskatchewan and Alberta.[29] In Prince Edward Island, no disciplinary power existed other than that which lay within the inherent power of the courts. In provinces where the law society did possess disciplinary powers, the Court of King's Bench generally retained co-extensive authority and was also authorized to hear appeals from suspended or disbarred lawyers. The Benchers in British Columbia enjoyed wide disciplinary powers subject to appeal to the Supreme Court Judges as Visitors.[30]

One Profession or Two?

It has been commonly assumed that the formal distinction of barrister from solicitor, still retained in name, has long been a dead letter in the common law provinces. Riddell's works leave this impression. American observer Alfred Reed concluded in 1921 that "[t]he distinction between the two branches ... is little more than nominal."[31] In certain respects, however, the distinction informed how Canadian lawyers thought about their profession. In each common law province except Alberta and Saskatchewan, it was possible for an individual to be either a barrister or a solicitor or both simultaneously. Even in Alberta and Saskatchewan, the distinct professions were recognized in name, every lawyer being both called to the bar and admitted as a solicitor. While most lawyers chose to be admitted to both branches of the legal profession simultaneously, this was not necessarily the case. Canadian lawyers were, after the Great War, acutely aware that "the legal profession in Canada is made up of two distinct professions, with different duties, different responsibilities and liabilities, different history and traditions and subject to different rules."[32]

Visions of Professionalism

The development of a code of professional ethics was strongly influenced by visions of professionalism promoted by elite lawyers. Early efforts to develop a code arose in Ontario,[33] Alberta,[34] and Saskatchewan,[35] and the Canadian Bar Association provided leadership in the field from its effective launch in 1915. They sought to cultivate a profession composed learned men (maleness was more or less a given) who could be trusted by the public, and who would care more for the advancement of the public good than for their own private gain. Hallowed professional traditions would help them to withstand temptation to behave in any other way. In his 1915 presidential address to the Canadian Bar Association, Sir James Aikins[36] claimed that "[f]aithful and efficient service has been and is a characteristic of our profession" and that lawyers were "certified to the people" as being of superior learning and "as worthy to be trusted, counsellors of persons in any occupation or in positions of authority."[37] The key distinguishing the profession of law from a mere "craft"[38] was said to be the professional's principled rejection of the profit motive:

> Few indeed have spent energy and time and money in the preparation for admission to the legal profession and have entered it with the primary object of thereby making money. Those who have done so have shewn at the outset

lack of judgment and good taste, both essentials of true professional success. It is not a calling or instrumentality suited to that purpose as is the business of the merchant, manufacturer or miner.[39]

Despite its supposed anti-commercial ethos, Aikins avoided portraying the profession as standing aloof from the concerns of ordinary people. His ideal lawyer was a useful man of the world. He combined pristine personal ethics with active, pragmatic, and "vigorous participation in affairs" and the "robust work of the world." Lawyers were practical individuals, and their role could be justified on the starkly utilitarian terms required of an early-twentieth-century North American democracy while they simultaneously embodied the contrary ideas of professional distance and public service. All things to all persons, the lawyer combined faithfully service of private interest with fidelity to the public good. Lawyers integrated the demands of individual liberty with the impulses of democracy, worked actively in commerce while resisting the taint of commercialization, served at once "the people," commerce, and the state – while remaining untarnished by overly close identification with any of these. Canadian lawyers were to embody the best ancient traditions while avoiding the scent of anachronism that hung over English barristers.[40]

Themes such as these recur time and again in the writings and speeches of Canadian lawyers during the half-decade beginning in 1915. Almost everyone was aware that legal professionals needed to actively justify their special privileges and exclusive roles (and incomes) in an evolving democratic state. Common justifications emphasized learning, practical usefulness,[41] dedication to public service, and purportedly superior moral sensibilities. Speaking to the Canadian Bar Association in 1915, E.F.B. Johnson, K.C., for example, emphasized the importance of lawyers in their local communities, in business, and in politics.[42] W.J. McWhinney, K.C., used his presidential address to the Ontario Bar Association the following year to stress the usefulness of lawyers to the age of commerce: "This is a business age, and business exigencies prevail, and in the main our Judges and lawyers are business men as distinguished from legal technical controversialists, and are expected to know and apply business principles in preference to merely establishing precedents."[43]

In an extraordinary address to the Canadian Bar Association in1919, Sir James Aikins developed a comprehensive theory of professionalism developed from the usefulness of lawyers in the pursuit of social well-being. This, he argued, justified a professional monopoly on the provision of legal services (something Canadian lawyers had not yet fully secured), more rigorous and exclusive legal education, and high professional fees; importantly, a developed notion of professionalism should be enforced by the guild. The first duty of the lawyer was to the state,[44] Aikins asserted. He continued:

> It is a false notion of democracy that the right to practice law should be free for all, that anyone can practice it, and without serious loss to the public, operate or help to operate the expensive and intricate machinery of justice which the State creates for its safety and well-being. The administration of justice has always touched the nadir of its decline when the profession has been lowest in morals and least educated. In such times there is seen a tendency on the part of practitioners to regard the work of the Bar as a trade and not a profession, a thing to be bartered and not a national service to be sought after; then also is found the pettifogger, the ambulance chaser, the fabricator of evidence and the trickster, and the man who is alien to the professional spirit and its traditions, destitute of gentlemanly instincts, disrespectful to his seniors, and a slanderer of Judges.[45]

The important social interests at stake made it essential, Aikins argued, that lawyers be highly educated. Of course, the well-educated deserved "adequate rewards for meritorious services"; hence, "Standard Solicitor's Tariffs" were necessary.[46] The object, for Aikins, was to "create a higher type of barrister and advocate, well skilled in the law, gentlemanly in conduct, kindly disposed to his fellow practitioners and of a public spirit." Socialization through frequent meetings of the members of each of the provincial bars would, he thought, tend to foster the appropriate culture of professionalism. He concluded that "[n]one can commend too highly the official law and Bar societies, those bulwarks protecting the people against incompetent and unscrupulous men posing as lawyers, and thus guarding the honour of the profession."[47]

The linkage of State, ethics, education, fees, elimination of unauthorized practice, expanded professional monopoly, and advance of the public interest forms a logical whole here. In the immediate postwar period, the Canadian Bar Association was actively and self-consciously engaged in a deliberate "professionalization project" of the sort sociologists and historians of the legal profession have more commonly identified *ex post facto*.[48]

It is apparent that the legal profession would not be given a free pass in the developing North American democracies of 1919.[49] The development of a code of professional ethics, the call for a bolstering of professional socialization, and the plea for extended professional education were all presented as means to improve the profession and, simultaneously, to provide public legitimation for regulated fee minimums and an expanded state-created monopoly.[50]

Winnipeg General Strike. *Library and Archives Canada, PA-163001*

Winnipeg was a focal point of radicalism in the postwar period, culminating in the General Strike of 1919. In Aikins it produced a president of the Canadian Bar Association who feared that a "false notion of democracy" might lead to the "intricate machinery of justice which the State creates for its safety and well-being" falling into the hands of the general public. The enthusiasm for democratic reform that characterized post–First World War Canada and the nearby US experiments with a radical democratization of legal professions combined to spur Canadian lawyers to professional reform.

The Spectre of Unprofessional Activity

A better understanding of the concerns of elite lawyers can be developed by considering the specific sorts of "unprofessional conduct" that caused them most distress. What comes into focus is an unpleasant mix of nativism, a sniffy disdain for the "commercialized" practices of non-elite practitioners, the sort of class bias that refuses to recognize as legitimate the legal claims of working people, and a vision of rule of law more oriented towards paternalism than the empowerment of the citizenry.

Elite and non-elite lawyers typically represent different clienteles, engage in different sorts of legal work, and come by their business in different ways. This is so much the case that a celebrated study of the Chicago Bar concludes with the suggestion that lawyers work in two distinct hemispheres with few points of contact.[51] Nominally anti-commercial professional ethics can line the pockets of elite practitioners, advance the interests of their clients, and simultaneously deprive less well-established attorneys of both the income and clientele that they can develop only through advertising, fee competition (denigrated as "ambulance chasing"), working for contingency fees, and other such commercialized practices.[52]

Certainly Sir James Aikins considered it to be a matter of principle that legal practice should not be "prostituted" for the crass purpose of making money. As the Canadian Bar Association began work on developing an ethical code in 1915, he warned Canadian lawyers:

> Persons who have thus sought to commercialize it [*i.e.*, the practice of law], to prostitute it to such an end in itself [*i.e.*, making money] have lowered the professional tone and so lost the respect and esteem of their fellow-practitioners and of the people. They take no interest in the advancement of our profession and do not possess its spirit.[53]

E.F.B. Johnson cautioned Canadian Bar Association members that "one of the most dangerous causes at work affecting the reputation of our Profession is the scheming for business," and proceeded to make abundantly clear that the real problem with commercialized legal practice was that it permitted injured workers, the poor, maimed, and injured to recover damages from big business:

> In most places particularly where there are large factories, electric railways and similar undertakings, involving great personal risk, there are always a certain number of lawyers who appear on the scene in company with the ambulance or the coroner. Men, not lawyers, have to my knowledge been employed by legal vultures, and have received a commission on bringing in the body dead or alive. Retainers are promptly obtained, and actions are brought again and again, on purely speculative grounds. Relying on the sympathy of a jury, defendants are put to heavy costs, with no chance of getting a dollar from the plaintiff, and with many chances in favour of a substantial verdict against them, particularly in actions against large corporations ... [there is then a discussion of Ontario legislation establishing

> workers' compensation and requiring trial by judge alone under the Ontario *Municipal Act*] ... If we could have continued the old experience of thirty or forty years ago with lawyers above suspicion, the jury system would still remain as it was intended to be – a bulwark against wrong-doing, and a tower of strength in the administration of justice. The soliciting of business in the manner I have indicated should disqualify any lawyer from ever practising again. And so with speculative litigation. Nothing is so destructive to the reputation of the solicitor, or to the legal profession generally, as the promoting and carrying on of cases on a purely speculative basis. It is unjust to the client, most dangerous to the community and absolutely demoralizing to our whole system of jurisprudence.[54]

There is little sense here that access to justice should be of concern to the legal profession, that the poor as well as the rich should be entitled to their day in court, that lawsuits to rectify injustice might be desirable, or that the rule of law should benefit even the most humble of citizens.

The vision of rule of law adhered to by many elite Canadian lawyers in the first quarter of the twentieth century was distinctly paternalistic. While historians such as E.P. Thompson and Greg Marquis have drawn attention to circumstances in which subordinate groups have employed the promise of equality before the law as sword and shield,[55] there is little sense of committed service to the client or of respect for client autonomy in the writings of Canadian lawyers at this time. One observer argued that it was improper for a lawyer to work for the acquittal of someone known to be guilty of an offence. He took the opportunity to pass comment critical of contingency fees as well.[56] Johnson argued that lawyers should maintain an impersonal, distanced position vis-à-vis their (subject) clients, declining to fight full-out on behalf of clients of whom they disapproved.[57]

Ominously, the Canadian Bar Association committee on legal ethics hinted that the practice of law might be falling into the wrong hands as young men not of Anglo-American origin entered into practice.

> In view of the changed and changing conditions of this country, and the large number of students now admitted to practice, many of whom come from various countries whose traditions and surroundings have not been similar to those of our own and the Motherland, the time may be considered as having arrived when it is necessary to reduce to writing for the information of members of the Bar and the guidance of our law students some of the most important general principles governing the conduct of the profession

> towards the Bench, the public, and their clients, setting forth among other things the ideals and standards of the profession, its honour, dignity and traditions.[58]

So-called ethnic Canadians could not be fully trusted.

To emphasize somewhat unsavoury motivations behind the development of ethical codes is, however, to present a partial and distorted impression. The American Bar Association's adoption of a code of professional conduct in 1908 was influential. There was also a very real idealism in wartime and immediate postwar Canada, producing genuinely held commitments to improve the institutions of the past and, in so doing, build a better Dominion. All of this intermingled in varying degrees with a nostalgic and inchoate sense that valued traditions were slipping away as the era of kings, queens, and principalities began drawing to a close after August 1914.

Developing the Code

Such concerns formed a background to the Canadian Bar Association's "Report of the Committee on Legal Ethics," which appeared in 1919.[59] Noting similar initiatives to define ethics in both the United States and Canada (Saskatchewan and Alberta and an attempt in Ontario), the committee called upon the president to appoint a select committee "to prepare such a statement of the principles of legal ethics as has been suggested in this report, using amongst other data the code of the American Bar Association supplemented by the draft code prepared for the Law Society of Alberta, as well as a similar code prepared some years ago and adopted by the Ontario Bar Association." They asked that the new committee report to the next meeting of the Canadian Bar Association.[60] The1919 Canadian Bar Association gathering heard about ethics from other sources as well. Dr. James Muir of Alberta presented his draft "Canons of Ethics" for consideration;[61] the Quebec Committee on Legal Ethics reported, encouraging "the adoption by all the provinces of Canada of the best means" to establish and maintain the "highest standards of professional ethics";[62] and the distinguished Ontario jurist William Renwick Riddell delivered an address on the topic of "A Code of Legal Ethics."[63]

Resistance

Riddell's contribution to the discussions is worthy of particular attention. He spoke against the idea of developing enforceable codes of ethics at a time when the notion was advancing with the speed of a prairie fire. Christopher Robinson, KC, had earlier dissuaded Ontario lawyers from following this course with the argument "that legal ethics could not be taught in that way, that it was merely a matter of mental and moral education, and not one that could be reached by the adoption of formal rules,"[64] but Mr. Justice Riddell failed to persuade in 1919. His objections are worthy of note, however. He was a reputable establishment figure and a highly informed individual. What he said represented a coherent inherited vision of professionalism. He expressed his views to confront a powerful counter-ideology of professionalism that was emerging as a new sort of "common sense" among elite lawyers.

A Supreme Court judge, Riddell had long been actively involved in providing instruction in professional ethics at the law school in Toronto.[65] The pre-eminent historian of the Ontario legal profession, he was well aware of its customs, traditions, and corporate values. Intriguingly, Riddell conducted a survey of "the Chiefs of Bench and Bar" in England, Ireland, and Scotland in the course of preparing his remarks, which provides us with a snapshot impression of elite British thought at the time. Like Riddell, they all opposed the development of a written code of professional ethics as a matter of principle (see Appendix).

Riddell stated six objections. These related to Canadian constitutionalism, the statutory limits of self-regulation, the limited value of a merely hortative code, the danger of "artificial conscience," fear that precise definition of prohibited conduct would erode ethical standards, and the impossibility of precision.

One of the strongest forces making the development of a written ethical code seem both logical and inevitable was the model of the United States. Riddell reported that "[m]ost of the Bar Associations of the various States of the Union have their formal Codes of Ethics" and that American lawyers exhibited an "almost universal approval of the written Code."[66] He recognized that "the usages of trade and of society, and the 'genius of the people'" in the United States were closer to those of Canadians than any other country.[67] Against this, Riddell presented Anglo-Canadian tradition, specific arguments on the merits, and an explanation for the mass psychosis that had apparently swept American lawyers. The "American mind," he asserted, sometimes deviated from common sense. While the US legal professions had in many instances concluded that codes of professional conduct were desirable, Riddell attributed this to a sort of juridical conditioning: "[I]n many instances that view is due in no slight degree to the fact that the United States and the separate States have all a written Constitution. The mind of the American lawyer naturally and instinctively inclines to written formulation of all precepts, all rules, all principles." Canada, of course, subscribed to "indefinite and indefinitely formulated principles upon which a British people should be governed."[68] Accordingly, Canadian lawyers should be inclined to follow an approach more compatible with British constitutionalism.

More substantively, he argued that the various Canadian law societies had neither statutory authority nor any inherent power to act as legislator, police officer, and judge in matters of professional ethics: "If it were proposed to make the Code a Penal Code violation of which would render the offender liable to disbarment, legislation would be necessary, and many considerations would arise ... which to my mind would be fatal to the proposition."[69] Conversely, a merely hortative code would be without benefit as being too "much like drawing up a Code of Etiquette to make a gentleman."[70] Lawyers should be encouraged through their training and formal education to behave as "liberal" and "learned" men and to aspire to the highest standard of conduct of a "scholar, gentleman, and Christian," Riddell said. That, however, was "the whole of the law and the prophets."[71]

A Code of Professional Conduct imposing only this general duty would be "superfluous, unnecessary."[72] Conversely, he argued that the precision aspired to by penal law was unattainable. First, "any attempts to particularize would be dangerous":[73] it would inevitably lead lawyers to conclude that anything not expressly prohibited was allowed. They would likely give themselves the benefit of doubt in construing ambiguity or omission, and "the dishonest lawyer's ingenuity will enable him to misconstrue language with some plausibility."[74] The broader the language used, the greater the danger of "fraud lurking in generalities";[75] yet highly precise language would seem to authorize behaviour falling below the standards of a "scholar, gentleman, and Christian."[76]

Riddell also feared "artificial conscience." This would arise if it were assumed that literally being in violation of a written rule "is morally wrong, however innocent it may be in fact."[77] Any code precise enough to give concrete guidance would create circumstances in which morality pointed in one direction while a specific rule pointed in another. In the hurly-burly of practice, he pointed out, "[c]ircumstances are so different that what looks like oppression in the abstract case is plain dealing and good business in the concrete."[78] Specific rules, whether developed as a matter of convenience or simply reflecting generally appropriate behaviour, cannot, by definition, do justice in extraordinary circumstances.[79] The particular examples Riddell cited in support of this line of argument indicate that significant concerns relating to civil liberties and class justice arise when ethical codes are enforced by the organized legal profession. Strict enforcement of general rules might lead to repression and social injustice. He pointed to four particular circumstances where problems might arise:

- a rule that, by appearing for a client, a lawyer represented his belief in the rightness of the cause
- a hypothetical situation in which a solicitor begins foreclosure proceedings for a twenty-five-cent shortfall in mortgage payments
- the rule against champerty
- the prohibition of contingent or conditional fees.

Each of Riddell's illustrations raised issues relating to fundamental civil liberties, the integrity of the legal system, or the capacity of law to deliver on its promise of equality for even the humblest persons.

Riddell strongly objected to one American bar association's rule that a lawyer's "appearance in Court should be deemed equivalent to an assertion on his honour that in his opinion his client's case is one proper for judicial determination." Any such rule could have a chilling effect on lawyers asked to represent unpopular clients and constrain them from pressing the limits of law (good or bad) in court. It would require lawyers to become, in effect, judges of their clients – judges who would hear no argument, who would not give reasons for their decisions, who may be biased for undisclosed reasons, and whose decisions were made in secret, without possibility of review. Riddell would have nothing to do with any such rule:

> [T]he client is entitled to the services of his lawyer to enforce any claim or defence which is not dishonest; the client is entitled to the full and candid opinion of his lawyer, but when that is given he is entitled to have his case put before the Court whatever may be the lawyer's opinion on the law. Neither Court nor client is at all concerned with the opinion of counsel – the client demands, the court enforces the law, as it is found to be – that is the duty of the Court, the right of the client.[80]

Identifying the lawyer with the client as closely as such a rule would suggest might deprive the accused of the cherished constitutional right to be presumed innocent until proven guilty. The consequences would likely be disproportionately felt by the poor or otherwise marginalized individuals and groups.

Addressing his second illustration, Riddell said that the behaviour of any solicitor who started foreclosure proceedings for a minuscule shortfall "would be strongly animadverted upon by the Code builders." Particular circumstances might render such action justifiable, however. The example he provided involved a hypothetical situation in which a mortgagor had long engaged in petty dishonesty by a "long series of attempts to defraud his creditor out of small sums." In such circumstances, the apparently malicious foreclosure action is in truth a matter of "simple self-defence."[81] In that case, the "unethical" foreclosure is necessary to protect the client and the legal system from the corrosive effects of petty dishonesty: professional "ethics" in such a case threatens system integrity.

The common law rule against champerty and related prohibitions on contingent or conditional fees were said to be "in the same category" and raise similar issues.[82] A situation might arise, he said, in which a poor person is unable to enforce a perfectly legitimate legal right because of costs unless a solicitor is willing to work in return for a portion of what might be won in litigation. Riddell observed that although "it may be good business and for the advantage in common of both parties, ... the Court says it is bad morals."[83] Such arrangements were then illegal in Ontario, but Riddell rejected the notion that an underlying ethical principle was at stake. It might be in the interest of the state that there be an end of lawsuits (*interest reipublicae ut sit finis litium*), but "that does not mean that it would be for the advantage of people at large, that there should be no law suits – so long as injustice prevails a lawsuit to end an injustice is infinitely better – and, I add, infinitely more in harmony with the genius of our people – than passive submission to injustice."[84] The class dimensions to the prohibitions on champerty, maintenance, and contingency fees – long noted by lawyers, historians, and legal scholars[85] – were thus clearly appreciated by Mr. Justice Riddell. The common law's promise of equality before the law rests on equality of access to legal services, and contingency fees are a powerful device in ensuring this. He acknowledged that different considerations might apply to the solicitors' and barristers' branches of the Canadian legal professions and that "there are reasons of prudence which may prevent the barrister from having anything to do with the subject matter of litigation or with contingent fees." Nonetheless, Riddell insisted that "the reasons are reasons of prudence and not of morals," even with respect to barristers.[86]

Codification

Despite Riddell's warnings, the Canadian Bar Association approved a code of professional ethics the following year. One thousand copies were disseminated.[87] Alberta and Manitoba made instruction in professional ethics a significant part of the curriculum for trainee lawyers, and the new code was distributed to law students, rapidly becoming part of legal education across the country.[88] In the first half of 1921, the Canadian Bar Association's Canons of Ethics were adopted by provincial law societies in British Columbia, Alberta, Saskatchewan, Manitoba, and Ontario.[89] In 1922, the Committee on Legal

Ethics stated that "[t]he value of the disciplinary powers cannot be overestimated" and that enforcement of the ethical rules was best left to "the Disciplinary Committees of the governing bodies of the various Law Societies of the different provinces."[90] The momentum was unstoppable.

The code had been drafted with Riddell's cautions in mind.[91] Of five short paragraphs in the preamble, the first three assert repeatedly that the specific duties outlined are not exhaustive of a lawyer's ethical duties. The Canons are premised on the understanding that a lawyer's special role as "a minister of justice, an officer of the Courts, his client's advocate, and a member of an ancient, honorable and learned profession"[92] requires ethical commitments beyond those of others. The code then sets out duties "To the State" (4 canons), "To the Court" (4 canons), "To the Client" (11 canons[93]), "To His Fellow Lawyer" (4 canons) and "To Himself" (7 canons[94]). A lawyer's "right to undertake the defence of a person accused of crime, regardless of his own personal opinion," was preserved.[95] Contingency fees and comparable arrangements continued to be prohibited unless "by law expressly sanctioned."[96]

The important issue for present purposes is not the content of the 1920 code[97] but how and why it came about at all. The forceful arguments of opponents in Canada and unanimous disapproval of the legal professions' leaders in the United Kingdom were insufficient to resist this innovation. The lack of any Canadian traditions of ethical policing makes the momentum all the more curious. In part, the answer is found in the forcefulness of the personalities involved. The efforts of individuals such as Sir James Aikins and Manitoba Chief Justice Mathers, and the advocacy of individuals such as E.F.B. Johnston[98] and Dr. James Muir,[99] were extraordinary. They were formidable individuals and persistent in pursuit of their goals. The persuasive influence of American innovations should not be underestimated, especially given deep connections between leading Canadian lawyers and their American counterparts.[100] Moreover, there had been significant earlier Canadian efforts in this direction. Many lawyers in the prairie west had supported the development of a code of ethics before the Canadian Bar Association emerged.[101]

The very idea of what it means to be a professional lay at the core. Professional prerogatives and privileges tend to be most questioned in times of populist politics. The rapidly changing social and economic conditions of the early twentieth century and the ascendance of populism (whether expressed in Progressive or United Farmer politics or in the sort of mass politics that generated the Winnipeg General Strike[102]) could not be ignored. The legal profession was called upon to justify itself to a wider public in new ways.[103] Like his British correspondents, Riddell assumed that lawyers' commitment to the collective good and their trustworthiness would be widely appreciated by society at large. His assumptions had deep roots, but no longer fit the temper of the times.

The more rule-bound approach favoured by the American Bar Association and its Canadian counterparts emerged from a recognition that old-style privileges and their traditional, paternalistic rationales were unlikely to withstand the cultural and political changes of the era.[104] In place of reliance upon a generalized professional culture and gentlemanly status as legitimating devices, reformers sought to substitute demonstrably rigorous education, more thorough training, "moral" screening, and ethical policing: if the new populism demanded that professions make good on their claims of superior expertise and high standards of conduct, lawyers were ready and able to respond.

It is no surprise that the momentum was greatest in the prairie west and most resisted in older, more settled places.[105] British traditions and institutions were most vulnerable in the new provinces of Canada. Although spurred on by populist politics, professional reform did not partake of its character. Reforming lawyers sought to ensure the continuation of cherished institutions in a new era. Their invocations of the democratic character of the age and the social fluidity of the new world pointed to the need for intelligent adaptation aimed at preservation, not destruction, of the profession they loved. Although "ethics policing" had a repressive side, this was no accident. As Riddell had sought to demonstrate, the new Canons, even with their nod to his concerns, reflected a conception of the ideal lawyer that was explicitly skewed against non-elite lawyers and thus their clients.[106] Both the fear that lawyers representing working-class clients besmirched professionalism and express nativism shaped the Canadian Bar Association's formulation of professional ethics. Thirty years after the first massive wave of European immigration to the prairie west, fear of the foreigner was rife.[107] The fear that inadequately socialized men of "foreign" stock would become lawyers followed anxiety about the immigrant. It was not all ethnocentrism, elitism, class bias, conservatism, and defensiveness in the face of profound democratic urgings, however. A genuine commitment to the ideal of ethical legal practice and a deeply felt series of commitments to both ethics and law, understood from their own British Canadian perspectives, motivated the lawyers who developed Canada's first code of professional conduct.

Drawing heavily on a new US-grown "common sense" about professionalism, the transformation of the Canadian legal professions from loose guilds to disciplinary regimes had begun.

Appendix: 1919 Survey of British Chiefs of Bench and Bar Regarding Codes of Professional Ethics

In 1919, Mr. Justice William Renwick Riddell conducted a survey of "the Chiefs of Bench and Bar" in England, Ireland, and Scotland, regarding codes of professional ethics. Below are key findings from this survey.[108]

England

Lord Chancellor:
The Lord Chancellor simply indicated that there was no written code governing the etiquette and conduct of English barristers. "[T]here is ... a considerable floating body of practice and tradition in these matters, which for the most part, is not committed to writing."

Lord Chief Justice:
"[N]o such written code of ethics exists in England, nor is His Lordship of opinion that there is any need for it."

Attorney-General:
"The Attorney-General does not think that a written code is desirable. Such a code could not be complete, because changing circumstances are bound to give rise to new questions from time to time."

Chairman of the General Council of the Bar:
The Chairman of the General Council of the Bar simply indicated that there was no written code governing the etiquette and conduct of English barristers.

Ireland

Lord Chancellor:
"[T]here are only a few rules, pertaining to retainers for the legal profession in Ireland, and ... he does not consider any further written code of ethics to be necessary."

Lord Chief Justice:
"There is no written code of ethics for the legal profession in Ireland, and the necessity for one has not been felt." He argued that there was an "esprit de corps" that enforced a "spirit of discipline which is absent in England."

Attorney-General:
"No code of legal ethics exists for the Irish Bar. The ethics of the profession are controlled by the public opinion of the Bar. The Benchers of the King's Inn exercise jurisdiction over members of the Bar in cases of violation of professional decorum. The standard of professional conduct is also reviewed by the Bar Council, but there is no coercive jurisdiction in that body."

Chairman, Incorporated Law Society:
"[T]here is no written code of ethics for the legal profession in Ireland, and the President does not approve of such a code."

Scotland

Lord Justice General:
"[T]here is no written code of legal ethics. There is, however, an unwritten code which is regarded by all Scottish lawyers as sufficient."

Lord Justice Clerk:
"We have no written code of ethics – our law of practice in the matter depends on practice and tradition ... Our Dean of Faculty is the arbiter for our Bar ... I think it would be very difficult, and I think somewhat dangerous, to formulate a written code of ethics."

Lord Justice Advocate:
"There is in existence no written code of ethics for the legal profession in Scotland. There are a few rules regulating counsel's retainers which ... have been more or less officially published ... but even these rules are no more than a formulation of professional custom ... I held office as Dean for several years; and, in accordance with the practice of my predecessors, I referred all cases of professional conduct which were referred to me, to solution in accordance with the simple rules of honour ... it is obvious that the application of the rules of strictly honourable conduct consorts very ill with any attempt to reduce the rules of honour to a written code."

Notes

An earlier version of this chapter appeared as "Becoming 'Ethical': Lawyers' Professional Ethics in Early Twentieth Century Canada" (1991) 20 Man. L.J. 227. It has been revised and reprinted here with permission.

1 As quoted in Canadian Bar Association, "Report of the Committee on Legal Education and Ethics" (1919) 4 Reports of the Canadian Bar Association 129 at 130-31.

2 *Ibid.*

3 "What Is a Profession? The Rise of the Legal Profession in Antiquity" (1944) Part 1 Notre Dame Lawyer 203 at 204.

4 *Ibid.* at 205.

5 *Ibid.* at 206. Compare E. Durkheim, *Professional Ethics and Civil Morals* (London: Routledge and Kegan Paul, 1957), esp. at 3-13.

6 H.W. Arthurs, "Code of Professional Ethics" in H.W. Arthurs, D.L. Mills, and G. Starr, "Materials on the Canadian Legal Profession" (York University School of Law, 1985) [unpublished] 247 at 247. S. Arthurs also argues that the service orientation, the notion of trust, and the abhorrence of *caveat emptor* as a foundation for client/professional relations create a radical distinction of "profession" from "business." See S. Arthurs, "Discipline in the Legal Profession in Ontario" (1970) 7 Osgoode Hall L.J. 235 ["Discipline"].

7 See, *e.g.*, R. Gordon, "The Independence of Lawyers" (1988) 68 B.U.L. Rev. 1; R.L. Abel, "Taking Professionalism Seriously" in *Annual Survey of American Law*, vol. 1 (New York: New York University School of Law, 1989) 41.

8 See A. Esau, "Teaching Professional Ethics and Responsibility at Law School: What, How, and Why?" in R. Matas and D. McCawley, eds., *Legal Education in Canada* (Montreal: Federation of Law Societies, 1987) 308; A. Esau, "Teaching Professional Responsibility in Law School" (1988) 11 Dal. L.J. 403.

9 E.N. Griswold, *Law and Lawyers in the United States: The Common Law under Stress* (London: Stevens and Sons, 1964); A.-H. Chroust, *The Rise of the Legal Profession in America*, vol. 2, *The Revolution and the Post-Revolutionary Era* (Norman: University of Oklahoma Press, 1965); T.J. Johnson, *Professions and Power* (London: Macmillan,1972); M.S. Larson, *The Rise of Professionalism: A Sociological Analysis* (Berkeley: University of California Press, 1979); ch. 7 in D. Boorstin, *The Americans: The Colonial Experience* (Harmondsworth, UK: Penguin, 1965); J.F. Kett, *The Formation of the American Medical Profession: The Role of Institutions, 1780-1860* (New Haven, CT: Yale University Press, 1968); R.L. Abel, *American Lawyers* (New York: Oxford University Press, 1989) at 10 and 40. Note, however, that "[a] revisionist historiography (Bloomfield, 1976; Calhoun, 1965) no longer uncritically accedes to Roscoe Pound's (1953) sweeping judgment that 'an Age of Decadence' reigned from ... 1836 to ... 1870" (*i.e.*, the period of Jacksonian attacks): W. Espeland and T.C. Halliday, *Resurrecting the Dead: Biography and Death Rituals in the Reconstruction of Professional Legitimacy by Chicago Lawyers, 1870-1900* (American Bar Foundation Working Paper Series, 1988).

10 See Chapters 4, 7, 8, and 11 in this volume.

11 P.L. Berger and T. Luckmann, *The Social Construction of Reality: A Treatise in the Sociology of Knowledge* (New York: Anchor Books, 1967); T.S. Kuhn, *The Structure of Scientific Revolutions*, 2d ed. (Chicago: University of Chicago Press,1970). Enormous schools of legal thought, including critical race theory, postcolonial legal studies, feminist legal studies, and critical inquiry, generally emphasize the extent to which social location matters in understandings of law and ethics.

12 J. Auerbach, *Unequal Justice: Lawyers and Social Change in Modern America* (New York: Oxford University Press, 1976); R.L. Abel, "Why Does the A.B.A. Promulgate Ethical Rules?" (1981) 59 Tex. L. Rev. 639; D.L. Rhode, "Why the A.B.A. Bothers: A Functional Perspective on Professional Codes" (1981) 59 Tex. L. Rev. 689; Deborah L. Rhode, *In the Interests of Justice: Reforming the Legal Profession* (Oxford: Oxford University Press, 2003); Deborah L. Rhode, *Access to Justice* (Oxford: Oxford University Press, 2004); Chapters 7 and 8 in this volume.

13 C.I. Kyer and J.E. Bickenbach, *The Fiercest Debate: Cecil A. Wright, the Benchers, and Legal Education in Ontario, 1923-1957* (Toronto: Osgoode Society for Canadian Legal History, 1987) at 72, regarding increasing standards of legal education: "The motives behind the movement towards higher uniform standards were not always above reproach. Jerold Auerbach has argued, for example, that the greatest part of the hostility felt by the academics and practising lawyers towards the 'propriety' of night schools was a resentment of foreign-born, Jewish, and black lawyers who had gained access to the profession through the less expensive night schools. If this is true of the United States ... there is almost no evidence to suggest that the Canadian attempts to standardize and upgrade legal education in the 1920s and later were similarly motivated by racism or xenophobia. [However] It is foolish to suggest that such attitudes were unknown in Canada, and it is not difficult to find in the Canada Law Times and other journals editorials warning of the 'dilution' of professional competence that would result if immigration policies were not tightened."

14 H. Arthurs, "Book Review of *Unequal Justice* by J.S. Auerbach" (1977) 27 U.T.L.J. 513; Francesca Barlett, Reid Mortensen, and Kieran Tranter, eds., *Alternative Perspectives on Lawyers and Legal Ethics: Reimagining the Profession* (London and New York: Routledge, 2011).

15 For a fascinating case study of the complex interrelationships between professional self-government and the larger community, with particular reference to developments in Western Canada, see P.J. Giffen, "Social Control and Professional Self-Government: A Study of the Legal Profession in Canada" in S.D. Clark, ed., *Urbanism and the Changing Canadian Society* (Toronto: University of Toronto Press, 1961) 117.

16 See W.W. Pue, "Rethinking Professionalism: Taking the Professions in Early Modern England Seriously" (1989) 4 C.J.L.S. 175.

17 See the work of American legal theorist C. Menkel-Meadow, "Exploring a Research Agenda of the Feminization of the Legal Profession: Theories of Gender and Social Change" (1989) 14 Law & Soc. Inquiry 289; Constance Backhouse, *Colour-Coded: A Legal History of Racism in Canada, 1900-1950* (Toronto: University of Toronto Press/Osgoode Society for Canadian Legal History, 1999); Harold J. Dick, *Lawyers of Mennonite Background in Western Canada before the Second World War* (Winnipeg: Legal Research Institute of the University of Manitoba, 1993); Carrie Menkel-Meadow and Michael Wheeler, eds., *What's Fair: Ethics for Negotiators*, 1st ed. (San Francisco: Jossey-Bass, 2004); César Arjona, Arif A. Jamal, Carrie Menkel-Meadow, Victor V. Ramraj, and Francisco Satiro, "Senses of Sen: Reflections on Amartya Sen's Ideas of Justice" (2012) 8 International Journal of Law in Context 155; Joan Brockman, "Racism and Legal Culture: Is There Room for Diversity in the Legal Profession?" (2008) 45 Alta. L. Rev. 75; Nick Blomley, "Homelessness, Rights and the Delusions of Property" (2009) 30 Urban Geography 577; I. Braverman, N. Blomley, D. Delaney, and A. Kedar, eds., *The Expanding Spaces of Law: A Timely Legal Geography* (Stanford, CA: Stanford University Press, 2014).

18 Generally useful sources on these matters include: W.R. Riddell, *The Legal Profession in Upper Canada in Its Early Periods* (Toronto: Law Society of Upper Canada, 1916); W.R. Riddell, "Women as Practitioners of Law" (1918) 18 Journal of Comparative Legislation and International Law 200; W.R. Riddell, *The Bar and Courts of the Province of Upper Canada or Ontario* (Toronto: Macmillan, 1928) [*Bar and Courts*]; Peter M. Sibenik, "The Doorkeepers: The Governance of Territorial and Alberta Lawyers, 1885-1928" (MA Thesis, University of Calgary, 1984); Peter M. Sibenik, "'The Black Sheep': The Disciplining of Territorial and Alberta Lawyers, 1885-1928" (1988) 3 C.J.L.S. 109; Curtis Cole, "A Developmental Market: Competition and Professional Standards in the Ontario Legal Profession, 1881-1936" (1983) 6 Can.-U.S.L.J. 125; Curtis Cole, "'A Hand to Shake the Tree of Knowledge': Legal Education in Ontario, 1871-1889, Symposium on Education and the Law" (1986) 17 Interchange 15; Curtis Johnson Cole, "'A Learned and Honourable Body': The Professionalization of the Ontario Bar, 1867-1929" (PhD Dissertation, University of Western Ontario, 1987).

19 There was, of course, an abortive effort to launch a Canadian Bar Association in the 1890s. See P. Girard, "The Roots of a Professional Renaissance: Lawyers in Nova Scotia, 1850-1910," in D. Gibson and W.W. Pue, eds., *Glimpses of Canadian Legal History* (Winnipeg: Legal Research Institute, 1991) 155.

20 See A.Z. Reed, *Bulletin 15: Training for the Public Profession of the Law: Historical Development and Principal Contemporary Problems of Legal Education in the United States with Some Account of Conditions in England and Canada* (New York: Carnegie Foundation, 1921) [*Bulletin 15*]; A.Z. Reed, *Bulletin 21: Present-Day Law Schools in the United States and Canada* (New York: Carnegie Foundation, 1928); J.P.S. McLaren, "The History of Legal Education in Common Law Canada" in R. Matas and D. McCawley, eds., *Legal Education in Canada* (Montreal: Federation of Law Societies, 1987) ["History of Legal Education"].

21 The Law Society of Upper Canada is arguably the oldest professional organization of lawyers in the common law world, tracing its origins to 1797: Riddell, *Bar and Courts, supra* note 18 at 47-89. To characterize the LSUC thus depends, of course, on how one interprets the variegated history of the English Inns of Court. See B. Abel-Smith and R. Stevens, *Lawyers*

and the Courts: A Sociological Study of the English Legal System, 1750-1965 (London: Heinemann, 1967).

22 Reed, *Bulletin 15, supra* note 20 at 26. This is an important point for it makes complete nonsense of any argument that fundamental democratic traditions make it important that the legal profession be immune from political governance. Whatever the merit of such arguments in the United Kingdom, the legal professions in Canada are, in their origins, entirely creatures of the state.

23 Riddell, *Bar and Courts, supra* note 18 at 112.

24 W.R. Riddell, "A Code of Legal Ethics" (1919) 4 Reports of the Canadian Bar Association 136 at 139 ["A Code of Legal Ethics"]; an analogous pattern of professional discipline appeared in matters relating to the English Bar during the nineteenth century. See Chapter 8 in this volume.

25 Appointed to the Manitoba bench in 1905, Mathers developed an excellent reputation as a trial judge and was elevated to the position of Chief Justice of the Court of King's Bench in 1910. He chaired the 1915 provincial inquiry into the construction of the Winnipeg Law Courts and the Legislative Building and a 1919 federal Royal Commission into the circumstances surrounding the Winnipeg General Strike. He played a leading role, with E.K. Williams, in the development of the Canadian Bar Association's Canons of Legal Ethics (adopted in 1920). Said to be a man of "uncompromising sternness," he died in 1927. See D. Gibson and L. Gibson, *Substantial Justice: Law and Lawyers in Manitoba, 1670-1970* (Winnipeg: Peguis, 1972) at 198, 201, 222-23, 236, 239, 251.

26 T.G. Mathers, "Legal Ethics" (Address to the Manitoba Bar Association, 19 May1920), Winnipeg, Archive of Western Canadian Legal History (Acc. No. 49.A2221) at 5. This paper was also presented at the 1920 meeting of the Canadian Bar Association: (1920) 5 Proceedings of the Canadian Bar Association 268.

27 *Ibid.*; "Report of the Committee of the Province of Quebec on Professional Ethics" (1919) 4 Reports of the Canadian Bar Association 132.

28 Gibson and Gibson, *Substantial Justice, supra* note 25 at 252, indicate: "The Manitoba Law Society's disciplinary powers were significantly strengthened in 1926 by an amendment authorizing the benchers to suspend or disbar members of the profession without prior judicial intervention. Previously, the benchers had been compelled to apply to a King's Bench judge if they wanted a lawyer suspended or disbarred; now they could do so on their own authority, subject only to an appeal to the Court of Appeal."

29 In 1921, Alberta began a long-drawn-out process of transferring disciplinary power from the courts to the Law Society, partly in response to a provincial Attorney-General's Department memorandum indicating that, absent active Law Society policing of its members, "the people will probably take the matter into their own hands and may possibly do some damage" (as quoted in Sibenik, "Doorkeepers," *supra* note 18 at 149). Grounds for suspension, or disbarment and striking from the rolls, in the early years included defalcation, criminal conviction, breach of legislation governing the professional activities of lawyers, any activity for which the English superior courts could strike a solicitor, "professional misconduct," and "conduct unbecoming an advocate" (*ibid.* at 145-47). See also Sibenik, "Black Sheep," *supra* note 18.

30 Mathers, *supra* note 26 at 5-6. For a very useful discussion of the course of professional development in Alberta, see Sibenik, "Doorkeepers," *supra* note 18; Sibenik, "Black Sheep," *supra* note 18.

31 Reed, *Bulletin 15, supra* note 20 at 26.

32 Mathers, *supra* note 26 at 6. For a comparative discussion, see J.R.S. Forbes, *The Divided Legal Profession in Australia: History, Rationalisation and Rationale* (Sydney: Law Book Company, 1979).

33 W.J. McWhinney, KC, "Ontario Bar Association" (1916) 52 Canadian Law Journal 1 at 4.

34 Under the leadership of Dr. James Muir, who drafted the earliest code of legal ethics intended for adoption by the governing body of any Canadian legal profession. Muir was then president of the Law Society of Alberta. The Alberta draft code is reproduced as "Suggested Canons of Ethics Prepared by James Muir, KIC, LL.D., President of the Law Society of Alberta" (1919) 4 Reports of the Canadian Bar Association 133 ["Suggested Canons of Ethics"].

35 Canadian Bar Association, *supra* note 1.

36 President of the Canadian Bar Association from 1915 until his death in 1929; Lieutenant-Governor of Manitoba from 1916. He has been described as follows: "A humourless man, of Methodist persuasion and consuming ambition, he almost invariably put business before pleasure, and found little time to develop close personal relationships. Although capable of impulsive generosity, he had a reputation for niggardliness. Nevertheless, there were few in the profession who would deny that he had been an uncommonly competent lawyer, or that he had devoted as much of his talent and energy to the interests of his province and his profession as to the amassing of personal wealth. Sir James Aikins' record of public service, as a bencher for fully fifty years (during which time he served as secretary, treasurer and president of the Law Society), as founder, long-time president, and generous patron of the Can. Bar Assn., and as Lieutenant-Governor of Manitoba, has few parallels." He also served as president of the Conference of Commissioners on Uniformity of Legislation in Canada from its origins in 1918 through 1923 (Gibson and Gibson, *Substantial Justice, supra* note 25 at 252, 255-56). An important study of Aikins's legal career is D. Gibson and L. Gibson, "Sir James Aikins' Seamless Web: Finding Fortune and Fame as a Lawyer in the Adolescent Canadian West" (1992) 21 Man. L.J. 161.

37 Sir James Aikins, "The Advancement of the Science of Jurisprudence in Canada" (1915) 51 Canadian Law Journal 161 at 162 ["Advancement"].

38 *Ibid.* at 165.

39 *Ibid.* at 162-63. Aikins was by this time a self-made millionaire – with the help of his father's influence.

40 *Ibid.* at 163-64: "Time was when the lawyer was regarded as aloof from the practical affairs of the world, as the learned and dignified aristocrat of society who did not concern himself with the daily duties of common life of the struggle of the people to improve their condition. Now, in our democratic country the members of the profession are not only with the people, but of the people, working among men, advising in their personal affairs, sympathising in their efforts, guiding in their business, aiding in their social movements for reform, taking share in all the departments of public government, yet, withal, maintaining the professional ideals of the past, their intellectual attainments, dignity, strength of honour and independence of character, which will not cringe before courts or be carried away by popular emotions or a hostile press." C. Berger, in *The Sense of Power: Studies in the Ideas of Canadian Imperialism, 1867-1914* (Toronto: University of Toronto Press, 1970), indicates that the sense that Canadians could lead the Empire by melding British tradition with the "genius" of a new, northern people was pervasive among early-twentieth-century English Canadian elites.

41 Utilitarian notions such as usefulness to the business community and practical learning were powerfully employed by English attorneys of the 1850s in their conflicts with the barristers' profession. See Chapter 4 in this volume.

42 E.F.B. Johnson, KC, "The Honour of the Profession" (1915) 51 Canadian Law Journal 178 at 178-79.

43 McWhinney, *supra* note 33 at 6.

44 The contrast with both British and American traditions, emphasizing the legal profession's role in protecting citizens from the state, is noteworthy.

45 Sir James Aikins, "The Legal Profession in Relation to Ethics, Education and Emolument" (1919) 55 Canadian Law Journal 335 at 335 (Presidential address to the Winnipeg meeting of the Canadian Bar Association).

46 *Ibid.* at 336.

47 *Ibid.* at 338.

48 R.L. Abel, "Comparative Sociology of Legal Professions: An Exploratory Essay" (1985) American Bar Foundation Research Journal 1; R.L. Abel, "Book Review of *The Rise of Professionalism* by M.S. Larson" (1976) 6 British Journal of Law and Society 82; M.S. Larson, *The Rise of Professionalism* (Berkeley: University of California Press, 1979); R.L. Abel, *The Legal Profession in England and Wales* (Oxford: B.H. Blackwell, 1988); R.L. Abel and P. Lewis, eds., *Lawyers in Society: The Common Law World* (Berkeley: University of California Press, 1988); R.L. Abel and P. Lewis, eds., *Lawyers in Society,* vol. 3 (Berkeley: University of California Press, 1989); R.L. Abel, *American Lawyers* (New York: Oxford University Press, 1989).

49 As a point of comparison, it is worth noting that the American Bar Association Canons of Ethics, which were reproduced in (1918) 4 Reports of the Canadian Bar Association 220 at 220, include the following as a preamble: "In America, where the stability of courts and of all departments of government rests with the approval of the people, it is peculiarly essential that the system of establishing and dispensing justice be developed to a high point of efficiency and so maintained that the public shall have absolute confidence in the integrity and impartiality of its administration. The future of the republic, to a great extent, depends upon our maintenance of justice pure and unsullied. It cannot be so maintained unless the conduct and the motives of the members of our profession are such as to merit the approval of all just men."

50 The extent of this concern is demonstrated by an article from *Law Notes,* reproduced in "Unauthorised Practice of Law" (1919) 55 Canadian Law Journal 375 and introduced as follows: "This Journal has always taken the ground and frequently referred to the wrongs suffered by the legal profession at the hands of the host of unlicensed practitioners and conveyancers. No remedy has been found, or rather none seems possible when many of our Provincial legislators are the robbers or are in various ways in alliance with them." The article reproduced from the US journal proceeded to protest the massive volume of real estate transactions documented by nonlawyers.

51 J.P. Heinz and E.O. Laumann, *Chicago Lawyers: The Social Structure of the Bar* (New York: Russell Sage Foundation, 1982).

52 Auerbach, *supra* note 12, esp. at 42ff. See Chapters 7, 8, and 11 in this volume. For a more recent British comparison, see Z. Bankowski and G. Mungham, *Images of Law* (London: Routledge and Kegan Paul, 1976), esp. ch.3, "Up Against the Law."

53 Aikins, "Advancement," *supra* note 37 at 162-63.

54 E.F.B. Johnson, *supra* note 42 at 184. Compare McWhinney, *supra* note 33 at 6: "The successful lawyer of to-day keeps his clients out of court unless the stake is worthwhile and the merits on his side. The speculator litigant as well as the legal ambulance chaser are few and much discouraged."

55 E.P. Thompson, *Whigs and Hunters: The Origin of the Black Act* (New York: Pantheon Books, 1975). For critiques of his rule-of-law thesis, see M.J. Horwitz, "The Rule of Law: An Unqualified Human Good?" (1977) 86 Yale L.J. 561; A. Merritt, "The Nature and Function of Law" (1980) 7 British Journal of Law and Society 194. See also G. Marquis, "Doing Justice to 'British Justice': Law, Ideology and Canadian Historiography" in W.W. Pue and B. Wright, eds., *Canadian Perspectives on Law and Society: Issues in Legal History* (Ottawa: Carleton University Press, 1988) [*Canadian Perspectives*].

56 "Professional Ethics" (1910) 46 Canadian Law Journal 531.

57 E.F.B. Johnson, *supra* note 42.

58 "Report of the Committee on Legal Ethics" (1919) 55 Canadian Law Journal 294 at 296-97. This comment is made just as the children of the first great waves of Eastern European immigration to the prairie west would have been establishing their careers and at the height of postwar xenophobia. For an intriguing general account of immigration and culture in the prairie west, see ch. 11, "Immigrant Communities 1870-1940: The Struggle for Cultural Survival" in G. Friesen, *The Canadian Prairies: A History* (Toronto: University of Toronto Press, 1987) 242. A full study of the ethnic demography of the profession remains to be undertaken. An account of the increasing ethnic tensions that characterized Winnipeg in the period leading up to the 1919 General Strike is found in D. Avery, "The Radical Alien and the Winnipeg General Strike of 1919" in C. Berger and R. Cook, eds., *The West and the Nation: Essays in Honour of W.L. Morton* (Toronto: McClelland and Stewart, 1976) 209.

59 Canadian Bar Association, *supra* note 1.

60 *Ibid.* at 131.

61 "Suggested Canons of Ethics," *supra* note 34.

62 "Report of the Committee of the Province of Quebec on Professional Ethics," *supra* note 27.

63 Riddell, "A Code of Legal Ethics," *supra* note 24.

64 Canadian Bar Association, *supra* note 1 at 130.

65 Along with Hamilton Cassels, Edwin Bell, and others: *ibid.* at 130.

66 "Suggested Canons of Ethics," *supra* note 34 at 138.

67 *Ibid.* at 137-38.

68 *Ibid.* at 138.

69 *Ibid.* at 139.

70 *Ibid.* This view was apparently shared by Dr. Scott of Edmonton, whom Riddell credits in a note.

71 *Ibid.* at 139. Riddell's audience would have recognized the biblical allusion: "Jesus said unto him, Thou shalt love the Lord thy God with all thy heart, and with all thy soul, and with all thy mind. This is the first and great commandment. And the second *is* like unto it, Thou shalt love thy neighbour as thyself. On these two commandments hang all the law and the prophets" (Matthew 22:37-40 [KJV]).

72 *Ibid.* at 140.

73 *Ibid.*

74 *Ibid.* at 141.

75 *Ibid.* Riddell expressed this concern with the Latin maxim *dolus latet in generalibus* (in generalities lurks deception).

76 Interestingly, Riddell pointed to corporate behaviour – considering themselves "justified in acting in any way not forbidden by the Companies Act" – and US constitutional practice as providing the foundation for this fear: *ibid.* at 148-49 nn. 5 and 6.

77 *Ibid.* at 141.

78 *Ibid.*

79 *Ibid.*: "It is well known that a statute against a particular course of conduct will inevitably bring about a state of public opinion that such conduct is morally wrong, however innocent it may in fact be."

80 "Suggested Canons of Ethics," *supra* note 34 at 140-41.

81 *Ibid.* at 141.

82 *Ibid.* at 143.

83 *Ibid.* at 142.

84 *Ibid.* 142.

85 See Chapters 8 and 11 in this volume. Auerbach, *supra* note 12; R.L. Abel, "Why Does the A.B.A. Promulgate Ethical Rules?" (1980-81) 59 Tex. L. Rev. 639.

86 "Suggested Canons of Ethics," *supra* note 34 at 149 n. 10.
87 "Report of the Committee on Legal Ethics" (1921) 6 Proceedings of the Canadian Bar Association 238 at 238.
88 *Ibid.*; "Report of the Committee on Legal Ethics" (1922) 7 Proceedings of the Canadian Bar Association 256; "Report of the Committee on Legal Ethics" (1923) 8 Proceedings of the Canadian Bar Association.
89 "Report of the Committee on Legal Ethics" (1921), *supra* note 87.
90 "Report of the Committee on Legal Ethics" (1922), *supra* note 88.
91 "Canons of Legal Ethics" (1920) 5 Proceedings of the Canadian Bar Association 261.
92 *Ibid.* at 261.
93 Four of which relate to permissible fee arrangements. Most of the rest more or less explicitly indicate that lawyers should not pursue their clients' interests too aggressively.
94 Including a prohibition on advertising, a duty to eradicate "unprofessional" practitioners, and a duty to hinder persons thought to demonstrate moral or educational deficiencies from being admitted to the Bar.
95 It is interesting, however, that this left it open to the interpretation that lawyers working in civil litigation might be taken as acting unethically when advancing causes that were of questionable merit: *expressio unius exclusio alterius* (to express one thing is to exclude another). Elsewhere, the canons prohibited stirring up litigation, especially in the area of personal injury claims. Given the importance of workplace injuries at the time, a class dimension is apparent.
96 Such arrangements were not expressly permitted under Canadian law at the time.
97 For an analysis of the code's provisions, see Mathers, *supra* note 26. See also Jonnette Watson Hamilton, "Metaphors of Lawyers' Professionalism" (1995) 33 Alta. L. Rev. 833.
98 E.F.B. Johnson, *supra* note 42.
99 "Suggested Canons of Ethics," *supra* note 34.
100 See, *e.g.*, "Address by Hon. William H. Taft on Legal Ethics" (1920) 5 Proceedings of the Canadian Bar Association 265. The influential "Report of the Committee on Legal Education and Ethics," *supra* note 1, demonstrates a considerable tone of intellectual deference to US leadership in this area. The ABA 1908 Canons were reproduced in (1918) 3 Reports of the Canadian Bar Association 220. See Bernard J. Hibbitts, "'Our Arctic Brethren': Canadian Law and Lawyers as Portrayed in American Legal Periodicals, 1829-1911" in Blaine Baker and Jim Philips, eds., *Essays in Canadian Law,* vol. 3, *In Honour of Richard Risk* (Toronto: University of Toronto Press, 1999); Philip Girard, "The Making of the Canadian Legal Profession: A Hybrid Heritage" (2014) 21 International Journal of the Legal Profession 145. L. Gibson's *A Proud Heritage: The First Hundred Years of Aikins, MacAulay and Thorvaldson* (Winnipeg: Aikins, MacAulay and Thorvaldson, 1993) points to Sir James Aikins's contacts with American Bar Association officials.
101 For example, on 15 April 1908, a Winnipeg newspaper reported: "BENCH SCORES BARRISTER, Judge Mathers in Setting Aside the Order for Substitution of Service's Case of *Czar v Proskouriakoff* Pleads for Code of Professional Conduct": in Law Society of Manitoba Scrapbook, 25 November 1907 to 31 December 1908 (Winnipeg, Manitoba Legal History Archives, Faculty of Law, University of Manitoba) at 52.
102 A useful overview of literature on the Winnipeg General Strike is provided in K. Kehler and A. Esau, "The Winnipeg General Strike Trials: Overview and Suggestions for Legal History Research" in K. Kehler and A. Esau, *Famous Manitoba Trials: The Winnipeg General Strike Trials – Research Source* (Winnipeg: Legal Research Institute, 1990) 1. See also Reihold Kramer and Tom Mitchell, *When the State Trembled: How A.J. Andrews and the Citizens' Committee Broke the Winnipeg General Strike* (Toronto: University of Toronto Press, 2010).
103 See Cole, "A Learned and Honourable Body," *supra* note 18.

104 For an intriguing comparative study, albeit one focused more on the intellectual structure of law, see D. Sugarman, "'A Hatred of Disorder': Legal Science, Liberalism and Imperialism" in P. Fitzpatrick, ed., *Dangerous Supplements* (London: Pluto, 1991) 34.

105 See R.L. Solomon, "Five Crises or One: The Concept of Legal Professionalism, 1925-1960" (American Bar Foundation Working Paper Series 9014) in Robert Nelson, David Trubek, and Rayman Solomon, eds., *Lawyers' Ideals and Lawyers' Practices: Professionalism and the Transformation of the American Legal Profession* (Ithaca, NY: Cornell University Press, 1992) 144.

106 The process is perhaps analogous to the larger process by which the "Enlightenment project" constructs an (abstracted) "ideal citizen" as a device that excludes others from participation in social and political life. Useful discussions that touch on this theme include: Sugarman, *supra* note 104; P. Fitzpatrick, "The Abstracts and Brief Chronicles of the Time: Supplementing Jurisprudence" in Fitzpatrick, *Dangerous Supplements, supra* note 104; P. Fitzpatrick, "'The Desperate Vacuum': Imperialism and Law in the Experience of Enlightenment" in A. Carty, ed., *Post-Modern Law: Enlightenment, Revolution and the Death of Man* (Edinburgh: Edinburgh University Press, 1990) 90.

107 Useful discussions of immigration patterns and ethnic relations are to be found in D.J. Hall, "Clifford Sifton: Immigration and Settlement Policy, 1896-1905" in H.D. Palmer, ed., *The Settlement of the West* (Calgary: University of Calgary, 1977); ch.1, "Strangers and Stereotypes: The Rise of Nativism, 1880-1920" in H. Palmer, *Patterns of Prejudice: A History of Nativism in Alberta* (Toronto: McClelland and Stewart, 1982) 17; Friesen, *supra* note 58 at 344-55, 404-7, 447.

108 Recorded in Riddell, "A Code of Legal Ethics," *supra* note 24 at 144-48.

PART 4

Challenging the Status Quo: Communists and Liberals

10

Gordon Martin, British Columbia Communist, 1948

Hindsight judges harshly.

Such has been the fate of those who blocked Gordon Martin's admission as a barrister a few years after the end of the war against fascism.[1] Martin held a recognized law degree, had served the required period of apprenticeship ("articles"), and met all other requirements for admission – save one. He was blacklisted by the organized legal profession's governing body (the Benchers) and the courts entirely because of his political beliefs. It was accepted that his "personal morals ... [could not] be questioned, that he was a hard worker at the University and conscientious in his work."[2] But he was a "Marxist communist."

The Benchers' judgment was severely criticized by some of their contemporaries, and history has condemned them.[3] One distinguished jurist, Roland Penner, criticized the incident as "a scandalous act of political discrimination ... [E]ven more scandalously, the courts in British Columbia upheld the Law Society's decision."[4] Vancouver lawyer Harry Rankin described the processes that left-wing applicants were put through as a "private inquisition," a "Star Chamber tribunal," a "witch hunt," and a "most undemocratic procedure ... simply political intimidation."[5] I have piled on too, accusing the Benchers of acting on a "whim" and the courts of substituting politics for legal reasoning and failing "miserably to live up to their role as guarantors of liberty."[6]

Such assessments bite, but they gloss far too quickly over the complicating contexts of mid-century administrative law and of then-prevalent notions of character and legal professionalism. An indication of the gap that separates their notions of character from ours is found in the words of the oaths required of new lawyers. Barristers were called upon to swear, "so help me God," their commitment to adhere to a distinct professional role:

> You are called to the degree of barrister to protect and defend the rights and interests of such persons as may employ you. You shall conduct all causes faithfully and to the best of your ability. *You shall neglect no man's interest, nor seek to destroy any man's property.* You shall not refuse causes of complaint reasonably founded, nor shall you promote suits upon frivolous pretences. You shall not pervert the law to favour or prejudice any man, but in all things shall conduct yourself truly and with integrity. In fine, the King's interests and your fellow subjects you shall uphold and maintain according to the constitution and the laws of this Province.[7]

Their oath (which was identical for solicitors) was in the following form:

> I, A.B. do sincerely promise and swear ... that I will be faithful and bear true allegiance to His Majesty King George VI as lawful Sovereign of Great Britain ... and of this Dominion of Canada, and that *I will defend him to the utmost of my power against all traitorous conspiracies* or attempts whatsoever which shall be made against his person, crown and dignity, and that *I will to my utmost endeavour to disclose and make known to His Majesty,* his heirs or successors, *all treasons or traitorous conspiracies and attempts which I shall know to be against him or any of them;* and all that I *do swear ... without any equivocation, mental evasion, or secret reservation. So help me God.*[8]

These words, along with the solicitors' special status as officers of the court and their understandings of the roles of the legal profession, steered the outcome. By contrast, today's Barristers' and Solicitors' Oaths in British Columbia expunge all reference to loyalty to Crown, country, or Constitution, along with obligations to "neglect no man's interest," to respect property, and to obstruct treason:

> Do you sincerely promise and swear (or affirm) that you will diligently, faithfully and to the best of your ability execute the offices of Barrister and Solicitor; that you will not promote suits upon frivolous pretences; that you will not pervert the law to favour or prejudice anyone; but in all things conduct yourself truly and with integrity; and that you will uphold the rule of law and the rights and freedoms of all persons according to the laws of Canada and of the Province of British Columbia?

The Benchers' Ruling

Martin's communism was beyond doubt. He had run for election to the provincial legislature as a Labour Progressive Party (Communist) candidate and

Gordon Martin. *Artray Studio photo (2360), courtesy of Vancouver Public Library*

was president of the University of British Columbia's student Communist Forum.[9] There was "nothing covert ... about him ... [H]e was a doctrinaire Communist."[10]

Upon applying for admission to the legal professions, Martin was called upon to demonstrate to the Benchers that he was a "fit and proper person." The Benchers' power was derived from the following provisions of the British Columbia *Legal Profession Act:*

> 39(3) They may call to the Bar and admit to practise as a barrister in British Columbia: –
>
> (*a*) Any person, being a British subject of full age and good repute, who ... [here follow the educational, age, and service requirements];
>
> (4) They may admit as solicitors of the Supreme Court: –
>
> (*a*) Any person, being a British subject of full age and good repute, who ... [here follow the educational and age requirements].[11]

Garfield A. King appeared to represent Martin, and a number of witnesses gave evidence as to his character. One of the witnesses, Lloyd McKenzie, recalled:

> He asked me, as president of the class, to speak on his behalf as a character witness, which I did, before the Benchers ... [A]nd I remember being cross-examined by Senator Farris ... He was questioning me, "Do you think he can take an oath of allegiance being a Communist and all that?" ... I was waiting outside the Benchers' room ... While I was out in the hall I was talking to John Stanton ... John Stanton was a Communist at that time and the *News Herald,* the morning paper of the day, had a headline story about this and said that two well-known Communists, Lloyd George McKenzie [certainly not a communist] and John Stanton, were waiting to give evidence.[12]

Although Martin admitted to being communist, he initially refused to answer questions about his views on the ground that the Benchers did not "have the authority to inquire into mine, nor anyone else's politics."

The Benchers took a simple view of their statutory obligations (a matter within the field that lawyers know as administrative law): the discretion to admit was entirely theirs. Their decision did not need to be based on evidence in any ordinary sense of the word, and their only duty was to "exercise their discretion honestly in the public interest and upon considerations of good sense."[13] Within those bounds, they said, they were immune from oversight. A bolder assertion of discretionary power and a narrower scope for external constraint can hardly be imagined: they believed themselves to be fully empowered as gatekeepers to the profession, and their decisions were irreversible as long as they did not act dishonestly or in deliberate bad faith.

Martin "adduced evidence in the form of statements, letters and statutory declarations" portraying him as "a man of good repute and ... a fit person to be called to the Bar and admitted to the practice of a solicitor in British Columbia."[14] The evidence of those who knew him was brushed aside, however, replaced by the opinion of those who did not. The Benchers doubted the "qualifications for the purpose" of the individuals attesting to his good repute[15] and emphasized that any testimony regarding his reputation for hard work, conscientiousness, or good personal morals was irrelevant to the question as to whether his communist beliefs *in themselves* constituted grounds for exclusion.

Martin testified that he could swear the necessary oaths in good faith[16] and that "the beliefs of the Communists in British Columbia do not entail adherence either to the Marxist doctrine of the overthrow of constituted authority by force or the subversive doctrines and activities of certain Communists in Canada."[17] That might have disposed of the objection. The Benchers, however, disregarded his stated beliefs in favour of their own conjecture. They thought his testimony "evasive"[18] and considered him tainted by association with convicted subversives: his testimony was deemed unbelievable.[19] Martin's efforts to explain the benign meaning of key passages in the writings of Marx and Engels, which seemingly advocate violent revolution and the abolition of private property, were dismissed as attempts "to show that they had a meaning other than what an ordinary reader would take from them."[20] In a word, Martin was a liar.

In remarkably circular reasoning, his claim that he could take the necessary oaths in good faith served to prove his dishonesty:

> When Mr. Martin states that he can conscientiously take such an oath, in view of his subscription to and general acceptance of the Marxist Manifesto, the Benchers find it difficult to believe in his sincerity or intellectual honesty.
>
> Their opinion is that in spite of his statements to the contrary he would be taking the oaths unscrupulously.[21]

And dishonesty in this regard negated all testimony as to his character:

> An applicant who takes such an oath unscrupulously is in their opinion not a person of probity or of good repute, regardless of the general opinion as to his character held by persons who know vaguely of his beliefs. Such persons cannot be expected to be aware of the incompatibility of those beliefs with the requirements of the oaths to be taken by a barrister and solicitor in the Province of British Columbia.[22]

The Benchers accepted as common knowledge the notion that communists are liars. Martin was an admitted communist. Hence, he was a liar and, *ipso facto*, not of good repute – matter disposed of. Once having admitted to being a communist, Martin could not shed the taint. The Benchers found that he had failed to satisfy them "that he is a person of good repute within the meaning and intent of the *Legal Professions Act*." Hence, he was "not a fit person to be called to the Bar or admitted as a solicitor of the Supreme Court of British Columbia."[23]

A storm ensued. Students at the University of British Columbia mobilized in his support, including "even members of the Young Liberals who had a sense of fair play."[24] The student newspaper attacked the Law Society,[25] and 1,500 students convened, passing a resolution asking "the Attorney-General to prevent any action by the society based on political discrimination against a legally-constituted organization"[26] such as the Labour Progressive Party.

Judicial Review in the Supreme Court of British Columbia

Although the *Legal Profession Act* of the day provided no avenue of appeal, Martin was able to bring the matter to the Supreme Court of British Columbia (immediately below the British Columbia Court of Appeal [BCCA]) through a process known as "judicial review." He hoped to persuade the court that the Benchers had acted outside the scope of their statutory powers.[27] Garfield A. King presented four arguments on Martin's behalf. First, he said that the Law Society could not demand an Oath of Allegiance of its applicants. Second, he asserted that an apprenticing lawyer (the technical terms are "articled clerk" on the solicitors' side and "student-at-law" on the barristers' side) was entitled to be dealt with under the procedures specified for the Law Society's Discipline Committee rather than directly by the Benchers. Both arguments failed on straightforward statutory interpretation.[28]

Martin's status as an articled clerk and student-at-law raised a more difficult, though subtle, point. Martin had enjoyed such status since 1945 on the basis of the Law Society's acceptance of the required certificate of good moral character. This, King argued, established an inchoate right to admission, triggering an obligation for the Benchers to act "judicially" and not with unbounded discretion. Having previously been deemed of "good character" and having completed three years of formal legal education and apprenticeship, Martin could, so the argument went, properly expect to become a lawyer. For the Benchers to deny him this as a result of changing their minds as to his character was, under the then prevailing understandings of administrative law and "natural justice" (due process), a very different matter from declining to grant a privilege: closer conformance to normal judicial standards of evidence and proof would be required,[29] and the outcome likely would have been different. There was no *evidence* that Martin was dishonest, treasonous, bent on violent overthrow of His Majesty's government, or anything other than a constitutionally minded, politically engaged, aspiring lawyer who happened to hold strong left-wing views. Mr. Justice Coady, however, held that the "certificate of good moral character" required on commencing apprenticeship was distinct from the "further evidence" required to satisfy the Benchers of the "good repute" needed for admission to the professions.[30] "Good repute" turns out to be both conceptually distinct from "good moral character" and a higher standard.

Who knew?

Much follows. Any *right* to become a lawyer, inchoate or otherwise, evaporates in the face of an explicit obligation imposed by statute on the Benchers to exercise their *discretion* in satisfying themselves as to this distinct requirement.

> They are not in such inquiry as they may conduct, bound by strict rules of evidence, nor do they require to have before them strict proof of every matter or thing which they are entitled to consider ... They are not deprived of their discretionary power by the enrolment of the applicant nor by the acceptance of the evidence of good moral character submitted at that time ... The statute here, rather than imposing a duty on, grants a power to the Law Society, which in turn is exercised by the Benchers. Notwithstanding the enrolment of a student-at-law or articled clerk, the discretionary power to call or admit is, it seems to me, in no way thereby curtailed or abrogated. It still remains in the absolute discretion of the Benchers and so long as that discretion is exercised honestly, fairly and reasonably, and from no indirect or improper motives and on no irrelevant or alien grounds, it is not open to review.[31]

King's final argument also failed. It asserted that the Benchers had taken "irrelevant or alien grounds" into consideration. In passing the *Legal Profession Act,* he argued, the legislature could not be presumed to have intended the Benchers to engage in political screening. This, he said, was because penalizing a person for his or her beliefs, opinions, or ideologies was a violation of the constitutional rights of a citizen. In pre-*Charter* days, a provincial legislature would likely have been able to do this had it *explicitly* stated that objective.[32] But the courts, so the argument went, should not import a legislative desire to violate fundamental freedoms into their reading of the statute. King argued that "the Benchers ... allowed extraneous and alien matters to affect their decision."[33] These are important terms of art. Any decision-making body resting its decision on irrelevant considerations proceeds unlawfully and can be corrected by the courts. Had this argument succeeded, the Benchers' decision would have been quashed, and Martin would have proceeded to his legal career. Coady J., however, would hear none of it: "It is not for the Court," his lordship said, "to substitute its view for that of the Benchers."[34] The Benchers would have the last word.

In the normal course of events, this should have been the end of the road. Martin had struck out both at the Law Society and on judicial review, and the relevant statute provided no avenue of appeal. The notoriety of the case, however, provoked amendments to the *Legal Profession Act.* Under the new legislation, "[a]ny person whom the Benchers have refused to call to the Bar or to admit as a solicitor may appeal from such refusal to the Court of Appeal ... [T]he Court of Appeal may, in whole or in part, either reverse or confirm the decision of the Benchers or refer the matter to the Benchers for further inquiry."[35] The new legislation opened a new opportunity for Martin to seek reversal of the Benchers' decision.

Martin's Day in the BC Court of Appeal

Martin's appeal was heard by five justices, each of whom wrote an opinion. The outcome is clear (all five ruled against Martin), but multiple judgments serve to obscure the legal principles relied upon. Three legal issues needed to be decided:

1 What was the proper role of the BCCA in reviewing the Benchers' decision?
2 Were the Benchers more properly characterized as an "administrative" body or as a "judicial" body whose decisions affected "rights"?
3 Had the Benchers conducted themselves properly in reaching the conclusion that Martin was unfit to become a barrister and solicitor?

Background understandings of communism mattered to all this. The Benchers' decision effectively created a class of individuals ineligible to become barristers or solicitors as they had come "to the conclusion that the Marxist philosophy of law and government, in its essence, is so inimical in theory and practice to our constitutional system and free society, that a person professing them is *eo ipso*, not a fit and proper person to practise law in this Province, and hence cannot be of 'good repute' within the meaning of the *Legal Professions Act.*"[36]

An extravagance of anticommunist rhetoric is the most memorable feature of the judgments. Chief Justice Sloan thought it an "alien philosophy,"[37] while Mr. Justice O'Halloran explained at great length that adherents to that "pernicious creed"[38] were determined to "weaken and destroy the foundations of our free society"[39] and help "Soviet Russia ... to obtain mastery of the world."[40] Marxism, he said, had a "strange power over its adherents" similar to the "blind passion" that had motivated Hitler's "Nazi youth."[41] Communists rejected "our conception of ethics and morality,"[42] and such a person was "little else than a fifth columnist (designedly or not) to assist an unfriendly country to destroy the rights and privileges a free people have established in Canada."[43] Mr. Justice Sidney Smith expressed agreement with the Benchers on the merits. He accepted that they were entitled to conclude that "it is one of the tenets of the

Communist movement that they be prepared to overthrow existing Governments by force if necessary."[44] Mr. Justice Robertson's judgment elaborated the evils of communism, barely touching on the legal issues before the court. Communist parties, Robertson said, were agents of "the Russian dictatorship."[45] As they sought violent revolution and conspired "to conquer and rule the world by any means,"[46] protestations of loyalty were not credible.[47] Mr. Justice Bird also believed that communists, operating as a "Fifth Column," were unworthy of trust.[48]

Sloan and Sidney Smith explicitly addressed the first of the legal questions. Each concluded that the matter was most properly treated as an appeal from the decision of an administrative body rather than as a retrial ("trial *de novo*"). This conclusion severely limited the scope of matters that the BCCA would consider:

> The amendment simply states that there shall be an appeal to this Court, and nothing more. Had it been the intention of the Legislature that we should embark on new proceedings, nothing would have been easier than to say so. The appeal is from a decision of the Benchers, and in my opinion the Benchers are an administrative body. That being so, the usual and well-known principles governing appeals from such bodies apply here; and so we can only interfere with their finding if their procedure was wrong, or if they acted in bad faith or against all reason or the public interest, or if they formed their opinion upon grounds never brought to appellant's notice.[49]

Chief Justice Sloan also viewed the new procedure as "an ordinary type of appeal from an administrative body,"[50] meaning that the only question for the court was "whether the discretion vested in the Benchers was properly exercised according to law."[51]

Three judges addressed the question of whether an applicant who met the statute's specified objective standards of education, training, and citizenship had a "right" to be admitted. Hoping to trigger an obligation to act judicially, Martin's counsel, John S. Burton, argued that Martin "had established the right to be called and admitted since he had complied with the academic and service requirements prescribed by the *Legal Profession Act* and had introduced evidence of his good character and repute."[52] Mr. Justice Sidney Smith rejected this argument:

> Ill repute completely disqualifies; but good repute is only the beginning of the matter. The truth is that there is nothing in the whole of the *Legal Professions Act* that entitles any person to be admitted to the Society (and

> in this I include call to the Bar). There are various sections stating that the Benchers may admit an applicant who complies with such and such conditions; but no section says that they must admit anyone. The whole is left to their discretion. And we must take the Act and the amendment as we find them. We cannot add to or detract from them ... [C]ompliance imposes no obligations on the Benchers.[53]

Mr. Justice Bird rejected the argument on similar grounds, viewing the applicant as having the onus of satisfying the Benchers as to his suitability for membership.[54] Mr. Justice O'Halloran also rejected the view that anyone might acquire a "right" to be admitted to the professions. The *Legal Profession Act* would not have conferred discretion on the Benchers if this was the legislature's intent, he thought. In any event, there was a logical need to protect the public from those who might use their influence as lawyers to "destroy our Canadian constitutional democracy."[55] The hardship to an applicant turned away after investing three years in training did not evoke the court's sympathy. The duty to protect the public interest was paramount. In any event, their lordships no doubt agreed with the Benchers that "any hardship is of his own creation."[56]

The characterization of the Benchers as "an administrative and not a judicial body" with a "wide discretion" in determining "the qualifications and disqualifications of those who seek the privilege of becoming a member of the Legal Profession"[57] dictated a light-touch review. Absent enormous procedural blunder (such as not giving Martin a chance to address the question of his fitness for the profession) or conduct tantamount to bad faith, the court would not interfere. The BC Court of Appeal implicitly endorsed the Benchers' understanding that, in "exercising a discretion which may depend upon considerations of policy and practical good sense ... they must, of course, act honestly. That is the total of their duty."[58]

More pointedly, they were not required to base their decision on a rational interpretation of evidence. They could, the court said, form their judgment on the basis of their own hunches about "matters of general information."[59] They had it on good authority that this would not be arbitrary "except in the sense in which many honest and sensible judgments are so. They express an intuition of experience which outruns analysis and sums up many unnamed and tangled impressions; impressions which may lie beneath consciousness without losing their worth."[60] Martin's supporters might be forgiven if they viewed this as licence for irrational bias.

The lowered threshold allowed the court to endorse the Benchers' intuition-based decision making. It also allowed a US Supreme Court decision finding no evidence that "Communists advocated the overthrow of Governments by force" to be distinguished from the circumstances before the court in Martin's case. A *judicial proceeding* involving depriving a person of vested rights, such as that before the US Supreme Court, required a different quality of proof than an *administrative decision* denying a "privilege to a Communist."[61] Mr. Justice Sidney Smith was prepared to assume an absence of evidence sufficient to "establish a conspiracy" against the government in a court of law. But, he said, "the Benchers do not require such evidence; they are entitled to exercise their evidence upon probabilities; and there is quite enough evidence on which an *administrative body* could reasonably hold that the Communist movement probably advocates the overthrow of government by force. The Benchers need go no further to justify their acts."[62]

The BC Court of Appeal was unanimous in upholding the Benchers' decision. In Sidney Smith's view:

> We have the right to override them if they act dishonestly against all reason or against the public interest. Appellant's counsel admitted below that he did not challenge their *bona fides.* And I find that I cannot say that their refusal to admit the appellant is either against all reason or against the public interest. Therefore I see no ground for interfering with their decision.[63]

Chief Justice Sloan thought their reasons reflected "the exercise of a proper discretion according to law,"[64] while Mr. Justice Bird agreed "that the findings made by them disclose a lawful and proper exercise of the discretion and public responsibility imposed upon them under the *Legal Professions Act*."[65] Mr. Justice Robertson endorsed the Benchers' conclusion and had "little to add to what has been said by them."[66]

Mr. Justice O'Halloran's reasons merit detailed consideration. His extensive comments about communism (bad) and Anglo-American political culture (good) provide little direct insight into his thoughts on the legal issues before the court. On those matters, it is reasonable to infer that he agreed with the comments of his colleagues, at least in broad outline. He emphasized that Martin had been heard personally and was represented by counsel before the Benchers and that they had issued "extended written reasons" for their decision.[67] The crux of the matter was of far greater importance than the minutiae of administrative law:

> I dismiss the appeal on the broad ground (although narrower grounds may be found) that a Marxist Communist *cannot be a loyal Canadian citizen;* at best his loyalty must be divided between Canada and the Communist

> leadership outside Canada which is engaged ideologically through him (whether he knows it or not) and others of like indoctrination in promoting disruptively in Canada and other countries what Lenin called "the class struggle of the proletariat" for the world revolution.
>
> I would dismiss the appeal.[68]

The legally minded reader will be intrigued by the possibilities suggested in the first parentheses and by the words I have rendered in italics, while those with insight into human psychology (Martin's and O'Halloran's) will be intrigued by the second parentheses. His lordship's apparent casualness about law is matched by his fear of an epidemic of virulent communist indoctrination, spreading invisibly and corrupting beyond even what its victims imagined. Only demonic possession bears comparison. Deep currents lie beneath these obviously troubled waters.

Mr. Justice O'Halloran and Anglo-American "Freedom"

Mr. Justice O'Halloran's judgment was, by far, the longest of the BCCA judgments.[69] Wide-ranging and unremitting in its excoriation of "Marxist Communism" (in contradistinction to "constitutional or Christian Socialist" politics),[70] it is clearly and colourfully expressed. The observation that "[f]or a Communist to talk about personal freedom of action, expression and thought is like the devil talking about the delights of Heaven"[71] is representative.

Intriguingly, much of the judgment is given over to fierce criticism of American thought. Thinking US cases unduly soft on communism, O'Halloran directly repudiated the "neutral and detached view of Communism" of "the majority of the United States Supreme Court, as it was constituted between 1937-1947."[72] The judges of that day were, he said, "quixotic," misled by an anti-authoritarian philosophy that supported "fictions and formulae difficult to reconcile with the realities of modern life." Judgments produced by "slim majorities" of a foreign court, produced in "disturbed periods," should be cautiously approached.[73]

Oliver Wendell Holmes, one of the most celebrated of US jurists, turns out to be the root of much evil. His lordship labelled Holmes as "something more than a constitutional Judge," a sort of judicial ideologue who "[w]ith John Dewey, Veblen, Beard and Robinson (see *Toronto Saturday Night* Editorial March 21, 1950) ... was the proponent of a distinctive American philosophy, which he introduced assiduously and vigorously."[74] These comments echo at a distance a breakthrough work in political theory that appeared in 1949.

Morton White's *Social Thought in America: The Revolt against Formalism* was a major contribution to scholarship:[75]

> White's demarcation of the major American thinkers of the late nineteenth century, including John Dewey, Charles Beard, Oliver Wendell Holmes, James Harvey Robinson, and Thorstein Veblen, as antiformalists marked the first work of intellectual history dedicated to a broad theorization of this period. He was the first to treat these individual critiques of historical analysis, philosophical speculation, and economic discourse as part of a shared intellectual project. What united these thinkers, according to White, was the growing sense that theirs was a period of transition, that the social revolution prompted by the corporate form had fundamentally altered the social and cultural framework of modern society. Consequently, all of these thinkers were preoccupied with delegitimating the standards of the past and projecting an outline for the future. The "revolt against formalism," then, entailed a rejection of "intellectual and moral rigidity" and an attachment to "the moving and the vital in social life."[76]

Each of these disparate thinkers rejected "the 'formalism' of abstract and deductive approaches to the study of philosophy, economics, law, politics, and history."[77] Holmes famously observed that "[t]he life of the law has not been logic: it has been experience."[78] It has been said that the larger group "realized that the life of the mind has not been logic but experience. As a result, they appreciated that thinking inevitably involves evaluating, willing, and acting to shape a culture's perception of itself rather than attempting to frame ideas according to presumably abstract and unchanging logical rules."[79] In short, they decoupled thought and policy making from claims of authority based on cultural inheritance, tradition, or God's will. Theirs was radical stuff, questioning all other faiths save their own profoundly deep faith in rationality, evidence, and reason.

Freedom of conscience, speech, and political commitment provided an acute focal point for such ideas. Two phrases from judgments of Mr. Justice Holmes caused especial offence. They were uttered in a case involving "Russian anarchists" prosecuted for seditious publications during the First World War and one involving a foreigner denied naturalization on the ground that her pacifism was inconsistent with an oath of allegiance to the United States. In those cases, Holmes endorsed "the principle of free thought – not free thought for those who agree with us but freedom for the thought that we hate," and asserted that "the best test of truth is the power of the thought to get itself accepted in the competition of the market."[80] The fuller context of these statements is as follows:

> If there is any principle of the Constitution that more imperatively calls for attachment than any other it is the principle of free thought – not free thought for those who agree with us but freedom for the thought that we hate ... I would suggest that the Quakers have done their share to make the country what it is ... I had not supposed hitherto that we regretted our inability to expel them because they believe more than some of us do in the teachings of the Sermon on the Mount.[81]

> If you have no doubt of your premises or your power and want a certain result with all your heart you naturally express your wishes in law and sweep away all opposition ... But when men have realized that time has upset many fighting faiths, they may come to believe even more than they believe the very foundations of their own conduct that the ultimate good desired is better reached by free trade in ideas – that the best test of truth is the power of the thought to get itself accepted in the competition of the market, and that truth is the only ground upon which their wishes safely can be carried out. That at any rate is the theory of our Constitution. It is an experiment, as all life is an experiment ... While that experiment is part of our system I think that we should be eternally vigilant against attempts to check the expression of opinions that we loathe and believe to be fraught with death ... Only the emergency that makes it immediately dangerous to leave the correction of evil counsels to time warrants making any exception to the sweeping command, "Congress shall make no law ... abridging the freedom of speech."[82]

These fuller passages locate the principle of free expression within a historical context. Free speech was a foundational rule that early-twentieth-century American liberals believed to be essential to the democratic governance of a pluralist society. And it offended Mr. Justice O'Halloran immensely.

"Should we not hate what is wrong?" O'Halloran asked.[83] O'Halloran located truth in a moral certitude derived from tradition, not in a process of continuous contestation of ideas: "the principles of constitutional democracy upon which free society is established, cannot be based upon pragmatic values, determinable by circumstance and consequentially variable. They must be based on certain absolute values, justice, truth and reason. That is why inalienable rights were written into the United States Constitution. That is why we have *Magna Carta*."[84] Holmes and his sort failed to "recognize moral limitations," producing an exaggerated tolerance for even the most offensive speech and thought. Holmes had failed to "recognize a distinction between propaganda as such, and *reasoned statements founded upon historical experience.*"[85] Communists cannot enjoy freedom of speech, his lordship declared, because we cannot "permit them to use it to destroy our constitutional liberties, by first poisoning the minds of the young, the impressionable and the irresponsible. Freedom of expression is not a freedom to destroy freedom."[86]

Holmes, we are told, was "so remote from the common currents of life that he did not read the newspapers."[87] His out-of-date "anti-authoritarian philosophy" had supported "fictions and formulae difficult to reconcile with the realities of modern life."[88] Confusing true freedom with the "unrestrained or abstract licence contained in the anti-authoritarian formula of liberty emotionalized by Rousseau," his approach "sought to elevate science almost into the position of religion."[89] Having retired from the bench at the age of ninety-one in 1932, Holmes could not have fully understood the course of history and "[t]he plain menace of the tyrant state and the conditions which beget it."[90] In any event, because materialist groundings were similar,[91] Marxist communism was a "logical product of the philosophy of Holmes, Dewey and Beard."[92] Unpleasant fellow travellers, indeed.

Mr. Justice O'Halloran and the Professionalism of Canadian Barristers or Solicitors

His lordship also elaborated on another aspect of British-Canadian distinctiveness – the role of the legal profession. "The Law," he declared, "is a profession; it is not a business or trade."[93] As such, it stands outside market relations:

> The law student's training is not manual training, but is training of the mind, not only in law, but if he wishes to be something more than a mere legal mechanic, he must study logic, history, in particular constitutional history, political science and economics, a certain amount of philosophy and acquire a reasonable familiarity with English literature, and know something at least of the literature of other countries. The job of the lawyer is basically to advise people upon all manner of things arising out of the complexities of life and the frailties of human nature. As such he cannot fail in time to acquire an influence upon others, impossible to reduce to purely material terms. It is not too much to say that the training and experience a lawyer undergoes fits him for leadership to a greater or less degree. Obviously such men should not be partial to political philosophies and movements that conflict with the interests of their own country.

> By reason of these things, all countries throughout the ages have given the lawyer a correspondingly high place in society – particularly so in the case of the lawyer who pleads in the higher Courts. The object of law training is to attract young men of high character, and to train them in a manner that they will be trustworthy, honourable and competent in the performance of their legal duties, and will use such influence as they may have to maintain and improve but not to destroy our Canadian constitutional democracy. They are to be the defenders and not the destroyers of liberty. They are expected to be sufficiently well-informed and experienced to distinguish between liberty and licence.
>
> If every person had the right to practice law upon passing the University law examinations, there would be no protection for the public. It is the duty of the Benchers to protect the public by refusing admission to the practice of law, not only the type of person who will prey upon the public for his own selfish ends, but also the type of person who professes a political philosophy alien to our free society, and who in a time of "cold war" is little else than a fifth columnist (designedly or not) to assist an unfriendly country to destroy the rights and privileges a free people have established in Canada.[94]

Three aspects stand out as particularly jarring to twenty-first-century sensibilities. First, O'Halloran thought it "obvious" that no lawyer should hold viewpoints "that conflict with the interests of their own country." Fair enough, perhaps, depending on what that means. But highly specific articles of faith were required:

> Those who accept common-law theory and practice confess to a belief in inherent rights of the individual diametrically opposed to the Hegelian and Marxist concepts of the state ... One dividing point appears clearly on the subject of inherent individual rights as adopted by Locke (who wrote the political philosophy of the Constitutional Revolution of 1688) and later with some variations, by Jefferson, when contrasted with the denial of these inherent rights by Hegel, Marx, Lenin and others upon whose political philosophy any type of totalitarian state is based. Hegel is the source of modern Fascist and Communist perversions.[95]

Lawyers, in short, were bound tightly to the existing British-Canadian constitutional structure, and communism was not a legitimate "political opinion" in the proper meaning of the term.[96] Holmes's notion of the Constitution as "an experiment" would have seemed as abhorrent as Martin's Marxism.

Second, O'Halloran thought that the Benchers' duty to "protect the public" was not limited – as we now generally think – to ensuring baseline competencies and screening out amoral individuals who might prey upon unsuspecting clients for their own selfish ends. High standards of personal integrity and ethics were required, but the leadership roles of lawyers demanded more: conformity to the requirements of "common-law theory and practice." The office of barrister or solicitor involved a positive and expansive duty to state and community not confined to narrow conceptions of role. Lawyers were not to be mere mouthpieces or guns for hire to do their clients' will. Protecting the public meant more than protecting clients.

And third, O'Halloran emphasized the moral role of lawyers in the community. His observation that their "influence over others" was "impossible to reduce to purely material terms" points to the importance of moral influence, broadly understood. Lawyers brought moral compass to bear in matters of business and in "the complexities of life and the frailties of human nature" in all their dimensions. A full-service paternalism that acknowledges clients as personal, familial, moral, social, economic, and spiritual beings puts lawyers' character into play in a way that simply cannot be imagined if the professional role is limited to serving instrumental or economic objectives in isolation.

When professionalism is so conceived, the conclusion that beliefs "inimical to his country" are "repugnant to the ancient and honourable profession of law" is inevitable.[97] And the exclusion of communists follows.

Historian as Quizmaster

How, then, are we to judge? The *Martin* case tests the limits of liberal tolerance for diversity of political viewpoints. A cliff edge is approached, and the possibility of extensive, privacy-intruding investigations of the personal opinions and characters of prospective lawyers looms. Historical context cannot excuse the judges and Benchers from blame. They were called upon to exercise judgment, and no outcome was predetermined by context. Their decisions were widely criticized by mainstream Canadians at the time as well as by adherents of far-left-wing politics and many subsequent commentators of diverse political stripes. Neither their peers elsewhere in Canada nor their immediate successors in British Columbia had the stomach for thoroughgoing ideological screening. No Canadian McCarthyism took seed; no subsequent case approached the abyss.

The university was a place of tolerance, and leftist students were able to pursue three years of legal studies without obstruction. At the University of British Columbia law faculty, they were able and willing to return as good as they received in political argument. Although some "professors were openly hostile" to Harry Rankin's leftist politics, "many could remain objective."[98] Well-known socialists such as Dalhousie's John Willis and McGill's Frank Scott ranked among the most capable and highly respected law teachers of the day, and it seems likely that most of the law-teaching profession had little taste for political repression.

Manitoba's lawyers declined to follow British Columbia's lead when a well-known young communist war veteran, Roland Penner (later provincial attorney general and dean of law at the University of Manitoba law faculty), decided to pursue a legal career.[99] British Columbia's Law Society continued to police the bounds of political belief but did so ineffectually. Immediately following Martin's exclusion, four law students were selected for a political inquisition of sorts, and each gained admission.[100] Rankin viewed the exercise as one in simple "political intimidation, the Law Society letting a whole generation of law students know that it was unacceptable to do any real thinking about change."[101] Sherwood Lett, who chaired the Law Society's credentials committee, required him to swear the following affidavit:

> I, Harry Rankin, do solemnly swear that I am not a communist or a member of any association holding communist views, that if called to the Bar I can take the Barristers' Oath without reservations of any kind and that I have no intention of following any communist association in the future.
>
> That I do not and will not advocate nor am I a member of any organization that advocates the overthrow of democratic government by force or violence or other constitutional means.[102]

Accepting that the Benchers and judges exercised choice in acting as they did, I suggest nonetheless that attention to context makes moral judgment more difficult than it might at first seem. By way of conclusion, I would emphasize, first, that the courts took the proper approach to reviewing the Benchers' decision; second, that, despite their rhetoric, there was less emotional irrationality to their anticommunism than seems; and, third, odd though it may now appear, that their expansive view of lawyers as especially charged with a mission in service of King and Constitution was the proper understanding of their time.

Each of the appellate judges emphasized his agreement with the Benchers' view that communists were *eo ipso* barred from admission to the legal profession. This view, and their lordships' many pages of impassioned, almost hysterical prose, distract from the formal reasons for decision (the *rationes decidendi*) of the case. The distinction is important. It is possible that their views on the essential nature of communism were wrong but that the legal decision to uphold Martin's exclusion was correct.

The legal outcome of the case before the courts was simply that the courts should not seek to second-guess the judgment of the Benchers, because the legislature had granted the latter a power to decide. The legislative scheme had to be respected. As there was no evidence of *mala fides* or improper motivation, and as Martin had been accorded an opportunity to explain himself, there was no reason to interfere. For a generation of lawyers with different attitudes towards administrative decision making and conditioned by the *Canadian Charter of Rights and Freedoms* to imagine that courts can always trump the legislature, this approach can be hard to appreciate. Current legal fashion does not imagine a bright-line distinction between "privileges" and "rights" and does not categorize tribunals as administrative or judicial. Twenty-first-century legal culture may take a more favourable attitude towards substituting the views of judges for the decisions of other bodies. Contemporary legal authority, however, supported the approach of the courts in *Martin*.[103] The narrow reasons for decision were certainly correct under the prevailing legal doctrine of the time.[104]

Seemingly eccentric understandings of the role of lawyers also appear less strange in context. Our generation is disinclined to view lawyers as anything other than commercial service providers who complete business transactions, do solicitors' work, and deal with the courts on behalf of their clients. Consequently, we view the ends of regulation as nothing more mystical than protecting clients from incompetent or unscrupulous individuals. Lawyers' ethical codes, like those of pharmacists and used-car salespersons, regulate a market for services. Massive transformations during the decades separating us from the *Martin* case have profoundly changed the character of the legal professions.[105] Viewed through our own demystified, democratized lenses, earlier understandings of lawyers' roles appear puffed up, inflated, arrogant, implausible, and even ridiculous. It matters little to us if a lawyer cannot honestly swear fidelity to the Queen – or that he or she might be disinclined to subvert "treasonous conspiracies."[106] However, the view that lawyers, through their mundane work, play a key role in social cohesion and constitutional governance, that their influence and importance cannot be reduced to "purely material terms," has an ancient lineage.[107] Indeed, the modern structures of Canadian legal professionalism, including self-regulation of the profession, codes of ethics, and patterns of legal education, were all derived from just such a professional ideology.[108] The views of Martin's antagonists were consistent in this regard with the highest aspirations for the legal professions as they were then understood. If those individuals are to be treated as objects of ridicule on this count, it can only be because we judge their time ridiculous.

What, then, are we to make of the legal establishment's vehement anti-communism? Both the vehemence and the "anti" are beyond doubt. Their passion seems irrational. Gordon Martin would engage in treason; it did not matter that his behaviour was exemplary or that he affirmed his good faith intentions to swear allegiance to His Majesty. Gordon Martin would seek to subvert "property"; it was irrelevant that he testified otherwise. Gordon Martin would act as a fifth columnist in the Russian cause; neither his denials nor the absolute absence of evidence mattered. The court offered its own interpretation of Marxist doctrine as authoritative, not Martin's. The fact that his explanation differed from that of the court could only be because he was lying or dangerously deluded. The notion that, *as a matter of definition,* a communist could not be a "good Canadian" verges on tautology. To elevate this to a common law rule seems ridiculous. All seven reasons for decision in the *Martin* cases are clear that "evidence" in any legal sense was neither required nor desired. Considering the case from the point of view of communists who aspire to become lawyers, the rationale and outcome are outrageous. The thought that a war veteran, the son of a prominent communist member of the Winnipeg city council, might be denied admission to the legal profession despite his personal and familial records of service to community and country seems repulsive.[109] The full horrors of Stalin and Mao were not yet fully appreciated, and many idealists had reason to imagine that Marxism might be liberating.

It does not, however, take enormous leaps of imagination to see things from the opposite viewpoint.[110] However unjust the outcome may have been, Gordon Martin was emphatically not the victim of a witch hunt, picked out for discriminatory treatment as a result of a search for "reds under the bed," on account of rumour and innuendo, loose associations, or involvement in unions. The Benchers had an authentic "red" before them. Moreover, communism then seemed frightening, just as, in more recent times, newer terrorist ideologies have seemed frightening. The war against the Nazis was only recently concluded, Nuremberg's trials had revealed the dangers of extremist political ideology, and the Soviet Union had mounted aggressive offensives against its former allies. The possibility of the Cold War's escalating to the battlefield would have seemed all too likely to a generation conditioned by the experience of two world wars. As Mr. Justice Bird points out, communist declarations of *bona fides* weighed lightly against the experience of the "developments which have occurred since the cessation of hostilities in 1945." He continues:

The revelations made in the Report of the Royal Commission on Communist Espionage in 1946 which discloses the debauching by Communist influences of Canadian public servants occupying positions of public trust, despite oaths of allegiance and office which they had taken, I am satisfied have created in the public mind an utter distrust of that philosophy as well as of its adherents. That distrust has been accentuated by the disclosure of similar activities in Great Britain, *i.e.*, the Fuchs case and also the Alger Hiss and other like proceedings in the United States.

Communism and all that pertains to that philosophy I think is now recognized as having a connotation equivalent to Fifth Column. It is common knowledge that Governments on this continent, public and private organizations, more particularly among Trades and Labour Unions, alive to the danger of Communist infiltration and influence are now alert to the menace, and are actively moving towards its elimination.[111]

Although the extent of a communist threat at the time remains unclear, British Columbia's legal authorities had reason to be concerned. Their views on the matter are intelligible. Just as the full evils of Stalin and Mao were not fully appreciated in 1950, so too the possibility of a democratic form of communism playing within the rules of constitutionalism had yet to be manifest.

It is possible that the Benchers drew the line in the wrong place. Certainly, the result was unjust to Gordon Martin. Hindsight, however, is perfect. Their field of vision was powerfully shaped by the dramatic events of their time. Only if we either dismiss their fears as palpably ridiculous or subscribe to Holmes's radical notion of a marketplace for ideas can we rush to judgment. If we allow that the political values of prospective lawyers might ever be properly taken into account, then things become more complex.[112]

Hindsight requires a degree of humility.

Postscript

Gordon Martin "found work for a few years as a faller and in a sawmill in Nanaimo before starting a television repair shop from home, Active TV service." An RCMP report in 1963 stated that he was a "good family man" with a successful business. Martin died of cancer in Nanaimo in 1974. Nearly a quarter-century later and fifty years after his exclusion from the legal profession, the Law Society of British Columbia issued a formal apology. In 1998, its treasurer (*i.e.*, president), Trudi Brown, said to the Victoria *Times Colonist*: "'It's a sorry tale,' ... But it could not happen now because 'we are only concerned if a person is competent.' A person could be a Communist or a Nazi and become a lawyer 'so long as they have not broken the law.'"[113]

Notes

An earlier version of this chapter appeared as "Banned from Lawyering: William John Gordon Martin, Communist" (2009) BC Studies 111. It has been revised and reprinted here with permission.

1 Lawyers in all common law provinces become barristers and solicitors virtually simultaneously now, with the result that few are aware that these are distinct professions with different roles and obligations. Lawyers in 1948 were more alive to this and, although little turned on it in the *Martin* case, addressed the requirements for call to the bar and enrollment as a solicitor as distinct matters.

2 *Re Legal Profession Act, Re Martin,* [1949] 1 D.L.R. 105 at 109 (Reasons of the Benchers of the Law Society of British Columbia) [Benchers' ruling]. The Benchers of the day were *R.H. Tupper; Sherwood Lett;* C.B. Garland, KC; *A.D. Crease, KC; Hon. J.W. de B. Farris, KC;* G. Roy Long, KC; T.R. Selkirk; *W.H.M. Haldane; Elmore Meredith; A.C. Des Brisay, KC; C.M. O'Brian, KC;* and *T.G. Norris, KC.* The Benchers' Minutes show unanimity among those taking part in the decision (shown in italics), with Lett and Norris being mandated to prepare a statement of reasons.

3 See Jamie Disbrow, *Exclusion by Due Process* – Martin v. Law Society of British Columbia: *A Cold War Eclipse of Civil Liberties* (MA Thesis, University of Ottawa, 1996).

4 Roland Penner, *A Glowing Dream: A Memoir* (Winnipeg: J. Gordon Shillingford Publishing, 2007) at 121. Penner had an intense personal interest in the matter during the 1950s, as he too was a communist who sought a career in law. Admitted without difficulty in Manitoba, his subsequent career included service as attorney general for Manitoba and as dean of law at the University of Manitoba.

5 H. Rankin, *Rankin's Law: Recollections of a Radical* (Vancouver: November House, 1975) at 65, 71, 72.

6 W. Wesley Pue, *Law School: The Story of Legal Education in British Columbia* (Vancouver: Continuing Legal Education Society of British Columbia/Faculty of Law, University of British Columbia, 1995) at 240-44. A fully documented version of this work can be found under the title *A History of Legal Education in British Columbia* at <http://papers.ssrn.com/sol3/papers.cfm?abstract_id=897084>.

7 Benchers' ruling, *supra* note 2 at 110 [emphasis in original].

8 *Ibid.* at 109-10 [emphasis in original].

9 "'Red' Law Student Okayed by Benchers: Secret Inquiry into Political Beliefs Clears Norm Littlewood" *Vancouver Sun* (31 July 1948).

10 Mr. Justice Lloyd McKenzie, interview by Professor Marilyn MacCrimmon, 24 May 1995 [McKenzie interview].

11 *Legal Profession Act*, R.S.B.C. 1936, c. 149, as cited in Benchers' ruling, *supra* note 2 at 106.

12 McKenzie interview, *supra* note 10.

13 Benchers' ruling, *supra* note 2 at 114.

14 *Ibid.* at 108.

15 *Ibid.* at 109.

16 *Ibid.* at 110. See also "'Red' Law Student," *supra* note 9.

17 Benchers' ruling, *supra* note 2 at 109.

18 *Ibid.* at 107.

19 *Ibid.* at 109.

20 *Ibid.* at 110. Anyone exposed to Marxist theory in graduate school – or anyone exposed to legal education, for that matter – might be somewhat more sympathetic to Martin on the matter of words meaning other than they seem.

21 *Ibid.*

22 *Ibid.* at 110-11.

23 *Ibid.* at 114.

24 Rankin, *supra* note 5 at 65.
25 "*Ubyssey* Hits Law Society" *Colonist* (Victoria) (29 September 1948) 1. It is reported that the student newspaper "strongly attacked action of the British Columbia Law Society in refusing Gordon Martin admission to the Bar ... Martin had stated he presumed the refusal was based on his political views."
26 "Students Ask Law Society to Explain Stand" *Colonist* (Victoria) (17 October 1948). About 1,500 students attended a meeting to protest the Law Society's refusal to admit Martin.
27 The form of proceeding was "by way of *mandamus* directed to the Law Society of British Columbia to show cause" why he should not be permitted to become a barrister and solicitor. See *Re Legal Profession Act, Re Martin,* [1949] 2 D.L.R. 559 at 559 at para. 1, per Coady J. [BCSC].
28 On the first argument, *ibid.* at para. 7: "s. 2 of the *Oaths of Allegiance Act* clearly indicates that the taking of the oath may be required as a statutory condition to the acceptance of the office." The reasoning on the second argument was in two parts. First, the Discipline Committee was engaged only in the face of a complaint, and there was no "complaint" against Martin. Second, status as an apprenticing lawyer did not make him a "member of the society" under the *Legal Profession Act.* Consequently, Martin remained an *applicant* for admission who bore the burden of persuading the Benchers of his fitness, not a member who was being subjected to discipline (at paras. 10-11).
29 *Ibid.* at para. 16.
30 *Ibid.* at para. 15.
31 *Ibid.* at para. 16.
32 Subject to questions relating to the division of powers between the provincial and Dominion tiers of government.
33 BCSC, *supra* note 27 at para. 17.
34 *Ibid.* at para. 18.
35 *Legal Profession Act,* s. 41A as enacted by 1949, c. 35, s. 2, as cited in *Martin v. Law Society of British Columbia,* [1950] 3 D.L.R. 173 at para. 2, per Sloan C.J.B.C. [BCCA].
36 BCCA, *ibid.* at para. 9.
37 *Ibid.* at para. 6.
38 *Ibid.* at para. 14, quoting Lord Chief Justice Goddard.
39 *Ibid.* at para. 12.
40 *Ibid.* at para. 13.
41 *Ibid.* at para. 17.
42 *Ibid.* at para. 23.
43 *Ibid.* at para. 54.
44 *Ibid.* at para. 77.
45 *Ibid.* at para. 63, quoting James Oneal and G.A. Werner, *American Communism: A Critical Analysis of Its Origins, Development and Programs* (New York: E.P. Dutton, 1947).
46 BCCA, *supra* note 35 at para. 61, quoting a pamphlet titled "Communism and Education," published in 1948 by the Committee on Un-American Activities, US House of Representatives.
47 BCCA, *ibid.* at para. 67.
48 *Ibid.* at paras. 98, 99.
49 *Ibid.* at para. 70, per Sidney Smith J.A.
50 *Ibid.* at para. 3, per Sloan C.J.B.C.
51 *Ibid.* at para. 4, per Sloan C.J.B.C.
52 *Ibid.* at para. 93, per Bird J.A.
53 *Ibid.* at paras. 71, 72, per Sidney Smith J.A.
54 *Ibid.* at para. 93, per Bird J.A.
55 *Ibid.* at paras. 50, 53, per O'Halloran J.A.

56 Benchers' ruling, *supra* note 2 at 113. Had the appellate justices been polled on the matter, it seems certain that O'Halloran and Robertson would have agreed. Their anticommunist fervour is beyond doubt. Although the other judgments make more of the limited role of an appellate court and the deference (not their language) to be accorded to the Benchers, each of the other justices went out of his way to indicate his agreement with the substantive outcome.
57 BCCA, *supra* note 35 at para. 4, per Sloan C.J.B.C.
58 *Leeds Corporation v. Ryder*, [1907] A.C. 420 at 423, per Lord Loreburn L.C., as cited in Benchers' ruling, *supra* note 2 at 107.
59 Benchers' ruling, *ibid.* at 107.
60 *Ibid.*, citing *Chicago, Burlington & Quincy R. Co. v. Babcock* (1907), 204 U.S. 585 at 598, per Holmes J., as quoted by Thorson P. in *Pure Spring Co. v. Minister of Nat'l Revenue,* [1947] 1 D.L.R. 501 at 522, 530 D.L.R. [Exchequer Court of Canada].
61 BCCA, *supra* note 35 at para. 78, per Sidney Smith J.A., referencing *Schneiderman v. U.S.* (1942), 320 U.S. 118.
62 BCCA, *ibid.* at para. 81, per Sidney Smith J.A. [emphasis added].
63 *Ibid.* at para. 82, per Sidney Smith J.A.
64 *Ibid.* at para. 7, per Sloan C.J.B.C.
65 *Ibid.* at para. 100, per Bird J.A.
66 *Ibid.* at para. 58, per Robertson J.A.
67 *Ibid.* at para. 8, per O'Halloran J.A.
68 *Ibid.* at paras. 57-58, per O'Halloran J.A. [emphasis added].
69 Forty-nine paragraphs and 6,506 words. *Cf.* Sloan C.J.B.C. (7 paragraphs, 522 words), Robertson J.A. (10 paragraphs, 1,049 words), Sidney Smith J.A. (14 paragraphs, 1,445 words), and Bird J.A. (16 paragraphs, 1,340 words).
70 BCCA, *supra* note 35 at para. 43, per O'Halloran J.A.
71 *Ibid.* at para. 20, per O'Halloran J.A.
72 *Ibid.* at para. 28, per O'Halloran J.A.
73 *Ibid.* at para. 38, per O'Halloran J.A.
74 *Ibid.*, citing "American Philosophy" *Saturday Night* (21 March 1950) 6.
75 Morton White, *Social Thought in America: The Revolt against Formalism* (New York: Viking, 1949).
76 Robert Genter, "The Challenge of Morton White and the Politics of Antiformalism," Book review of *Social Thought in America: The Revolt against Formalism,* by Morton White, *H-Ideas* (July 2000), online: Humanities and Social Sciences Net <http://www2.h-net.msu.edu/reviews/showrev.php?id=4345>.
77 James T. Kloppenberg, "Morton White's *Social Thought in America*" (1987) 15:3 *Reviews in American History* 508.
78 Oliver Wendell Holmes, *The Common Law* (Boston: Little, Brown, 1881) at 1.
79 Kloppenberg, *supra* note 77 at 512.
80 As quoted in BCCA, *supra* note 35 at para. 31, per O'Halloran J.A.
81 *United States v. Schwimmer* (1929), 279 U.S. 644 at 654-55, per Holmes J. Holmes's contemporaries would have understood the reference to chs. 5-7 of St. Matthew's Gospel and the implicit pacifism of the Sermon on the Mount, including especially Matthew 5: 9, "Blessed are the peacemakers: for they shall be called the children of God"; 5: 38-39, "Ye have heard that it hath been said, An eye for an eye, and a tooth for a tooth: But I say unto you, That ye resist not evil: but whosoever shall smite thee on thy right cheek, turn to him the other also"; and 5:44, "But I say unto you, Love your enemies, bless them that curse you, do good to them that hate you, and pray for them which despitefully use you, and persecute you."
82 *Abrams et al. v. United States* (1919), 250 U.S. 616 at 630-31, per Holmes J.

83 BCCA, *supra* note 35 at para. 33, per O'Halloran J.A.
84 *Ibid.* at para. 34, per O'Halloran J.A.
85 *Ibid.* at para. 32, per O'Halloran J.A. [emphasis added].
86 *Ibid.* at para. 34, per O'Halloran J.A.
87 *Ibid.* at para. 32, per O'Halloran J.A. The quotation is attributed to Mr. Justice Frankfurter. Although not sourced in Mr. Justice O'Halloran's judgment, it appears to be from *Craig v. Harney* (1947), 331 U.S. 367 at 391-92, per Frankfurter J., dissenting.
88 BCCA, *supra* note 35 at para. 38, per O'Halloran J.A.
89 *Ibid.* at para. 39, per O'Halloran J.A.
90 *Ibid.* at para. 40, per O'Halloran J.A.
91 See *ibid.* at para. 41, per O'Halloran J.A., pointing to "Pandit Nehru, Einstein, and Mauriac" in a critique of Soviet and US materialism.
92 *Ibid.* at para. 43, per O'Halloran J.A.
93 *Ibid.* at para. 50, per O'Halloran J.A.
94 *Ibid.* at paras. 52-54, per O'Halloran J.A.
95 *Ibid.* at para. 48, per O'Halloran J.A.
96 *Ibid.* at para. 45, per O'Halloran J.A.
97 *Ibid.* at para. 46, per O'Halloran J.A.
98 Rankin, *supra* note 5 at 62. Mr. Justice O'Halloran criticized the universities for their different understandings. See BCCA, *supra* note 35 at paras. 45, 46.
99 Penner, *supra* note 4 at 125.
100 Norman Littlewood, Harold Dean, Ike Shulman, and Harry Rankin.
101 Rankin, *supra* note 5 at 62.
102 As quoted in *ibid.* at 70.
103 And, it must be noted, even modern Canadian administrative law finds ways of carving out a wide swath of deference to the substantive decisions of certain administrative tribunals.
104 The substantial legal argument put forward by Martin's counsel turned on the harm that Martin suffered in being denied entry to the legal profession after having invested three years in training and then having his "inchoate right" interfered with. The practical consequence of this argument, if successful, would have been to turn the matter from an administrative decision into a judicial one, triggering a higher standard of review. This was in essence an argument to transform settled authority, however, and the earlier BC case of *Hagel v. Law Society of British Columbia*, in *Re Hagel and Law Society of British Columbia*, [1922] B.C.J. No. 33; 31 B.C.R. 75 (March 1922), per Hunter C.J.B.C., was treated as determinative of the rights/privilege matter: "[I]t was the intention of the Legislature to entrust the decision to the Benchers, and therefore in the absence of any power being given to review their decision, the Court has no jurisdiction to substitute its own view for what is sufficient proof for that [good character and reputation] of the Benchers" (at para. 2).
105 See, for example, Constance Backhouse and W. Wesley Pue, eds., *The Promise and Perils of Law: Lawyers in Canadian History* (Toronto: Irwin Law, 2009).
106 The citizenship requirement was done away with only in 1989, and then by a majority Supreme Court of Canada decision that turned on *Charter* analysis in *Law Society British Columbia v. Andrews*, [1989] 1 S.C.R. 143 (Dickson C.J. and McIntyre, Lamer, Wilson, Le Dain, La Forest, and L'Heureux-Dubé JJ.).
107 See, for early expressions of this view in relation to the English legal profession, Chapter 4 in this volume.
108 See, for example, W. Wesley Pue, "The Canadian Legal Profession: The Historical Context" in Alice Woolley, Brent Cotter, Iwan Saunders, and Richard Devlin, eds., *Professional Responsibility in Canada* (Markham, ON: LexisNexis Canada, 2008) at 93-128.

109 Penner, *supra* note 4.

110 The context is explained in Thomas Berger's thoughtful treatment in "The Communist Party and the Limits of Dissent" in his *Fragile Freedoms: Human Rights and Dissent Canada* (Toronto/Vancouver: Clarke, Irwin, 1981) at 127-62.

111 BCCA, *supra* note 35 at paras. 98-99, per Bird J.A.

112 *Cf.* the decision of the Illinois State Bar to exclude one Matthew Hale on the ground that his racist beliefs rendered him unfit for the profession. See *Hale v. Committee on Character and Fitness of the Ill. Bar,* 99-1349, Supreme Court of the United States, 530 U.S. 1261; 120 S. Ct. 2716; 147 L. Ed. 2d 982; 2000 U.S. Lexis 4348; 68 U.S.L.W. 3789; and Theresa Keeley, "Comment: Good Moral Character: Already an Unconstitutionally Vague Concept and Now Putting Bar Applicants in a Post-9/11 World on an Elevated Threat Level" (2004) 6 U. Pa. J. Const. L. 844; Melissa Rourke and Meredith Schoenfeld, "The Honesty Standard and the Need for a More Stringent Standard: An Update on Model Rule 8.1" (2002) 15 Geo. J. Legal Ethics 895; Carol M. Langford, "Barbarians at the Bar: Regulation of the Legal Profession through the Admissions Process" (2008) 36 Hofstra L. Rev. 1193; Leslie C. Levin, "The Folly of Expecting Evil: Reconsidering the Bar's Character and Fitness Requirement" (2014) 2014 B.Y.U.L. Rev. 775.

113 Roger Stonebanks, "Law Society's Apology Comes 50 Years Late" *Times Colonist* (Victoria) (19 December 1998) B1.

11

Liberal Entrepreneurship Thwarted

CHARLES RANN KENNEDY AND THE FOUNDATIONS OF ENGLAND'S MODERN BAR

The professional battles of a brilliant but obscure nineteenth-century English barrister represent crucial turning points in the evolution of the modern bar. For over a decade in the mid-nineteenth century, Charles Rann Kennedy was more or less constantly engaged in a struggle to reconstitute professional practice in ways compatible with the new political economy – and with his own business needs. His approach combined commonplace nineteenth-century world-views with elements derived from an inherited ideology of legal professionalism. Kennedy fought mostly losing battles. He is a founder of the modern bar, nonetheless, for his losing struggles illustrate historical might-have-beens. The fact that he fought them at all forced change on the profession at large, although the reforms provoked in response ran in directions entirely opposite to those he sought.

Kennedy became a sort of folk devil within the Bar. He served as one of a few "visible reminders of what we should not be."[1] As Stanley Cohen has it, "the successful creation of folk devils rests on their stereo-typical portrayal as atypical actors against a background that is overtypical."[2] His meteor-like flash of prominence ended up confirming the established leadership of the Bar and cast the die decisively. His struggles gave sharp definition to debates about professionalism, forcing results where others may have preferred drift. In the end, choice was limited, debate constrained, and innovation confined within one channel where previously there had been many.

Professional Struggles of Charles Rann Kennedy

Charles Rann Kennedy was an unlikely candidate for the role of folk-devil. He was the son of a prominent Birmingham priest, Rann Kennedy.[3] His brother, Benjamin Hall Kennedy, was a priest, classicist, and educator who became a prominent advocate of women's admissions to Cambridge University.[4]

Subsequent generations of the family produced Lord Justice of Appeal William Rann Kennedy and County Court Judge Alfred Ravenscroft Kennedy. Charles won medals in Greek and Latin at Cambridge before his election as a fellow of Trinity College, Cambridge, in 1831.[5] He was president of the Union in 1832,[6] and in 1835 was called to the bar of Lincoln's Inn. His legal publications included *New Rules of Pleading* in 1838, *The Privileges of the House of Commons* in 1841, *A Treatise on Annuities* in 1846, and an analysis (summary of legislation) to Burchall's *Joint-Stock Companies Registration Act* in 1844.[7] He was a classical scholar of distinction[8] and contemporaries described him as "a scholar of the very first class,"[9] "a man of great learning in his profession,"[10] and "a man of highest attainments and of transcendent ability."[11] Despite his manifest abilities and privileged background, however, Kennedy did not achieve the success he might have expected in his profession. He was unsuccessful in practice (if income is the marker), ostracized from professional association, and ultimately vilified both by the leaders of bar and bench and by middle-class public opinion.

In 1850, the board of Queen's College, Birmingham, created a law department and named Kennedy as their first Professor of Law.[12] His willingness to take the position signalled professional failure, for university law teaching was not a desirable career option.[13] His poetry reveals a degree of discomfort with Birmingham,[14] and a contemporary records that "when he came to compete with the heterogeneous mass of trained and untrained, of skilled and stupid, of clever and impudent, of weak and strong, of good and bad, which makes up the body of men called 'the Bar,' he found himself out-distanced and absolutely over-looked."[15] Kennedy wrote that on moving to Birmingham he had to "abandon the Home Circuit, which I had formerly attended without success."[16]

It is unclear why Kennedy's intellectual abilities were not matched by success in practice. His lack of success cannot be attributed to any deficiency in the learning or, perhaps, the other skills required of a barrister. Sir John Romilly offered the opinion that Kennedy had knowledge and abilities sufficient to "eminence in the profession,"[17] while the Lord Chief Justice of England praised his abilities as a lawyer and orator,[18] and the *Birmingham Post* described him as a man of "noble intellect and vast acquirements."[19] Passage of the *County Courts Act* in 1846 may have hurt him, as it did others.[20] Rann Kennedy explained his son's lack of success as resulting from poor health,[21] while an obituary in *Aris's Birmingham Gazette* attributed it to high virtue: "[H]e had not the trick of bringing himself down to the level of the people among whom he had to practice, and his style of speaking, though terse and perspicuous to a degree seldom met with, lacked the delicate flavour of clap-trap which takes with the *profanum vulgus*."[22] There was also some suggestion – repudiated in the pages of the *Legal Observer* – that he lacked sufficient personal connections of the sort that might steer barristers' work towards him.[23]

Establishing a practice in Birmingham proved difficult. An obstacle immediately arose when the Midland Circuit Mess rejected his application for membership. The stated reason was that they were merely applying a general rule against barristers' moving to new circuits.[24] Kennedy believed he had been rejected for unworthy reason. Displaying considerable facility with legal argument, he argued that there *was* no such general rule, that there *should* be no such rule, and that, even if such a rule had in fact been applied in previous cases, there were sufficient distinguishing features to make it inapplicable to his circumstances.[25]

Kennedy thought the decision was driven by self-interest and that members of the Mess sought to preserve their monopoly.[26] "By what title do my opponents claim a freehold in the practice of this county? For what crime would they drive me from the town of Birmingham? The only crime I have committed is that I come to fish in the same free waters as themselves."[27]

Elsewhere he complains that "a liberal profession is not exempt from the most illiberal jealousies ... that a barrister's union may be no better than a trade's union."[28] He also developed an extensive argument to show that barristers who change circuits would not hurt the business of established practitioners.[29] There may well have been more to the matter than simple commercial interest, however. In a letter to the Lord Chancellor, Kennedy called "upon all good men to shut their ears against private whisperings, and not to be deterred by any malignant influence from doing me justice."[30] The nature of those "private whisperings" is unclear.

Although Kennedy enjoyed the support of leading barristers at the time of his application for appointment as Professor of Law,[31] it is possible the Mess thought of him as a troublemaker or simply preferred not to associate with him for other reasons.[32] He had begun legal work in Birmingham without waiting for admission to the Mess. This would have been quite acceptable only twenty years earlier,[33] but Bar messes had attained a more formalized existence in recent years and at least nominal participation in their activities was expected of lawyers attending Assize Courts.[34] He explained his decision to begin work before concluding professional niceties:

> My opinion was, and is, that the efficiency of a lecturer would be greatly diminished, if he entirely neglected to attend courts of law, and to keep up his knowledge of legal practice. Having become a resident in this town [*i.e.*, Birmingham], it became necessary for me to abandon the Home Circuit,

> which I had formerly attended without success, and to choose one in this neighbourhood. I chose the Midland, in which Birmingham is situated, and immediately began to attend the sessions of the town. The disputes to which this gave rise between my brother barristers and myself, and the annoyance to which I have been subjected, it is needless to enlarge upon.[35]

Kennedy saw the matter largely in terms of the freedom of barristers to practise without inhibition from their professional institutions. He seems to have longed for the days of his early career when the mess was little more than a dining club.[36] His prime affront to his colleagues may have been precisely this attitude: "If the decrees of these men are to have the effect they desire, the thing is reduced to this – that, before I accepted the situation of Professor at Queen's College, I ought to have asked permission of the Midland Circuit, to practise in their district."[37] It is possible too that some barristers may have disapproved of his work as a law teacher. The creation of a college department of law was an extraordinary event. The College Council believed they were leading the nation in a new path of formal legal education as part of a larger program of establishing practical, "scientific" education in Birmingham.[38] Kennedy's strong local connections may have helped in securing the appointment, and it is possible that his availability helped to nudge the College to create its law department.[39] The creation of a law department was a good fit with the vision of W. Sands Cox, who had originally founded Queen's College precisely so that "men in Birmingham who wished to take up the medical profession should have an opportunity of training near their homes and at moderate cost."[40]

The character of legal education was neither fixed nor without controversy. The Select Committee on Legal Education[41] had called for major changes in the method of legal education in England in its 1846 report, including recommending the establishment of a "Law University." Under the editorial direction of Edward Cox, the *Law Times* more or less constantly called for major reforms in the training of barristers, and *The Times* itself frequently criticized the Bar.[42] Barristers were not generally enthusiastic for more structured legal education, however. The Inns responded only modestly to calls for improved education[43] and arguments were mustered in defence of the status quo.[44] Some were anxious about a scholarly legal education because, "just as lawyers might relate law to philosophy and history and so on, they might also go on to do the reverse and question law and legal technique in the light of philosophy."[45] The Bar celebrated the "Virtues of Practical Men."[46] Moreover, discussions of legal education inevitably led to questions concerning the status (and competitive position) of solicitors.[47]

By stepping into his new role at Queen's College, Kennedy sided with innovation in education and profession alike. At the time "[t]here was virtually no legal education at the universities."[48] It was the career choice of a reformer as well as a scholar. The course of instruction that he developed was intended for those set on a career as a solicitor as well as for aspiring barristers.[49] Kennedy's program combined formal instruction with gentlemanly learning as a common core intended for both branches of the legal profession. Some viewed the very idea as an affront to the dignity of the Bar. One contemporary feared that improving the solicitors' education would lead to either fusion of the professions or to inter-branch tensions: "This restless spirit of ambition on the part of solicitors will grow in proportion as they become more highly educated ... This is the argument against making [their] examination too stiff ... Who will perform the drudgery of the law?"[50] Kennedy complained to the Lord Chancellor "that my election to that office [*i.e.*, Professor of Law at Queen's College] would have been but a poor recommendation to the favour of the *Circuit Court*."[51] He had even "heard of such a thing as a barrister being prohibited from lecturing on his circuit."[52] Members of the Mess may have disliked the idea of formalized legal education altogether, or simply that it was conducted independently of the organized Bar. Kennedy observed that "[i]t is possible, indeed, that the Council, [of Queen's College] by special favour, may come to some arrangement, which may satisfy circuit *etiquette;* by either transferring the patronage into the hands of its leaders, or appointing, under their sanction, some man, who will give no alarm to professional jealousy."[53]

At any rate, conflict with the Midland Circuit Mess accompanied Kennedy's move to Birmingham. It was a turning point in his relations with his fellow barristers, who were faced with a choice between smoothing things over or confronting the Mess. By being excluded from the Mess, he said, he was "discountenanced and annoyed in every possible way," ranging from being "deprived of the honour of dining with the judges" and being "outcast from the society of your fellow barristers" to economic blacklisting. Most members of the Mess would refuse to hold briefs with an excluded barrister. That, in turn, would "prevent solicitors from employing him in any cause which requires the assistance of more than one counsel." The reputational damage was even worse: "[T]he excommunication of a man from society excites a universal prejudice against him, and few solicitors will venture to give a brief to one upon whom his own profession have fixed a stigma."[54]

While exclusion from the Mess inflicted damage, there was nothing in the Mess's power to prevent Kennedy from practising law as he saw fit. The Inns of Court too were ineffective as organs of professional discipline in this period. When the Mess excluded him, the organized legal profession lost all further influence over how he practised his profession. Thus freed, Kennedy opted for innovation. In the area of barristers' work, "there were some clear rules that were almost invariably obeyed but there was no proper code and the real sanction behind the rules was professional opinion."[55] Barristers' professional "etiquette" (the word is revealing) was inchoate. Even the contours of etiquette were open to debate, and it was understood that it existed as social convention rather than enforceable rule. There is a world of difference between mid-nineteenth-century barristers' etiquette and modern codes of professional conduct published by state-empowered professional associations and backed by sanctions administered by them. Dicey observed in 1867:

> The Bar rules are regulations which have a twofold aim: firstly, to promote honourable conduct; secondly, to check competition. All the rules which have the first aim may be summed up under the one law – thou shalt not hug attorneys. Under this head must be brought many minor regulations, such as rules against frequenting public coffee-rooms, or unduly cultivating the society of attorneys during circuit. No doubt these rules are extremely indefinite. No two lawyers will agree as to exactly what they are. Pedants and purists will enumerate a hundred little rules of etiquette, some of which they impose upon themselves, and all of which they are ready to impose on the less experienced and more docile members of circuit. Men of more sense and vigour do not pay much attention to the minutiae of the professional code. Still, all persons will acknowledge that there are some social rules of the kind referred to which it would be well for any barrister to observe who did not wish to incur considerable odium.[56]

The general import of etiquette was that barristers were not engaged in a trade. As gentlemen they were expected to be concerned with loftier matters than the active pursuit of legal business. Rules obliged barristers to practise in particular areas (their chosen "circuits"), prohibited fee competition, designated circumstances in which two barristers would have to be retained where one would do, and so on. The barrister was not to solicit clients either directly or indirectly by "hugging" attorneys. Rather, the barrister was to sit in "chambers" (gentlemen did not – and still do not – work in "offices"), waiting for legal business to present itself. It was to be brought only by an attorney or solicitor.[57] Barristers were to avoid meeting directly with clients; they would take their instructions from an attorney who would be the guiding legal mind in the conduct of a suit and who would negotiate the appropriate remuneration. Payment was regarded as an honorarium and not as a fee for contracted services. Barristers could not also be an attorney, act as an attorney, or work in partnership with an attorney.

Although general rules such as these were widely known, the lack of an enforcement mechanism kept things fluid at the edges. The minutiae were subject to discussion. Barristers were generally kept within the ill-defined bounds of etiquette by the weight of professional feeling. Exclusion from a circuit mess was rare, and even this did not prevent the individual from continuing to practise.[58] Paradoxically, Kennedy's exclusion from the Midland Circuit Mess in 1850 freed him entirely from the constraints of professional opinion for the next decade. He charged furiously through the gap thus opened.

Professional Isolation

Throughout the 1850s, Kennedy more or less disregarded established patterns of practice, whether in relation to clients, solicitors, other barristers, or judges. For the most part, he gave up trying to persuade the Bar leadership to mend its ways, appealing rather to "failing barristers" (who, he estimated, composed three-fourths of the Bar)[59] and to a broader public. The organized Bar had no tradition of dealing punitively with such an individual and left things alone. It intervened only much later, after his attacks became highly publicized, personal, vitriolic, and threatening to bench as well as bar. Throughout the intervening period, Kennedy actively challenged the conventional division of barristers from solicitors.[60] He offended the Metropolitan and Provincial Law Association (an early solicitors' association and onetime rival to the London-based Law Society),[61] and in 1852 launched a campaign that the *Law Times* viewed as an attack on the attorneys' (solicitors') branch.[62] Kennedy justified his actions simply on the grounds that "etiquette" did not serve the interests of ordinary barristers. He articulated his reasons and flouted the rules, acting out his position that professional organizations had no moral or legal right to set or enforce standards of practice.[63]

In particular, he confronted the Bar's leadership over practice in the County Courts, established in 1846 to hear cases involving sums up to twenty pounds (increased to fifty pounds in 1850). The legislation opened barristers to competition from the "lower branch" of the profession by creating a right of audience for attorneys. This had a devastating effect on the practices of a large number of barristers.[64] In 1851, "the 'Grand Court' of the Northern Circuit 'passed a resolution' that there was no rule of professional etiquette to prevent a barrister holding a brief in a County Court without a special fee; but that, on the contrary, any Barrister might accept and hold a brief in any of those courts with a fee of one guinea, if he thought fit to do so."[65] This was not enough for Kennedy. Showing both boldness and imagination, he advertised the formation of a "Mutual Law Association" in 1852. Its purpose was to provide members of the society with his legal services at an affordable rate.[66] He could do so in part because he lived and worked out of Birmingham rather than London.[67] Second, he would ignore rules purporting to prohibit fee competition. Kennedy scandalized the *Law Times* by being "all for free trade and competition in law,"[68] which he justified through appeal to capitalist principles:

> The price of every commodity adjusts itself. Leave counsels' fees to find their natural level, and find it they will. To fix anything of the kind at an artificial standard, is contrary to every maxim of political economy and common sense. A rule that counsel should never receive less than a guinea, is about as wise as a rule that no man shall sell a pound of sugar for less than eighteen pence.[69]

He was unapologetic about his self-interest ("Guinea-rules will never bring real guineas into *my* pocket"[70]), and his views probably reflected those of many underemployed barristers. The attack was not primarily on the elite of the Bar, however much it may have disquieted them. Rather, he argued that "[t]he only persons who benefit by this assumed standard are the attorneys." This was because artificially high barristers' fees made those of attorneys seem reasonable in comparison. Moreover, whereas the *County Courts Act* gave clients the option of being represented by an attorney alone, etiquette required that barristers could be hired only by a solicitor or attorney on the client's behalf.[71]

Cutting out unnecessary solicitor intermediaries was the third means of reducing costs. Sidestepping etiquette, Kennedy announced he would engage in direct contact with his clients: "If the attorney *were only the barrister's clerk*, as *under a good system he should be*, there would be no harm in his introducing the case *to his master;* but a person who requires an additional fee, and has power to intercept the case without letting it reach the barrister, answers little useful purpose that I can see."[72] He also intended to encroach more directly upon the more routine work of solicitors:

> I seek to do for law what Cobden has done for corn – to make it cheap and reasonable. *By law I do not mean litigation;* the less of that the better. *I mean legal advice, instruction, assistance.* The County Courts have brought the administration of justice to the poor man's door; but you want more than that. You want to have within your reach a class of honourable advocates

> and faithful interpreters of the law. In plain English, you want a Bar; but a Bar accessible and useful to the people.[73]

The scope of work for his Mutual Law Association was to encompass legal work that solicitors saw as theirs alone. The threat to solicitors' incomes and to the persistence of a divided profession was clear. Kennedy had no doubt as to the competitive ability of barristers operating in the same market as the "lower branch" of the profession, and relied heavily on the traditional status crutches of the Bar in marketing *his* services. Counsel, he said, were "more far-seeing" than other legal practitioners. He took pride that "[w]e barristers are gentlemen and scholars – as a class we are above the attorneys; we have better education, higher thoughts, greater capabilities."[74]

While these proposals scandalized the editors of the *Law Times* (an unofficial voice of attorneys[75]) and clearly breached etiquette,[76] no direct action was taken during the 1850s, probably because none was possible. Prompted by the complaint of a Birmingham solicitor,[77] the Benchers of the Inner Temple persuaded Kennedy to discontinue the Mutual Law Association. Nonetheless, he continued to charge fees as he thought fit, continued to practise in County Courts, continued to engage in direct client contact, and generally persisted in engaging in a practice that blurred, if it did not obliterate, the barrister/attorney demarcation. Reflecting upon his professional attainments as of 1855, he was pleased to have achieved an income of £800 to £900 a year, "not of a high character but chiefly in the inferior courts,"[78] up from £500 or £600 in 1854. These figures represented a reasonable though unspectacular income. While successful junior barristers might earn as much as £2,000 per annum in the late 1850s, "the more usual income from the rank and file was in the region of £500 to £1,200 yearly."[79] Kennedy's unorthodox practice signalled a plausible road to financial security for ordinary barristers.

In 1856, however, he commenced work on matter that was to exacerbate his conflict with the Bar. It ultimately resulted in his ruin, and gave impetus to major changes in how the organized Bar operated.

Exorcism

A mutual friend introduced Kennedy to Patience Swinfen in April 1856.[80] Mrs. Swinfen asked his opinion about litigation that had been concluded at the Stafford assizes on 15 March. She had been named beneficiary of a sizable estate in the will of her father-in-law, Samuel Swinfen. Upon his death, Samuel's nephew and heir-at-law, Captain Frederick Hay Swinfen, "filed a bill in Chancery, praying (among other things) for an issue to try the competency of the testator."[81] The matter came before Justice Cresswell Cresswell and a special jury at the Stafford assizes. Mrs. Swinfen's lead barrister was the former solicitor-general, Sir Frederick Thesiger (later Lord Chelmsford). While the matter was before the court, Thesiger concluded a compromise of the action *against the express wishes of his client.* He told her that "he had received a private intimation from high quarters, that she would lose the case, and that she had better save something from the wreck."[82] Kennedy observed that "[w]hat this meant was plain enough,"[83] and everyone took it to refer to a private conversation between Thesiger and the judge.[84]

As a result of their meeting, Kennedy undertook to represent Mrs. Swinfen in an attempt to overturn the compromise and prove the will. Subsequently, the mission extended to suing Thesiger for damages arising from his violation of his client's instructions. This was explosive. It challenged the integrity of a senior lawyer. Founded on the principle that litigants should have final say in the conduct of their own causes, it called into question the general scope of *authority* of barristers in relation to clients. The challenge tainted an eminent judge, Sir Cresswell Cresswell, with the imputation of impropriety, and consequently cast doubt on the fairness of the courts more generally. As the litigation proceeded, Cresswell suffered the indignity of being called to testify about his management of the case.[85] Worse still, Thesiger had been created Baron Chelmsford, Lord Chancellor, in the interim. Thus, the theory of the case was either that the Lord Chancellor and a senior judge had conspired illegally to deprive a widow of her inheritance or that the Lord Chancellor had deliberately misled a client.[86] Neither construction added lustre to the public face of the bench:

> If Sir Frederick Thesiger had the intimation from high quarters which he said he had, and if it exercised the slightest influence upon his mind, I need not say, the compromise was illegal. Yet it is hardly possible to conceive such a thing. If he slandered the high personage alluded to, he must have had some improper motive for intimidating his client, and the court can never uphold an agreement concluded under such circumstances ... the case is fraught with treachery.[87]

The litigation drew public attention to the nature of the working relationship between judicial bench and bar in spectacular fashion. Arrangements such as those alleged may have provided a degree of common-sense flexibility to the common law's legendary "rigidity" (prior to fusion with equity), however unseemly this particular arrangement seemed. Compromise in the midst of a trial permitted substantively fair outcomes where "law" permitted only formally "just" ones. Whereas the court could impose only either/or solutions, a compromise, even one encouraged surreptitiously by a judge, might award liabilities and benefits between the parties more fairly, deciding "matters that could not have been dealt with by the Court itself."[88] The widow and daughter-in-law, in other words, did not have to be left impoverished in order for the heir-at-law to inherit. It seems clear that some such system of compromise was frequently resorted to. The much-valued trust between barrister and judge may have been especially useful in all of this. In his argument against Kennedy, a Mr. Whateley, appearing for Chelmsford, stated that if counsel did not have such authority, the "business of the country could not be carried on."[89] This made the matter a test case of sorts:

> This constant bargaining at *Nisi Prius* lowers the dignity of counsel, and leads them to forget their duties. They are negotiating compromises when they should be pleading in Court; they are making arrangements for their own convenience, when they should be advocating the cause of their clients ... We cannot be blind to what is going on around us. If the present had been a solitary instance of a counsel betraying his client by a compromise, there would have been a universal outcry against him at the English Bar. It is because such things have been perpetrated before, that the same thing has been attempted now. The evil is a growing one, and requires a check: the abuse is notorious, and requires to be discountenanced.[90]

Kennedy added the telling comment that "[n]o barrister but one holding a high rank in the profession would dare to do such an act as Mrs. Swinfen's counsel has done."[91] He saw himself in a heroic role, saying he "had to maintain a doctrine of law novel and obnoxious in Westminster Hall, to meet the frowns of eminent judges, and to support her charges against the most distinguished advocates."[92]

The offence caused to prominent barristers did not end with scandalous allegations against a Queen's Counsel and an eminent judge or with the challenge to barristers' authority in general. Kennedy's unorthodox professional relationship with his client, too, was an affront. The combination of both with Kennedy's aggressive advocacy was volatile. His flouting of the ordinary rules of behaviour and immunity to the constraints of mess opinion served to confirm the leaders of the Bar in their commitment to conventional professional etiquette. Kennedy simultaneously challenged the integrity of leading barristers[93] and judges, the authority of barrister over client, and, consequently, the legitimacy of the English court system[94] measured on its own terms of openness, rigorous advocacy,[95] and judicial impartiality.[96] This raised the question of what could be done to control barristers such as Kennedy, and provoked reconsideration of the discipline required by a changing profession.

The opportunity to resolve all these issues came to a head when Kennedy's client refused to pay him for his services. He sued her for his legal fees, putting his behaviour as both an advocate and a private person on trial. Ultimately, this led to his destruction and to the delineation of a crucial new legal rule.

Kennedy had dealt with Patience Swinfen directly, without the mediation of an attorney.[97] The terms and conditions of his employment were negotiated directly with her, and, while attorneys were employed in the course of litigation, Kennedy "inverted the usual order of things, and became what the attorney commonly is, the *dominus litis*,[98] taking "complete control over the cause, over both counsel and attorneys."[99] This opened the possibility that he had been "acting as an attorney."[100] Mr. Macaulay commented on his handling of the Swinfen litigation that "he conducted it in a disgraceful manner, acting as attorney and counsel and everything."[101] So great was this offence that he was threatened with disbarment.[102]

Both the process and the outcome of his fee negotiations with Patience Swinfen were said to have breached professional etiquette. Fees were not marked on his briefs in the usual way,[103] and Kennedy agreed to payment after the legal work had been done rather than in advance (as was the usual practice).[104] Kennedy understood Mrs. Swinfen's inability to pay upfront[105] and also knew that she would never be able to pay him unless they were successful to some degree in litigation.[106] Extraordinary services were provided. Kennedy said: "I quitted my practice, gave myself up to her service, supported and comforted her through the whole of her struggles, shrank from no personal danger, freely spent my money, offered to pledge my all as security for her, and risk the bread of my family."[107] The services offered went far beyond the normal barrister's work. He wrote newspaper articles[108] and pamphlets,[109] published reports of the litigation,[110] and relocated his family from Birmingham to London.[111]

Kennedy's conduct and tone seemed almost calculated to offend. He did give qualified support to the view that counsel owed a duty to the court as well as to his client:

> It has been sometimes suggested, that an advocate ought to be a perfectly indifferent person, an assistant of the court, or a minister of justice, rather than a partisan of his client. This view is erroneous, contrary both to the theory and the practice of advocacy. To exclude from the counsel's mind all spirit of partisanship, is neither possible nor desirable ... You have a right to

> expect that a counsel will conduct causes temperately and discreetly, but you have no right to demand an absence of zeal, which is not only natural but justifiable.[112]

It must have seemed doubtful to observers that Kennedy displayed discretion or acted temperately in his conduct of the Swinfen litigation.

His critics thought he engaged in a "violent course of invective" that involved unnecessarily "hard words and vituperation,"[113] and it was said that he displayed "malignity" towards Sir Frederick Thesiger.[114] In an early proceeding, Kennedy had spoken of Thesiger's "disgraceful" conduct,[115] and the "treachery"[116] to which Mrs. Swinfen had been exposed by her "betrayer."[117] He complained of the "nisi Prius juggler," who as a class would "shirk the performance of their duty"[118] for the "love of gain and the love of ease."[119] Other lawyers involved in the case complained that he had launched an "attack [upon] persons superior to himself without cause."[120] At a minimum, what he said "may not have been in perfect good taste."[121] Crowder J. criticized Kennedy's "unmeasured and unwarrantable language,"[122] and Cresswell J. complained that Thesiger had been "most unsparingly and unjustifiably assailed."[123]

Others were wary of his excessive partisanship. When Kennedy first attempted to overturn the compromise, London attorneys John and Charles Cole rigorously resisted taking any affidavit from Mrs. Swinfen impugning Judge Cresswell.[124] Attorneys were reluctant to be involved at all in the case against Lord Chelmsford.[125] There was little in the cause that was immediately attractive from a professional viewpoint. It involved speculative litigation with little likelihood of success, pursued against the great and powerful, and with no hope of remuneration if the case was lost. *The Times,* which during the 1850s and 1860s was more or less continuously engaged in campaigns against the leaders of the Bar, hesitated.[126]

Kennedy's invective was not limited to the courts. His satirical poem "The Reference" describes a judge who persuades a sergeant-at-law to force a compromise on his reluctant client because he does not wish to miss a dinner engagement.[127] Kennedy sought to communicate the evils of the Bar leadership to the widest possible audience through newspaper articles and his own published reports of the litigation. These usually just reproduced argument, testimony, and affidavit evidence given in court, broadcasting his unrestrained invective to a much larger audience than would otherwise have been reached. For added effect, the preface to the first of his published pamphlets on the cases, "To Patience Swinfen," attacked Thesiger and Cresswell in language considered by many to be unfair:[128]

> Thine was a courage singly to exclaim 'Gainst Might perverting justice.
> ...
> The canting tones of dull servility
> In halls of Themis shall be heard no more;
> And tricksters shall unlearn their crafty lore:
> So potent is thy spell! At sight of thee
> Behold where treason skulks with conscious dread,
> And base corruption hangs her guilty head.

Flogging the obvious point, Kennedy explained in a subsequent collection of poetry that for "an explanation of this sonnet" readers should look at his report of *Swinfen v. Swinfen* as "[a] perusal of the affidavits ... will enable my readers to appreciate the calumnious attack made upon me, and the motives of those who made it. I trust that neither calumnies nor menaces (even from *High Quarters*) will ever deter me from doing my duty."[129]

For those who found his ardour on behalf of his client and his vitriolic attacks on leading barristers and judges distasteful, Kennedy's *de facto* immunity from professional discipline seemed regrettable. He had entered into the work and conducted the cause in breach of ordinary professional etiquette. However, as long as he continued to act on behalf of his client, presenting legal claims in a representative capacity, there was little that could be done to restrain him. The Inns of Court were notoriously poorly organized and ineffective disciplinary bodies,[130] the Mess had no more hold over him, and Kennedy's view that professional etiquette was not legally enforceable was plausible.[131] Provided he appeared in court as counsel, there was little the judicial bench or Benchers of the Inns could do to restrain him. Any further action by judges would run into the prevalent professional ideology's celebration of the advocate as a vigorous and selfless defender of the client. A legislative response was difficult in itself and not something the Inns wished to invite: it was important to them to preserve their status as independent self-governing bodies.[132]

The opportunity to act against him arose in 1861. By then Kennedy had represented Patience Swinfen in court on at least fourteen separate occasions and been remarkably successful in his efforts.[133] Thesiger's compromise was overturned and Samuel Swinfen's will upheld, with the result that Patience Swinfen inherited a property valued at some £60,000.[134] Kennedy's only significant failure was the action against Lord Chelmsford (the former Sir Frederick Thesiger) for legal malpractice. Though he had good arguments and a seemingly strong evidentiary foundation for the claim, the judges created a rule of barristers' immunity in order to decide for Chelmsford (adding, for good measure, that their colleague had acted *bona fide* throughout).

Importantly, however, Kennedy had done all of this as an advocate advancing the interests of his client. That changed in 1861. Patience Swinfen returned from holiday, married Charles Broun (also known as Brown), and refused to pay Kennedy the fees to which he felt entitled under the contract of his employment. He sought to recover his fees in court but quickly found himself on the defensive, having to justify and explain his every action. He had to defend his failure to use a solicitor as an intermediary, his assumption of the role of *dominus litis,* his failure to obtain fees in advance, and his partisan zeal. He justified his behaviour on the grounds that the case "could not have been won by an adherence to the rules of etiquette."[135] Mrs. Swinfen, he argued,

> was unreasonable enough to desire that her cause should be won ... to have a counsel who would be, not her attorney's tool, but her own champion; not a counsel whose fee was paid beforehand – for that would not help her much – but one who was properly armed beforehand, by due preparation for the conflict – armed with thought and study and research, and a mind capable of using such weapons; and further, with that zeal which identifies itself with the client, and a resolution to fight her battle without regard to personal consequences. This was what she wanted, and what I supplied. Perhaps I violated rules; I offended great people, her adversaries; but I accomplished the desired object.[136]

It was suggested that the action against Lord Chelmsford had been pursued at Kennedy's insistence as a personal vendetta,[137] and Kennedy had to answer to charges of both champerty and maintenance[138] (because he was to have been paid after a successful outcome of the litigation) and of infringing on the monopoly of attorneys.[139] Moreover, he was accused of abusing his professional relationship with Mrs. Swinfen by fraudulently persuading her to execute a deed in his favour valued at £20,000.[140] Each of these arguments was effectively met. Mrs. Swinfen's testimony demonstrated that she was no helpless widow tricked into agreements she didn't understand by an unscrupulous barrister.[141] The charges of champerty and maintenance were legally vulnerable,[142] and defending against them provided Kennedy with yet another opportunity to cast himself heroically as Swinfen's champion.[143] Finally, the allegation that Kennedy had "acted as an attorney" ran into serious factual and legal difficulties (not the least of which involved the problem of defining precisely the difference between solicitors' and barristers' work).[144]

During the trial of the action at Warwick, it was the judge, Cockburn L.C.J., who raised the issue that was to prove ultimately fatal to Kennedy's case. It also created an enduring deterrent to other counsel tempted to circumvent etiquette, and provided a simple and convenient mechanism of policing the dividing line between the two branches of the legal profession. At the close of evidence, Mr. Macaulay, appearing for Mrs. Broun, moved to dismiss the case on the ground that "there was no proof of an account stated."[145] Cockburn ruled:

> I think there is evidence for the jury, but I will give you leave to move. I think the objection lies still deeper. In my opinion there is no substratum of a contract, because I hold that the plaintiff acted as a counsel, and his fees must have been an honorarium. I do not agree with certain recent cases, in which it has been said that there may be a special contract for such fees. However, those points shall be reserved for you.[146]

The Lord Chief Justice of England reserved a point that had not been raised. He did more than this to drive the outcome. A jury decision against Kennedy would have ensured his personal financial ruin and provided effective retribution for his indiscretions, but it would have left the *law* untouched. Anxious to ensure that the substantive issues touching on barristers' practice would be definitively resolved, Cockburn wanted more. A jury verdict *for* Kennedy was required before there could be an authoritative judicial ruling *against* what he represented.

Cockburn summed up so as to achieve this result. He reminded the jurors of the legal points reserved and instructed them to decide narrowly on the facts:

> [Y]ou have nothing to do with the legal questions; you will have to determine, whether in point of fact the defendant admitted that she owed a certain sum for services, and promised to pay it; whether there was a contract for the services before they were performed, and a subsequent acknowledgment of liability.[147]

The jury, in short, was to consider the matter precisely as if it were any other action for an account stated, disregarding the peculiarities of legal practice or the rectitude of Kennedy (who had been called "diabolical," "disgraceful," and "base" by his opponents[148]). Pointedly, Cockburn made it quite clear that he felt Kennedy's version of events was to be believed over Mrs. Swinfen's (Broun's),[149] and that Kennedy had performed valuable services for her. She was made to seem like a selfish ingrate:

> Signal indeed those services were. The litigation in which Mr. Kennedy embarked in her behalf was one of fearful hazard, and nothing but the high

> attainments, the energy, perseverance, unflinching courage, and great powers of advocacy of Mr. Kennedy, could have achieved the victory. The value of his services was fully appreciated by his client and her letters were produced to show this.[150]

The jury understood what they were to do and quickly returned the verdict Cockburn sought. Leave to move was granted to Mrs. Broun "on the two grounds: whether it was an account stated, and whether there was valid consideration."[151]

The stage was now set for the Court of Common Pleas to review the nature of barristers' practice, the relationship between barristers and their clients, and the relative roles of barrister and attorney. *The Times* expressed its disapproval of the jury verdict in Kennedy's favour. It accused him of "pecuniary meanness" and "unmanly behaviour," and dared the Benchers of Lincoln's Inn and members of the Home Circuit to take action. "[T]he Bar," it said, "would be a curse to society if such things were tolerated in its members, and the public have a right to appeal to the Benchers of the Inns of Court for protection against practices which, if recognized by the inaction of these bodies, must deprive litigants of all confidence in members of the Bar."[152] Similar disapproval was quickly registered by the *Daily News,* the *Morning Post,* and the *Birmingham Daily Post.*[153]

A turning point had been reached. Kennedy had previously courted publicity in order to carry his arguments to a broader public; that support was now diminished. The condemnation of the organized profession by the respectable press heightened the sense of crisis felt by the Inns on account of the introduction only a fortnight previously of Sir George Bowyer's "Bill for the Better Government of the Inns of Court, and for the Discipline of the Bar."[154] This strengthened the hand of those within the Inns who were resolved to implement a more rigorous disciplinary structure, *and* likely set the ground for the judges to enforce the etiquette of the Bar insofar as it lay within their power.

From this point onward, it became difficult to support Kennedy's commercial and utilitarian concept of barristerial practice without also appearing to condone deception, fraud, and immorality. Circumstances peculiar to this one case came to stand for the evils of deviance from professional etiquette in general. Most damaging was the revelation that Kennedy had been involved in an adulterous affair with his client. In a stunning strategic blunder, Kennedy himself had introduced extensive evidence of their love affair.[155] Bad enough that they were having sex outside of marriage; their sin was compounded as Kennedy was a married man. The press was scandalized. *The Times* commented that "the history of human baseness does not offer an instance previous to this trial wherein an Englishman, while attempting to substantiate a money claim against a woman, has sought to make the woman confess in the witness-box that she has indulged in familiarities from which the act of adultery might be inferred."[156] The *Birmingham Daily Post* also denounced the introduction of evidence of sexual intimacy and observed:

> Had the trial turned simply upon the question of money, Mr. Kennedy might have suffered in reputation, and might have exposed himself to the censure of the bar, but he would not have made the utter shipwreck of his name and fortune which he has now to lament. As it is, he is simply a ruined man. It is more than doubtful if he will be permitted to derive any benefit from the verdict given in his favour. It is probable ... that he will no longer be allowed to practise at the English bar.[157]

How heavily this revelation weighed in the minds of judges and leading barristers is unclear. The nature of the relationship with Mrs. Swinfen neatly translated into a parable of the dangers of breach of professional etiquette. An image of femininity helpless before exploitive man was evoked by the *Birmingham Daily Post* in its observation that "[i]t was strange and unprecedented that a counsel should bargain with his client – and that client a woman – for an equal share of the property he had undertaken to recover on her behalf." The paper pointed out that "the stipulated sum of £20,000 was an enormous reward to extract," and implied that it had been agreed because of the couple's overly intimate relationship. The *Post* was not under any delusions as to Mrs. Swinfen's "helplessness," however. She was, in its view, one of those "women who, whatever their character, are evidently possessed of acute [*sic*] and energy far out of proportion to the ordinary members of their sex," and who had "extraordinary self-possession, unbounded fertility of resource, and unshakable determination."[158]

It was but a small step to conclude that what had *really* started things off poorly in the whole affair was Kennedy's direct contact with his client. *The Times* opined that if barristers were to negotiate fees directly with their clients, the Bar would become "a disreputable body of purveyors to attorneys."[159] The newspaper commented that Kennedy's "professional remuneration was properly to be fixed by the attorney, and not by the client. Thus, and thus only, the amount could be brought under proper professional supervision and taxation, and could be removed from the suspicion of extortion or undue influence."[160] It was suggested too that the litigation would not even have been commenced had not Kennedy intruded himself in Mrs. Swinfen's affairs.[161] Prompting other people's litigation was then, as now, thought to be a bad thing. It was clearly stated by Kennedy's opponents that he had persuaded Mrs. Swinfen to engage in litigation that was not genuinely in her interest and that he did so solely "for the purpose of satisfying his own ambition."[162]

Such themes, raised in court and reiterated in the press, were given authoritative legal expression by the judges of the Common Pleas in *Kennedy v. Broun*. In form, the court was deliberating the merits of Cockburn's suggestion that barristers could not contract for their fees. Their decision served to legislate the nature of legal practice in years to come. The matter was not entered into lightly by the judges, nor was the resolution an obvious one. Although the Court of Common Pleas ruled that "the relation of counsel and client renders the parties mutually incapable of making any contract of hiring and service concerning advocacy in litigation,"[163] only three years earlier Chief Baron Pollock had assumed the opposite.[164] In no sense was the matter settled law. The difficulty was such that a decision was handed down over two months after the conclusion of argument. The judgment was written in advance and delivered by the Chief Justice *per curiam*.[165]

Three background considerations operated: (1) the perceived need to protect judges and courts from assaults on their legitimacy through litigation such as this; (2) the need to preserve attorneys as a distinct class of legal professionals and to preserve the Bar's elite status; and (3) the need to offer an explanation of the financial failure of the majority of barristers not attributable to their profession's restrictive etiquette.

None of these could be pursued fully. In the age when "freedom of contract"[166] ruled, any restrictions on agreements respecting legal services needed to be justified. Only four years before *Kennedy v. Broun*, John Stuart Mill had famously written that

> the sole end for which mankind are warranted, individually or collectively, in interfering with the liberty of action of any of their number, is self-protection. That the only purpose for which power can be rightfully exercised over any member of a civilised community, against his will, is to prevent harm to others. His own good, either physical or moral, is not a sufficient warrant ... It is, perhaps, hardly necessary to say that this doctrine is meant to apply only to human beings in the maturity of their faculties.[167]

Unsurprisingly, the judges in *Kennedy v. Broun* rested their decision on prevention of harm to third parties and protection of the vulnerable. The paternalistic rationale found its grounding in the fear that clients entering into litigation are peculiarly vulnerable to being taken advantage of by selfish barristers. The *Birmingham Daily Post*'s portrayal of helpless femininity was transformed by their Lordships to a more general concern for defenceless lay clients:

> The facts of the present case forcibly shew some of the evils which would attend both on the advocate and the client if the hiring of counsel was made binding. In this case, the advocate, by disclosing words of infinite confidence which passed in moments of helpless anxiety, has raised the phantom of a contract for a sum of monstrous amount; and of this we hope we may say that there is no one in the profession of the plaintiff who would be willing to accept from him this verdict for £20,000 as a gift. In the present case, too, if the client compares the competence and peace secured for her by her former advocate with the perils and miseries of wearisome litigation derived from her later advocate, the contrast may suggest to her that gratuitous advocacy is preferable to contract as a mode of remunerating advocates.[168]

The outcome was also rationalized by Erle C.J. as required for the protection of innocent third parties. The most obvious were the attorneys whose "rights and duties" had become established over time[169] for very good reason: "if contracts for hire could be made by advocates, an interest in litigation might be created contrary to the policy of the law against maintenance; and the rights of attornies might be materially sacrificed, and their duties be imperfectly performed by unscrupulous advocates."[170] In other words, the preservation of a distinct attorneys' profession was at stake and justice required a division of legal labour. While Erle C.J. spoke of preserving the rights and privileges of the attorneys, equilibrium between the two branches of the legal profession more generally turned on the outcome. Blurring of the distinction would tend to corrode the authority of the mess, the circuit system, the centralized bar, and its social homogeneity. The Benchers' leadership and all the informal mechanisms of social control for a tight-knit professional community were at risk. Elite barristers, too, might find that their competitive ability rested on claims to expertise and status unlikely to prove sustainable in a free market for legal services.

This takes us to the third reason why the judges of the Common Pleas ruled as they did. The problem was both simple and obvious. As has been noted, many barristers had suffered economically following the creation of County Courts in 1846,[171] and Kennedy's unorthodox practice indicated a path to their financial salvation. The judges' explanation for inequality of wealth and status among barristers somewhat ironically rested on free market principles:

> We are aware that, in the class of advocates, as in every other numerous class, there will be bad men, taking the wages of evil, and therewith also for the most part the early blight that awaits upon the servants of evil. We are aware also that there will be many men of ordinary powers, performing ordinary duties without praise or blame. But the advocate entitled to permanent success must unite high powers of intellect with high principles of duty. His faculties and acquirements are tested by a ceaseless competition proportioned to the prize to be gained, that is, wealth and power and honour without, and active exercise for the best gifts of mind within.[172]

Where, then, did Kennedy fit? He obviously had not attained permanent success. Nor, however, was he an "ordinary" man performing "ordinary duties." Even his detractors recognized his great learning, eloquence, and perseverance. Conveniently, his failures could be attributed to moral weakness, an impression consistent with both his demonstrated professional arrogance and his illicit love affair with a client. Henceforth, Kennedy's unorthodox approach to practice lost its respectable veneer. Dissent from etiquette was rendered not just unprofitable but socially deviant and, explicitly here, tantamount to engaging in the service of the devil. Every perceived excess from Kennedy's high fee and "unmanly" exploitation of a "helpless" female, through to his adulterous affair and his vitriolic attack on respected barristers and judges, could be traced back to his original sin of deviating from professional norms.

Kennedy's wrongdoing was not seen as simply an individual failing, however. Rather, the whole political community was said to have suffered. This, the court said, was because "[t]he incapacity of the advocate in litigation to make a contract of hiring affects the integrity and dignity of advocates, and so is in close relation with the highest of human interests, viz. the administration of justice."[173] The judges emphasized that the legitimacy of law itself rested upon the character of barristers:

> He [the barrister] is trusted with interests and privileges and powers almost to an unlimited degree. His client must rely on him at times for fortune and character and life. The law trusts him with a privilege in respect of liberty of speech which is in practice bounded only by his own sense of duty; and he may speak upon subjects concerning the deepest interests of social life, and the innermost feelings of the human soul. The law also trusts him with

> a power of insisting on answers to the most painful questioning; and this power, again, is in practice only controlled by his own view of the interests of truth. It is of the last importance that the sense of duty should be in active energy proportioned to the magnitude of these interests.[174]

Here, too, Kennedy failed. While the client ought to be able to trust her lawyer for fortune and character, Kennedy had claimed a very large proportion of Mrs. Swinfen's wealth as his own and had assailed her character in the most public fashion possible.[175] While the law trusted Kennedy with a liberty of speech bounded by his sense of duty, he had slandered judges and prominent lawyers, and pursued the most painful questioning of all concerned for reasons having little to do with the pursuit of the "best interests of truth." Kennedy had failed miserably at fulfilling his twofold duty, "that is to say, duty to his client, binding him to exert every faculty and privilege and power in order that he may maintain that client's right, together with duty to the court and himself, binding him to guard against abuse of the powers and privileges intrusted to him, by a constant recourse to his own sense of right."[176]

It was greed that had caused Kennedy to fail, unleashing destructive force on Patience Swinfen, Frederick Thesiger, and Cresswell Cresswell. Erle C.J. reasoned as follows:

> But, if the law allowed the advocate to make a contract of hiring and service, it may be that his mind would be lowered, and that his performance would be guided by the words of his contract rather than by principles of duty, that words sold and delivered according to contract, for the purpose of earning hire, would fail of creating sympathy and persuasion in proportion as they were suggestive of effrontery and selfishness; and that the standard of duty throughout the whole class of advocates would be degraded. It may also be that, if contracts for hire could be made by advocates, an interest in litigation might be created contrary to the policy of the law against maintenance; and the rights of attorneys might be materially sacrificed, and their duties be imperfectly performed by unscrupulous advocates.[177]

Kennedy had shifted from merely eccentric to dangerous. Moreover, the danger he presented did not arise from want of learning or an idiosyncratic personality. Rather, danger was omnipresent, found in every corridor and in every drawing room in which a barrister might contract directly with a client. Infringement of the rules of etiquette henceforth became deviant, not merely eccentric.

Given the pervasiveness of the danger, it is not surprising that other responses were provoked. Kennedy had shown the ineffectiveness of the organized Bar by flouting its etiquette for over a decade. The spectacular revelations of the original Swinfen litigation occurred in the context of mounting criticism of the Bar. The Kennedy affair crystallized many concerns and removed barriers to reforms aimed at preserving professional form, protecting etiquette, and strengthening the power of the organized Bar over its members. One local manifestation was a rejuvenation of the bar mess – still the most effective locus of discipline – in the Midlands. The Midland Circuit Mess minute book reveals a revival of interest in disciplinary matters that had been lacking since the fuss about the Mutual Law Association a decade earlier. In the spring of 1863, the Staffordshire Circuit Mess began to keep formal minutes of its meetings for the first time.[178] In London, the Benchers of Inner Temple began proceedings to disbar Kennedy, an attempt that was never successfully concluded.[179]

Something else happened, however, that was to produce more far-reaching results for bar organization in England. The introduction of Sir George Bowyer's bill in March 1862 set the stage for reforms that followed. These emphasized discipline but recognized the interests of non-elite barristers to the extent of acknowledging a need for more democratic governance. The preamble to the bill observed that "it is desirable to amend the Constitution of the Four Inns of Court ... for the purpose of giving to the Barristers of those Societies a share in and Control over their Government ... and also to provide a fit tribunal, with the necessary Powers, for maintaining the Discipline of the Bar."[180] Provisions were made for a power to disbar or suspend any deviant barrister. While the bill failed to pass, "in reality the damage to the old way of doing things was irreparable."[181] Kennedy's escapades were not solely responsible for bringing about Bowyer's bill, but his example contributed significantly to a general concern about the Bar.[182] *Kennedy v. Broun* ramped up concerns dramatically. The case provided a neat moral narrative that had previously been lacking. It became a parable in support of conventional etiquette, which now, for the first time, required efficient enforcement mechanisms. A turning point had been reached. Reforms previously impossible to achieve now appeared necessary.

Conclusion

How, then, are the professional adventures of Charles Rann Kennedy to be interpreted with regard to the transition to the modern bar? His career provided impetus to a transformation of legal practice and professional organization. New elements suffused established structures in metasomatic processes.

Kennedy sought a liberalization of barristers' practice and a loosening of etiquette, but brought about its opposite. In response to the economic challenges faced by barristers, he offered a program whereby new markets for their services could be tapped. His proposals were well grounded in the ideology of *laissez-faire* and justified explicitly on that basis. His approach to advocacy was also nested solidly within the traditional ideology of professionalism. It would never have occurred to him that barristers were anything other than men of refined intellect, "gentlemen and scholars – as a class ... above the attorneys."[183] Barristers' traditional status were integral to Kennedy's worldview. He believed in a bar composed of rugged, fearless individuals who played a central role in advancing individual freedom by protecting their clients from abuse.

His program came off the rails not because it was implausible but as a result of the particular circumstances within which it was advanced and defended. While his ideas were likely quite palatable to many barristers,[184] they were anathema to the Bar leadership and to the judiciary. A competing paradigm was developing that was inclined to more, not less, "professional" control over practice at the Bar. The twin innovations represented by *Kennedy v. Broun* and Bowyer's bill shaped the modern bar. Many of the features that Larson and her followers have identified as a market control project are manifest in this sequence of events. There could be no clearer assertion of a professional's right to define a layperson's needs for his or her service than in Thesiger's handling of Mrs. Swinfen's original case. The identification of barristers' services as a distinct commodity had been threatened by Kennedy's Mutual Law Association and by his assumption of the role of *dominus litis* in the Swinfen litigation. Conventional approaches of the bar elite were dramatically entrenched in the outcome. The dual problem of creating an exclusive demand for barristers' services and dealing with unlicensed competitors was resolved in *Kennedy v. Broun*'s articulation of distinct roles for barristers and attorneys. That judgment and consequent developments were carefully calculated to preserve the Bar's claim of a "monopoly of credibility" by projecting an "ethical," "public spirited" image that was ensured by rules of etiquette, now for the first time enforced by courts.[185] In the battle of competing professional forms, the ultimate victory went to the powerful and the well-connected – to the Benchers and the bench. Kennedy was ruined.

None of this was inevitable. The very fact that Kennedy was able to champion an alternative vision of practice for nearly a decade and a half indicates the nineteenth century's openness to professional innovation. In the end, it was only peculiar and unpredictable circumstances that facilitated the consolidation of professional reform instituting novel central controls over the practices of individual barristers. A process of change was begun (though not completed) only when Kennedy became notorious, exposed, and vulnerable. As much as any other, his story provided the parable and moral lesson impelling professional innovation in exactly the opposite direction to that for which he fought.

The Bar retained its essential structures, including the Inns of Court, circuit messes, rules of etiquette, and divisions of labour. The turn towards regularized and intrusive discipline, however, transformed these structures in their essence,[186] just as completely as metasomatic processes transform geology.

The trajectory of the modern bar and its understandings of professionalism had begun.

Notes

An earlier version of this chapter appeared as "Exorcising Professional Demons: Charles Rann Kennedy and the Transition to the Modern Bar" (1987) 15:1 Law and History Review 135. It has been revised and reprinted here with permission.

1 Stanley Cohen, *Folk Devils and Moral Panics: The Creation of the Mods and Rockers* (Oxford: Oxford University Press, 1980) at 10.

2 *Ibid.* at 61. Profoundly important examples of such a process are documented in Paul Boyer and Stephen Nissenbaum, *Salem Possessed: The Social Origins of Witchcraft* (Cambridge, MA: Harvard University Press, 1974), and Arthur Miller, *The Crucible* (1953). A similar process is documented in relation to the United States legal profession in ch. 4, "Cleansing the Bar," in J. Auerbach, *Unequal Justice: Lawyers and Social Change in Modern America* (New York: Oxford University Press, 1976). For an example of the process, see P.A. Thomas, Helen Power, and Robert East, "The British Miners' Strike" (1985) 5 Windsor Y.B. Access Just. 181. In the history of crime, Daniel Pick has said that "the designation of the criminal is bound up, in complex ways, with the opposing but reciprocal process of defining the good citizen, or the good subject, in specific, in particular periods," in "The Faces of Anarchy: Lombroso and the Politics of Criminal Science in Post-Unification Italy" (1986) 21 History Workshop 61.

3 See Conrad Gill, *History of Birmingham*, 2 vols. (Oxford: Oxford University Press, 1952) 1: 375; Frederic Boase, *Modern English Biography*, 6 vols. (London: Netherton and Worth, 1897) 2:195.

4 Sir Leslie Stephen and Sir Sidney Lee, eds., *The Dictionary of National Biography*, 22 vols. (Oxford: Oxford University Press, 1973) [*Dictionary of National Biography*].

5 *Ibid.*

6 J.A. Venn, *Alumni Cantabrigienses* (Cambridge: Cambridge University Press, 1951).

7 *Dictionary of National Biography*, supra note 4.

8 See "Mr. Kennedy's Testimonials for the Vacant Chair of Greek at the University of Edinborough," B.L. 8366, 6633 ["Mr. Kennedy's Testimonials"].

9 *The Times* (2 April 1862).

10 (1863) 2 (n.s.) The Jurist 20.

11 Lord Chief Justice of England, in Charles Rann Kennedy, *The Great Swinfen Case: Report of the Extraordinary Trial at Warwick in the Matter of Kennedy v. Brown and Wife* (London: n.p., 1862) 44 [Kennedy, *The Great Swinfen Case*].

12 See *The Times* for the following dates: 9 March 1849 at 6, 3 October 1849 at 5, 3 January 1850 at 6. The story of the Queen's College Law Department is set out more fully in Chapter 4.

13 Dicey himself was a failed barrister. See Richard A. Cosgrove, *The Rule of Law: Albert Venn Dicey, Victorian Jurist* (London: Macmillan, 1980). Kennedy may in fact have had higher scholarly ambitions. Less than two years later, he applied for the chair of Greek in Edinburgh. See "Mr. Kennedy's Testimonials," *supra* note 8. By this time, however, it would have been clear that the Queen's College program in law was floundering. See "Mr. Kennedy's Manifesto" *Law Times* 20 (30 October 1852) 58.

14 See "The Roses' Address on Her Ninth Birthday" in C.R. Kennedy, *Poems: Original and Translated* (London: William Walker, 1857) 31 [*Poems*]. Note also the juxtaposition of "My Cottage in Hertfordshire" with "View of a Manufacturing Town" at 90-91 of the same collection.

15 *E.g.*, John Pym Yeatman, *The Professorship of the Law Department of the Queen's College, Birmingham: A Letter to the Council and Governors* (Birmingham: M. Maher and Son, 1869) at 5.

16 Charles Rann Kennedy, *A Letter to the Lord Chancellor on the Subject of Circuit Leagues* (Birmingham: George Bell, 1850) 4 [*Circuit Leagues*].

17 In *Broun v. Kennedy*, 33 Beav. 133, 152, 55 E.R. 317, 325.

18 In Kennedy, *The Great Swinfen Case, supra* note 11 at 44.

19 *Birmingham Daily Post* (3 April 1862) at 2.

20 See Brian Abel-Smith and Robert Stevens, *Lawyers and the Courts* (London: Heinemann, 1967) at 53-62; Raymond Cocks, *Foundations of the Modern Bar* (London: Sweet and Maxwell, 1983) at 86-87; Patrick Polden, *A History of the County Court, 1846-1971* (Cambridge and New York: Cambridge University Press, 1999).

21 "Testimonial to the Rev. Rann Kennedy, M.A." *Aris's Birmingham Gazette* (26 November 1849) at 1, col. 3.

22 "The Death of Mr. Kennedy" *Aris's Birmingham Gazette* (21 December 1857) at 6, col. 7.

23 "The Bar and the Attorneys. Mr. Rann Kennedy's Birmingham Speech" *Legal Observer* 45 (6 November 1852) 12.

24 Kennedy, *Circuit Leagues, supra* note 16.

25 *Ibid.* Daniel Duman, however, offers evidence suggesting that such a rule came to be generally enforced by circuit messes during the 1850s: *The English and Colonial Bars in the Nineteenth Century* (London: Croom Helm, 1983) at 47. The status of such a rule cannot be known with certainty until the history of each mess is written. Cocks argues that such restrictions did not appear in the Home Circuit until 1856 or in the Norfolk Circuit until 1872. See Raymond Cocks, "The Bar at Assizes: Barristers on Three Nineteenth Century Circuits" (1976) 6 Kingston L. Rev. 36 at 45 ["The Bar at Assizes"].

26 *Ibid.* at 12

27 *Ibid.* at 15.

28 *Ibid.* at 11.

29 *Ibid.* at 8-12.

30 *Ibid.* at 14-15.

31 On the one hand, Kennedy received testimonials from distinguished individuals prior to his election as Professor of Law at Queen's College: Sir Frederick Thesiger, M.D. Hill, R.B. Crowder, W.H. Watson, W. Shateley, W. Shee, C. Whitehurst, S. Martin, M. Chambers, A.E. Cockburn, J. Manning, and T.S. Murphy. See *Aris's Birmingham Gazette* (12 November 1849) at 3, col. 2. On the other hand, it seems that Kennedy had previously run afoul of the profession in London: "The Bar and the Attorneys," *supra* note 23.

32 Simple social incompatibility cannot be ruled out entirely. As late as the 1870s, the Home Circuit debated "whether or not social incompatibility was sufficient grounds for blighting a man's career": See Cocks, *Foundations of the Modern Bar, supra* note 20 at 147-48.

33 *Ibid.* at 16-17.

34 See, for example, Archer Polson, *Law and Lawyers,* 2 vols. (London, 1840) 1:136, cited in Cocks, *ibid.* at 31. In *Law Times* 3 (1844) 501, the bar mess is presumed to serve a useful disciplinary role. Cocks, *ibid.* at 80. See *ibid.* at 147ff for a discussion of the bar mess in the 1870s.

35 Kennedy, *Circuit Leagues,* supra note 16 at 4.

36 See generally Cocks, *Foundations of the Modern Bar, supra* note 20 at 15, who finds the first evidence of mess organization in 1836. Kennedy, in *Circuit Leagues, supra* note 16 at 6, describes the bar mess as "an association ... the proper character of which, as its name imports, is that of a private club, for convivial and social purposes; and which, if entrance to it were purely voluntary, and if it were confined to legitimate objects, would be a pleasant and harmless thing enough."

37 Kennedy, *Circuit Leagues, ibid.* at 15.

38 United Kingdom, *Report of the Select Committee on Legal Education* (25 August 1846) [*Select Committee on Legal Education*]. See discussions in Cocks, *Foundations of the Modern Bar, supra* note 20; Peter Stein, "Legal Theory and the Reform of Legal Education in Mid Nineteenth Century England" in *L'Educazione Giuridica* (Perugia, 1979) at 185-206. On the objectives of the Council of Queen's College generally and with regard to the Department of Law in particular, see "The Queen's College, Birmingham" *Aris's Birmingham Gazette* (12 May 1851) at l, col. 3; J.T.J. Morrison, *William Sands Cox and the Birmingham Medical School* (Birmingham: Cornish Brothers, 1926); William Sands Cox, ed., *Annals of the Queen's College, Birmingham,* 4 vols. (Birmingham: L.W.H. and L. Collingridge, 1873) i-iv.

39 Reverend Rann Kennedy, his father, was a benefactor of Queen's College. See *The Times* (3 January 1850). His brother, Benjamin Hall Kennedy, was at the time headmaster of Shrewsbury School. Both were well connected in Birmingham. See E. Edwards, *Personal Recollections of Birmingham and Birmingham Men* (Birmingham: Midland Educational Trading Company, 1877).

40 Gill, *History of Birmingham, supra* note 3 at 1:397.

41 *Select Committee on Legal Education, supra* note 38.

42 See Cocks, *Foundations of the Modern Bar, supra* note 20 at 69ff, 8, and 88ff.

43 Abel-Smith and Stevens, *supra* note 20 at 65-66; A.H. Manchester, *A Modern Legal History of England and Wales, 1750-1950* (London: Butterworths, 1980) at 58.

44 *Law Times* 1 (1843) 42, quoted in Cocks, *Foundations of the Modern Bar, supra* note 20 at 69.

45 *Ibid.* at 38.

46 *Ibid.* at 177.

47 Although he sought to provide an education for students destined for both branches of the legal profession, Kennedy clearly did not see them as equal and understood them to be in competition. See Kennedy, *Circuit Leagues,* supra note 16 at 10. Competitive pressures resulting at least in part from court reorganization were clearly hurting the Bar in the 1840s and 1850s. See Abel-Smith and Stevens, *supra* note 20 at 53-62; Cocks, *Foundations of the Modern Bar, supra* note 20 at 86-87.

48 Abel-Smith and Stevens, *supra* note 20 at 69.

49 *The Times* (3 January 1850) 6. *Aris's Birmingham Gazette* (25 February 1850) at 2, cols. 2-3, under the heading "Queen's College, Birmingham," carries a report indicating that the founders of the law department hoped to educate both aspiring barristers and aspiring solicitors in one program.

50 *Law Times* 20 (1852) 85, as quoted in J.R.S. Forbes, *The Divided Legal Profession in Australia* (Sydney: Law Book Company, 1979) at 16.

51 Kennedy, *Circuit Leagues, supra* note 16 at 15 [emphasis in original].

52 *Ibid.* at 16. One background concern may have been the sense that this would curry favour with solicitors, leading to unfair competition by a barrister well connected with attorneys and solicitors. Duman, *supra* note 25 at 46.
53 Kennedy, *Circuit Leagues, supra* note 16 at 15 [emphasis in original].
54 *Ibid.* at 7.
55 Cocks, *Foundations of the Modern Bar, supra* note 20 at 128 (see also 2, 22).
56 Albert V. Dicey, "Legal Etiquette" *Fortnightly Review* 8 (1 August 1867) 173.
57 The attorneys' and solicitors' branches of the legal profession were largely fused by an Act of 1751, although the use of a common title, "solicitor," was not formally sanctioned until the *Judicature Act, 1873,* s. 87. See Abel-Smith and Stevens, *supra* note 20 at 15, 53n.
58 See generally Cocks, *Foundations of the Modern Bar, supra* note 20; Duman, *supra* note 25; Dicey, *supra* note 56.
59 Kennedy, *Circuit Leagues, supra* note 16 at 11. Duman, *supra* note 25 at 4-9, 143-68, is generally supportive of Kennedy's assertion, indicating that a large number of "barristers" did not in fact earn their living in English legal practice. In "The New Era," the *Law Times* 20 (3 July 1852) 10 at 10, estimated that nine-tenths of the Bar "will be unable to live by it."
60 At a later time, and when it very much served his interests to appear as something other than a renegade barrister, Kennedy vehemently denied the allegation of having done the work of an attorney. See Kennedy, *The Great Swinfen Case, supra* note 11 at 43. See, however, "The Bar and the Attorneys," *supra* note 23 at 74; "The Junior Bar and the Attorney" *Law Times* 20 (27 November 1852) 110.
61 Abel-Smith and Stevens, *supra* note 20 at 57.
62 "The Attack on the Attorneys" *Law Times* 20 (9 October 1852) 25; "Mr. Kennedy's Manifesto" *Law Times* 20 (30 October 1852) 58.
63 Kennedy, *Circuit Leagues, supra* note 16 at 5, 7.
64 Cocks, *Foundations of the Modern Bar, supra* note 20 at 86-88; Abel-Smith and Stevens, *supra* note 20 at 32-37. See also discussion in Chapter 7 in this volume.
65 "Etiquette of the Bar" *Law Times* 17 (30 August 1851) 209. The previous self-denying rule of etiquette was threatening to the Bar's distinctiveness as it opened the door to a new type of attorney. The *Law Times* observed that specialist County Court advocates had begun to appear: "[T]he abolition of the old restriction may also be objected to by that small section of the other branch of the Profession whose practice consists, not in acting within the honourable and comprehensive province which legitimately belongs to the Solicitor and Attorney, but in devoting their whole attention to the conduct of such small debt cases as the existing system prevents Barristers being engaged in."
66 See generally "The Attack on the Attorneys," *supra* note 62 at 25.
67 See *ibid.* at 26 and "The Profession in the County Courts" *Law Times* (26 June 1852) at 101-2 (expressing disapproval of "local Barristers").
68 "The Attack on the Attorneys," *supra* note 62 at 25.
69 Pamphlet of C.R. Kennedy, quoted in *ibid.*
70 *Ibid.* [emphasis in original].
71 *Ibid.*
72 *Ibid.* [emphasis in original]. Many junior barristers apparently held similar views: "The Profession in the County Courts," *supra* note 67 at 101-2.
73 "The Attack on the Attorneys," *supra* note 62 at 25-26 [emphasis added]. The fear that all this might lead to fusion of the two professions was expressed in "The Bar and the Attorneys," *supra* note 23 at 74.
74 "The Attack on the Attorneys," *ibid.* at 26.
75 See Cocks, *Foundations of the Modern Bar, supra* note 20 at 64ff for a discussion of the readership and editorial policies of the *Law Times* in this period.

76 *Ibid.* at 87, however, reports that young barristers generally sought direct access to clients and that in one case "a Mess actually encouraged them to break the traditional rules of etiquette and approach clients directly." See *Law Times* 17 (12 July 1851) 209.
77 Inner Temple, *Bench Table Orders*, 5 November 1852 (recording letter from Thomas S. James).
78 Kennedy, *The Great Swinfen Case, supra* note 11 at 10.
79 Duman, *supra* note 25 at 144. Duman also observes (at 146) that "the figure of £500 probably referred to men who had established permanent practices," and that this may be a generous estimate. See H. Byerley Thomson, *The Choice of a Profession* (London: Chapman and Hall, 1857) at 94, 97-98.
80 The account that follows is largely based on material found in Kennedy, *The Great Swinfen Case, supra* note 11 at 36. See also Chapter 8 in this volume. Other accounts of these events are in published law reports, newspapers, other publications of C.R. Kennedy, and documents held in the Staffordshire County Record Office: Broun v. Kennedy, Bill of Complaint; Answer; Affidavits 0858/2/2. General accounts of the litigation are found in "Mrs. Patience Swinfen versus Barristers" (1974) 2 Queensland Lawyer 40, and J.R. Lewis, *The Victorian Bar* (London: Robert Hale, 1982) 95; Howard Clayton, *The Great Swinfen Case* (London and New York: Regency Press, 1980).
81 C.R. Kennedy, *Swinfen v. Swinfen: Report of the Argument in the Common Pleas, in Michaelmas Term, 1856* (London: Richard Hatton, 1857) at 3 [Kennedy, *Swinfen v. Swinfen*].
82 *Ibid.* at 4, 29.
83 *Ibid.* at 29
84 Kennedy, *The Great Swinfen Case, supra* note 11 at 13.
85 *Swinfen v. Lord Chelmsford* (1860) 5 Hurlstone and Normans' Reports 890 [*Swinfen v. Lord Chelmsford*]; *The Times* (6 July 1859) 11.
86 Illegal conspiracy was specifically alleged by Kennedy: *The Times* (5 July 1859) 11; *Swinfen v. Lord Chelmsford, supra* note 85.
87 Kennedy in Kennedy, *Swinfen v. Swinfen, supra* note 81 at 30.
88 *Ibid.* at 21.
89 Quoted in *ibid.* at 44.
90 Kennedy, quoted in *ibid.* at 19.
91 *Ibid.*
92 Kennedy, *The Great Swinfen Case, supra* note 11 at 37.
93 Other barristers involved included W.J. Alexander, QC and Attorney General to H.R.H. the Prince of Wales, Whitmore, and John Gray, Treasury Solicitor for Patience Swinfen. Sir Alexander Cockburn, QC, Attorney-General and subsequently Chief Justice of England, was lead counsel on the other side.
94 See generally Kennedy, *Swinfen v. Swinfen, supra* note 81 at 35-36.
95 *Ibid.* at 36. Kennedy expresses a longing for "the fearless, the trustworthy, the independant advocate" of "half a century ago."
96 A core principle strongly affirmed in *Dimes v. Grand Junction Canal*, [1853] 3 H.L.C. 759 (H.L.).
97 Kennedy, *The Great Swinfen Case, supra* note 11 at 5-6.
98 C.R. Kennedy, *Mr. Kennedy's Argument in the Common Pleas against the Rule Obtained by the Defendants in Kennedy v. Broun & Wife* (Birmingham: S.B. Howell, 1862) at 56 [*Mr. Kennedy's Argument*].
99 Kennedy, *The Great Swinfen Case, supra* note 11 at 7.
100 Kennedy, *Mr. Kennedy's Argument, supra* note 98 at 59.
101 Macaulay in Kennedy, *The Great Swinfen Case, supra* note 11 at 25. Kennedy defended himself against this charge on the grounds that he did not in fact "act as an attorney" and

that even if he did, this was a matter of etiquette not enforceable by the courts. According to Raymond Cocks there was no firm rule requiring a solicitor intermediary in barristers' dealings with lay clients until 1888. See Cocks, "The Bar at Assizes," *supra* note 25 at 36 and 46. See Kennedy, *The Great Swinfen Case, supra* note 11 at 43; Kennedy, *Mr. Kennedy's Argument, supra* note 98 at 56. Two elite barristers of the day agreed that there was no *universal* rule on this matter: "County Courts Extension Bill" *Law Times* 20 (26 June 1852) 102 (Lord Brougham); "Lord Denman's Letter" *Law Times* 20 (6 November 1852) 73. In any event, powerful interests held sway over the logic he was able to muster. See *Kennedy v. Broun* (1863) 13 C.B. (N.S.) 677 at 736ff; 143 E.R. 268 at 291ff per Erle C.J.; see also Cockburn C.J., quoted in Kennedy, *Mr. Kennedy's Argument, supra* note 98 at 7 (the excerpt here is somewhat different from that of the same passage in Kennedy, *The Great Swinfen Case, supra* note 11 at 44-45).

102 Kennedy, *The Great Swinfen Case, ibid.* at 43.
103 *Ibid.* at 7
104 *Ibid.* at 7, 14, 23; Kennedy, *Mr. Kennedy's Argument, supra* note 98 at 14.
105 Kennedy, *The Great Swinfen Case, ibid.* at 7.
106 *Ibid.* at 10.
107 *Ibid.* at 39.
108 *Ibid.* at 6, 13, 14; Kennedy, *Mr. Kennedy's Argument, supra* note 98 at 3.
109 Kennedy, *The Great Swinfen Case, ibid.* at 14.
110 *Ibid.* at 9, 11; Kennedy, *Mr. Kennedy's Argument, supra* note 98 at 3.
111 Kennedy, *The Great Swinfen Case, ibid.* at 9, 10; Kennedy, *Mr. Kennedy's Argument, ibid.* at 26.
112 Kennedy, *Mr. Kennedy's Argument, ibid.* at 55.
113 Mr. Whateley, quoted in Kennedy, *Swinfen v. Swinfen, supra* note 81 at 37.
114 *Ibid.* at 40.
115 *Ibid.* at 7.
116 *Ibid.* at 30.
117 *Ibid.* at 35.
118 *Ibid.* at 36.
119 *Ibid.* at 18, 19.
120 Keating, quoted in *ibid.* at 46.
121 E. James, quoted in *ibid.* at 51.
122 *Ibid.* at 53.
123 *Ibid.* at 60.
124 Kennedy, *The Great Swinfen Case, supra* note 11 at 8.
125 *Ibid.* at 16; Clayton, *supra* note 80.
126 *The Times* (26 November 1859) at 11, reported that in *Swinfen v. Lord Chelmsford* "Mr. Kennedy commenced his arguments in this case ... and had not concluded when the Court rose. The further hearing of the case was adjourned till the sitting of the Court on the first day of the next term. We therefore reserve our report of Mr. Kennedy's argument, as it would be unfair to that learned gentleman to publish it in an unfinished state." *The Times* never followed through on this commitment.
127 Kennedy, *Poems, supra* note 14 at 107-12.
128 See Kennedy, *The Great Swinfen Case, supra* note 11 at 22. At a later date, Kennedy apparently "repudiated any intention to charge either Mr. Justice Cresswell or Sir F. Thesiger with corrupt motives," and "regretted the attack he had made." *The Times* (31 March 1862) at 11, 12.
129 Kennedy, *Swinfen v. Swinfen, supra* note 81 at 2. The explanation appears in Kennedy, *Poems, supra* note 14 at 88.
130 Cocks, *Foundations of the Modern Bar, supra* note 20 at 2, 22, 128; Duman, *supra* note 25 at 34-40.

131 See Kennedy, *Circuit Leagues, supra* note 16; Kennedy, *Mr. Kennedy's Argument, supra* note 98 at 45, 56.
132 Cocks, *Foundations of the Modern Bar, supra* note 20 at 121; Abel-Smith and Stevens, *supra* note 20 at 53ff; Duman, *supra* note 25 at 55, 62.
133 *Swinfen vs. Swinfen* (11 June 1856) 18 C.B. 485; 139 E.R. 1459 (show-cause for attachment to enforce compromise entered into by Thesiger); *Swinfen vs. Swinfen* (12 January 1857) 1 C.B. (N.S.) 364; 140 E.R. 150 (motion for attachment against Patience Swinfen for contempt of court in refusing to abide by the compromise); *Swinfen vs. Swinfen* (7-10 November 1857) 24 Beav. 549; 53 E.R. 470 (ordering a trial on the issue of the competency of the testator and declining to specifically enforce the compromise entered into by Thesiger); *Swinfen vs. Swinfen* (22 April 1858) 2 DE G. & J . 381; 44 E.R. 1037 (judgment of 24 Beav. 549 affirmed on appeal); *Swinfen vs. Swinfen* (Stafford Summer Assizes, 1858) 1 F. & F. 584; 175 E.R. (trial of issue of the testamentary capacity of Samuel Swinfen. Verdict in favour of Will whereby Patience Swinfen inherited estate); *Swinfen vs. Swinfen* (No. 1) (12 January 1859) 27 Beav. 148; 54 E.R. 57 (motion in Chancery by heir-at-law seeking a retrial of the issue of testamentary capacity refused); *Swinfen v. Swinfen* (28, 30 March 1859), 1 SW & TR. 283; 164 E.R. 730 (on the question of costs to Captain Frederick Swinfen. No order as to costs made); *Swinfen v. Lord Chelmsford* (Trinity Term, 1859) 1 F. & F. 619; 175 E.R. (trial of action against Sir Frederick Thesiger for "improperly, fraudulently and without authority" entering into a compromise – directed verdict for defendant); *Swinfen v. Lord Chelmsford, supra* note 85 (directed verdict for defendant upheld on appeal, establishing the rule that barristers are immune from suit for incompetence or neglect); *Swinfen v. Bacon* (21 November 1860) 6 H. & N. 184; 158 E.R. 76 (on a subsidiary issue of debt owing to Patience Swinfen from an overholding tenant on the Swinfen estate); *Swinfen v. Swinfen* (No. 3) (5 December 1860) 29 Beav. 199; 54 E.R. 603; *Swinfen v. Swinfen* (No. 4) (5 December 1860) 29 Beav. 207; 54 E.R. 606; *Swinfen v. Swinfen* (No. 5) (5 December 1860) 29 Beav. 211; 54 E.R. 608 (on subsidiary estate issues); *Swinfen v. Bacon* (15 May 1861) 6 H. & N. 846; 158 E.R. 349 (proceeding in error from 21 November 1860 judgment of the Court of Exchequer).
134 Kennedy, *The Great Swinfen Case, supra* note 11 at 38.
135 Kennedy, *Mr. Kennedy's Argument, supra* note 98 at 60, side-note.
136 *Ibid.* at 60-61.
137 See Kennedy, *The Great Swinfen Case, supra* note 11 at 18, 26, 34; Kennedy, *Mr. Kennedy's Argument, ibid.* at 5, 12; Clayton, *supra* note 80.
138 Kennedy, *The Great Swinfen Case, ibid.* at 9ff, 18; Kennedy, *Mr. Kennedy's Argument, ibid.* at 11ff, 13, 14, 15, 50, 56.
139 Kennedy, *Mr. Kennedy's Argument, ibid.* at 44, 59.
140 Kennedy, *The Great Swinfen Case, supra* note 11 at 16-17, 20-22, 25, 27, 28.
141 *Ibid.* at 26-35.
142 Kennedy, *Mr. Kennedy's Argument, supra* note 98 at 11-18.
143 Kennedy, *The Great Swinfen Case, supra* note 11 at 18.
144 *Ibid.* at 43; Kennedy, *Mr. Kennedy's Argument, supra* note 98 at 9.
145 Kennedy, *The Great Swinfen Case, ibid.* at 25.
146 *Ibid.*
147 *Ibid.* at 44.
148 *Ibid.* at 25.
149 *Ibid.* at 45.
150 *Ibid.* at 44.
151 *Ibid.* at 45, per Cockburn L.C.J.
152 *The Times* (2 April 1862) 9.
153 See *Birmingham Daily Post* (3 April 1862) 2.

154 Bowyer's bill is discussed in Duman, *supra* note 25 at 56-57. See Sessional Papers 1862. II.383, printed 18 March 1862. The chronology was as follows:

Autumn 1861. Kennedy decides to sue Mrs. Broun.
19 March 1862. 1st reading of Bowyer's bill; 2d reading set for 2 April 1862.
29-30 March 1862. *Kennedy v. Brown* trial and verdict.
2 April 1862. *The Times* editorial attacking Kennedy; Bowyer's bill 2d reading deferred.
24 April 1862. Rule *nisi* to set aside judgment in favour of Kennedy.
25 April 1862. Special Council of Benchers of Lincoln's Inn strikes committee to discuss Bowyer's bill with other Inns (Lincoln's Inn, *The Black Books*).
13 May 1862. Lincoln's Inn Council reads resolution of the four Inns attacking Bowyer's bill (Lincoln's Inn, *The Black Books*).
13 June 1862. Shew-cause commenced to set aside rule *nisi* in favour of Patience Broun.
11-12 November 1862. *Kennedy v. Broun* argued in Common Pleas.
25 November 1862. Bench of Common Pleas announces delay in giving judgment in *Kennedy v. Broun*.
17 January 1863. Judgment of Common Pleas in *Kennedy v. Broun*.

155 Kennedy, *The Great Swinfen Case, supra* note 11; *The Times* (31 March 1862) at 11, 12.
156 *The Times* (2 April 1862) 9.
157 *Birmingham Daily Post* (3 April 1862) 2.
158 *Ibid.*
159 *The Times* (2 April 1862) 9.
160 *Ibid.*
161 *Ibid.; The Times* (24 April 1862) 11 (reporting *Kennedy v. Broun* per Macaulay Q.C.).
162 *Ibid.;* Clayton, *supra* note 80.
163 *Kennedy v. Broun* (1863) 13 C.B. (N.S.) 677 at 727; 143 E.R. 268 at 287, per Erle C.J. for the court.
164 *Swinfen v. Lord Chelmsford, supra* note 85 at 919, 921. Quoted in Kennedy, *Mr. Kennedy's Argument, supra* note 98 at 46.
165 A rule *nisi* was granted to the defendants in April 1862 (*The Times* [24 April 1862] 11) and Kennedy began his show cause nearly two months later (*The Times* [13 June 1862] 11). Further hearings took place during June and November (*The Times* [17 June 1862] 13, [11 November 1862] 9, [12 November 1862] 11, and [14 November 1862] 8-9). Over two weeks following the last hearing, *The Times* reported (25 November 1862 at 11) that "[t]he Chief Justice announced that in this case the Court would not be ready to give judgment this term, as they wished to look into the authorities." The written judgment of the court was ultimately read by the Chief Justice only in January 1863: *The Times* (17 January 1863) 11.
166 P.S. Atiyah, *The Rise and Fall of Freedom of Contract* (Oxford: Oxford University Press, 1979).
167 John Stuart Mill, "On Liberty" in Mary Warnock, ed., *Utilitarianism and Other Writings* (New York: Meridian, 1974) 135.
168 *Kennedy v. Broun* (1863) 13 C.B. (N.S.) 677 at 736; 143 E.R. 268 at 291, per Erle C.J.
169 *Ibid.* at 731; 143 E.R. 268 at 289.
170 *Ibid.* at 738; 143 E.R. 268 at 292.
171 Cocks, *Foundations of the Modern Bar, supra* note 20 at 86-89; Abel-Smith and Stevens, *supra* note 20 at 55-57.
172 *Kennedy v. Broun* (1863) 13 C.B. (N.S.) 677at 737; 143 E.R. 268 at 291.
173 *Ibid.*
174 *Ibid.*

175 In addition to the proceedings themselves, Kennedy had prepared a pamphlet titled "The Serpent of Swinfen." See Kennedy, *The Great Swinfen Case, supra* note 11 at 20; Clayton, *supra* note 80.

176 *Kennedy v. Broun* (1863) 13 C.B. (N.S.) 677 at 737-38; 143 E.R. 268 at 291.

177 *Ibid.* at 738; 143 E.R. 268 at 291-92.

178 The Staffordshire Sessions Bar Mess minute book begins on 6 April 1863. The Midland Circuit Mess Minutes and the Staffordshire Sessions Bar Mess Minutes are held by the Department of Western Manuscripts, Bodleian Library, Oxford.

179 Inner Temple, *Bench Table Orders.*

180 Sessional Papers 1862.II.383.

181 Cocks, *Foundations of the Modern Bar, supra* note 20 at 121.

182 *E.g., Solicitor's Journal* (12 April 1862) 427; *Daily News* (1 April 1862) at 4, cols. 5-6; Chapter 8 in this volume.

183 Quoted in *Law Times* 20 (9 October 1852) at 26.

184 See the evidence discussed in *supra* note 59. For a US comparison, see Auerbach, *supra* note 2.

185 Magali Sarfatti Larson, *Rise of Professionalism: A Sociological Analysis* (Berkeley/Los Angeles: University of California Press, 1977). *Cf.* Maureen Cain, "The General Practice Lawyer and the Client: Towards a Radical Conception" (1979) 7 Int'l J. Soc. L. 331 (who, however, fails to adequately take account of the distinctiveness of the *barristers'* function. R.L. Abel, *Legal Profession in England and Wales* (Oxford: Blackwell, 1988).

186 For an account of subsequent developments, see Abel, *ibid.* See also Abel-Smith and Stevens, *supra* note 20.

PART 5

Dominion and Colonial Lawyering

12

Christ, Manhood, and Empire

THE CASE METHOD OF LEGAL EDUCATION IN CANADA, 1885-1931

Reflecting on the first eight decades of Ukrainian settlement in the Canadian prairies, Methodius Nychka recalled:

> The Anglo-Saxon majority in this area seemed quite hostile to the Slavs. They regarded them as people capable only of low servile manual tasks. Anglo-Saxons considered themselves the masters of this country, the country which they hoodwinked from the Indians. Our people, although poor, conquered this Canadian soil, not through war, but through tireless, stubborn toil. They dried out swamps, bridged roads, built railroads, cut down forests. Our pioneer slowly rooted himself into the new land, tamed her wild nature, made her cultivable, fertile.[1]

This passage serves as a valuable reminder of the central place perceptions of ethnicity have played in the history of western Canada. Its metaphoric construction of colonization as sexual conquest remind us too that cultural presuppositions about masculinity and gender pervade narratives of colonization and settlement. In this chapter, I explore the relationship that existed in the minds of elite reformers of the Canadian legal profession between the Socratic method of legal education and the effective colonization of Canadian space. It matters that their deliberations concerning legal education took place in a context within which assumptions regarding ethnicity, masculinity, class, progress, and colonization constituted common sense.

Introduction

Although ultimately part of a much larger story concerning the processes of "civilization" and of the incorporation of distant spaces and diverse peoples alike into the Canadian polity, my immediate focus is the mundane internal affairs of a particular legal profession. I am concerned here with developments during the first third of the twentieth century, and especially with the decade and a half starting in 1914. This is the period in which legal education's cultural role in state formation came into sharpest focus as the cultural movements surrounding lawyering took institutional form in a new national organization. The Canadian Bar Association (CBA), which met for the first time in 1914,[2] provided a vehicle through which professional visions could be expressed, particular matters debated, reports issued, and plans laid for the implementation of reforms.

The Canadian Bar Association was (and is) an entirely voluntary elite institution. It has never played any formal role in the governance of Canadian lawyers and is closer in spirit to gentlemen's clubs than to regulatory bodies on the model of either the late-nineteenth-century English Inns of Court[3] or the provincial law societies ("integrated Bars") that exist in each common law Canadian jurisdiction.[4] Existing within civil society, the association's ethos is that of volunteerism and public service, not regulation in the ordinary sense of the word. One seemingly small feature of its early years is important: the prime movers in this key moment of lawyers' professionalization were Western Canadian – and especially Manitoban – lawyers.[5] During the period addressed in this chapter, *all* major initiatives in professionalization of Canadian lawyers originated in the prairie west.

The suggestion that some significant connection exists between modes of qualification for legal practice, on the one hand, and issues surrounding colonization, empire, and culture, on the other, is, admittedly, somewhat counterintuitive. Bearing in mind, however, Gauri Viswanathan's urging that educational history needs to be understood not just in terms of institutional growth or curriculum development but also within its "expressive context,"[6] two contexts become important in relation to early-twentieth-century Canadian legal education. First, it is important to appreciate the centrality of law in imperial processes. Second, I wish to point to some reasons why Canada's full incorporation of the west seemed problematic in the first third of the twentieth century. The ways in which the problems of Empire were understood by influential British Canadians are centrally important.

After lightly sketching these contexts, I briefly describe significant developments relating to professional qualification taking place during the decade and a half starting in 1914. Finally, early-twentieth-century Canadian lawyers' understandings of the relations between legal education, colonization, and governance of Canada's space are described.

Law and Empire

It may indeed be the case, as Césaire has it, that the "decisive actors" in colonization were not missionaries, judges, lawyers, or teachers, but rather "the adventurer and the pirate, the wholesale grocer and the shop owner, the gold digger and the merchant."[7] Nonetheless the ideological or discursive universes that enveloped imperial expansion required some level of self-justification. Imperial apologetics was always more than mere propaganda, myth, or illusion. It consisted, loosely and to varying degrees, of belief in the inevitability of "progress," "scientific" racism, confidence in the inevitability of "progress," commitment to a "civilizing" mission, and an intense sense of moral obligation to bear the "White Man's Burden." Members of the Round Table Movement, to take but one early-twentieth-century example, shared "a belief in the political wisdom of the British and their system of government. Many believed the British had a duty and a moral responsibility to educate 'the backward peoples' of the world to an understanding of the British system."[8] Such attitudes, commonplace within Empire's mentality, were neither empty rhetoric nor a false consciousness cynically put about in service of material ends.

Imperialists often thought of themselves as transmitting great gifts to the world.[9] Foremost among these were technology, Christianity, rational social organization, law, progress, and liberty. Each element of "civilization" was significant. Such notions were not neatly severable one from the other, nor even analytically distinct in any rigorous fashion, and any attempt to place them in rank order of importance is futile. English "law," to take but one example, was widely thought to be infused with Christian principles, and was considered the essence of liberty, the principal foundation for rational social order and hence the key to "progress."[10] It was also, however, considered the cornerstone of secular rationality: nineteenth-century bourgeois Europeans as diverse as Sir Henry Maine, Max Weber, and Karl Marx perceived some relationship between legal form, social progress, capitalism, and economy.[11]

Although the growth of cultural studies, postcolonialism, and related intellectual interests has cut a wide swath through scholarship, analyses of the role of law in the imperial project are not as plentiful as one might hope. This is the more curious perhaps in light of the many, obvious, and intersecting roles law plays in relation to colonialism. Martin Chanock has aptly observed that law is the cutting edge of colonialism,[12] while Sally Merry accords law central place in "the colonizing process."[13] Both within metropolitan states and among their colonial outposts, law is simultaneously an exercise of force, "schoolmaster,"[14] cultural arena, referee as commercial interests, discursive field, legitimating device, focal point of resistance, disciplinary technique,

Statues of Moses, Jesus, and King Solomon on top of Royal Courts of Justice, opened by Queen Victoria, 1882. *Conway Library, The Courtauld Institute of Art, London*

ideological state apparatus, shaper of souls, and semi-autonomous social field (no doubt among many others). More specifically, "law" or some notion of it is clearly central to British identities, to Anglo-American self-image.[15] It certainly seems plausible that the contributions of Anson or Dicey or Langdell have had more profound impact on twentieth-century Anglo-American cultures and their imperialist legacies than F.R. Leavis or Joseph Conrad, or even William Shakespeare. No such position could be sustained, however, from any random literature review or citation count in scholarship on post-colonial or cultural studies themes.[16]

Peter Fitzpatrick has argued that Enlightenment European law actively defined itself in *opposition* to the "other."[17] Western law, and for our purposes British law in particular, makes peculiar claims to secular rationality, in presumed contradistinction to the laws of the "other." Native law may amount only to "Khadi" justice. It may be irrational, inconsistent, corrupt, unwholesome, biased, unpredictable, founded on superstition or charisma, parochial, incompetently administered, primitive, and unreliable. British law, however, defines itself *against* these. It represents itself as the accumulated wisdom of the ages, the pinnacle of civilization, the summit of liberty, and the reconciliation of freedom with order. Superior even to the laws of other European peoples, British law has often appeared to its subjects as the key to progress. A common juridical terrain resting on "a rational method, a unified science and an exact language" (misappropriating here Rorty's words[18]), British law was thought of as a very special social tool uniquely capable of transcending the fragmenting and destructive centrifugal forces of religion, class, ethnicity, and locality. Imperialism and the common law appeared to offer a truly transcendental secular rationality.[19] This not inconsiderable gift could not, however, be distributed as one offers loaves to the hungry, shelter to the homeless, or blankets to the freezing. Rather, it had to be carefully transported, implanted, and nurtured in foreign soils. Awkwardly, not all peoples were immediately pre-adapted to appreciate the liberties, freedoms, and progress British law held out to them. Recalcitrant individuals and entire populations often failed to even perceive the superiority of British ways over their own superstitions and rituals – failed to understand that "[u]niversal becoming is the prerogative of the West."[20] In early-twentieth-century Canada, knowledge of the intrinsic superiority of British ways, the virtues associated with British law, and confidence in the transformative vision of Empire virtually *defined* respectability.

The task of transforming unruly peoples around the world into civilized individuals capable of assuming the privileges, rights, and responsibilities of self-governance was the central mission of Empire. Complexly, British justice was both a tool used to achieve this result and the desired end itself. "Law" and Britishness were co-extensive, the apex of cultural evolution. "Law," like the study of "English literature," sought nothing less than the transformation of souls.[21]

With this object in mind, British law itself became transformed. The lines between state and civil society blurred as law intervened in areas previously relatively untouched by the *State* writ large. A reworking of administrative structures and court systems[22] was accompanied by the development of assorted "*regulatory agents* who are charged with an array of functions ranging from the collection and recording of information, inspection, surveillance, reporting, initiation of enforcement action, and a host of other activities."[23] The central object of law became regulation in the sense of "preserving and shaping something and not merely suppressing it."[24] Science, law, bureaucratic rationality, Britishness, masculinity – all in peculiar and varying mixes with religious faith – guided "repeated attempts by those who would manage the areas of legality and culture to establish a single coherent order based on the certainty of knowledge, the conventions of mankind, or the unique inheritance of a national culture."[25]

Peculiar features of Anglo-American North America rendered it particularly problematic, almost ungovernable in principle. The differences between places where status claims based on class, race, or other ascriptive traits are tolerated (or, minimally, taken for granted as social facts) and newer, "settler" societies like Canada and the United States, where class claims did not enjoy immediate legitimacy, where class relations had not yet congealed, where ethnicities interacted unpredictably, are profoundly important. De Tocqueville's well-known observations that lawyers were the only available "counterbalance to democracy" in the United States, and that the "legal spirit" was uniquely adapted "to neutralize the vices inherent in popular government,"[26] develop from this insight. In adopting this well-known formulation, de Tocqueville verbalized a "common sense" about the governance of the New World that most of Anglo-America's respectable classes shared. Well before de Tocqueville's travels, Ontario's Archdeacon John Strachan had noted the impossibility of establishing a fully British constitution in the absence of a landed aristocracy (impossible to establish in the Canadas), and he too had hoped that lawyers would fill the constitutional void. Early plans to develop a college of law at Toronto's Osgoode Hall, loosely modelled on the English Inns of Court, were similarly directed towards socializing a legal elite and shaping "their students into learned and honourable members of their gentlemanly profession."[27] For both observers, the socialization of lawyers provided a key to social well-being.

Canada and the Prairie West, 1900-30

Canada, an American nation,[28] presented peculiar problems of governance. "British" though distant from the British Isles, "in" but not entirely "of" North America, Canada's place within Empire and continent has never been lacking in ambiguity.

In 1913, an American observer recorded that "[t]hose who really are at the head of local affairs" in Canada "echo, practically unanimously, the sentiment of Sir John A. Macdonald: 'A British subject I was born; a British subject I will die!'"[29] In many important ways, however (population density, climate, landscape, availability of cheap land, social diversity, class structure, and the sheer extent of space, to name just a few), "Canadian society resembled American rather than British society."[30] Canada's Britishness, subjected to considerable pressures, was actively, creatively, and constantly renegotiated. The powerful influence of the republic to the south should never be underestimated. Smith has pointed to pervasive cultural influences from the United States and speculated that this had a profound effect on the transformation of Anglo-Canadian culture over the nineteenth century. Early in that century, "British culture and civilization was the *élan vital*. The job of those in the wilderness was to unleash its power as quickly and fully as possible." By the beginning of the twentieth century, however, even staunchly British Canadians (it bears emphasis that "Britishness" was *the* hallmark of respectability) had come "to view themselves not as the agent of an Old World culture charged with civilizing the New, but as beings uplifted and restored by their New World environment whose duty it was to regenerate the Old."[31]

Of particular importance in the dual mission of "civilizing the New" and "regenerating the Old" was Canada's own imperial expansion. Canada embarked upon its own version of "manifest destiny" in 1869, when Britain ceded the Northwest Territories to the Canadian Parliament (then representing only Ontario, Quebec, Nova Scotia, and New Brunswick). Prime Minister John A. Macdonald's National Policy sought, *inter alia,* to incorporate a vast new northwestern space into its territory. The clear intent was to develop the west in "the interests of 'Old Canada' ... and Canadian policy was oriented around the plan to establish a new 'investment frontier' that would open the west and enrich the east in one fell swoop."[32] Canada's incorporation of the Hudson's Bay Company territories and the former colonies of British Columbia and Vancouver Island became the story of Ontario's colonial ambitions. In this confident era, English Canadians had few doubts about their ability to rise to the considerable challenges involved. At century's end, they were confident in their ability to incorporate the west, develop their economy, improve on inherited traditions, and – soon, they thought – lead the Empire.

Confidence was an indispensable asset. The challenges were profound. Planting British civilization required massive investment in infrastructure and institutions, but the prior condition on which all else rested was the European settlement of the region. This was a considerable challenge. The area that forms the contemporary Prairie provinces of Manitoba, Saskatchewan, and Alberta alone covers some 750,000 square miles (larger than the combined area of Germany, France, and Spain in Europe or the US states of Texas, New Mexico, Arizona, and California – or nearly one-fourth the size of Australia).[33] Faced with a need for huge numbers of immigrants and the ever-present threat of annexation by the United States, the Canadian government actively sought immigrant settlers in unorthodox places. Policies established by Clifford Sifton, Manitoba Member of Parliament and federal Minister of the Interior from 1896 to 1905, transformed Canada. Although Sifton shared common assumptions that "blacks, Italians, Jews, Orientals, and urban Englishmen ... would not ... succeed on farms," his department otherwise actively encouraged a wide and diverse range of non-British to immigrate. An enormous influx of Eastern Europeans followed. Sifton's waves of immigrants transformed Prairie Canada. Population growth was explosive.[34]

Now, the attempt to *instantly* re-create the culture, institutions, and ethos of another place is inherently problematic. On the one hand, this influx of settlers illustrates that "the promise of the west became the promise of Canada."[35] At a cultural level, Canada's National Policy was driven by people "who sought to reproduce" in the West "what they believed to be the best characteristics of Eastern Canadian life." More precisely, "their intention in Western Canada was, if not to create a new Jerusalem, at least to build a better Ontario."[36] Sifton's immigration policies, however, rendered the region ethnically diverse, polyglot, and altogether quite "unBritish" and "unOntarian." At the outbreak of the First World War, nearly half of the region's residents had been born in another country. Previous prairie residents (who traced their origins variously to First Nations, Métis, French, Québecois, British, American, or Icelandic ancestry) had been joined by Germans, Poles, Scandinavians, Ukrainians, Hutterites, Mennonites, Jews, Doukhobors, Ontarians, Maritimers,[37] and more British and Americans, among others. Huge ethnic block settlements developed. Even today a "little Ukraine" stretches almost uninterrupted from just northwest of Winnipeg to the outskirts of Edmonton. The ethnic map of the rural prairies, past and present, reveals a pattern of sizable, discrete, often barely overlapping ethnic block settlements. A trip through the region in 1920 (or even in 1960) took the traveller through extensive areas where English was rarely spoken. T.C. Byrne reported that in 1937 "knowledge of Ukrainian [was] as indispensable" in east central Alberta "as French in Quebec or English in Ontario."[38] Icelandic, Cree, German, Dakota, Ukrainian, Sarcee, Polish, French, Swedish, Dene, Dutch, and Russian, among others, predominated in other areas. In 1931, only about 50 percent of the population of the prairies claimed British origins.[39]

The cities too were transformed. Winnipeg, the region's railway centre and metropolis, looked across the Red River to western Canada's historic French capital of St. Boniface. An impressive French Catholic cathedral faced off across the river from Winnipeg's commercial centre, providing a striking visual reminder of Britishness's tenuous hold on this part of Empire. Winnipeg's explosive growth[40] produced an urban centre unlike any other in British North America. To arrive at Winnipeg's Canadian Pacific Railway Station was to enter

> an international bazaar: the noise of thousands of voices and a dozen tongues circled the high marble pillars and drifted out into the street ... this was not a polite and ordered society but rather was customarily described as Little Europe, Babel, New Jerusalem, or the Chicago of the North.[41]

Social diversity was manifest in innumerable ways throughout the region. In town and country alike, the institutions and customs of different communities engaged with each other but remained distinct: shops, trade, recreation, news media, associational life, and religion were, to varying degrees, ethnically and/or linguistically segregated. So, too, expectations regarding the way business should be conducted, marriages formalized, interpersonal disputes resolved, and children raised varied with ethnicity and community. A multitude of informal legal regimes occupied this new Canadian space, even in its urban core. Sometimes alternative legalities were barely informal at all. Many First Nations communities remained significantly self-governing, living in accordance with their own norms, values, political structures, and legal systems long after the colonial state formally asserted authority over them.[42] The same was true of most immigrant communities. Long after the Canadian state fancied itself as having asserted effective legal control over its territory, Doukhobors and Mennonites, for example, enjoyed territorial integrity, shared language, religion, ethnicity, and distinct economic structures. Both groups were surprisingly resilient in sustaining "legal" systems that governed almost all aspects of life. They did so without deference to the Canadian state or its norms.[43] Issue after issue, time after time, and place after place, leaders of diverse communities across the prairie region worked to preserve their nationality. Religious organizations, alongside more secular forms of association, provided institutional habitats in which informal law flourished. A dense associational life existed, revolving variously around gender, ethnicity, religion, interests, politics, sports, labour, economics, and class.

One significant manifestation of civil society took place at the intersection of class, politics, and work. The combination of utopian spirit and rapid change proved fertile ground for both trade union activity and radical politics. Irritated by more or less conventional labour and class issues, urban workers flexed their muscles towards the end of the First World War. A burst of radicalism "more pervasive in the west than in the rest of Canada or North America" occurred.[44] Mounting labour discontent produced a modestly impressive strike in Winnipeg in 1918 and the Western Labour Conference of March 1919, and culminated later that spring in the great Winnipeg General Strike. This marked a turning point in Canadian history. From 15 May to 23 June, Winnipeg was virtually shut down. Necessary services continued only at the sufferance of a Strike Committee, and members of the respectable classes feared that effective governance of one of the Empire's great industrial cities had been usurped by working-class radicals bent on revolution, threatening everything respectable British Canada stood for.

Winnipeg and Canadian elites viewed the strike "as a pivotal moment in labour-capital relations, not just for Winnipeg but for the nation and the continent. Huns, Bolsheviks, aliens – in short, revolutionaries – were threatening to destroy their dreams."[45] The coincidence of Bolshevik revolution in Russia with labour radicalism among an ethnically diverse working class in Canada

Permit poster issued by Strike Committee, 1919. *Archives of Manitoba/Archives du Manitoba, Winnipeg Strike 2, N488*

persuaded respectable British Canadians that labour's discontent manifested a foreign disease. One police magistrate remarked upon the "large extent" to which "Bolsheviki ideas are held by the Ruthenian, Russian and Polish people, whom we have in our midst."[46] Such views held firm despite the demonstrable fact that labour's leadership was resolutely British.

The great strike provided dramatic focus for those concerned about the future of British civilization in this new land, but the concerns it brought to a head had been long developing. British Canadians' understandings of the problems of governance in the west drew upon a tradition that included de Tocqueville and Strachan, combined with growing xenophobia and severely eroded faith in the assimilative power of Britishness. The Canadian West represented an especially unruly space whose peculiar challenges to the advance of British civilization had reached a crisis point. Although the immediate crisis, the 1919 strike, was resolved by the deployment of armed force in support of the State's order, respectable opinion knew well that political power cannot grow permanently from the barrel of a gun.

They perceived the regulation of psychic space as the "last frontier" in domesticating unruly populations. Modernity's urge to control, regulate, domesticate, confine, and render all humanity predictable played itself out in Western Canada in a series of attempts to remake the individual.[47] Respectable British Canadians had long felt that, without discipline from within or (as necessary) imposed from without, the individual threatened the body politic, society at large, and ultimately *civilization* itself: "an individual without character ... was a miniature mob: disorganized, immoral, and unhealthy as well as an inefficient member of the collectivity."[48] Canada's "founding fathers sought to create a 'Moral Dominion' premised on strong central government,

Anti-strike veterans prepare to march, 4 June 1919. *Archives of Manitoba/Archives du Manitoba, Winnipeg Strike, N12295*

individualism, hierarchical social relations, capitalism, self-discipline, and family patriarchy."[49]

Canadian legal education took shape in this context in early-twentieth-century Prairie Canada, developed by men who shared such background assumptions.

Law and Empire: Canada, circa 1919

Not surprisingly, British Canadian lawyers shared the world-view of the respectable classes regarding Britishness, civilization, the progress of Empire, and the challenges it faced. For them law was both end and means of Empire. Speaking in Winnipeg to the Canadian Bar Association shortly after the General Strike, Winnipeg lawyer, Manitoba Lieutenant-Governor, *and* Canadian Bar Association president James Aikins expressed the hope that socialism, anarchy, Bolshevism, and other similar "recrudescences of an old disease"[50] would be utterly destroyed, as anathema to law. Tellingly, his notion of law was inseparable from his conceptions of Britishness, Christianity, and civilization. The "fundamental British principles" that he thought constituted the distilled essence of law included "protection of person and property, fair and prompt trial of offences and disputes by a system of qualified Judges, of advocates and juries, freedom of religious worship, of speech, of press, of assemblage, government of people by themselves and indeed all those things which pertain to our civilization, a civilization which rests upon Christianity."[51]

Sir James Aikins. *Topley Studio Fonds, Library and Archives Canada, PA-033981*

Choosing his words carefully, Aikins explained that "state paternalism" (socialism) was un-British, un-Christian, and hence unlawful in the true sense of that term. It was, he said,

> an endeavour to rest everything upon law or government, overlooking the fact that for Canadians the law should fix the minimum demands of social and business duties, and that all requirements between that and the perfect law of liberty should be left to the enlightened conscience and Christian character of the individual. If, in the ultimate, Christian democracy rests upon the moral character of its citizens, clearly the first aim of all law should be to develop the highest type of human entity, and as far as is consistent with the rights of others leave him unfettered in thought and action.[52]

These remarks reveal much. Theorists have pointed to the existence of a theoretical infrastructure that binds particular visions of law to national and imperial projects.[53] Aikins's comments illustrate that this is no mere theoretical conceit. These linkages were at the forefront of thought among one influential sort of British colonial lawyer in the early twentieth century.

Bolshevism was, no doubt, also in his mind as this Winnipeg lawyer delivered his speech.[54] While local deviations from British social organization would also have been of concern, the distance between prairie society and proper principles of social organization would have seemed immense. In identifying contemporary political and social visions as manifestations of an "old disease," Aikins sought to consign them to history's trashcan. Particularly out of place in the New World, perhaps, such notions were anachronistic, the enemy of progress. So, Aikins believed, the course of history had decreed. This formulation disposed simultaneously of Marxist communism but also of Christian communism such as that of the prairie region's Mennonites, Hutterites, and Doukhobors, and of the collective sharing of wealth and resources customary in many First Nations communities.[55]

Disease is a powerful metaphor.[56] Aikins, like other leading figures, perceived of "society," "nation," or "state" as analogous to a natural organism. Properly cared for, appropriately disciplined (just as the individual had to limit alcohol consumption, regulate diet, control sexual urges, and exercise regularly), the organic state could grow and thrive, expand in size in proportion to its destiny ("manifest destiny" in the United States, *lebensraum* for Nazis, the National Policy's designs of westward and northward expansion in Canada), and provide well for all its parts.[57] As an organism, however, states, like individuals, were susceptible to disease. Bad ideas, bad people, and immoral individuals were like bacterial invasions, open sores, or cancers. None could be tolerated; any, however seemingly insignificant, could become fatal to the organism as a whole.[58] Medical science, informed by germ theory and rapidly developing surgical techniques, provided a host of analogies whose relevance to social policy seemed commonsensical.

If law was to be used to shape the highest human entity, it is clear that Aikins understood the desirable end product to be rather like the ideal/typical moral, Christian Britisher (or, more likely, *British Canadian*). Britain, British commerce, British technology, British government, British law, and British Empire represented a sort of endpoint in human history: any future progress would develop from the British baseline, not in contradiction of it. Taken together, then, this lawyer's professional speech draws upon and reinforces many of the conceptual underpinnings of colonialism, including a racial hierarchy that located the British (and, only then, other northwestern Europeans) above others, a preference for Protestantism over Catholicism, and *certainly* of Christianity over other religions – hence, a judgment *against* Confucianism (and Confucians), Judaism (and Jews), Hinduism (and Hindus), First Nations spirituality (and unassimilated First Nations peoples), and so on. Aikins's world-view was premised on a belief in the inevitability of progress and, concomitantly, the necessity of destroying – albeit "humanely" – those who would not embrace its promise. Policies of assimilation, social control, and ultimately destruction of the unassimilable flowed from these assumptions about the course of history, as did a subsidiary belief that good government required

Cartoon of Sir James Aikins, published c. 1909, by the Newspaper Cartoonists' Association of Manitoba. *From* Manitobans as We See 'Em, *c. 1908. Courtesy the Manitoba Historical Society*

potentially invasive moral regulation. Outside of this intrusive realm, however, competitive capitalism and *laissez-faire* individualism were believed to be the *only* acceptable principles for social organization.

Expressed with unusual clarity and coherence, perhaps, Aikins's views were nonetheless commonplace. They are noteworthy in two respects. First, he offered these views not as abstract social theory or in defence of Imperial policy but rather in explanation of his vision of law. The law/not-law distinction, as H.L.A. Hart reminds us,[59] is culturally defined and Aikins's comments illustrate the clarity and specificity with which elite British Canadian lawyers once understood these matters. A century later, our understandings of law tend to be formal, processual, or functional, but Aikins's conception was substantive as well. There was *substantive content* in his notions of law, as well as procedural commitment to due process and the formal requirements of the rule of law. Aikins's reflections on law, Bolshevism, and labour unrest are thoroughly infused with assumptions concerning morality, immigration, ethnic diversity, citizenship, and the assimilation of both immigrants and Aboriginal peoples. Human culture does not come neatly packaged in severable bundles. Neither does law. Although our intellectual positions about such topics are typically presented in falsely tidy bundles, it is important to recall always that the connections, the legal and linguistic slippages or points of connection between them, are perhaps more important than the particular features of each taken on its own.

The second noteworthy point is simply this: although Aikins's views may have been unremarkable, they were expressed not merely as one private citizen to others but by the Lieutenant-Governor of Canada's "keystone" province *in his capacity as president and leader of the Canadian Bar Association.* They bespoke an understanding of law backed by the Dominion's leading institution of lawyers' professionalization. Such notions constituted both a "respectable" common sense about matters social or political and the *sine qua non* of legal professionalism. The expertise of lawyers, in short, was understood as *a cultural attainment, over and above the presumed narrowly specialist knowledge of the words of judges, the texts of statutes, legal procedures, or law office forms.* The true lawyer was an entirely cultural product, never to be confused with individuals who had merely mastered a certain examinable knowledge or practical know-how.[60] The package, emphatically, was British, gentlemanly, Christian. And it nested within and defined the economic and political mainstream.

Legal Education and Cultural Attainment

Now, how was the future "cultural attainment" of lawyers to be ensured, and how did that connect with service to law and Empire in early-twentieth-century Canada? In investigating this, the meteoric rise and fall of the Manitoba Law School from 1914 to 1930 needs to be considered. Often overlooked in histories of legal education in Canada, this period was a crucial formative era. Current models of legal education were first developed at this time, most fully in Manitoba. Manitoba's legal profession was the first in Canada to require full-time attendance at a university-affiliated law school for a significant portion of its novitiates, and the first to seek to abolish qualification by apprenticeship. Its was the earliest formal endorsement *by an organized legal profession* of what is known in Canada as "cultural" legal education (conventionally understood in curriculum terms, involving subjects such as public international law and legal history).[61] The Manitoba Law School, created as a partnership between the Law Society of Manitoba and the University of Manitoba, moved rapidly to raise admission requirements. It was the first in the Dominion of Canada to make the case method (teaching law through study of decided cases) central to its program. Such initiatives, endorsed by a number of legal and academic commentators across the country, were carried furthest and fastest by the Manitoba Law School.[62]

Although at the forefront, the school was not off on a lark of its own. In this period, new university law schools were also founded at the University of Saskatchewan and the University of Alberta; new professional schools of law begun in Regina, Vancouver, and Victoria; and significant changes in staffing, curriculum, pedagogy, or entrance requirements implemented at Osgoode

Hall, McGill, Dalhousie, and the University of New Brunswick.[63] The intent behind all such reforms was to turn out lawyers who would understand law and lawyers' professional functions in ways roughly consonant with views such as those of James Aikins and his peers (who called their own views "ethical").

This involved reformers in attempts to restrict legal education to individuals pre-adapted by class background, ethnicity, or in some other way to the mental world of their professional leaders. Aikins's long-time ally in educational reform, H.A. Robson, approved the "pious fraud" by which one US law school deployed increased admissions standards with the hidden objective of deterring men of "an undesirable class" from entering the profession.[64] To similar effect, Aikins argued that only those possessing "the qualifications of mind and character" that could be formed into true lawyers should be permitted to begin legal studies.[65] Given the right student intake and the right form of legal education, it seemed that the appropriate character-moulding process could be assured. In such circumstances, it was assumed that law schools could not graduate anything less than appropriately socialized gentlemen lawyers.

The Embodiment of Law and Its Integrative Functions

Before turning to address the forms of education they had in mind, one more connection must be made: the connection between what lawyers thought – or what sort of men they were – and the law's integrative functions. From our perspective it is perhaps difficult to perceive any connection at all between a belief that the substantive law should be anti-Bolshevist, British, or something else and an educational mission aimed at the pre-selection and gentlemanly socialization of lawyers. This is because *our* habits of thought intrude, creating the sense that a conceptual Berlin Wall of sorts exists between positive law (what the law is) and the personnel of the legal system (who the lawyers are). Separating these, we imagine that the substance of the law exists independently of the actions, values, or thoughts of lawyers. In this view, it seems logical to assume that law is made by judges and legislatures but that ordinary lawyers are more or less irrelevant to the state of the law. Our culture perceives lawyers as mechanics of legality, picking bits of law off the parts shelves and sticking them where they need to go in order to serve the client's objective best interest.

If it seems to us that there is no connection between "law" and "lawyers," however, it may be that it is we who suffer from simple-mindedness. In sharp contrast, the generation who developed the template for modern Canadian legal education were fully aware of law's embodiment: that it has no meaning whatsoever other than that which is absorbed, reflected by, and exuded from lawyers. MacKay thought that "[t]he law is what the consensus of legal opinion in the community believes it to be, first the judges, next the lawyers, and finally the mass of intelligent laymen who direct the organized activities of the state."[66] LAW writ large is not self-enacting, does not implement itself, controls no one, influences nothing. MacKay's understandings were close to what we now think of as legal pluralism (although he assigned greater urgency to bringing "one law" into being than most contemporary legal pluralist scholars consider necessary or desirable). The real law – living law – existed, he thought, in consensus of opinion. Without professional consensus both case law and statute were mere abstractions ("Statute law is as much a creation of the judiciary and the lawyers as case law"[67]). Hence, British law was brought into place not by assertions of sovereignty or legal reception but rather as part of daily routine whenever lawyers acted. Its values were inculcated in the community at large as lawyers went about their work and participated in community life, generally acting as stabilizing influences in all their multitudinous individual formal or informal, big or small, legal interventions. Early-twentieth-century legal reformers believed that order, community, and State were the cumulative result of just such infinite, repeated, micro-level interventions:

> The lawyer's office is unquestionably the most important office in the community, and that for the obvious reason that the lawyer is really the only man in the community who really makes it his business to understand the delicate and complex organization of government and law by which the community directs its activities for common ends ... The state itself is an edifice constructed solely out of legal material. It is literally made of law.[68]

Clearly, if the state is made of law and law is made of professional consensus, then it matters tremendously not only what lawyers know in their minds but also what they know in their hearts.[69] This mattered deeply. Informed gentlemen of MacKay's era felt that a consensus of legal opinion was necessary in order to "create the state; allow it to perish and peace, good order, and good government must perish with it."[70] Professional consensus, in short, was the condition precedent to everything they held dear.

Clearly, the geographic and cultural circumstances of early-twentieth-century Canada – huge spaces, a diverse and undersocialized population – militated against the development of professional consensus.[71] Professional consensus, indispensable yet seemingly incapable of spontaneous generation, had to be consciously transplanted, nurtured, and developed if British civilization was to flourish in this new land (as Europeans considered it). Crudely (and admittedly taking something of a shortcut through the logic of elite Canadian lawyers), if the imminent demise of "peace, good order, and good government" was the problem, then legal education was the answer.[72] Only the creation of the right kind of law schools could ensure a "uniform standard of legal opinion," a "professional consensus of opinion and a professional esprit de corps."[73]

This aspect of the twentieth century's quest for legal education has not been subjected to any sustained analysis. One suspects that similar concerns and processes must have been at play in the United States, and probably also in other "British Diaspora" lands.[74] If so, however, understandings such as MacKay's, Aikins's, and Robson's have been largely overlooked, possibly squeezed out of historical studies developed within other conceptual frames.[75] There are hints of an awareness of similar issues in some US writings, but that is all.[76] Robert Gordon, for example, characterizes the late-nineteenth-century Harvard revolution in legal education (the shift to a case method of law teaching) as a repudiation of older models: "Law schools like Columbia and Yale at first tried to hold out against the pull of the Harvard model in order to preserve an older conception of the law school as designed to train generalist lawyer-statesmen."[77] The Canadian experience indicates, however, that adoption of the case method might be more accurately understood *not* as a repudiation of the lawyer-statesmen (or gentlemanly lawyer) ideal but rather as a new technique for inculcating virtue in neophyte lawyers.

The Manitoba Law School provides a unique access point for understanding the origins of the common law world's predominant twentieth-century method of law teaching. The creators of this made-in-Canada professional school had looked closely at alternative models of legal education in both the United Kingdom and the United States. They did not for a moment doubt that they were working at the forefront of legal education in Empire and continent alike. It remains possible that they deluded themselves and that they did not understand fully what they were about, but this seems unlikely. Their research, learning, social networks, travels, scholarship, and contributions to public life suggest otherwise. It is at least as probable that their work provides a source of insight into contemporary US developments and into the thinking and cultural presuppositions that lay behind them. The experiences of the periphery, in other words, might illuminate the centre.

Now, how and what did they teach? And what does that tell us about the character of early-twentieth-century legal education?

Case Method and the Political Economy of Law

The case method was the mind, heart, and soul of the Manitoba Law School's golden age innovations. Studied, assessed, announced, promulgated, published, celebrated, and taught by Manitobans in this period, it became the centrepiece of their state-of-the-art law school's curriculum.[78] This much is clear. We also know that this generation of legal reformers counted upon law school to do a tremendous work of state formation. By first selecting then developing appropriately gentlemanly lawyers who would, upon obtaining professional qualification, be sent out to their lives' work across the State's territory, they hoped to save Dominion and Empire from disintegration in the face of seemingly overwhelming centrifugal forces, ethnic divisions, and the rest. One key piece of the puzzle is still missing, however: how exactly did they expect the case method to achieve such important results? Where was the magic in studying cases?

US writings are generally not very helpful in addressing such questions. The cultural mission of legal education needs to be understood as something other than a "status project" of elite lawyers,[79] more important than superior technical training,[80] wider in import than the project of educating "lawyer-statesmen,"[81] and greater than mere "practical training."[82] Looking back, it is easy to assume that the case method came into being primarily because it is an excellent technique for teaching the skills in doctrinal analysis that underlie appellate litigation (if not the social sciences skills that "Brandeis Briefs" require). Viewing matters in this light, Robert Gordon has concluded:

> For all the noise about how practical the case method was, it was also a decision to refuse to train lawyers for – or even to acknowledge the existence of – all the new tasks that required an understanding of statutes, administrative records and procedures, financial structures of corporations, large-scale transactional work such as mergers and reorganizations, conducting trials, drafting documents, and arguing appeals. Intellectually, the decision was an act of self-mutilation, a deliberate cutting off of "pure" legal science from contemporary legal economics and the comparative history and sociology of law.[83]

This, certainly, is the way the case method appears from a position in early-twenty-first-century North America. We need to remember, however, that the men who created Canadian legal education anew in the early twentieth century considered a *proper* understanding of law to be synonymous with a series of underlying knowledges, beliefs, faith, or understandings regarding economy, public administration, constitution, corporate behaviour, and so on. Bearing this in mind, assertions or exhortations such as the following need to be accorded central place in our efforts to understand early-twentieth-century Canadian legal education:

- an exhortation to law students "not only to aspire to be the thorough lawyer, but to be the best Canadian"[84]
- informing law students that their duty was "to create a sentiment and ideals among the people with whom you come into contact which will place them upon a higher level and justify your influence. You should aim to be leaders in thought, promoters of the intellectual and moral development of our young nation, so that it may become a strong and forceful leader in the Empire"[85]
- assertions that the purpose of a law school was to teach "law in a big way," promoting "profound knowledge" and creating "an inextinguishable desire to become perfect as students, ambitious to know thoroughly the law"[86]
- explicit contempt for "smartness" unencumbered "by any other knowledge than the latest edition of the Digest, the last Consolidated Statutes, and a text book on some particular branch of the law"[87]
- belief in the necessity of "bigness" in legal learning, implying: (1) "culture" (obtained by "a broad study of subjects which are more or less connected with the law"); (2) a concern with "the highest interests of man in practical affairs"; and (3) a certain "dignity of moral feeling and profound knowledge"[88]
- promotion of the view that the goal of legal education was to educate "jurists rather than mere lawyers, having in mind the thought that a jurist seeks to conform law to current ideas of moral rectitude, while a lawyer is too prone to perpetrate existing monstrosities of artificial wrong"[89]
- faith that legal education could instill "the vision of a divine justice transcending the imperfections of human justice"[90]
- confidence that a "scientific" approach to legal education would enlarge "the mental horizon" and quicken "understanding"[91]
- belief that a key duty of legal educators was to develop in students "a sense of professional honour and of civic duty; ... legal education should be directed to producing not only competent practitioners, but men who by their wise and sympathetic handling of the problems of our national life, will add to the dignity and influence of the great profession of the Law."[92]

Such observations are not atypical. Further examples could easily be multiplied on both sides of the forty-ninth parallel.[93] Taking such rhetorical plays seriously and not disparagingly, another obvious question arises: how did these reformers think that adopting the case method would make "better men," teach law in a "big" way, enlarge "mental horizon," instill a sense of "professional honour" or "civic duty," promote "moral" development, or anything else? Looking back, it is easy to think that the method in fact achieved opposite results.[94]

When one looks for evidence of the case method's actual implementation in the early Manitoba Law School, the relationship between reformers' aspirations and their educational achievement is at first hard to discern. The first problem, simply, is that evidence as to how the method was in fact taught is rather thin. There are no first-hand accounts of law teaching in this period, almost no reflections by law teachers as to what they thought they were doing, and no recollections by students of what they felt their teachers were doing to them. There are no diaries, class notes, law students' annuals, or similar materials available.[95] Three types of sources exist to indicate how the method was implemented: curriculum guides (which consisted only of lists of cases), selected published casebooks, and casebooks developed by Manitoba Law School faculty. Each source falls well short of providing what we would hope to know about the use of the case method. Any teacher or student knows that there can be a huge disconnect between course guides, selected books, and other documentation reflecting what a course is about and the actual teaching of it. Early-twentieth-century Oxford, to take one example, could provide an extraordinarily well-rounded education in law and policy despite a curriculum and teaching materials that, in retrospect, seem to indicate the narrowest of "black letter" instruction: the real education came from close interaction in and out of formal teaching situations of students with instructors who were widely read, well-rounded intellectuals.[96]

All indications are that the actual substance of information conveyed by case teaching constituted a thinner gruel than one might have expected given the ambitions of its Canadian fathers. The two commercially published casebooks developed by Manitoba law teachers in this period fail by almost any early twenty-first-century academic, intellectual, or professional standard. Both appeared in 1916. Each was jointly compiled by J.B. Hugg and H.A. Robson, neither of whom was a bush-league lawyer by any standard. The table of contents for their *Leading Cases on Public Corporations* has only one substantive heading ("Leading Cases"). *Cases on Company Law* is slightly further developed. The co-editors expended little effort on creative taxonomy. Cases are presented unadorned, explained only by a brief parenthetical note indicating the principle of law addressed. One case is presented in support of each legal principle, and the excerpts are brief. The volumes lack the point/counterpoint presentation of inconsistent or hard-to-reconcile cases that subsequent generations have taken to constitute the (realist) core of the case method. There is no reference to secondary literature, no discussion of policy matters, no editorial note, comment, critique, or recommended further readings. The cases reproduced were selected for the clarity with which they stated legal principles.[97] Robson and Hugg expressed their belief in "[t]he desirability of placing actual cases ... before law students."[98] They thought it appropriate to mix cases from several jurisdictions despite variations in statutes. Each statutory scheme, they said, was undergirded by "the same solid body of general principles as expressed in a thoroughly matured jurisprudence." Confident in the existence of an underlying *ius gentium*, they considered the smallish variations of *lex locii* to be of secondary importance: "[t]he differences in the organic provisions and in the details of regulation" were "easy to grasp."[99] The editors explained that, by reading excerpts from actual judgments, students would develop a broader "comprehension than would be indicated merely by the topic under which the case is usually cited. The disquisitions of learned Judges are more illuminating than a text writer's epitomes."[100]

Let us pause here for a moment's reflection. It is precisely this confidence in the "illuminating" character of the "disquisitions of learned Judges" that now seems hardest to comprehend. It should be clear that the casebooks actually developed for Manitoba's law students could not plausibly have been thought more illuminating than anything else available on account of either the amount of reading they imposed (slim) or the conceptual difficulty the material presented (low). Both are rather unpretentious, even somewhat simplistic volumes: spoon-feeding efforts, really. Something else was at play.

Judicial Disquisitions as Medicine for the Soul

What could that be? If the casebooks themselves were sparse, amounting to little more than structured black letter statements (the headings), backed, digest-like, with short excerpts from a single relevant case, what do they provide that a textbook couldn't? In what way could they be said to amount to anything greater than a guidebook to legal rules?

The necessity of considering questions such as these marks the gap in mentality between our world and theirs, for the answers are neither modern nor rational (in any way we would understand those terms). In sum, all that the books provided was direct exposure to the words of the judges – legal oracles. The operational logic within which these educators operated was not that of legal realism, scientific rationality, or modernity. It was, rather, the rationality of culture, an "irrational" logic founded on odd notions that exposure to "great" literatures *in their original* would make not just better scholars (or lawyers) but also better people, better gentlemen, better "souls."

Why? Because the great judges of the past were both learned in law and, by definition, distinguished gentlemen. Given sufficient – and sufficiently direct – exposure, it was assumed that their greatness would rub off. There is a direct analogy between what early-twentieth-century Canadian lawyers thought and widely accepted views about the virtues of great literature. In 1960, for example, Clifton Fadiman wrote that reading the great books of the western canon made the reader "feel buoyed up by the noble stream of Western civilization."[101] The Great Books, Fadiman said, helped make "interior life more meaningful,"[102] "enlarged" the reader, and served as "tools of self-enhancement" and "self-discovery," working mysteriously on the innermost being "like a developing fluid on film."[103] Good books, in short, transform the soul.[104]

Similar sentiments were taken for granted among the Canadian lawyers who created twentieth-century legal education. It is precisely because their understanding of the mysterious mechanisms by which a reading program (in this case a guided reading of case law) made *better men* were commonly shared in the society of which they were part that they left their views on these matters largely unarticulated. Distinct parallels existed in other areas of Canadian educational and scholarly life, for such assumptions pervaded Canada's polite classes. John Watson, one of Canada's most influential teachers of philosophy at the turn of the century, provides one example. He believed that "if students of philosophy were to pass from a lower to a higher plane of thought they must read the classical texts for themselves. He would set his own class of more advanced students at work upon extracts from the philosophy of Kant, watch them as they struggled with its perplexities, and give helpful instruction only when it was needed."[105] In the same way that faithfully reading the Bible's genealogies (the "begats") as part of a Bible study program was thought by some Christians to be improving, so too their contemporaries perceived a mystical quality that attached to the reading of original sources of philosophy or law.

Religious analogies are doubly apt. First, because secular and religious learning did not then live in hermetically sealed boxes: philosopher John Watson, for example, has been identified as providing philosophical roots for the social gospel, and James Aikins was a life-long Sunday school teacher who explicitly modelled legal education on the institutional structures of Manitoba theological colleges.[106] Secular and religious knowledge were thoroughly intertwined.[107] Second, the mission of legal education, like that of Christian indoctrination, was at core a project concerned with transforming souls, not minds: its elements included pre-selection of the elect (requiring "pious fraud" in admissions requirements), acculturation and character development (full-time law schools to serve as seminaries of law), and a Great Mission (as gentlemen lawyers dispersed throughout the land working their British cultural mission among the polyglot non-British population).

It is noteworthy that significant aspects of educational vision were shared between the Manitoba Law School, circa 1923, and an interdenominational evangelical school of the same period. Prairie Bible Institute (PBI), located in Three Hills, Alberta, provided Bible instruction as a core part of its curriculum. Biblical truths were conveyed to PBI students through a series of questions that, the school's catalogue said, were

> designed to enable the student to sound the depths of God's Word as an organic body of revelation. The teacher refrains from coming between the student and his subject. The student, by personal first-hand research, but under careful guidance, is pushed into rich original findings. The result is that the Bible is not mediumized to the student, but the student has his own revelation and his own message of the truth.[108]

In language strikingly reminiscent of James Aikins's comments on legal education, Prairie Bible Institute promised that its educational system would lead the student to "secure the Book as *his own possession – his very own.* This is the culminating object of the school."[109]

I do not intend by noting such similarities to suggest in the least either that the Manitoba Law School was modelled on Prairie Bible Institute or (much less) that Christian institutions took their bearings from innovations in legal education. Both, however, existed in a time and a place where similar background assumptions about the nature of learning, the ends of education, and the formation of character constituted the larger ambient environment. The PBI comparison is relevant not just for the importance attached to the reading of original texts but also for its emphasis on teaching the truth of God's Word through a series of discussion questions intended to lead each student to "his own revelation and his own message of the truth." Although God's Word was not to be "mediumized" by man, PBI assumed that each student assisted in this way would come to his own understanding of a singular truth. The method was not founded on the presumption that any joyous anarchy of meaning was tolerable or possible. Each individual student was expected to find "Truth" in the singular, to come to an understanding in all respects identical to that of the larger community of privileged interpreters. Theirs was a truth for the world at large.[110] It was authoritatively true, conservative. New interpretations, novel "truths" were not within the realm of contemplation.

Socratic Method, Inner Transformation, and Revealed Truth

There is, of course, a remarkable similarity with the case method. In its classic form, cases were taught through the so-called Socratic method, which, like PBI's Bible teaching, proceeded through a series of carefully constructed questions. The ideal type of Socratic law school instructor is a man (more on the method's masculinity below) who peppers students with questions, telling them nothing, refusing to assume the role of an authoritative lecturer, leading them to discern their own legal truths. All the while, however, he – like Prairie Bible Institute's instructors – understands that students will be examined on the basis of conformity with the views held by a privileged community of legal interpreters.

Unfortunately, lack of direct evidence means that we are unable to know what actually took place in the Manitoba Law School's classrooms. It seems likely, however, that some form of question-and-answer approach to legal education had been contemplated from the beginning; even if this had not been the case, the Socratic method would have influenced the school's pedagogic strategy by the mid-1920s at the latest. At that time, Thaddeaus Hébert had become Canada's outstanding master of Socratic teaching in neighbouring Saskatchewan, where he practised Socratic method as a high art. In classic Socratic style, Hébert called upon students at the University of Saskatchewan for case briefs, questioned them on their reports, called for reconciliation of apparent inconsistencies in case law, challenged their views by offering hypothetical cases for analysis, and in general creatively worked the material so as to leave the class confused. Raising questions but declining to convey "truth" directly, Hébert quite deliberately forced students to struggle on their own in the search for meaning within the original texts of law. One of Hébert's students, J.A. Corry, humorously described his students as "victims" of the teaching method.[111] A "victim" himself, Corry thought they all derived a good deal of benefit from the experience.

It seems reasonable to assume that similar approaches to classroom teaching would have been tried at the Manitoba Law School. Certainly, C. Rhodes Smith (hired in 1925) was no fan of the lecture method of instruction. Lectures, he said, tended "to degenerate into dictation of notes by the lecturer, written down at breakneck speed by the students." Even at its best, he thought that "the formal lecture ... does very little to develop the power of analysis and gives little practice in expression and argument."[112]

We simply do not know enough to be certain about how law teaching played out in the classroom. There would inevitably have been variations in teaching style from teacher to teacher and from year to year, but some form of Socratic method or question-and-answer teaching to accompany the reading of cases seems likely. The circumstantial evidence is strong. Their deep familiarity with legal education in the United States (where Socratic teaching defined the case method), practices at the law school in the next province, and C.R. Smith's views on the poverty of lecture-based teaching all point in this direction. This suggests a second mechanism at play in the manufacture of gentlemanly, lawyerly souls.

Just as Prairie Bible Institute's teachers thought that having students read divinely inspired texts on their own, guided by a series of questions focused on the texts, would produce an inner – hence, enduring – revelation of Truth, so too law school teachers believed self-discovery of legal principles aided by interrogation of qualified teachers would led to a deep, enduring conversion to legal orthodoxy. Neither institution seriously contemplated the possibility that its students might find heresy, not Truth, through such processes. The method was assumed to produce inner transformation, understandings of self so intimately bound with doctrinal truth (legal or Christian) that the transformation would endure for a lifetime, withstanding all temptation, being immunized from challenge by those who understood not. More than memorization or learning or even literacy training was at stake – the process was intended to be life transforming.

Socratic Education as Rite of Masculine Passage

> [A] law course is a serious matter. An arts course is intended for boys, a law course forms men.[113]

A second aspect of cultural transformation, not as directly related to doctrinal orthodoxy, is also relevant. Law's cultural project was a *manly endeavour.* I do not mean this only in the superficial sense that almost all lawyers of the period were men (they were) or that many had misogynist inclinations (they did).[114] Australian scholar Margaret Thornton has argued both that contemporary professional culture casts "benchmark men" as the norm and that this orientation has deep historical roots. "Benchmark" males, she says, are "invariably" of British ethnic origin, "[w]hite ... heterosexual, able-bodied, middle-class." They are individuals who espouse "middle-of-the-road political and religious beliefs"[115] and who enjoy participation in a "culture of fraternity" that draws strongly on "the imagined masculine of liberalism." This imagined masculinity conceives of itself as consisting in equal parts of atomized, self-interested individuals[116] *and* the sorts of intimate bonds fostered by sports and club life. Powerful notions of gentlemanliness pervade respectable clubs, informing understandings of masculinity. In early-twentieth-century Canada, as in

Australia and the United States, the admission of a few women lawyers "did not change the fundamental nature of the bar as a male fraternity."[117]

The Socratic method contributed to masculine cultures of fraternity in at least two ways. Most obviously, the method's reliance on repeated struggles between professors and students led to its being considered a more virile system of education than instruction by lecture.[118] Classroom battles of wits and aggressive contests for "true" understandings dramatized professional processes of survival of the fittest. The Socratic method drew upon and contributed to a larger social common sense in which social Darwinism was important and in which military metaphors informed notions of masculinity and professional virtue alike. Although it seems odd to us, virtue and war were not then seen as opposed ideals, aggression and friendship were not incompatible. In this period, it was widely thought that war itself should – and could – be constrained by the gentlemanly instincts of the officer class. Moreover, the cultural ideal of the "Christian soldier" was an important component of respectable male self-image.[119] In such contexts, the particular ebb and flow of intellectual exchange, terror, battle, and gentlemanly swordplay that characterized Socratic classrooms spoke to the moral development of students at least as much as it did to their intellectual growth. Cultural understandings surrounding masculinity, military virtue, gentlemanliness, and Christianity coalesced in this new educational method.[120] *Everything* about the Socratic engagement was masculine.[121]

Further, the method reproduced masculine culture by association: it imported and reproduced key features of male associational life in the university environment. Rotundo describes a wide field of "young men's organizational culture," including literary societies, debating societies, and the like. In each of these, "[t]he endless process of competitive evaluation that was involved in these verbal clashes represented another refinement of a habit bred by boy culture. Boys constantly evaluated one another on the basis of physical skills. After they grew to be young men, they judged their peers by verbal and intellectual standards instead of physical ones."[122] The Socratic classroom's "verbal clashes" – and their cultural import – would have been familiar to young men of this era precisely because they replicated patterns of self-improvement common in many other masculine sites. Such clashes, which, depending on context and nuance, covered the entire range from playful fencing bouts to something akin to total war, formed the core of a distinctly male culture.

Understood in this way, one of the more mysterious aspects of the case method is intelligible. Legal educators commonly note that Socratic teaching is a notoriously inefficient means of conveying information. Even simple legal arrangements that might be taught in an hour or two of lectures or a few pages of a textbook (for example, that valid contracts require offer, acceptance, and consideration) take weeks or months of classroom time when the case method is used. Law students not infrequently complain that teachers deliberately try to confuse them rather than assisting their learning. One conventional explanation is indeed plausible: that information obtained through such deliberately painful processes is more permanently etched in the mind than that communicated through lectures or text reading. There is, in fact, however, no solid evidence to substantiate this view. The educational leaps involved are those of intuition or faith, not science.

Viewed through the lens of masculinity and in relation to projects of personal character formation, however, the case method makes a good deal of sense. Its mimicry of positivist science and commitment to "facts" reflects "a 'masculine' readiness to look brute reality unblinkingly in the face ... and to embark upon the strenuous, tough-minded, intellectual path."[123] It is active (male) learning, not passive (female).[124] The *very fact* that it is artificially difficult becomes virtue once we understand that it is the *struggle itself* that is thought to be character building. Success requires hard slogging in a trench warfare of the mind. It is the tempering fire of struggle, not the transmission of information, that ensures that lawyers will be tough, disciplined, manly, and capable of forgoing the many temptations of life in order to focus on the higher goal, the longer-term objective. Legal education, rendered sufficiently difficult, becomes training in impulse control – an indispensable component of character.[125]

Summary and Conclusions

This chapter has argued that law has a central place in colonizing processes and that British imperialists saw the transplantation of their law – which, though infused with British Christianness, they considered a transcendent secular rationality – to new lands as a key component of their larger "civilizing" mission. Canadian lawyers, like others in the British world, believed in "the encompassing ability of law to make or re-make society totally."[126] In pursuit of this civilizing mission, law's role included the tasks of negotiating, managing, confining, and – ultimately – destroying the *de facto* legal pluralism of colonial spaces. Because legal pluralism at this level emerged not from State decree but directly from the unruly human raw material of Empire, it was necessary for law to transform colonial subjects themselves if the body politic was to be inoculated "against the virus of difference."[127]

For a number of reasons Canadian social space – and Western Canada's in particular – was particularly unruly, posing special problems for law's civilizing mission during the first three decades of the twentieth century. Aware that powerful centrifugal forces were at play, Canadian lawyers believed the state to be an edifice made of law, and that law was itself nothing other than the consensus of opinion. In order to nurture an appropriately lawful, British consensus of opinion among Canada's diverse peoples, some elite Canadian lawyers sought means of implanting appropriately cultured lawyers who would carry law with them to even the remotest nooks and crannies of this new land. Consequently, a "cultural legal education" was developed so as to nurture lawyers capable of bearing this important integrative mission. This, in turn, required new entry standards for legal education, the creation of full-time seminaries of law, and new methods of instruction. Foremost among those new educational approaches were the case method and its near-twin, Socratic teaching. The significance of both lay not in anything we would now consider rational or scientific but in their presumed ability to effect transformations of soul and the development within their students of gentlemanly character and a virile masculinity.

That said, it is important to emphasize again what this chapter is not about. This has been a descriptive endeavour of modest proportions. I have not sought to pass judgment on the historical actors I have discussed. Nor would I wish to argue either that the way in which they saw the world is more accurate than any other, or that their cultural missions were in fact as important as they thought. I do not wish to assert that Canadian lawyers were particularly *effective* imperialists, or that they were more important to projects of imperialism than anyone else, or even that their efforts had any significant impact beyond their own professional world. This chapter addresses *their* world, *their* culture, *their* mentality. It is an attempt to document what they fancied themselves as achieving. As such, it is an essay on the internal culture of lawyers, only peripherally concerned with what they may in fact have contributed to refashioning the larger culture of which they were part. It remains possible that the case method did not in fact save Canada or the United States or the British Empire from dissensus, legal pluralism, the tug of centrifugal forces, anarchy. To properly assess any such claims would require a rather different project.

Moreover, I have not sought to argue that the impetus behind the case method or Socratic instruction was the same in all places and all times. Nor do I wish to assert that the case method has any timeless character or cultural essence: even identical texts and course structures perform remarkably varied cultural work in different contexts.[128] There *is* good reason to think that Canadian initiatives were heavily influenced by common-sense assumptions about legal education in the United States. Consequently, Canadian understandings in these respects may cast some light on the history and culture of legal education south of the forty-ninth parallel. That possibility too, however, requires another, very substantial research project if it is to be properly assessed.

Nonetheless, some patterns discernible in the history of Canadian legal education do resonate elsewhere. The developments, thought processes, and cultures described here can be understood as part of the history of governance.[129] Reflecting on the processes of British imperialism, Corrigan and Sayer have asserted that

> it took a national culture of extraordinary self-confidence and moral rectitude to construe such imperialism as a "civilizing mission" (and in fact to rule with surprisingly little use of direct armed force, in comparative terms, from the "Mother Country") ... Beside the greed and butchery we must put the reading matter on the East India Company ships, the ethos of the district commissioners and the Indian civil service; not in order to write off (or excuse) the former, but rather to understand the cultural forms, the energizing vision, that could animate and legitimate it notwithstanding ... cultural forms were key forms of rule.[130]

Like the reading matter on ships, the books assigned to law students, the reading material of lawyers, and the ethos of the legal profession must be understood in relation to imperialism at least as much as in relation to the internal dynamics of a professional guild.

More than any other arena, more than any other profession, law and lawyers can provide insight into the ways in which "the transcendent symbols of nationhood" connect "with the humdrum, ordinary and every day, in such a way that the former can be claimed as representing the latter."[131]

Notes

An earlier version of this chapter appeared as "British Masculinities, Canadian Lawyers: Canadian Legal Education, 1900-1930" in Robert McQueen and W. Wesley Pue, eds., *Misplaced Traditions: The Legal Profession and the British Empire* (1999) 16 Law in Context 80 [Special Issue]. It has been revised and reprinted here with permission.

1 Rev. M. Nychka, OSBM, "Mundare Yesterday and Today," trans. by Rev. G. Siermachewsky, in Fr. S. Yakymyshyn et al., eds., *Mundare Yesterday and Today* (Toronto: Basilian Press, 1969) 97 at 109.

2 I ignore here a pre-history of the *idea* of creating a national bar association that included a failed initiative originating in Nova Scotia in the late nineteenth century. See Philip Girard, "The Roots of a Professional Renaissance: Lawyers in Nova Scotia 1850-1910" (1966) 20 Man. L.J. 654; Philip Girard, "'His Whole Life Was One of Continual Warfare': John Thomas Bulmer, Lawyer, Librarian and Social Reformer" (1990) 13 Dal. L.J. 396; Philip Girard,

Lawyers and Legal Culture in British North America: Beamish Murdoch of Halifax (Toronto: University of Toronto Press/Osgoode Society for Canadian Legal History, 2011).

3 The qualification in this sentence is important: the English Inns of Court were in no respect prototype regulatory bodies in the modern sense until well into the nineteenth century. See, *e.g.*, Chapters 2 and 8 in this volume; W.W. Pue "Trajectories of Professionalism: Legal Professionalism after Abel" in A. Esau, ed., *Manitoba Law Annual, 1989-1990* (Winnipeg: Legal Research Institute, 1991) 57, reprinted from (1990) 19 Man. L.J. 384 ["Trajectories of Professionalism"]. Each of the Inns resisted taking on the character of anything resembling a regulatory body well into the twentieth century. See Chapter 9 in this volume; R.L. Abel, *The Legal Profession in England and Wales* (Oxford: B.H. Blackwell, 1988).

4 For histories of Canadian law societies, see C. Moore, *The Law Society of Upper Canada and Ontario's Lawyers, 1797-1997* (Toronto: University of Toronto Press, 1997); D. Gibson and L. Gibson, *Substantial Justice: Law and Lawyers in Manitoba, 1670-1970* (Winnipeg: Peguis Publishers, 1972); A. Watts, *History of the Legal Profession in British Columbia, 1869-1984* (Vancouver: Law Society of British Columbia, 1984, 1986).

5 See Chapters 3, 5, 6, and 9 in this volume.

6 G. Viswanathan, *Masks of Conquest: Literary Studies and British Rule in India* (New York: Columbia University Press, 1989) at 4.

7 A. Césaire, excerpt from "Discourse on Colonialism," as reproduced in P. Williams and L. Chrisman, eds., *Colonial Discourse and Post-Colonial Theory: A Reader* (New York: Columbia University Press, 1994) 172 at 173.

8 J. Kendle, *The Round Table Movement and Imperial Union* (Toronto: University of Toronto Press, 1975) at xv.

9 Fitzpatrick has trenchantly described imperialists as conceiving of law as a "gift we gave them": P. Fitzpatrick, "'The Desperate Vacuum': Imperialism and Law in the Experience of Enlightenment" in A. Carty, ed., *Post-Modern Law: Enlightenment, Revolution and the Death of Man* (Edinburgh: Edinburgh University Press, 1990) 90 at 99 ["Desperate Vacuum"]; *cf.* P. Fitzpatrick, *The Mythology of Modern Law* (London: Routledge, 1992) at 107-8 [*Mythology*].

10 An intriguing account of mid-nineteenth-century English attitudes towards their constitution and "progress" ("the major metanarrative beyond politics at this time") is provided by P. Joyce, "The Constitution and the Narrative Structure of Victorian Politics" in J. Vernon, ed., *Re-reading the Constitution: New Narratives in the Political History of England's Long Nineteenth Century* (Cambridge: Cambridge University Press, 1996) 179 at 189. The religious underpinnings of law, even in the United States, are discussed in S. Siegel, "Joel Bishop's Orthodoxy" (1995) 13 L.H.R. 215-59. See also W.P. LaPiana, *Logic and Experience: The Origin of Modern American Legal Education* (New York: Oxford University Press, 1994) at 55ff. LaPiana's views are critiqued by R.W. Gordon on the grounds that the books of the period reveal only a small role for natural law reasoning: R.W. Gordon, "The Case for (and against) Harvard" (1995) 93 Mich. L. Rev. 1231 at 1251-52. With respect, this seems to overlook the possibility that religious thought, albeit not worn on the sleeve, might influence legal writing – in precisely the same way that Gordon asserts that the categories of classical legal thought came to pervade all legal thinking, even in those who were not sympathetic to the project in the first place (at 1244- 45). If all law can be "ideological," then all law can be "religious" too.

11 See, *e.g.*, P. Corrigan and D. Sayer, *The Great Arch: English State Formation as Cultural Revolution* (Oxford: Basil Blackwell, 1985). See especially "Afterthoughts" at 182-208 for a useful discussion of major sociologists. On Maine, see A. Diamond, ed., *The Victorian Achievement of Sir Henry Maine: A Centennial Reappraisal* (Cambridge: Cambridge University Press, 1991); R. Cocks, *Sir Henry Maine: A Study in Victorian Jurisprudence*

(Cambridge: Cambridge University Press, 1988); Nick O'Brien, "'Something Older than Law Itself': Sir Henry Maine, Niebuhr, and 'the Path Not Chosen'" (2005) 26 J. Legal Hist. 229; Raymond Cocks, *Sir Henry Maine: A Study in Victorian Jurisprudence* (Cambridge: Cambridge University Press, 1988). On Weber and Marx, see Max Weber, "Part VI. The Nation, the Modern State, and Modern Law" in Stephen Kalberg, ed., *Max Weber: Readings and Commentary on Modernity* (Oxford: Blackwell Publishing, 2005); ch. 7, "Rationality and Law" in Peter Ghosh, *Max Weber and "the Protestant Ethic": Twin Histories* (Oxford: Oxford University Press, 2014); Raymond Wacks, *Understanding Jurisprudence: An Introduction to Legal Theory*, 4th ed. (Oxford: Oxford University Press, 2015); Hong Qian and Haiyan Xu, "From the Comparison between Karl Marx and Marx [*sic*] Weber to the Solution to Human Beings' Problems" (2014) 11 US-China L. Rev. 1192; Martti Koskenniemi, "What Should International Lawyers Learn from Karl Marx?" in Susan Marks, ed., *International Law on the Left: Re-examining Marxist Legacies* (Cambridge: Cambridge University Press, 2008).

12 M. Chanock, *Law, Custom, and Social Order: The Colonial Experience in Malawi and Zambia* (Cambridge: Cambridge University Press, 1985) at 4 [*Law, Custom, and Social Order*].

13 S.E. Merry, "Law and Colonialism" (1991) 25 Law & Soc'y Rev. 889 at 891.

14 A. Sachs, *Justice in South Africa* (Berkeley: University of California Press, 1973) at 43.

15 Social historians have been especially good at putting these matters on the intellectual agenda: E.P. Thompson, *Customs in Common: Studies in Traditional Popular Culture* (New York: New Press, 1993); C. Hill, *Liberty against the Law: Some Seventeenth Century Controversies* (London: Penguin Books, 1996); D. Hay, P. Linebaugh, and E.P. Thompson, *Albion's Fatal Tree: Crime and Society in Eighteenth Century England* (London: Allen Lane, 1975); P. Romney, "From Constitutionalism to Legalism: Trial by Jury, Responsible Government, and the Rule of Law in the Canadian Political Culture" (1989) 7 L.H.R. 121.

16 The relationship of law to imperial ambitions is, however, increasingly recognized by lawyers, historians, and others seeking to understand the legal side to momentous changes that precipitated or followed European colonial expansion, and the various processes caught under the rubric of decolonization. See, *e.g.*, Ian Duncanson, *Historiography, Empire and the Rule of Law: Imagined Constitutions, Remembered Legalities* (London: Routledge, 2013); Martin Chanock, *The Making of South African Legal Culture 1902-1936: Fear, Favour and Prejudice* (Cambridge: Cambridge University Press, 2001); Martin Chanock, "Constitutionalism, Democracy and Africa: Constitutionalism Upside Down" (2010) 28 Law in Context 126; Douglas Harris, *Fish, Law, and Colonialism: The Legal Capture of Salmon in British Columbia* (Toronto: University of Toronto Press, 2001); Douglas C. Harris, *Land, Fish, and Law: The Legal Geography of Indian Reserves and Native Fisheries in British Columbia, 1850-1927* (PhD Dissertation, York University, 2004); Jonathan Goldberg-Hiller and Neal Milner, "'Feeble Echoes of the Heart': A Postcolonial Legal Struggle in Hawai'i" (2008) 4 Law, Culture and Humanities 224; Merry, *supra* note 13; H. Foster, "Long-Distance Justice: The Criminal Jurisdiction of Canadian Courts West of the Canadas, 1763-1859" (1990) 34 Am. J. Legal Hist. 1; Chanock, *Law, Custom, and Social Order*, *supra* note 12; F. MacKenzie, "Gender and Land Rights in Murang'a District, Kenya" (1990) 17 Journal of Peasant Studies 609; Renisa Mawani, *Colonial Proximities: Crossracial Encounters and Juridical Truths in British Columbia, 1871-1921* (Vancouver: UBC Press, 2009); Renisa Mawani, "Law and Colonialism: Legacies and Lineages" in Austin Sarat and Patricia Ewick, eds., *Law and Society Handbook* (Malden: John Wiley and Sons, 2015) 417; Renisa Mawani, "Law as Temporality: Colonial Politics and Indian Settlers" (2014) 4 U.C. Irvine L. Rev. 101; Renisa Mawani, "'Half-Breeds,' Racial Opacity, and Geographies of Crime: Law's Search for the 'Original' Indian" (2010) 17 Cultural Geographies 487; Renisa Mawani and Iza Hussin, "The Travels of Law: Indian Ocean Itineraries" (2014) 32 L.H.R. 733; S.F. Moore, *Social Facts and Fabrications: Customary Law on Kilimanjaro, 1880-1980*

(Cambridge: Cambridge University Press, 1986); P. Fitzpatrick, "Crime as Resistance: The Colonial Situation" (1989) 28 Howard Journal 272; P. Fitzpatrick, "Marxism and Legal Pluralism" (1983) 1 Austl. J. Law & Soc'y 45 ["Marxism and Legal Pluralism"]; S. Banner, "Written Law and Unwritten Norms in Colonial St. Louis" (1996) 14 L.H.R. 33; Stuart Banner, *Legal Systems in Conflict: Property and Sovereignty in Missouri, 1750-1860* (Norman: University of Oklahoma Press, 2000); E.P. Thompson, *supra* note 15; T. Loo and L. McLean, eds., *Historical Perspectives on Law and Society in Canada* (Toronto: Copp Clark Longman, 1994); Ronen Shamir, *The Colonies of Law: Colonialism, Zionism and Law in Early Mandate Palestine* (Cambridge: Cambridge University Press, 2000); Ronen Shamir, "Nation-Building and Colonialism: The Case of Jewish Lawyers in Palestine" (2001) 8 International Journal of the Legal Profession 109; W. W. Pue and Rob McQueen, eds., *Law's Empire* (2007) 16 Social Identities 685 [Symposium Issue]; W.W. Pue, ed., *Postcolonial Legal Studies* (2003) Law, Social Justice and Global Development [Symposium Issue], online: Faculty of Law, University of Warwick <http://elj.warwick.ac.uk/global/ >; Robert McQueen and W. Wesley Pue, eds., *Misplaced Traditions: British Lawyers, Colonial Peoples* (1999) 16 Law in Context [Special Issue]. Pooja Parmar's work on the complex relationships of imperial law in post-independence India charts promising new paths: *Indigeneity and Legal Pluralism in India: Claims, Histories, Meanings* (Cambridge: Cambridge University Press, 2015). See also Mitra Sharafi, "Justice in Many Rooms since Galanter: De-romanticizing Legal Pluralism through the Cultural Defense" (2008) Law and Contemporary Problems 139; Antony Anghie, *Imperialism, Sovereignty and the Making of International Law* (Cambridge: Cambridge University Press, 2007); Preeti Nijhar, *Law and Imperialism* (London: Pickering and Chatto, 2009); Jonathan Goldberg-Hiller, "Persistence of the Indian: Legal Recognition of Native Hawaiians and the Opportunity of the Other" (2011) 33 New Political Science 23; Jonathan Goldberg-Hiller, "Reconciliation and Plasticity in a Postcolonial Hawai'i" (2012) 8 Law, Culture and the Humanities 485; Jonathan Goldberg-Hiller, "The Cultivation of Resentment: Treaty Rights and the New Right. By Jeffrey R. Dudas" (2009) 43 Law & Soc'y Rev. 451; Stuart Banner, *How the Indians Lost Their Land: Law and Power on the Frontier* (Cambridge, MA: Harvard University Press, 2005); Stuart Banner, "Two Properties, One Land: Law and Space in Nineteenth-Century New Zealand" (1999) 24 Law & Soc. Inquiry 807; Stuart Banner, "Why Terra Nullius? Anthropology and Property Law in Early Australia" (2005) 23 L.H.R. 95; P.G. McHugh, *Aboriginal Societies and the Common Law: A History of Sovereignty, Status, and Self-Determination* (Oxford: Oxford University Press, 2005); Ronen Shamir, "The Comrades Law of Hebrew Workers in Palestine: A Study in Socialist Justice" (2002) 20 L.H.R. 279.

17 Fitzpatrick, *Mythology, supra* note 9.

18 R. Rorty, *Philosophy and the Mirror of Nature* (Oxford: Blackwell, 1986) at 1063, as cited in I. Duncanson, "Cultural Studies Encounters Legal Pluralism: Certain Objects of Order, Law and Culture" (1997) 12 C.J.L.S. 115 at 122ff ["Cultural Studies"]

19 The character of law's engagement with the Enlightenment project is developed and critiqued in Fitzpatrick "Desperate Vacuum," *supra* note 9. See also Fitzpatrick, *Mythology, supra* note 9.

20 Fitzpatrick, *Mythology, ibid.* at 41.

21 See, *e.g.*, Viswanathan, *supra* note 6 at 55-56; I. Duncanson, "The Ends of Legal Studies" (1997) Web Journal of Current Legal Issues, online: <http://webjcli.ncl.ac.uk>; Duncanson "Cultural Studies," *supra* note 18.

22 D.E. Chunn, *From Punishment to Doing Good: Family Courts and Socialized Justice in Ontario, 1880-1940* (Toronto: University of Toronto Press, 1992); D.E. Chunn "Maternal Feminism, Legal Professionalism and Political Pragmatism: The Rise and Fall of Magistrate Margaret Patterson, 1922-1934" in W. Pue and B. Wright, eds., *Canadian Perspectives on Law and Society: Issues in Legal History* (Ottawa: Carleton University Press, 1988); D.E.

Chunn, "For God, Country, and the Public Purse: 'Liberal' Politics and the Campaign for Family Courts in British Columbia, 1939-1945" in H. Foster and J. McLaren, eds., *Essays in the History of Canadian Law: British Columbia and the Yukon* (Toronto: University of Toronto Press/Osgoode Society for Canadian Legal History, 1995) 423; J. McLaren, "Maternal Feminism in Action – Emily Murphy, Police Magistrate" (1988) 8 Windsor Yb. Access Just. 234. A number of the "institutional histories" contributed to W.W. Pue with D. Guth, eds., *Canada's Legal Inheritances* (1995) 23 Man. L.J. [Symposium Issue], touch on these issues. See also R. Smandych and K. Sacca, "The Development of Criminal Law Courts in Pre-1870 Manitoba" in A. Esau, ed., *Manitoba Law Annual* (1996) 24 Man. L.J. 201 [Symposium Issue], and the sources cited therein.

23 A. Hunt, *Explorations in Law and Society: Toward a Constitutive Theory of Law* (New York: Routledge, 1993) at 316.

24 M. Valverde, *The Age of Light, Soap and Water: Moral Reform in English Canada, 1885-1925* (Toronto: McClelland and Stewart, 1991) at 33.

25 Duncanson, "Cultural Studies," *supra* note 18 at 117. On the relation of law and science, see Fitzpatrick, "Marxism and Legal Pluralism," *supra* note 16 at 54-55; D. Sugarman, "'A Hatred of Disorder': Legal Science, Liberalism, and Imperialism" in P. Fitzpatrick, ed., *Dangerous Supplements* (London: Pluto, 1991) at 34-67. On the intermixing of religious and "scientific" thought, see R. Cook, *The Regenerators: Social Criticism in Late Victorian English Canada* (Toronto: University of Toronto Press, 1985); Valverde, *supra* note 24.

26 A. de Tocqueville, *Democracy in America*, trans. by G. Lawrence, ed. by J.P. Mayer (New York: Harper Perennial, 1988) at 268.

27 Moore, *supra* note 4 at 88, 67-98. See also G.B. Baker, "The Juvenile Advocates' Society, 1821-26: Self-Proclaimed Schoolroom for Upper Canada's Governing Class" in Canadian Historical Association, *Historical Papers* (Ottawa: Canadian Historical Association, 1985) at 74-101.

28 See A. Smith, *Canada – An American Nation? Essays on Continentalism, Identity, and the Canadian Frame of Mind* (Montreal and Kingston: McGill-Queen's University Press, 1994) [*An American Nation?*].

29 J.K. Goodrich, *The Coming Canada* (Chicago: A.C. McClurg, 1913) at 300.

30 Romney, *supra* note 15 at 122.

31 A. Smith, "American Culture and the Concept of Mission in Nineteenth-Century English Canada" in Smith, *An American Nation? supra* note 28 at 31. See also C. Berger, *The Sense of Power: Studies in the Ideas of Canadian Imperialism, 1867-1914* (Toronto: University of Toronto Press, 1970). Canadian culture had also long been influenced strongly by immigration of people from the democratic and un-British American republic. P. Romney has done an admirable job of capturing southern influences on Ontario legal culture in the early nineteenth century, in Romney, *supra* note 15.

32 G. Friesen, *The Canadian Prairies: A History* (Toronto: University of Toronto Press, 1987) at 162.

33 Figures taken from Friesen, *ibid.* at 5 for the prairie west; and from World Atlas 3 and US Atlas 3 (1991-92), Software Toolworks Atlas Pack MPC, Software Toolworks.

34 See generally Friesen, *ibid.* Some aspects of this history are covered in Gibson and Gibson's *Substantial Justice, supra* note 4. On Clifford Sifton, see also "Time Links, Sir Clifford Sifton," online: Time Links <http://timelinks.merlin.mb.ca/refernc/db0053.htm>. See also J.M. Bumsted, *The Peoples of Canada: A Post-Confederation History* (Toronto: Oxford University Press, 1992) [*Peoples of Canada*]; R.D. Francis and Chris Kitzan, *The Prairie West as Promised Land* (Calgary: University of Calgary Press, 2007).

35 Friesen, *supra* note 32 at 340.

36 R.C. Macleod, "Canadianizing the West," as excerpted in R. Francis, R. Douglas, and Howard Palmer, eds., *The Prairie West: Historical Readings*, 2d ed. (Edmonton: Pica Pica Press, 1992) 225 at 226.

37 *I.e.*, residents of Canada's Atlantic provinces: Nova Scotia, Prince Edward Island, and New Brunswick (Newfoundland had not yet joined Confederation).

38 T.C. Byrne, *The Ukrainian Community in North Central Alberta* (MA Thesis, University of Alberta, 1937) at 41.

39 For discussions of prairie ethnicity and settlement patterns, see C.A. Dawson, *Group Settlement – Ethnic Communities in Western Canada* (Toronto: Macmillan, 1936); Friesen, *supra* note 32 at 242-73; W. Eggleston, "The People of Alberta" (1937) 15 Canadian Geographical Journal 212; V.L. Hull, *A Geographic Study of the Impact of Two Ethnic Groups on the Rural Landscape in Central Alberta* (MA Thesis, University of Alberta, 1965); W.H. Jackson, *Ethnicity and Areal Organisation among French Canadians in the Peace River Region, Alberta* (MA Thesis, University of Alberta, 1970); V.J. Kaye, *Early Ukrainian Settlements in Canada, 1895-1900* (Toronto: University of Toronto Press, 1964); V.J. Kaye, "Three Phases of Ukrainian Immigration" in Y. Slavutych, R.C. Elwood, V.J. Kaye, and J.M. Kirschbaum, eds., *Slavs in Canada*, vol. 1 (Edmonton: Inter-University Committee on Canadian Slavs, 1967) 36; H.L.P. Stibbe, *The Distribution of Ethnic Groups in Alberta, Canada, According to the 1961 Census* (MSc Thesis, University of Alberta, 1967); G.M. Stubbs, *The Geography of Cultural Assimilation in the Prairie Provinces* Oxford: (DPhil Thesis, Oxford University, 1965).

40 241 in 1871, 3,700 in 1874, 26,000 in 1891, 42,000 in 1900, 90,000 in 1906, 150,000 in 1913, and 179,087 by 1921. Figures from Bumsted, *Peoples of Canada, supra* note 34 at 75; Gibson and Gibson, *supra* note 4 at 113; Friesen, *supra* note 32 at 274; J.M. Bumsted, *The Winnipeg General Strike of 1919: An Illustrated History* (Winnipeg: Watson and Dwyer Publishing, 1994) at 10 [*Winnipeg General Strike*]; A.F.J. Artibise, "Boosterism and the Development of Prairie Cities, 1871-1913" in A.FJ. Artibise, ed., *Town and City: Aspects of Western Canadian Urban Development* (Regina: Canadian Plains Research Center, 1981) 209, as excerpted in Francis et al., *supra* note 36 at 516.

41 Friesen, *supra* note 32 at 243.

42 See, *e.g.*, James Youngblood Henderson's contribution to Pue and Guth, *Canada's Legal Inheritances, supra* note 22; John Borrows, *Canada's Indigenous Constitution* (Toronto: University of Toronto Press, 2010); John Borrows, *Recovering Canada: The Resurgence of Indigenous Law* (Toronto: University of Toronto Press, 2002).

43 See, *e.g.*, J. Peters, *The Waisenamt: A History of Mennonite Inheritance Custom* (Steinbach, MB: Mennonite Village Museum, 1985); H. Dick, *Lawyers of Mennonite Background in Western Canada before the Second World War* (Winnipeg: Legal Research Institute, 1993); J. McLaren, "Creating 'Slaves of Satan' or 'New Canadians'? The Law, Education, and the Socialization of Doukhobor Children, 1911-1935" in Foster and McLaren, *supra* note 22 at 352-85.

44 Friesen, *supra* note 32 at 358.

45 Friesen, *ibid.* at 361. See Reinhold Kramer and Tom Mitchell, *When the State Trembled: How A.J. Andrews and the Citizen's Committee Broke the Winnipeg General Strike* (Toronto: University of Toronto Press, 2010). For a useful review of historiography and of archival records relating to the Winnipeg General Strike, see K. Kehler and A. Esau, *Famous Manitoba Trials: The Winnipeg General Strike Trials – Research Resource* (Winnipeg: University of Manitoba, Legal Research Institute, 1990). See also Bumsted, *Winnipeg General Strike, supra* note 40; D.J. Bercuson, *Confrontation at Winnipeg: Labour, Industrial Relations, and the General Strike*, rev. ed. (Montreal and Kingston: McGill-Queen's University Press, 1990).

46 As quoted in Bumsted, *Peoples of Canada, supra* note 34 at 67. Original source: D. Avery, "The Radical Alien and the Winnipeg General Strike of 1919" in J.M. Bumsted, ed., *Interpreting Canada's Past II* (Toronto: Oxford University Press, 1986) at 222-39.

47 See W.W. Pue, "Revolution by Legal Means" in P. Glenn, ed., *Contemporary Law/Droit contemporain* (Montreal: Editions Yvons Blais, 1994) 1.

48 Valverde, *supra* note 24 at 27.
49 Ch. 1 in T. Loo and C. Strange, *Making Good* (Toronto: University of Toronto Press, 1997).
50 J. Aikins, "Address of the President" (1919) 39 Canadian Law Times 537 at 539 ["Canadian Bar Association Presidential Address"].
51 J. Aikins, "The President's Address" (1920) 56 Can. L.J. 308 at 310.
52 Aikins, "Canadian Bar Association Presidential Address," *supra* note 50 at 543.
53 See especially Fitzpatrick, *Mythology, supra* note 9 at 111-18.
54 James Aikins's close personal assistant, E.H. Coleman, travelled with the White Russian forces, documenting first-hand accounts of encounters with Bolshevism in a pamphlet published upon his return.
55 See, *e.g.*, D. Cole and I. Chaikan, *An Iron Hand upon the People* (Vancouver: Douglas and McIntyre, 1990). J. McLaren has addressed clashes between Doukhobor and British Canadian cultural values in "The Doukhobor Belief in Individual Faith and Conscience and the Demands of the Secular State" in J. McLaren and H. Coward, eds., *Religious Conscience, the State and the Law: Historical Contexts and Contemporary Significance* (Albany: State University of New York Press, 1999). "Family" sharing presumably remained acceptable, but only if family was taken to be a nuclear family amputated from the extended kinship lines that have served to organize many sorts of human societies other than the one Aikins sought to advance. See also A. Esau, "Communal Property and Freedom of Religion: *Lakeside Colony of Hutterian Brethren v. Hofer*" in McLaren and Coward, *ibid.* at 97-116, and J. [Sakej] Y. Henderson, "The Struggle to Preserve Aboriginal Spiritual Teachings and Practices" in McLaren and Coward, *ibid.* at 168-88.
56 "Disease" was connected to, and associated with, another powerful metaphor in this period: "degeneration." See D. Pick, *Faces of Degeneration: A European Disorder, c.1848-c.1918* (Cambridge: Cambridge University Press, 1993). The publisher's write-up explains: "This book investigates the specific conception and descent of a language of 'degeneration' from 1848-1918, with particular reference to France, Italy and England. Daniel Pick shows how in the refraction and wake of evolution and naturalism, new images and theories of atavism, 'degenerescence' and socio-biological decline emerged in European culture and politics. He indicates the wide cultural and political importance of the idea of degeneration, whilst showing that the notion could mean different things at different times in different places." See also W. Greenslade, *Degeneration, Culture and the Novel: 1880-1940* (Cambridge: Cambridge University Press, 2010).
57 In retrospect, we can appreciate that their views were midway on an intellectual trajectory that culminated in Nazi geopolitics. R. Muir, *Modern Political Geography* (London: Macmillan, 1975), discusses the scholarship of Friedrich Ratzel (1844-1904), Kjellen, and Nazi geopolitician Haushofer, concluding that Nazi geopolitics was "an amalgamation of the organic state notions of Ratzel, Mackinder's global system and heartland thesis, macro-regionalism, postwar paranoia and the supposed German right to *Lebensraum*" (at 6). It is noteworthy that, despite repeated attempts to treat geopolitics as a German corruption of science, the work of British scholar Halford Mackinder (founder of Geographical Studies at Oxford University) was central to Nazi geopolitical thought. Such ideas, their reliance on biological metaphors, and their relation to social Darwinism were simply "in the air" at this time.
58 The rhetoric, language, and policies around eugenics in Canada are but one dramatic manifestation of this conception of the state. See A. McLaren, *Our Own Master Race: Eugenics in Canada, 1885-1945* (Toronto: McClelland and Stewart, 1990).
59 See Fitzpatrick, *Mythology, supra* note 9 at 116.
60 See Chapter 5 in this volume.
61 See J. Willis, *A History of Dalhousie Law School* (Toronto: University of Toronto Press, 1979).
62 These points are developed in more detail in Chapters 5 and 6 in this volume.

63 I touched lightly on these developments and referenced the literature in *Law School: The Story of Legal Education in British Columbia* (Vancouver: Continuing Legal Education Society of British Columbia/University of British Columbia Faculty of Law, 1995), also "published" at <http://faculty.law.ubc.ca/pue/historybook/> [*Law School*]; Chapters 5 and 6 in this volume.

64 Memo, Robson to MacLean, 22 April 1914, University of Manitoba Archives, UA20, Box 10, Folder 5.

65 Aikins, "Canadian Bar Association Presidential Address," *supra* note 50 at 546.

66 I.A. MacKay, "The Education of a Lawyer" [speech delivered in December 1913 to the Third Annual Meeting of the Law Society of Alberta] (1940-42) Alta. L. Q. 103 at 108. See also J.C. Gray's 1883 observation that "the opinions of judges and lawyers as to what the law is *are* the law" (as quoted in Gordon, *supra* note 10 at 1239).

67 MacKay, *ibid.* at 108.

68 *Ibid.* at 115.

69 Newer scholarship has occasionally focused on similar understandings, albeit motivated by rather different concerns. See, for example, the essays collected in W.W. Pue, ed., *Lawyering for a Fragmented World* (1998) 5 International Journal of the Legal Profession [Symposium Issue]. A massive body of literature that focused on the representativeness of bar or bench in terms of gender, racial, ethnic, or religious composition was also motivated, at least in part, by such considerations.

70 MacKay, *supra* note 66 at 115. There are cross-border parallels that are interesting and deserving of further exploration. These include the American Law Institute's Restatement projects, which "supposed that disinterested legal minds could identify a core of national common law principles that rose above both variations in state law and mere politics." This and similar views suggest an integrative or state-formation function of the legal profession, albeit not as explicitly as among the Canadian professional reformers. See Gordon, *supra* note 10 at 1235 (source of quotation; referencing LaPiana, *supra* note 10). See also G.E. White, "The American Law Institute and the Triumph of Modernist Jurisprudence" (1997) 15 L.H.R. 1.

71 MacKay, *ibid.* at 107-8.

72 *Ibid.* at 110.

73 *Ibid.* at 110-11.

74 For a historiographic review of literature on the concept of a British Diaspora, see P. Lyon, "On Diasporas – The Jewish, the British and Some Others: A Note" in *The Diaspora of the British*, Collected Seminar Papers No. 31 (London: University of London, Institute of Commonwealth Studies, 1982) at 72-80. The notion has recently been developed in legal history by P. Karsten, "Cows in the Corn, Pigs in the Garden, and 'the Problem of Social Costs': 'High' and 'Low' Legal Cultures of the British Diaspora Lands in the 17th, 18th, and 19th Centuries" (1998) 32 Law & Soc'y Rev. 63.

75 Predominantly, the "frames" of "trait theory" of professions, market control theory (and its "jurisdictional" cousin, ethnic discrimination). Leading literature working these veins include R.L. Abel, "Revisioning Lawyers" in R.L. Abel and P.S.C. Lewis, eds., *Lawyers in Society: An Overview* (Berkeley: University of California Press, 1995) 1; M.S. Larson, *The Rise of Professionalism: A Sociological Analysis* (London: University of California Press, 1977); R.L. Abel, *Legal Profession in England and Wales, supra* note 4; R.L. Abel, *American Lawyers* (New York: Oxford University Press, 1989); R.L. Abel and P.S.C. Lewis, eds., *Lawyers in Society*, vol. 3, *Comparative Theories* (Berkeley: University of California Press, 1989); H. Arthurs, R. Weisman, and F. Zemans, "Canadian Lawyers: A Peculiar Professionalism" in R.L. Abel and P.S.C. Lewis, eds., *Lawyers in Society*, vol. 1, *The Common Law World* (Berkeley: University of California Press, 1988) at 123-85; J.S. Auerbach, *Unequal Justice: Lawyers and Social Change in Modern America* (New York: Oxford University Press, 1976); A. Abbott,

The System of Professions: An Essay on the Division of Expert Labor (Chicago: University of Chicago Press, 1988). For discussions of such theories and how they have influenced histories of legal education and legal professions, see Chapter 5 in this volume and Pue, "Trajectories of Professionalism," *supra* note 3.

76 See, *e.g.*, LaPiana, *supra* note 10; Gordon, *supra* note 10. The expectations that de Tocqueville and Strachan had of the legal professions (discussed above) are well known, for example, but the generation of Aikins and Robson provides greater insight into the way in which law was to work its projects in the realms of cultural and state transformation. Although R.A. Ferguson's *Law and Letters in American Culture* (Cambridge, MA: Harvard University Press, 1984) deals with different issues in a different time, it, too, is suggestive.
77 Gordon, *supra* note 10 at 1235.
78 See Chapter 6 in this volume.
79 Gordon, *supra* note 10 at 1232-33, 1234-35, 1241.
80 *Ibid.* at 1234.
81 *Ibid.* at 1235.
82 *Ibid.* at 1236, 1242.
83 *Ibid.* at 1260.
84 J. Aikins, "Formal Opening of the Manitoba Law School, Inaugural Address to the Students by Sir James Aikins, K.C., M.P." (1914) 34 Canadian Law Times 1183 at 1190 ["Inaugural Address to the Students"].
85 *Ibid.* at 1190.
86 *Ibid.* at 1188-89.
87 *Ibid.* at 1188.
88 *Ibid.* at 1187, 1188.
89 C.A. Boston, "Some Neglected Fields in Legal Education. Address of Chairman. Delivered before the Section of Legal Education of the American Bar Association at Washington, D.C., Oct. 20, 1914" (1914) 34 Canadian Law Times 1081 at 1091.
90 R.W. Lee, "Legal Education, Old and New, III" (1916) 36 Canadian Law Times 109 at 114.
91 *Ibid.*
92 R.W. Lee, "Legal Education: A Symposium" (1919) 39 Canadian Law Times 138 at 141. For further assessment of Lee's contribution, including the cultural urgings underlying his attempt to establish common law education in Québec, see R. Macdonald, "The National Law Programme at McGill" (1990) 13 Dal. L.J. 211.
93 For more on this, see Chapter 5 in this volume.
94 M. Thornton, *Dissonance and Distrust: Women in the Legal Profession* (Melbourne: Oxford University Press, 1996) [*Dissonance*]; D. Kennedy, "Legal Education as Training for Hierarchy" in D. Kairys, ed., *The Politics of Law: A Progressive Critique*, 3d ed. (New York: Basic Books, 1998) 54; R. Wilkins, "The Person You're Supposed to Become: The Politics of the Law School Experience" (1987) 45 U.T. Fac. L. Rev. 98.
95 Surprisingly, more material of this sort survives with respect to the rather less prestigious, less ambitious Vancouver Law School. See Pue, *Law School, supra* note 63.
96 I am grateful to the University of British Columbia's founding law dean, Dean George Curtis, for drawing this to my attention during the course of extensive discussions concerning the legal education he received at Oxford.
97 H.A. Robson, K.C. Hugg, and J.B. Hugg, *Leading Cases on Public Corporations* (Toronto: Carswell, 1916), Preface.
98 H.A. Robson and J.B. Hugg, *Cases on Company Law* (Toronto: Carswell, 1916), Preface.
99 *Ibid.* at 8.
100 *Ibid.* at 9. For a fuller discussion of these casebooks, see Chapter 6 in this volume.
101 C. Fadiman, *The Lifetime Reading Plan* (New York: World Publishing, 1960) at 18.
102 *Ibid.* at 19.

103 *Ibid.*

104 See A. Bloom, *The Closing of the American Mind: How Higher Education Has Failed Democracy and Impoverished the Souls of Today's Students* (New York: Simon and Schuster, 1987).

105 J.A. Irving, "The Development of Philosophy in Central Canada from 1850 to 1900" (1950) 31 Canadian Historical Review 252 at 274. I am grateful to Lyndsay Campbell for bringing this to my attention.

106 See Chapter 6 in this volume; D. Gibson and L. Gibson, "Sir James Aikins' Seamless Web: Finding Fortune and Fame as a Lawyer in the Adolescent Canadian West" (1992) 21 Man. L.J. 161.

107 See, *e.g.*, Cook, *supra* note 25.

108 As quoted in J.G. Stackhouse Jr., *Canadian Evangelicalism in the Twentieth Century: An Introduction to Its Character* (Toronto: University of Toronto Press, 1993) at 73.

109 *Ibid.* at 78.

110 "But Prairie at no time seemed to recognize the basic epistemological contradiction between claiming pure inductivism and having study guided by direct questions. Nor did it seem to allow for the prospect that a student might come up with something truly 'original' – something that might contradict Prairie's own statement of faith. In all of this of course, Prairie was not exceptional but rather typical of evangelicals. As has been noted, this 'cognitive style' in Canada awaits further study, but on this sort of epistemological naiveté in Britain and America, see [sources cited]": Stackhouse, *ibid.* at 237.

111 J.A. Corry, *My Life and Work: A Happy Partnership (Memoirs of J.A. Corry)* (Kingston, ON: Queen's University Press, 1981).

112 C.R. Smith, "Legal Education: A Manitoba View" (1935) Can. Bar Rev. 404 at 408. Smith was a lecturer at the Manitoba Law School at the time.

113 MacKay, *supra* note 66 at 108.

114 For discussions of gender and the legal profession in this period, see Pue, *Law School, supra* note 63; J. Brockman, "'Not by Favour but by Right': The History of Women and Visible Minorities in the Legal Profession of British Columbia" in J. McLaren and H. Foster, eds., *Essays in the History of Canadian Law*, vol. 6, *The Legal History of British Columbia and the Yukon* (Toronto: Osgoode Society for Canadian Legal History, 1995); L.K. Yorke, "Mabel Penery French (1881-1955): A Life Re-Created" (1993) 42 U.N.B.L.J. 3.

115 Thornton, *Dissonance, supra* note 94 at 40. For further development of these concepts, see M. Thornton, "'Liberty, Equality and?' Endowing Fraternity with Voice" (1996) 18 Sydney L. Rev. 555.

116 Thornton, *Dissonance, supra* note 94 at 8.

117 E.A. Rotundo, *American Manhood: Transformations in Masculinity from the Revolution to the Modern Era* (New York: Basic Books, 1993) at 213. For a remarkable effort by women law students to redefine professional understandings on their own terms, see *Vancouver Law Students' Annual*, 1919-20, as discussed in Pue, *Law School, supra* note 63 at 225ff.

118 Rotundo, *ibid.* at 8.

119 "A lawyer ... by taking up arms as a Christian soldier, could purify his wealth and power by using it to godly ends ... Historian Robert Crunden has observed that many notable progressives came from religious families that cultivated stern Protestant consciences. Resisting pressure to follow careers in the ministry or missionary work, these devotees of reform found secular channels for their evangelical impulses, launching crusades to save society from its worldly sins." Rotundo, *ibid.* at 173.

120 See, generally, J.W. Hamilton, "Metaphors of Lawyers' Professionalism" (1995) 33 Alta. L. Rev. 833, for an outstanding assessment of the interplay of metaphorical networks relating to masculinity, Christianity, and war in Canadian lawyers' professional self-understandings. On "discipline," "stability," "self-reliance," and "masculinity" as components of British national

identity, legal thought, and legal education, see D. Sugarman, "Great Beyond His Knowing: Morton Horwitz's Influence on Legal Education and Scholarship in England, Canada and Australia" in Daniel W. Hamilton and Alfred L. Brophy, eds., *Transformations in American Legal History II – Essays in Honor of Morton J. Horwitz* (Cambridge, MA: Harvard University Press, 2011) at 504-42.

121 The Socratic method bears comparison with a number of rites of masculine formation on both sides of the Atlantic, including French fencing studios, English public school education, bourgeois sporting culture, and Canadian private schools. The point cannot be developed at length here. See R.A. Nye, *Masculinity and Male Codes of Honor in Modern France* (New York: Oxford University Press, 1993); J.A. Mangan, "Social Darwinism and Upper-Class Education in Late Victorian and Edwardian England" in J.A. Mangan and J. Walvin, eds., *Manliness and Morality: Middle-Class Masculinity in Britain and America 1800-1940* (Manchester: University of Manchester Press, 1987) 135; J. Walvin, "Symbols of Moral Superiority: Slavery, Sport and the Changing World Order, 1800-1940" in Mangan and Walvin, *ibid.* at 242; J.A. Barman, *Growing Up British in British Columbia: Boys in Private School, 1900-1950* (PhD Dissertation, University of British Columbia, 1982).

122 Rotundo, *supra* note 117 at 70. See also Lani Guinier, Michelle Fine, and Jane Balin, *Becoming Gentlemen: Women, Law School, and Institutional Change* (Boston: Beacon Press, 1997); Walter Bennett, *The Lawyer's Myth: Reviving Ideals in the Legal Profession* (Chicago: University of Chicago Press, 2001).

123 Gordon, *supra* note 10 at 1240. Gordon portrays "scientific" approaches as being an attempt to throw off the shackles of religion and moral sentiment in approaching law. This, I think, overlooks the close and complicated relationships between empiricism, science, and God in this period, but this is not the place to explore such themes in any depth. My selective quotation from Gordon's work is deliberate and not intended to be misleading.

124 For a useful general discussion of the cultural construction of masculinity and femininity in western culture, see M. Thornton, "Authority and Corporeality: The Conundrum for Women in Law" (1998) 6 Feminist Legal Studies 147.

125 Rotundo, *supra* note 117 at 73, observes that "books of sermons appeared less often during the second half of the century, when they were replaced by a moralistic secular literature (usually scientific or medical) that echoed most of the themes of impulse control that had dominated the preaching of earlier generations." Understanding legal education against this background helps to make sense of James Aikins's address at the opening of the Manitoba Law School, a large part of which was dedicated to imploring students to apply themselves fully to the study of law, to "control" themselves, avoid "excesses" (including alcohol), and manifest the virtues of "integrity," "moral fibre," "character," "honour," and the "habit of industry." Aikins, "Inaugural Address to the Students," *supra* note 84 at 1183-87.

126 Fitzpatrick, *Mythology*, *supra* note 9 at 56.

127 Duncanson, "Cultural Studies," *supra* note 18 at 116.

128 *Cf.* Viswanathan, *supra* note 6, for an analogous treatment of English literature studies.

129 See, *e.g.*, Hunt, *supra* note 23 at 306: "Central to this conception of 'governance' is the idea that government is not only the work of 'Governments'; central to the projects of government are the key institutionalized professions – such as the medical profession – that stand between Government and the population. Or to put it in different terms, this conception of 'governance' traverses the distinction between state and civil society; it is to be found on both, not just on one side, of this evocative dichotomy." That said, it is odd that even sociologists of law have tended to underestimate (or simply ignore) the roles of the legal profession in relation to governance so construed.

130 Corrigan and Sayer, *supra* note 11 at 194.

131 *Ibid.* at 196.

13

Lawyers' Professionalism, Colonialism, State Formation, and National Life in Nigeria, 1900-60

"THE FIGHTING BRIGADE OF THE PEOPLE"

Co-authored with Chidi Oguamanam

A common conceit of organized legal professions is that lawyers play central roles in state formation, state re-formation, and nation building. The fact that lawyers imagine their profession in such a fashion approaches a universal truth as closely, perhaps, as any social observation. Lawyers tend to think of their profession as operating as a kind of social "glue," serving as an indispensable conduit of values, and binding societies and countries together. Simultaneously, the legal profession thinks of itself as a key agent in the cause of liberty.

Arrogant though it may be, such self-perceptions are indeed grounded in a reality of sorts. Lawyers, indeed, *are* always "there," serving, variously, the causes of independence movements, revolution, authoritarian rule, sovereign statehood, or colonial administrations. Law is Janus-faced, promising both liberty and order. Because "law" is conventionally thought to play essential roles in constituting a desirable, perhaps *necessary* uniformity of governance across state territory, lawyers have often emphasized their own roles in state formation. The lawyers' professional work includes bringing law equally to all portions of state territory[1] *and* active involvement in myriad cultural projects by which central legal values are transmitted to all of the state's peoples and cultures. Law, in a word, "civilizes" provincials. Lawyers often, perhaps always, view themselves as key agents in this civilizing mission.

This is certainly a viable interpretation of the work of lawyers and the organized legal profession in the mainland United Kingdom and also in Ireland.[2] Projects of state formation connote rather different things, however, in diverse contexts. When we think of Ireland, for example, rather than the English homeland, projects of "nation building" or "state formation" take on different colourings. Processes viewed with equanimity at home form part and parcel of "colonization" or "colonialism" abroad. Such words carry rather different connotations than the more neutral-sounding languages of state integration that seem appropriate descriptors of the lawyerly role at home.

Surprisingly, perhaps, these cultural or political processes and the associated self-images advanced by organized legal professions remain very largely unstudied. Most scholarship about lawyers since the late twentieth century has placed primary emphasis on "market control" or "monopoly" theory. Dictated by a paradigm generated within a larger body of scholarship on the sociology of professions, this approach assumes that people become professionals so as to become rich and, further, that they *organize their profession* in such a way as to advance this goal through collective action. Unsurprisingly, researchers have been able to find evidence confirming their assumptions. Viewed through such lenses, all of the conventional traits of professionalism appear to have been developed in the cause of monopoly. Entry standards, educational requirements, qualification procedures, practice rules, ethical codes, and the very notion of self-regulation can all be reduced to fit the interpretive frame.[3]

More recent scholarship loosened the grip of market control theory, opening scholarship about professions to a significantly widened range of insights. One new approach offers instead a more or less functionalist understanding of lawyers' roles in relation to liberal politics.[4] It avoids the extreme reductionism of market-control theory and develops important perspectives on the origins of constitutionally bound moderate states in post-Enlightenment European traditions. It suffers, however, from overlooking the dark side of liberalism more than it ought. Research in this vein has also tended to look more to the work of lawyers or to their specific causes rather than to the organizational principles of the legal profession *as a profession*.[5] As a result, lawyers' agency in larger cultural projects has been mostly overlooked, even as intense concern about the "politics" of lawyers has emerged.[6]

The centrality of cultural projects vis-à-vis state integration or colonial governance has not been treated as a closely guarded secret by legal professionals. The importance of these missions is apparent on the face of professional apologetics in many places and at many times. By and large, it is only by *reading past* what professionals have said and written in articulating their professional vision that we can avoid noticing the pervasive moral vision at the heart of professionalism. The involvement of legal professionals in advancing the cause and course of colonial state formation is apparent in the cases of South Africa, Australia, Canada, and British Palestine, no doubt among many others.[7]

One of the first acts of the British Empire in Palestine focused on the task of imposing "new laws and new legal institutions" along with

> educating the "native" lawyers, be they Arabs or Jews, and regulating their activities. Beginning in the early 1920s, the colonial state launched a quite assertive programme of professionalisation in law. The Jerusalem law-school, the first and only such school in the country, was inaugurated by the colonial government in 1920, when the British civil administration of Palestine barely began to function.[8]

The legal education provided was carefully calibrated according to the future role and tasks imagined for the student. A basic curriculum, taught in Hebrew or Arabic, was intended to prepare students for work as lawyers, but not for a law degree as such. The degree program, taught only to English speakers, included core common law subjects, international law, and jurisprudence. Educational developments such as these, combined with the 1922 *Advocate's Ordinance* definitions established a two-tiered legal profession. "Gentlemanly" knowledge of the British sort was privileged. The result was a form of professionalization that

> set the conditions for legitimate juridic participation in the Palestinian politicolegal sphere on the basis of the commitment of lawyers to English law and on the basis of their ability to develop expert-based ties to the institutions and officialdom of the colonial state.
>
> The advent of the professionalisation project is key to understanding the *habitus* of Jewish lawyers, particularly their attitude towards the place of law in the nation-building project.[9]

India, the jewel of the Empire's crown, raises a series of difficult questions regarding both the colonial state and the nation-building project that displaced it. British imperialism carried peculiar burdens of history and practice in relation to the many diverse local cultures of that subcontinent. The longevity of British rule in India, combined with the more or less complete absence of "settlers" (as such), produced a cultural context quite distinct from both Palestine and the "*Statute of Westminster*" colonies (Newfoundland, South Africa, New Zealand, Canada, and Australia). Even the category of "Indian lawyer" is complexly layered, for we need to distinguish, at a minimum, between "Indian lawyers" (barristers or solicitors), expatriate lawyers working in India, and Indians working in traditional roles that western secular law denotes as "legal." It is an untidy fact that "Indian lawyers" in the first sense simultaneously played important roles in two aspects of Congress Party politics at the turn of the twentieth century. They were legendary figures who struggled against British rule and *also* served the cause of internal state consolidation, "modernization," and secularization, seeking to bind the huge territory and diverse peoples of India into one.[10] Elsewhere, processes such as these might be termed "internal colonization." Moreover, as Shamir reminds us, drawing on Partha Chatterjee's account of "the trajectory of Indian nationalism under British imperialism ... bourgeois opposition to colonialism has always been ambiguous. There is a history of collaboration between the colonial state and the educated classes, he writes, 'sealed by the marriage of law and literacy.'"[11]

In this chapter, we explore a few key questions relating to the relationships between lawyers and colonialism in Nigeria. What role did lawyers play in relation to colonialism or decolonization in Nigerian history? How did they conceive of their job and themselves as a profession and as professionals? What professional self-images did they carry as they went about their work? What peculiar modalities did they employ in advancing cultural and political causes dear to their hearts? What circumstances and opportunities did they exploit in the process? Following Adewoye, we treat British colonial Nigeria's history in two phases.[12]

Empire

Between 1880 and 1939, the British sought to establish effective governance over diverse national and ethnic configurations that later became Nigeria. A form of culturally and spatially segregated legal pluralism was constructed as imperial authorities sought to contain Nigerian issues to "native courts," while shielding British commercial interests from indigenous legal challenge. Native involvement in the legal profession was discouraged. Following patterns similar to those playing out in India at the same time, many Nigerians sought to establish a pan-Nigerian nationalism *within* the British Empire. Nigerian lawyers became agents for both westernization and self-determination. "Law" carried tremendous symbolic power in the myriad cultural and political struggles that ensued. From one side, British rule imposed law's majesty on colonial subjects. Law's promise of justice, however, dramatically empowered the colonized, who invoked their masters' tools in the form of British law, in resistance to the Empire. As early as the first decade of the twentieth century, legal practitioners in Lagos were politically active, "being looked upon for leadership and as 'the fighting brigade of the people.'"[13]

Decolonization

Beginning in the 1930s but accelerating dramatically after 1945, British colonial policy in Nigeria shifted focus from maintaining Empire to establishing the groundwork for Nigeria's independence. Independence came much more quickly than earlier generations had anticipated, in 1960. The fading Empire's

A Priceless Heritage

Published in the *Vancouver Sun* on 18 August 1938, this cartoon illustrates the central role that colonists thought "British Law" played in the imperial project.

officialdom scrambled, making desperate haste to launch the processes of state formation and to establish durable western institutions in the soon-to-emerge nation. Dramatically reversing their earlier policies, the British took steps to instantly create a westernized local elite. As a result, larger numbers of indigenous lawyers appeared. Many became agents for a western style of pan-Nigerian nationalism.

Empire and Liberal Nationalism

Two moments of colonial Nigeria's history provide valuable insight into the relationships between lawyering, culture, and Empire, illustrating the transformative consequences that political trials can have on processes of cultural formation. In both the Eleko of Lagos case in the south (*Eshugbayi Eleko v. Officer Administering the Government of Nigeria and Another*) and litigation affecting the Emir of Kano in the north, traditional authority figures found themselves enmeshed in forensic battles constructed within British imperialism. Among Europe's imperialisms, the British variant exceeded all others in seeking to justify its rule through an ostentatious embrace of the rhetoric, languages, and political ideologies of the rule of law. Just as Hay, Marquis, and Thompson have found in England and Canada, an announced commitment to the rule of law actually constrains power.[14] If "law" permits the subaltern to speak,[15] it also provides tools, forums, and languages through which local elites can express their resistance to colonial subjugation. The appropriation of the masters' tools for one's own ends is never an innocent project, however. Colonized peoples' *legal* resistance to colonialism is most often at once a project *without* European liberalism and deeply imbricated *within* it. Struggles to resist Europe's imperial pretensions through law coexisted with an overlapping project. Deploying rights claims cast within western liberalism's classic legal form, that project sought to secure a single Nigerian nationalism that would bind diverse and far-flung peoples into a sovereign Westphalian-style state.

Recognizing this draws us towards the vision of lawyers and politics close to that which emerges from the collaborations of Lucien Karpik and Terence Halliday. Their subtle, historically grounded model of professionalism posits a legal professionalism that *tends,* because of the representative function that lies at the heart of lawyering, towards rights consciousness, participation in public discourses, and the constitution of a "public" through legal engagements. The rituals and sanctity of the courtroom render it a privileged place in which powerful discourses of resistance, appropriately cast in the "languages of state"[16] not only *can* but *must* be expressed. Lawyers, protected by the privilege that attaches to the forum itself and to their profession, are free to speak to the audience immediately present. Through their role in that venue, they address the larger audiences of the public at large. What happens in the courtroom can reverberate throughout society, echoing loudly and long as events are reported in the media, dissected, analyzed, and debated in other public venues, and discussed in pepper soup joints, village squares, marketplaces, coffee-houses, pubs, homes, and other gathering places. The courtroom combines the language of rights, special privileges of free expression, and high visibility. It is, in a word, entirely political. What's more, forensic contests pit rights against power, employ the language of justice, and, where state power is involved, begin the process of constituting those subject to state power as rights-bound citizens.

Where foreign imperialisms are challenged, the mix can be explosive, for Empire is anchored in perceptions of prestige and infallibility on the part of the imperial authorities as much as in the image of the rule of law. When imperial authority is questioned in courts of law, one or other anchor will slip. Ironically, traditional political institutions, symbolized by traditional rulers coopted to serve Empire, provided important sites for challenging the imperial authority. This was demonstrated in the cause célèbre involving the traditional ruler of Lagos, Eshugbayi Eleko, and the colonial Officer Administering the Government of Nigeria. A man with strong personality, the Eleko was not the typical sort of native ruler with whom the colonial master would be well pleased. The Empire reacted, however, only when he resisted the colonial authority's efforts to have him curtail one of his prominent subjects, an individual who was the symbol of a rising professional and political class opposed to the colonialism. The *Eleko* case sparked the early fire of Nigeria's decolonization. Lawyers, both as professionals and as politicians, were central to the process. This conflict took place in one region of Nigeria between the Empire and an icon of Britain's indirect rule. It demystified the colonial establishment, simultaneously rallying local folks and bolstering their confidence in traditional indigenous authority.

Primacy of Traditional Authorities and Indirect Rule

In traditional Nigerian societies, the social structures of family, kinship, religion, traditional institutions, and belief systems perform many of the sorts of functions involved in adjusting claims or settling disputes that take place through law in western state structures. Colonial authorities in Nigeria knew full well that traditional rulers played key roles in all of this, and that the accustomed recourse of the people of Nigeria in times of conflict or social stress was not to law *per se*.[17] Having learned elsewhere that British dominance was secured most rapidly, most effectively, and at the lowest cost by governing at a distance, Britain's colonial administration preferred to work through traditional rulers, institutions, and modalities of justice wherever possible. Successful empires are not uncertain as to their objectives, however. In the final instance, the preservation of indigenous traditional authorities depended on their willingness to adapt and mould themselves to British ends. Local authority insufficiently aligned with the colonial agenda could be dangerous, and in such situations the Empire viewed the sacrifice of a traditional institution as the lesser of two evils.

Moreover, while indirect rule bestowed enormous powers upon the village chiefs and local heads or emirs (especially in Northern Nigeria), two peculiar features need to be noted. First, there were limits on what could be delegated. "Framework" political and judicial powers were not up for grabs and, whatever might be "ruled" indirectly from place to place, the British Resident and District Officers' ultimate authority was never in question. With regard to judicial functions, the British did not at first seek to substitute their own legal system for those already in place in Nigeria. What emerged in most of the territory was a type of a quasi-judicial arrangement working in alliance with the traditional establishment in the form of the Native Courts operating without a professional bar.

Second, indirect rule could never work through authentically traditional power structures, rulers, or offices, for the traditional was profoundly altered when it became enmeshed in the ends of Empire. Even where it was most successful, indirect rule warped the character of traditional institutions, creating fractures along new social or political fault lines, distorting native confidence in the institutions, and weakening cultural and social cohesion generally.[18]

The success of indirect rule as a governance strategy varied widely in the different territories that later became Nigeria. A huge success in the North and somewhat successful in the Southwest (the Lagos area), indirect rule failed to take hold in the Southeast. The peoples of that region were essentially republican in their political outlook, and lacked strong, centralized traditional institutions of the sort that indirect rule relied upon. The failure of British efforts to fill their need by creating so-called warrant chiefs was demonstrated dramatically in the Aba women's riots of 1929. This amounted to a two-month insurrection (December 1929 to January 1930) by some 25,000 women of the Southeast's Aba area (including the present Abia and parts of Cross River and Akwa-Ibom States) against the colonial imposition of warrant chiefs and the corruption and burdensome taxation that came with them. Over fifty women were killed during this period of resistance.[19] Even in the protectorates of Southern and Northern Nigeria and the Lagos colony, where indirect rule worked better, the Empire's romancing of traditional institutions could alienate ordinary people from traditional rulers, who, from one perspective, could appear as conspirators, collaborators, and *de facto* agents of the British administration. Traditional rule balanced on a razor's edge, teetering precariously between tradition and Empire.

Two pivotal moments reveal the foundational incoherence involved in structuring imperial rule through traditional leaders and also the different relationships that the North and South of Nigeria had with the colonial administration. The knock-on effects were felt powerfully in the post-independence era, and the craft management of North/South relations remains a delicate matter to this day.

British-Style Judicial System

A British-style legal system did take root, however. It emerged first in the commercial capital and then extended outward across the Nigerian space. The increasingly cosmopolitan nature of the colony of Lagos, including the development of thriving commercial concerns by both colonialists and returning slaves (mainly from Sierra Leone), made the establishment of British-style courts a compelling need. Colonial administrators were determined, however, not to allow the full operation of British justice. Apart entirely from questions of cultural "fit," British justice was simply too risky. "In far-off England ... robust judicial independence [and rule of law] might be welcome, so the colonial administration seemed to think, but not in a colony where British authority was as yet not fully established."[20]

Initiated as an urban affair dealing mostly with commercial matters, a legal system modelled on that of England took form around the establishment of the Supreme Court system in Lagos. This was followed in due course by its extension into other urban and commercial centres in the Southern provinces. Colonial policy, however, drew a sharp line delineating a geography of law. British law was "zoned" to commercial centres only. Barristers were prohibited from going into hinterland regions out of fear that the law they carried with them might undermine the peace in areas governed by indirect rule. In such regions, law came in the form of British officials presiding over Native Courts. Ironically, perhaps, it was the western Supreme Court system, not the modified Native Courts, that proved more credible to Nigerians. Although favoured by the colonial administration, Native Courts were widely disdained as both corrupt and tainted by their association with traditional rulers, who increasingly came to be seen as overly compliant with the demands of imperial authority.

Lawyers as Incongruous Elements

In all probability, British fear of an independent bar was well founded. When confidence in traditional authority was eroded, non-elite natives were inclined to look to lawyers as a counterpoise of sorts to the alien administration. Lawyers could enjoy popular support and a high media profile, filling the vacuum left as the legitimacy of traditional authorities faded. Sometimes popularly imagined to be more powerful than the British political heads themselves, lawyers appeared threatening from the perspective of hinterland colonial officials. "The fear that lawyers might bully political officers administering justice without formal training ... underlay much of the antagonism toward members of the legal profession,"[21] but there was greater cause for concern too. The political damage lawyers might work in a colonial context was dramatically illustrated in 1913. In that year a Southern Nigerian expatriate lawyer "strayed" into the peaceful enclave of Kano, a region where traditional institutions and colonial administration had struck a rhythm in the practice of indirect rule.

In 1913, Nigeria was, for all practical purposes, administered as two entities: the Northern and Southern groups of provinces. The two entities had come under one colonial administration the year before, however, in a step preparatory to unification. At ease in the mainly Islamic regions of Northern Nigeria, the colonial administration capitalized on strong traditional authority to perpetuate the system of indirect rule. Here, the British sought to shield traditional authorities from untoward anxieties, including the difficulties that might be wrought by southern lawyers (expatriate and indigenous) who might seek to introduce elements of a British-style justice system into the region. The South was another matter, and Adewoye reports that before the start of the Great War, "the legal profession, properly so called, was establishing itself in Southern Nigeria" to such an extent that "there were about twenty-five qualified legal practitioners, concentrated mainly in Lagos and Calabar."[22]

Daring to Subpoena the Emir of Kano

A significant legal and political test of colonial arrangements came to a head in April 1913, when the Northern Nigeria government sought to acquire a piece of property owned by Messrs L and K (Kano), an expatriate company. The company retained the services of a Lagos-based expatriate lawyer, Sir William Geary, who duly moved from Lagos to Zungeru Divisional Court to represent his clients. Geary and his junior, Joshua John Peele, took on the case. Peele was an English solicitor living in Kano. He had enrolled to practise law in Nigeria in December 1912, and was the only legal practitioner in the whole of Northern Nigeria at the time. Their main objective was to establish the firm's title to the land, and the value of the firm's real and personal property at the particular location. These were noncontentious matters and the Chief Justice of Northern Nigeria had proposed arbitration as a means of determining the amount of compensation due to the company. On the substance of the matter, Geary succeeded in getting a satisfactory deal for his client. He secured a new trading site for the company and a payment of two thousand naira in compensation for the site acquired by the government.

The course of Nigerian legal history turned sharply, however, when Geary dared to subpoena the revered traditional ruler, the Emir of Kano, to give evidence in an open court. The Emir was said to have leased the property to the company.[23] The colonial administration was outraged. The lawyers had not consulted the British Resident before taking this dramatic step, which simultaneously caused affront to British Resident and offended the dignity of a revered traditional ruler upon whom the British relied. Fearing that the peace and tranquillity of the potentially volatile Islamic North was threatened by the "rude interference" of lawyers and other foreigners from the South, colonial authorities reacted with sweeping judicial reforms aimed at circumscribing the nascent legal profession's scope of activity and influence. These came into effect just as the amalgamation of the two Nigerias came about in 1914. Ironically, these reforms enhanced the popular opinion of lawyers, and, contrary to intent (as seems the rule in imperial overreactions), spurred the development of anticolonial sentiments. "The people," indigenous lawyers, and anti-imperialism fed off each other.

Baring Colonial Fangs against Lawyers: The Unintended Consequences

There was little scope for legal practice in Northern Nigeria in 1900. Provincial Courts were presided over by the provincial commissioners (the political heads of the colonial administration) and operated without the services of trained lawyers. British commerce had not yet intruded to any significant degree, and local life continued to be governed in accordance with long-established patterns of regulation and dispute resolution, mostly without regard to British law. Not surprisingly, there were almost no lawyers in the North and legal work (in the western sense) was mostly confined to commercial matters in the urban centres – and mostly undertaken by Southern-based lawyers.

In 1913, Northern Nigeria's colonial administration reacted to the Emir incident by seeking to prevent Southern lawyers from straying into the native towns of the Northern provinces. With the federation of the two Nigerias in 1914, the Provincial Courts system was extended to Southern Nigeria. As a result, for almost two decades thereafter, lawyers were prevented from providing advocacy services anywhere in Nigeria other than in cases before the Supreme Court in Lagos and a few other commercial centres.[24] In Adewoye's view:

> The judicial reforms were triggered by colonial panic over the now evident role of lawyers in public affairs, which tended almost always to cast the administration in a negative light. Lawyers penetrated even the traditional chiefs who appeared to enjoy the confidence of the colonial masters, some of them were their legal advisers ... If the educated elite were the *bête noire* of the colonial administration, the lawyer in particular seemed like a menace. Not only would he make a living independently of his white overlords, his position in [and out of courtroom] ... touched on sensitive aspects of colonial administration.[25]

Curiously, it was the status accorded legal professionals by British law that made them so dangerous. When lawyers criticized colonial power, they did so from a position of privilege and authority: "The esteem in which lawyers were generally held was bound to affect the position of colonial authorities."[26] The colonial administration, however, failed to appreciate the weight its Nigerian subjects accorded to the promises of British justice and the rule of law. These particular cultural transplants took root quickly, providing rallying points for opposition to colonial authority in Nigeria and giving colonials a language of resistance that was intelligible, palatable, and persuasive "at home." Local colonial administrators were surprised by the magnitude of opposition to its anti-lawyer judicial reforms. Indigenous and non-Nigerian lawyers worked together, mobilizing powerfully to create a sustained protest against the anti-lawyer reforms that ultimately provoked a crisis of colonial rule. On his return to England, William Geary was instrumental in bringing the question of judicial reforms in Nigeria before the House of Commons,[27] leading to the lawyer-friendly reforms that prevailed from 1933 to 1962. It was precisely because Empire's legitimacy rested so much on the ideology of the rule of law that "no other measure" in the history of colonial Nigeria "aroused so much opposition and protest as the judicial reorganization."[28] The attempt to deny Nigerians access to professional legal services sparked wider ripples of resistance as lawyers mobilized other professional and elite groups in Nigeria against the colonial administration. In a pattern also seen elsewhere, lawyers took steps towards professional organization.

In this wider series of struggles, one incident provided a flashpoint. Nothing did so much to entrench the image of lawyers as the "fighting brigade of the people" as the Eleko case.

The Eleko Case: Lawyers' Political Opportunism

The Emir of Kano invoked his traditional and religious authority in a fashion that ensured the political tranquillity desired by Nigeria's colonial masters. The traditional ruler of Lagos, Eshugbayi Eleko, was another matter, however. The Eleko did not fit the stereotype of traditional authority of the sort that could be easily hijacked by the colonialists. Highly distrusted by the British for his perceived unwillingness to cooperate with the colonial rulers, the Eleko was correspondingly popular among his own people. The local elite, lawyers, and other professionals held him in high regard as a symbol of uncompromised traditional authority. The oppositional stance was well ingrained and conflict characterized the relationship between the Eleko's Ruling House of Dosunmu and the colonial administration from 1908 to 1931. Eshugbayi Eleko's independence on a variety of issues, including, notably, lack of support for the administration's imposition of water rates on his subjects in 1915, made him unpopular with the colonial administration.

In a move widely perceived as "an affront to native custom," the colonial administration "suspended" the Eleko from office in 1916.[29] His humiliation stung Britain's colonial subjects, many of whom wondered by what right an alien power arrogated to itself the authority to alter a *traditional* institution, to appoint or remove the people's natural ruler and the symbol of traditional authority. Indigenous law recognized the removal of an Eleko only by the action of a majority of the representative members of the families in the House of Docemo-Oyekan, the Royal House of Lagos. Otherwise the Lagos elite rallied to the support of their traditional ruler and the Eleko Question became the most pressing political issue in Nigeria. Leading indigenous lawyers such as Joseph Eagerton Shyngle, Adeyemo Alakija, and Bright Wilson, went with prominent politicians and other educated Nigerians in delegation to the Colonial Governor, Sir Hugh Clifford. Through their intercessions, the suspension order was withdrawn.[30] Although it proved fleeting, this victory boosted the popular influence and esteem of lawyers enormously. The Empire had been made to bow.

Accommodation between the Eleko and the British was short-lived. In 1920, one of the Eleko's most valued subjects and staunchest supporters sparked another round of controversy while visiting London. Sir Herbert Macaulay, Nigeria's foremost nationalist politician, made remarks during the course of an interview that were highly critical of the colonial administration. Macaulay carried the Eleko's official staff, and Nigeria's colonial administration understood him to have spoken in a quasi-official capacity on behalf of the traditional leader. When the Eleko refused British demands to denounce Macaulay publicly the colonial authorities again withdrew their recognition of his status and role. Relations deteriorated further until the Eleko was sent into internal exile at Oyo in 1925.

The colonial administration attempted to link its Eleko problem to a crisis internal to the Lagos ruling house, claiming that it had merely sanctioned "the deposition of Esugbayi from his position as the head of the House of Docemo" and consequently authorized his removal from the office of Eleko.[31] Exile, in its view, was more generous than the traditional means of removing the Eleko: death. He was detained and forcibly exiled to Oyo, where he was put on a government stipend conditioned on good behaviour. This was deeply humiliating for a man who was an uncompromising symbol of indigenous traditional authority and who enjoyed the confidence of all sectors of his Yoruba nation, including professional elites. The Eleko did not submit willingly.

Indigenous lawyers took up the *Eleko* cause in defence of the institutional autonomy of traditional authority, native custom, and the rule of law. The

Eleko's legal battle took shape around an application for *habeas corpus*. It played out over a sustained period, and was continually before the courts between 1925 and 1928.[32] Two indigenous Nigerian lawyers, Eric Moore and Shyngle,

> appeared for the Eleko at the initial hearings of what was to become the most celebrated political case of in the colonial era. At this point lawyers as professionals took over from lawyers as politicians. The case [twice] reached as far as the Privy Council in London, but the Eleko Question was ultimately settled politically. Eleko Eshugbayi did not reign long after he was allowed to return in Lagos. He died in October 1932.[33]

The political vacuum created when traditional institutions were suppressed (the Eleko) or warped to imperial ends (the Emir) was filled by lawyers. Lawyers were feared by imperial authorities in equal proportion to their status as heroic figures among colonial subjects. The Empire's fear of indigenous lawyers, manifest in sustained antagonism towards the legal profession and formal restrictions on lawyers' professional activities, worked against the colonial administration. By apparently revealing hypocrisy at the heart of Britain's much-vaunted commitment to the rule of law, anti-lawyer actions eroded the legitimacy of Empire. In the minds of ordinary people and Nigerian elites alike, the Eleko question dramatized a powerful symbolic degradation of both local authority and local culture. The case demonstrated the excesses of a colonial administration operating without checks and balances. The moral tale of unaccountable colonial authority was reiterated and reinterpreted time and again as developments in the case were reported, discussed, and assessed in all quarters. Lawyers, more than any other group, rose to the occasion, helping to define the issues, participating in strategic mobilizations, feeding interpretations of events and issues to the media, and of course joining battle directly in the courtroom.

There, they fought on the terrain of British law, using the rhetoric, language, and promises of the Empire to contain it. In popular conception, lawyers became "fighting heroes," larger-than-life characters who, with impunity, tweaked the nose of an Empire on which the sun never set. Muttering law's unusual incantations, embodied simultaneously as native and British, covered with the full dignity conferred by the wig and gown, dark suits, and immaculate white bibs, lawyers demonstrated that the component parts of the Empire's majesty were rather underwhelming: the enemies they engaged in forensic battle were revealed as more or less ordinary, fallible human beings. A lawyer "could put the white official in the dock and cross-examine him," and could use court proceedings to "challenge the administrative acts of the colonial rulers."[34] Precisely because Britain said – *and believed* – that it was fully committed to the rule of law, lawyers who played within the rules enjoyed immunity from imperial retribution. Consequently, they came to assume a mythical and enigmatic status in the reckoning of the majority of Nigerians. The lawyer challenged arbitrary power, asserted local values, and played to, but also promoted, the development of Nigeria's incipient public – all with the active collaboration of a vibrant indigenous press.[35] *Eleko* cast lawyers in a heroic role like no other. It positioned them as dependable defenders of cultural institutions and authority and worthy champions of independence and decolonization in the struggles that were unfolding.

Summary and Conclusions

It is apparent, then, that the legal profession in Nigeria, like its counterparts elsewhere, played key roles in the development of political liberalism and in advancing cultural projects considered foundational to political and constitutional order. Although its roles took on particular features in colonial Nigeria, they are recognizably of a kind with the roles played by the Paris *avocats* and the English Bar (to pick but two well-studied examples) in establishing government within the framework of the rule of law and, importantly, a politics committed to this. In an overseas colonized land, all such issues were refracted through the lens of imperialism. The defining struggles were about the principles of constitutionalism that should be operative within the framework of a far-flung Empire, rather than governance principles at home.

Two consequences flowed from this. First, constitutionalism required a defence of traditional and local nodes of power in a way that was not characteristic of kindred movements in Europe or in settler colonies. Second, and somewhat paradoxically, native lawyers played on a new terrain. Their roles were played out on a Nigerian "national" stage that itself was a product of Empire. In this, they helped to foster a degree of pan-Nigerian nationalism beyond anything the colonial administrators could have desired.

The Emir of Kano incident triggered sweeping judicial reforms, which revealed a brittleness of Empire. The colonial administration had become resentful of indigenous lawyers and, indeed, of any indigenous agency not confined to officially sanctioned channels. More importantly, it demonstrated the lengths that the administration could go to "preserve at least the outward façade of the authority of the indigenous traditional authorities"[36] when they were content to do imperial bidding. Conversely, *Eleko* and other politically ripe legal causes[37] highlight the peculiar strategic position lawyers assumed in the absence of an indigenous political leadership. This gap presented an opportunity for lawyers as professionals, politicians, and cultural agents to take on the role of the "fighting brigade of the people." The case provides Nigerian history's "classic example of African lawyers taking the leading part in defence of their traditional institution against rude assault by alien rulers."[38]

Empires are built on the illusion of omnipotence. One crucially important consequence of legal interventions was that the "the aura of unassailability" that surrounded whites in colonial Africa began to yield to the growing prestige of the local elite.[39] Lawyers, more than any other group, dispelled the illusion and made the most of the changed circumstances.

The period following *Eleko* was foundational for the struggle for political independence that took place only three decades later. The case mobilized the support of educated Nigerians in many walks of life, including the press, in support of lawyer-friendly judicial reorganizations from 1933 to 1962. In this period, authorities reversed the changes triggered by the Emir of Kano case, expanded the jurisdiction of the Supreme Court, and abolished the Provincial Court system. The unfettered legal profession that emerged was well placed to wage the political struggle that culminated in Nigeria's independence in October 1960.

Postscript

Ironically, it was only when they were most circumscribed professionally that Nigerian lawyers came most fully into their own. Politically mobilized and professionally effective, indigenous lawyers were a Frankenstein creation of the colonial administration, doing much to dislodge the colonial establishment that gave their profession life.

The same is true to some extent in the Nigerian legal profession's relationship with military dictatorships in the post-independence period. In this period, lawyers have often remained remarkably faithful to their historical commitment to the rule of law, tackling a different kind of enemy in the form of military dictatorships. The results are difficult to gauge, with evidence of lawyers acting as both defenders of civil liberties and the rule of law in many cases *and* willing accomplices of the military in others. The Nigerian legal profession struggles constantly for its collective soul, not infrequently seeking to rediscover itself by reconnecting with its glorious history.

Notes

An earlier version of this chapter appeared as "Lawyers' Professionalism, Colonialism, State Formation, and National Life in Nigeria, 1900-60: 'The Fighting Brigade of the People'" (2007) 13 Social Identities: Journal for the Study of Race, Nation and Culture 769 (co-authored with Chidi Oguamanam). It has been revised and reprinted here with permission.

1 *E.g.*, G. Price, "The North" in W.W. Pue and D. Guth, eds., *Canada's Legal Inheritances* (Winnipeg: Canadian Legal History Project, Faculty of Law, University of Manitoba, 2001) 352.

2 D. Hay, "Property, Authority, and the Criminal Law" in D. Hay, P. Linebaugh, J.G. Rule, E. Thompson, and C. Winslow, eds., *Albion's Fatal Tree: Crime and Society in Eighteenth-Century England* (London: A Lane, 1975) 17; D. Hay, P. Linebaugh, J.G. Rule, E. Thompson, and C. Winslow, eds., *Albion's Fatal Tree: Crime and Society in Eighteenth-Century England* (London: A Lane, 1975); E. Thompson, *Customs in Common* (London: Merlin Press, 1991).

3 W.W. Pue, "Trajectories of Professionalism: Legal Professionalism after Abel" in A. Esau, ed., *Manitoba Law Annual, 1989-1990* (Winnipeg: Legal Research Institute, 1991); reprinted from (1990) 19 Man. L.J. 384.

4 T. Halliday and L. Karpik, "Politics Matter: A Comparative Theory of Lawyers in the Making of Political Liberalism" in T. Halliday and L. Karpik, eds., *Lawyers and the Rise of Western Political Liberalism* (Oxford: Clarendon Press, 1997) 15; T. Halliday, L. Karpik, and M. Feeley, eds., *The Fates of Political Liberalism in the British Post-Colony: The Politics of the Legal Complex* (Cambridge: Cambridge University Press, 2012); T. Halliday and L. Karpik, eds., *Colonialism's Legacies: Variations on the Theme of Political Liberalism in the British Post-Colony* (Cambridge: Cambridge University Press, 2012); T. Halliday, "'The Conscience of Society?' The Legal Complex, Religion, and the Fates of Political Liberalism" in Scott L. Cummings, ed., *The Paradox of Professionalism: Lawyers and the Possibility of Justice* (Cambridge: Cambridge University Press, 2011); Susan Block-Lieb, Terence C. Halliday, and Josh Pacewicz, "Who Governs? Delegations in Global Trade Lawmaking" (2013) 7 Regulation and Governance 279; Terence C. Halliday, "Legal Yardsticks: International Financial Institutions as Diagnosticians and Designers of the Law of Nations" in Kevin Davis, Angelina Fisher, Benedict Kingsbury, and Sally Engle Merry, eds., *Governance by Indicators: Global Power through Quantification and Rankings* (Oxford: Oxford University Press, 2012) 180; Terence C. Halliday, Lucien Karpik, and Malcolm M. Feeley, eds., *Fighting for Political Freedom: Comparative Studies of the Legal Complex and Political Change* (Oxford: Hart Publishing, 2007); Terence C. Halliday, Lucien Karpik, and Malcolm M. Feeley, "Struggles for Political Liberalism: Reaching for a Theory of the Legal Complex and Political Mobilisation" in Halliday, Karpik, and Feeley, *Fighting for Political Freedom, ibid.*; Bruce Carruthers and Terence C. Halliday, "Law, Economy and Globalization: How Modern International Financial Institutions Embraced Adam Smith and Accidently Discovered Max Weber" in Richard Swedberg and Victor Nee, eds., *The Spirit of Global Capitalism* (Stanford, CA: Stanford University Press, 2007) 128; Terence Halliday, "Incrementalisms in Global Lawmaking" (2007) 42 Tex. Int'l L.J. 481.

5 L. Karpik, *French Lawyers: A Study in Collective Action, 1274-1994* (Oxford: Clarendon Press, 1999), and K.F. Ledford, *From General Estate to Special Interest: German Lawyers, 1878-1933* (New York: Cambridge University Press, 1996), are notable exceptions.

6 R.L. Abel, "Lawyers for Liberalism: Axiom, Oxymoron, or Accident?" (1998) 1:8 Books-on-Law, online: Pitt Law <http://jurist.law.pitt.edu/lawbooks/revnov98.htm#Abel>; L. Karpik and T. Halliday, "Reply Essay: Can Lawyers Be Committed to Political Liberalism? (2001) 4:4 Books-on-Law, online: Pitt Law <http://jurist.law.pitt.edu/lawbooks/ revapr01.htm#KarpikHalliday>; S. Scheingold, "Taking Weber Seriously: Lawyers, Politics, and the Liberal State Lawyers and the Rise of Western Political Liberalism: Europe and North America from the Eighteenth to Twentieth Centuries" (1999) 24:4 Law & Soc. Inquiry 1061.

7 M. Chanock, *The Making of South African Legal Culture 1902-1936: Fear, Favour, and Prejudice* (Cambridge: Cambridge University Press, 2001); W.W. Pue, "Planting British Legal Culture in Colonial Soil: Legal Professionalism in the Lands of the Beaver and Kangaroo" in L. Cardinal and D. Headon, eds., *Shaping Nations: Australia and Canada, 1851-2001* (Ottawa: Institute of Canadian Studies/University of Ottawa Press, 2001) 91;

W.W. Pue, “Cultural Projects and Structural Transformation in the Canadian Legal Profession” in W.W. Pue and D. Sugarman, eds., *Lawyers and Vampires: Cultural Histories of Legal Professions* (Oxford: Hart Publishing, 2003) 367; A. Sachs, *Justice in South Africa* (Berkeley: University of California Press, 1973); Chapters 5, 6, and 12 in this volume.

8 R. Shamir, “Nation-Building and Colonialism: The Case of Jewish Lawyers in Palestine” (2001) 8:2 International Journal of the Legal Profession 109 at 111-12.

9 *Ibid.* at 112.

10 *E.g.*, B. Chandra, *India's Struggle for Independence*, 3d ed. (New Delhi: Penguin Books, 1989); M.K. Gandhi, *An Autobiography: Or, the Story of My Experiments with Truth* (Ahmedabad: Navajivan Publishing House, 1969); M. Sharafi, *Bella's Case: Parsi Identity and the Law in Colonial Rangoon, Bombay, and London, 1887-1926* (PhD Dissertation, Princeton University, 2006); M. Sharafi, “Lawyers' Empire II: A New History of Colonial Lawyering?” (Paper presented at the Critical Legal Conference, National Academy for Legal Study and Research, Hyderabad, India, September 2006).

11 Shamir, *supra* note 8 at 109.

12 O. Adewoye, *The Legal Profession in Nigeria, 1865-1962* (Ikeja, Nigeria: Longman, 1977).

13 “Editorial” *Lagos Weekly Record* (2 February 1907), as quoted in *ibid.* at 153.

14 Hay, *supra* note 2; G. Marquis, “Doing Justice to British Justice: Law, Ideology and Canadian Historiography” in W.W. Pue and B. Wright, eds., *Canadian Perspectives on Law and Society: Issues in Legal History* (Ottawa: Carleton University Press, 1988) 43; Thompson, *supra* note 2.

15 F.J. Ghazoul, “When the Subaltern Speaks” *Al-Ahram Weekly*, online: <http://weekly.ahram.org.eg/1999/417/cu1.htm>; G.C. Spivak, Can the Subaltern Speak?” in C. Nelson and L. Grossberg, eds., *Marxism and the Interpretation of Culture* (Urbana: University of Illinois Press, 1988) 271.

16 M. Cain, “The General Practice Lawyer and the Client: Towards a Radical Conception” (1979) 7:3 Int'l J. Soc. L. 331 at 335.

17 Adewoye, *supra* note 12 at 16.

18 D. Anderson, *Histories of the Hanged: The Dirty War in Kenya and the End of Empire* (New York: W.W. Norton, 2005).

19 OnWar.com, “The Women's Wars in Nigeria 1929-1930” (2006), online: <http://www.onwar.com/aced/data/whiskey/womens1929.htm>.

20 Adewoye, *supra* note 12 at 72.

21 *Ibid.* at 179.

22 *Ibid.* at 34.

23 W. Geary, *Nigeria under British Rule* (London: Frank Cass, 1965).

24 Supreme Court Ordinance no. 6, 1914.

25 Adewoye, *supra* note 12 at 67.

26 *Ibid.* at 71.

27 Geary, *supra* note 23.

28 Adewoye, *supra* note 12 at 76.

29 *Ibid.* at 159.

30 *Ibid.*

31 *Eshugbayi Eleko v. Officer Administering the Government of Nigeria and Another* (1931), 6 N.L.R. 65; A.C. 662 at 666.

32 T.O. Elias, *Law in a Developing Society* (Benin City, Nigeria: Ethiope Publishing, 1972).

33 Adewoye, *supra* note 12 at 160.

34 *Ibid.* at 40.

35 The first major indigenous newspaper was the *West African Pilot*, which was established by Nigeria's foremost nationalist, US-trained journalist Dr. Nnamdi Azikiwe. Popularly called “Zik of Africa,” he became Nigeria's first president in 1960. The *West African Pilot* was a

pro-independence and anticolonial newspaper with a blend of radical politics and firebrand nationalism.

36 Adewoye, *supra* note 12 at 62.

37 See *ibid.* at 181, discussing in particular *Amodu Tjani v. Secretary of Southern Nigeria*, [1921] 2 A.C. 399.

38 *Ibid.* at 158.

39 *Ibid.*

Index

Note: Page numbers in *italics* indicate illustrated material.

M

Printed and bound in Canada by Friesens
Set in Univers Condensed and Minion by Artegraphica Design Co. Ltd.
Copy editor and proofreader: Francis Chow
Indexer: Lillian Ashworth
Cover designer: Alexa Love